START SMART

Back to School Refresher

QUICK CHECK

Problem Solving

IMAX® Theatre

FUN facts

DID YOU KNOW?

The IMAX® Theatre at the Maryland Science Center, has a giant screen that is 70 feet high. The theatre seats up to 400 people. It is designed to make the people watching the screen feel as if they are part of the action.

Read

Read the problem. Look for important information. Then see what you need to find.

Your class is going to a show in your town. You and 5 friends want to sit in the same row. Can all of you sit in Row E?

Yes

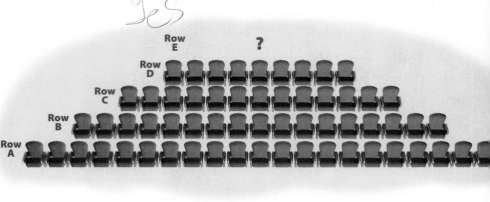

You can use a four-step process to solve many math problems. Read below to find out how to use each step.

1. What do you know?
2. What do you need to find?

Plan

3. How many seats are in Row A?
4. How many seats are in Row B?
5. How many seats are in Row C?

Solve

You and your 5 friends equals 6.

$$1 \quad + \quad 5 \quad = \quad 6$$

6. What is the pattern of the seats? Explain.
7. How many seats does Row E have?

Look Back

8. Is your answer reasonable? Explain why.

Take Your Seat, Please

9. **Write About It** What if a row of seats was added in front of Row A? How many seats would that row have if the same pattern continued?

At the Book Fair

Addition and Subtraction

Raul's school is having a book fair. The fair lasts all week.

DID YOU KNOW?

Reading can be lots of fun. The Parent Teacher Associations in New Jersey hold book fairs in schools. The money raised at these book fairs is used for special school projects.

1. The books for the fair arrived in two boxes. One box had 63 books. The other box had 78 books. How many books were there in all?

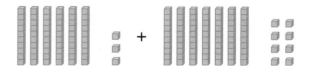

2. On Thursday, 89 books were sold at the book fair. On Friday, 53 books were sold. How many more books were sold on Thursday than on Friday?

3. On Friday, 74 fiction books are left. There are also 35 science books left. How many more fiction books are left than science books?

4. Raul's library has 83 books about animals. Keisha's library has 31 books about animals. How many books about animals do they have in all? Use mental math. Add tens, then ones. Write the number sentences.

5. Durwen's class library has 112 books. At the end of the year, 8 students each take 2 books to keep. How many books are left in Durwen's class library? Use mental math. Count back by twos. Write to show your thinking.

Estimating

At the Madison School book fair, 219 books were sold on Thursday. On Friday, 428 books were sold.

6. Rachel says that more than 600 books were sold in all. Estimate to see if Rachel's answer is reasonable. Round the number of books sold to the nearest hundred. Add. Show your work.

7. Rachel says about 200 more books were sold on Friday than on Thursday. Is she correct? Round the number of books sold to the nearest hundred. Subtract. Show your work.

Book Fair Problem

8. Write a problem using addition and subtraction. Draw pictures or use models to solve it. Give your problem to a partner to solve.

Algebraic Thinking

Hot Ice

FUN facts

DID YOU KNOW?

Ice hockey is a popular sport in Pennsylvania. The Pittsburgh Penguins and Philadelphia Flyers are Pennsylvania's professional ice hockey teams. They play each other a few times a year.

Comparing Numbers

Compare the numbers. Use <, >, or =. Complete

ITEMS	PITTSBURGH PENGUINS	PHILADELPHIA FLYERS
Team Jerseys	287	291
CD Holders	299	311
Sports Bags	267	276

the number sentence.

1. Compare the number of jerseys the fans of each team bought. **291 ● 287**

2. Compare the number of CD holders that the fans bought. **299 ● 311**

3. Compare the number of sports bags that the fans bought. **267 ● 276**

Solve Number Sentences

In each of these hockey games, the total number of goals scored equaled 10. The Penguins' scores are given. Find the scores of the Flyers. Write the number sentence. Write who won the game.

4. 6 + ■ = 10

5. 3 + ■ = 10

6. 5 + ■ = 10

7. How many goals in all were scored by the Penguins?

8. How many goals in all were scored by the Flyers?

Solve Real-World Problems

9. Kathy spent $7 on food and $7 on a jersey while at a Penguins game. Jasper spent $4 on food, $7 on a jersey, and $2 on a team booklet while at a Flyers game. Who spent more? Write a number sentence using <, >, or =. Explain.

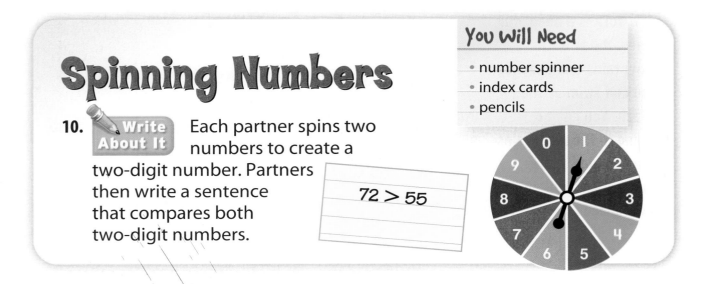

Spinning Numbers

You Will Need
- number spinner
- index cards
- pencils

10. **Write About It** Each partner spins two numbers to create a two-digit number. Partners then write a sentence that compares both two-digit numbers.

72 > 55

Summer Days

DID YOU KNOW?

New York is a beautiful state. It has both mountains and beaches. You can swim at the beach. You can go hiking in the mountains. You can play sports, such as baseball, in most places.

Venn Diagram

Justin made a Venn diagram to show the results of his survey about summer activities.

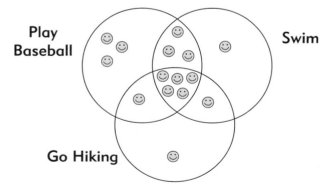

Play Baseball

Swim

Go Hiking

1. Each ☺ stands for a student in the class. How many students swim, play baseball, and go hiking during the summer?

2. How many take part in only one activity during the summer?

3. Explain how you find the total number of students that go hiking during the summer.

Bar Graphs and Pictographs

Justin made these graphs. It shows how many students take part in the summer activities.

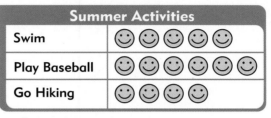

Summer Activities

	1	2	3	4	5	6	7	8	9	10	11	12	13	14
Swim														
Play Baseball														
Go Hiking														

Number of Students

Summer Activities

Swim	😊 😊 😊 😊 😊
Play Baseball	😊 😊 😊 😊 😊 😊
Go Hiking	😊 😊 😊 😊

😊 = 2 students

4. In which activity does the greatest number of students take part?

5. How many fewer students swim than play baseball?

6. Compare the two graphs. How are they the same? How are they different?

Create a Graph

7. Choose three summer activities. How many students in your class take part in these activities? Collect the data. Show what you find out. Choose a type of graph and make it.

8. **Write About It** Write a sentence that tells about your graph.

Air and Space in Arizona

DID YOU KNOW?
Each year, many families tour the Pima Air and Space Center in Tucson, Arizona. Visitors to the museum can see 250 different kinds of aircraft. The museum offers many programs and classes to teach children more about airplanes and space flight.

Time

On a clock there are 15 minutes in each quarter of an hour. There are 5 minutes between numbers.

1. The Chan family went to the Pima Air and Space Center in the morning. What time did they leave? Use the clock.

2. The Chan family wanted to get to the Pima Air and Space Center at 9:15 A.M. They were a quarter of an hour late. Which clock shows what time they arrived?

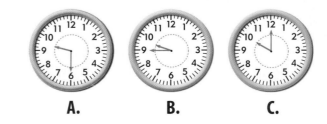

A.   B.   C.

Temperature

Nights can be cool in Tucson during the winter. The temperature can sometimes get down to the 30s Fahrenheit. However, Tucson is best known for its hot weather. On summer days, the temperature is often over 100 degrees Fahrenheit. Even at night, it can still be in the 80s or 90s.

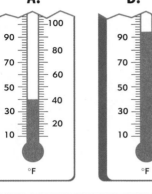

3. Which thermometer shows a warmer temperature?

THINK SOLVE EXPLAIN
4. Which thermometer shows the temperature on a warm summer night in Tucson? Tell how you know.

THINK SOLVE EXPLAIN
5. Which thermometer shows a cooler temperature? Could this be a normal winter temperature in Tucson? Explain.

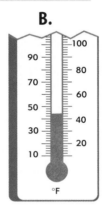

THINK SOLVE EXPLAIN
6. Do either of the thermometers show a summer temperature in Tucson? Explain.

Saturday at the Center

7. **Write About It** Suppose that next Saturday you are going to visit the Pima Air and Space Center. What might your day be like from when you wake up until the time you go to bed? Write down 5 things you will do that day. Then draw clock faces and hands to show the times at which you will do them.

A Day at the Museum

DID YOU KNOW?
It's fun to visit the Cleveland Museum of Natural History in Ohio. There are models of dinosaurs that lived 160 million years ago. Some of these creatures measured up to 70 feet long!

Length

Use the picture for problem 1.

1. The picture of the ticket below is about 5 buttons long. About how many buttons wide is it?

Customary Units

2. Some dinosaurs had sharp teeth over 6 inches long. The tooth in the picture below is about how many inches long?

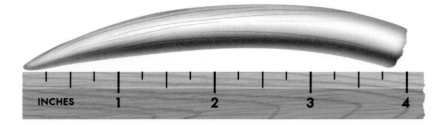

Metric Units

3. The picture is about how many centimeters long?

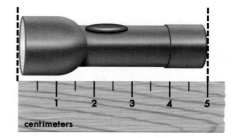

Estimate the length of each picture. Then use a metric ruler to measure. Write your estimate and the measure.

	Estimate	Measure

4. _____ _____

5. _____ _____

6. _____ _____

Measuring Up

7. **Write About It** Find something in your classroom you would measure in yards. Measure it. Record your measurement. Draw a picture.

8. Find something in your classroom you would measure in meters. Measure it. Record your measurement. Draw a picture.

The Butter Cow

DID YOU KNOW?

The Illinois State Fair is held in Springfield every August. Each year, an artist at the fair makes a life-sized sculpture of a cow, from 500 pounds of butter!

3-Dimensional Figures

Choose the name of the correct figure.

1. What shape is this?

  A. cylinder   **B.** sphere   **C.** cone

2. What shape is this?

  A. cone   **B.** sphere   **C.** cube

3. What shape is this?

  A. cylinder   **B.** cube   **C.** pyramid

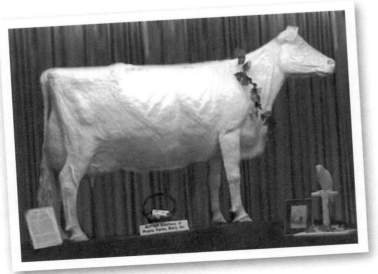

Write the name of each figure. Write how many faces, vertices, and edges each one has.

		Name	Faces	Vertices	Edges
4.					
5.					

2-Dimensional Figures

Write the name of the shape that does not belong. Tell how you know.

THINK
SOLVE
EXPLAIN

6.

Write the name of each figure. Write how many sides and angles each one has.

		Name	Sides	Angles
7.		Triangle	3	3
8.		Pentagon	5	5

Supermarket Geometry

9. Can you think of something from the supermarket with the shape of a sphere? Can you think of a supermarket item with the shape of a rectangular prism? Draw pictures of these objects.

10. **Write About It** Explain how a cube and a rectangular prism are different.

Fact File: Climate

MISSOURI

Missouri's weather can sometimes be extreme. It can get very hot in the summer, and very cold in the winter.

What Is the Highest Temperature Ever Recorded?

The highest temperature ever recorded in Missouri is 118°F, most recently in 1954.

What Is the Greatest Rainfall Ever Recorded?

Can you imagine a foot of rain in just 42 minutes? That's what happened in the town of Holt on June 22, 1947. It was the heaviest rainfall ever recorded in Missouri.

What Are Average Monthly Temperatures?

St. Louis and St. Joseph Average High and Low Temperatures by Month (rounded to the nearest °Fahrenheit)												
St. Louis	Jan.	Feb.	Mar.	Apr.	May	June	July	Aug.	Sept.	Oct.	Nov.	Dec.
High	40	45	52	67	77	86	89	87	80	70	55	43
Low	25	28	34	48	59	67	71	69	62	51	38	28

St. Joseph	Jan.	Feb.	Mar.	Apr.	May	June	July	Aug.	Sept.	Oct.	Nov.	Dec.
High	35	41	55	67	76	86	90	86	79	69	53	39
Low	16	21	32	43	54	63	67	64	55	43	32	21

Source: High Plains Regional Climate Center

MACMILLAN/McGRAW-HILL
Math

Mc
Graw
Hill **Macmillan**
McGraw-Hill

PROGRAM AUTHORS

Douglas H. Clements, Ph.D.

Professor of Mathematics Education

State University of
New York at Buffalo

Buffalo, New York

Carol E. Malloy, Ph.D.

Assistant Professor of
Mathematics Education

University of North Carolina
at Chapel Hill

Chapel Hill, North Carolina

Lois Gordon Moseley

Mathematics Consultant

Houston, Texas

Yuria Orihuela

District Math Supervisor

Miami-Dade County Public Schools

Miami, Florida

Robyn R. Silbey

Montgomery County Public Schools

Rockville, Maryland

SENIOR CONTENT REVIEWERS

Gunnar Carlsson, Ph.D.

Professor of Mathematics

Stanford University

Stanford, California

Ralph L. Cohen, Ph.D.

Professor of Mathematics

Stanford University

Stanford, California

The *McGraw·Hill* Companies

Macmillan McGraw-Hill

Published by Macmillan/McGraw-Hill, of McGraw-Hill Education, a division of The McGraw-Hill Companies, Inc., Two Penn Plaza, New York, New York 10121.

Foldables™, Math Tool Chest™, Math Traveler™, Mathematics Yes!™, Yearly Progress Pro™, and Math Background for Professional Development™ are trademarks of The McGraw-Hill Companies, Inc.

Printed in the United States of America

ISBN 0-02-104004-4/3
8 9 027/055 08 07 06

learning through listening

Students with print disabilities may be eligible to obtain an accessible, audio version of the pupil edition of this textbook. Please call Recording for the Blind & Dyslexic at 1-800-221-4792 for complete information.

CONTRIBUTING AUTHORS

Mary Behr Altieri

1993 Presidential Awardee

Putnam/Northern Westchester BOCES

Yorktown Heights, New York

Ellen C. Grace

Educational Consultant

Albuquerque, New Mexico

Dinah Zike

Dinah Might Adventures

Comfort, Texas

CONSULTANTS

ASSESSMENT

**Lynn Fuchs, Ph.D.,
and Douglas Fuchs, Ph.D.**

Department of Special Education

Vanderbilt University

Nashville, Tennessee

PROFESSIONAL DEVELOPMENT

Nadine Bezuk, Ph.D.

Director, School of Teacher Education

San Diego State University

San Diego, California

READING AND MATH

Karen D. Wood, Ph.D.

Professor, Dept. of Reading and
  Elementary Education

University of North Carolina
  at Charlotte

Charlotte, North Carolina

ESL

Sally S. Blake, Ph.D.

Associate Professor,
  Teacher Education

The University of Texas at El Paso

El Paso, Texas

Josefina Villamil Tinajero, Ed.D.

Professor of Bilingual Education

Dean, College of Education

The University of Texas at El Paso

El Paso, Texas

Contents

LOG ON

Activities referenced on pp. 1, 20, 23, 38, 49

e-Journal pp. 29, 45

www.mmhmath.com

Technology

Math Tool Chest, pp. 13, 46

Math Traveler, p. 46

Multimedia Glossary, pp. 648–658

HANDS ON

For More Activities, See Index Listings.

x ALGEBRA

UNIT 2

CHAPTERS 3-4

THEME: CREATURE FEATURES

LOG ON

Activities referenced on pp. 51, 68, 71, 82, 93

ⓔ-Journal pp. 75, 89

www.mmhmath.com

Technology

Math Tool Chest, pp. 59, 90
Math Traveler, p. 90
Multimedia Glossary, pp. 648–658

HANDS ON

For More Activities, See Index Listings.

ⓧ ALGEBRA

v

UNIT 3

CHAPTERS 5-6

THEME: LET IT GROW

LOG ON

Activities referenced on pp. 95, 110, 113, 126, 137

e-Journal pp. 123, 133

www.mmhmath.com

Technology

Math Tool Chest, p. 105

Math Traveler, p. 134

Multimedia Glossary, pp. 648–658

HANDS ON

For More Activities, See Index Listings.

x ALGEBRA

UNIT 4

CHAPTERS 7-8

THEME: ALL ABOUT YOU

LOG ON

Activities referenced on pp. 139, 156, 159, 176, 187

e-Journal pp. 165, 183

www.mmhmath.com

Technology

Math Tool Chest, pp. 167, 169, 184
Math Traveler, p. 184
Multimedia Glossary, pp. 648–658

HANDS ON

For More Activities, See Index Listings.

x **ALGEBRA**

UNIT 5

CHAPTERS 9-10

THEME: PERFORMING ARTS

LOG ON

Activities referenced on pp. 189, 200, 203, 218, 229

e-Journal pp. 207, 225

www.mmhmath.com

Technology

Math Tool Chest, pp. 191, 196, 211, 226

Math Traveler, p. 226

Multimedia Glossary, pp. 648–658

HANDS ON

For More Activities, See Index Listings.

x **ALGEBRA**

UNIT 6

CHAPTERS 11–12

THEME: HERE, THERE, AND EVERYWHERE

LOG ON

Activities referenced on pp. 231, 246, 249, 264, 275

ⓔ-Journal pp. 259, 271

www.mmhmath.com

Technology

Math Tool Chest, pp. 233, 257
Math Traveler, p. 272
Multimedia Glossary, pp. 648–658

HANDS ON

**For More Activities,
See Index Listings.**

ⓧ ALGEBRA

UNIT 7

CHAPTERS 13-14

THEME: OUTER SPACE

LOG ON

Activities referenced on pp. 277, 292, 295, 310, 321

 e-Journal pp. 303, 317

www.mmhmath.com

Technology

Math Tool Chest, pp. 279, 318

Math Traveler, p. 318

Multimedia Glossary, pp. 648–658

HANDS ON

For More Activities, See Index Listings.

x **ALGEBRA**

x

UNIT 8
CHAPTERS 15-16

THEME: OUR EARTH

Activities referenced on pp. 323, 338, 341, 354, 365

ⓔ-Journal pp. 345, 361

www.mmhmath.com

Technology

Math Tool Chest, pp. 335, 351, 362

Math Traveler, p. 362

Multimedia Glossary, pp. 648–658

HANDS ON

For More Activities, See Index Listings.

x **ALGEBRA**

UNIT 9
CHAPTERS 17-18

THEME: COOL COLLECTIONS

LOG ON

Activities referenced on pp. 367, 378, 381, 396, 407

e-Journal pp. 387, 403

www.mmhmath.com

Technology

Math Tool Chest, pp. 369, 383, 404
Math Traveler, p. 404
Multimedia Glossary, pp. 648–658

HANDS ON

For More Activities, See Index Listings.

x ALGEBRA

UNIT 10
CHAPTERS 19-20

THEME: ARTS AND CRAFTS

LOG ON

Activities referenced on pp. 409, 426, 429, 440, 451

e-Journal pp. 430, 447

www.mmhmath.com

Technology
Math Tool Chest, pp. 410, 419, 448
Math Traveler, p. 448
Multimedia Glossary, pp. 648–658

HANDS ON
**For More Activities,
See Index Listings.**

x ALGEBRA

UNIT 11

CHAPTERS 21-22

THEME: SPORTS AND FITNESS

LOG ON

Activities referenced on pp. 453, 468, 471, 488, 499

e-Journal pp. 487, 495

www.mmhmath.com

Technology

Math Tool Chest, p. 496
Math Traveler, p. 496
Multimedia Glossary, pp. 648–658

HANDS ON

For More Activities, See Index Listings.

x ALGEBRA

UNIT 12

CHAPTERS 23-24

THEME: HOUSES AND HOMES

LOG ON

Activities referenced on pp. 501, 520, 523, 540, 551

 e-Journal pp. 537, 547

www.mmhmath.com

Technology

Math Tool Chest, p. 548

Math Traveler, p. 548

Multimedia Glossary, pp. 648–658

HANDS ON

For More Activities, See Index Listings.

UNIT 13

CHAPTERS 25-26

THEME: LET'S EAT

Activities referenced on pp. 553, 572, 575, 592, 603

ⓔ-Journal pp. 585, 599

www.mmhmath.com

Technology

Math Tool Chest, pp. 559, 569, 600
Math Traveler, p. 600
Multimedia Glossary, pp. 648–658

**For More Activities,
See Index Listings.**

UNIT 14

CHAPTERS 27–28

THEME: SUMMER FUN

LOG ON

Activities referenced on pp. 605, 620, 623, 636, 647

e-Journal pp. 629, 643

www.mmhmath.com

Technology

Math Tool Chest, p. 607

Math Traveler, p. 644

Multimedia Glossary, pp. 648–658

HANDS ON

For More Activities, See Index Listings.

Amazing Math!

Hot Enough to Fry an Egg!

The hottest temperature ever recorded on Earth is 136°F! That is hot enough to fry an egg on a rock. What kind of clothing might you wear on such a hot day?

Learn more about temperature in Chapter 22.

Psst! Rise and shine!

How Much Sleep?

A giraffe sleeps only 4 hours a day! A koala, however, sleeps 22 hours a day! How much longer does a koala sleep than a giraffe?

Learn more about subtraction in Chapter 5.

Bamboo Shoots!

Bamboo is the fastest-growing plant. It can grow as much as 3 feet in one day! How many feet can bamboo grow in 2 days?
Learn more about addition in Chapter 3.

Grab a Slice!

Over 7 million pizzas are eaten every day in America! What shape is closest to a pizza? What shape is closest to a slice of pizza?
Learn more about geometry in Chapter 23.

What Do I Need to Know?

At the party, Jon has a piñata with 95 objects inside. How many tens and ones are there in 95?

Place Value and Money

What Will I Learn?

In this chapter you will learn to

- understand number patterns
- explore numbers through hundred thousand
- count money and make change
- use skills and strategies to solve problems

How Do I Read Math?

When you read a mathematics book, sometimes you read words and symbols, and sometimes you read only symbols.

All of these represent 274:

- **two hundred seventy-four**
- **$200 + 70 + 4$**
- **2 hundreds, 7 tens, 4 ones**

VOCABULARY

- even number
- odd number
- place value
- whole number
- digit
- standard form
- expanded form
- word form
- period

Foldables

Use your Foldables to help you with chapter concepts.

1. Fold a 2–inch tab along the long edge of a paper.
2. Fold the paper into 3 parts to make three pockets.
3. Glue the outside edges of the pockets together.
4. Label as shown. Record what you learn.
5. Take notes and write numbers on index cards.

1.1 Counting and Number Patterns

Learn

Look at each team's uniforms. The numbers form a number pattern. What pattern do you see?

Find the number pattern in this hundreds chart.

Even numbers have 0, 2, 4, 6, or 8 in the ones digit. **Odd numbers** have 1, 3, 5, 7, or 9 in the ones digit.

Use a Hundreds Chart

1	2	3	4	5	6	7	8	9	10
11	12	13	14	15	16	17	18	19	20
21	22	23	24	25	26	27	28	29	30
31	32	33	34	35	36	37	38	39	40
41	42	43	44	45	46	47	48	49	50
51	52	53	54	55	56	57	58	59	60
61	62	63	64	65	66	67	68	69	70
71	72	73	74	75	76	77	78	79	80
81	82	83	84	85	86	87	88	89	90
91	92	93	94	95	96	97	98	99	100

Players on the purple team have even numbers. Players on the yellow team have odd numbers.

Even and odd numbers are one kind of number pattern.

Try It Find the missing numbers. Tell what pattern you used.

1. 10, 15, 20, 25, 30, 35

2. 9, 12, 15, 18, 21, 24, 27

3. 20, 30, 40, 50, 60, 70, 80

4. 5, 7, 9, 11, 13, 15, 17

5. ✏️ **Write About It** **Explain** the pattern that you see for odd and even numbers in problem 1.

Practice and Problem Solving

Find the missing numbers. Tell what pattern you used.

6. 20, 22, 24, 26, 28, 30, 34   7. 55, 50, 45, 40, 35, 30, 25

8. 24, 28, 32, 36, 40, 44, 48   9. 33, 36, 39, 41, 45, 48, 51

10. 55, 65, 75, 85, 95, 105, 115   11. 820, 720, 620, 520, 420, 320

Tell whether the number is *odd* or *even*.

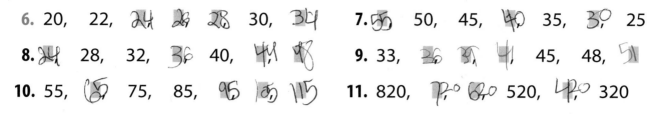

12. 9 odd   13. 15 odd   14. 18 even

15. 26 even   16. 31 odd   17. 52 even

18. 56 even   19. 47 odd   20. 29 odd

★ 21. 745 odd   ★ 22. 1,004 even   ★ 23. 4,778 even

Solve.

24. Start at 6. What pattern could you use to get to 21? What are the numbers? Are the numbers even or odd?

25. Johanna is playing a board game. She has to skip-count by fours to move the pieces. She is at the 8th space and moves 6 skips. What space does she land on?

THINK SOLVE EXPLAIN
26. Becky's home address is 425 Pine Street. Is the number odd or even? Explain.

★ 27. **Logical Reasoning** Kenny started at 20. He skip-counted until he got to 36. Could he be counting by threes? Why or why not? THINK SOLVE EXPLAIN

✓ Spiral Review and Test Prep

28. Isabelle has 3 computer games and 5 board games. How many games does she have in all?

    A. 2 games   **C.** 5 games

    B. 3 games   **D.** 8 games

29. How many pennies make a nickel?

    F. 100 pennies   **H.** 5 pennies

    G. 25 pennies   **I.** 2 pennies

30. $5 + 5 = 10$ 31. $9 + 3 = 12$ 32. $8 - 3 = 5$ 33. $14 - 7 = 7$

1.2 Explore Place Value

Hands On Activity

Whole numbers are numbers in the set, 0, 1, 2, 3, 4, and so on. You can use models to show the number 126.

Show 126 in more than one way.

VOCABULARY
place value
whole number

You Will Need
- place-value models

Use Models

Use hundreds, tens, and ones models to show 126.

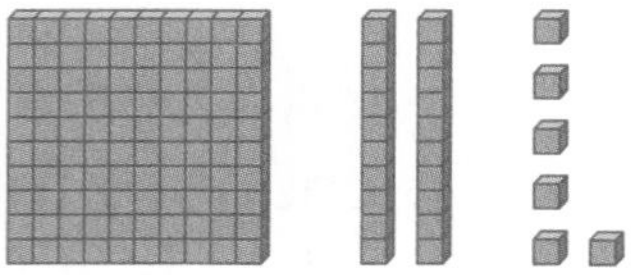

These models show the **place value** for the number 126.

Use only tens and ones models to show 126.

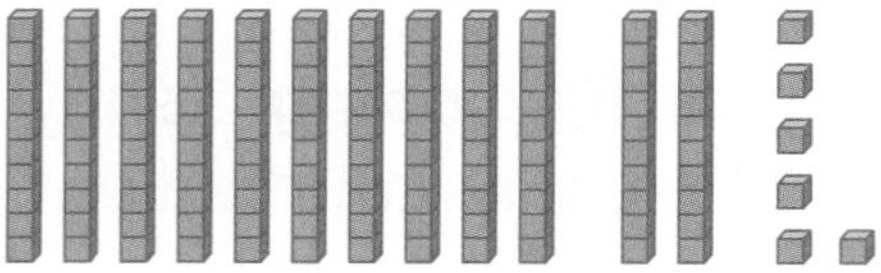

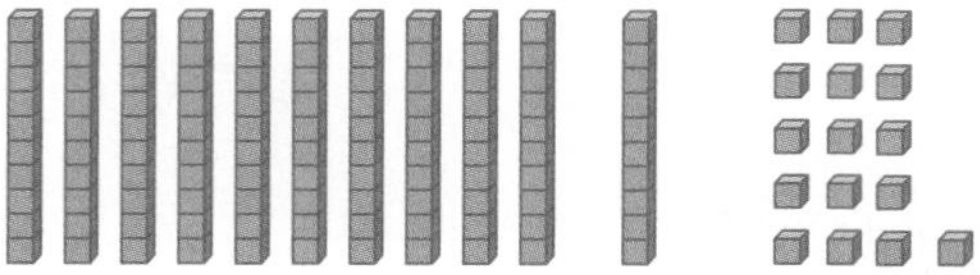

Explain Your Thinking

1. How many hundreds, tens, and ones do you use to show 126 when you use hundreds, tens, and ones?

2. How many tens and ones do you use when you use only tens and ones models?

3. **What If** You can use only ones models. How would you show 126?

4. How do place-value models help you better understand numbers?

Your Turn

Write each number.

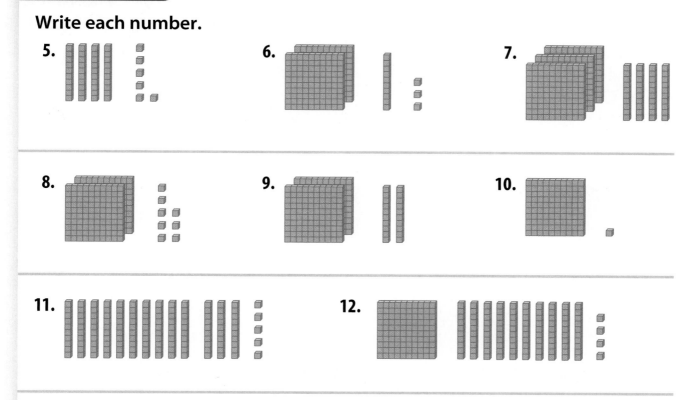

5.

6.

7.

8.

9.

10.

11.

12.

Use place-value models to show each number.

13. 102   14. 230   15. 400   16. 309

17. **Write About It** **Explain** how the ones, tens, and hundreds are related in the number 214.

1.3 Place Value Through Thousands

Learn

A prize-winning dogsled racer once fell and had to run to catch up to her dogs! She ran 2,643 feet. What is the value of each digit in 2,643?

A **digit** is any of the symbols used to write numbers 0, 1, 2, 3, 4, 5, 6, 7, 8, 9.

Show 2,643 to find the value of each digit.

Let's see how to connect place-value models to a place-value chart.

Make Connections

Models

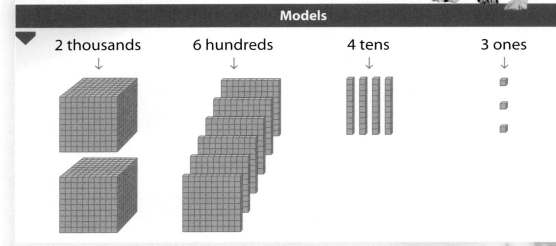

2 thousands   6 hundreds   4 tens   3 ones

Place-Value Chart

Thousands	Hundreds	Tens	Ones
2	6	4	3

↑ The value of the 2 is **2,000**.

↑ The value of the 6 is **600**.

↑ The value of the 4 is **40**.

↑ The value of the 3 is **3**.

Three friends each have a dog. One day they decided to have a race running with their dogs. They ran 1,385 feet.

Show 1,385 in different ways.

Finish 1,385 feet

There's More Than One Way!

Standard Form
1,385

A comma separates the thousands and the hundreds.

Standard form is a way of writing a number that shows only its digits.

Expanded Form
1,000 + 300 + 80 + 5

Expanded form is a way of writing a number as the sum of the value of its digits.

Word Form
One thousand, three hundred eighty-five

Word form is a way of writing a number using words.

Try It

Write each number in standard form.

1.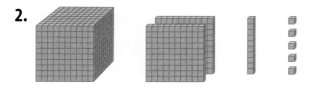

2.

3. 3 thousands, 4 hundreds, 5 ones

4. 700 + 40 + 1

5. 6,000 + 500 + 10 + 9

6. four hundred twenty-two

7. **Write About It** **Explain** when to use a zero when writing a number in standard form.

Practice and Problem Solving

Write each number in standard form.

8.

9.

★ **10.** 30 + 4 + 400 + 2,000

★ **11.** 800 + 7,000 + 30 + 2

Write each number in word form and expanded form.

12. 561   **13.** 1,243   **14.** 8,054   **15.** 408   **16.** 4,320

Solve.

17. What number has 4 thousands, 3 more hundreds than thousands, 2 more tens than hundreds, and no ones?

18. Make It Right Here is how Daren wrote the number 4,011 in expanded form. Tell what mistake he made. Explain how to correct it.

$$4,000 + 100 + 10$$

Link to MUSIC

The biggest game of musical chairs was played in Singapore on August 5, 1989. There were 8,238 people in the game.

19. Write the number of people in expanded form and word form.

Spiral Review and Test Prep

20. What is the value of 2 quarters, 1 nickel, and 1 penny?

A. 61¢   **C.** 56 ¢

B. 59 ¢   **D.** 31¢

21. Matt wakes up at 8:15 A.M. School starts 1 hour later. At what time must Matt be at school?

F. 9:15 A.M.   **H.** 8:30 A.M.

G. 9:00 A.M.   **I.** 7:15 A.M.

Skip-count to find each missing number. (p.2)

22. 19, ■, 23, ■, 27

23. 144, ■, ■, 444, 544

24. 90, 85, 80, ■, ■

8   **Self-Check**   8. 231   12. Five hundred sixty-one; 500 + 60 + 1   **Extra Practice** page 20, Set B

Practice at School ★ Practice at Home

CHANGE ONE DIGIT

Use a calculator to find a new number.

Ready

Players: 2
You Will Need: a calculator, paper and pencil

GO!

► Player 1 writes a new 4-digit number under the 1,000. This number is different from 1,000 by 1 **digit** only. At no time can the number of digits be more or less than 4.

► Player 2 uses the calculator as the referee. Add or subtract a number that will make the written number true. Press the = sign. If the display matches the number, Player 2 gets 1 point.

► Player 2 writes a new number underneath the last one that is different by 1 digit only.

Set

Enter the number 1,000 into the calculator. Write 1,000 at the top of your paper.

► Player 1 uses the calculator as the referee. Add or subtract 1 number. Press the = sign. If correct, Player 1 gets a point.

► Continue taking turns.

► After 10 rounds, the player with more points is the winner. A draw is possible.

I'll add 200 to change 1,000 to 1,200.

1.4 Place Value Through Hundred Thousands

Learn

The chart shows the sales of 3 toys. What is the value of each digit in the number of Robot Dogs sold?

Use a place-value chart to find the value of each digit.

VOCABULARY
period

TOYS SOLD

Toy	Number of Toys
Dinosaurs	753,543
Dolls	923,162
Robot Dogs	529,355

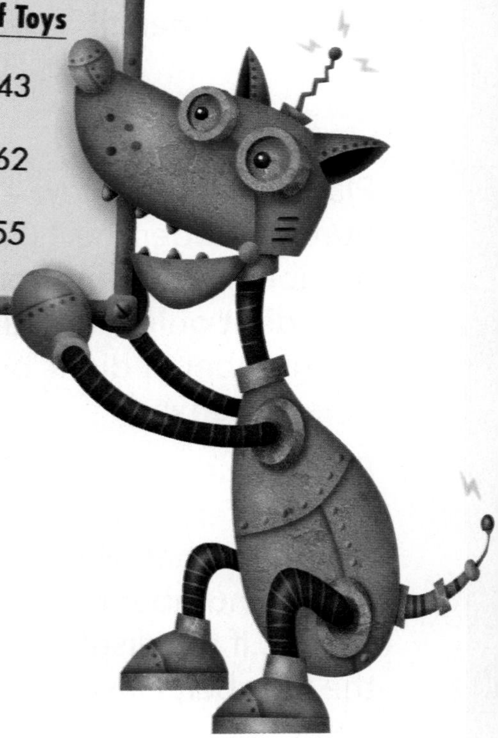

Use a Place-Value Chart

The chart shows the value of each digit in 529,355.

Thousands			Ones		
Hundreds	Tens	Ones	Hundreds	Tens	Ones
5	2	9	3	5	5

A **period** is each group of 3 digits in a place–value chart.

You can use expanded form to show each digit's value:
500,000 + 20,000 + 9,000 + 300 + 50 + 5

Try It
Write the value of each underlined digit. Use a place-value chart to help.

1. 2,456
2. 8,358
3. 5,582
4. 83,035

5. 876,654
6. 263,475
7. 341,567
8. 543,654

9. **Write About It** How does place value help you find the value of the 6 in 236,234?

Practice and Problem Solving

Write the value of each underlined digit.

10. 2̲3

11. 4̲56

12. 80̲7

13. 1̲,543

14. 2,45̲6

15. 2̲1,435

16. 35̲,666

17. 1̲00,765

18. 987,6̲54

19. 43̲2,543

Write the value of 5 in each number.

20. 35

21. 502

22. 52,312

23. 256,762

24. 512,478

Write the digit in each place named.

25. 659 (hundreds)

26. 123,476 (tens)

27. 34,782 (ten thousands)

ⓧ Algebra Complete the table.

28. What number is 1,000 more?

Input	2,987	4,321	7,001
Output			

★29. What is 10,000 less?

Input	21,098	43,145	90,500
Output			

Solve.

30. Flight Maker sells 196,227 computer games. Write this number in expanded form.

★31. Name a 6-digit number in which the sum of its digits is odd and less than 6.

THINK
SOLVE
EXPLAIN

Spiral Review and Test Prep

32. Amy, Bob, and Carl are standing in line. Nobody else is in line with them. How many different ways can they stand in line?

   A. 4 ways   **C.** 6 ways

   B. 5 ways   **D.** 8 ways

33. April caught 4 fish. Oscar caught 6 fish. How many fish did they catch in all?

   F. 2 fish   **H.** 10 fish

   G. 8 fish   **I.** 24 fish

34. $9 + 3$

35. $18 - 9$

36. $13 - 4$

37. $6 + 4$

1.5 Explore Money

Hands On Activity

Suppose you and a friend are buying a toy that costs $3.57. What bills and coins would you use to buy it? How much change will you receive?

Work with a partner. Take turns being the buyer and cashier.

You Will Need
- Play money

Use Models

STEP 1

The buyer purchases the toy.

STEP 2

The cashier gives the change.

STEP 3

The buyer counts the change.

STEP 4

Copy and complete to record your work in a table.

Cost of Item	Amount Paid	Change in Bills and Coins
$3.57	$5.00	

Explain Your Thinking

1. What is the cost of the toy?

2. How did you pay for the toy?

3. How much change did you get back?

4. Which bills and coins did you get back?

5. What is another way to show the value of the change?

6. **What If** You use a ten-dollar bill to pay for the toy. What change will you receive?

Technology Link

Use the money tool in **Math Tool Chest** to show money amounts and make change.

Your Turn

Find the change.
List the bills and coins of the change.

7. You paid with $5.00.

8. You paid with $10.00.

$2.85

$8.27

Complete the table. Use play money to help.

	Cost of Item	Amount Paid	Change: Bills and Coins
9.	$4.66	$5.00	
10.	$3.25	$10.00	

11.  **Write About It** **Explain** how you could use only quarters and pennies to give change for the binoculars.

1.6 Count Money and Make Change

Learn

Ben wants to buy a present for his sister. He buys the stuffed animal for $7.79. He gives the cashier a ten-dollar bill. How much change should he receive?

Find the change.

Let's see how to connect counting up to counting the change.

Make Connections

Count up

▼ The cashier can find the change by counting up from $7.79 to $10.00.

Start at $7.79 → $7.80 → $7.90 → $8.00 → $9.00 → $10.00

Count the change

Then Ben can check his change by counting from greatest to least value.

Start at $1.00 → $2.00 → $2.10 → $2.20 → $2.21

Ben should receive $2.21 in change.

14

Henry and Jackie are at the store to buy a jumprope. They use a ten-dollar bill. How much change should they receive?

You can show the change in different ways.

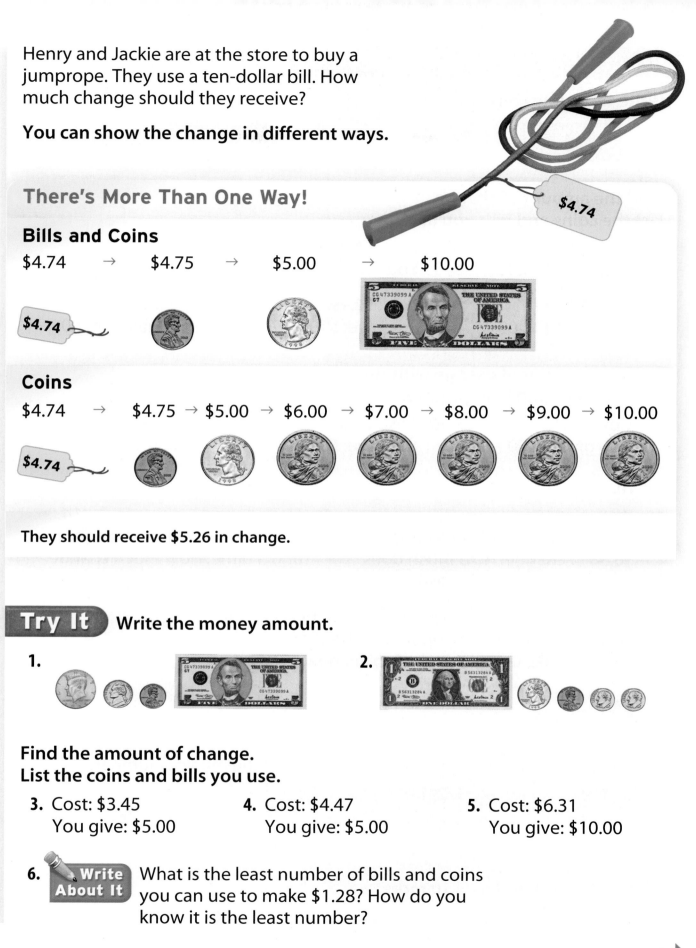

There's More Than One Way!

Bills and Coins

$4.74 → $4.75 → $5.00 → $10.00

Coins

$4.74 → $4.75 → $5.00 → $6.00 → $7.00 → $8.00 → $9.00 → $10.00

They should receive $5.26 in change.

Try It Write the money amount.

1.

2.

Find the amount of change.
List the coins and bills you use.

3. Cost: $3.45
   You give: $5.00

4. Cost: $4.47
   You give: $5.00

5. Cost: $6.31
   You give: $10.00

6. **Write About It** What is the least number of bills and coins you can use to make $1.28? How do you know it is the least number?

Practice and Problem Solving

Write the money amount.

7.

8.

Find the amount of change.
List the coins and bills you use.

9. Cost: $8.88
   You give: $10.00

10. Cost: $4.09
    You give: $5.00

11. Cost: $2.13
    You give: $5.00

12. Cost: $4.19
    You give: $10.00

13. Cost: $2.99
    You give: $10.00

14. Cost: $7.02
    You give: $10.00

Find the amount of change without using quarters.
List the coins and bills you use.

★ 15. Cost: $1.19
      You give: $2.00

★ 16. Cost: $3.07
      You give: $5.00

★ 17. Cost: $4.25
      You give: $10.00

Solve.

18. You use $10.00 to pay for a crossword puzzle. You receive $6.58 in change. How much does the crossword puzzle cost?

19. Holly buys a jump rope for $4.06. She pays with a five-dollar bill and a dime. How much change should she receive?

20. **Make It Right** Marco paid $1.00 to buy a ball for $0.40. Camille counted up to find the change. Tell what mistake Camille made. Explain how to correct it.

THINK
SOLVE
EXPLAIN

Spiral Review and Test Prep

21. Which shows all odd numbers? (p. 2)

    A. 1, 2, 3   C. 3, 2, 1

    B. 9, 7, 5   D. 3, 4, 5

22. Find the missing number.
    $5 + 6 + 3 = \blacksquare + 3 + 5$

    F. 8   H. 5

    G. 6   I. 3

Write the number that is 10 more. (p. 6)

23. 45   24. 90   25. 134   26. 431   27. 709

Extra Practice   page 20, Set D

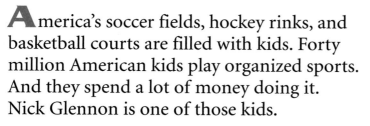

PAY TO PLAY

America's soccer fields, hockey rinks, and basketball courts are filled with kids. Forty million American kids play organized sports. And they spend a lot of money doing it. Nick Glennon is one of those kids.

To play his favorite sport, Nick has to buy the basic gear. That includes shin pads, knee pads, hip pads, gloves, elbow pads, shoulder pads, a helmet, skates, a hockey stick, and a hockey puck.

IT ALL ADDS UP

Experts say the average child spends well over $500 each year playing sports. Why so expensive? Equipment, gear, clothes, and traveling costs add up fast.

Kids who play sports say the joy of the game can't be measured in dollars and cents. "It's my life," says Aidan Wolfe, 10. Aidan plays soccer in Portland, Oregon. "I love soccer!"

Average Cost of HOCKEY GEAR

Helmet $49.99

Stick $49.90

Protective Pad Set $99.90

Skate Lace Tightener $1.90

Skates $89.90

Puck $8.99 for 12

Problem Solving

Reading Skill **Main Idea** What is the main idea of this article?

1. Nick buys 12 hockey pucks. He pays with a ten-dollar bill. How much change should he get back?

2. The coach tells Nick to buy a skate lace tightener. Nick has 5 dollars. How much will he have left?

1.7 Problem Solving: Skill
Using the Four-Step Process

Read

Yoko buys this toy. She gets back $2.52 in change.

How much did she give to the cashier to pay for the toy?

Plan

Use the four-step process to solve.

Read the problem to: See what you need to find. Identify information that will help you find it.

- **What do you know?**
  the price of the toy; the amount of change
- **What do you need to find?**
  the amount she gave to pay for the game

Make a plan. Decide what strategy you will use. Follow your plan.
Solve the problem.

Look back to see if your answer makes sense.

Count up $2.52 from the price of the toy to solve.

$7.48

Solve

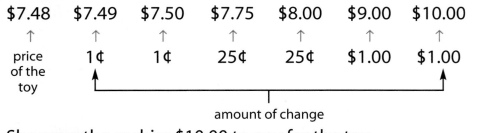

$7.48	$7.49	$7.50	$7.75	$8.00	$9.00	$10.00
↑	↑	↑	↑	↑	↑	↑
price of the toy	1¢	1¢	25¢	25¢	$1.00	$1.00

amount of change

She gave the cashier $10.00 to pay for the toy.

Look Back

Does your answer make sense?

1. **Write About It** **Explain** how using the four-step process helped you to solve this problem.

Practice

Solve. Use the four-step process.

2. Justin wants to buy a yo-yo that costs $1.25. He has 3 quarters and 2 dimes. How much more does he need to buy the yo-yo?

3. Lon has 350 points. Hanna has 200 more points than Lon. Toni has 100 points less than Lon. How many points does each player have?

Mixed Strategy Review

4. Christina buys a baseball glove that costs $11.34. She uses a ten-dollar bill and a five-dollar bill. What should her change be?

5. Art's game piece is on box 10 of a board game. He moves it ahead 10 boxes, and then 10 more boxes. Where is his game piece now?

6. Logical Reasoning What is the greatest 4-digit number using the digits 5, 2, 8, and 0?

Choose a Strategy

- Logical Reasoning
- Draw a Picture or Diagram
- Make a Graph
- Act It Out
- Make a Table or List
- Find a Pattern
- Guess and Check
- Write an Equation
- Work Backward
- Solve a Simpler Problem

Use data from the table for problems 7–10.

7. Tami plays 3 more games. She gets 100 points added to her score for each game. What is her new score?

8. How do you write Ben's score in expanded form?

9. Which person's score has a 2 in its hundreds place?

Student Scores	
Name	**Score**
Ben	780 points
Ed	640 points
Suni	820 points
Tami	230 points

10. ✎ **Write a problem** using the data from the table. Solve it. Ask others to solve it.

Problem Solving

Set A Find the missing numbers. Tell what pattern you used. (pp. 2–3)

1. 30, ▊, 40, 45, ▊, 55, ▊

2. 27, 33, ▊, 45, 51, ▊, 63, ▊

Set B Write each number in expanded form. (pp. 4–8)

3. 5,146   **4.** 379   **5.** 4,600   **6.** 405   **7.** 6,038

Write the word name for each number.

8. 683   **9.** 2,490   **10.** 8,761   **11.** 3,019   **12.** 570

13. 491   **14.** 7,030   **15.** 1,565   **16.** 92,102   **17.** 324

Set C Write the value of the underlined digit. (pp. 10–11)

18. 49   **19.** 325,000   **20.** 3,562   **21.** 24,032   **22.** 985

Write the value of the digit 3 in each number.

23. 163,402   **24.** 377   **25.** 325,000   **26.** 232,601   **27.** 37

Write the digit in each place named.

28. 6,742 (hundreds)   **29.** 30,740 (ten thousands)   **30.** 146,198 (tens)

31. 15,302 (thousands)   **32.** 340,002 (hundred thousands)   **33.** 519 (ones)

Set D Find the amount of change. List the coins and bills. (pp. 12–16)

34. Cost: $3.87 You give: $5.00   **35.** Cost: $2.76 You give: $5.00   **36.** Cost: $4.08 You give: $5.00

37. Cost: $8.42 You give: $10.00   **38.** Cost: $7.15 You give: $10.00   **39.** Cost: $3.56 You give: $10.00

Set E Solve. Tell how you used 4 steps to solve. (pp. 18–19)

40. Jeri buys a game for $3.25. She gets $0.75 back. How much did Jeri use to pay for the game?

41. Harry has 580 points. He loses 300 points in his next turn. What is his new score?

Review/Test

Find the missing numbers.

1. 21, ▮, 25, 27, ▮, 31

2. 115, 110, ▮, ▮, 95, 90

Write the word name for each number.

3. 342   **4.** 506   **5.** 2,220   **6.** 3,508   **7.** 4,071

Write the value of each underlined digit.

8. 3,4_9_7   **9.** 1_2_,489   **10.** 2_3_4,558   **11.** _4_98,641

Write the money amount.

12.

13.

14. 1 five-dollar bill, 4 one-dollar bills, 4 dimes

15. 2 one-dollar bills, 5 quarters, 2 pennies

Find the amount of change. List the coins and bills you use.

16. Cost: $2.56
You give: $5.00

17. Cost: $3.19
You give: $5.00

18. Cost: $8.34
You give: $10.00

Solve.

19. Here is a number sentence:
$3,000 + ▮ + 70 + 8 = 3,578$.
What is the missing number?

20. **Write About It** **Explain** how you can show $1.47 using 2 different sets of bills and coins.

Do I Need Help?

Exercises	Review Concepts	Use Extra Practice Set
1–2	pp. 2–3	Set A
3–7, 19	pp. 4–8	Set B
8–11	pp. 10–11	Set C
12–18	pp. 12–16	Set D
20	pp. 18–19	Set E

Foldables Use your Foldables to help you review.

What Do I Need to Know?

Nathan scored 1,412 points playing a video game. What is the value of the 4 in his score?

Numbers and Money

What Will I Learn?

In this chapter you will learn to

- compare and order numbers and money
- estimate quantities
- round whole numbers and money
- use skills and strategies to solve problems

How Do I Read Math?

When you read a mathematics book, sometimes you read words and symbols, and sometimes you read only symbols.

These symbols are used to compare numbers and money:

- < means "is less than"
- > means "is greater than"
- = means "is equal to"

VOCABULARY

- benchmark number
- round

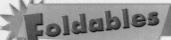

Foldables

Use your Foldables to help you with chapter concepts.

1. Fold a 2–inch tab along the long edge of a paper.
2. Fold the paper into 3 parts to make 3 pockets.
3. Glue the outside edges of the pockets together.
4. Label as shown. Record what you learn.
5. Take notes on index cards.

2.1 Compare Numbers and Money

Learn

The chart shows information about 2 toys on sale at a store. Which toy had greater sales?

Toys	Cost	Number Sold
Truck	$7.51	114
Race Car	$7.58	110

Compare: 114 and 110

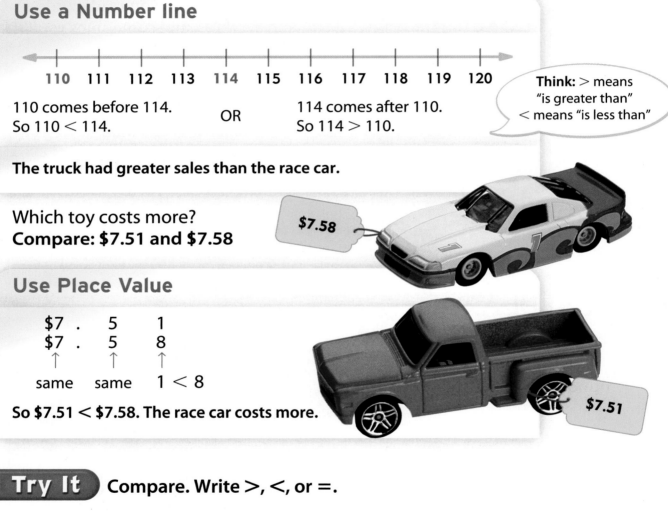

Use a Number line

110 111 112 113 **114** 115 116 117 118 119 120

110 comes before 114.
So 110 < 114.

OR

114 comes after 110.
So 114 > 110.

Think: > means "is greater than" < means "is less than"

The truck had greater sales than the race car.

Which toy costs more?
Compare: $7.51 and $7.58

$7.58

Use Place Value

$7 . 5 1
$7 . 5 8
↑   ↑   ↑
same   same   1 < 8

So $7.51 < $7.58. The race car costs more.

$7.51

Try It   Compare. Write >, <, or =.

1. 67 ● 76

2. 116 ● 99

3. 544 ● 544

4. 193 ● 139

5. $5.51 ● $1.55

6. $1.21 ● $1.12

7. $7.08 ● $7.80

8. **Write About It** Is a 2-digit whole number always less than a 3-digit number? Explain how you know.

Practice and Problem Solving

Compare. Write >, <, or =.

9. 55 ⬤ 44

10. 103 ⬤ 93

11. 66 ⬤ 616

12. 128 ⬤ 128

13. 804 ⬤ 488

14. 997 ⬤ 979

15. 101 ⬤ 110

16. 701 ⬤ 770

17. $4.41 ⬤ $1.44

18. $2.32 ⬤ $2.23

19. $6.09 ⬤ $6.90

20. $7.99 ⬤ $7.99

21. $0.98 ⬤ $1.11

22. $3.33 ⬤ $3.30

★23. 3 ⬤ 2 ⬤ 1

★24. 14 ⬤ 12 ⬤ 17

★25. 24 ⬤ 21 ⬤ 28

Solve.

26. Megan scored 125 points in a board game. Leroy scored 152 points. Who scored higher? How can you tell?

27. Which of these 2 prizes is greater: two thousand, five hundred fifty dollars or $2,550? Explain.

28. Steven saved $2.33 to buy a game. The money shown is the amount Bill saved. Who has more money? How can you tell?

★29. **Logical Reasoning** Use the 4 digits listed below to make the greatest whole number. Use each digit only once. Explain your reasoning.

| THINK SOLVE EXPLAIN |

| 5 | 8 | 9 | 7 |

Spiral Review and Test Prep

30. Meg is taller than Kim. Sue is shorter than Bob and Kim, but not taller than Meg. Who is the shortest?

   A. Meg   **C.** Kim

   B. Sue   **D.** Bob

31. Greg has a one-dollar bill, 3 nickels, and 2 pennies. How much money does he have? (p. 14)

   F. $1.50   **H.** $1.21

   G. $1.32   **I.** $1.17

What is the missing number? (p. 2)

32. 99, ▮, 103, 105, 107

33. 70, 75, ▮, ▮, 90, 95

Extra Practice page 38, Set A

2.2 Order Numbers and Money

Learn

The chart lists 3 players and their scores for the *Catch the Caterpillar* game.

List the scores in order from greatest to least.

Highest Game Scores

Players	Scores
Cecilia	953
Molly	1004
Lúis	989

There's More Than One Way!

Use a Number Line

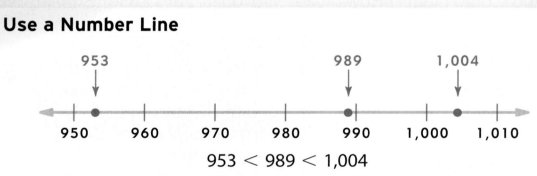

$$953 < 989 < 1,004$$

Use a Place-Value Chart

thousands	hundreds	tens	ones
	9	5	3
1	0	0	4
	9	8	9

↑ 1,004 is the greatest number.

↑ Compare the tens. 9 = 9

↑ 5 < 8 So 953 < 989.

↑ Since you know that 50 < 80, you do not need to compare the ones.

List in order from greatest to least:
Molly 1,004   Lúis 989   Cecilia 953

Adam is at the store to buy a video game. Three hand-held video games are on sale at Games Galore. Which game costs the least? Which game costs the most?

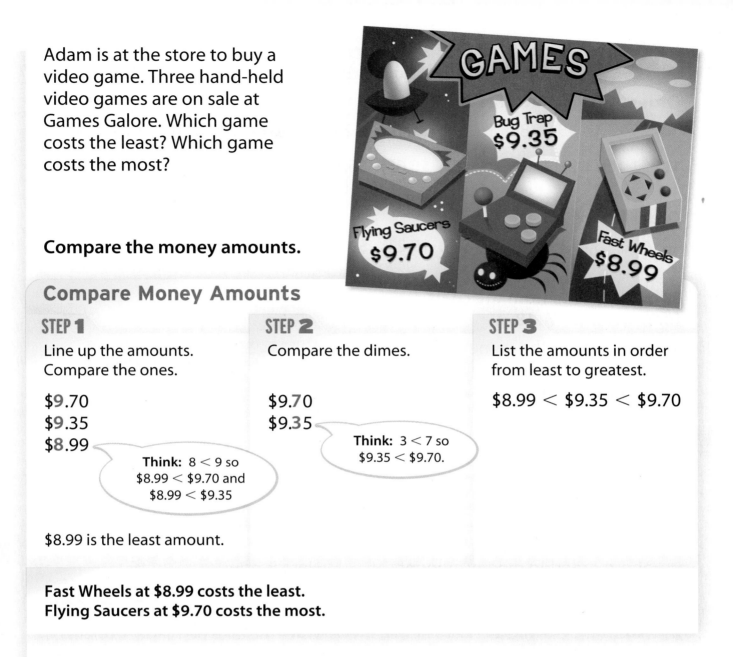

Compare the money amounts.

Compare Money Amounts

STEP 1

Line up the amounts. Compare the ones.

$9.70
$9.35
$8.99

Think: 8 < 9 so $8.99 < $9.70 and $8.99 < $9.35

$8.99 is the least amount.

STEP 2

Compare the dimes.

$9.70
$9.35

Think: 3 < 7 so $9.35 < $9.70.

STEP 3

List the amounts in order from least to greatest.

$8.99 < $9.35 < $9.70

Fast Wheels at $8.99 costs the least.
Flying Saucers at $9.70 costs the most.

Try It Order from least to greatest.

1. 2,312; 2,245; 1,765   2. 8,099; 8,136; 8,089   3. 6,324; 6,257; 6,145

Order from greatest to least.

4. $5.62; $7.12; $4.32   5. $6.75; $6.82; $6.63   6. $8.29; $8.49; $8.19

7.  **Write About It** Order these 3 numbers from greatest to least: 547; 598; 2,001. Explain how you can tell right away which is the greatest number.

Practice and Problem Solving

Order from least to greatest.

8. 234; 1,245; 789   **9.** 2,010; 2,245; 2,209   **10.** 4,110; 4,101; 4,001

11. $1.16; $2.09; $1.46   **12.** $6.65; $6.82; $6.63   **13.** $1.25; $5.21; $2.51

Order from greatest to least.

14. 678; 3,411; 2,187   **15.** $9.21; $9.12; $9.09   **16.** $0.96; $1.16; $1.06

Solve. Use data from the chart for problems 17–18.

17. Miko played the game that took the longest time to finish. Which game did Miko play?

18. Analyze How can you tell which game took the least amount of time without comparing the value of each digit?

Chess Game Time Records

Game Number	Minutes from Start to Finish
1	109
2	98
3	120

19. **Write a Problem** that asks about ordering money amounts. Solve it. Have a classmate solve it.

20. Make It Right Here is how Parth ordered 3 numbers. Tell what mistake he made. Explain.

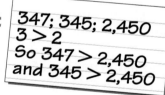
347; 345; 2,450
3 > 2
So 347 > 2,450
and 345 > 2,450

Spiral Review and Test Prep

21. Which number has 3 tens and no hundreds? (p. 4)

  A. 301   **C.** 37

  B. 103   **D.** 3

22. Which is the standard form for 100 + 50 + 4? (p. 6)

  F. 514   **H.** 154

  G. 415   **I.** fifty-four

Find the change. (p. 14)

23. Cost of item: $2.99
You paid: $5.00

24. Cost of item: $6.33
You paid: $10.00

Writing for Math

A card game costs $4.64. Tia pays with a ten-dollar bill. What change will she receive? Explain your thinking.

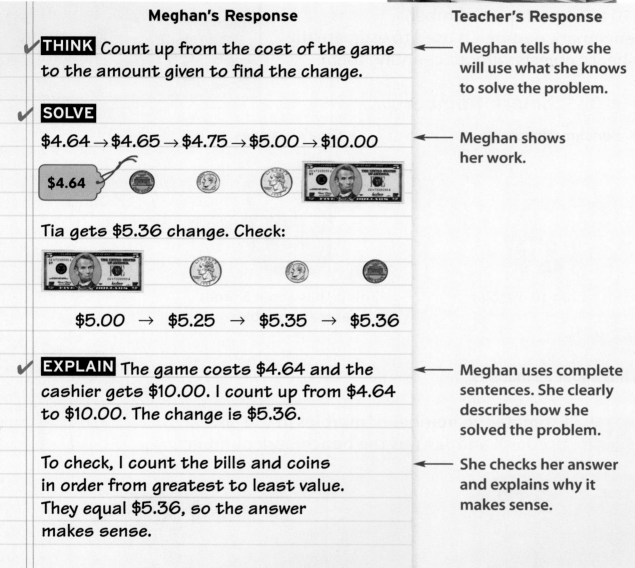

Meghan's Response

✓ **THINK** Count up from the cost of the game to the amount given to find the change.

✓ **SOLVE**

$4.64 → $4.65 → $4.75 → $5.00 → $10.00

$4.64

Tia gets $5.36 change. Check:

$5.00 → $5.25 → $5.35 → $5.36

✓ **EXPLAIN** The game costs $4.64 and the cashier gets $10.00. I count up from $4.64 to $10.00. The change is $5.36.

To check, I count the bills and coins in order from greatest to least value. They equal $5.36, so the answer makes sense.

Teacher's Response

← Meghan tells how she will use what she knows to solve the problem.

← Meghan shows her work.

← Meghan uses complete sentences. She clearly describes how she solved the problem.

← She checks her answer and explains why it makes sense.

Writing

Solve. Use Meghan's work as a guide.

1. Frank buys a book for $3.49 and pays with a $5 bill. How much change does he receive?

2. Sandy has 2 $1 bills, 5 quarters, and 1 dime. Sasha has $3.50. Who has more money?

2.3 Estimate Quantities

Learn

Gina places a bag of marbles in a glass jar. About how many marbles does she have?

Use 10 as a benchmark number. A **benchmark number** is used to estimate the number of objects without counting them.

Use a Benchmark Number

Benchmark number

This jar has 10 marbles.

Gina's marbles

This jar has about 5 times as many marbles.

Gina has about 50 marbles.

Try It

Estimate the number of marbles in the jar. Use Jar X and Jar Y as the benchmark numbers.

Jar X
20 marbles

Jar Y
100 marbles

1. 10 or 40

2. 80 or 200

3.  **Explain** why you would estimate a number instead of counting.

Practice and Problem Solving

Use the benchmark numbers to estimate the number of objects.

10 beads

50 beads

4.
100 or 300

5.
40 or 80

★**6.**
100 or 150

Choose 10, 100, or 1,000 to estimate.

7. the number of visitors to a zoo in a month

8. the number of pages in your notebook

9. the number of pencils in a pack

10. the number of paper clips in a box

Solve.

THINK SOLVE EXPLAIN

11. Peter would like to buy about 500 marbles. How can he use a benchmark instead of counting 1 by 1 to 500?

12. Victoria has 2 five-dollar bills, 1 quarter, and 3 nickels. How much money does Victoria have?

Spiral Review and Test Prep

13. Which is the greatest number? (p. 26)

    A. 1,006   C. 860

    B. 992   D. 583

14. Cory needs one more nickel in order to buy an eraser for 50¢. How much change does Cory have? (p. 14)

    F. 35¢   H. 45¢

    G. 40¢   I. 60¢

Write the value of the 4 in each number. (p. 10)

15. 482   16. 25,849   17. 48,002   18. 58,924

Extra Practice page 38, Set C

2.4 Round to Tens and Hundreds

Learn

A pinball machine keeps track of the number of times it has been played each week. About how many times has each game been played?

Round each number to the nearest ten and hundred. To **round** is to find the value of a number based on a given place value.

VOCABULARY
round

Use a Number Line

Round to Nearest Ten

212 is closer to 210 than to 220.
So, 212 rounds to 210.

248 rounds to 250.

273 rounds to 270.

Round to Nearest Hundred

212 is closer to 200 than to 300.
So, 212 rounds to 200.

248 rounds to 200.

273 rounds to 300.

To the nearest ten, the number of games played rounds to 210, 250, and 270.
To the nearest hundred, the number of games played rounds to 200, 200, and 300.

Try It Round to the nearest ten or ten dollars.

1. 33 **2.** 49 **3.** $14 **4.** 126 **5.** $469

Round to the nearest hundred or hundred dollars.

6. 459 **7.** $381 **8.** $901 **9.** $1,254 **10.** 6,782

11. **Write About It** **Explain** how the number 158 can be rounded to 160 or to 200.

Practice and Problem Solving

Round to the nearest ten or ten dollars.

12. 48 **13.** 89 **14.** $70 **15.** 148 **16.** $451

17. 592 ★**18.** 1,234 ★**19.** $5,001 ★**20.** 1,193 ★**21.** 9,892

Round to the nearest hundred or hundred dollars.

22. 312 **23.** $782 **24.** 201 **25.** $911 **26.** 555

★**27.** 8,067 ★**28.** $4,029 ★**29.** $7,777 ★**30.** 11,742 ★**31.** 24,567

x **Algebra Find the missing digit to make the sentence true.**

32. 3▉7 rounds to 320.

33. 5, ▉56 rounds to 5,000.

Solve.

34. Albert is up to page 103 in his book. To the nearest hundred, about how many pages has Albert read?

35. Discount Toys sold 192 talking bears last week. To the nearest hundred, about how many bears were sold?

36. Analyze Anne rounds a number with the digits 6, 2, and 8. To the nearest hundred, the number rounds to 900. What is the number?

37. Health Sam learned that boys his age should eat about 2,800 calories each day. He usually eats about 100 fewer calories. How many calories does Sam eat each day?

Spiral Review and Test Prep

38. What is the value of the 4 in 5,422? (p. 6)

A. 4,000 **C.** 40

B. 400 **D.** 4

39. Which is not equal to 14?

F. $10 + 3$ **H.** $7 + 7$

G. $8 + 6$ **I.** $5 + 9$

Write the number that is 100 more. (p. 10)

40. 45 **41.** 390 **42.** 901 **43.** 2,437

Extra Practice **page 38, Set D**

2.5 Round to the Nearest Thousand

Learn

A total of 2,184 Basketball Shootout games were played. To the nearest thousand, how many games were played?

Round 2,184 to the nearest thousand.

There's More Than One Way!

Use a Number Line

2,184

2,000   2,500   3,000

2,184 is closer to 2,000 than to 3,000.
So 2,184 rounds to 2,000.

Use Rounding Rules

STEP 1	STEP 2	STEP 3
Find the place you want to round.	Look at the digit to its right.	If the digit is **less than 5**, the place you want to round remains the same. If the digit is **5 or greater**, add 1 to the place you want to round.
2,184	2,184	1 < 5
		So 2,184 rounds to 2,000

About 2,000 Basketball Shootout games were played.

Try It   Round to the nearest thousand or thousand dollars.

1. 3,541   **2.** $1,254   **3.** 8,932   **4.** 21,562   **5.** $76,123

6. 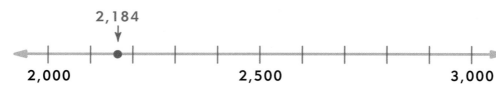 **Write About It** **Explain** how you would use rounding rules to round 2,831 to the nearest thousand.

34

Practice and Problem Solving

Round to the nearest thousand or thousand dollars.

7. 3,842   **8.** $2,234   **9.** 8,912   **10.** 1,510   **11.** $7,223

12. $25,673   **13.** 12,371   **14.** 55,555   **15.** $10,934   **16.** 89,954

17. 999   **18.** 7,482   **19.** 29,521   **20.** $12,401   **21.** 47,099

★**22.** 182,592   ★**23.** $244,209   ★**24.** $799,999   ★**25.** $412,098   ★**26.** 982,500

Solve. Use data from the table for problems 27–29.

27. Suppose in Week 3 there are 100 more visitors than in Week 2. To the nearest thousand, how many visitors are there in Week 3?

BETTY'S ARCADE

WEEK	NUMBER OF VISITORS
1	2,770
2	3,095

28. What is the number of visitors in Week 1 rounded to the nearest thousand?

29. What is the number of visitors in Week 2 rounded to the nearest hundred?

THINK SOLVE EXPLAIN

30. Generalize Write about why population numbers are more likely to be rounded than exact.

★**31.** Rounded to the nearest ten, hundred, and thousand, the number is 921,000. What is the greatest possible number?

Spiral Review and Test Prep

32. Which number has 8 in the thousands place? (p. 6)

  A. 8,456   **C.** 3,850

  B. 4,678   **D.** 2,848

33. What is 840 rounded to the nearest ten? (p. 32)

  F. 840   **H.** 850

  G. 841   **I.** 900

Compare. Write >, <, or =. (p. 24)

34. 36 ⬤ 62   **35.** $120 ⬤ $99   **36.** 2,001 ⬤ 2,100   **37.** 7,823 ⬤ 877

2.6

Problem Solving: Strategy
Make a Table

Read

Mr. Bing has to pick a game for his gym class to play. He knows the class's 3 favorite games. Which game should he pick?

- **What do you know?**
  The class's 3 favorite games

- **What do you need to find out?**
  Which game he should pick

Plan

Collect and organize data to find out which game the students like most.

Solve

Organize the results in a table.

Survey Results		
Game	Tally	Number
Kickball	卌 IIII	9
Dodgeball	卌 III	8
Soccer	卌 卌 II	12

Soccer has the greatest number of votes.
Mr. Bing will pick soccer.

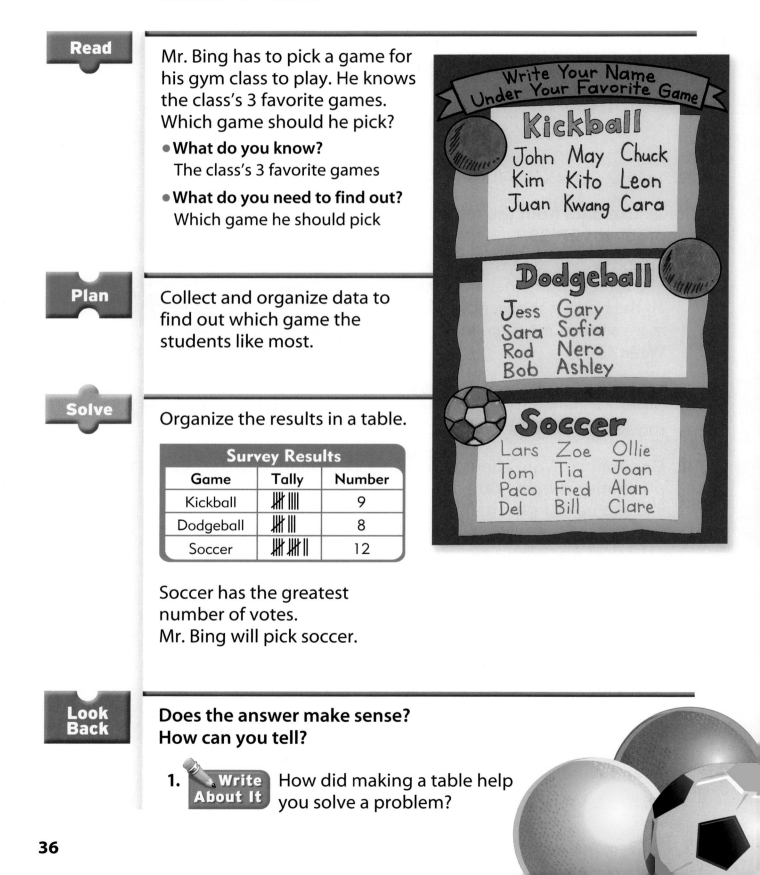

Write Your Name Under Your Favorite Game

Kickball
John May Chuck
Kim Kito Leon
Juan Kwang Cara

Dodgeball
Jess Gary
Sara Sofia
Rod Nero
Bob Ashley

Soccer
Lars Zoe Ollie
Tom Tia Joan
Paco Fred Alan
Del Bill Clare

Look Back

Does the answer make sense? How can you tell?

1. **Write About It** How did making a table help you solve a problem?

Practice

Use the data for problems 2–4.

2. Make a table for the data.

3. Which day had the least sign-ups? The most?

4. **What If** 5 more students sign up for Wednesday. Then which day will have the most sign-ups? The least?

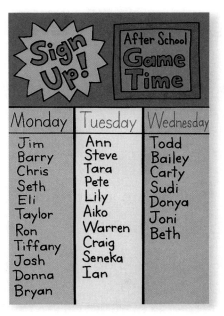

Mixed Strategy Review

Use data from the table on page 36 for problems 5–8.

5. How many more votes did the most popular game get than the least popular game?

★ 6. Some students changed their minds about which game to play. Now there is a tie between 2 of the games. How could the votes change so that 2 games are tied?

Choose a Strategy
- Logical Reasoning
- Draw a Picture or Diagram
- Make a Graph
- Act It Out
- Make a Table or List
- Find a Pattern
- Guess and Check
- Write an Equation
- Work Backward
- Solve a Simpler Problem

7. How many students voted in the survey?

8. ✎ **Write a problem** using the data in the table. Solve the problem and show your work.

9. **Collect data** for your own survey. Ask friends to name their favorite outdoor game. Make a table to organize your data. Create a problem that uses the data. Ask a friend to solve it.

★ 10. **Social Studies** In the year 2010, Lake Compounce Amusement Park, the oldest amusement park in the United States, will be 164 years old. How old was it in the year 2002?

Extra Practice

Set A Compare. Write >, <, or =. (pp. 24–25)

1. 89 ● 98　　　**2.** 391 ● 319　　　**3.** 420 ● 42　　　**4.** 532 ● 532

5. $0.76 ● $0.67　　**6.** $5.64 ● $5.46　　**7.** $1.20 ● $0.12　　**8.** $8.54 ● $8.54

Set B Order from least to greatest. (pp. 26–28)

9. 132; 3,210; 689　　　**10.** 4,345; 4,145; 5,621　　　**11.** 3,609; 3,215; 3,208

12. 5,988; 5,918; 5,889　　**13.** 6,034; 6,430; 6,403　　**14.** 8,060; 8,600; 8,006

Set C Use the benchmark to estimate. (pp. 30–31)

15.　**16.**

10 beads　　　　　20 or 50　　　　　100 or 200

Set D Round to the nearest ten or ten dollars.
　　　Then round to the nearest hundred or hundred dollars. (pp. 32–33)

17. $86　　**18.** 153　　**19.** 366　　**20.** 6,008　　**21.** $4,391

22. $4,038　**23.** 7,662　　**24.** 8,728　　**25.** $15,648　**26.** 32,774

Set E Round to the nearest thousand or thousand dollars. (pp. 34–35)

27. 3,625　　**28.** $5,489　**29.** 7,362　　**30.** $1,552　**31.** 6,214

32. 14,724　**33.** 28,841　**34.** $62,457　**35.** 33,118　**36.** $88,701

Set F Use data from the table for problems 37–38. (pp. 36–37)

37. Which player got the
most points?

38. Write the scores in order from
least to greatest.

Math Game Scores	
Players	Scores
Alano	2,134
Ben	2,314
Carol	2,431

Review/Test

Compare. Write, $>$, $<$, or $=$.

1. 44 ⬤ 84   **2.** 92 ⬤ 103   **3.** 300 ⬤ 30   **4.** $1.41 ⬤ $1.14

Write in order from greatest to least.

5. 3,105; 2,756; 4,567   **6.** 1,345; 1,435; 2,451   **7.** $3.21; $3.12; $3.31

Choose 100 or 500 to estimate each number.

8. the number of sheets in a package of art paper

9. the number of students in your school

Round each to the nearest ten and the nearest hundred.

10. 85   **11.** 831   **12.** 592   **13.** 6,102

Round each to the nearest thousand or thousand dollars.

14. $4,831   **15.** 9,431   **16.** $78,357   **17.** 83,560

Solve. Copy and complete the data for problems 18–20.

18. Which team won the most baseball games?

19. Which team won the fewest baseball games?

20. **Write About It** **Explain** how using a table helps you solve a problem.

Number of Baseball Games Won		
Team	**Tally**	**Number**
Cardinals	卌 卌 ‖	12
Royals	卌 卌 卌	▉
Tigers	卌 卌 卌 卌 卌	▉

Do I Need Help?

Exercises	Review Concepts	Use Extra Practice Set
1–4	pp. 24–25	Set A
5–7	pp. 26–28	Set B
8–9	pp. 30–31	Set C
10–17	pp. 32–35	Sets D and E
18–20	pp. 36–37	Set F

Foldables Use your Foldables to help you review.

Assessment

Decision Making

Broadway Elementary School is having a toy sale. Hector and Dora each have money to buy toys and games.

Should Hector and Dora put their money together and share what they buy? Or should they each buy their own toys and games?

TOY SALE

All Board Games	$ 1.25
All Computer Games	$ 7.50
All Video Games	$10.00
Yo-Yos	$ 0.75
Balls	$ 0.25
All other games and toys	$ 0.50-$3.00

You Decide!

What will they do with their money?

Hector's money

Dora's money

Read for Understanding

1. How much money does Hector have? How much money does Dora have?

2. Which games or toys cost the most? Which cost the least?

3. Can Dora buy a computer game? Why or why not? Can Hector?

4. Can Hector buy a video game? Why or why not? Can Dora?

Make Decisions

5. If Dora and Hector put their money together, how much will they have all together?

6. What are some games and toys Dora and Hector can buy and share together?

7. **What If** Dora decides to buy her own toys and games. Which kinds can she buy? Which can't she buy?

8. **What If** Hector decides to buy his own toys and games. Which kinds can he buy? Which can't he buy?

9. What are some reasons for Dora and Hector to put their money together? What are some of the reasons not to?

10. What should Hector and Dora ask each other before they decide if they should share their money?

11. Hector has a computer. He is getting a video game player next month. Should he put his money together with Dora's? Why or why not?

12. If you had the same amount of money as Hector, which game or toy would you buy?

13. Dora does not own a computer. She does have a video game player. Should she put her money together with Hector's? Why or why not?

Your Decision!

THINK
SOLVE
EXPLAIN

What do you think Dora and Hector should do? Explain.

Unit Study Guide and Review

Vocabulary

Complete. Use a word from the list.

1. The ___ for 340 is 300 + 40.

2. The ___ for five hundred two is 502.

3. Each group of 3 digits in a place-value chart is called a ___.

VOCABULARY

digits
expanded form
period
standard form

Skills and Applications

Understand number patterns. (pp. 2–3)

Find the missing numbers.
    8, 10, ■, 14, ■

Solution
Skip-count by twos from 8.
8, 10, 12, 14, 16

Find the missing numbers.

4. 3, ■, 9, ■, 15

5. 10, ■, ■, 25, 30

Read and write whole numbers. (pp. 4–11)

Write the number 124,673 in expanded form and word form.

Solution
Show the number in a place-value chart.

Thousands			Ones		
Hundreds	Tens	Ones	Hundreds	Tens	Ones
1	2	4	6	7	3

100,000 + 20,000 + 4,000 + 600 + 70 + 3 is the expanded form.
One hundred twenty four thousand, six hundred seventy-three is the word name.

Write each number in standard form.

6. three thousand, forty-five

7. one thousand, four hundred seventy-four

8. eighteen thousand, ninety-seven

Write the expanded form for each number.

9. 1,532   10. 81,479

Find the value of each underlined digit.

11. 65,1<u>9</u>3   12. <u>2</u>31,768

Foldables Use your Foldables to help you review.

Count money and make change. (pp. 12–16)

Cost: $3.74 You give: $5.00

What is your change?

Solution

Count up from $3.74 to $5.00.

$3.75 → $4.00 → $5.00
Change: $1.26

Find the change.

13. Cost: $1.78
You give: $5.00

14. Cost: $4.52
You give: $5.00

15. Cost: $8.89
You give: $10.00

16. Cost: $3.72
You give: $10.00

Compare, order, and round whole numbers and money. (pp. 24–35)

Write in order from least to greatest.
2,176; 1,892; 2,078

Solution

Line up the numbers. Compare the digits, one place at a time.

2,176
1,892 1 < 2 so 1,892 is least.
2,078 2,078 1 > 0 so 2,176 is greatest.

Least to greatest: 1,892; 2,078; 2,176

Write in order from least to greatest.

17. 689; 547; 559

18. $356; $3,800; $3,785

19. 2,576; 2,412; 1,999

Round to the nearest hundred.

20. 859   **21.** 547

22. 3,642   **23.** $4,623

Use skills and strategies to solve problems. (pp. 18–19, 36–37)

Which game had the most players?

Solution
Look at the table.

217 > 175;
217 > 215

217 is next to the game tag.

Tag had the most players.

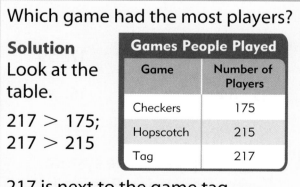

Games People Played

Game	Number of Players
Checkers	175
Hopscotch	215
Tag	217

Use data from the table for problems 24–25.

24. Which game had the least number of players?

25. Write the number of players who played tag in expanded form.

Enrichment

Roman Numerals

In Ancient Rome people used letters to name numbers.

I	V	X	L	C
1	5	10	50	100

When the same letters appear together, add to find the number.

II	XX	III
Think: $1 + 1 = 2$	**Think:** $10 + 10 = 20$	**Think:** $1 + 1 + 1 = 3$

When a letter (or letters) of lesser value is to the right of a letter of greater value, add.

VI	XII	LXI
Think: $5 + 1 = 6$	**Think:** $10 + 1 + 1 = 12$	**Think:** $50 + 10 + 1 = 61$

When a letter of lesser value is to the left of a letter of greater value, subtract.

IV	IX	XL
Think: $5 - 1 = 4$	**Think:** $10 - 1 = 9$	**Think:** $50 - 10 = 40$

Write the number.

1. VII
2. XXIV
3. LVI
4. XLI
5. XIX
6. LXIII
7. LII
8. LXXIV

Write the Roman numeral.

9. 4
10. 36
11. 53
12. 59
13. 90
14. 73
15. 64
16. 81

Solve.

17. Write and solve an addition problem using Roman numerals.

18. How is our place value system different from using Roman numerals? In which system is it easier to write numbers?

Performance Assessment

How Do You Count by 2s, 5s, and 10s?

Design a game for your class. Here are the facts you need to make the game.

- The game board is a 10-by-10 grid with the squares numbered from 1 to 100.

- There are 2 sets of game cards numbered by 2s from 2 to 20. One set is red. The other set is yellow. Each card has 1 number.

- There are 2 sets of game cards numbered by 5s from 5 to 25. One set is red. The other set is yellow. Each card has 1 number.

- Use a number cube with numbers 1–6 and small objects for playing pieces.

Include in your directions:

- Rules about who goes first
- Rules about how to win

Choose at least 2 more:

- Counting by 2s and 5s
- Counting by 10s
- Forward and backward moves
- Rounding

Hint: You may want to test out your game with a friend before handing in your final copy.

Tips For A Good Answer

- Have clear rules for the game.
- Show a game board that is correctly numbered.
- Be sure it can really be played and won!

PORTFOLIO

You may want to save this work in your portfolio.

Assessment

TECHNOLOGY Link

Place-Value Models

Tricia has 1,254 stickers in her album. How many thousands of stickers does she have? How many hundreds? How many tens? How many ones?

You can use place-value models from the *Math Tool Chest CD-ROM* to build a model.

- Start with the 4. Stamp out that many ones.
- Stamp out 5 tens.
- Stamp out 2 hundreds.
- Stamp out 1 thousand.

The number box keeps count as you stamp.

How many thousands does she have? How many hundreds? How many tens? How many ones?

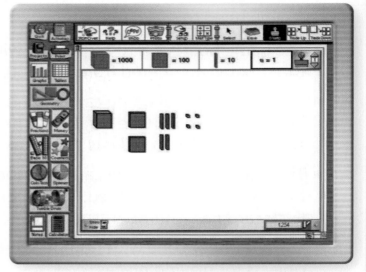

Math Tool Chest CD-ROM

Use the computer to model each number. Then name the value of each digit.

1. 1,432
2. 2,581
3. 4,173
4. 6,108

Solve.

5. Mrs. Arnold's class has collected 2,315 nuts for a class project. How many thousands of nuts do they have? How many hundreds? How many tens? How many ones?

6. **Analyze** How does using the model help you name the value of each digit in the number?

 For more practice, use Math Traveler™.

Test-Taking Tips

Sometimes you have answers to choose from when you take a test. It helps to get rid of, or eliminate, the answers that you know right away are not correct. This is called the **process of elimination**.

Cara has 100 beads on her necklace. Every tenth bead is blue. What number bead is the sixth blue bead?

A. 20 **C.** 60

B. 45 **D.** 62

You know that the answer has to be a ten. You can eliminate choices B and D.

Now you have only 2 choices, A and C. This gives you a better chance of choosing the correct answer, C.

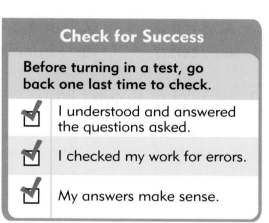

Check for Success

Before turning in a test, go back one last time to check.

✓ I understood and answered the questions asked.

✓ I checked my work for errors.

✓ My answers make sense.

Read each problem. Eliminate any answer choices you know are wrong. Choose the best answer.

1. 88 is less than ▮.

   A. 42   **C.** 82
   B. 55   **D.** 98

2. Which is 100 more than 5,421?

   F. 6,421   **H.** 5,431
   G. 5,521   **I.** 5,321

3. 487 rounded to the nearest ten is ▮.

   A. 400   **C.** 490
   B. 450   **D.** 500

4. Which is not less than 4,127?

   F. 105   **H.** 2,063
   G. 697   **I.** 5,111

5. What number is missing?
   15, 20, 25, 30, ▮, 40

   A. 10   **C.** 45
   B. 35   **D.** 62

6. $892 rounded to the nearest hundred dollars is ▮.

   F. $1,000   **H.** $900
   G. $982   **I.** $800

Test Prep

PART 1 • Multiple Choice

Choose the best answer.

1. Which is the greatest number? (p. 4)

   A. 8 tens   **C.** 8 hundreds
   B. 9 tens   **D.** 9 hundreds

2. Skip-count to complete the pattern. (p. 2)

   35, 40, 45, ▮, 55, 60

   F. 65   **H.** 48
   G. 50   **I.** 30

3. Jenna is playing a game with her brother. Which game piece is shaped like a rectangle?

   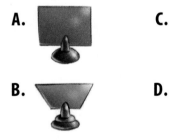

   A.   **C.**

   B.   **D.**

4. What counting pattern does this number line show? (p. 2)

   0   2   4   6   8   10

   F. Adding 1
   G. Skip-counting by twos
   H. Skip-counting by fives
   I. Skip-counting by tens

5. Which is true about this figure?

   A. It is a square.
   B. It is a trapezoid.
   C. It has 3 sides.
   D. It has 4 sides.

6. Game cards follow this pattern: 10, 20, 30, 40, and so on. Which of the following cards could be part of the game? (p. 2)

   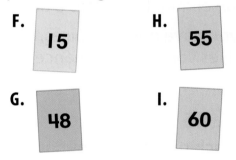

   F. 15   **H.** 55

   G. 48   **I.** 60

7. Which item weighs less than 1 pound?

   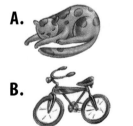

   A.   **C.**

   B.   **D.**

8. Find the missing number.

   18, 21, ▮, 27, 30

   F. 22   **H.** 26
   G. 24   **I.** 28

PART 2 • Short Response/Grid In

Record your answers on the answer sheet provided by your teacher or on a sheet of paper.

9. Players can score 12 points in the first round and 12 points in the second round. How many points can players score in these 2 rounds?

THINK SOLVE EXPLAIN

10. What is the rule for this table?

Input	1	3	5	7
Output	8	10	12	14

11. Write the amount. (p. 14)

12. What time is shown on this clock?

13. Write the number 4,732 in word form. (p. 6)

Use data from the table for problems 14–15.

Points Scored in Kickball

Class	Number of Points
Room A	9
Room B	5
Room C	4
Room D	7

14. Which class scored the least number of points? (p. 26)

15. List the room numbers in order from least to greatest number of points. (p. 26)

16. Chantel scored 94 points in a game. Steven scored 104 points. How can you tell quickly who scored more points without comparing each digit? (p. 26)

PART 3 • Extended Response

Record your answer on a sheet of paper. Show your work.

THINK SOLVE EXPLAIN

17. The player with the most points is the winner. Which player came in second place? Explain your answer.

Carlos	136
Chun	156
Brooke	132
Devon	158

Test Prep

What Do I Need to Know?

There are 2 clownfish in one tank. There are 5 clownfish in another tank. How many clownfish are there in all?

Addition Properties and Strategies

What Will I Learn?

In this chapter you will learn to

- use the properties of addition
- add 2- and 3-digit numbers
- estimate sums
- use skills and strategies to solve problems

How Do I Read Math?

When you read a mathematics book, sometimes you read words and symbols and sometimes you read only symbols.

Here are different ways to read the addition sentence, $13 + 25 = 38$.

- **13 plus 25 equals 38.**
- **The sum of 13 and 25 is 38.**

VOCABULARY

- addend
- sum
- Commutative Property
- Identity Property
- Associative Property
- pattern
- regroup
- estimate

Foldables

Use your Foldables to help you with chapter concepts.

1. Fold a sheet of paper into 3 parts.
2. Open. Fold again, 1 inch from the top.
3. Unfold and draw lines along the folds.
4. Label as shown. Record what you learn.

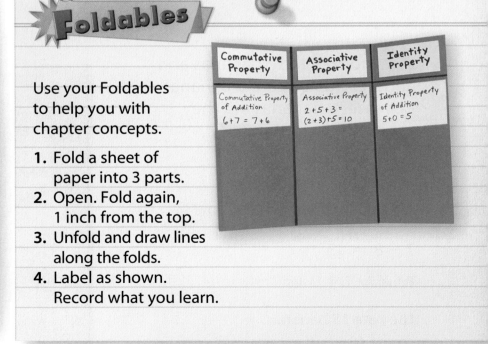

Commutative Property	Associative Property	Identity Property
Commutative Property of Addition $6+7 = 7+6$	Associative Property $2+5+3 = (2+3)+5=10$	Identity Property of Addition $5+0 = 5$

3.1

Algebra: Addition Properties

Learn

At the Indianapolis Zoo in Indiana, 15 monkeys were doing tricks. Then the 2 monkeys shown in the picture joined them. How many monkeys were doing tricks in all?

Find: 15 + 2

Use a Number Line

Think: Start at 15. Count on 16, 17.

Count on mentally.

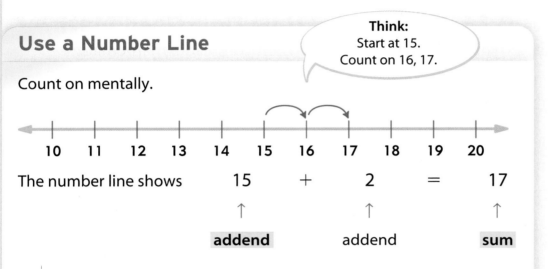

The number line shows   15   +   2   =   17

        ↑   ↑   ↑

    addend   addend   **sum**

There were 17 monkeys doing tricks.

One monkey ate 7 bananas and another monkey ate 8 bananas. How many bananas did they eat in all?

Find: 7 + 8

Use Doubles Plus One

$7 + 8 = 15$

Think: $7 + 7 = 14$ and 1 more is 15.

They ate 15 bananas.

What If 3 monkeys are doing tricks and 5 more monkeys join them. No more monkeys come. How many monkeys are doing tricks?

Use these addition properties to help you add mentally.

Use Properties

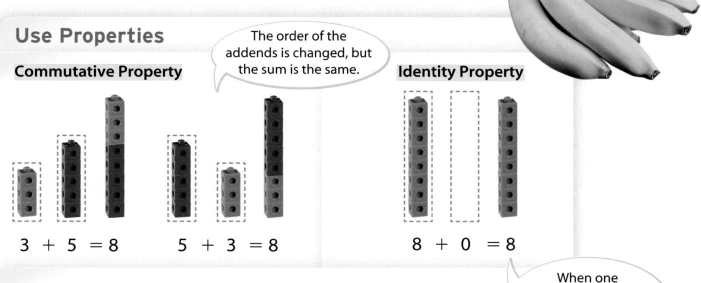

Commutative Property

The order of the addends is changed, but the sum is the same.

$3 + 5 = 8$ $5 + 3 = 8$

Identity Property

$8 + 0 = 8$

When one addend is zero, the sum is the same as the other addend.

There are 8 monkeys doing tricks.

Suppose 3 monkeys join the 8 monkeys. Then 2 more monkeys come. How many monkeys are doing tricks now?

Find: 8 + 3 + 2

Use Properties

$8 + 3 + 2 =$

$3 + 8 + 2 =$ ← Use the Commutative Property to change the order.

$3 + (8 + 2) =$ ← Use the **Associative Property** which states that grouping the addends does not change the sum. Use parentheses. Look for ways of making a ten.

$3 + 10 = 13$

There are 13 monkeys doing tricks.

Try It **Add. Show how you used strategies and properties.**

1. $7 + 2$ **2.** $6 + 3 + 5$ **3.** $6 + 5$ **4.** $0 + 9$ **5.** $4 + 0 + 6$

6. 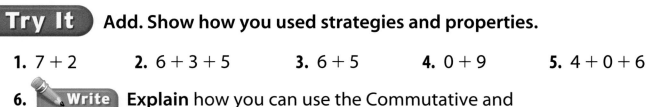 **Write About It** **Explain** how you can use the Commutative and Associative Properties to add $6 + 8 + 4$ mentally.

Practice and Problem Solving

Add. Show how you use strategies and properties.

7. $7 + 4$ 8. $9 + 4$ 9. $23 + 7$ 10. $6 + 0$ 11. $14 + 8$

12. $4 + 22$ 13. $9 + 7$ 14. $8 + 8$ 15. $6 + 14$ 16. $7 + 0$

17. $3 + 5 + 3$ 18. $8 + 5 + 2$ 19. $4 + 3 + 6$ 20. $5 + 7 + 5$

21. $6 + 2 + 4 + 1$ 22. $1 + 7 + 1 + 3$ 23. $2 + 6 + 8 + 0$ 24. $1 + 2 + 9 + 2$

ⓧ Algebra Find each missing number.

25. $9 + 1 = 1 + \blacksquare$ 26. $4 + \blacksquare = 4$ 27. $7 + \blacksquare + 9 = 16$

28. $\blacksquare + 6 + 2 = 6 + 10$ 29. $(5 + 4) + (2 + 6) = 10 + \blacksquare$

Solve.

THINK SOLVE EXPLAIN

30. **Analyze** Which property can you use to find the missing number? Explain how.
$4 + 7 + 8 = 7 + 4 + \blacksquare$

31. In Iria's classroom the Animal Corner has 4 fish, 3 turtles, 6 mice, and 2 parakeets. How many animals are there in all?

32. **Career** On Monday Pat walks 5 dogs. On Tuesday he walks 2 more dogs than on Monday. How many dogs does he walk in all? Explain.

33. **Make It Right** Tami added 9 and 8. Tell what mistake she made, then correct it.

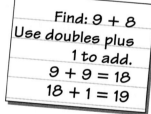

Find: $9 + 8$
Use doubles plus 1 to add.
$9 + 9 = 18$
$18 + 1 = 19$

THINK SOLVE EXPLAIN

✓ Spiral Review and Test Prep

34. What is the missing number? (p. 53)
$\blacksquare + 6 = 13$ $6 + \blacksquare = 13$
A. 19   C. 7
B. 8   D. 3

35. Which has a sum of 12? (p. 52)
F. $7 + 7$ H. $8 + 3$
G. $6 + 7$ I. $5 + 7$

Round to the nearest hundred. (p. 32)

36. 549   37. 791   38. 1,297   39. 3,333   40. 23,764

Extra Practice page 68, Set A

BASEBALL BATS

TIME FOR KIDS

Where there's a baseball team, there are usually bats. But the New York Mets once found themselves with nearly 30,000 bats too many. These bats weren't made of wood, however. They were alive! The team's spring-training stadium in Port St. Lucie, Florida, was home to a colony of Brazilian free-tailed bats.

How did thousands of furry bats end up in a stadium? In Florida, buildings are replacing forests where bats live. So bats are being forced to live closer to people.

HOME SAFE

The 4-inch bats were making a giant mess in the stadium. They produced several inches of droppings each day. So, one night while the bats were out, special screens were put up in the stadium to keep them from returning. That left many bats without a home.

To save them, the town built a bat house in the stadium. It has 160 spaces in which the creatures live. Up to 15,000 bats can live comfortably there. The Bat House is a home run with bats!

Problem Solving

Reading Skill **Problem and Solution** What problem is presented in this article? What is the solution?

1. A Brazilian free-tailed bat measures 4 inches long. About how much do 2 bats measure?

2. The Bat House was built to house up to 15,000 bats. Write that number in expanded form.

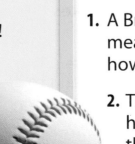

3.2

Algebra: Addition Patterns

Learn

Marisa learned that ants are social insects. They live in communities or groups. She estimates there are 800 ants in one colony and 500 in another colony. How many ants are there in all?

VOCABULARY

pattern

Find: 800 + 500

Facts and Patterns

$8 + 5 = 13$
$80 + 50 = 130$
$800 + 500 = 1,300$

Think: 8 ones + 5 ones = 13 ones
8 tens + 5 tens = 13 tens
8 hundreds + 5 hundreds = 13 hundreds

A **pattern** is a series of numbers or figures that follows a rule.

There are 1,300 ants in both colonies.

Try It

Write the number that makes each sentence true.

1. $4 + 5 = \blacksquare$
$40 + 50 = \blacksquare$
$400 + 500 = \blacksquare$

2. $\blacksquare + 4 = 11$
$\blacksquare + 40 = 110$
$\blacksquare + 400 = 1,100$

3. $3 + \blacksquare = 8$
$30 + \blacksquare = 80$
$300 + \blacksquare = 800$

4. **Write About It** **Describe** how you use facts and patterns to find $500 + 500$ mentally.

Practice and Problem Solving

Write the number that makes each sentence true.

5. $3 + 6 = $ ▮
   $30 + 60 = $ ▮
   $300 + 600 = $ ▮

6. ▮ $+ 7 = 15$
   ▮ $+ 70 = 150$
   ▮ $+ 700 = 1,500$

7. $4 + $ ▮ $= 8$
   $40 + $ ▮ $= 80$
   $400 + $ ▮ $= 800$

Add. Use mental math.

8. $200 + 800$

9. $200 + 900$

10. $700 + 600$

11. $800 + 800$

12. $4,000 + 1,000$

13. $3,000 + 4,000$

14. $500 + 60 + 20$

15. $300 + 70 + 30$

Find the missing digit.

★16. 6▮$+ 34 = 94$

★17. $30 + $▮$1 = 121$

★18. ▮$30 + 700 = 1,430$

Solve. Use data from the bar graph for problems 19–21.

19. **Mental Math** Which 2 animals got 1,000 votes in all?

20. Which animal got the most votes? How do you know?

21. Which group has more votes, dogs and cats or horses and cows?

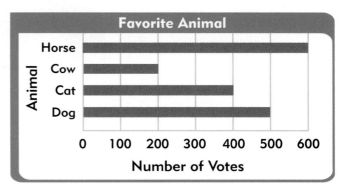

22. **Analyze** How would you add $300 + 72$ mentally?

23. Beth had 105 dog stickers and 50 cat stickers. How many items did she have altogether?

Spiral Review and Test Prep

24. Laura buys a pet toy. She pays with a one-dollar bill and gets back a quarter and a dime for change. How much did the toy cost? (p.14)

    A. $0.35
    B. $0.65
    C. $0.70
    D. $1.00

25. What is the value of the underlined digit in $5\underline{4},048$? (p. 6)

    F. 40,000
    G. 4,000
    H. 400
    I. 40

26. $8 + 4$

27. $3 + 6$

28. $9 + 7$

29. $6 + 9$

30. $2 + 5$

3.3 Explore Regrouping in Addition

Hands On Activity

You can use place-value models to explore addition with regrouping. When you **regroup**, you rename a number in a different way.

Find: 154 + 258

VOCABULARY
regroup

You Will Need
• place-value models

Use Models

STEP 1

Show 154 as 1 hundred, 5 tens, 4 ones and 258 as 2 hundreds, 5 tens, 8 ones.

STEP 2

Combine the ones models. Regroup if necessary.

STEP 3

Combine the tens models. Regroup if necessary.

STEP 4

Combine the hundreds models. Find the sum.

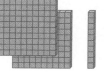
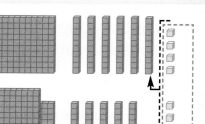

Explain Your Thinking

1. How do you model each addend?

2. Is it necessary to regroup the ones? How do you know?

3. Is it necessary to regroup the tens? How do you know?

4. Is it necessary to regroup the hundreds? How do you know?

5. What is the sum of 154 and 258?

Technology Link

Use the place-value tool in **Math Tool Chest** to add whole numbers.

Your Turn

Find each sum.

6. 61 + 13

7. 46 + 104

8. 215 + 36

9. 154 + 327

10. 282 + 119

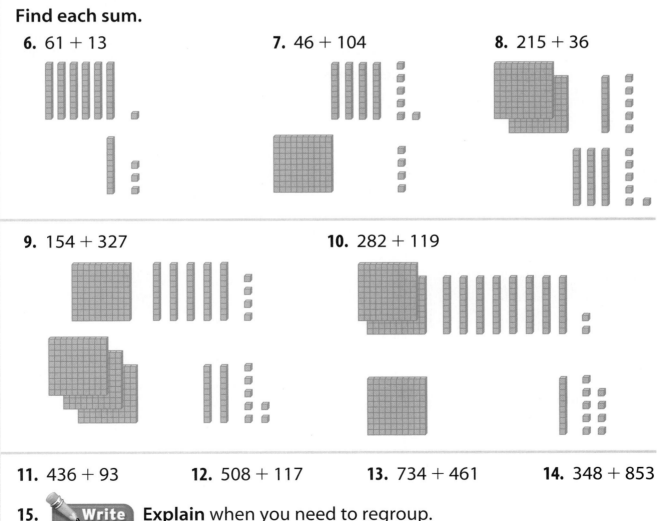

11. 436 + 93

12. 508 + 117

13. 734 + 461

14. 348 + 853

15. **Write About It** **Explain** when you need to regroup.

3.4 Add Whole Numbers

Learn

Alligators can be dangerous when protecting their nests. In Central Florida, 278 American alligator nests were counted. In South Florida, 456 American alligator nests were counted. How many nests were counted in all?

Find: 456 + 278

Let's see how to connect models to paper and pencil.

278 nests

456 nests

Make Connections

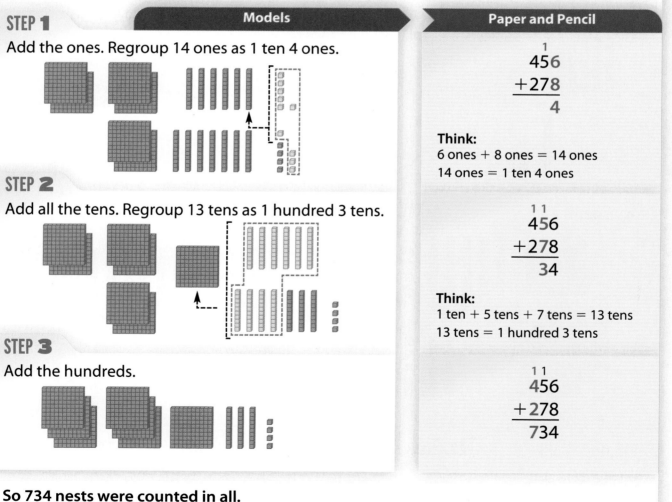

	Models	**Paper and Pencil**
STEP 1 Add the ones. Regroup 14 ones as 1 ten 4 ones.		$\begin{array}{r} {}^{1} \\ 456 \\ +278 \\ \hline 4 \end{array}$ **Think:** 6 ones + 8 ones = 14 ones 14 ones = 1 ten 4 ones
STEP 2 Add all the tens. Regroup 13 tens as 1 hundred 3 tens.		$\begin{array}{r} {}^{1\,1} \\ 456 \\ +278 \\ \hline 34 \end{array}$ **Think:** 1 ten + 5 tens + 7 tens = 13 tens 13 tens = 1 hundred 3 tens
STEP 3 Add the hundreds.		$\begin{array}{r} {}^{1\,1} \\ 456 \\ +278 \\ \hline 734 \end{array}$

So 734 nests were counted in all.

A nature photographer spent $978 on new equipment.
He spent $94 on film. How much did he spend in all?

Find: $978 + $94

Add Dollar Amounts

STEP 1

Add the ones.
Regroup if necessary.

$$\begin{array}{r} ^{1} \\ \$978 \\ +94 \\ \hline 2 \end{array}$$

Think:
12 ones = 1 ten 2 ones

STEP 2

Add all the tens.
Regroup if necessary.

$$\begin{array}{r} ^{1\,1} \\ \$978 \\ +94 \\ \hline 72 \end{array}$$

Think:
17 tens = 1 hundred 7 tens

STEP 3

Add all the hundreds.
Regroup if necessary.

$$\begin{array}{r} ^{1\,1} \\ \$978 \\ +94 \\ \hline \$1,072 \end{array}$$

Think:
10 hundreds = 1 thousand

The nature photographer spent $1,072 in all.

Add Dollars and Change

Add as you would
whole numbers.

You can also
use a calculator.

Write the dollar sign
and the decimal point
in the sum.

$$\begin{array}{r} ^{1} \\ \$2.12 \\ +5.78 \\ \hline \$7.90 \end{array}$$

Try It Find each sum.

1. $\begin{array}{r} 44 \\ +26 \\ \hline \end{array}$

2. $\begin{array}{r} 23 \\ +74 \\ \hline \end{array}$

3. $\begin{array}{r} 905 \\ +812 \\ \hline \end{array}$

4. $\begin{array}{r} \$8.74 \\ +7.29 \\ \hline \end{array}$

5. $\begin{array}{r} \$9.83 \\ +9.76 \\ \hline \end{array}$

6. $\begin{array}{r} 689 \\ +49 \\ \hline \end{array}$

7. $\begin{array}{r} 857 \\ +603 \\ \hline \end{array}$

8. $\begin{array}{r} \$6.50 \\ +2.75 \\ \hline \end{array}$

9. $\begin{array}{r} \$3.92 \\ +3.92 \\ \hline \end{array}$

10. $\begin{array}{r} 404 \\ +782 \\ \hline \end{array}$

11. **Write About It** **Explain** the steps you would use
to add 365 + 208.

Practice and Problem Solving

Find each sum.

12. 472	13. $512	14. 905	15. 485	16. $7.73
+803	+ 309	+398	+ 80	+ 6.94

17. $9.76+$5.40   **18.** 167+708   **19.** $156+$999   **20.** $8.87+$2.05

21. $76.40+$34.27   **22.** 789 + 657   **23.** 870+456   **24.** 456+654

(x) Algebra Find each missing digit.

25. 456	26. ▉27	27. 7▉2	28. 5▉8
+65▉	+670	+594	+ ▉4▉
1,110	1,197	1,376	1,187

Solve.

29. Career Anna works as a tour guide at the zoo. She earned $547 in July and $568 in August. How much did she earn in all?

30. Jon bought a frame for $2.78 and a picture for $3.65. What is the total cost?

★31. Number Sense Sue gets 300 when she rounds a number to the nearest hundred. What is the least number it could be? What is the greatest number it could be?

32. Make It Right Look at Hal's work. What was his mistake? Show how to correct it.

THINK SOLVE EXPLAIN

```
   1
  936
 +599
 1,525
```

Spiral Review and Test Prep

33. Pete has $10 to buy 2 toys at $4 each. How much will be left? (p. 14)

    A. $8   **C.** $4

    B. $6   **D.** $2

34. Order from least to greatest. 564; 463; 465 (p.26)

    F. 564; 463; 465 **H.** 465; 564; 463

    G. 463; 465; 564 **I.** 463; 564; 465

Find each missing number. Tell what property you used. (p. 52)

35. ▉ + 0 = 5   **36.** 2 + (3 + 4) = 2 + (4 + ▉)   **37.** (5 + 6) + ▉ = 5 + (▉ + 7)

12. 1,275 17. $15.16 25. 4

Extra Practice page 68, Set C

LEAST SUM GAME

Pick digits for addends to create the least sum.

Ready

Players: 2 or more
You will need:
Digit Deck, paper, pencil

Set

Shuffle the Digit Deck cards and place the deck face down.

Make a game sheet and scorecard for each player.

GO!

▶ Player 1 picks a card and each player records the number in any one of the boxes. If a wild card is drawn, each player can choose any digit.

▶ Do not let the other player see where you write the number. Once the digit is written in the box, you cannot change or erase it.

▶ Players take turns picking cards and recording in boxes.

▶ When all boxes are filled, each player finds the sum.

▶ The player with the least sum gets 1 point.

▶ If the sums are the same, each player gets 1 point.

▶ The first player to get 5 points wins.

3.5 Estimate Sums

Learn

Veterinarians took care of 349 animals in one week and 364 animals another week. About how many animals did they care for in 2 weeks?

Sometimes an exact sum is not needed. You can **estimate** by finding an answer that is close to the exact answer.

Estimate: 349 + 364

VOCABULARY
estimate

Use Rounding

STEP 1

Round each addend to the nearest hundred.

$$349 \rightarrow 300$$
$$+364 \rightarrow +400$$

STEP 2

Add to find the estimated sum.

$$\begin{array}{r} 300 \\ +400 \\ \hline 700 \end{array}$$

The veterinarians saw about 700 animals.

Round to . . .

the nearest ten.

$$89 \rightarrow 90$$
$$+902 \rightarrow +900$$
$$\overline{\ \ 990}$$

the nearest thousand.

$$1,543 \rightarrow 2,000$$
$$+2,087 \rightarrow +2,000$$
$$\overline{\ \ 4,000}$$

Think: 1,543 is between 1,000 and 2,000. It is closer to 2,000.

Try It Estimate each sum. Tell how you rounded.

1. 46 + 38

2. 112 + 95

3. 220 + 370

4. 1,345 + 2,507

5. **Write About It** How can you estimate 278 + 79 two different ways?

Practice and Problem Solving

Estimate each sum. Tell how you rounded.

6. $13 + 72$

7. $417 + 523$

8. $345 + 710$

9. $781 + 15$

10. $1,432 + 6,573$

11. $5,385 + 3,710$

12. $6,321 + 515$

13. $387 + 166$

★14. $23,034 + 12,987$

★15. $31,256 + 57,009$

★16. $87,231 + 10,123$

(X) Algebra Estimate. Write $>$ or $<$ to make true sentences.

17. $48 + 17$ ● 70

18. $376 + 497$ ● 800

19. $613 + 821$ ● $1,500$

Solve.

20. **Analyze** Sam says that $108 + 55$ is about 170. Would 200 also be a reasonable estimate? Explain.

21. Ms. Lin spends $158 on medicine and $95 on pet treats. About how much does she spend in all?

Link to SCIENCE

Over short distances, cheetahs can reach speeds of up to 113 kilometers an hour, making them the fastest animals on land.

22. **What If** A cheetah could keep up that speed. About how many kilometers would it travel in 2 hours? Explain.

Spiral Review and Test Prep

23. Which problem has a sum of about 500? (p. 64)

    A. $297 + 352$ C. $520 + 189$

    B. $387 + 365$ D. $198 + 267$

24. There are 9 fish and 4 frogs in a tank. Which shows how many animals in all? (p. 52)

    F. $9 + 4 = 13$ H. $13 + 4 = 17$

    G. $13 + 9 = 22$ I. $9 + 5 = 14$

Describe and complete the skip-counting pattern. (p. 2)

25. 100, ■, 90, ■, 80, ■, 70

26. 11, ■, 15, 17, 19, ■, ■

3.6

Problem Solving: Skill
Estimate or Exact Answer

Read

There are 212 pigs at a farm. There are also 199 chickens and 98 ducks. About how many animals are at the farm?

- **What do you know?**
  The number of each animal

- **What do you need to find?**
  About how many animals are at the farm

Plan

Since the problem asks "**about** how many," you do not need to find the exact number of animals. You can **estimate**.

Solve

Round each number to the nearest hundred. Then add.

$$212 + 199 + 98$$
$$\downarrow \quad\quad \downarrow \quad\quad \downarrow$$
$$200 + 200 + 100 = 500$$

There are about 500 animals at the farm.

▶ **Sometimes an exact answer is needed.**

The farmer wants to get a tag for each animal. How many tags should he buy?

Since the farmer does not want to have too many tags, an exact answer is needed.

$$212 + 199 + 98 = 509$$

The farmer needs to buy 509 tags.

Look Back

Are your answers reasonable?

1. **Write About It** **Explain** when you would need an exact answer or an estimated answer.

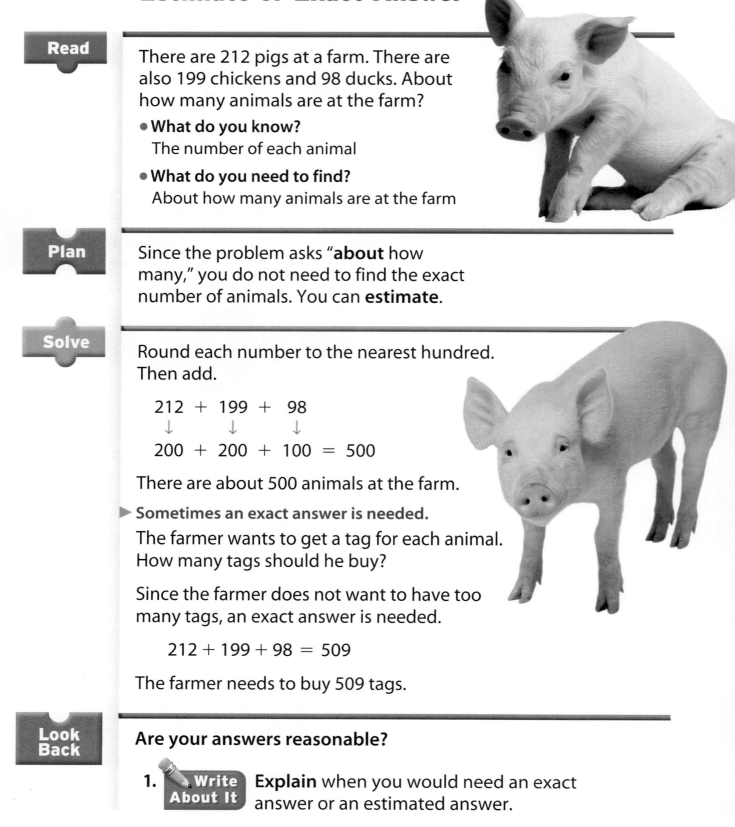

Solve. Explain why your answer is an estimate or exact answer.

2. Last month the farmer had 262 chicken eggs and 179 duck eggs. In all, how many eggs does the farmer have?

3. The farmer bought 19 cows in May and 22 in June. In July he bought only 9 cows. Did the farmer buy more than 40 cows in all?

Mixed Strategy Review

4. Ms. Jenkins has 94 books about parrots and 128 books about owls. How many books does she have in all on the 2 types of birds?

5. Stanley wants to buy a fish that costs $5.28. He uses a ten-dollar bill to pay for the fish. How much change should Stanley get back?

6. ✎ **Write a problem** using this addition sentence: $167 + 184 = 351$

Choose a Strategy
- Logical Reasoning
- Draw a Picture or Diagram
- Make a Graph
- Act It Out
- Make a Table or List
- Find a Pattern
- Guess and Check
- Write an Equation
- Work Backward
- Solve a Simpler Problem

Use data from the table for problems 7–10.

7. Find the sum of the number of horses and cows.

8. Risha feeds the chickens and ducks each day. Does she feed more than 400 of them a day? Explain.

9. About how many animals are at Green Willow Farm?

10. ✎ Write About It Rewrite problem 8 so an exact answer is needed. Explain why it is needed.

GREEN WILLOW FARM

Animal	Number of Animals
Chicken	203
Cow	62
Duck	231
Horse	89
Pig	208
Sheep	197

Problem Solving

Extra Practice

Set A **Add.** (pp. 52–54)

1. $7 + 5$	**2.** $9 + 7$	**3.** $8 + 3$	**4.** $6 + 0$
5. $16 + 4$	**6.** $6 + 3$	**7.** $8 + 9$	**8.** $13 + 6$
9. $3 + 8 + 4$	**10.** $6 + 8 + 4$	**11.** $9 + 3 + 4 + 1$	**12.** $7 + 5 + 7 + 2$
13. $3 + 7 + 6$	**14.** $5 + 6 + 7$	**15.** $4 + 9 + 6$	**16.** $8 + 8 + 4$

Set B **Write the number that makes each sentence true.** (pp. 56–57)

17. $5 + 6 =$ ▦
 $50 + 60 =$ ▦
 $500 + 600 =$ ▦

18. $6 + 8 =$ ▦
 $60 + 80 =$ ▦
 $600 + 800 =$ ▦

19. $3 +$ ▦ $= 12$
 $30 +$ ▦ $= 120$
 $300 +$ ▦ $= 1,200$

Set C **Add. Check for reasonableness.** (pp. 58–62)

20. $\begin{array}{r} 385 \\ +611 \\ \hline \end{array}$	**21.** $\begin{array}{r} \$324 \\ +108 \\ \hline \end{array}$	**22.** $\begin{array}{r} \$7.22 \\ +5.68 \\ \hline \end{array}$	**23.** $\begin{array}{r} 795 \\ +462 \\ \hline \end{array}$
24. $\begin{array}{r} \$2.31 \\ +2.04 \\ \hline \end{array}$	**25.** $\begin{array}{r} 275 \\ +718 \\ \hline \end{array}$	**26.** $\begin{array}{r} 425 \\ +819 \\ \hline \end{array}$	**27.** $\begin{array}{r} 298 \\ +801 \\ \hline \end{array}$
28. $\begin{array}{r} 562 \\ +498 \\ \hline \end{array}$	**29.** $\begin{array}{r} 705 \\ +\ \ 68 \\ \hline \end{array}$	**30.** $\begin{array}{r} 299 \\ +560 \\ \hline \end{array}$	**31.** $\begin{array}{r} 948 \\ +763 \\ \hline \end{array}$

Set D **Estimate each sum. Tell how you rounded.** (pp. 64–65)

32. $21 + 67$	**33.** $339 + 578$	**34.** $683 + 509$	**35.** $458 + 27$
36. $789 + 667$	**37.** $1,567 + 4,356$	**38.** $3,780 + 5,705$	**39.** $8,425 + 378$

Set E **Solve.** (pp. 66–67)

40. Nan had a 6-inch snake. It grew 2 inches, then 2 more inches. How long is it now?

41. A lion weighs 432 pounds. A tiger weighs 661 pounds. About how much do both weigh together?

LOG ON www.mmhmath.com
For more practice and Chapter Self-Check Test

Add.

1. 19 + 9

2. 8 + 7

3. 0 + 6

4. 14 + 6

5. 15 + 6

6. 9 + 0

7. 3 + 5 + 7

8. 5 + 0 + 2

Write the number that makes each sentence true.

9. $6 + 2 = \blacksquare$
$60 + 20 = \blacksquare$
$600 + 200 = \blacksquare$

10. $4 + \blacksquare = 13$
$\blacksquare + 90 = \blacksquare$
$\blacksquare + \blacksquare = 1{,}300$

11. $5 + \blacksquare = 12$
$50 + \blacksquare = \blacksquare$
$\blacksquare + \blacksquare = 1{,}200$

Add.

12. 24 + 53

13. $25 + $758

14. 412 + 591

15. 645 + 291

16. $5.39 + $2.61

17. 581 + 476

18. 359 + 582

19. 673 + 172

Estimate each sum.

20. 19 + 71

21. 527 + 563

22. 457 + 810

23. 483 + 15 + 42

Solve.

24. Kyle has 6 clown fish and 7 guppies in his fish tank. Ralph has 3 more fish than Kyle. How many fish does Ralph have?

25. **Write About It** The pet shop groomed 246 dogs in June and 372 dogs in July. Is the total number of dogs groomed more than 600? Explain.

Do I Need Help?

Exercises	Review Concepts	Use Extra Practice Set
1–8	pp. 52–54	Set A
9–11	pp. 56–57	Set B
12–19	pp. 58–62	Set C
20–23	pp. 64–65	Set D
24–25	pp. 66–67	Set E

 **Foldables** Use your Foldables to help you review.

What Do I Need to Know?

The female porcupine weighs 25 pounds. The male porcupine weighs 12 pounds more. How many pounds does the male porcupine weigh?

Add Greater Numbers

What Will I Learn?

In this chapter you will learn to

- find the sum of greater numbers
- add more than two numbers
- use skills and strategies to solve problems

How Do I Read Math?

When you read a mathematics book, sometimes you read words and symbols and sometimes you read only symbols.

These number sentences show how numbers are related:

- $8 + 2 = 10$
- $80 + 20 = 100$

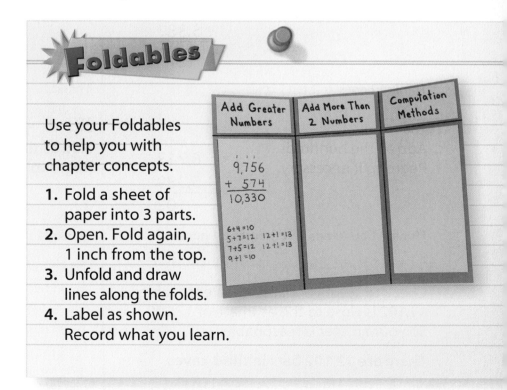

Use your Foldables to help you with chapter concepts.

1. Fold a sheet of paper into 3 parts.
2. Open. Fold again, 1 inch from the top.
3. Unfold and draw lines along the folds.
4. Label as shown. Record what you learn.

4.1 Add Greater Numbers

Learn

Little brown bats sleep as they cling to the ceilings of caves. There are 6,713 bats in a cave. In another cave nearby there are 5,389 bats. How many bats live in the 2 caves in all?

Find: 6,713 + 5,389

Estimate:

$$6{,}713 \rightarrow 7{,}000$$
$$+5{,}389 \rightarrow +5{,}000$$
$$12{,}000$$

Use Paper and Pencil

STEP 1
Add the ones.
Regroup if necessary.

$$\overset{1}{6{,}713}$$
$$+5{,}389$$
$$2$$

Think: 12 ones = 1 ten 2 ones

STEP 2
Add all the tens.
Regroup if necessary.

$$\overset{1\,1}{6{,}713}$$
$$+5{,}389$$
$$02$$

Think: 10 tens = 1 hundred 0 tens

STEP 3
Add all the hundreds.
Regroup if necessary.

$$\overset{1\,1\,1}{6{,}713}$$
$$+5{,}389$$
$$102$$

Think: 11 hundreds = 1 thousand 1 hundred

STEP 4
Add all the thousands.
Regroup if necessary.

$$\overset{1\,1\,1}{6{,}713}$$
$$+\;5{,}389$$
$$12{,}102$$

Think: 12 thousands = 1 ten thousand 2 thousands

Check to see if your answer is reasonable.
12,102 is close to the estimate of 12,000.
So your answer is reasonable.

There are 12,102 bats in the 2 caves.

Ms. Beatty films bats in caves. She spends $75.82 for equipment at one store and $89.20 at another store. How much money does Ms. Beatty spend in all on equipment?

Find: $75.82 + $89.20

There's More Than One Way!

Use Paper and Pencil

STEP 1

Line up the decimal points to line up the place value.

Add as you would whole numbers.

$75.82
+ 89.20

STEP 2

Regroup each place if necessary.

Write a dollar sign and decimal point in the answer.

$$\begin{array}{r} {\scriptstyle 1\,1} \\ \$75.82 \\ +\ \ 89.20 \\ \hline \$165.02 \end{array}$$

Use a Calculator

Press:

[7] [5] [.] [8] [2] [+] [8] [9] [.] [2] [0] [=]

Display:

```
75.82+89.20=
        165.02
```

Write a dollar sign in the answer.

Ms. Beatty spends $165.02 on equipment.

Try It Add. Check for reasonableness.

1. 2,345
   +1,423

2. 2,538
   + 974

3. $36.55
   + 28.99

4. $56.76
   + 74.28

5. 3,492
   + 131

6.  **Write About It** **Explain** how finding the sum of 3-digit numbers is similar to and different from finding the sum of 4-digit numbers.

Practice and Problem Solving

Add. Check for reasonableness.

7.	8.	9.	10.	11.
3,434 +2,324	4,567 +2,837	5,856 +7,594	3,685 + 886	9,756 + 574

12.	13.	14.	15.	16.
$65.64 + 47.73	$64.87 + 8.36	9,475 +8,869	$87.89 + 15.47	9,758 + 876

17. $4{,}251 + 6{,}729$ **18.** $\$53.62 + \$8.38$ **19.** $9{,}762 + 5{,}618$

★**20.** $34{,}364 + 77{,}612$ ★**21.** $\$476.39 + \$86.43$ ★**22.** $245{,}769 + 84{,}967$

ⓧ Algebra Complete. Write > or <.

23. $5{,}324 + 6{,}912 \ \bullet \ 4{,}798 + 8{,}145$ **24.** $4{,}813 + 5{,}124 \ \bullet \ 3{,}789 + 5{,}485$

25. $9{,}352 + 1{,}942 \ \bullet \ 8{,}978 + 2{,}003$ **26.** $6{,}786 + 987 \ \bullet \ 997 + 7{,}034$

Solve.

27. Hank pays $1,198 for some new cameras and $976 for a night lens. How much did he spend in all?

28. ✎ **Write About It** **Explain** how estimation might help to check the reasonableness of your answer. *THINK SOLVE EXPLAIN*

29. Science A bottlenosed dolphin may dive up to 1,476 feet below the ocean's surface. How deep is that to the nearest 10? Nearest 1,000?

30. Make It Right Here is how Keith added $3{,}494 + 5{,}298$. Tell what mistake he made. Explain how to correct it. *THINK SOLVE EXPLAIN*

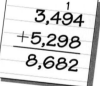

$$\begin{array}{r} \overset{1}{3{,}494} \\ +5{,}298 \\ \hline 8{,}682 \end{array}$$

✔ Spiral Review and Test Prep

31. What is the missing number? (p. 52)

$\blacksquare + 6 = 14 \quad 6 + \blacksquare = 14$

A. 19 **C.** 7

B. 8 **D.** 3

32. Which is another name for 120? (p. 6)

F. $12 + 10$ **H.** $100 + 2$

G. $10 + 20$ **I.** $100 + 20$

Round to the nearest thousand. (p. 34)

33. 5,497 **34.** 791 **35.** 1,697 **36.** 3,333 **37.** 23,764

> ꞏ23. 12.$113.37 7. 5,758

Extra Practice page 82, Set A

Writing for Math

The number of tickets sold for the dog show on Friday is 2,345. For Saturday 2,971 tickets were sold. The dog show organizers estimate that 5,000 programs should be enough for these 2 days. What do you think? Explain.

Jillian's Response

✓ **THINK** Estimate, then add to find the number of programs needed. Compare the actual sum with 5,000.

✓ **SOLVE** Estimate:

$$
\begin{array}{r}
2,345 \\
+\ 2,971 \\
\end{array}
\rightarrow
\begin{array}{r}
2,000 \\
+\ 3,000 \\
\hline
5,000 \\
\end{array}
$$

Find the actual sum.
2,345 + 2,971 = 5,316 > 5,000
5,000 programs will not be enough.

✓ **EXPLAIN** I used rounding. The estimated sum was 5,000. Then I added 2,345 and 2,971 to get 5,316. 5,316 is greater than 5,000. There will not be enough programs.

To check, I used the Commutative Property. 2,971 + 2,345 = 5,316, so my answer makes sense.

Teacher's Response

← Jillian explains how she will use what she knows to solve the problem.

← Jillian shows her work.

← Jillian compares her answer to the estimated sum and explains why it is not reasonable.

← Jillian checks her answer for accuracy and reasonableness.

THINK SOLVE EXPLAIN

Solve. Use Jillian's work as a guide.

1. The pet store has 2,398 bones, and 337 more balls. How many balls does the pet store have?

2. Gina wants a pair of athletic socks for $5.95 and a T-shirt for $14.50. Will $20.00 be enough?

4.2 Add More Than Two Numbers

Learn

Whoa! Rory's cattle ranch has 1,887 cows, 165 horses, and 463 calves. How many animals are on the ranch?

Find: 1,887 + 165 + 463

Estimate:
1,887 + 165 + 462

$\downarrow$ $\downarrow$ $\downarrow$

2,000 + 200 + 500 = 2,700

Use Paper and Pencil

STEP 1

Add the ones. Regroup if necessary.

$$\begin{array}{r} \overset{1}{}1,887 \\ 165 \\ +463 \\ \hline 5 \end{array}$$

Think: Make a ten.
7 + 5 + 3 = 7 + 3 + 5
           = 10 + 5
           = 15

STEP 2

Add all the tens. Regroup if necessary.

$$\begin{array}{r} \overset{2\,1}{}1,887 \\ 165 \\ +463 \\ \hline 15 \end{array}$$

Think: Use doubles.
 6 + 6 = 12
12 + 8 = 20
20 + 1 = 21

STEP 3

Add all the hundreds. Regroup if necessary.

$$\begin{array}{r} \overset{1\,2\,1}{}1,887 \\ 165 \\ +463 \\ \hline 515 \end{array}$$

Think: Make a ten.
 2 + 8 = 10
 1 + 4 = 5
10 + 5 = 15

STEP 4

Add all the thousands. Regroup if necessary.

$$\begin{array}{r} \overset{1\,2\,1}{}1,887 \\ 165 \\ +463 \\ \hline 2,515 \end{array}$$

Think:
1 + 1 = 2

You can also use a calculator.

Check for reasonableness. 2,515 is reasonably close to 2,700.

There are 2,515 animals on the ranch.

Try It Add. Check for reasonableness.

1. 97 + 423 + 89

2. 348 + 192 + 674

3. 5,782 + 348 + 230

4. **Write About It** Does it matter which number you add first in each place? Why or why not?

Practice and Problem Solving

Add. Check for reasonableness.

5. 545
    102
    +733

6. $6,145
        39
    + 462

7. $7.04
    2.64
    + 5.39

8. 8,276
    114
    + 894

9. 473
    68
    +7,272

10. $5.97 + $6.73 + $5.89

11. 510 + 630 + 6,865

12. 49 + 9,911 + 97 + 98

(X) **Algebra** Find each missing number so that the sum of all the numbers is 1,030. Use a calculator to help.

★**13.** 255 261 ▇ 250

★**14.** ▇ 256 253 263

Solve.

THINK
SOLVE
EXPLAIN

15. Analyze Explain how you can check the sum in an addition problem with more than 2 numbers.

THINK
SOLVE
EXPLAIN

16. ✎ **Write a problem** adding more than 2 numbers. Solve it. Ask others to solve it.

Link to SCIENCE

The smallest breed of cattle is the Ovambo. Bulls weigh about 496 pounds and cows weigh about 353 pounds.

17. Estimate how much 1 bull and 1 cow would weigh together. How did you make your estimate?

Spiral Review and Test Prep

18. What is another name for 205? (p. 6)

A. 20 + 5
B. 200 + 5
C. 200 + 50
D. 20 + 50

19. Which is the missing number? (p. 2)

25, ▇, 21, 19, 17, 15

F. 23
G. 22
H. 20
I. 18

Write each missing number in the counting patterns. (p. 2)

20. 56, 57, ▇, 59

21. 777, 778, ▇, 780

22. 989, ▇, 991, 992

4.3

Problem Solving: Strategy
Draw a Diagram

Read

There are 45 people in the Dog and Cat Club. Twenty-one people only have dogs. Eighteen people only have cats. Six people have both as pets. How many people have a dog?

- **What do you know?**
  45 people in the club;
  21 only have dogs;
  18 only have cats;
  6 have both

- **What do you need to find out?**
  How many people have a dog

Plan

You can use a Venn diagram to solve the problem.

Solve

Show the information you know on the Venn diagram.

Add the number of people who have only dogs and the number of people who have both.

$$21 + 6 = 27$$

So, 27 people have a dog.

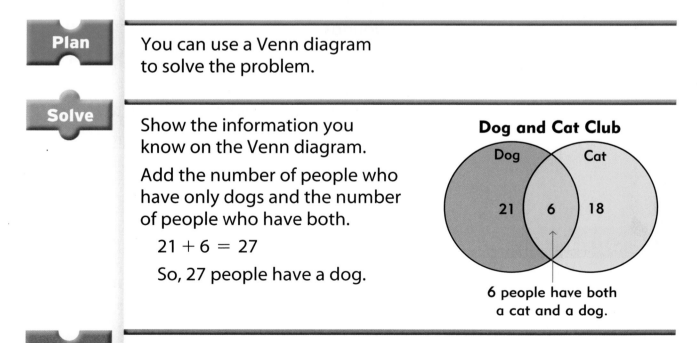

Dog and Cat Club

Dog   Cat

21   6   18

6 people have both
a cat and a dog.

Look Back

Does your answer make sense?

1. **Write About It** **Explain** how a Venn diagram helps you solve the problem.

Practice Use the Venn diagram to solve problems 2–4.

2. How many birds are listed in this Venn diagram?

3. How many animals that do not fly are listed in this Venn diagram?

4. How many are birds, but are also animals that do not fly?

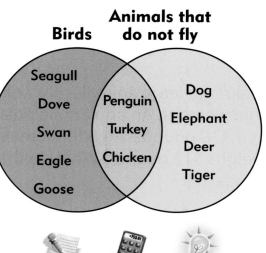

Birds   **Animals that do not fly**

Seagull
Dove
Swan
Eagle
Goose
Penguin
Turkey
Chicken
Dog
Elephant
Deer
Tiger

Mixed Strategy Review

5. Meg gave water to 46 dogs and 56 cats. How many animals received water?

6. Mila saw 7 birds and then 8 more birds. Then she saw 6 more birds. How many birds did she see in all?

Use the table for problems 7–9.

7. Show one way to organize the results of the survey.

8. How many pets are there in all?

9. List the pets in order from greatest number to least.

10. **Collect data** from your classmates about the kinds of pets they have. How will you organize your results?

11. ✏ **Write a problem** that must be solved by writing a number sentence with the data you collected. Solve it. Ask others to solve it.

Choose a Strategy

• Logical Reasoning
• Draw a Picture or Diagram
• Make a Graph
• Act It Out
• Make a Table or List
• Find a Pattern
• Guess and Check
• Write an Equation
• Work Backward
• Solve a Simpler Problem

Survey	
What pets do you have?	
Jan	2 dogs
Randy	1 cat
Allan	1 dog
Len	1 goldfish
Phil	5 goldfish
Sara	2 dogs
Anita	3 cats
Yoshi	3 dogs

Problem Solving

4.4 Choose a Computation Method

Learn

Polar bears are large animals that adapt to very cold weather. An adult male polar bear weighs 1,438 pounds. An adult female polar bear weighs 512 pounds. What do the 2 bears weigh together?

Find: 1,438 + 512

There's More Than One Way!

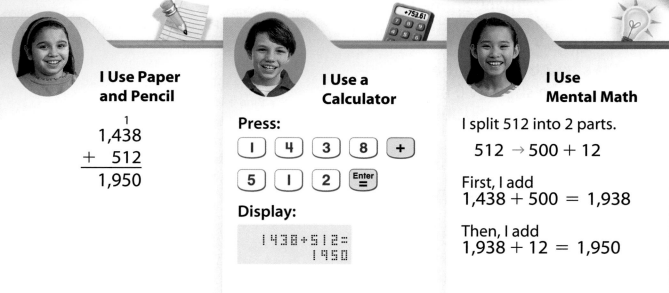

I Use Paper and Pencil

$$\begin{array}{r} \overset{1}{1{,}438} \\ +\ \ 512 \\ \hline 1{,}950 \end{array}$$

I Use a Calculator

Press:

1 4 3 8 +

5 1 2 Enter =

Display:

1438+512=
1950

I Use Mental Math

I split 512 into 2 parts.

512 → 500 + 12

First, I add
1,438 + 500 = 1,938

Then, I add
1,938 + 12 = 1,950

The 2 bears weigh 1,950 pounds.

Try It   Add. Tell which method you use.

1. 3,582 + 3,008   **2.** 8,205 + 1,736   **3.** 1,274 + 5,866   **4.** 6,000 + 3,500

5. 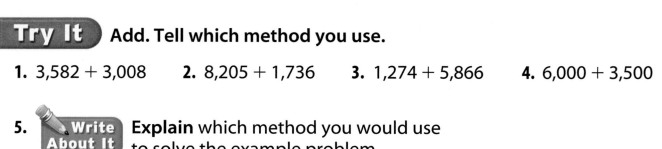 **Write About It** **Explain** which method you would use to solve the example problem.

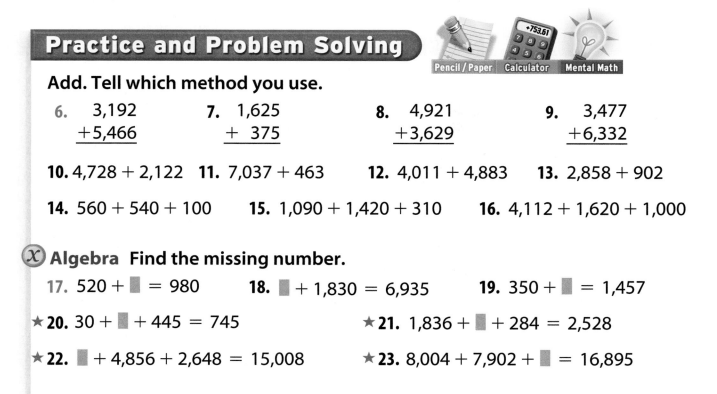

Pencil / Paper   Calculator   Mental Math

Add. Tell which method you use.

6. $\begin{array}{r} 3{,}192 \\ +5{,}466 \\ \hline \end{array}$ 7. $\begin{array}{r} 1{,}625 \\ +\ \ 375 \\ \hline \end{array}$ 8. $\begin{array}{r} 4{,}921 \\ +3{,}629 \\ \hline \end{array}$ 9. $\begin{array}{r} 3{,}477 \\ +6{,}332 \\ \hline \end{array}$

10. $4{,}728 + 2{,}122$ 11. $7{,}037 + 463$ 12. $4{,}011 + 4{,}883$ 13. $2{,}858 + 902$

14. $560 + 540 + 100$ 15. $1{,}090 + 1{,}420 + 310$ 16. $4{,}112 + 1{,}620 + 1{,}000$

$\mathcal{X}$ **Algebra** **Find the missing number.**

17. $520 + \blacksquare = 980$ 18. $\blacksquare + 1{,}830 = 6{,}935$ 19. $350 + \blacksquare = 1{,}457$

★20. $30 + \blacksquare + 445 = 745$ ★21. $1{,}836 + \blacksquare + 284 = 2{,}528$

★22. $\blacksquare + 4{,}856 + 2{,}648 = 15{,}008$ ★23. $8{,}004 + 7{,}902 + \blacksquare = 16{,}895$

Explain.

THINK SOLVE EXPLAIN

24. A female polar bear is 96 inches tall. A male polar bear is 36 inches taller than the female bear. What is their combined height? Explain.

25. Polar bears travel an average of 5,500 miles a year. How many miles do they travel in 2 years?

26. Suppose a polar bear travels 5,981 miles in 1 year. What is this number rounded to the nearest ten? To the nearest hundred? To the nearest thousand?

27. ✏ **Write a problem** in which it is easier to find the sum using mental math than paper and pencil. Solve the problem. Then give it to a classmate to solve.

THINK SOLVE EXPLAIN

Spiral Review and Test Prep

28. To the nearest hundred, which number rounds to 500? (p. 32)

   A. 431   C. 566
   B. 495   D. 585

29. What is the value of the 9 in 2,936? (p. 6)

   F. 9,000   H. 90
   G. 900   I. 9

Compare. Write $>$ **,** $<$ **, or** $=$ **.** (p. 24)

30. 54 ⬤ 34   31. 103 ⬤ 301   32. 284 ⬤ 289   33. 4,910 ⬤ 4,091

Chapter 4

Extra Practice

Set A Add. Check for reasonableness. (pp. 72–74)

1. 3,126
    +2,324

2. $80.76
    + 16.06

3. 4,005
    +3,687

4. $35.13
    + 15.41

5. 7,651
    +1,368

6. $27.65
    + 37.31

7. 9,241
    +1,436

8. $56.78
    + 24.29

Set B Add. Check for reasonableness. (pp. 76–77)

9. $136 + 27 + 251

10. 4,229 + 303 + 464

11. $0.42 + $1.30 + $1.25

12. $3.19 + $0.47 + $2.51

13. 5,365 + 59 + 432

14. $0.63 + $3.84 + $7.85

15.   394
    7,778
    + 466

16.   811
      347
    +633

17. $2.47
      6.33
    + 0.70

Set C Use the data from the Venn diagram for problems 18–19. (pp. 78–79)

18. How many land animals are listed? How many water animals are listed?

19. How many are both land and water animals?

Land Animals **Water Animals**

Tiger
Sheep
Cow
Pig

Seal
Penguin
Turtle
Frog

Starfish
Dolphin
Goldfish
Shark

Set D Add. Tell which method you use. (pp. 80–81)

20. 834
    +258

21. 1,340
    +5,600

22. 3,859
    +3,071

23. 4,865
    + 765

24. 3,590
    +2,550

25. 2,999
    +6,742

LOG ON www.mmhmath.com
For more practice and Chapter Self-Check Test

Review/Test

Add. Check for reasonableness.

1. $125 + 895$

2. $4,826 + 596$

3. $7,538 + 493$

4. $\$1,164 + \$906$

5. $3,425 + 1,082$

6. $4,124 + 3,245$

7. $5,436 + 6,982$

8. $\$10.35 + \$27.04$

9. $7,432 + 1,672$

10. $34 + 509 + 162$

11. $1,072 + 97 + 440$

12. $\$787 + \$84 + \$142$

13. $\$18.50 + \$1.05 + \$10.17 + \$0.33$

Add. Tell which method you use.

14. $3,570 + 2,500$

15. $2,786 + 7,943$

16. $3,002 + 4,738$

Solve.

17. There are 945 customers at a store on Monday, 832 on Tuesday, and 915 on Wednesday. How many customers were in the store in those 3 days?

18. Ned needs 275 pounds of chicken feed. It comes in 75-pound, 125-pound, and 175-pound sacks. Which sacks should he buy so that he has enough?

19. Matt and Guy want to buy a book about animals. Each boy agrees to chip in $7.75 for the book. What is the most they could pay for the book?

20. **Write About It** **Summarize** How do you decide when to add mentally, estimate a sum, or use paper and pencil to add?

Do I Need Help?

Exercises	Review Concepts	Use Extra Practice Set
1–9	pp. 72–74	Set A
10–13	pp. 76–77	Set B
14–16	pp. 80–81	Set D
17–20	pp. 78–79	Set C

Assessment

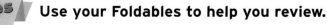

Foldables **Use your Foldables to help you review.**

Reading Math and Science
Build a Tall Tower

The Washington Monument, in Washington, D.C., was completed in 1884. At 550 feet (168 meters), it is the tallest masonry structure in the world. A masonry structure is built from blocks, usually brick or stone. Tall structures have been made from stone for centuries. The trick is to build the walls thick enough and to make the structure wide enough that it won't fall down.

The Washington Monument has a wide base. It also tapers toward the top. This means that it decreases in thickness the higher it gets. There is less weight on top that the bottom must support.

In this activity you will build a tower. You will experiment with ways to make it tall and strong.

Activity

Hypothesize

Study the blocks you have. Talk with your group. Plan how to make the tallest tower that won't fall down.

You Will Need
- 80 cube-shaped blocks

	Cubes used	Height (in cubes)
Tower 1		
Tower 2		
Tower 3		
Tower 4		

Procedure

1. Build a tower as tall as possible. Use as many pieces as you can. Copy the chart to record your data.

2. Record the number of blocks you used. Record how many blocks tall your tower is.

3. Try several times until you think you can't make it taller.

Conclude and Apply

1. **Observe** Which tower was the tallest?

2. Which tower used the most cubes? Explain.

3. **Measure** How tall would a tower be if you combined your 3 tallest towers?

4. Describe the building strategy that worked best for making your tower.

Going Further: Use your blocks and your textbook to make a strong bridge. How many textbooks long can you make the bridge if it is at least 3 blocks high? What is your strategy?

Problem Solving

Unit Study Guide and Review

Vocabulary

Complete. Use a word or words from the list.

1. The ___ of $6 + 7$ is 13.

2. The ___ shows that $7 + 8 = 8 + 7$.

3. The ___ shows that when zero is added to a number the answer is always that number.

4. You can round the numbers, then add to ___ a sum.

5. To add 3 or more numbers, use the ___.

VOCABULARY

Associative Property
Commutative Property
estimate
Identity Property
regroup
sum

Skills and Applications

Use the properties of addition. (pp. 52–54)

Add. Tell what properties you used.
$$2 + 5 + 8$$

Solution
Use the Commutative Property.
$$2 + 8 + 5$$

Use the Associative Property.
$$(2 + 8) + 5$$
$$10 + 5 = 15$$

Add. Then write a different addition sentence.

6. $15 + 0$

7. $5 + 3 + 2$

Add. Tell what properties you used.

8. $8 + 0 + 12$

9. $3 + 8 + 7 + 5$

Add using mental math strategies. (pp. 56–57)

Find: $800 + 700$

Solution
Use basic facts and patterns to add mentally.

Think:
$$8 + 7 = 15$$
$$80 + 70 = 150$$
$$800 + 700 = 1,500$$

Add. Use mental math.

10. $90 + 10$

11. $120 + 40$

12. $800 + 400$

13. $1,300 + 700$

Foldables **Use your Foldables to help you review.**

Estimate sums, including money amounts. (pp. 64–65)

Estimate: 281 + 637

Solution
Round each number.

Think: 281 + 637
$$\downarrow \quad \downarrow$$
300 + 600 = 900

So 281 + 637 is about 900.

Estimate each sum.

14. 482 + 135

15. 2,062 + 817

16. $9.98 + $8.25

17. $4.78 + $2.23

Find the sums of whole numbers. (pp. 58–62, 72–77)

Find: 674 + 148

Solution

Add the numbers in each place.
Regroup if necessary.

$$\begin{array}{r} {}^{1\,1} \\ 674 \\ +148 \\ \hline 822 \end{array}$$

Add.

18. 546 + 178

19. 3,845 + 7,629

20. 764 + 187 + 32

21. 467 + 77 + 1,012

22. $605 + $234 + $371

23. $2.65 + $0.43 + $13.39

Use skills and strategies to solve problems. (pp. 66–67, 78–79)

At the zoo, Carmen saw 7 animals that only eat plants and 12 animals that only eat meat. She also saw 4 animals that eat both plants and meat. How many animals eat plants?

Solution

Look at the Venn diagram.
7 + 4 = 11

11 animals eat plants.

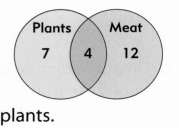

Use the data from the Venn diagram for problems 24–25.

24. How many animals eat meat?

25. How many animals do not eat both meat and plants?

Enrichment

Front-End Estimation

You know how to use rounding to estimate sums.
Here is another way to estimate.

Front-end estimation is a way of estimating a number using the digit in the greatest place.

Look at the digit in the greatest place. Think of it as the "front" digit. The underlined digits in the numbers below are the "front" digits.

<u>2</u>3   <u>9</u>9   <u>1</u>56   <u>3</u>48   <u>8</u>01

Here's how to use front-end estimation

Estimate: 423 + 766 + 528

423 + 766 + 528   Find the front digits.

↓   ↓   ↓   Rewrite the numbers using
                         only the front-end digits.
400 + 700 + 500   Use zeros for the other digits.

400 + 700 + 500 = 1,600   Add to find the estimate.

Estimate each sum. Use front-end estimation.

1. 39 + 31

2. 44 + 92

3. 75 + 22

4. 54 + 85 + 13

5. 56 + 23

6. 67 + 11 + 34

7. 506 + 243

8. 56 + 23 + 93 + 81

9. 180 + 420 + 310

10. 491 + 350 + 207

Solve.

11. Generalize Will a front-end estimation be greater or less than the actual sum? Explain.

12. Give an example of when you might use front-end estimation. When would using front-end estimation not make sense?

Performance Assessment

How Do You Make a Budget?

The children's museum is planning to add an exhibit of stuffed animals.

During the next 3 years the museum will add animals every year. The budget limit for each year is $555.

Here is the beginning of Amy's plan for the first year of buying the stuffed animals.

Name	Price	Total
Cat	$65	$65
Bear	$94	$159

$65 + $94 = $159

Stuffed Animal Price List

Name	Price
Cat	$65
Bear	$94
Horse	$48
Dog	$36
Snake	$47
Tiger	$82
Turtle	$65
Duck	$34
Elephant	$72
Lion	$63
Fox	$54
Swan	$79

Choose the animals and show the budget for the next 3 years. Use the Stuffed Animals Price List as a guide. Try to use up as much of the budget each year as you can.

- How much could be spent in all?

- After making your choices, add up the total for all 3 years. Is there any money left? Can you buy another toy?

Tips For A Good Answer

- Have a completed chart for each of 3 years.

- Show the total spent after each animal.

- Show a complete total for each year.

- Show a grand total after 3 years.

- Spend as much of the budgeted money as possible.

$34

You may want to save this work in your portfolio.

Assessment

TECHNOLOGY Link

Model Properties of Addition

Ramón has 17 apples in one bag and 5 apples in another bag. Write 2 different number sentences that show the total number of apples.

You can use counters ★🔔 in the *Math Tool Chest CD-ROM* to stamp out a model of $17 + 5$ and $5 + 17$.

- Use a mat with 2 sections open.

- In the top section, stamp out 17 apples in the first row.

- Stamp out 5 apples in the second row.

- In the bottom section, stamp out 5 apples in the first row.

- Stamp out 17 apples in the second row.

Math Tool Chest CD-ROM

The number boxes keep count as you stamp. What pair of addition sentences can you write?

Use the computer to find the missing numbers.

1. $10 + 4 = \blacksquare$
$4 + 10 = \blacksquare$

2. $8 + 15 = \blacksquare$
$15 + 8 = \blacksquare$

3. $4 + 16 = \blacksquare$
$16 + 4 = \blacksquare$

4. $6 + 18 = \blacksquare$
$18 + 6 = \blacksquare$

Solve.

5. Miguel has 16 marbles in one box and 9 marbles in another. Write 2 different number sentences that show the total number of marbles.

6. Analyze How does using the model help you decide if the order of the addends changes the sum?

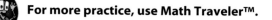 **For more practice, use Math Traveler™.**

Test-Taking Tips

When you are taking a test, it is important to **read carefully**. It helps to read each item more than once.

Sparkle design pencils cost $0.75 each. They are also sold in packs of 3 for $2.00. What is the least amount of money 5 pencils can cost?

A. $3.00   C. $3.50
B. $3.25   D. $3.75

When you read the problem the first time, you might think the answer is choice D, $3.75.

$0.75 + $0.75 + $0.75 + $0.75 + $0.75 = $3.75

If you read the problem again, you might notice that you can buy 3 pencils for $2.00.

$2.00 + $0.75 + $0.75 = $3.50

The correct choice is C.

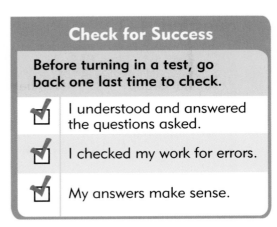

Check for Success

Before turning in a test, go back one last time to check.

☑ I understood and answered the questions asked.

☑ I checked my work for errors.

☑ My answers make sense.

Read each problem carefully. Think about how you would answer it. Then read the problem again. Choose the best answer.

Number line: 0 2 4 6 8 10 12 14 16 18 20 (arrow pointing to 17)

1. Look at the number line. Which number is the arrow pointing to?

    A. 5   C. 20
    B. 17   D. 22

2. Dena had 2 cents on Monday. She doubled it every day after that. How much did she have on Friday?

    F. $0.04   H. $0.32
    G. $0.10   I. $0.64

3. The number 111 is 10 more than which number?

    A. 10   C. 101
    B. 91   D. 110

4. What is the eighth number in this skip-counting pattern?
    3, 6, 9, 12, 15, 18

    F. 19   H. 24
    G. 21   I. 27

Test Prep

PART 1 • Multiple Choice

Choose the best answer.
Use data from the table for questions 1–3.

Species of Reptiles

Animal Group	Number of Species
Turtles/Tortoises	215
Crocodiles/Alligators	25
Lizards	3,000
Snakes	2,700

1. Which group has the least number of species? (p. 26)
   A. Lizards
   B. Turtles/Tortoises
   C. Snakes
   D. Crocodiles/Alligators

2. How many species of snakes and lizards are there? (p. 72)
   F. 5,700   H. 2,725
   G. 3,215   I. 240

3. Which is the closest estimate for the number of species of reptiles in all? (p. 64)
   A. 6,500   C. 5,900
   B. 6,300   D. 5,700

4. Which basic fact could you use to find the sum of 200 + 700? (p. 56)
   F. 7 + 7   H. 20 + 700
   G. 200 + 70   I. 2 + 7

5. A haddock fish is about 100 centimeters in length and a cod fish is about 200 centimeters. The length of an Atlantic salmon is between these two lengths. What could the length of an Atlantic salmon be? (p. 24)
   A. 210 centimeters
   B. 205 centimeters
   C. 150 centimeters
   D. 98 centimeters

6. Will's father is building a pen for turtles. He has two 5-foot-long pieces and two 3-foot-long pieces of wood. Which shows how much wood Will's father has? (p. 52)
   F. 5 + 3   H. 5+3+5+3
   G. 5 × 3   I. 5×3×5×3

7. A number has 3 digits. The ones digit is greatest. The tens digit is 2 times the hundreds digit. What is the number? (p. 4)
   A. 242   C. 449
   B. 368   D. 638

8. Which symbol makes the number sentence true? (p. 24)

   3,658 ⬤ 3,685

   F. >   H. =
   G. <   I. +

Record your answers on the answer sheet provided by your teacher or on a sheet of paper.

9. Cara has the money shown. How much does she have? (p. 14)

10. Find the missing number. (p. 52)

$$32 + \blacksquare = 12 + 32$$

THINK SOLVE EXPLAIN

11. Pat buys new fish for her tank each week. The first week she bought 4 fish, the second week she bought 8 fish, and last week she bought 12 fish. If the pattern continues, how many fish will she buy this week? Explain (p. 2)

12. At the aquarium there is an adult male sea lion that weighs 678 pounds. What is its weight rounded to the nearest hundred? (p. 32)

13. Write 9,064 in expanded form and word form. (p. 6)

14. The table below shows the number of baby animals born each year at a zoo. If this pattern continues, how many babies will be born in the fifth year? (p. 2)

Number of Animals Born					
Year	1	2	3	4	5
Number of babies	5	10	15	20	

15. Kelly uses a twenty-dollar bill to buy a stuffed tiger that costs $14.99. Explain how to use mental math to find out Kelly's change. (p. 14)

16. At Eleanor Elementary School there are 167 third graders, 184 fourth graders, and 178 fifth graders. How many students are in those 3 grades? (p. 76)

Record your answer on a sheet of paper. Show your work.

17. One sea turtle nest had 185 hatched eggs. Another nest had 145 hatched eggs. About how many turtles hatched in all? Explain. (p. 60)

Test Prep

What Do I Need to Know?

There are 17 petals on the flower.
If 5 petals fall off, how many
petals are left on the flower?

Subtraction Strategies

What Will I Learn?

In this chapter you will learn to

- relate addition and subtraction
- find missing addends
- subtract multiples of 10, 100, and 1,000
- subtract 2- and 3-digit numbers
- use skills and strategies to solve problems

How Do I Read Math?

When you read a mathematics book, sometimes you read words and symbols, and sometimes you read only symbols.

All of these represent forty-one minus twenty-three equals eighteen:

- $41 - 23 = 18$
-
$$\begin{array}{r} 41 \\ -23 \\ \hline 18 \end{array}$$

VOCABULARY

- related facts
- fact family
- difference
- equation
- inverse operations

Foldables

Subtraction Strategies

$$\begin{array}{r} {\scriptstyle 3\ 10} \\ 540 \\ -217 \\ \hline 323 \end{array}$$
Regroup is to rename a number in a different way.

Use your Foldables to help you with chapter concepts.

1. Fold two sheets of notebook paper in half like hamburgers.
2. Cut the first sheet 1–inch along the fold at both ends at the margin.
3. Cut the second sheet along the fold between the margins.
4. Roll up the first sheet. Slip it halfway through the cut in the second sheet. Open it up.
5. Fold the bound pages in half to make a bound journal. Label as shown. Record what you learn.

www.mmhmath.com
For Real World Math Activities

5.1 Algebra: Relate Addition and Subtraction

Learn

Ian picks 11 tomatoes and 4 green peppers. How many vegetables did he pick? How many more tomatoes than green peppers did he pick?

You can use related facts , or basic facts using the same numbers.

VOCABULARY
difference
equation
fact families
inverse operations
related facts

Use Related Facts

Add to find how many vegetables he picked.

$11 + 4 = 15$ or $4 + 11 = 15$

Ian picked 15 tomatoes and green peppers.

Subtract to find how many more tomatoes than green peppers he picked.

$$11 \quad - \quad 4 \quad = \quad 7$$

$\uparrow$
difference

Ian picked 7 more tomatoes than green peppers.

Use Fact Families

Fact families are made from related sentences.

$7 + 6 = 13$ $13 - 6 = 7$
$6 + 7 = 13$ $13 - 7 = 6$

$18 + 0 = 18$ $18 - 0 = 18$
$0 + 18 = 18$ $18 - 18 = 0$

Think: Addition and subtraction are opposite, or **inverse** , **operations** .

$15 + 15 = 30$
$30 - 15 = 30$

What If 8 of 17 vegetables are ready to be picked. How many vegetables are not ready to be picked?

You can use an equation to solve this problem. An **equation** is a number sentence that shows 2 amounts are equal.

Use an Equation

STEP 1

Use a ■ to represent how many vegetables are not ready to be picked.

$8 + ■ = 17$

STEP 2

Use a related subtraction fact.

$17 - 8 = 9$

So $■ = 9$

There are 9 vegetables not ready to be picked.

Try It Write a fact family for each group of numbers.

1. 5, 8, 13   **2.** 5, 0, 5   **3.** 6, 6, 12   **4.** 23, 9, 14   **5.** 7, 13, 20

Identify if each is an equation.

6. $4 + 3 = 7$ **7.** $5 + 2$ **8.** $16 - 8$ **9.** $24 - 5 = 19$

10. $4 + 6 = 10$ **11.** $9 - 7$ **12.** $4 + 0 = 4$ **13.** $27 - 9$

Find each missing addend.

14. $8 + ■ = 12$ **15.** $■ + 14 = 20$ **16.** $5 + ■ = 12$ **17.** $■ + 12 = 19$

18.
$$\begin{array}{r} ■ \\ +13 \\ \hline 22 \end{array}$$

19.
$$\begin{array}{r} ■ \\ +5 \\ \hline 11 \end{array}$$

20.
$$\begin{array}{r} 8 \\ +■ \\ \hline 16 \end{array}$$

21.
$$\begin{array}{r} 15 \\ +■ \\ \hline 20 \end{array}$$

22. **Write About It** **Explain** why using related facts helps to solve a problem.

Practice and Problem Solving

Write a fact family for each group of numbers.

23. 7, 11, 18   **24.** 4, 9, 13   **25.** 9, 9, 18   **26.** 2, 2, 0   **27.** 6, 21, 15

Identify if each is an equation.

28. $15 - 4$ **29.** $9 + 0 = 9$ **30.** $16 + 8$ **31.** $22 - 7 = 15$

Find each missing addend.

32. $7 + \blacksquare = 12$ **33.** $\blacksquare + 7 = 14$ **34.** $8 + \blacksquare = 15$ **35.** $\blacksquare + 6 = 14$

★**36.** $292 + \blacksquare = 321$ ★**37.** $982 + \blacksquare = 1{,}090$ ★**38.** $\blacksquare + 191 = 458$ ★**39.** $854 + \blacksquare = 919$

Solve.

40. Make It Right
Hans wrote
this fact family.
Tell what mistake
he made. Explain
how to correct it.

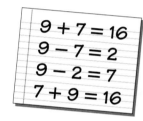

$9 + 7 = 16$
$9 - 7 = 2$
$9 - 2 = 7$
$7 + 9 = 16$

41. ✎ **Write a problem** that
can be solved by addition. Then
change the problem so it can be
solved using a related fact.

Link to SCIENCE

The largest flower in
the world belongs to
a kind of rafflesia
plant. The pink
flower can grow up
to 36 inches wide
and weigh as much
as 15 pounds. Each of its 5 petals is
about 1 inch thick and 18 inches long.

42. How many petals would 3
rafflesia flowers have in all?

✔ Spiral Review and Test Prep

43. What number will make the
number sentence true? (p. 52)
$(5 + 3) + \blacksquare = 5 + (3 + 8)$
- **A.** 3
- **B.** 7
- **C.** 5
- **D.** 8

44. Skip-count to find the missing
number: 21, 18, 15, $\blacksquare$ (p. 2)
- **F.** 10
- **G.** 12
- **H.** 13
- **I.** 14

Write the change. (p. 14)

45. Cost: $2.85
You give: $5.00

46. Cost: $0.32
You give: $1.00

47. Cost: $3.79
You give: $4.00

Problem Solving: Reading for Math

GREEN ALERT!

Many plants on our planet are in trouble. At least 1 out of 8 plant types in the world may soon disappear. The news is even worse in the United States. Here, nearly 1 out of 3 plants is at risk of being lost forever. One list of plants in danger has about 34,000 plants on it!

HELP IS ON THE WAY

Public gardens across the United States are pitching in to help save the plants. The New York Botanical Garden cares for 19 different plant collections. One of its collections features endangered plants from the Northeast U.S. The North Carolina Botanical Garden has 15 collections, including the largest meat-eating plant collection in the country! The State Botanical Garden of Georgia has set up 10 gardens to show off its plant life.

How do botanical gardens help endangered plants? The gardens grow endangered plants so scientists can study them. The gardens also teach people about the importance of protecting plant life.

A meat-eating plant being tended by a worker at The State Botanical Garden of Georgia.

Problem Solving

Reading Skill **Draw Conclusions** What conclusion can you make after reading this story? List one fact to support your conclusion.

1. North Carolina's Botanical Garden has 15 collections. Georgia's has 10 collections. How many collections do both gardens have in all?

2. How many more collections does New York's Botanical Garden have than Georgia's?

5.2 Problem Solving: Skill
Identify Extra Information

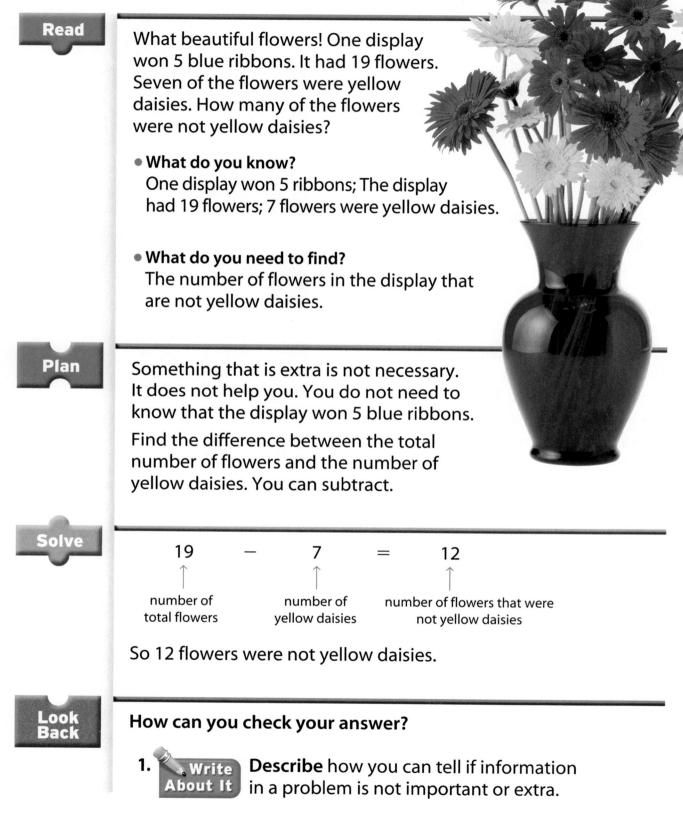

Read

What beautiful flowers! One display won 5 blue ribbons. It had 19 flowers. Seven of the flowers were yellow daisies. How many of the flowers were not yellow daisies?

- **What do you know?**
  One display won 5 ribbons; The display had 19 flowers; 7 flowers were yellow daisies.

- **What do you need to find?**
  The number of flowers in the display that are not yellow daisies.

Plan

Something that is extra is not necessary. It does not help you. You do not need to know that the display won 5 blue ribbons.

Find the difference between the total number of flowers and the number of yellow daisies. You can subtract.

Solve

$$19 \quad - \quad 7 \quad = \quad 12$$

number of total flowers | number of yellow daisies | number of flowers that were not yellow daisies

So 12 flowers were not yellow daisies.

Look Back

How can you check your answer?

1. **Write About It** **Describe** how you can tell if information in a problem is not important or extra.

Practice

Solve. Identify the extra information.

2. The Garden Club made 18 displays for the show. One is a flag made with 17 red, white, and blue flowers. There are 6 red flowers and 8 white flowers. How many blue flowers are there?

3. Another display at the show has the same number of daisies and buttercups. Daisies at the show cost $1.00 each. There are 18 flowers in the display. How many buttercups are in this display?

Mixed Strategy Review

4. Brian has 5 quarters, 2 dimes, 7 nickels, and 2 pennies. He wants to buy a sandwich for $2.00. Explain if Brian has enough money.

5. There were 209 people at the museum on Saturday and 299 people at the museum on Sunday. How many people in all were at the museum last weekend?

Choose a Strategy
- Logical Reasoning
- Draw a Picture or Diagram
- Make a Graph
- Act It Out
- Make a Table or List
- Find a Pattern
- Guess and Check
- Write an Equation
- Work Backward
- Solve a Simpler Problem

Use data from the Garden Club News for problems 6–10.

6. How many more maple trees than oak trees are at the show?

7. How many more maple trees than cherry trees are at the show?

8. How many fruit trees are there in all?

9. Which 2 kinds of trees equal the number of maple trees?

Garden Club News	
Tree	Number of Trees
Apple	26
Cherry	8
Peach	8
Maple	35
Oak	9

10. **Write About It** Write a problem using the data from the chart. Solve it. Ask others to solve it.

Problem Solving

5.3 Algebra: Subtraction Patterns

Learn

There are still 300 tickets left for Sunday's Orchid Show. How many tickets have already been sold?

Find: 800 − 300

Orchid Show

Tickets:
$5.25 adults
$4.75 children under 12

Limited
800 tickets available for Sunday's show

Use Facts and Patterns

$$8 - 3 = 5$$
$$80 - 30 = 50$$
$$800 - 300 = 500$$

Think: 8 ones − 3 ones = 5 ones
8 tens − 3 tens = 5 tens
8 hundreds − 3 hundreds = 5 hundreds

A total of 500 tickets have been sold.

Facts and Patterns with Zero

$$20 - 10 = 10$$
$$200 - 100 = 100$$
$$2,000 - 1,000 = 1,000$$

Think: 20 ones − 10 ones = 10 ones
20 tens − 10 tens = 10 tens
20 hundreds − 10 hundreds = 10 hundreds

Try It

Write the number that makes each sentence true.

1.
$$7 - 5 = \blacksquare$$
$$70 - 50 = \blacksquare$$
$$700 - 500 = \blacksquare$$

2.
$$9 - 4 = \blacksquare$$
$$90 - 40 = \blacksquare$$
$$900 - 400 = \blacksquare$$

3.
$$13 - \blacksquare = 8$$
$$130 - \blacksquare = 80$$
$$1,300 - \blacksquare = 800$$

4. **Write About It** **Explain** how to use subtraction facts and patterns to find 700 − 400 mentally.

Practice and Problem Solving

Write the number that makes each sentence true.

5. $7 - 6 = \blacksquare$
   $70 - 60 = \blacksquare$
   $700 - 600 = \blacksquare$

6. $8 - 2 = \blacksquare$
   $80 - 20 = \blacksquare$
   $800 - 200 = \blacksquare$

7. $40 - 10 = \blacksquare$
   $400 - 100 = \blacksquare$
   $4,000 - 1000 = \blacksquare$

Subtract mentally.

8. $1,400 - 700$

9. $780 - 600$

10. $120 - 60$

11. $624 - 300$

12. $80 - 20$

13. $1,100 - 1,100$

14. $640 - 400$

15. $937 - 607$

Find the missing digit.

★16. $\blacksquare31 - 200 = 731$

★17. $120 - \blacksquare0 = 50$

★18. $1,\blacksquare30 - 700 = 630$

Solve. Use data from the table for problem 19.

19. **Career** Jared hoped to work 110 hours during June. Did he work more or fewer hours than he hoped? How many more or fewer hours?

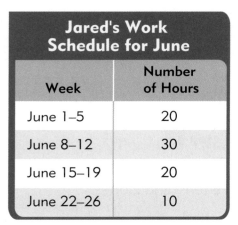

Jared's Work Schedule for June	
Week	Number of Hours
June 1–5	20
June 8–12	30
June 15–19	20
June 22–26	10

20. **Write a problem** that can be solved by subtracting mentally. Solve it. Ask others to solve it.

★21. Rick's father bought 1 adult ticket at $5.25 and 1 child's ticket at $4.75 for the Orchid Show. How much change did his father get if he paid for the tickets with a twenty-dollar bill?

Spiral Review and Test Prep

22. Which number is closest to this sum? $49 + 37$ (p. 60)
   - **A.** 70
   - **B.** 80
   - **C.** 90
   - **D.** 100

23. Mr. Harper works in his garden for 45 minutes every day. How long did he work in 3 days? (p. 60)
   - **F.** 45 minutes
   - **G.** 90 minutes
   - **H.** 135 minutes
   - **I.** 145 minutes

24. $9 + 4$ (p. 52)

25. $18 + 0$ (p. 52)

26. $8 + 8 + 3$ (p. 52)

27. $2 + 12 + 1$ (p. 52)

5.4 Explore Regrouping in Subtraction

Hands On Activity

You can use place-value models to explore regrouping in subtraction.

Find: 362 − 148

You Will Need
• place-value models

Use Models

STEP 1
Show 362 as 3 hundreds, 6 tens, and 2 ones.

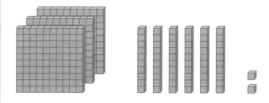

STEP 2
Subtract the ones. There are not enough ones to subtract 8. You need to regroup 1 ten and 2 ones into 12 ones.

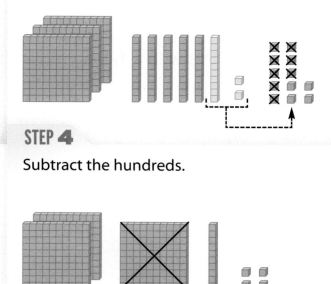

STEP 3
Subtract the tens. You do not need to regroup.

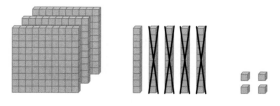

STEP 4
Subtract the hundreds.

104

Explain Your Thinking

1. How do you model the numbers in the subtraction problem?

2. Why do you regroup?

3. How many tens and hundreds do you have to regroup?

4. How many ones, tens, and hundreds do you subtract?

5. What is 362 − 148?

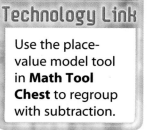

Technology Link

Use the place-value model tool in **Math Tool Chest** to regroup with subtraction.

Your Turn

Use models to subtract.

6. 163 − 128

7. 207 − 138

8. 137 − 49

9. 322 − 148

10. 280 − 94

11. 351 − 247

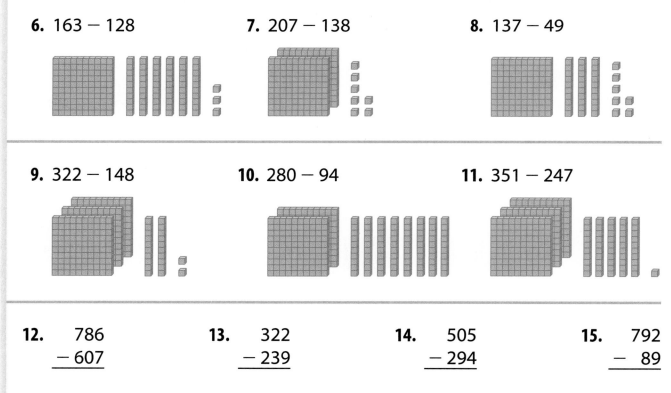

12.
$$\begin{array}{r} 786 \\ -\ 607 \\ \hline \end{array}$$

13.
$$\begin{array}{r} 322 \\ -\ 239 \\ \hline \end{array}$$

14.
$$\begin{array}{r} 505 \\ -\ 294 \\ \hline \end{array}$$

15.
$$\begin{array}{r} 792 \\ -\ 89 \\ \hline \end{array}$$

16.  **Explain** why you should start subtracting with the models that have the least place value.

5.5 Subtract Whole Numbers

Learn

Strangler fig vines climb on trees in order to reach for the sun. If a tree is 267 feet tall and the strangler fig vine has climbed 196 feet, how much farther does it have to climb?

Subtract to find the difference.

Find: 267 − 196

Let's see how to connect models to using paper and pencil.

strangler fig vine

tree

Make Connections

STEP 1	Models	Paper and Pencil
Model 267. Subtract the ones.		Subtract the ones. $\begin{array}{r} 267 \\ -196 \\ \hline 1 \end{array}$ **Think:** 7 ones − 6 ones = 1 one

STEP 2	Models	Paper and Pencil
Regroup and subtract the tens.		Regroup and subtract the tens. $\begin{array}{r} {}^{1\,16}\\ 2\!\!\!/67 \\ -196 \\ \hline 71 \end{array}$ **Think:** 16 tens − 9 tens = 7 tens

STEP 3	Models	Paper and Pencil
Subtract the hundreds.		Subtract the hundreds. $\begin{array}{r} {}^{1\,16}\\ 2\!\!\!/67 \\ -196 \\ \hline 71 \end{array}$ **Think:** 1 hundred − 1 hundred = 0 hundred

The vine has to climb 71 more feet.

Today ticket sales were $938 for the forest exhibit at the nature preserve. Yesterday they were $719. How much more money was collected today?

Find: $938 − $719

Subtract Money Amounts

STEP 1

Subtract the ones. Regroup if necessary.

$$
\begin{array}{r}
\overset{2\,18}{\$9\cancel{3}\cancel{8}} \\
-\ 7\,1\,9 \\
\hline
9
\end{array}
$$

Think: 3 tens 8 ones = 2 tens 18 ones

STEP 2

Subtract the tens. Regroup if necessary.

$$
\begin{array}{r}
\overset{2\,18}{\$9\cancel{3}\cancel{8}} \\
-\ 7\,1\,9 \\
\hline
1\,9
\end{array}
$$

STEP 3

Subtract the hundreds. Regroup if necessary.

$$
\begin{array}{r}
\overset{2\,18}{\$9\cancel{3}\cancel{8}} \\
-\ 7\,1\,9 \\
\hline
\$2\,1\,9
\end{array}
$$

You can also use a calculator to subtract.

Add to check: $219 + $719 = $938.
Ticket sales were $219 more today.

Another Example

$$
\begin{array}{r}
\overset{6\,16}{\$7.\cancel{6}8} \\
-\ 1.9\,7 \\
\hline
\$5.7\,1
\end{array}
$$

You can subtract money the same way you would whole numbers. Be sure to write the dollar sign and the decimal point.

Try It Subtract. Check your answer.

1. $\begin{array}{r} 525 \\ -169 \\ \hline \end{array}$

2. $\begin{array}{r} \$917 \\ -\$473 \\ \hline \end{array}$

3. $\begin{array}{r} \$7.34 \\ -\$2.86 \\ \hline \end{array}$

4. $\begin{array}{r} \$7.14 \\ -\$5.57 \\ \hline \end{array}$

5. 651 − 392

6. $812 − $576

7. $9.06 − $5.92

8. $5.31 − $4.99

9. **Write About It** Make up a subtraction problem in which you subtract two 3-digit numbers and must regroup the tens and the hundreds. **Explain** how to solve the problem.

Practice and Problem Solving

Subtract. Add to check.

| 10. | 764
 −592 | 11. | 552
 −493 | 12. | $347
 −256 | 13. | 992
 −985 | 14. | 556
 −357 |

15. $9.13 − $4.79   16. 887 − 708   17. 672 − 486   18. $938 − $692

x **Algebra** Find each missing digit.

| 19. | 616
 − 34■
 269 | 20. | ■43
 −430
 113 | 21. | 5■3
 −465
 48 | ★22. | ■6■
 −1■9
 573 |

Solve. Use data from the table for problems 23–24.

23. List the vegetables in order from greatest to least number of calories in a cup.

24. For lunch Andy had a hamburger, a cup of black beans, and a cup of mashed potatoes. The meal had 745 calories. How many calories did the hamburger have?

Calorie Count	
Vegetable (1 cup)	**Calories**
green beans	35
black beans	225
green peas	125
mashed potatoes	160

Source: World Almanac and Book of Facts

25. Each year the Pottstown Garden Club collects $1,245 in dues. So far it has collected $848. How much more must the club collect?

26. **Make It Right** This is how Earl subtracted. Tell what mistake he made. Show how to correct it.

$$
\begin{array}{r}
^{12}\\
^{2}11\\
4\cancel{3}1\\
-192\\
\hline
339
\end{array}
$$

THINK SOLVE EXPLAIN

Spiral Review and Test Prep

27. Which number is the same as 40,000 + 2,000 + 600 + 7? (p. 10)

   A. 402,607   C. 42,607
   B. 42,670   D. 42,067

28. Find the missing number. 6,783 + ■ = 6,793 (p. 72)

   F. 0   H. 100
   G. 10   I. 6,783

29. 15 − 8 (p. 96)   30. 11 − 9 (p. 96)   31. 13 − 8 (p. 96)   32. 14 − 7 (p. 96)

Extra Practice page 110, Set D

FIND THE DIFFERENCE

Use the Digit Deck to get the greatest number and find the difference.

Ready

Players : 2 to 4
You Will Need: Digit Deck, paper and pencil

GO!

► Each player starts with 900 points.

► One player chooses 2 cards from the Digit Deck.

► Each player uses those 2 cards to make a 2-digit number, not letting others see the number.

► All players subtract the 2-digit number from 900.

► Another player picks 2 cards from the Digit Deck. Each player uses those 2 cards to make another 2-digit number.

Set

Shuffle the cards and place them face down.

Write 900 at the top of your paper.

► All players subtract the new number from the number of points remaining.

► Play 3 more rounds.

► The player with the lowest final difference wins.

Extra Practice

Set A Write a fact family for each group of numbers. (pp. 96–99)

1. 15, 4, 19   **2.** 3, 9, 12   **3.** 5, 5, 10   **4.** 7, 9, 16

Find the sum or difference. Write a related addition or subtraction fact.

5. $24 + 7$ **6.** $7 + 1$ **7.** $38 - 2$ **8.** $9 - 0$

Set B Solve. Identify the extra information. (pp. 100–101)

9. Paul picks 14 apples from 1 tree and 9 apples from another. He picks 8 pears and 10 peaches. How many more apples did he pick than pears?

10. Mrs. Katz won 14 ribbons. Mr. Sands won 15 first-prize ribbons and 2 second-prize ribbons. How many ribbons did Mr. Sands win in all?

11. A bush has 12 flowers and 10 buds. If 5 buds open, how many buds are left unopened?

12. Nany uses 43 roses and 36 daisies to make a display. She finishes at 3:00 P.M. How many flowers did she use?

Set C Write the number sentence that makes each sentence true. (pp. 102–103)

13.
$$9 - 5 = \blacksquare$$
$$90 - 50 = \blacksquare$$
$$900 - 500 = \blacksquare$$

14.
$$12 - 3 = \blacksquare$$
$$120 - \blacksquare = 90$$
$$\blacksquare - 300 = 900$$

15.
$$\blacksquare - 3 = 8$$
$$110 - \blacksquare = 80$$
$$1{,}100 - 300 = \blacksquare$$

Set D Subtract. Check your answer. (pp. 104–109)

16. $333
      $-\ 101$

17.   48
      $-\ 24$

18. $312
      $-\ 73$

19.   848
      $-\ 653$

20. $768
      $-\ \$215$

21.   648
      $-\ 325$

22.   842
      $-\ 273$

23.   3,478
      $-\ 565$

LOG ON   www.mmhmath.com
For more practice and Chapter Self-Check Test

Subtract.

1. 12
    − 8

2. 14
    − 9

3.   4
    −4

4. 20
    − 1

Write a fact family for each group of numbers.

5. 6, 8, 14

6. 12, 7, 19

7. 4, 8, 12

8. 4, 17, 13

Write the number sentence that makes each sentence true.

9. $9 - 4 = \blacksquare$
     $90 - 40 = \blacksquare$
     $900 - 400 = \blacksquare$

10. $\blacksquare - 7 = 1$
     $\blacksquare - 70 = 10$
     $\blacksquare - 700 = 100$

11. $10 - \blacksquare = 4$
     $100 - \blacksquare = 40$
     $1,000 - \blacksquare = 400$

Subtract.

12.   63
     − 22

13. 587
     − 503

14. 215
     − 90

15. $8.31
     − 2.53

16. 542
     − 521

17. 957
     − 78

18. $6.23
     − 3.98

Solve.

19. One day a plant nursery sold 34 small trees, 125 flowering plants, and 47 cactus plants. How many flowering plants and cactus plants were sold in all?

20. **Write About It** **Summarize** How does knowing one addition fact help you subtract?

Do I Need Help?

Exercises	Review Concepts	Use Extra Practice Set
1–8	pp. 96–99	Set A
9–11	pp. 102–103	Set C
12–18	pp. 104–109	Set D
19–20	pp. 100–101	Set B

Foldables Use your Foldables to help you review.

What Do I Need to Know?

Tamyra counts 23 ripe apples and 16 unripe apples. How many more ripe apples are there than unripe apples?

Subtract Greater Numbers

What Will I Learn?

In this chapter you will learn to

- subtract across zeros
- estimate differences
- subtract greater numbers
- use skills and strategies to solve problems

How Do I Read Math?

When you read a mathematics book, sometimes you read words and symbols, and sometimes you read only symbols.

All of these represent 175 subtracted from 900 equals 725:

- **nine hundred minus one hundred seventy-five equals seven hundred twenty-five**
- **$900 - 175 = 725$**

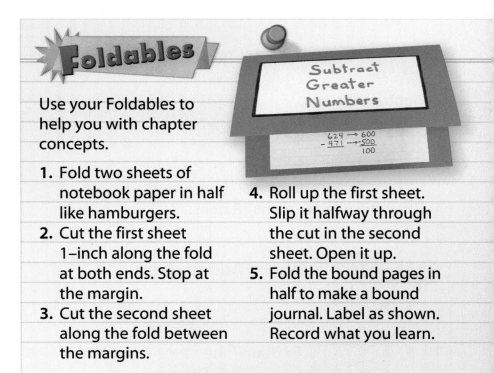

Foldables

Use your Foldables to help you with chapter concepts.

1. Fold two sheets of notebook paper in half like hamburgers.
2. Cut the first sheet 1–inch along the fold at both ends. Stop at the margin.
3. Cut the second sheet along the fold between the margins.
4. Roll up the first sheet. Slip it halfway through the cut in the second sheet. Open it up.
5. Fold the bound pages in half to make a bound journal. Label as shown. Record what you learn.

6.1 Regroup Across Zeros

Learn

The Ecology Club members plant trees to block pollution. They need to plant 203 trees this year. If they have already planted 125 trees, how many trees do they still need to plant?

Find: 203 − 125

Use Paper and Pencil

STEP 1

Subtract the ones.
No tens to regroup.
So regroup the hundreds.

$$\begin{array}{r} {}^{1\ 10}\cancel{2}\cancel{0}3 \\ -125 \\ \hline \end{array}$$

Think: 2 hundreds 0 tens = 1 hundred 10 tens

STEP 2

Regroup the tens.

$$\begin{array}{r} {}^{9}_{1\ \cancel{10}13}\cancel{2}\cancel{0}\cancel{3} \\ -125 \\ \hline \end{array}$$

You can also use a calculator.

Think: 10 tens 3 ones = 9 tens 13 ones

STEP 3

Subtract the ones, tens, and hundreds.

$$\begin{array}{r} {}^{9}_{1\ \cancel{10}13}\cancel{2}\cancel{0}\cancel{3} \\ -125 \\ \hline 78 \end{array}$$

Add to check:
$$\begin{array}{r} 78 \\ +125 \\ \hline 203 \end{array}$$

They still need to plant 78 trees.

Try It   Subtract. Add to check.

1. 307 − 39

2. $2.07 − $0.35

3. 302 − 199

4. 409 − 285

5. 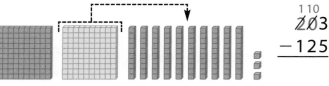 **Explain** the steps to subtract 506 − 248. Then solve.

Practice and Problem Solving

Subtract. Add to check.

6.	106	7.	703	8.	$201	9.	500	10.	506
	− 27		−147		− 31		−317		−257

11. $605 − $339

12. 600 − 312

13. 401 − 294

14. 205 − 118

15. 401 − 57

16. 802 − 704

x **Algebra** Use the rule to find the difference.

17.

Rule: Subtract 445

Input	851	704	900
Output			

18.

Rule: Subtract 354

Input	412	603	701
Output			

Solve. Use data from the table for problems 19–21.

19. How many more people prefer to grow annual flowers rather than perennials?

THINK SOLVE EXPLAIN
★20. **What If** 40 people who chose vegetables change their minds and vote for perennials. How will this change the survey results?

21. **Mental Math** Which 2 kinds of plants earned 500 votes?

Which Do You Prefer to Grow? Survey Results

Kind of Plants	Number of Votes
Annual Flowers	300
Perennial Flowers	270
Vegetables	230

Spiral Review and Test Prep

22. Which belongs in the same fact family as 6 + 3 = 9? (p. 96)

 A. 9 + 3 = 12   C. 12 − 3 = 9

 B. 9 − 3 = 6   D. 6 − 3 = 3

23. Which has an estimated sum of 400? (p. 64)

 F. 191 + 231   H. 270 + 301

 G. 312 + 287   I. 221 + 115

What is the value of the underlined digit in each number? (p. 10)

24. 4<u>2</u>1

25. <u>6</u>,302

26. 13,<u>0</u>31

27. 1<u>2</u>4,512

Extra Practice page 126, Set A

6.2 Estimate Differences

Learn

Enrique researches information on 2 kinds of trees, the pecan hickory and the eastern redbud. About how much taller than the eastern redbud is the pecan hickory?

Estimate: 148 − 47

eastern redbud
47 feet

pecan hickory
148 feet

Round to the Nearest Ten

Round each number to subtract mentally.

$$148 - 47$$
$$\downarrow \qquad \downarrow$$
$$150 - 50 = 100$$

The pecan hickory is about 100 feet taller than the eastern redbud.

Round to . . .

the Nearest Hundred

$$388 - 159$$
$$\downarrow \qquad \downarrow$$
$$400 - 200 = 200$$

the Nearest Thousand

$$6{,}843 - 3{,}087$$
$$\downarrow \qquad \downarrow$$
$$7{,}000 - 3{,}000 = 4{,}000$$

Try It

Estimate each difference. Tell how you rounded.

1. 49 − 31   **2.** 420 − 170   **3.** 1,450 − 607   **4.** 8,513 − 2,807

5.  **Write About It** **Estimate** 386 − 75 using 2 strategies. Tell which strategy you prefer and explain your choice.

Practice and Problem Solving

Estimate each difference.

6. $83 - 62$

7. $616 - 423$

8. $1,245 - 710$

9. $381 - 15$

10. $1,144 - 272$

11. $4,432 - 1,673$

12. $9,385 - 5,730$

13. $4,211 - 115$

14. $3,024 - 917$

15. $9,256 - 7,009$

16. $7,512 - 2,097$

17. $5,193 - 3,579$

ⓧ Algebra Write $>$ or $<$ to make a true sentence.

18. $38 - 17 \bullet 30$

19. $416 - 197 \bullet 300$

20. $1,121 - 612 \bullet 400$

★21. $94 - 36 \bullet 83 - 39$

★22. $84 - 21 \bullet 77 - 36$

★23. $156 - 85 \bullet 178 - 93$

Solve.

THINK
SOLVE
EXPLAIN

24. **Analyze** Sandy estimates $872 - 312$ is about 600. How did she round the numbers? Is this estimate greater or less than the exact answer? Explain.

25. Pablo saw 98 flowering desert bushes and Jamie saw 133. How many did they see altogether?

Link to SCIENCE

The Saguaro cactus can live up to 200 years and grow to 50 feet tall.

26. One Saguaro cactus is 103 years old. About how many more years might it live? Explain.

Spiral Review and Test Prep

27. Greg planted 15 tulips one day and 7 tulips another day. Which shows how many tulips he planted? (p. 60)

    A. $15 - 7 = 8$ C. $7 + 8 = 15$

    B. $15 - 8 = 7$ D. $15 + 7 = 21$

28. Tim drives 482 miles. What is that number rounded to the nearest hundred? (p. 32)

    F. 500   H. 480

    G. 490   I. 400

29. $\blacksquare + 7 = 11$ (p.52)

30. $3 + 4 + \blacksquare = 12$ (p.52)

31. $\blacksquare + 6 + 2 = 18$ (p.52)

6.3 Problem Solving: Strategy
Write an Equation

Read

Eric is growing 2 flowers in his garden. One flower is 78 centimeters tall and the other flower is 100 centimeters tall. He wants to know how much taller one plant is than the other.

- **What do you know?**
  The heights of the flowers

- **What do you need to find?**
  The difference between the heights of the 2 flowers

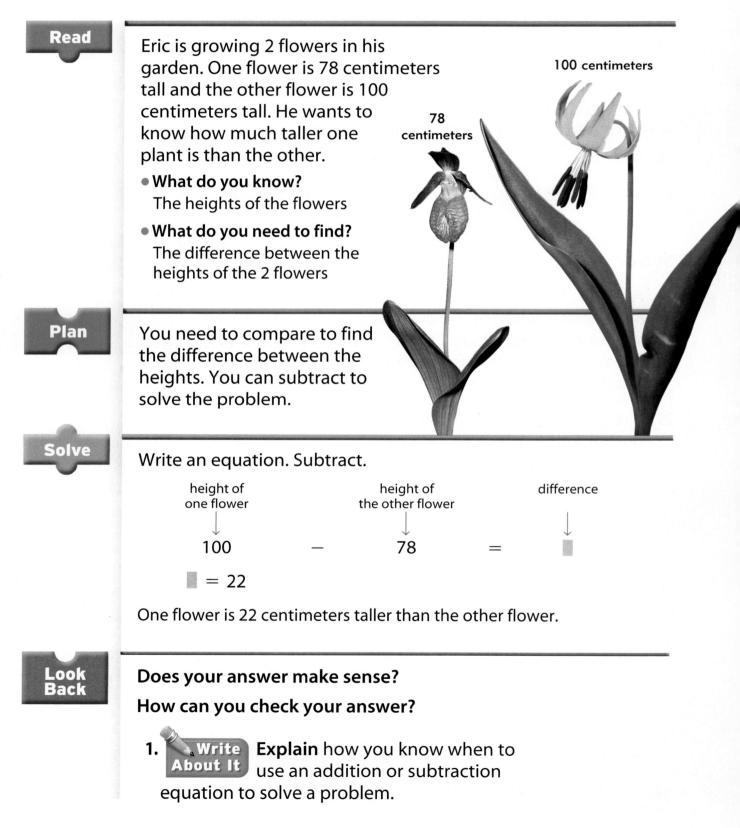

100 centimeters

78 centimeters

Plan

You need to compare to find the difference between the heights. You can subtract to solve the problem.

Solve

Write an equation. Subtract.

height of one flower		height of the other flower		difference
↓		↓		↓
100	−	78	=	�a

▪ = 22

One flower is 22 centimeters taller than the other flower.

Look Back

Does your answer make sense?

How can you check your answer?

1. **Write About It** **Explain** how you know when to use an addition or subtraction equation to solve a problem.

2. A Douglas fir is 100 meters tall and a ponderosa pine is 68 meters tall. How much taller is the Douglas fir than the ponderosa pine?

3. A grand fir tree can grow to be 72 meters tall. The coast redwood tree can grow to be 17 meters taller. How tall can the coast redwood tree grow?

4. Last year students raised $1,016 for the library. They hope to raise at least $175 more this year. What is the least amount they can raise to meet their goal?

5. In Littleton Park there are 1,128 trees. Clarksville Common has 840 trees. How many fewer trees are in Clarksville Common?

Mixed Strategy Review

6. Laura uses a dollar to buy a packet of seeds. She gets back 35¢ change. How much did the seeds cost?

Use data from the survey for problems 7–9.

7. How many more votes did the winning flower get than the one with the least number of votes?

★ 8. If you round all the votes to the nearest hundred, can you still tell which flower won? Can you tell which came in second? Why or why not?

9. ✎ **Write a problem** using the information from the chart. Solve it. Then give it to a friend to solve.

Choose a Strategy
- Logical Reasoning
- Draw a Picture or Diagram
- Make a Graph
- Act It Out
- Make a Table or List
- Find a Pattern
- Guess and Check
- Write an Equation
- Work Backward
- Solve a Simpler Problem

Watertown Official Town Flower Survey

Flower	Number of Votes
Rose	1,345
Tulip	978
Daisy	1,008
Tiger Lily	749

6.4

Subtract Greater Numbers

Learn

The Botanical Gardens creates a special display with 2,238 red roses and 1,319 pink roses. How many more red roses are there than pink roses?

Find: 2,238 − 1,319

Estimate:

$$\begin{array}{r} 2,238 \longrightarrow 2,000 \\ -1,319 \longrightarrow -1,000 \\ \hline 1,000 \end{array}$$

Use Paper and Pencil

STEP 1

Subtract the ones. Regroup if necessary.

$$\begin{array}{r} \overset{2\ 18}{2,2\cancel{3}\cancel{8}} \\ -1,319 \\ \hline 9 \end{array}$$

Think:
3 tens 8 ones = 2 tens 18 ones

STEP 2

Subtract the tens. Regroup if necessary.

$$\begin{array}{r} \overset{2\ 18}{2,2\cancel{3}\cancel{8}} \\ -1,319 \\ \hline 19 \end{array}$$

STEP 3

Subtract the hundreds. Regroup if necessary.

$$\begin{array}{r} \overset{1\ \ 12\ 2\ 18}{2,\cancel{2}\cancel{3}\cancel{8}} \\ -1,319 \\ \hline 919 \end{array}$$

Think:
2 thousands 2 hundreds =
1 thousand 12 hundreds

STEP 4

Subtract the thousands.

$$\begin{array}{r} \overset{1\ \ 12\ 2\ 18}{2,\cancel{2}\cancel{3}\cancel{8}} \\ -1,319 \\ \hline 919 \end{array}$$

The answer of 919 is close to the estimate of 1,000. The answer is reasonable.

There are 919 more red roses than pink roses.

Admission to the Botanical Gardens is $10.00. Carlos has a discount coupon worth $2.25 off the price. How much will Carlos pay?

Find: $10.00 − $2.25

Estimate: $10.00 − $2.25
  ↓   ↓
$10.00 − $2.00 = $8.00

There's More Than One Way!

Use Paper and Pencil

STEP 1

Line up the decimal points.

$10.00
−   2.25

STEP 2

Subtract as you would whole numbers.

Regroup if necessary.

```
    9  9
  0 10 10 10
$ 1 0 . 0 0
−     2 . 2 5
      7 . 7 5
```

STEP 3

Write the dollar sign and decimal point in the difference.

```
    9  9
  0 10 10 10
$ 1 0 . 0 0
−     2 . 2 5
    $ 7 . 7 5
```

Use a Calculator

Press: [1] [0] [.] [0] [0] [−] [2] [.] [2] [5]

Display: 10.00 − 2.25 =
                    7.75.

The answer of $7.75 is close to the estimate of $8.00. The answer is reasonable.

Carlos will pay $7.75 for admission.

Try It

Subtract. Check that each answer is reasonable.

1. 2,346 − 1,538   **2.** 8,139 − 893   **3.** $60.77 − $33.45   **4.** $70.98
                                                                                 −   4.99

5. **Write About It** **Describe** how subtracting 4-digit numbers and subtracting 3-digit numbers are similar.

Practice and Problem Solving

Subtract. Check that each answer is reasonable.

6.	4,568	7.	3,567	8.	8,435	9.	3,574	10.	6,251
	−2,423		−1,887		−7,598		−896		−6,251

11. $75.53 − $38.75

12. $62.74 − $7.55

13. 8,004 − 7,695

★ 14. 100,000 − 99,348   ★ 15. $400.48 − $176.49   ★ 16. 142,075 − 78,294

X **Algebra** Write + or − to make a true number sentence.

17. 3,945 ⬤ 396 = 3,549

18. 4,003 ⬤ 2,673 = 6,676

Solve. Use data from the sign for problems 19–20.

19. Paul buys one of each type of plant. He gives the clerk $30. How much change should he get?

Plant Sale
Tulips $11.35
Violets $8.75
Daisies $7.35

THINK
SOLVE
EXPLAIN

20. **Write a problem** using the data from the table. Solve it. Ask others to solve it.

THINK
SOLVE
EXPLAIN

21. **Logical Reasoning** How many cuts are needed in a log to get 4 pieces? 5 pieces? 6 pieces? What do you notice? Predict the number of cuts needed to get 27 pieces.

22. **Make It Right** Here is how Helen subtracted 3,002 − 1,764. Tell what mistake she made. Show how to correct it.

THINK
SOLVE
EXPLAIN

✓ Spiral Review and Test Prep

23. Which number has exactly 1 hundred thousand, 1 ten thousand, and 1 hundred? (p. 10)

 A. 111,001   C. 100,100

 B. 110,100   D. 10,100

24. It is 8 o'clock now. Pete will walk his dog in 2 hours. At what time will Pete walk his dog? (p. 52)

 F. 1 o'clock   H. 9 o'clock

 G. 2 o'clock   I. 10 o'clock

Write the digit in the thousands place. (p. 6)

25. 5,604   26. 9,428   27. 10,641   28. 248,007

Extra Practice page 126, Set D

Writing for Math

A plant store sold $1,109 worth of flowers and trees. They sold $768 in trees. How much did they sell in flowers? Explain.

Jorge's Response

Teacher's Response

✔ **THINK**

Subtract to find the difference between the amount sold in trees and the amount sold in flowers and trees.

← Jorge explains how he will use what he knows to solve the problem.

✔ **SOLVE**

Subtract:
They sold $341 of flowers.

$$\begin{array}{r} \overset{10}{\cancel{0}}\,\overset{0}{\cancel{1}}\overset{10}{\cancel{0}}9 \\ \$1,109 \\ -\quad 768 \\ \hline \$341 \end{array}$$

← Jorge shows his work.

✔ **EXPLAIN**

The store sold $768 in trees. I subtracted that amount from $1,109, the total sale of flowers and trees, to find out how much they sold in flowers. The difference is $341, so they sold $341 of flowers.

← Jorge uses appropriate math terms, such as **subtract** and **difference**. He clearly explains *why* he subtracted to solve the problem.

To check, I added $341 to $768, the amount of trees sold. The sum is $1,109, the total of flowers and trees sold. So my answer makes sense.

$$\begin{array}{r} \$341 \\ +\ 768 \\ \hline \$1,109 \end{array}$$

← Jorge uses the add-to-check strategy to check his answer for accuracy and reasonableness.

THINK SOLVE EXPLAIN

Solve. Show your work and tell why your answer makes sense. Use Jorge's work as a guide.

1. A new TV costs $549. If Bonnie uses a "$150-off" coupon, how much will she need to pay for the TV?

2. Hector has $10.00. If he buys a magazine for $4.17, will he have enough left to buy a card game for $6.00?

6.5 Choose a Computation Method

Learn

At the Agricultural County Fair, 2,017 people attended on the first day and 1,713 people the second day. How many fewer people attended on the second day than the first day?

Find: 2,017 − 1,713

Estimate: 2,200 − 1,700 = 300

There's More Than One Way!

I use Paper and Pencil

$$
\begin{array}{r}
{\scriptstyle 1\ \ 10} \\
2,\cancel{0}17 \\
-\ 1,713 \\
\hline
304
\end{array}
$$

I use a Calculator

Press:

2 0 1 7 −

1 7 1 3 Enter =

Display:

2017-1713=
304.

I use Mental Math

I split both 2,017 and 1,713 into 2 parts.
2,017 → 2,000 + 17
1,713 → 1,700 + 13

First, I subtract.
2,000 − 1,700 = 300

Then 17 − 13 = 4

Last, I add
300 + 4 = 304

There were 304 fewer people that attended on the second day.

Try It Tell which method you use.

1. 5,482 − 3,209 **2.** 809 − 768 **3.** 8,500 − 4,300 **4.** 7,082 − 3,098

5. **Write About It** **Explain** which method you would use to solve the example problem.

Pencil / Paper   Calculator   Mental Math

Subtract. Tell which method you use.

6. $557 - 409$ **7.** $398 - 87$ **8.** $430 - 304$ **9.** $746 - 564$

10. $5,284 - 674$ **11.** $6,153 - 4,298$ **12.** $7,500 - 2,300$ **13.** $1,278 - 1,185$

14. $9,000 - 4,076$ **15.** $3,988 - 3,049$ **16.** $2,093 - 1,578$ **17.** $9,204 - 5,214$

★**18.** $45,841 - 32,293$ ★**19.** $80,469 - 76,558$ ★**20.** $45,876 - 23,940$

$\boxed{x}$ **Algebra Find the missing number.**

21. $670 - \blacksquare = 340$ **22.** $\blacksquare - 100 = 540$ **23.** $8,900 - \blacksquare = 5,005$

Solve. Use data from the table for problems 24–25.

24. How many more visitors were at the State Fair on Saturday than on Sunday?

25. About how many visitors were at the State Fair all 3 days?

State Fair Visitors

Friday: 1,098
Saturday: 1,934
Sunday: 1,061

THINK SOLVE EXPLAIN

26. Generalize When is it easier to use a calculator to solve a problem than using paper and pencil or mental math?

27. **Write a problem** with subtraction using numbers in the thousands where using mental math is the easiest way to solve the problem.

THINK SOLVE EXPLAIN

Spiral Review and Test Prep

28. Which number is greater than 8,458? (p. 24)

  A. 7,980   **C.** 8,390

  B. 8,299   **D.** 8,548

29. Which number rounds to 3,000? (p. 34)

  F. 2,498   **H.** 3,602

  G. 2,744   **I.** 3,999

30. $47 + 38 + 95$ (p. 76)   **31.** $59 + 73 + 185$ (p. 76)   **32.** $145 + 99 + 153$ (p. 76)

Chapter 6

Extra Practice

Set A **Subtract. Check your answer.** (pp. 114–115)

| 1. | 302 − 19 | 2. | 404 − 269 | 3. | $3,050 − 299 | 4. | 8,000 − 4,233 |

5. 302 − 58   **6.** $4,008 − $279   **7.** 6,020 − 3,654   **8.** 950 − 472

Set B **Estimate each difference.** (pp. 116–117)

| 9. | 972 − 513 | 10. | 334 − 178 | 11. | 668 − 26 | 12. | 8,237 − 3,890 |

13. 841 − 589   **14.** 356 − 24   **15.** 1,538 − 589   **16.** 3,038 − 1,950

Set C **Write an equation to solve.** (pp. 118–119)

Use data from the table for problems 17-19.

17. How many more species of beech are there than magnolias?

18. How many fewer species of dogwoods are there than willows?

19. How many more species of willows are there than magnolias?

Tree Species

Tree	Estimated Number of Species
Magnolia	230
Beech	900
Willow	500
Dogwood	110

Set D **Subtract.** (pp. 120–122)

| 20. | $0.72 − 0.38 | 21. | $263.89 − 134.95 | 22. | $7.12 − 2.65 | 23. | $842.23 − 599.57 |

24. $6,365 − $407   **25.** 5,224 − 567   **26.** 7,548 − 892

Set E **Subtract. Tell which method you use.** (pp. 124–125)

27. 708 − 288   **28.** 1,987 − 782   **29.** 5,193 − 4,893   **30.** 2,800 − 1,783

31. 2,003 − 1,962   **32.** 1,543 − 98   **33.** 8,937 − 6,467   **34.** 792 − 74

LOG ON www.mmhmath.com
For more practice and Chapter Self-Check Test

Subtract. Add to check.

1. 50 − 27 **2.** 405 − 25 **3.** 860 − 114 **4.** 702 − 331

5. 501 − 306 **6.** 634 − 100 **7.** 980 − 90 **8.** 756 − 206

Estimate each difference.

9. 75 − 58 **10.** 832 − 309 **11.** $3,364 − $609 **12.** 289 − 37

Subtract. Check that each answer is reasonable.

13. 606 − 89 **14.** $6,340 − $284 **15.** 4,875 − 3,168

16. 882 − 256 **17.** 3,515 − 1,863 **18.** 943 − 678

19. 407
− 89

20. $21.90
− 11.75

21. $7.46
− 3.39

Solve.

22. An oak tree is 78 feet tall. The fir tree next to the oak is 122 feet tall. How much taller is the fir tree? Write an equation.

23. A large bouquet of flowers costs $8.49. A small bouquet sells for $5.75. How much money will you save if you buy a small bouquet?

24. A nursery has 2,468 bushes in stock. At the end of the season there are 386 bushes left. Show how to estimate the number of bushes the nursery sold.

25. **Write About It** What are 3 different methods you can use to solve a subtraction problem?

Do I Need Help?

Exercises	Review Concepts	Use Extra Practice Set
1–8	pp. 114–115	Set A
9–12	pp. 116–117	Set B
13–21	pp. 120–122	Set D
22–24	pp. 118–119	Set C
25	pp. 124–125	Set E

Foldables Use your Foldables to help you review.

Decision Making

Aaron wants to plant vegetables in his garden. He has $10 to spend on plants. He will use seedlings that have already started growing.

144 inches

120 inches

You Decide!

Which vegetable plants should he buy and how can he arrange them?

Vegetable Plants for Sale

Mix and Match Plants
$2.25 for a tray of 16
or $0.25 for 1

Beefsteak Tomatoes
Plant 36 inches apart

Bell Peppers
Plant 12 inches apart

Lettuce
Plant 15 inches apart

Cherry Tomatoes
Plant 18 inches apart

Read for Understanding

1. How long is Aaron's garden? How wide is it?

2. How far apart should beefsteak tomatoes be planted?

3. What is the total cost of 2 trays of plants?

4. Which needs more space between each plant, lettuce or bell peppers?

Make Decisions

5. Which vegetables can be planted closest together?

6. Which vegetables must be planted with the most space between them?

7. How much more space is needed between beefsteak tomatoes than between cherry tomatoes?

8. Is Aaron's garden long enough to plant 4 beefsteak tomato plants in a row? Explain.

9. Can Aaron buy 4 trays of plants? How can you tell?

10. If Aaron buys 4 trays of plants, how much money will he have left?

11. How many lettuce plants can Aaron fit in 1 row of his garden if he starts in a corner?

12. What if Aaron wants to buy only cherry tomato plants. How many plants can he fit in his garden?

13. If you plant 3 lettuce plants and 3 cherry tomato plants in 1 row, how long will that row be?

14. Should Aaron place plants in the corners of his garden? Why or why not?

15. What are some reasons for and against buying only 1 kind of vegetable plant for Aaron's garden?

Your Decision!

THINK
SOLVE
EXPLAIN

Which plants should Aaron buy? How should he arrange them in his garden? Draw a diagram to show your decision.

Problem Solving

Vocabulary

Complete. Use a word from the list.

1. The answer in subtraction is the ___.

2. To ___ a difference you can round the number, then subtract.

3. ___ are made up of related facts.

VOCABULARY
difference
estimate
fact families
related facts

Skills and Applications

Relate Addition and Subtraction. (pp. 96–99)

Find the missing addend:
■ + 5 = 12

Solution
Use the related subtraction fact.

$12 - 5 = 7$, so $7 + 5 = 12$
■ = 7

Write a fact family.

4. 2, 6, 8   5. 8, 8, 16

Find each missing addend.

6. ■ + 4 = 11   7. 6 + ■ = 14

8. ■ + 7 = 7   9. 5 + ■ = 11

Use Subtraction Patterns. (pp. 102–103)

Find: 1,300 − 700

Solution
Use patterns to subtract mentally.

$13 - 7 = 6$
$130 - 70 = 60$
$1,300 - 700 = 600$

Subtract. Use mental math.

10. 70 − 40   11. 90 − 50

12. 50 − 40   13. 120 − 40

14. 800 − 400   15. 1,100 − 600

16. 1,300 − 800   17. 1,800 − 900

Foldables Use your Foldables to help you review.

Subtract whole numbers. (pp. 104–108, 114–115, 120–122)

Find: 614 − 148

Solution
Subtract. Regroup if necessary.

$$\begin{array}{r} \overset{\scriptstyle 10}{\underset{}{}} \\ \overset{5\ \cancel{0}\ 14}{\cancel{6}\cancel{1}\cancel{4}} \\ -148 \\ \hline 466 \end{array}$$

Check:
466 + 148 = 614

Subtract. Check your answer.

18. 456 − 187

19. 2,345 − 709

20. $605 − $234

21. 5,070 − 651

22. 642 − 98

23. 1,012 − 78

24. $8.24 − $3.19

25. $4.02 − $0.87

Estimate Differences. (pp. 116–117)

Estimate: 821 − 367

Solution
Round each number.

Think: 821 − 367
$$\downarrow\downarrow$$
$$800 − 400 = 400$$

So 821 − 367 is about 400.

Estimate each difference.

26. 678 − 324

27. 842 − 513

28. 1,380 − 564

29. 1,602 − 178

30. $6.98 − $2.85

31. $8.74 − $3.23

Use skills and strategies to solve problems. (pp. 100–101, 118–119)

A farmer has room to plant 523 rows of corn. So far she has planted 187 rows. How many more rows of corn can she plant?

Solution
Write an equation.
523 − 187 = ▇
523 − 187 = 336
She can plant 336 more rows of corn.

Solve.

32. The florist ordered 124 roses, 276 tulips, and 178 carnations. How many more carnations than roses were ordered?

33. A seed catalog offers 1,246 kinds of flower seeds and 382 kinds of vegetable seeds. About how many more kinds of flower seeds are offered?

Enrichment

Odd or Even Sums and Differences

Odd numbers end in 1, 3, 5, 7, or 9. An example is 27.
Even numbers end in 0, 2, 4, 6, or 8. An example is 46.

Write if the number is odd or even.

1. 45   **2.** 1   **3.** 127   **4.** 94   **5.** 328

When you add or subtract even and odd numbers, can you predict what the sum will be? Will you get an odd or even number? You can make a table to look for patterns.

6. Make a table like the one below to find sums.

Numbers	Example	Sum	Odd or Even?
odd + odd	43 + 21		
odd + odd	11 + 85		
even + even	32 + 12		
even + even	44 + 30		
odd + even	15 + 8		
even + odd	16 + 33		

7. Make a table like the one below to find differences.

Numbers	Example	Difference	Odd or Even?
odd - odd	15 − 3		
odd - odd	67 − 41		
even - even	88 − 14		
even - even	96 − 30		
odd - even	13 − 4		
odd - even	25 − 22		
even - odd	14 − 7		
odd - even	17 − 12		

Use models. Write if the sum is *odd* or *even*.

8.

9.

10. Generalize What did you discover? Write a paragraph.

11. How can you use these generalizations to check that a sum or difference is reasonable?

Performance Assessment

Which Items Can You Buy?

Dave has $475 to spend on his garden this year. He wants to have between $30 and $35 left to paint the garden fence. Look at the items on sale at the garden shop. Which items can Dave buy?

Make a chart like the one below to help you keep track of how much money is left. Make your chart as long as you need to.

Use your chart to help you answer these questions.

- How many different items can Dave buy?
- How much money does he have left?

Item	Cost	Money Left

$55

$220

$69

$23

$129

$49

$49

$17

$20

Tips For A Good Answer

- Show a chart that is clearly filled in.
- Show the steps you followed to find the money left after each purchase.
- Show the correct amount left.

You may want to save this work in your portfolio.

ⓔ-Journal www.mmhmath.com
Write about math. Unit 3 **133**

Assessment

TECHNOLOGY Link

Error Corrections

Ryan was checking his subtraction problems using his calculator. He entered 382 − 285. He should have entered 382 − 275. How can he fix the mistake without starting over? What is the difference?

Using the TI-15

To correct a mistake, enter the following:

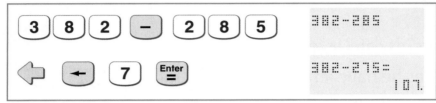

Ryan fixed the mistake by using the ⬅ key to move the cursor back 1 space and the ← to delete the 8.

The difference is 107.

Enter the problem into your calculator, then correct the problem by entering the number in brackets. Find the difference.

1. 485 − 63 [93]

2. 518 [548] − 134

3. 572 − 84 [54]

4. 603 [613] − 76

5. 291 [591] − 88

6. 840 [841] − 87

7. 762 [752] − 112

8. 157 − 85 [55]

9. 350 [340] − 95

Solve.

10. Joyce was checking her subtraction problem of 296 − 38. She entered 296 − 35 into her calculator. What is the correct difference?

11. Todd was using his calculator to subtract 458 − 96. He made a mistake and entered 478 − 96. How many times must he press the left arrow key to change the 7 to a 5? Explain.

For more practice, use Math Traveler™.

Test-Taking Tips

In a multiple choice test, you can eliminate choices by first **estimating the answer**.

Carl spent $3.47 at the store. How much change should he get from $5.00?

A. $0.98   **C.** $1.63

B. $1.53   **D.** $2.53

Estimate the answer by rounding $3.47 to $3.50.

$5.00 − $3.50 = $1.50

You can eliminate choices A and D. Now find the exact answer.

$5.00 − $3.47 = $1.53.

B is the correct choice.

Check for Success

Before turning in a test, go back one last time to check.

☑ I understood and answered the questions asked.

☑ I checked my work for errors.

☑ My answers make sense.

Use estimation to eliminate choices. Choose the best answer.

1. 399 + 802

 A. 403   **C.** 1,191
 B. 1,101   **D.** 1,201

2. 119 less than 450 is ▨.

 F. 331   **H.** 349
 G. 341   **I.** 569

3. Val got $3.76 in change from a ten-dollar bill. How much did she spend?

 A. $4.24   **C.** $6.24
 B. $5.34   **D.** $6.34

4. 538 − 82

 F. 456   **H.** 610
 G. 506   **I.** 620

5. 822 − 396

 A. 426   **C.** 536
 B. 526   **D.** 1,208

6. There were 324 people at the concert on Tuesday, 478 people on Wednesday, and 389 on Thursday. How many people went to the concert during the 3 days?

 F. 1,071   **H.** 1,191
 G. 1,091   **I.** 1,312

Test Prep

PART 1 • Multiple Choice

Choose the best answer.

1. On Saturday at the Flower Show, Joe made $886 selling plants. On the next 2 days he made $679 and $528. About how much did he make all together? (p. 72)

   A. $1,800   **C.** $2,000
   B. $1,900   **D.** $2,100

2. What is the missing number? (p. 56)

   $$7 + 5 = 12$$
   $$70 + 50 = 120$$
   $$700 + \blacksquare = 1,200$$

   F. 50   **H.** 500
   G. 70   **I.** 700

3. When Marco planted a tomato plant in the ground it was 8 inches high. Seven weeks later the plant was 56 inches high. How much did the plant grow in those seven weeks? (p. 106)

   A. 7 inches   **C.** 49 inches
   B. 48 inches   **D.** 64 inches

4. Write 32,506 in expanded form. What number is missing? (p. 10)

   $$30,000 + \blacksquare + 500 + 6$$

   F. 20,000   **H.** 200
   G. 2,000   **I.** 2

5. By mistake Tracy erased part of her subtraction problem. What is the missing digit? (p. 120)

   $$4\blacksquare6 - 149 = 287$$

   A. 6   **C.** 3
   B. 2   **D.** 4

6. Scarlett writes a 4-digit odd number. The sum of the digits is an even number. Which of the following could be her number? (p. 52)

   F. 1,345   **H.** 3,002
   G. 2,583   **I.** 45,917

7. Danny lives on the right side of Oliver Street. His house is the fifth one on that side. The first two houses on the right side have the addresses 2043 and 2045. Which of the following could be Danny's house? (p. 2)

   A. 2046   **C.** 2051
   B. 2047   **D.** 2069

8. What is the value of 7 in the number 576,890? (p. 10)

   F. thousands
   G. hundred thousands
   H. ten thousands
   I. tens

Record your answers on the answer sheet provided by your teacher or on a sheet of paper.

9. What operation makes this number sentence true? (p. 106)

88 ● 4 = 84

THINK SOLVE EXPLAIN
10. Each trip to Joe's Plant Store and back takes Kim 20 minutes. One day Kim made 3 trips to the plant store. How long did it take her all together? Explain. (p. 76)

11. Subtract. Then add to check your work. (p. 114)

$4,002
−   964

12. On Saturday about 1,645 people attended the Flower Show. On Sunday about 1,654 people attended. On Monday 1,564 people attended. List the days in order of greatest to least attendance. (p. 26)

13. What is the total amount? (p. 14)

Use the table for questions 14–16.

Flowering Herbs		
Name	Height	Month It Flowers
Lavender	30 in.	June-July
Borage	16 in.	June-August
Catnip	14 in.	July-September
Chives	24 in.	June
Sage	18 in.	June

14. How many plants flower only in the month of June? (p. 36)

15. Which is the tallest herb that flowers in July? (p. 26)

THINK SOLVE EXPLAIN
16. How much taller are the chives than the catnip? Explain. (p. 106)

THINK SOLVE EXPLAIN
Record your answer on a sheet of paper. Show your work.

17. Mitchell has $40.00 to spend on school supplies. He needs to buy 2 notebooks for $1.39 each, a package of pencils for $1.89, a backpack for $15.99, and 5 folders for $0.75 each. How much change will Mitchell have after his purchases? Explain how you know. (p. 120)

Test Prep

What Do I Need to Know?

Tim wants to go to the playground at the time shown. What time is shown on the clock?

Time

What Will I Learn?

In this chapter you will learn to

- tell time
- convert measures of time
- find elapsed time and ending time
- use a calendar
- use a time line
- use skills and strategies to solve problems

How Do I Read Math?

When you read a mathematics book, sometimes you read words and symbols, and sometimes you read only symbols.

All of these represent the time shown on the clock below:

- **2:30**
- **two-thirty**
- **half past two**
- **thirty minutes after two o'clock**

VOCABULARY

- A.M.
- P.M.
- minute
- hour
- half hour
- quarter hour
- elapsed time
- week
- month
- ordinal number
- time line

Foldables

Use your Foldables to help you with chapter concepts.

1. Place two sheets of paper an inch apart.
2. Roll up the bottom edges of the papers. Stop them 1–inch from the top edges.
3. When all tabs are about the same size, crease the paper to hold the tabs in place.
4. Staple along the fold.
5. Label as shown. Record what you learn.

Half hour = 30 minutes   2 half hours = 1 hour

7.1 Tell Time

Learn

The clocks below show when Tara ate breakfast, lunch, a snack, and dinner one day. What time did Tara eat breakfast? Lunch? A snack? Dinner?

VOCABULARY

A.M.
P.M.
minute (min)

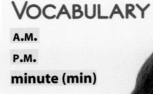

Read and Write Time

Breakfast Time	**Lunch Time**	**Snack Time**	**Dinner Time**
7:30	12:00	3:45	6:15

Read:
• seven-thirty A.M.
• half past seven
• thirty minutes after seven

Read:
• twelve o'clock P.M.
• twelve noon

Read:
• three forty-five P.M.
• forty-five minutes after three
• a quarter to four

Read:
• six-fifteen P.M.
• a quarter after six
• fifteen minutes after six

> A.M. is a name for time from 12 midnight to 12 noon.

Write: 7:30 A.M.

Write: 12:00 P.M.

Write: 3:45 P.M.

Write: 6:15 P.M.

> P.M. is a name for time from 12 noon to 12 midnight.

Tara ate breakfast at 7:30 A.M., lunch at 12:00 P.M., a snack at 3:45 P.M., and dinner at 6:15 P.M.

These clocks show the time Tara arrives at school and when she leaves school. Read the clocks to find out when Tara arrives at and leaves school.

Tell time to the nearest 5 minutes and the nearest minute. A **minute** is a unit of time.

Arrives   Leaves

8:35   3:03

Count by 5s

The hour hand points to 8 o'clock.

Start at the 12 and count by 5s.
This clock shows 8:35.

Think: There are 5 minutes between each number.

Tara arrives at school at 8:35 A.M.

Count by 1s

The hour hand points to 3 o'clock.

Start at the 12 and count by 1s.
This clock shows 3:03.

Think: There is 1 minute between each tick mark.

She leaves school at 3:03 P.M.

Try It   Write each time using A.M. or P.M. Then write the time in 2 ways.

1.

2.

3.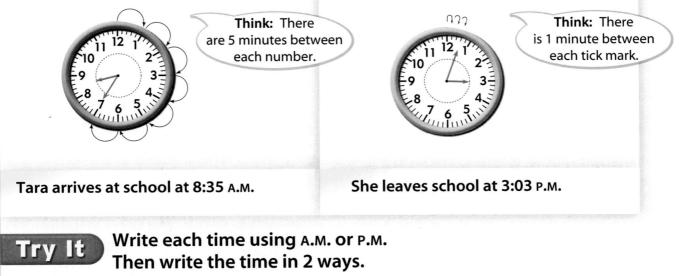

4.

5.  **Explain** where the hour and minute hands are when the time is 7:45.

Practice and Problem Solving

Write the time in 2 different ways. Include A.M. and P.M.

6.

7.

ⓍAlgebra Fill in the missing digits on the digital clocks.

8.
5: 0

9. **6:3**

★ 10. **:**

Solve.

11. **Language Arts** Write a description of something you usually do at 7:30 A.M. Then write about something you do at 7:30 P.M.

12. **Compare** Why is it necessary to use A.M. and P.M.?

13. **Make It Right** Eric made a mistake. Tell what mistake he made and explain how to correct it.

10 minutes after 4

Link to SOCIAL STUDIES ★

This famous clock in London, England, is known as "Big Ben." The name "Big Ben" actually refers to the bell inside the tower, not to the clock.

14. What hour is shown on Big Ben in this picture? Do you think it is A.M. or P.M.? Why?

Spiral Review and Test Prep

15. Which is in the ones place in 45,876? (p. 6)

   A. 4   **B.** 8   **C.** 7   **D.** 6

16. Which is the greatest number? (p. 26)

   F. 4,404   **H.** 4,000 + 40
   G. 4,044   **I.** 44 hundred

17. 30 + 40 (p. 56)   18. 150 − 50 (p. 102)   19. 700 + 400 (p. 56)   20. 130 − 70 (p. 102)

6. 4:45 P.M., forty-five minutes past four   8. 4

Extra Practice page 156, Set A

TELLING TIME

Use analog clocks to display time.

Ready

Players: 2 or more
You Will Need: analog clocks, 10 index cards

Set

Make 10 time cards with times like 4:48 and 12:19.

Mix the cards and place them face down.

GO!

▶ Each player has an analog clock.

▶ One player picks a card.

▶ Each player sets their clock to the time shown on the card.

▶ The first player done shows his or her clock. If correct, that player earns a point. If not, the other player may steal the point by showing the correct time.

▶ The other player picks another card, and play repeats.

▶ The first player with 10 points wins.

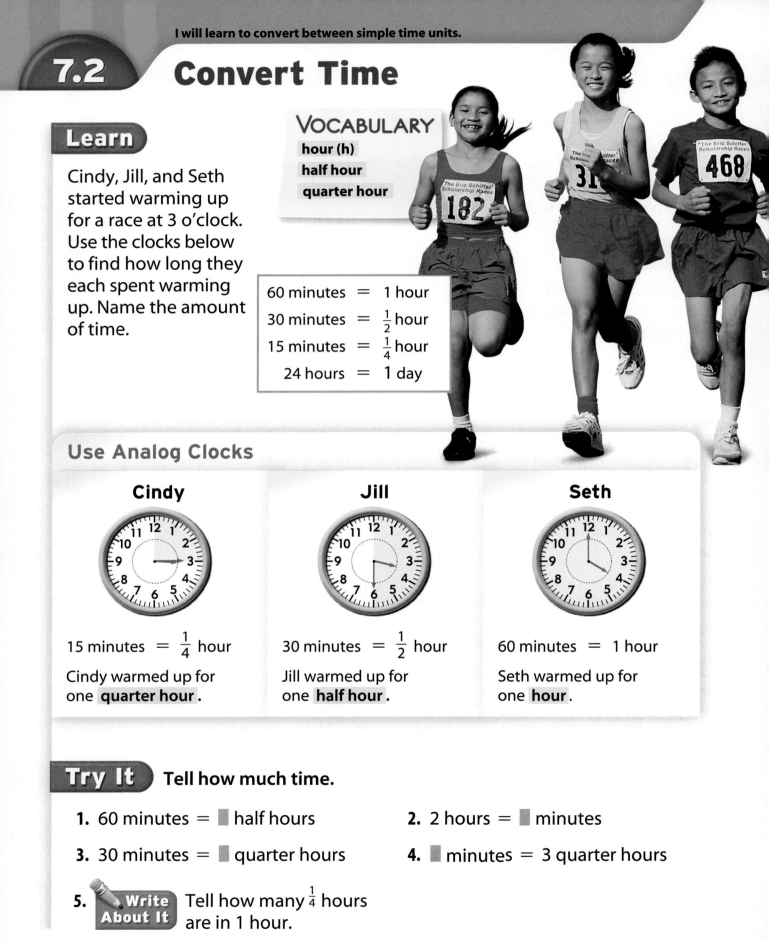

7.2 Convert Time

Learn

Cindy, Jill, and Seth started warming up for a race at 3 o'clock. Use the clocks below to find how long they each spent warming up. Name the amount of time.

Vocabulary
- hour (h)
- half hour
- quarter hour

60 minutes	= 1 hour
30 minutes	= $\frac{1}{2}$ hour
15 minutes	= $\frac{1}{4}$ hour
24 hours	= 1 day

Use Analog Clocks

Cindy

15 minutes = $\frac{1}{4}$ hour

Cindy warmed up for one **quarter hour**.

Jill

30 minutes = $\frac{1}{2}$ hour

Jill warmed up for one **half hour**.

Seth

60 minutes = 1 hour

Seth warmed up for one **hour**.

Try It — Tell how much time.

1. 60 minutes = ▮ half hours

2. 2 hours = ▮ minutes

3. 30 minutes = ▮ quarter hours

4. ▮ minutes = 3 quarter hours

5. **Write About It** Tell how many $\frac{1}{4}$ hours are in 1 hour.

Tell how much time.

6. 2 half hours = ▉ minutes

7. 2 quarter hours = ▉ half hour

8. $\frac{1}{2}$ hour = ▉ minutes

9. 3 hours = ▉ minutes

10. 3 days = ▉ hours

★ 11. 10 minutes = ▉ seconds

Solve. Use data from the table for problems 12–14.

12. **Health** A 100-pound woman walks 15 minutes on day 1 and bikes for 15 minutes on days 2 and 4. She skates for 15 minutes on days 3 and 5. How many calories has she used in the 5 days?

13. In 15 minutes, how many more calories does a 100-pound person use skating than walking?

14. You want to exercise for 1 hour. You want to use at least 200 calories. Which exercise could you do?

Calories Used
by a 100 Pound Person

Exercise	Length of Time	Calories Used
Walking	15 minutes	41
Bicycling	15 minutes	45
Skating	15 minutes	54

★ 15. **Generalize** How do fractions help you tell time?

THINK
SOLVE
EXPLAIN

16. Jen's school day is 335 minutes long. How many minutes is that rounded to the nearest 10? (p. 32)

   A. 300   **C.** 340

   B. 330   **D.** 400

17. Which is the best estimate for 7,457 − 2,876? (p. 116)

   F. 6,000   **H.** 3,000

   G. 4,000   **I.** 2,500

18. 3,744 (p. 72)
    +2,189

19. 900 (p. 114)
    − 769

20. $9,456 (p. 120)
    − 8,976

21. 1,245 (p. 72)
    + 890

22. 456 + 108 (p. 60)

23. $372 + $159 (p. 60)

24. 45 + 125 + 650 (p. 76)

7.3 Elapsed Time

Learn

Celina lives in a tower by the water. She spends her vacation with her family, looking for storms and reporting them. Suppose Celina's shift is from 10:45 A.M. to 12:15 P.M. How long is her shift?

You can find elapsed time to solve this problem. **Elapsed time** is the amount of time it takes to go from start to finish.

VOCABULARY
elapsed time

Use Skip-Counting

Think: From 10:45 to 11:45 is 1 hour.

Think: Skip-count from 11:45 by 5s to 12:15.

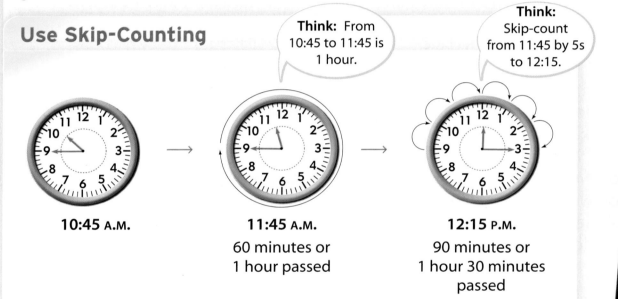

10:45 A.M.

11:45 A.M.
60 minutes or
1 hour passed

12:15 P.M.
90 minutes or
1 hour 30 minutes
passed

Celina's shift is 90 minutes or 1 hour and 30 minutes.

What If Celina begins her shift at 10:00 A.M. and is on lookout for 2 hours and 45 minutes. What time will Celina finish her shift?

Skip-count by the hour and by 5 minutes to solve.

Find the Ending Time

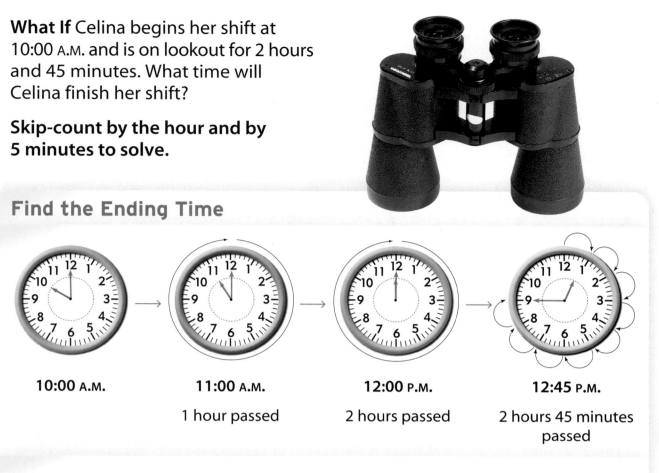

10:00 A.M.	11:00 A.M.	12:00 P.M.	12:45 P.M.
	1 hour passed	2 hours passed	2 hours 45 minutes passed

Celina would finish her shift at 12:45 P.M.

Try It

How much time has passed?

1. Begin: 11:20 A.M.
   End: 1:40 P.M.
2. Begin: 12:35 P.M.
   End: 1:50 P.M.
3. Begin: 9:55 P.M.
   End: 11:25 P.M.
4. Begin: 9:10 A.M.
   End: 1:10 P.M.

What time will it be in 1 hour and 15 minutes?

5.

6.

7. `3:10`

8.  **Write About It** **Describe** how you can find the time it will be 3 hours after any given time.

Practice and Problem Solving

How much time has passed?

9. Begin: 3:10 A.M.
 End: 3:40 A.M.

10. Begin: 7:05 A.M.
 End: 12:25 P.M.

11. Begin: 11:30 A.M.
 End: 6:40 P.M.

What time will it be in 2 hours and 30 minutes?

12.

13.

★ **14.**

Estimate how much time it takes for each activity. Write *1 minute, 10 minutes, 1 hour.*

15. run across the playground

16. eat a bowl of cereal

Solve. Use data from the schedule for problems 17–18.

THINK SOLVE EXPLAIN

17. Allie needs an hour to finish her art project. Can she finish it in art class today? Why or why not?

THINK SOLVE EXPLAIN

18. ✏ **Write a problem** about elapsed time using the information in the schedule. Solve it. Ask others to solve it.

★ **19.** You are taking a field trip to the zoo. The bus leaves school at 8:15 A.M. and returns at 2:45 P.M. Create a schedule for your trip.

Daily Schedule		
Subject	**Begin**	**End**
Reading	8:45	10:00
Math	10:05	11:15
Art	11:20	12:00
Lunch	12:05	12:40
Social Studies	12:45	1:20
Science	1:25	2:15
Gym	2:20	2:55

Spiral Review and Test Prep

20. Which related fact can help to find $15 - 7$? (p. 96)

 A. $15 + 7 = 22$ **C.** $8 - 7 = 1$

 B. $22 - 5 = 7$ **D.** $8 + 7 = 15$

21. You pay for a $4.55 book with a five-dollar bill. How much change should you get back? (p. 14)

 F. $0.45   **H.** $1.45

 G. $0.55   **I.** $1.55

22. $459 - 156$ (p. 106)

23. $\$321 + \$157$ (p. 60)

24. $1,402 - 345$ (p. 114)

9. 30 minutes   12. 5:50

Extra Practice page 156, Set C

Problem Solving: Reading for Math

DAY BY DAY

Arthur Barbosa de Asunçao (ah-soon-SOW) lives in Brazil, a country in South America. His day is filled with activities. Arthur's mom wakes him up at 6:45 A.M. so he can get ready for school.

Thirty minutes after he wakes up, Arthur begins school. What's his favorite subject? "Portuguese!" he says. Portuguese is the native language of Brazil. "I also like to learn about the Indians in the Amazon."

SCHOOL'S OUT!

Unlike kids in the U.S., Arthur goes to school for only 4 hours and 45 minutes a day. At noon Arthur heads to the beach, where he plays soccer for an hour. Then he heads home for lunch.

From 2:00 P.M. to 6:00 P.M., Arthur plays with his friends or goes biking with his dad. Two hours later, Arthur starts his homework. Family dinner is at 9:00 P.M.. "Before bed, I watch television," Arthur says. One hour later, it's bedtime.

 Reading Skill

Compare and Contrast In what ways is Arthur's day different from yours? How is it similar?

1. Arthur wakes up at 6:45 A.M. to get ready for school. He is in school 30 minutes later. What time does Arthur start school?

2. Arthur eats breakfast at 7:00 A.M. and lunch an hour after school is done. How much time has passed between the two meals?

Eight-year-old Arthur and his pet dog, Miranda.

Problem Solving

7.4 Calendar

Learn

The calendars below show your schedule for 2 **months**. If today is September 24, how many days is it until your next baseball game? How many weeks?

VOCABULARY
- week
- month
- ordinal number

Time Facts

7 days	=	1 week
28 to 31 days	=	1 month
about 4 weeks	=	1 month
12 months	=	1 year
52 weeks	=	1 year
365 days	=	1 year
366 days	=	1 leap year

Use a Calendar

The next baseball game is October 11.

Count the days from September 24 to October 11.

It is 17 days, or 2 weeks and 3 days, before your next game.

The baseball game is on the second Monday of October. Second is an ordinal number.

You can use ordinal numbers to read dates.

An **ordinal number** tells order or position.

Write and Read Dates

What is the date for the first Tuesday of October?

Write: October 5   **Read:** October fifth

Try It Use the calendars above.

1. What is the date for the first Tuesday in September?

2. What day does the twenty-fourth of October fall on?

3. **Write About It** **Explain** how you use ordinal numbers on a calendar.

September

SUN	MON	TUES	WED	THURS	FRI	SAT
			1	2	3	4
5	6	7	8	9	10	11
12	13 Ballet Class	14 Piano Recital	15	16	17	18
19	20 Ballet Class	21	22	23	24	25
26	27 Ballet Class	28	29	30		

October

SUN	MON	TUES	WED	THURS	FRI	SAT
					1	2
3	4	5	6	7	8	9
10	11 Baseball Game	12	13	14	15	16
17	18	19	20	21	22	23
24 31	25	26	27	28	29	30

Practice and Problem Solving

Use the calendars for problems 4–7.

4. How many weeks are there from January 6 through February 17?

5. How many days are there from New Year's Day through Groundhog Day?

6. Sara has an art class on the second Thursday of each month. What is the date of the class for January?

7. For how many weeks are students back in school before the Martin Luther King, Jr. holiday?

| January |||||||
Sun	Mon	Tue	Wed	Thu	Fri	Sat
				1 New Year's Day	2	3
4	5 Back to School	6	7	8	9	10
11	12	13	14	15	16	17
18	19 Martin Luther King, Jr. Day	20	21	22	23	24
25	26	27	28	29	30	31

Solve.

8. **Music** The last Broadway performance of *A Chorus Line* was September 29, 1983. Mr. Holt saw the musical 2 weeks before its last performance. On what date did Mr. Holt see the musical?

| February |||||||
Sun	Mon	Tue	Wed	Thu	Fri	Sat
1	2 Groundhog Day	3	4	5	6	7
8	9	10	11	12	13	14 Valentine's Day
15	16 President's Day	17	18	19	20	21
22	23	24	25	26	27	28

★ 9. **Spatial Reasoning** Trace this figure. Do not lift the pencil from the paper. Do not retrace any lines. Begin with the first letter you touch and list the letters you touch in order.

Spiral Review and Test Prep

10. Steve was 47 inches tall when he was 7 years old. He is now 9 years old and 4 inches taller. How tall is Steve? (p. 52)

    A. 56 inches   **C.** 51 inches

    B. 54 inches   **D.** 43 inches

11. Which symbol can make this number sentence true? (p. 102)
    $$15 - 7 \; \bullet \; 12 - 5$$

    F. $<$ **H.** $=$

    G. $>$ **I.** $\times$

12. $0.93 - $0.59 (p. 106)

13. $5.23 + $9.45 (p. 60)

14. $2.87 - $0.41 (p. 106)

7.5 Time Lines

Learn

Byron made a time line showing some important events in his life. What year was he born?

Use a time line to solve this problem.

VOCABULARY
time line

Use a Time Line

Read the time line from left to right.

Think: The years at the left happened first.

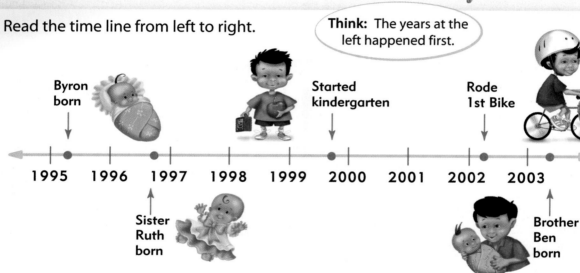

Byron born

Sister Ruth born

Started kindergarten

Rode 1st Bike

Brother Ben born

1995 1996 1997 1998 1999 2000 2001 2002 2003

Byron was born in 1995.

Try It Use the time line above for problems 1–3.

1. What happened between 1999 and 2002?

2. What happened after Byron was born and before he started kindergarten?

3. What happened most recently in Byron's life?

4. **Write About It** **Explain** how a time line can help you compare dates and events.

Practice and Problem Solving

Use Tina's time line for problems 5–9.

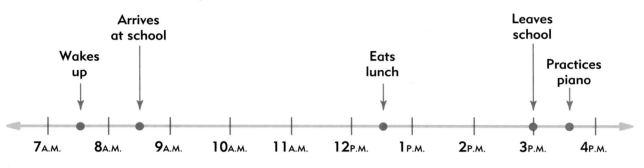

5. What happens at 8:30 A.M.?

6. What time does Tina eat lunch?

7. What does Tina do between lunchtime and piano practice?

★ **8.** Tina goes to sleep at 9:00 P.M. What could happen between piano practice and bedtime?

★ **9.** Recess time is at 10:45 A.M. Where does it belong on the time line?

Solve.

THINK
SOLVE
EXPLAIN

10. Logical Reasoning On a time line showing toy inventions, the rollerskate is to the left of the teddy bear. The model rocket is to the right of the teddy bear. Write the inventions in order from earliest to latest. Explain how you solved the problem.

THINK
SOLVE
EXPLAIN

11. Collect Data Find out the birth years of several students in your school. Make a time line using the data.

12. Create a time line of important events in your life.

Spiral Review and Test Prep

13. What is the missing number?
■ + 4 = 12 (p. 52)

A. 8   **C.** 16

B. 12   **D.** 22

14. Which is another name for 1,000 + 200 + 6? (p. 10)

F. 1,260   **H.** 1,026

G. 1,206   **I.** 126

Round to the nearest hundred. (p. 32)

15. 387   **16.** 89   **17.** 1,709   **18.** 733

7.6 Problem Solving: Skill
Identify Missing Information

Read

Wednesday was busy for Lita! From 3:00 P.M. to 4:15 P.M. she practiced the piano. She did homework until she went to soccer practice. She practiced for 45 minutes until 6:15 P.M. How long did Lita work on homework?

► **What do you know?**

piano practice 3:00 P.M. to 4:15 P.M.; soccer practice for 45 minutes to 6:15 P.M.

► **What do you need to find?**

How much time Lita spent on homework

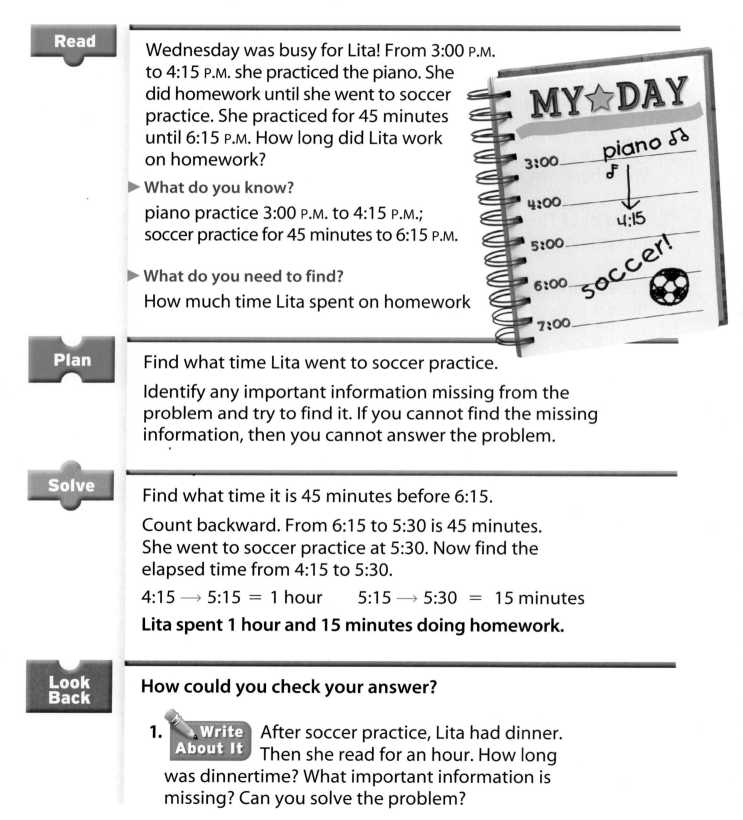

MY☆DAY
3:00 ___ piano ♫
4:00 ___
4:15
5:00 ___ soccer!
6:00 ___
7:00 ___

Plan

Find what time Lita went to soccer practice.

Identify any important information missing from the problem and try to find it. If you cannot find the missing information, then you cannot answer the problem.

Solve

Find what time it is 45 minutes before 6:15.

Count backward. From 6:15 to 5:30 is 45 minutes. She went to soccer practice at 5:30. Now find the elapsed time from 4:15 to 5:30.

4:15 → 5:15 = 1 hour   5:15 → 5:30 = 15 minutes

Lita spent 1 hour and 15 minutes doing homework.

Look Back

How could you check your answer?

1. **Write About It** After soccer practice, Lita had dinner. Then she read for an hour. How long was dinnertime? What important information is missing? Can you solve the problem?

Practice Solve. Identify the missing information.

2. The team starts practice at 9:00 A.M. by jogging for 20 minutes. Then they practice passing the ball before learning new plays from 10:00 A.M. to 11:30 A.M. How long do they practice passing the ball?

3. Lita played a soccer game that began at 9:15 A.M. When the game ended, she went directly to a 1-hour team meeting that ended at 11:45 A.M. How long was the game?

Mixed Strategy Review

4. Logical Reasoning Julia has some money in her pocket. She spends 25¢ on an apple. Then she finds 75¢ in her purse. Now she has a total of $1.20. How much money did she have in her pocket before she bought the apple?

5. Lionel went to the library from 11:30 A.M. until 2:10 P.M. How long did he spend at the library?

Choose a Strategy
- Logical Reasoning
- Draw a Picture or Diagram
- Make a Graph
- Act It Out
- Make a Table or List
- Find a Pattern
- Guess and Check
- Write an Equation
- Work Backward
- Solve a Simpler Problem

Use data from the class schedule for problems 6–9.

6. How much time does the class spend on Language?

7. At what time does lunch end?

8. How many minutes pass from the beginning of Math class to the beginning of lunch?

9. ✏ **Write a problem** using data from the Daily Schedule. Solve it. Ask others to solve it.

Daily Schedule		
Subject	**Begin**	**End**
Art	8:45 A.M.	9:30 A.M.
Math	9:30 A.M.	10:35 A.M.
Language	10:35 A.M.	11:30 A.M.
Lunch	11:30 A.M.	12:15 P.M.
Physical Education	12:15 P.M.	1:00 P.M.
Social Studies	1:00 P.M.	1:40 P.M.
Reading	1:40 P.M.	2:45 P.M.

Extra Practice page 156, Set F

Extra Practice

Set A Write each time in 2 ways. Include A.M. or P.M. (pp. 140–142)

1.

2.

Set B Tell how much time. (pp. 144–145)

3. $\frac{1}{4}$ hour = ▉ minutes   **4.** 3 hours = ▉ $\frac{1}{2}$ hours   **5.** 2 hours = ▉ $\frac{1}{4}$ hours

Set C How much time has passed? (pp. 146–148)

6. Begin: 2:05 A.M. End: 2:25 A.M.   **7.** Begin: 4:30 A.M. End: 4:30 P.M.

Set D Use data from the calendar for problems 8–9. (pp. 150–151)

What is the date for. . .

8. the second Tuesday in March?

9. the third Friday in March?

			March			
Sun	Mon	Tue	Wed	Thu	Fri	Sat
	1	2	3	4	5	6
7	8	9	10	11	12	13
14	15	16	17	18	19	20
21	22	23	24	25	26	27
28	29	30	31			

Set E Use the time line. (pp. 152–153)

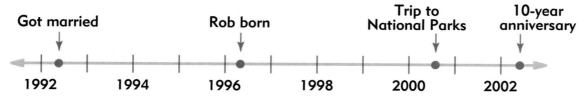

10. What year did Rob's parents marry?   **11.** What happened in 1996?

Set F Solve. Identify the missing information. (pp. 154–155)

12. Mac went to a basketball game at 1:30 P.M. The game lasted 2 hours. Then Mac went home. How long did Mac take to get home from the game?

13. On May 4 Beth was in an all-star game. Two weeks later she played another game. That was 3 days ago. Today is Friday. What day of the week was May 4?

LOG ON www.mmhmath.com
For more practice and Chapter Self-Check Test

Review/Test

Write each time using A.M. or P.M.

1.

2.

Tell how much time.

3. 3 hours = ▮ minutes

4. $\frac{1}{2}$ hour = ▮ minutes

How much time has passed?

5. Begin: 4:21 A.M. End: 12:21 P.M.

6. Begin: 9:05 A.M. End: 10:15 P.M.

Use the calendar to solve problems 7–8.

7. What date is the second Friday?

8. Sam takes ballet lessons on the first and third Mondays of each month. What are the dates?

July						
Sun	Mon	Tue	Wed	Thu	Fri	Sat
				1	2	3
4	5	6	7	8	9	10
11	12	13	14	15	16	17
18	19	20	21	22	23	24
25	26	27	28	29	30	31

Solve.

9. Marie jumps rope for 8 minutes, then jogs for 15 minutes without a break. She stops at 4:00 P.M. What time did she begin?

10. **Write About It** **Explain** how you find the name of the day for any given date.

Do I Need Help?

Exercises	Review Concepts	Use Extra Practice Set
1–2	pp. 140–143	Set A
3–4	pp. 144–145	Set B
5–6	pp. 146–148	Set C
7–8	pp. 150–151	Set D
9–10	pp. 154–155	Set F

Foldables Use your Foldables to help you review.

What Do I Need to Know?

How many carrots did Gena's rabbit eat?

Number of Carrots Eaten

Gena's rabbit	🥕🥕🥕
Joe's rabbit	🥕🥕🥕🥕🥕

🥕 = 1 carrot eaten

Data and Graphs

What Will I Learn?

In this chapter you will learn to

- collect and organize data
- find range, median, and mode
- interpret data in graphs
- identify and locate points on a grid
- use skills and strategies to solve problems

How Do I Read Math?

When you read a mathematics book, sometimes you read words and symbols, and sometimes you read only symbols.

All of these represent the number 5:

- **five**
- ||||

VOCABULARY

- survey
- tally
- line plot
- median
- mode
- range
- key
- pictograph
- bar graph
- scale
- ordered pair
- line graph

Foldables

Use your Foldables to help you with chapter concepts.

1. Place two sheets of paper an inch apart.
2. Roll up the bottom edges of the paper. Stop them 1–inch from the top edges.
3. When all tabs are about the same size, crease the paper to hold the tabs in place.

Data and Graphs

8.1 Collect and Organize Data
Range- the difference between the largest and smallest
8.2 Find Median, Mode and Range
8.3 Explore Pictographs
8.4 Explore Bar Graphs
8.5 Problem Solving Strategy: Work Backward
8.6 Coordinate Graphs
8.7 Interpret Line Graphs

4. Staple along the fold.
5. Label as shown. Record what you learn.

LOG ON
www.mmhmath.com
For Real World Math Activities

8.1 Collect and Organize Data

VOCABULARY
survey
tally
line plot

Learn

A **survey** is a method of gathering data by asking people questions. Mrs. Marshall's class did a survey about the number of brothers and sisters each student has. Which number of brothers or sisters had the greatest number of responses?

You can organize the results in a **tally** chart or **line plot**.

Numbers of Brothers and Sisters

1 0 2 1 4 2 1
1 5 2 1 1 0 3
0 3 2 0 2 1 2 1

Use a Chart and Line Plot

Show a tally mark for each response.

Tally Chart

Brothers or Sisters	Tally	Number of Responses
0	IIII	4
1	HHT III	8
2	HHT I	6
3	II	2
4	I	1
5	I	1

Mark an X above each number for each response.

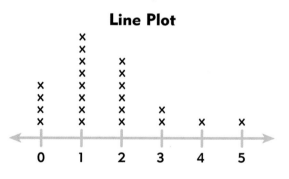

More students have 1 brother or sister than any other number of brothers and sisters. You can tell because 1 received the most responses.

Try It Make a tally chart and line plot for these responses.

1. Lengths of pencils in inches: 4, 5, 4, 3, 6, 6, 6, 4, 5, 3, 5, 5, 5, 6, 6

2. **Write About It** **Explain** which makes it easier to compare data, a tally chart or a line plot.

Practice and Problem Solving

Make a tally chart and line plot from the data in problem 3. Use the data to answer problems 4–6.

3. Age of club members: 10, 10, 8, 9, 7, 8, 10, 10, 10, 9, 8, 7, 7, 8, 10, 10, 8, 10, 9, 10, 7, 10

4. How many members are either 8 years old or 9 years old?

5. How many more members are 7 years old than are 9 years old?

★ 6. Next week, 2 members have birthdays. How does this change the tally chart and line plot?

Solve. Use data from the tally chart for problems 7–10.

7. Make a line plot to show the data in the tally chart. At which 2 times do the most students eat dinner?

8. How many students eat at half past the hour?

THINK SOLVE EXPLAIN

9. Three students no longer eat at 6:00 P.M. They eat at 5:00 P.M. How does this change the line plot?

Dinner Time

Time	Tally	Number of Students
5:00 P.M.	$\cancel{||||}\ ||$	7
5:30 P.M.	$\cancel{||||}$	5
6:00 P.M.	$|||$	3
6:30 P.M.	$\cancel{||||}\ |||$	8

★ 10. When combined, the number of students who eat dinner at 5:30 P.M. and 6:00 P.M. is the same number of students at which time? Write an equation.

11. **Collect Data** Survey your class for their shoe sizes. Make a tally chart and a line plot to show the results. Draw a conclusion about the most common shoe size.

THINK SOLVE EXPLAIN

Spiral Review and Test Prep

12. Which number rounds to 800 when rounded to the nearest ten? (p. 32)

   A. 819   C. 809

   B. 815   D. 795

13. Which number is greater than 9,101? (p. 24)

   F. 9,010   H. 9,100

   G. 9,099   I. 9,111

14. $0.87 − $0.29 (p. 106)   15. $6.13 + $2.45 (p. 60)   16. $7.01 − $1.25 (p. 114)

8.2 Find Median, Mode, and Range

Learn

The members of the chess club were asked to mark their ages on a tally chart. How can you describe this set of data?

First write each number in order from least to greatest to solve the problem.

8, 8, 8, 9, 9, 9, 9, 9, 10, 10, 10, 11, 11

VOCABULARY

median
mode
range

CHESS CLUB

AGE	8	9	10	11
TALLY	|||	ⅢⅠ	|||	||

Find the Median

Find the **median** by looking for the middle number.

8,   8,   8,   9,   9,   9,   **9**,   9,   10,   10,   10,   11,   11

> This is the median.

The median is 9.

Find the Mode

Find the **mode** by looking for the number that occurs most often.

8,   8,   8,   **9**,   **9**,   **9**,   **9**,   **9**,   10,   10,   10,   11,   11

> This is the mode.

The mode is 9.

> You can also use a calculator.

Find the Range

Find the **range** by subtracting the least number from the greatest.

8,   8,   8,   9,   9,   9,   9,   9,   10,   10,   10,   11,   **11**

$11 - 8 = 3$

The range is 3.

> The range is the difference of 11 and 8.

The line plot shows the number of visitors who come to see the chess competition each week.

Find: the mode.

Number of Visitors

```
              x     x
     x        x     x
     x        x     x     x
     x        x     x     x     x
  ←──┼─────┼─────┼─────┼─────┼──→
    15    20    25    30    35
```

Use Paper and Pencil

STEP 1

First order the data from least to greatest.

15,   15,   20,   20,   20,   25,   25,   25,   30,   30,   35

STEP 2

Find the mode by looking for the number or numbers that occur most often.

15,   15,   **20,   20,   20,   25,   25,   25,**   30,   30,   35

In this case, there are 2 modes.

The modes are 20 and 25.

Try It

Find the range, median, and mode.

1. 8, 5, 5, 3, 6, 9, 6, 8, 5

2. 3, 2, 1, 1, 2, 2, 3, 3, 1, 3

3. 15, 10, 15, 10, 20, 10, 10

4. 40, 50, 40, 30, 40, 30, 30, 30, 40

5.  **Analyze** What do range, median, and mode tell you about a set of data?

Practice and Problem Solving

Find the range, median, and mode.

6. 2, 5, 7, 6, 2

7. 5, 5, 8, 8, 5, 5, 8, 8, 5

8. 16, 18, 12, 18, 13

9. 50, 52, 54, 56, 50, 54, 53

Solve. Use data from the tally chart for problems 10–12.

10. What is the range of the data?

11. What is the median of the data?

12. What is the mode of the data?

Number of Water Skiers	
Day	Number
Monday	卌 |||
Tuesday	卌 ||
Wednesday	||||
Thursday	卌 ||
Friday	卌	

THINK SOLVE EXPLAIN
13. **Analyze** How can the median be the greatest number in a set?

★14. **Logical Reasoning** Juan found the range, median, and mode of five 1-digit numbers. If the range was 3, the median was 5, and the mode was 5, what could be the five 1-digit numbers?

15. **Make It Right** Here is how Maddy found the median of 5, 4, 3, 2, and 4. What mistake did Maddy make? Explain how to correct it.

2, 3, ⑤, 4, 4
5 is the median.

THINK SOLVE EXPLAIN

Spiral Review and Test Prep

16. Tonya began practice at 4:00 P.M. She ended practice at 5:15 P.M. How many minutes did she practice? (p. 144)

   A. 60 minutes   C. 70 minutes
   B. 65 minutes   D. 75 minutes

17. Mike had 304 stamps in his collection. He gave away 72 stamps. How many stamps does Mike have now? (p. 114)

   F. 376 stamps   H. 242 stamps
   G. 262 stamps   I. 232 stamps

What time will it be in 1 hour and 40 minutes? (p. 146)

18. 4:40 P.M.

19. 11:35 A.M.

20. 6:40 P.M.

21. 12:10 A.M

6. range-5, median-7, mode-2   10. 4   Extra Practice page 176, Set A

Writing for Math

Rob's math scores are 78, 79, 95, 82, 79, 88, and 92. His math grade will be either the median or the mode. Which is higher, the median or the mode? Explain in a letter to Rob which is the higher grade.

Jen's Response

Teacher's Response

✓ **THINK** Find the mode. It is the score listed most often. Find the median by listing the scores in order and finding the middle score. Compare to decide which score is greater.

← Jen explains how she will use what she knows to solve the problem.

✓ **SOLVE** Numbers in order:
78, 79, 79, 82, 88, 92, 95
Mode: 79   Median: 82

← Jen shows her work.

✓ **EXPLAIN**   November 15, 2003
Dear Rob,
The median, or middle score, is 82. The mode, or score listed most often, is 79. Since the median is greater than the mode, ask your teacher to use the median score for your grade.

Sincerely,
Jen

← Jen uses appropriate math terms, such as **median** and **mode**. Jen advises Rob to use the median and explains why it is greater than the mode.

THINK SOLVE EXPLAIN

Solve. Show your work and tell why your answer makes sense. Use Jen's work as a guide.

1. The heights in centimeters of a group of third grade students are: 100, 102, 105, 108, 110, 110, and 113. Is the mode or the median greater?

2. A fitness group jogs 3 miles every week. Today, their times in minutes are: 19, 25, 28, 31, 35, 41, and 45. What is the range of times for the group?

8.3 Explore Pictographs

Hands On Activity

The chart shows the number of books read in a Read–a–Thon. How can you display the data another way?

You Will Need
- graph paper
- ruler

VOCABULARY

key
pictograph

You can use a pictograph to display data. A **pictograph** is a graph that shows data using symbols.

Read-a-Thon

Month	Number of Books Read
September	45
October	25
November	40
December	60
January	80

Use Models

STEP 1

Write the title at the top of the graph.

Write a label for each row.

Read-a-Thon

September	
October	
November	
December	
January	

A **key** tells how many items each symbol represents.

STEP 2

Use 1 picture of the book for every 10 books read. Use a half picture of the book for every 5 books read.

Decide how many symbols to draw for each month. Complete the graph.

Read-a-Thon

September	▮▮▮▮▮
October	▮▮▮
November	
December	
January	

Each ▮ represents 10 books.
Each ▮ represents 5 books.

Explain Your Thinking

1. What does each symbol represent?

2. How did you decide how many symbols to draw?

3. Why is it important to have a title for the graph?

4. How many more books were read in January than in October?

Technology Link

Use the calculator tool in **Math Tool Chest** to compare data.

Follow these directions to make a pictograph.

Make Connections

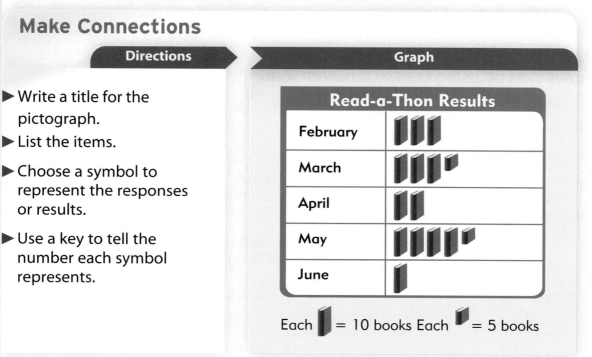

| Directions | Graph |

▶ Write a title for the pictograph.
▶ List the items.
▶ Choose a symbol to represent the responses or results.
▶ Use a key to tell the number each symbol represents.

Read-a-Thon Results

February	
March	
April	
May	
June	

Each ▮ = 10 books Each ▮ = 5 books

Your Turn

Use data from the pictograph above for problems 5–7.

5. **What If** 30 books were read in June. How would the pictograph change?

6. How many books were read in March?

7. Use a calculator to compare the number of books read in April and May.

8. **Write About It** **Explain** why you need a key for a pictograph.

8.4 Explore Bar Graphs

Hands On Activity

The chart shows some favorite weekend activities. How can you display the data another way?

Weekend Activities	
Activity	**Number of Students**
Hike	卌 |||
Picnic	卌 卌 |||
Shop	||||
Circus	卌 卌 卌	
Movies	卌 卌

You Will Need
- graph paper
- ruler

VOCABULARY
bar graph
scale

You can use a bar graph to display data. A **bar graph** shows data by using bars of different lengths.

Use Models

STEP 1

Write the title and the labels for the left and bottom sides of the graph. Decide on a scale to use. Write the numbers on the left side. Label the activities along the bottom.

A **scale** is a set of numbers, spaced equally, along a side of a graph.

Weekend Activities

Number of Students: 20, 16, 12, 8, 4, 0

Activity: Hike, Picnic, Shop, Circus, Movies

STEP 2

Draw bars for each activity to show the number of students. Complete the graph.

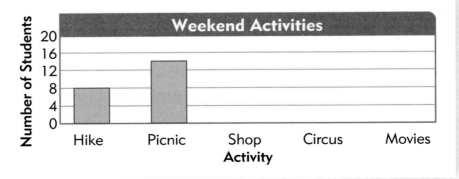

Weekend Activities

Number of Students: 20, 16, 12, 8, 4, 0

Activity: Hike, Picnic, Shop, Circus, Movies

Explain Your Thinking

1. Why does the scale show every fourth number?

2. How do you decide the height of the bars?

3. How do you show 14 students on the bar graph?

4. How many fewer students like to shop than to go to the movies?

Technology Link

Use the graph tool in **Math Tool Chest** to graph data.

Follow these directions to make a bar graph.

Make Connections

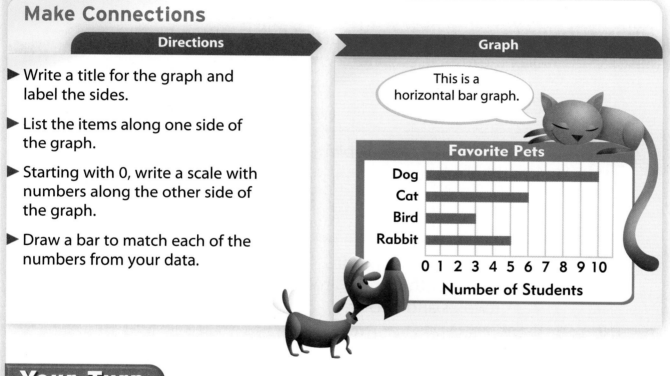

Directions	Graph

▶ Write a title for the graph and label the sides.

▶ List the items along one side of the graph.

▶ Starting with 0, write a scale with numbers along the other side of the graph.

▶ Draw a bar to match each of the numbers from your data.

This is a horizontal bar graph.

Favorite Pets

Dog, Cat, Bird, Rabbit

0 1 2 3 4 5 6 7 8 9 10

Number of Students

Your Turn

Use data from the bar graph above for problems 5–6.

5. Which pet is the most popular?

6. How could you change the graph to show that 4 students like rabbits?

7. **Write About It** **Explain** how a graph changes when you change its scale.

Extra Practice page 176, Set B

8.5 Problem Solving: Strategy
Work Backward

Read

Alani asks 5 people in her ballet class the number of years they have been dancing. After she gathers her data, Alani finds that the median is 3. The range is 2. The modes are 2 and 3. What are the responses?

- **What do you know?**
  There are 5 responses; the median is 3; the range is 2; the modes are 2 and 3.

- **What do you need to find out?**
  All of the responses

Plan

One way to solve this problem is to work backward.

Solve

Step 1: Start with the modes. There are 5 responses. Since both 2 and 3 are modes, there are two 2s and two 3s.

2,　　　2,　　　3,　　　3,　　　■

Step 2: Since the range is 2, find what number minus 2 equals 2.

$■ - 2 = 2$　　　$4 - 2 = 2$

The responses are 2, 2, 3, 3, 4

> Since the median is 3, the missing number must be greater than 3.

Look Back

Is your answer reasonable? How can you tell?

1. **Write About It** **Explain** how working backward helped you solve this problem.

Practice

Work backward to solve.

2. Alani pays for a new tutu with a hundred dollar bill. With her change, she buys ballet slippers for $19. She has $17 left. How much is the tutu?

3. On weekends, Alani practices 45 minutes each day. She finishes at 12:30 P.M. What time does she begin ballet practice?

Mixed Strategy Review

4. You spend $40 on a shirt and hat. The shirt costs $12 more than the hat. How much does the shirt cost?

5. Marge's new puppy gained 3 pounds in January. This is half as much weight as the puppy gained in February. In March the puppy gained 1 pound. How many pounds has the puppy gained?

6. Number Sense Name a 3-digit number that has twice as many ones as tens and half as many hundreds as ones.

Choose a Strategy
- Logical Reasoning
- Draw a Picture or Diagram
- Make a Graph
- Act It Out
- Make a Table or List
- Find a Pattern
- Guess and Check
- Write an Equation
- Work Backward
- Solve a Simpler Problem

Use data from the sign for problems 7–8.

7. Time It is 2:45 P.M. when you get in line for the amusement park ride. At what time will you get on the ride?

8. You see that your friends are getting on the ride now. It is 12:30 P.M. What time did they first get in the line?

From here:
35 minutes

9. ✎ **Write a problem** about time that can be solved by working backward. Solve it. Ask others to solve it.

8.6 Coordinate Graphs

Learn

Here is a map of Elm Elementary School. Where is the Computer Room? What is located at (4, 4)?

You can use ordered pairs.

An **ordered pair** is a pair of numbers that gives the location of a point on a map or grid.

VOCABULARY
ordered pair

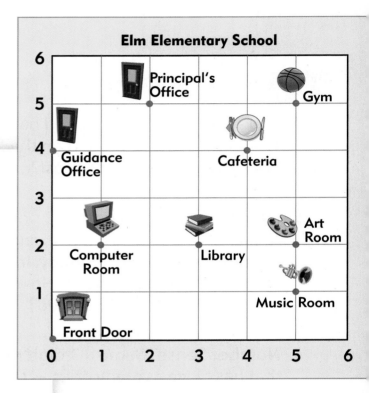

Elm Elementary School

Use a Coordinate Graph

▶ Start at 0. Go 1 space to the right.

▶ Go up 2 spaces. Now you are at the Computer Room.

The Computer Room is at (1, 2).

▶ The first number tells you how many spaces to count right. The second number tells you how many spaces to count up.

▶ Go 4 spaces to the right and 4 spaces up. Now you are at the cafeteria.

The Cafeteria is located at (4, 4).

Try It Use the map above to write the location.

1. Gym   **2.** Music Room   **3.** Principal's Office   **4.** Computer Room

Name the place at each location on the map.

5. (3, 2)   **6.** (5, 2)   **7.** (0, 0)   **8.** (0, 4)

9. **Write About It** Are (4, 3) and (3, 4) the same place on a map? Why or why not?

Practice and Problem Solving

Use the map to write the location.

10. Track

11. Nurse's Office

12. Principal's Office

13. Baseball Field

Name the place at each location on the map.

14. (3, 3)

15. (0, 3)

16. (2, 0)

17. (5, 3)

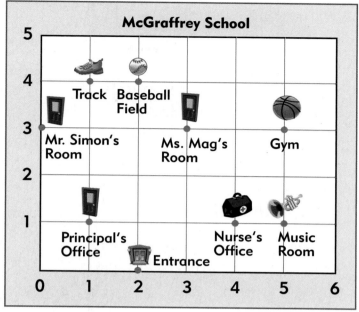

McGraffrey School

Solve. Use data from the map for problems 18–22.

18. You want to go from the Gym to the Principal's Office. From which point will you start? Where will you end?

19. **Analyze** If you connect points (1, 1), (2, 4), and (1, 4), what shape will you draw?

20. If you connect the ordered pairs (1, 2), (1, 5), (5, 2), and (5, 5), what shape will you see?

21. **Write a problem** about a place on the map. Solve it. Ask others to solve it.

THINK
SOLVE
EXPLAIN

★ **22.** Name 4 points on the map that form a square when connected.

Spiral Review and Test Prep

23. $1{,}378 - \blacksquare = 0$. What value for $\blacksquare$ makes the equation true? (p. 96)

   A. 0   **C.** 945

   B. 378   **D.** 1,378

24. $4{,}764 + \blacksquare = 4{,}764$ (p. 52)

   F. 4,764   **H.** 1

   G. 4,674   **I.** 0

Write each number in expanded form. (p. 10)

25. 4,254

26. 15,098

27. 28,090

8.7 Interpret Line Graphs

Learn

Mike recorded the temperatures one day in March in Daytona Beach, Florida. What is the temperature at 8 A.M.?

You can solve this problem by interpreting the line graph.

A **line graph** shows how something changes over time.

VOCABULARY

line graph

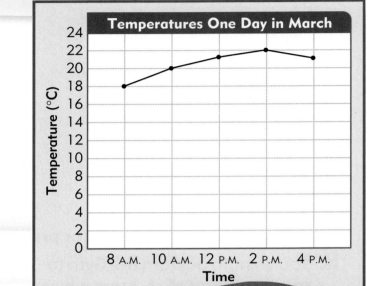

Temperatures One Day in March

Use the Line Graph

STEP 1

Find the time labeled 8 A.M.

Follow that line up to the point.

STEP 2

Move left to the scale and read the temperature.

The temperature at 8 A.M. is 18°C.

Try It

For problems 1–4, use the line graph above.

1. What is the temperature at 12 P.M.?

2. Which time has the temperature of 20°C?

3. Which time has the highest temperature?

4.  **Generalize** Based on the temperatures shown on this graph, what do you think the temperature was at 6 A.M.?

Practice and Problem Solving

Solve. Use the line graph for problems 5–9.

5. How much snow has fallen at 9 A.M.?

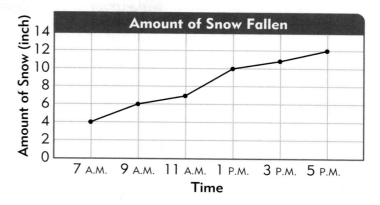

6. Between which 2 times did the amount of snow change 3 inches?

7. At which time is the amount of snow at 11 inches?

8. How many more inches is the amount of snow at 5 P.M. than at 7 A.M.?

★ 9. How much snow has fallen at 12 P.M.?

10. Gigi had a puzzle of Daytona Beach with 850 pieces in it. She put together 437 pieces already. How many pieces still need to be put together?

11. **Analyze** Ana sees a number with the digits 4, 8, and 2. To the nearest hundred, the number rounds to 400. What is the number?

12. **Write About It** **Generalize** Based on the temperatures shown on the graph above, what do you think the amount of snow will be at 7 P.M.?

THINK
SOLVE
EXPLAIN

Spiral Review and Test Prep

13. Which fact is in the same family as $16 - 7 = 9$? (p. 96)

   A. $9 + 7 = 16$ **C.** $16 - 8 = 8$

   B. $9 \times 7 = 63$ **D.** $9 - 7 = 2$

14. Louis had 387 cards in his collection. Round this number to the nearest hundred. (p. 32)

   F. 200 cards   **H.** 400 cards

   G. 300 cards   **I.** 500 cards

Find 100 less than the given number. (p. 6)

15. 450

16. 922

17. 109

18. 703

Set A Use the following data for problems 1–4. (pp. 160–161; 162–164)

Number of Homework Assignments that Students Have

1, 4, 2, 2, 4, 1, 2, 3, 4, 2, 1, 3, 2, 1, 4, 1, 3, 4, 2, 1, 2, 3.

1. Make a tally chart of the data.

2. Make a line plot of the data.

3. What is the range?

4. What is the mode?

Set B Use the data from the table for problems 5–7. (pp. 166–167; 168–169)

5. Make a pictograph of the data.

6. Make a bar graph of the data.

7. How many fewer laps were there in Week 1 than in Week 2?

Swim Club	
Week	Number of Laps
1	10
2	15
3	13

Set C Work backward to solve. (pp. 170–171)

8. Nicole has soccer practice 45 minutes each day. She finishes at 4:15 P.M. What time does she start soccer practice?

9. Derek gave Cam $6.00. Matt gave Cam $4.00 more than Derek did. Sam gave him $10.00 more than Derek. How much did Cam get?

Set D Use the map for problems 10–13
Write the location or the object. (pp. 172–173)

10. Sneaker

11. Camera

12. (2, 4)

13. (3, 2)

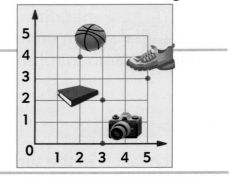

Set E Use the line graph for problems 14–15. (pp. 174–175)

14. How many visitors went to the museum on Friday?

15. Between which 2 days did the number of visitors decrease?

LOG ON www.mmhmath.com
For more practice and Chapter Self-Check Test

Use the following data for problems 1–4.

Number of turns as room leader:

5, 3, 3, 5, 2, 3, 4, 3, 2, 3, 6, 5, 4, 3, 5, 5, 3, 2, 3, 4, 5, 3, 3, 1, 3

1. Use the data to make a tally chart and a line plot.

2. What was the least number of turns?

3. What is the range, median, and mode of the data?

4. Use the data to make a bar graph and pictograph.

Use the map to write the location.

5. Birds

6. Petting Zoo

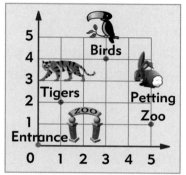

Use the graph for problems 7–9.

7. Which months have the average temperatures below 40°F?

8. Between which 2 months did the temperature rise 1°F?

9. School starts at 9:15 A.M. Carl takes 50 minutes to get ready and walk to school. What time should he start to get ready?

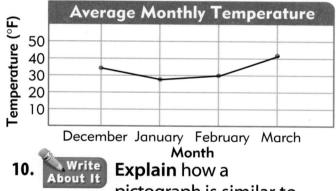

10. **Write About It** **Explain** how a pictograph is similar to and different from a bar graph.

Do I Need Help?

Exercises	Review Concepts	Use Extra Practice Set
1–3	pp. 160–164	Set A
4, 10	pp. 166–169	Set B
5–6	pp. 172–173	Set D
7–8	pp. 174–175	Set E
9	pp. 170–171	Set C

 Use your Foldables to help you review.

Applying Math and Science
How Does Exercise Change Your Breathing?

Y̲ou have just finished running a race. What do you notice about your breathing?

When you exercise, your lungs work harder to help bring oxygen to your muscles. In this activity you will discover what happens to your breathing when you exercise.

Hypothesize

Make a hypothesis about what happens to your breathing when you exercise. One breath means breathing in and out.

You Will Need
• stopwatch

Procedure

1. Work with a partner. Copy the chart on the next page. Record the number of breaths after each step.

2. Count how many times you breathe in 60 seconds.

3. Run in place for 60 seconds.

4. Count how many times you breathe in 60 seconds after exercising.

5. Rest for a few minutes until your breathing returns to normal.

6. Repeat steps 2-5 two more times.

Conclude and Apply

THINK
SOLVE
EXPLAIN

1. **Observe** What happened to your breathing when you exercised? How do you know?

2. **Interpret data** Look at your data in the first trial. How many more breaths did you take after exercise?

3. Use the data from the whole class to make a bar graph that shows how many people had an increase of 1, 2, 3, 4, 5, 6, and 7 breaths.

4. **Communicate** Explain why you think you breathe more often during exercise.

Going Further Repeat the activity, but measure your heart rate per minute before and after exercise. How does your heart rate change?

	Normal	After Exercise
1		
2		
3		

Problem Solving

Unit Study Guide and Review

Vocabulary

Complete. Use a word from the list.

VOCABULARY

median
mode
pictograph
quarter hour
week

1. 15 minutes equals a ___.

2. A ___ is 7 days.

3. The ___ is the number or numbers that occur most often in a set of data.

4. A ___ is a graph that uses symbols to show data.

Skills and Applications

Tell, write, and convert time and find elapsed time. (pp. 140–142; 144–145; 146–148)

How much time has passed?

Begin	End

Solution From 3:45 to 4:45 is 1 hour. From 4:45 to 5:00 is 15 minutes.

1 hour and 15 minutes has passed.

Tell how much time has passed.

5. Begin: 11:00 A.M. End: 4:00 P.M.

6. Begin: 3:25 P.M. End: 7:04 P.M.

Tell how much time.

7. 60 minutes = ■ $\frac{1}{2}$ hours

8. $\frac{1}{2}$ hour = ■ minutes

9. 30 minutes = ■ $\frac{1}{4}$ hours

Organize and interpret data. (pp. 160–161; 162–164)

Organize the data in a line plot.
Number of People in Family
3, 5, 2, 4, 6, 2, 4, 5, 2, 3, 4

Number of People in Family

```
      x           x
      x     x     x
      x     x     x     x
  |   |     |     |     |     |
  1   2     3     4     5     6
```

Use the data and line plot to solve.

10. Make a tally chart using the data.

11. What is the range?

12. What is the mode?

13. What is the median?

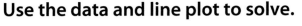 Use your Foldables to help you review.

Interpret and make graphs. (pp. 166–167; 168–169; 174–175)

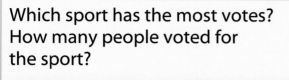

Which sport has the most votes? How many people voted for the sport?

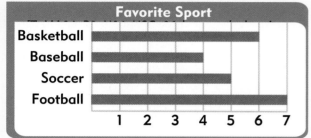

Favorite Sport

	1	2	3	4	5	6	7
Basketball							
Baseball							
Soccer							
Football							

Solution

Find the longest bar. Move down to the scale and read the number.

Football has the most votes. Seven people voted for football.

Use the graph for problems 14–18.

14. How many more people voted for basketball than baseball?

15. How would the graph change if 1 more person voted for soccer?

16. Draw a pictograph using the same data.

17. Explain why a line graph would not be a good way to represent the data.

18. Explain why a line graph would not be a good way to represent the data in the line plot.

Use skills and strategies to solve problems. (pp. 154–155, 170–171)

Rosie runs laps at the track for 45 minutes after school. She has just finished and it is 4:00 P.M. What time did she begin running?

Solution
Work backward.

Skip-count backward by 5s to 45 to find the time that Rosie began running.

Think: 4:00, 3:55, 3:50, 3:45, 3:40, 3:35, 3:30, 3:25, 3:20, 3:15

Rosie started running at 3:15 P.M.

Solve.

19. You leave your cousin's house on June 15. You have visited her for one week. On what day of the week did you arrive? Explain.

20. Robert walks home from his friend Tom's house for dinner with his older brother. He is home by 6:30 P.M. His walk is 20 minutes. He stopped on his way to buy a popsicle and that took 5 minutes. What time did Robert leave Tom's house?

Enrichment

Circle Graphs

A circle graph is another way of showing data. It is also known as a pie graph or pie chart.

The graph shows the results of a survey on people's favorite time of day. The entire circle represents the votes of 100 people. Each section tells you the number of people who voted for each time of the day.

Favorite Time of Day

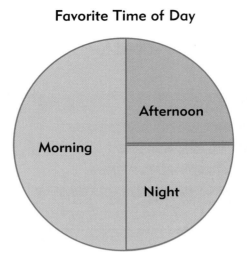

You can tell that morning has the most votes because that is the largest part of the graph. Since the whole circle represents 100 votes and 50 + 50 = 100, morning has 50 votes.

1. How many people voted for afternoon? Explain how you know.

2. How many people voted for night? Explain how you know.

3. Now make your own circle graph using this data: Survey of 100 people about favorite primary color: Red 50 votes; Blue 25 votes; Yellow 25 votes.

4. Use the graph you made in Problem 3 to make a statement about the votes.

5. **Analyze** Where have you seen examples of circle graphs? What kinds of data did they show?

Performance Assessment

How Do You Show Data on a Graph?

How much time do you spend watching TV? You might be surprised at the answer!

Keep track of the time you spend watching TV for a week. Then show the data on a graph.

Make a bar graph like the one started below. Be sure to:

• give your graph a title.

• see that the graph is correctly labeled.

• check that the bars show the data correctly.

Write 2 questions that can be answered by reading your graph.

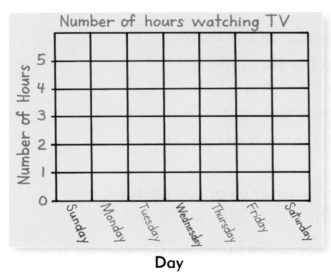

Day

Tips For A Good Answer

• Show the list of the data you collected.

• Show a graph that is properly labeled.

• List questions that can be answered from the graph.

You may want to save this work in your portfolio.

e-Journal www.mmhmath.com
Write about math.
Unit 4   **183**

Assessment

TECHNOLOGY Link

Make Graphs

Students at Central Elementary School are planting trees as a school project. They planted 52 trees the first week, 36 trees the second week, and 48 trees the third week. During which week did they plant the most trees?

You can use the *Math Tool Chest CD-ROM* to graph the data 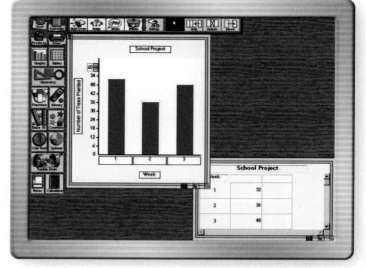.

Math Tool Chest CD-ROM

- Choose Bar Graph. Enter the graph title and the label for each side.

- Change the scale on the vertical side so the greatest number is 60.

- Click on the link at the bottom of the graph.

- Choose Table. Enter the data for the number of trees planted in the second column.

- The bars are drawn as you enter the data.

During which week did they plant the most trees?

Take a class survey. Use the computer to graph each set of data. Look for patterns in the data. Discuss the results with your classmates.

1. Ask classmates how they get to school—by bus, car, bike, or walk.

2. Ask classmates what their favorite pizza topping is.

3. **Analyze** How does using the computer help you redraw a bar graph when the data changes?

For more practice, use Math Traveler™.

Test-Taking Tips

Some of the questions you find on tests deal with graphs. You use the information shown in the table to **make a graph** and solve the problem.

Here is a survey on favorite colors. Use the data to make a bar graph.

Favorite Color

Color	Number of Students
Purple	16
Orange	5
Red	8
Green	10

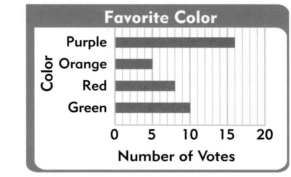

Use the data to make a bar graph. Label your graph. Then use it to answer the questions.

Favorite Pet

Pets	Cats	Dogs	Fish	Gerbils
Number of Students	21	33	17	5

1. How many students answered the survey?

2. Write a statement describing the data in the graph.

Use the data to make a bar graph. Label your graph. Then use it to answer the questions.

Favorite Sport

Sport	Soccer	Baseball	Ice Skating	Basketball
Number of Students	25	19	10	22

3. How many more students play soccer than play basketball?

4. Draw a conclusion based on the graph.

PART 1 • Multiple Choice

Choose the best answer.

1. Which fact could you use to check $7 - 4 = 3$? (p. 96)

   A. $7 + 4 = 3$ C. $3 + 7 = 10$
   B. $3 + 4 = 7$ D. $4 - 3 = 1$

2. Darin is waiting in a line with 15 people. There are 5 people ahead of him. How many people are behind Darin? (p. 2)

   F. 10 people   H. 8 people
   G. 9 people   I. 5 people

3. Which number would *not* round to 2,500 when rounding to the nearest hundred? (p. 32)

   A. 2,446   C. 2,504
   B. 2,475   D. 2,544

4. Jerry's brother Dan is 14. His sister is 2 years older than Jerry and 3 years younger than Dan. How old is Jerry? (p. 52)

   F. 9 years old   H. 11 years old
   G. 10 years old   I. 12 years old

5. You spend $3.78 on a new toy. You pay with a five-dollar bill. What is your change? (p. 14)

   A. $0.22   C. $1.32
   B. $1.22   D. $2.22

6. You are skip-counting, starting with 0. First you get an odd number, then an even number, then an odd number, and so on. What could you be doing? (p. 2)

   F. Skip-counting by 2s
   G. Skip-counting by 5s
   H. Skip-counting by 4s
   I. Skip-counting by 10s

7. Frank has 4 jacks. Hanna has 7 jacks. Which equation shows the total number of jacks? (p. 118)

   A. $7 - 4 = 3$ C. $7 - 3 = 4$
   B. $7 + 4 = 11$ D. $4 + 3 = 7$

8. Find the rule. (p. 106)

Input	900	850	800	750
Output	850	800	750	700

   F. Add 50.
   G. Subtract 50.
   H. Subtract 500.
   I. Subtract 100.

9. A number machine always puts out a number that adds 3. If the number 11 is put into the machine, what number is put out? (p. 52)

   A. 8   C. 14
   B. 11   D. 17

PART 2 • Short Response/Grid In

Record your answers on the answer sheet provided by your teacher or on a sheet of paper. Use the table for problems 10–14.

Albert's Schedule

7:30	Eat breakfast
8:00	Get ready for school
8:20	Leave for bus stop
8:30	Get on bus
8:45	Get to school

10. How much time does it take Albert to get ready for school? (p. 146)

11. How much time has passed from the time Albert eats breakfast to the time he gets on the bus? (p. 146)

12. How long is the bus ride? (p. 146)

13. First class starts at 9:10. How much time does Albert have before his first class? Explain. (p. 146)

THINK SOLVE EXPLAIN

14. Albert makes a pictograph of his schedule. Each symbol stands for 5 minutes. How many symbols would he need to show the amount of time he spends on the bus? (p. 146)

15. Zach's favorite number is 17. The number on his hockey jersey is 25 more than his favorite number. What is the number on his hockey jersey? (p. 60)

16. Dolores has $52.50. Does she have enough to buy a sweater and a pair of shoes? Explain. (p. 26)

THINK SOLVE EXPLAIN

skirt	$22.98
shirt	$23.75
sweater	$29.28
shoes	$24.99

17. What number is missing in this skip-counting pattern? (p. 2)

3, 6, 9, 12, ▆, 18

18. Chris collected 573 bottle caps. This is 34 bottle caps more than what his brother collected. To the nearest ten, how many bottle caps did his brother collect? (p. 32)

PART 3 • Extended Response

Record your answer on a sheet of paper. Show your work.

THINK SOLVE EXPLAIN

19. The change in Matthew's pocket totals $0.39. What are the fewest coins he can have? Explain how you know. (p. 14)

What Do I Need to Know?

Your family buys 4 tickets to your school play. Each ticket costs $3. How much money does your family spend?

Understand Multiplication

What Will I Learn?

In this chapter you will learn to

- relate multiplication and addition
- use arrays to explore multiplication
- use skills and strategies to solve problems

How Do I Read Math?

When you read a mathematics book, sometimes you read words and symbols, and sometimes you read only symbols.

All of these represent three groups of two equals six:

- **3 times 2 equals 6**

- **3 × 2 = 6**

- $$\begin{array}{r} 2 \\ \times 3 \\ \hline 6 \end{array}$$

VOCABULARY

- multiplication
- factor
- product
- multiplication sentence
- multiple
- array
- Commutative Property of Multiplication

Foldables

Use your Foldables to help you with chapter concepts.

1. Fold a 2–inch tab along the long edge of the paper.
2. Fold the paper in half like a hamburger to make two pockets.
3. Glue the outside edges of the pockets together.
4. Label as shown. Record what you learn.
5. Take notes on index cards.
6. Sort and store note cards in your Foldable pocket book.

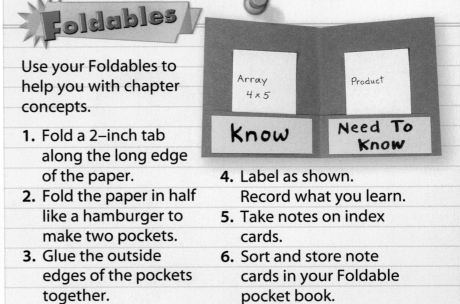

9.1 Explore the Meaning of Multiplication

Hands On Activity

Multiplication is an operation on 2 numbers to find the total.

You can use models to find how many are in 4 groups of 6.

You Will Need
• connecting cubes

VOCABULARY
multiplication

Use Models

STEP 1

To model multiplication show 4 groups of 6 cubes.

STEP 2

Make a table like the one shown.

Record the number of groups and the number in each group. Record the total number.

Explore other ways to group 24.

Number of Groups	Number in Each Group	Total

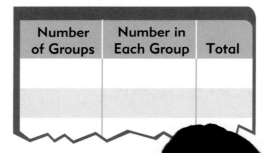

Explain Your Thinking

1. How did you model the numbers in the multiplication problem?

2. How did you find the total number?

3. How can you use addition to find the total number?

4. How many cubes are in 4 groups of 6?

Technology Link

Use the place value tool in **Math Tool Chest** to explore multiplication.

Your Turn

Use models to find the total number.

5. 3 groups of 5

6. 6 groups of 2

7. 2 groups of 7

8. 8 groups of 1

9. 1 group of 3

10. 3 groups of 3

11. 5 groups of 6

12. 2 groups of 5

13. 9 groups of 2

14. 5 groups of 5

15. 8 groups of 3

16. 4 groups of 3

17. 3 groups of 8

18. 2 groups of 9

19. **Write About It** **Explain** how multiplication is like addition.

9.2 Algebra: Relate Multiplication and Addition

Learn

Have you ever had to practice an instrument? If you practice 2 hours a day for 6 days, how many hours will you practice in all? Find 6 groups of 2.

Find: 6 × 2

Let's see how to connect models and paper and pencil.

VOCABULARY
multiplication sentence
factor
product
multiple

Make Connections

Models

There are 2 cubes in each group. There are 6 groups.

Paper and Pencil

Addition

You can add 2 six times.

2 + 2 + 2 + 2 + 2 + 2 = 12

You can also use a calculator.

Multiplication

You can also multiply 6 times 2.

6 × 2 = 12

You will practice for 12 hours.

What If You practice 3 times a week for 7 weeks. How many times will you practice in all?

Find: 7 × 3

There's More Than One Way!

Use Repeated Addition

Add.

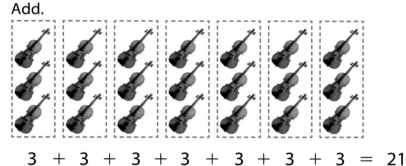

3 + 3 + 3 + 3 + 3 + 3 + 3 = 21

Use a Multiplication Sentence

When the groups are equal, you can write a **multiplication sentence**.

> **Remember:**
> A number sentence is also an equation.

Number of weeks		Number of practices a week		Total number of practices
7	×	3	=	21
↑		↑		↑
factor	×	**factor**	=	**product**

```
  3  ← factor
× 7  ← factor
___
 21  ← product
```

21 is a **multiple** of 3.

You will practice 21 times in all.

Try It Write an addition and a multiplication sentence.

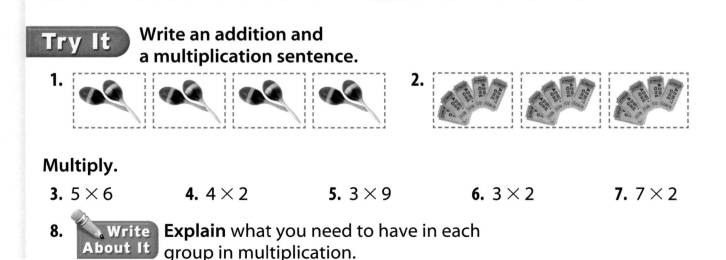

1.

2.

Multiply.

3. 5 × 6   **4.** 4 × 2   **5.** 3 × 9   **6.** 3 × 2   **7.** 7 × 2

8. **Write About It** **Explain** what you need to have in each group in multiplication.

Practice and Problem Solving

Write an addition and a multiplication sentence.

9.

Multiply.

10. $3 \times 2 = 6$ 11. $4 \times 5 = 20$ 12. $2 \times 9 = 18$ 13. $6 \times 2 = 12$ 14. $4 \times 7 = 28$

15. $2 \times 8 = 16$ 16. $3 \times 3 = 9$ 17. $5 \times 5 = 25$ 18. $2 \times 4 = 8$ 19. $4 \times 3 = 12$

x Algebra   **Describe and complete each skip-counting pattern.**

20. 3, 6, 9, 12, 15, 18, __21__

21. 4, 8, 12, 16, __20__, 24

Solve.

22. An artist takes 5 minutes to sketch each dancer's face. How many minutes would it take to sketch 5 faces? 25 faces

★ 23. Tickets for the school play cost $5 for adults and $2 for students. How much do 3 adult and 2 student tickets cost? Explain. 19 dollars

THINK SOLVE EXPLAIN

24. **Make It Right** Here is how Henry showed 3 groups of 4. Tell what mistake he made. Show how to correct it.

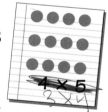

Link to MUSIC

Professional ballerinas can go through about 3 pairs of pointe shoes in 1 week of performances.

25. About how many pairs of pointe shoes does a ballerina need for 3 weeks of performances?

Spiral Review and Test Prep

26. You read a book for 45 minutes. What is another way to show how long you read? (p. 144)
 - **A.** two $\frac{1}{2}$ hours
 - **B.** one hour
 - **C.** two $\frac{1}{4}$ hours
 - **D.** three $\frac{1}{4}$ hours

27. Andy's party is December 18. Today is December 3. How long is it until Andy's party? (p. 150)
 - **F.** 22 days
 - **G.** 3 weeks
 - **H.** 2 weeks
 - **I.** 15 days

28. $5,687 - 367$ (p. 102)

29. $14 + 29$ (p. 58)

30. $468 + 174$ (p. 58)

9. $4 + 4 + 4 + 4 = 16$; $4 \times 4 = 16$ 10. 6

Extra Practice   page 200, Set A

Problem Solving: Reading for Math

QUEEN OF THE JUNGLE

How do you make a Broadway show out of a story that doesn't have a single human character? Ask Julie Taymor. She turned *The Lion King* movie into a Broadway show. She put a jungleful of animals onstage. Julie couldn't use real lions and elephants, however. She found a way for human actors to play animal roles.

WILD THINGS

Julie and her crew designed costumes to look like wildlife. The costumes were made of masks, body paints, and bright fabrics. On stage, masked dancers on high stilts play giraffes. A life-sized elephant lumbers along. It's moved by actors who walk under each of its legs.

The cast gives 2 performances each on Wednesdays, Saturdays, and Sundays. They also give 1 performance on Thursdays and Fridays. Each show runs for 2 hours and 40 minutes, with a 20-minute break. But their hard work pays off! The show has won 25 major awards.

Actors become animals in *The Lion King*.

Problem Solving

Reading Skill

Summarize Summarize this article in 3 sentences or less.

1. How many performances does the cast give on Wednesdays, Saturdays, and Sundays combined?

2. If you saw all the shows on Wednesday, Thursday, and Friday, how many hours would you have spent in all?

9.3 Explore Multiplication Using Arrays

Hands On Activity

You can make arrays to explore multiplication.

Find: 3 × 5

You Will Need
- counters
- graph paper

Use Models

STEP 1

Start making the **array** with rows.

Use 3 counters to begin each row.

rows

STEP 2

Use 5 counters in each row to show columns.

columns

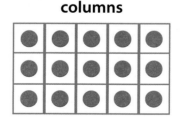

STEP 3

Count to find the total number of counters, or the product of 3 × 5.

Explain Your Thinking

1. How many rows and columns did you make?

2. What is the total number of counters?

3. **What If** You make an array for 5 × 3. How many rows and columns will you make?

Technology Link

Use the counters tool in **Math Tool Chest** to make arrays.

Find: 6 × 4

Let's see how to connect models to paper and pencil.

Make Connections

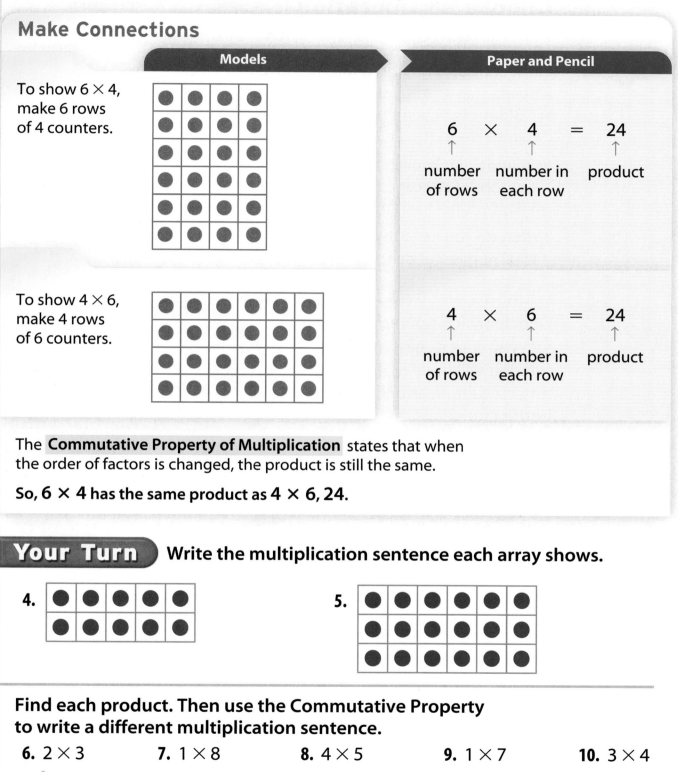

Models		Paper and Pencil

To show 6 × 4, make 6 rows of 4 counters.

$$6 \times 4 = 24$$

number of rows   number in each row   product

To show 4 × 6, make 4 rows of 6 counters.

$$4 \times 6 = 24$$

number of rows   number in each row   product

The **Commutative Property of Multiplication** states that when the order of factors is changed, the product is still the same.

So, 6 × 4 has the same product as 4 × 6, 24.

Your Turn   **Write the multiplication sentence each array shows.**

4.

5.

Find each product. Then use the Commutative Property to write a different multiplication sentence.

6. 2 × 3   **7.** 1 × 8   **8.** 4 × 5   **9.** 1 × 7   **10.** 3 × 4

11. **Write About It** **Explain** how the arrays for 4 × 5 and 5 × 4 are related to the Commutative Property.

Extra Practice page 200, Set B

9.4

Problem Solving: Skill
Choose an Operation

Read

Clark School is having a talent show. One act has 4 groups of dancers. There are 3 dancers in each group. How many dancers are in the act?

- **What do you know?**
  4 groups of dancers;
  3 dancers in each group

- **What do you need to find?**
  Total number of dancers

Plan

Decide which operation to use.

You can add to find the total, but you will have to add many times. Multiplication is the better choice.

Solve

Write an equation.

There are 4 groups of dancers, 3 dancers in each group.

| 4 | × | 3 | = | ■ |

| groups of dancers | | dancers in each group | | total |

| 4 | × | 3 | = | 12 |

There are 12 dancers in the act.

Look Back

Does your answer make sense?

1. **Write About It** **Explain** how you decide whether to add or multiply to solve a problem.

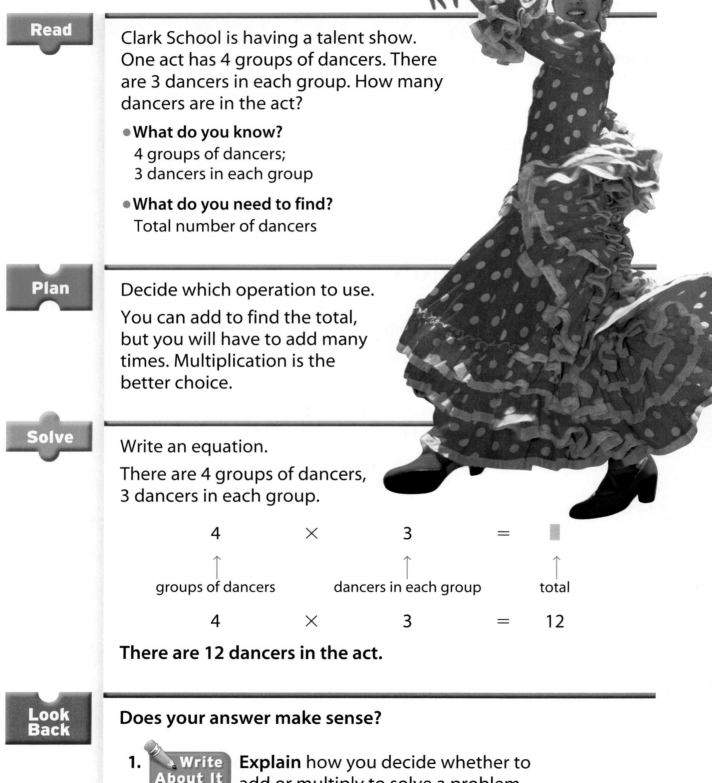

Practice Solve. Explain why you chose the operation.

2. A juggling act has 5 groups of jugglers. Each group has 2 jugglers. How many jugglers are in the juggling act?

3. The balcony has 3 rows of seats. There are 6 seats in each row. How many seats are in the balcony?

Mixed Strategy Review

4. The Music Club raised $305. They used $195 to buy new instruments. They used the rest of the money to buy music books. How much did they spend on music books?

5. Danielle danced for 45 minutes and sang for 35 minutes one day. The next day, she danced for 30 minutes. How much time did she spend dancing on those 2 days?

Choose a Strategy
- Logical Reasoning
- Draw a Picture or Diagram
- Make a Graph
- Act It Out
- Make a Table or List
- Find a Pattern
- Guess and Check
- Write an Equation
- Work Backward
- Solve a Simpler Problem

Use the Talent Show program for problems 6–12.

6. How many students are in Act 3?

7. How many students are in Act 1?

8. How many students are in the skit performed as Act 4?

9. How many more students are in Act 4 than in Act 2?

10. All together, how many students are in Acts 1 and 3?

11. What is the total number of students in the talent show?

CLARK SCHOOL TALENT SHOW

Act 1 Song 3 groups of 3 students
Act 2 Skit 9 male students and 7 female students
Act 3 Dance 6 groups of 2 students
Act 4 Skit 7 third grade students and 11 fourth grade students

12. ✏️ **Write a problem** where you have to choose an operation to solve. Use the data from the program. Solve it. Ask others to solve it.

Extra Practice page 200, Set C

Problem Solving

Set A Find each total. Write an addition and a multiplication sentence. (pp. 190–191; 192–194)

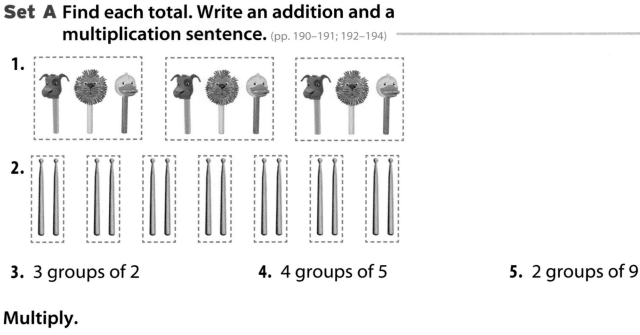

1.

2.

3. 3 groups of 2   **4.** 4 groups of 5   **5.** 2 groups of 9

Multiply.

6. 2×2 **7.** 5×3 **8.** 4×6 **9.** 2×1 **10.** 4×3

Set B Write the multiplication sentence each array shows. (pp. 196–197)

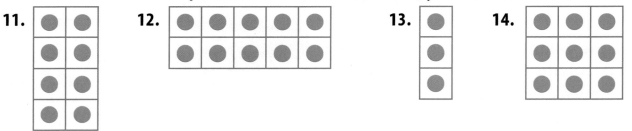

11.   **12.**   **13.**   **14.**

Find each product. Then use the Commutative Property to write a different multiplication sentence.

15. 5×6 **16.** 2×4 **17.** 7×3 **18.** 4×8 **19.** 3×6

Set C Solve. Tell how you choose the operation. (pp. 198–199)

20. There are 24 students in one chorus. Another chorus has 17 students. If the two groups do a show together, how many students are in the show?

21. The Maple Elementary School puppet show has 6 puppets in each act. There are 3 acts. How many puppets are used in the show?

Write an addition and a multiplication sentence.

1.

2.

Multiply.

3. 3×2 **4.** 2×8 **5.** 5×6 **6.** 7×5 **7.** 7×2

8. 8×2 **9.** 2×4 **10.** 6×2 **11.** 2×1 **12.** 5×5

13. 8×5 **14.** 4×2 **15.** 9×5 **16.** 5×4 **17.** 2×2

18. $\begin{array}{r} 2 \\ \times\, 5 \\ \hline \end{array}$ **19.** $\begin{array}{r} 5 \\ \times\, 1 \\ \hline \end{array}$ **20.** $\begin{array}{r} 5 \\ \times\, 3 \\ \hline \end{array}$ **21.** $\begin{array}{r} 7 \\ \times\, 0 \\ \hline \end{array}$

Solve.

22. The chorus bus has 5 rows of seats. Each row has 4 seats. If 1 singer sits in each seat, can 18 singers fit on the bus? How do you know?

23. Pablo and his 3 friends saw their favorite movie twice this week. Use addition and multiplication to find the total number of movie tickets they bought this week.

24. A marching band has 5 rows with 3 band members in each row. How many members are in the band?

25. **Write About It** **Analyze** what pattern do you find in the numbers when you skip-count by 2s?

Do I Need Help?

Exercises	Review Concepts	Use Extra Practice Set
1–2	pp. 190–194	Set A
3–21, 25	pp. 196–197	Set B
22–24	pp. 198–199	Set C

 **Use your Foldables to help you review.**

Assessment

What Do I Need to Know?

There are 4 rows of chairs on
stage for your recital. Each row
has 5 chairs. How many chairs are
there in all?

Multiplication Facts to 5

What Will I Learn?

In this chapter you will learn to

- multiply by 2, 3, 4, and 5
- identify and use the Identity and Zero Properties of Multiplication
- use skills and strategies to solve problems

How Do I Read Math?

When you read a mathematics book, sometimes you read words and symbols, and sometimes you read only symbols.

All of these represent two times two equals four:

- **the product of 2 and 2 is 4**

- **2 × 2 = 4**

- $\begin{array}{r} 2 \\ \times 2 \\ \hline 4 \end{array}$

VOCABULARY

- Identity Property of Multiplication
- Zero Property of Multiplication

Foldables

Pockets Full of Multiplication Facts

8 =

Use your Foldables to help you with chapter concepts.

1. Fold a 2–inch tab along the long edge of the paper.
2. Fold the paper in half like a hamburger to make two pockets.
3. Glue the outside edges of the pockets together.
4. Label as shown. Record what you learn.
5. Make three pockets and glue them together.

This forms a Foldable with six pockets.

6. Take notes and write facts on index cards.
7. Sort and store fact cards in your Foldable pocket book.

10.1 Multiply by 2 and 5

Learn

The Young Dancers are practicing for tonight's show. How many dancers are in the dance group if there are 2 rows of 4 dancers?

You can multiply to solve this problem.

Find: 2 × 4

There's More Than One Way!

Use Skip-Counting

Skip-count by 4s to find the total number of dancers.

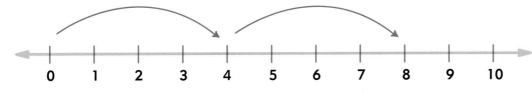

The number line shows $2 \times 4 = 8$.

Use an Array

To show 2×4, make 2 rows of 4 counters.

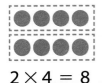

$2 \times 4 = 8$

There are 8 dancers in the dance group.

There are 3 shows a week. The show runs for 5 weeks.
How many shows are there in all?

Find: 5 × 3

There's More Than One Way!

Use Models

There are 5 groups and 3 in each group.

There are 15 total cubes.

You can also use a calculator.

Use an Equation

Number of weeks		Number of shows in a week		Total number of shows
5	×	3	=	15

$$3 \leftarrow \text{factor}$$
$$\underline{\times\ 5} \leftarrow \text{factor}$$
$$15 \leftarrow \text{product}$$

There are 15 shows in all.

Try It

Find each product.

1. 8 ×5	**2.** 1 ×2	**3.** 3 ×5	**4.** 2 ×2	**5.** 2 ×6
6. 4 ×5	**7.** 9 ×5	**8.** 8 ×2	**9.** 1 ×5	**10.** 7 ×5

11. 4 × 2   **12.** 3 × 2   **13.** 6 × 5   **14.** 7 × 2   **15.** 2 × 9

16.  **Describe** the methods you can use to remember facts for multiplying 2. Give an example for each method.

Practice and Problem Solving

Find each product.

17. 5
    ×5

18. 7
    ×5

19. 4
    ×2

20. 9
    ×5

21. 8
    ×2

22. 2
    ×2

23. 2×7

24. 2×1

25. 2×4

26. 5×3

27. 9×2

28. 6×5

29. 2×3

30. 5×4

31. 3×5

32. 8×5

★33. $(2 + 1) \times 2$

★34. $(1 + 1) \times 5$

★35. $(5 + 1) \times 2$

x **Algebra Complete the tables.**

36.

Rule: Multiply by 5			
Input	3	5		
Output			35	45

37.

Rule: Multiply by 2			
Input		4	6	
Output	4			16

Solve.

38. There are 8 girls in a ballet class. Each girl needs ballet slippers. How many ballet slippers do they need all together?

39. **Write About It** **Explain** the strategies you use to help you remember facts for 5. Give an example.

THINK SOLVE EXPLAIN

40. **Collect data** from your friends about favorite music groups. Show your data in a pictograph. Write a problem that uses the data. Ask another student to solve it.

41. **Make It Right** Here's how Henry multiplied 7×2. Tell what mistake he made. Explain how to correct it.

THINK SOLVE EXPLAIN

$7 \times 2 = 12$

Spiral Review and Test Prep

42. Round the number 2,431 to the nearest hundred. (p. 32)

   A. 2,400   **C.** 2,000

   B. 2,300   **D.** 400

43. What is the missing number? (p. 56)

   123, 223, ▮, 423, 523

   F. 233   **H.** 333

   G. 323   **I.** 343

44. $579 - 154$ (p. 102)

45. $2,009 - 456$ (p. 114)

46. $3,891 + 768$ (p. 72)

Extra Practice page 218, Set A

Writing for Math

A group of 6 children each need 5 markers and 3 sheets of paper for a project. How many markers are needed in all? Explain your thinking.

Jeff's Response	Teacher's Response
✓ **THINK**	
I can draw a diagram to find the number of markers needed for all 5 children.	← Jeff explains what he knows and decides which strategy he needs to solve the problem.
✓ **SOLVE**	
Draw a diagram to show the problem. Then skip-count to solve.	← Jeff shows his work.
x x x x x x x x x x x x x x x 5 10 15 x x x x x x x x x x x x x x x 20 25 30 Check: $5 + 5 + 5 + 5 + 5 + 5 = 30$	
✓ **EXPLAIN**	
I drew a picture to show the markers for each child. Then I skip-counted to find the total. So, 30 markers are needed.	← Jeff uses complete sentences. He clearly describes how he solved the problem.
To check, I can use repeated addition. $5 + 5 + 5 + 5 + 5 + 5 = 30$. The sum matches the product, so my answer makes sense.	← Jeff uses repeated addition to make sure his answer is reasonable.

THINK SOLVE EXPLAIN

Solve. Show your work and tell why your answer makes sense. Use Jeff's work as a guide.

1. Ethan has 3 nickels. If he trades in his nickels for pennies, how many pennies will he get?

2. How many 2 pound weights are needed to balance the scale with a 10 pound ball on 1 side?

Writing

10.2 Problem Solving: Strategy
Find a Pattern

Read

The Frost School Chorus lines up in 7 rows. There are 5 students in the 1st row, 10 in the 2nd row, 15 in the 3rd row, and 20 in the 4th row. If the number of students in each row keeps increasing by the same amount, how many students will be in the 7th row?

- **What do you know?**
  The number of rows; the number in each row

- **What do you need to find?**
  The number in the 7th row

Plan

One way to solve this problem is to find a pattern. Then use the pattern to solve the problem.

Solve

Look at how the numbers change.

The numbers are increasing by 5. They are all multiples of 5.

$$+5 \qquad +5 \qquad +5$$

5	10	15	20
1st row	**2nd row**	**3rd row**	**4th row**
5×1	5×2	5×3	5×4

You can multiply the number of the row by 5 to find the number of students in that row.

$5 \times 7 = 35$

There are 35 students in the 7th row of the chorus.

Look Back

How else could you solve this problem?

1. **Write About It** **Explain** how finding a pattern helps you solve problems.

208

Practice

Find a pattern to solve.

2. The 24 dancers in a show dance in 1 long chorus line. Every third dancer wears a red costume. All of the others wear blue. Kitty is the 14th dancer. What color costume does she wear?

3. During August there is a concert in the park each week. So far the concerts have been on August 1st, 8th, and 15th. On what date will the 5th concert most likely be?

Choose a Strategy

- Logical Reasoning
- Draw a Picture or Diagram
- Make a Graph
- Act It Out
- Make a Table or List
- Find a Pattern
- Guess and Check
- Write an Equation
- Work Backward
- Solve a Simpler Problem

Mixed Strategy Review

4. Dimitrius was 34 inches tall at 4 years old. He is now 42 inches tall at 8 years old. If he grows the same number of inches each year, how many inches did he grow each year? Describe the change.

★ 5. Miguel wants to learn to play the flute. A new flute costs $475. He can save $280 if he buys a used flute. Miguel decides to buy the used flute and a $29 carrying case. How much does he spend?

6. Look at the picture of the chairs. There is 1 more row of chairs that will be set up in the back. If the pattern continues, how many more chairs are needed for the new row? How many more music stands are needed for the new row?

7. ✎ **Write a problem** that can be solved by finding a pattern. Solve it. Ask another student to solve it.

Problem Solving

10.3 Multiply by 3 and 4

Learn

Have you ever been in a play? Each of these actors wears 3 costumes during the play. How many costumes are needed for the actors?

You can multiply to solve this problem.

Find: 4×3

There's More Than One Way!

Double a Known Fact

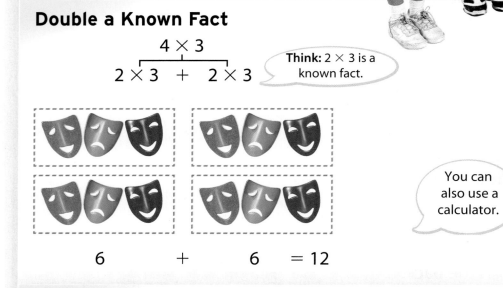

$$4 \times 3$$
$$2 \times 3 \quad + \quad 2 \times 3$$

Think: 2×3 is a known fact.

$$6 \quad + \quad 6 \quad = 12$$

You can also use a calculator.

Use Skip-Counting

Skip-count by 3 to find the total number of costumes.

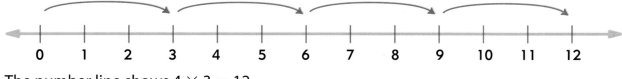

0 1 2 3 4 5 6 7 8 9 10 11 12

The number line shows $4 \times 3 = 12$.

The actors need 12 costumes.

How many people watch the play if there are 3 rows of 5 chairs each?

Find: 3 × 5

Technology Link

Use the place-value models in **Math Tool Chest** to find products.

There's More Than One Way!

Use an Array

The array shows 3 rows of 5 counters. There are 15 counters.

Use a Number Line

Skip-count by 5 to find the total number of people.

The number line shows 3 × 5 = 15.

There are 15 people watching the play.

Try It

Find each product.

1. 5 ×4	**2.** 7 ×4	**3.** 2 ×4	**4.** 6 ×4	**5.** 4 ×4
6. 5 ×3	**7.** 3 ×3	**8.** 2 ×3	**9.** 6 ×3	**10.** 7 ×3

11. **Write About It** **Explain** how knowing 3 × 4 can help you figure out 3 × 8.

Practice and Problem Solving

Multiply.

12. $\begin{array}{r} 4 \\ \times 2 \\ \hline \end{array}$ **13.** $\begin{array}{r} 7 \\ \times 3 \\ \hline \end{array}$ **14.** $\begin{array}{r} 4 \\ \times 4 \\ \hline \end{array}$ **15.** $\begin{array}{r} 3 \\ \times 4 \\ \hline \end{array}$ **16.** $\begin{array}{r} 5 \\ \times 4 \\ \hline \end{array}$

17. 3×1 **18.** 3×3 **19.** 3×2 **20.** 3×6 **21.** 4×7

22. 3×9 **23.** 3×5 **24.** 3×8 **25.** 3×4 **26.** 3×2

★**27.** $4 \times (4 - 1)$ ★**28.** $4 \times (2 - 1)$ ★**29.** $3 \times (5 - 2)$ ★**30.** $4 \times (5 - 3)$

Solve. Use data from the chart for problems 31–33.

THINK
SOLVE
EXPLAIN

31. Each actor in the play needs 4 scarves. If there are 8 actors in the play, will they use all the scarves? Why or why not?

32. The play has 3 acts. Each act needs 7 gold wands. How many gold wands will not be used?

★**33.** **Measurement** An actor ties 3 scarves together. Each scarf is 36 inches long. He uses 3 inches from each scarf to make the knots. How long are the knotted scarves? Draw a picture.

Props Available for the Play

Item	Number
Colored scarves	35
Hats	112
Gold Wands	26

THINK
SOLVE
EXPLAIN

34. **Make It Right** Here's how Suzanne multiplied 4×5. Tell what mistake she made. Explain how to correct it.

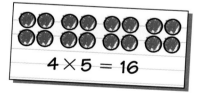

$4 \times 5 = 16$

✔ Spiral Review and Test Prep

35. What is the median? (p. 162)

2, 5, 6, 2, 5

A. 2   **C.** 5

B. 4   **D.** 22

36. What is the range? (p. 162)

7, 1, 10, 1, 2, 11

F. 11   **H.** 2

G. 10   **I.** 1

37. $56 + 78$ (p. 58)   **38.** $1,433 - 375$ (p. 104)   **39.** $775 + 420$ (p. 58)

Extra Practice page 218, Set C

GRID PRODUCTS

Use arrays to show multiplication facts.

Ready

Players: 2 to 4 teams of 2 players each

You Will Need: graph paper for each team, crayons, and part of the Digit Deck — cards with the digits 1–5 (4 of each), 2 zeros and 2 "wild" cards

Set

Each team outlines an area to be filled as instructed by the teacher. (10-by-12 for example)

Mix the cards.

GO!

▶ Take two cards from the top of the deck and place face up for all to see.

▶ Each team decides where on the larger area it wants to box, label, and color that array on its grid. For example, if 3 and 4 are drawn, outline and color a 3-by-4 area. Label it 3 × 4 = 12.

▶ Repeat, choosing 2 new cards from the top of the deck. If there is not enough space in a team's grid to draw its fact, the team may split it or skip a turn. For example, 4 x 3 can be split into 2 × 3 and 2 × 3.

▶ When the deck is done, reshuffle and continue.

▶ Play continues until a team has filled the entire outlined grid. That team is the winner.

10.4 Algebra: Multiply by 0 and 1

Learn

Sometimes only 1 group of 4 players is needed to play a song. How many players is this?

VOCABULARY

Identity Property of Multiplication

Zero Property of Multiplication

Use the Identity Property

The **Identity Property of Multiplication** states that when you multiply 1 by a number, the product is that number.

$1 \times 4 = 4$

There are 4 players.

When the players are finished, there are 0 groups of 4 players. How many players is this?

Use the Zero Property

The **Zero Property of Multiplication** states that when you multiply 0 by a number, the product is 0.

$0 \times 4 = 0$

There are 0 players.

Try It

Find each product. Write the property you used.

1. 2×0
2. 8×1
3. 7×0
4. 6×1
5. 3×0

6. **Write About It** **Explain** why it is easy to solve $6{,}789{,}342 \times 0$.

Practice and Problem Solving

Find each product.

7.	1	8.	4	9.	3	10.	5	11.	8
	$\times 7$		$\times 0$		$\times 0$		$\times 1$		$\times 0$

12. 6×0 **13.** 0×5 **14.** 1×2 **15.** 1×9 **16.** 1×7

17. 0×9 **18.** 1×3 **19.** 8×1 **20.** 1×6 **21.** 0×7

Ⓧ **Algebra** **Find each missing number.**

22. $\blacksquare \times 5 = 0$ **23.** $4 \times \blacksquare = 4$ **24.** $1 \times 5 = \blacksquare$

★**25.** $\blacksquare \times 131 = 131 \times 9$ ★**26.** $1{,}236 \times \blacksquare = 0$ ★**27.** $\blacksquare \times 287 = 287$

Solve.

28. Science The sound of a musical instrument can travel through the air at 1,125 feet each second. How far does the sound travel in 0 seconds? How can you tell?

29. The drum players in a band march in 2 rows with 4 players in each row. If they switch and march in 4 rows, how many players would be in each row? Explain. THINK SOLVE EXPLAIN

30. A trumpet music book costs $9.95. The band leader bought 2 trumpet music books. How much did they cost all together?

31. Write About It **Explain** 2 different strategies you can use to find 6×4. THINK SOLVE EXPLAIN

✔ Spiral Review and Test Prep

32. Which shows numbers in order from least to greatest? (p. 6)

A. 1,110; 1,091; 1,121; 1,099

B. 2,020; 2,220; 2,202; 2,222

C. 3,111; 3,131; 3,113; 3,099

D. 4,040; 4,104; 4,400; 4,440

33. Which data set has a range of 4? (p. 162)

F. 1, 3, 5, 6, 7, 9

G. 5, 3, 4, 5, 6, 7

H. 5, 5, 6, 7, 8, 8

I. 1, 6, 6, 9, 9, 3

34.	$6.75 (p. 60)	35.	$2.46 (p. 104)	36.	$8.42 (p. 60)	37.	427 (p.60)
	$+ 6.75$		$- 0.97$		$+ 6.99$		$+540$

Multiplication

1.   4
  ×4

2.   4
  ×1

3.   5
  ×2

4.   6
  ×3

5.   2
  ×2

6.   9
  ×3

7.   1
  ×2

8.   6
  ×4

9.   9
  ×5

10.   8
  ×3

11.   5
  ×0

12.   3
  ×3

13.   5
  ×1

14.   6
  ×5

15.   2
  ×4

16.   9
  ×4

17.   7
  ×2

18.   6
  ×3

19.   4
  ×5

20.   0
  ×8

21.   5
  ×7

22.   2
  ×5

23.   3
  ×9

24.   8
  ×2

25.   5
  ×6

26.   4
  ×4

27.   2
  ×3

28.   4
  ×7

29.   7
  ×3

30.   5
  ×5

31.   4
  ×9

32.   6
  ×1

33.   2
  ×6

34.   3
  ×4

35.   9
  ×2

36.   7
  ×4

PICK A FACT

Match factor cards with product cards to make multiplication facts.

Ready

Players: 2
You Will Need: index cards

Set

Each student makes 2 matching cards for each of 10 multiplication facts. One card has the problem; the other card has the answer.

Mix cards and lay them face down in a 4-by-5 array.

GO!

▶ The first player turns over 2 cards. If the cards make a true multiplication fact, keep the cards and choose again. If not, put the cards back. Take turns.

▶ Play until all cards are matched. Each pair of cards gets 1 point.

▶ The player with the most points wins.

Extra Practice

Set A Find each product. (pp. 204–206)

1. 4 ×2	2. 8 ×5	3. 8 ×2	4. 5 ×5	5. 6 ×5

6. 7 ×2	7. 9 ×2	8. 2 ×3	9. 2 ×7	10. 2 ×5

11. 2×8 **12.** 2×1 **13.** 6×2 **14.** 2×2 **15.** 7×5

Set B Use the table for problems 16–17. (pp. 208–209)

16. The table shows the number of tickets sold each week for a new popular movie. What number pattern do you see in the ticket sales each week?

17. If this skip-counting pattern continues, what could the ticket sales be in week 4?

Ticket Sales	
Week	Tickets Sold
1	8 Million
2	6 Million
3	4 Million

Set C Find each product. (pp. 210–212)

18. 4 ×4	19. 8 ×3	20. 6 ×4	21. 3 ×4	22. 5 ×3	23. 7 ×4	24. 6 ×3

25. 3×4 **26.** 3×1 **27.** 9×3 **28.** 3×6 **29.** 4×4

30. 4×5 **31.** 4×9 **32.** 3×2 **33.** 7×3 **34.** 3×3

Set D Find each product. (pp. 214–215)

35. 0×3 **36.** 1×6 **37.** 0×4 **38.** 9×1 **39.** 7×0

Find each missing number.

40. $\blacksquare \times 3 = 0$ **41.** $4 \times \blacksquare = 4$ **42.** $0 \times 7 = \blacksquare$ **43.** $\blacksquare \times 9 = 9$

LOG ON www.mmhmath.com
For more practice and Chapter Self-Check Test

Review/Test

Multiply.

1. 4
×2

2. 3
×8

3. 5
×4

4. 7
×3

5. 7
×0

6. 5
×1

7. 3
×2

8. 4
×4

9. 3
×2

10. 4
×3

11. 3
×5

12. 6
×0

13. 9×1

14. 4×6

15. 3×3

16. 8×4

Find each product. Write the property you used.

17. 9×0
18. 1×7
19. 4×0
20. 9×1
21. 8×0

Solve.

22. There are 12 dancers. How can you arrange them on stage in equal rows?

23. One band has 4 guitar players. Each guitar has 6 strings. How many strings are there in all?

24. The chorus lines up in 7 rows. The 1st row has 3 singers, the 2nd row has 6 singers, and the 3rd row has 9 singers. If this pattern continues, how many singers will be in the 7th row?

25. **Write About It** **Analyze** What pattern do you find in numbers when you skip-count by 4s starting at zero?

Do I Need Help?

Exercises	Review Concepts	Use Extra Practice Set
1–16, 23	pp. 204–206, 210–212	Sets A and C
17–22	pp. 214–215	Set D
24–25	pp. 208–209	Set B

 Use your Foldables to help you review.

Decision Making

Lights! Camera! Action! You are the student director of the spring show, which will be in 5 weeks. You must decide whether to have a puppet show, a dance show, or a musical.

You Decide!

Which show do you want to present? Why?

PUPPET SHOW

Practice time: 4 times a week after school.

Practice length: 1 hour

Performers: 3 students

Backstage help: 0 students

Puppet makers: 4 students

DANCE SHOW

Practice time: 5 times a week after school.

Practice length: 1 hour

Performers: 5 students

Backstage help: 3 students

MUSICAL

Practice time: 3 times a week after school.

Practice length: 2 hours

Performers: 7 students

Backstage help: 2 students

Read for Understanding

1. How long would the practice for each show be for 1 week?

2. How many students would be involved in each show?

3. Which show does not need any help backstage?

4. Which show needs the most backstage help?

Make Decisions

5. Each performer and backstage helper invites 2 guests to the show. How many guests will be in the audience for each show?

6. Each performer in the musical changes costumes 3 times during the show. What is the total number of costumes needed for the show?

7. Each dancer wears 4 different pairs of shoes during the dance show. How many pairs of shoes are needed in all?

8. It takes 4 hours to make each puppet. The show needs 4 puppets. How many hours does it take to make all of the puppets?

9. A backstage helper cannot practice more than 90 minutes on a school day. Which shows can he work on? Why?

10. Some students cannot practice on Tuesdays and Thursdays. Which show could these students work on? Why?

11. What would be some reasons to direct the puppet show? What would be some reasons not to direct?

12. What would be some reasons to direct the dance show? What would be some reasons not to direct?

13. What would be some reasons to direct the musical? What would be some reasons not to direct?

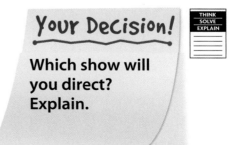

Your Decision!

THINK
SOLVE
EXPLAIN

Which show will you direct? Explain.

Vocabulary

Complete. Use a word from the list.

1. If you know 5 × 7 = 35, the ___ of Multiplication can help you find 7 × 5.

2. The answer in a multiplication sentence is called the ___.

3. If one ___ of a multiplication sentence is zero, the product is always zero.

4. You can use the ___of Multiplication to mentally find 1 × 1,247.

VOCABULARY

Commutative Property
factor
Identity Property
product
Zero Property

Skills and Applications

Multiply facts through 5. (pp. 190–194, 204–206, 210–212)

Find: 4 × 2

Solution
Use equal groups:

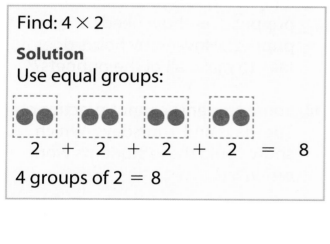

2 + 2 + 2 + 2 = 8

4 groups of 2 = 8

Find each product.

5. 2 × 6   6. 3 × 5

7. 4 × 4   8. 3 × 7

9. 2 × 2   10. 8 × 3

11. 3 × 3   12. 4 × 8

13.   4   14.   3
    ×5   ×2

15.   6   16.   4
    ×3   ×7

17.   3   18.   5
    ×4   ×1

19.   9   20.   8
    ×4   ×2

Foldables Use your Foldables to help you review.

Use properties of multiplication. (pp. 196–197, 214–215)

Find: 9×2

Solution
Use the Commutative Property:

$2 \times 9 = 18$, so
$9 \times 2 = 18$

Multiply. Tell which property you used.

21. $9 \times 3 = $ ▮

22. ▮ $\times 8 = 8$

23. $6 \times$ ▮ $= 0$

24. $7 \times 5 = $ ▮

25. $8 \times$ ▮ $= 0$

26. ▮ $\times 1 = 9$

27. $4 \times$ ▮ $= 4$

28. ▮ $\times 5 = 0$

29. $6 \times 3 = $ ▮

30. $1 \times$ ▮ $= 7$

Use skills and strategies to solve problems. (pp. 198–199, 208–209)

Kayla is saving for a new pair of tap shoes. She starts on the first day by saving 2 cents. The second day she saves 4 cents and the third day she saves 6 cents. If this pattern continues, how much will she save on the sixth day?

Solution
Find the pattern:

Day	1	2	3	4	5	6
Cents	2	4	6	▮	▮	▮

The amount increases by 2 each time.

The pattern is 2, 4, 6, 8, 10, 12.

She will save 12 cents on the sixth day.

Solve.

31. The band is setting up 16 chairs in rows. The bandleader wants all of the rows to have the same number of chairs. How many chairs will be in each row? How many rows will there be?

32. There are 4 members in the band who play the clarinet. Two times as many girls play the trumpet. How many girls play the trumpet?

33. At each concert, the band raffles 3 prizes. How many prizes are raffled at 4 concerts?

Enrichment

Intersection Models

You have seen how to use arrays to show multiplication. Here is another kind of model. Here is how to multiply 2×3 using an intersection model.

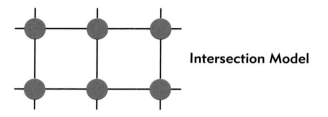

Intersection Model

1. Which part of the model shows the first factor in 2×3?

2. Which part of the model shows the second factor?

3. How do you find the product?

Write the multiplication fact.

4.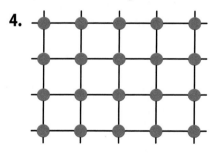

5.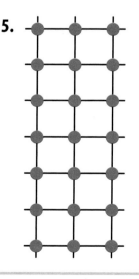

Draw a model for each.

6. 9×2 **7.** 3×5 **8.** 6×8 **9.** 3×4

10. **Write About It** **Compare** how an intersection model and an array are alike and different.

Performance Assessment

What Is the Total Cost?

Your school is putting on a play! To help raise money, the drama club is selling blank pages in the play program book.

Each page that you buy has an array of boxes. You can fill the boxes with drawings or messages.

Plan 2 pages that your class wants to buy. To set up a page, you need to make some choices.

- Choose 2, 3, or 4 boxes across.

- Choose 3, 4, or 5 boxes up and down.

- Write an equation that tells the number of boxes on each of the pages.

- Use the Price List chart to determine the total cost of each page.

- Determine the total cost of the 2 pages.

- Decide what will go in the boxes.

Price List	
Boxes Per Page	Cost Per Box
6–8	$5
9–12	$4
13–16	$3
17–20	$2

Tips For A Good Answer

- Show the correct cost for each page.

- Show the correct total for the 2 pages.

 You may want to save this work in your portfolio.

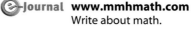

TECHNOLOGY Link

Model Multiplication

Marta's Pet Store has new puppies. Marta put the puppies in 4 different beds. There are 3 puppies in each bed. How many puppies does Marta have?

You can use counters 𝄫 from the *Math Tool Chest CD-ROM* to stamp out a model of 4 groups of 3 puppies.

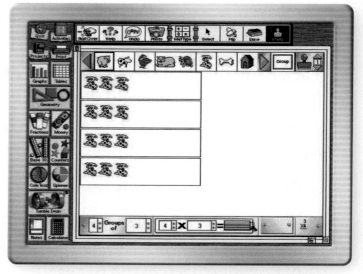

Math Tool Chest CD-ROM

- Choose multiplication for the mat type.

- At the bottom of the screen, choose 4 in the box on the left and 3 in the box on the right.

The number boxes show that you are finding 4 groups of 3, or 4 × 3.

How many puppies does Marta have?

Use the computer to model each fact. Find the product.

1. 3 × 5   **2.** 8 × 2   **3.** 5 × 6   **4.** 7 × 3

Solve.

5. Kendra has 8 packages of baseball cards. There are 5 cards in each package. How many baseball cards does she have?

6. Mr. Montgomery has 4 cartons of water. There are 6 bottles in each carton. How many bottles of water does he have?

7. Analyze How does using the models help you multiply?

 For more practice, use Math Traveler™.

Test-Taking Tips

Some test questions are easier to answer if you **draw a picture**.

Robyn is using this pattern of tiling:
1 red, 1 blue, 1 green, 1 red, 1 blue, 1 green.
Then she repeats the pattern several times.
What color is the 14th tile?

A. blue   **C.** yellow

B. red   **D.** green

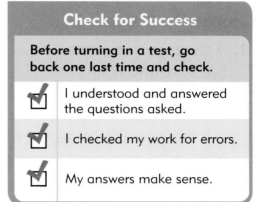

Check for Success

Before turning in a test, go back one last time and check.

☑ I understood and answered the questions asked.

☑ I checked my work for errors.

☑ My answers make sense.

You can draw a picture to find out:

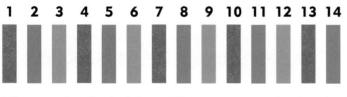

The 14th tile is blue. The correct choice is A.

Draw a picture to help you choose the best answer.

1. Jean has 4 quarters, 2 dimes, and 11 nickels. How many groups worth $0.35 can she make?

   A. 3 groups   **C.** 7 groups
   B. 5 groups   **D.** 9 groups

2. Karen has 2 guppies on Monday. Each day the number of guppies in her tank doubles. How many guppies could she have on Friday?

   F. 5 guppies   **H.** 32 guppies
   G. 18 guppies   **I.** 64 guppies

3. There are 15 cans that need to be stacked in rows. How many rows will there be if each row has one less than the row before?

   A. 4 rows   **C.** 6 rows
   B. 5 rows   **D.** 9 rows

4. Douglas is making a quilt using this pattern for the squares: 2 red, 2 yellow, 2 orange. Then he repeats the pattern. What color is the 18th square?

   F. red   **H.** orange
   G. yellow   **I.** green

Test Prep

PART 1 • Multiple Choice

Choose the best answer.

1. A theater club is making a background for a play. The background can be no wider than 108 inches. Which of these is not a possible measurement for the background? (p. 24)

   A. 180 inches

   B. 104 inches

   C. 98 inches

   D. 89 inches

2. Materials come in measures that are multiples of 100. Singh measures the background at 98 inches. What is the number to the nearest hundred? (p. 32)

   F. 90   **H.** 190

   G. 100   **I.** 200

3. You know that $2 \times 6 = 12$. Use this to find the product of 4×6. (p. 210)

   A. 24   **C.** 16

   B. 18   **D.** 10

4. Which is the same as 3×5? (p. 197)

   F. $3 + 5$ **H.** 5×3

   G. $3 \div 5$ **I.** $5 + 3$

5. What is the missing number in this pattern? (p. 2)

   $3, $6, $9, ▮, $15

   A. $10   **C.** $12

   B. $11   **D.** $18

6. Find the rule. (p. 52)

Input	3	5	7	9
Output	7	9	11	13

   F. Add 3   **H.** Add 4

   G. Subtract 3   **I.** Subtract 4

7. A recipe states that there are 4 servings in 1 quart of punch. How many servings are there in 4 quarts of punch? (p. 210)

   A. 4 servings   **C.** 12 servings

   B. 8 servings   **D.** 16 servings

8. The school band performs a concert. Which is a reasonable length of time for the concert? (p. 142)

   F. 50 minutes   **H.** 50 seconds

   G. 50 hours   **I.** 5 days

9. What is the total amount? (p. 14)

   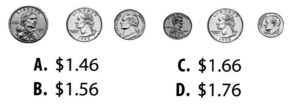

   A. $1.46   **C.** $1.66

   B. $1.56   **D.** $1.76

Record your answers on the answer sheet provided by your teacher or on a sheet of paper.

10. There were 1,267 tickets sold for the concert. What is this number rounded to the nearest hundred? (p. 32)

11. Mrs. Thomson has 5 rows of 3 thimbles in her display case. How many thimbles does she have in all? (p. 212)

12. It takes Jen 45 minutes to get ready for school. How many quarter hours is this? (p. 144)

13. Find the range for the set of data.
2, 4, 3, 1, 7, 9 (p. 162)

THINK
SOLVE
EXPLAIN
14. There are 2,942 ants in an ant farm and 3,478 ants in another. About how many ants are there in all? Explain how you got your estimate. (p. 64)

15. What is the difference?
7,208 − 977 (p. 114)

16. Piere's favorite song is 3 minutes and 20 seconds long. Jennie's favorite song is 4 minutes long. How much longer is Jennie's song than Piere's? (p. 106)

Use the graph for problems 17–19.

Theater Club Attendance	
Week	Number of Students
1	☆ ☆ ☆ ☆ ☆ ☆
2	☆ ☆ ☆ ☆ ☆
3	☆ ☆ ☆ ☆
4	☆ ☆ ☆ ☆ ☆

Each ☆ = 2 students

17. How many students attended the Theater Club in week 1? (p. 166)

18. Cara brought cookies for a snack for week 3. Each member of the club got 2 cookies. How many cookies did they get in all? Explain. (p. 204)

THINK
SOLVE
EXPLAIN

19. How many more members attended in week 1 than week 3? (p. 166)

PART 3 • Extended Response

Record your answer on a sheet of paper. Show your work.

THINK
SOLVE
EXPLAIN

20. A cheerleading squad has 29 members. To enter a future show, they need to have twice as many members. How many cheerleaders do they need in all? Explain how you solved this problem.

Test Prep

What Do I Need to Know?

There are 3 hot air balloons.
Each balloon has 4 people inside.
How many people are there in
the 3 balloons?

Multiplication Facts and Strategies

What Will I Learn?

In this chapter you will learn to

- find square numbers
- multiply by 6, 7, and 8
- find missing factors
- use skills and strategies to solve problems

How Do I Read Math?

When you read a mathematics book, sometimes you read words and symbols, and sometimes you read only symbols.

All of these describe 4 groups of 6 equals 24:

- **The product of 4 and 6 is 24**
- $4 \times 6 = 24$

$$\begin{array}{r} 6 \\ \times 4 \\ \hline 24 \end{array}$$

VOCABULARY

- square number
- variable

Foldables

Use your Foldables to help you with chapter concepts.

1. Fold a 2–inch tab along the long edge of the paper.
2. Fold the paper in half like a hamburger to make two pockets.
3. Glue the outside edges of the pockets together.
4. Label as shown. Record what you learn.
5. Make two Foldables and glue them together.
6. Take notes and write facts on index cards.
7. Sort and store fact cards in your Foldable pocket book.

11.1 Explore Square Numbers

Hands On Activity

You can use grids to explore square numbers.

How many small squares are there in a grid 3 squares long and 3 squares wide?

You Will Need
- graph paper
- crayons or markers

Use Models

STEP 1

Draw a square on graph paper that is 3 small squares wide and 3 small squares long.

A square has the same number of ☐ on each side.

3 squares wide

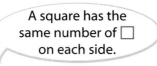

3 squares long

STEP 2

Record your work.
Show each factor and the product.

Number of Rows (Factor)		Number in Each Row (Factor)		Total (Product)
3	×	3	=	9

STEP 3

Repeat steps 1 and 2 for other different sized squares.

Explain Your Thinking

1. How many rows did you draw in your square in Step 1?

2. How many ☐ are in each row?

3. How many ☐ in all?

4. How do you decide how many rows?

Technology Link

Use the counters tool in **Math Tool Chest** to model square numbers.

Find: 4 × 4

Let's see how to connect models to paper and pencil.

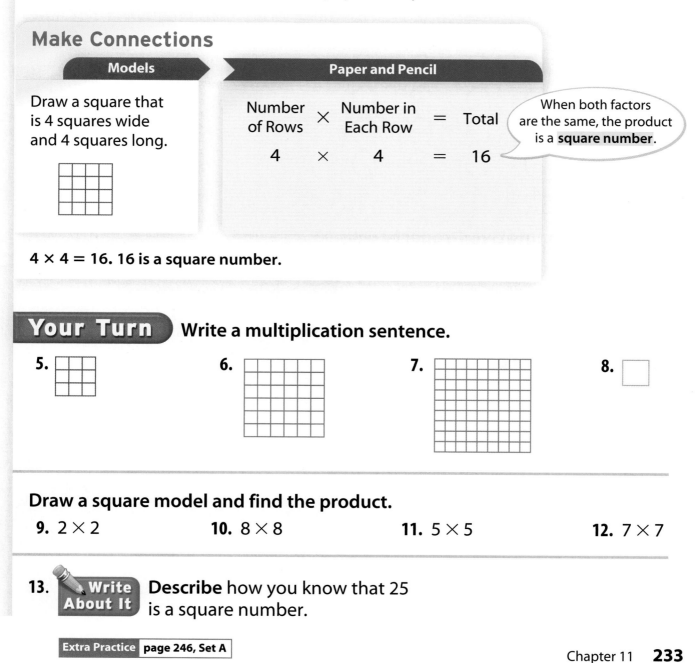

Make Connections

Models	Paper and Pencil

Draw a square that is 4 squares wide and 4 squares long.

Number of Rows	×	Number in Each Row	=	Total
4	×	4	=	16

When both factors are the same, the product is a **square number**.

4 × 4 = 16. 16 is a square number.

Your Turn Write a multiplication sentence.

5.

6.

7.

8.

Draw a square model and find the product.

9. 2 × 2

10. 8 × 8

11. 5 × 5

12. 7 × 7

13. **Write About It** **Describe** how you know that 25 is a square number.

11.2 Multiply by 6 and 8

Learn

You can see many things while riding horses. Suppose there are 6 groups on the trail. Each group has 4 riders. How many people are on the trail ride?

Find: 6 × 4

There's More Than One Way!

Use Repeated Addition

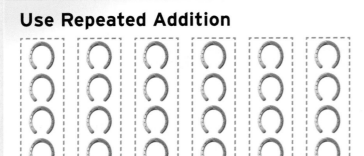

4 + 4 + 4 + 4 + 4 + 4 = 24

Use the Commutative Property

You know that
4 × 6 = 24,
so, 6 × 4 = 24.

> **Think:** The order of the factors does not change the product.

Double a Known Fact

4 × 6 = (3 × 4) + (3 × 4)

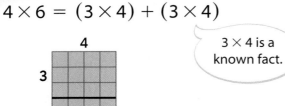

> 3 × 4 is a known fact.

12 + 12 = 24

There are 24 people on the trail ride.

234

Tourists are traveling through Africa with 8 camels. Each camel carries 9 sacks of supplies. How many sacks are the camels carrying in all?

Find: 8 × 9

Double a Known Fact

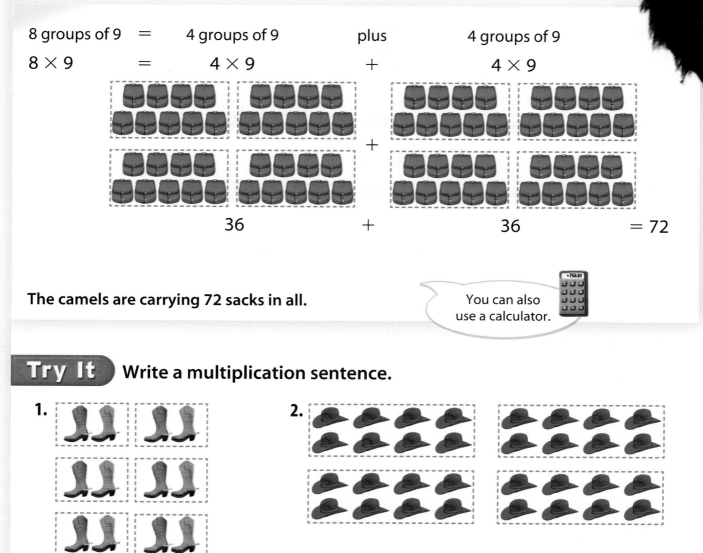

8 groups of 9 = 4 groups of 9 plus 4 groups of 9

8 × 9 = 4 × 9 + 4 × 9

36 + 36 = 72

The camels are carrying 72 sacks in all.

You can also use a calculator.

Try It **Write a multiplication sentence.**

1.

2.

Find each product.

3. 6 × 2　　　**4.** 6 × 4　　　**5.** 6 × 6　　　**6.** 8 × 5　　　**7.** 8 × 7

8. **Write About It** **Discuss** with your classmates about strategies used to multiply 8 × 4. Explain which strategy you prefer.

Practice and Problem Solving

Write a multiplication sentence.

9.

Find each product.

10. 5
   ×6

11. 7
   ×8

12. 8
   ×8

13. 6
   ×8

14. 9
   ×6

15. 1 × 8

16. 0 × 6

17. 4 × 8

18. 5 × 8

19. 0 × 8

★20. (3 + 1) × 6

★21. (2 + 1) × 6

★22. (3 + 3) × 6

Solve.

23. Ted has 7 boxes of lunches. Each box has 8 lunches. How many lunches does Ted have?

24. **Write a problem** using the equation 6 × 7 = 42.

25. **Time** It takes 45 minutes to drive from home to a friend's house. How many hours does it take to drive there and back home?

26. **Make It Right** Here's how Jamie multiplied 8 × 7. Describe what mistake he made. Explain how to correct it.

THINK
SOLVE
EXPLAIN

(8 × 7)
(2 × 7) + (4 × 7)
= 14 + 28 = 42

Spiral Review and Test Prep

27. A road map costs $1.75. How much change should you get if you pay with a five-dollar bill? (p. 114)

   A. $3.25   C. $4.25

   B. $3.75   D. $4.75

28. Which is the same as four quarter hours? (p. 144)

   F. 15 minutes   H. 45 minutes

   G. 30 minutes   I. 60 minutes

29. 342 + 113 (p. 60)

30. 686 − 259 (p. 104)

31. 492 + 173 (p. 60)

Extra Practice page 246, Set B

Practice at School ★ Practice at Home

FACTOR FIND

Use arrays and mental math to name factors.

Ready

Players: 2
You Will Need: index cards, markers, graph paper

Set

On each card, write a product from the facts you have learned.

Shuffle the cards and place them face down.

GO!

▶ Player 1 picks a card and names 2 factors whose product is the same as the number on the card.

▶ Player 1 outlines that array on a piece of graph paper.

▶ Player 2 counts the number of squares inside the outlined area.

▶ If the number outlined matches the number on the card, player 1 gets a point.

▶ The player with the most points after 10 rounds is the winner.

11.3 Multiply by 7

Learn

The Indiana Transportation Museum has many model trains on display. One display has 7 trains, each with 6 cars. How many cars are there in all?

Find: 7 × 6

There's More Than One Way!

Add on to a Known Fact	Double a Known Fact

Add on to a Known Fact

7 groups of 6 = 6 groups of 6, plus 6

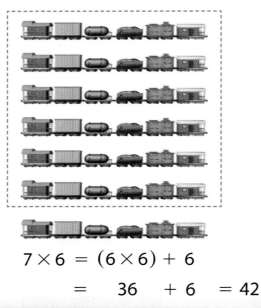

$7 \times 6 = (6 \times 6) + 6$

$= 36 + 6 = 42$

Double a Known Fact

> Think: 3×7 is a known fact. $3 \times 7 = 7 \times 3$

$7 \times 6 = (7 \times 3) + (7 \times 3)$

$= 21 + 21$

$= 42$

There are 42 cars in all.

Try It Find each product.

1. 7×1 **2.** 7×4

3. 7×2 **4.** 7×5

5. **Write About It** **Explain** how knowing other facts can help you find facts for 7.

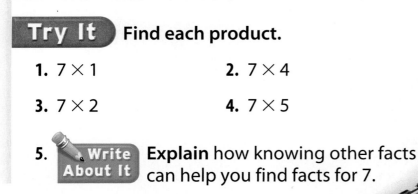

Practice and Problem Solving

Write a multiplication sentence.

6.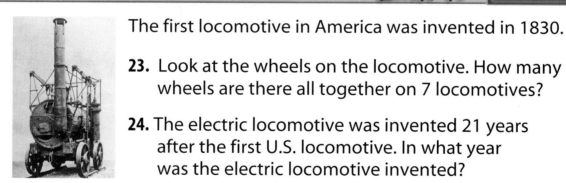

7.

Find each product.

8. 6×7 9. 4×7 10. 7×3 11. 5×7 12. 7×8

13. 7×1 14. 7×7 15. 5×4 16. 0×7 17. 3×4

★18. $(1 + 1) \times 7$ ★19. $(2 + 2) \times 7$ ★20. $(3 + 3) \times 7$

ⓧ Algebra Complete the table.

21.

Rule: Multiply by 7				
Input	1	3		8
Output	7		42	

22.

Rule:			
Input	2	3	5
Output	14	21	35

Link to ⭐ SOCIAL STUDIES ⭐

The first locomotive in America was invented in 1830.

23. Look at the wheels on the locomotive. How many wheels are there all together on 7 locomotives?

24. The electric locomotive was invented 21 years after the first U.S. locomotive. In what year was the electric locomotive invented?

✓ Spiral Review and Test Prep

25. There are 3 passengers in each of 8 rows on a train car. How many passengers are there in all? (p. 210)

   A. 11 riders   **C.** 21 riders
   B. 16 riders   **D.** 24 riders

26. Which comes next in this skip-counting pattern?
   20, 24, 28, ▮ (p. 2)

   F. 29   **H.** 32
   G. 30   **I.** 34

27. $22 + 45 + 476$ (p. 76)   28. $3,419 - 326$ (p. 120)   29. $209 + 775 + 98$ (p. 76)

11.4 Algebra: Find Missing Factors

Learn

A kayak seats 2 people. A group of 10 people wants to rent kayaks. How many kayaks do they need to rent?

Find the number of groups of 2 when the total is 10.

VOCABULARY

variable

Use a Known Fact

⬛ groups of 2 equals 10

⬛ × 2 = 10

List the 2s facts until you reach 10.

$1 \times 2 = 2$

$2 \times 2 = 4$

$3 \times 2 = 6$

$4 \times 2 = 8$

$5 \times 2 = 10$

They need to rent 5 kayaks.

240

Larger boats are also available. There are 5 boats for a group of 20 people. The same size group has to be on each boat. How many people are on each boat?

Write an equation to solve.

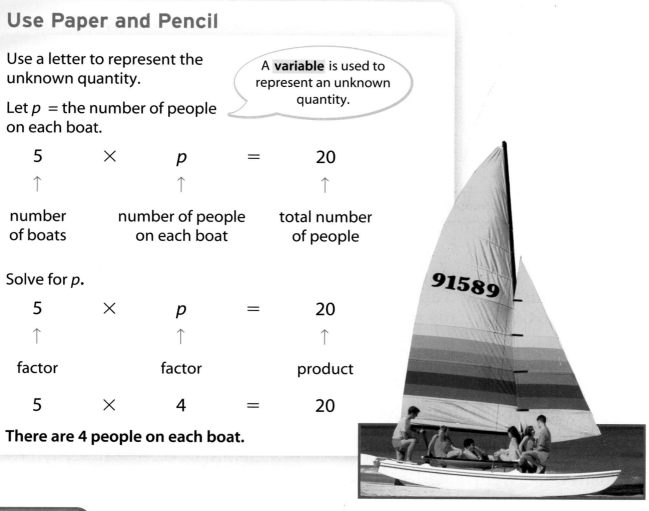

Use Paper and Pencil

Use a letter to represent the unknown quantity.

A **variable** is used to represent an unknown quantity.

Let p = the number of people on each boat.

$$5 \quad \times \quad p \quad = \quad 20$$
↑   ↑   ↑

number of boats   number of people on each boat   total number of people

Solve for p.

$$5 \quad \times \quad p \quad = \quad 20$$
↑   ↑   ↑

factor   factor   product

$$5 \quad \times \quad 4 \quad = \quad 20$$

There are 4 people on each boat.

91589

Try It

Find the missing factor.

1. ▉ groups of 8 is 16   2. 6 groups of ▉ is 54   3. 3 groups of ▉ is 15

4. $t \times 2 = 14$ 5. $4 \times y = 16$ 6. $3 \times b = 27$ 7. $s \times 6 = 48$

8. **Write About It** **Explain** how to find the missing factor d in $3 \times d = 12$ using a different strategy than the ones shown.

Practice and Problem Solving

Find the missing factor.

9. ▮ groups of 4 is 8   10. 6 groups of ▮ is 24   11. 3 groups of ▮ is 18

12. $7 \times d = 28$ 13. $5 \times w = 15$ 14. $2 \times a = 2$ 15. $9 \times v = 18$

16. $k \times 5 = 0$ 17. $7 \times l = 35$ 18. $n \times 8 = 56$ 19. $2 \times h = 12$

★20. $(v + 1) \times 3 = 9$ ★21. $(j + 4) \times 2 = 16$ ★22. $5 \times (3 + y) = 35$

Ⓧ **Algebra** Complete each table.

23.

Number of boats	1	2	3	4
Total number of people	4			

24.

Number of rowboats	2	4	6	8
Total number of oars	4			

Solve.

25. The product of 8 and another factor is 64. What is the missing factor?

26. It takes Ken 2 hours to clean a boat. How many boats would he have cleaned after 14 hours?

27. On Sunday and Monday, 12 boats were rented on each day. On each of the other days of the week, 8 boats were rented. How many boats were rented in all?

28. **Make It Right** Here's how Ray found the missing factor. Describe what mistake he made. Explain how to correct it.

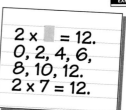

THINK
SOLVE
EXPLAIN

2 × ▮ = 12.
0, 2, 4, 6,
8, 10, 12.
2 × 7 = 12.

Spiral Review and Test Prep

29. Round 658 to the nearest hundred. (p. 32)

    A. 600   **C.** 655

    B. 650   **D.** 700

30. It is 10:30 A.M. What time will it be in 12 hours? (p.146)

    F. 10:42 A.M.   **H.** 10:30 P.M.

    G. 12:00 P.M.   **I.** 10:42 P.M.

31. $248 + 827$ (p. 60)   32. $4,073 - 983$ (p. 114)   33. 7×3 (p. 238)

Extra Practice page 246, Set D

Problem Solving: Reading for Math

HISTORY ON WHEELS

The first cable car, or trolley, was created in San Francisco, California, on August 2, 1873. Trolleys could chug along at 20 miles an hour. They could easily climb the city's steep hills. But when automobiles were invented, many trolley cars were no longer used.

BRINGING THEM BACK

One group, the Market Street Railway, helps keep San Francisco's trolleys running. The group's members spend time fixing old trolley cars. So far, the group has brought dozens of trolleys back to the city's streets—and they're restoring more.

One of those trolleys is Car #162. It first ran in 1915, taking people to school, stores, and work. Like most trolleys, it had benches for people to sit on. Those benches—and lots of other things—now need to be fixed. Volunteers plan on restoring 2 center benches and 8 end seats. Once it is restored, Car #162 will once again travel the streets of San Francisco. That's great news for riders!

Cable cars: A San Francisco treat.

Problem Solving

 Reading Skill

Fact and Opinion What are 3 facts mentioned in the story?

1. Car #162 has 8 end seats that need to be fixed. Suppose 2 volunteers work on each seat. How many volunteers will work on the end seats in all?

2. Long trolley benches can seat 4 people comfortably. Smaller benches can seat 2 people. If Car #162 has 4 long benches and 2 small benches, how many people can sit down in the trolley?

11.5

Problem Solving: Skill
Solve Multistep Problems

Read

Mr. and Mrs. Li are taking 5 student members of the drama club on a bus trip to tour theaters. How much will the bus ride cost?

- **What do you know?**
  Number of tickets needed; cost of each ticket

- **What do you need to find?**
  Total cost of the tickets

BUS TICKETS

ADULTS	$8.00
STUDENTS	$3.00

Plan

Some problems take more than 1 step to solve. You must decide how to solve each step and in what order.

First, multiply to find the cost of each type of ticket. Then, add the products to find the total cost of the tickets.

Solve

Step 1 They need 2 adult tickets.
$2 \times \$8 = \$16$

Step 2 They need 5 student tickets.
$5 \times \$3 = \$15$

Step 3 Add the products to find the total.
$(2 \times \$8) + (5 \times \$3) =$
   $\$16 \quad + \quad \$15 \quad = \$31$

The bus tickets cost $31.

Look Back

Is your answer reasonable?

1. **Write About It** **Explain** why you cannot add the total cost of each type of ticket first.

244

2. Two families go on a boat tour. There are 3 children and 4 adults. Children's tickets cost $4 and adult tickets cost $7. How much will the boat ride cost?

3. The science club goes on a trip to a museum. There are 3 cars of 5 people each and 4 vans of 7 people each. How many people go on the trip?

4. Amy walked 1 block to the bus stop. Then she rode a bus 4 blocks to the theater. Later, she went home the same way. How many blocks did Amy travel on her entire trip?

5. John and Tina are buying lunch. Drinks cost $2 each and salads cost $4. John has 1 drink and 2 salads. Tina has 1 drink and 1 salad. How much does their lunch cost?

Mixed Strategy Review

6. A minibus only fits 10 people. There are 25 people. How many buses do you need?

7. Ming leaves home at 8:15 A.M. He arrives at school 40 minutes later. What time does he get to school?

Use data from the map for problems 8–10.

8. May walked from the post office to the bank, then to the police station. Sue walked from the library to the post office, then to the bank. Who walked farther?

9. Starting at the bank, describe the shortest route to visit all 5 buildings.

10. ✎ **Write a problem** using the data from the map.

Choose a Strategy
- Logical Reasoning
- Draw a Picture or Diagram
- Make a Graph
- Act It Out
- Make a Table or List
- Find a Pattern
- Guess and Check
- Write an Equation
- Work Backward
- Solve a Simpler Problem

Problem Solving

Chapter 11

Extra Practice

Set A Draw the model and find the product. (pp. 232–233)

1. 3×3 **2.** 6×6 **3.** 4×4 **4.** 5×5 **5.** 2×2

Set B Write a multiplication sentence for the picture. (pp. 234–236)

6.

Find each product.

7. $\begin{array}{r} 6 \\ \times 4 \\ \hline \end{array}$ **8.** $\begin{array}{r} 3 \\ \times 8 \\ \hline \end{array}$ **9.** $\begin{array}{r} 2 \\ \times 6 \\ \hline \end{array}$ **10.** $\begin{array}{r} 8 \\ \times 6 \\ \hline \end{array}$ **11.** $\begin{array}{r} 9 \\ \times 8 \\ \hline \end{array}$

12. $\begin{array}{r} 5 \\ \times 6 \\ \hline \end{array}$ **13.** $\begin{array}{r} 7 \\ \times 6 \\ \hline \end{array}$ **14.** $\begin{array}{r} 8 \\ \times 8 \\ \hline \end{array}$ **15.** $\begin{array}{r} 0 \\ \times 6 \\ \hline \end{array}$ **16.** $\begin{array}{r} 1 \\ \times 8 \\ \hline \end{array}$

17. 8×4 **18.** 6×3 **19.** 8×0 **20.** 8×2 **21.** 6×9

Set C Find each product. (pp. 238–239)

22. $\begin{array}{r} 7 \\ \times 7 \\ \hline \end{array}$ **23.** $\begin{array}{r} 2 \\ \times 7 \\ \hline \end{array}$ **24.** $\begin{array}{r} 5 \\ \times 7 \\ \hline \end{array}$ **25.** $\begin{array}{r} 8 \\ \times 7 \\ \hline \end{array}$ **26.** $\begin{array}{r} 3 \\ \times 7 \\ \hline \end{array}$

27. $\begin{array}{r} 4 \\ \times 7 \\ \hline \end{array}$ **28.** $\begin{array}{r} 6 \\ \times 7 \\ \hline \end{array}$ **29.** $\begin{array}{r} 9 \\ \times 7 \\ \hline \end{array}$ **30.** $\begin{array}{r} 0 \\ \times 7 \\ \hline \end{array}$ **31.** $\begin{array}{r} 1 \\ \times 7 \\ \hline \end{array}$

Set D Find the missing factor. (pp. 240–242)

32. $t \times 4 = 12$ **33.** $5 \times m = 10$ **34.** $d \times 6 = 18$ **35.** $3 \times y = 27$

Set E Solve. (pp. 244–245)

36. Jack walked 2 blocks to the store, then 5 blocks to the library. Later, he walked home the same way. How many blocks did he walk?

37. Terrance buys 3 train tickets for $8 each. Gina buys 4 train tickets for $7 each. Who spent more money? How much more?

LOG ON www.mmhmath.com
For more practice and Chapter Self-Check Test

Review/Test

Draw the model and find the product.

1. 7×7 **2.** 5×5 **3.** 8×8 **4.** 1×1 **5.** 4×4

Find each product.

6. 6×4 **7.** 7×6 **8.** 8×3 **9.** 6×6

10. $\begin{array}{r} 8 \\ \times 5 \\ \hline \end{array}$ **11.** $\begin{array}{r} 6 \\ \times 1 \\ \hline \end{array}$ **12.** $\begin{array}{r} 7 \\ \times 0 \\ \hline \end{array}$ **13.** $\begin{array}{r} 3 \\ \times 8 \\ \hline \end{array}$

14. $\begin{array}{r} 7 \\ \times 2 \\ \hline \end{array}$ **15.** $\begin{array}{r} 6 \\ \times 5 \\ \hline \end{array}$ **16.** $\begin{array}{r} 8 \\ \times 9 \\ \hline \end{array}$ **17.** $\begin{array}{r} 6 \\ \times 0 \\ \hline \end{array}$

Find the missing factor.

18. $h \times 5 = 45$ **19.** $3 \times n = 21$ **20.** $6 \times w = 24$ **21.** $p \times 8 = 48$

Solve.

22. Janell drove 8 hours each day for 2 days. Then she drove 4 hours each day for 3 days. How many hours did she drive all together?

23. Joe and Nina each have 4 bags of treats. Ling has 3 times as many bags as Joe's and Nina's combined. How many bags do they have in all?

24. A train conductor works 7 hours each day. One week she worked 5 days. The next week she worked 3 days. How many more hours did she work the first week than the second week?

25. **Write About It** **Analyze** When you forget a multiplication fact, what method do you prefer to use to figure it out?

Do I Need Help?

Exercises	Review Concepts	Use Extra Practice Set
1–5	pp. 232–233	Set A
6–17	pp. 234–236; 238–239	Sets B and C
18–21	pp. 240–242	Set D
22–25	pp. 244–245	Set E

Foldables Use your Foldables to help you review.

Erin went to Alaska for vacation. She spent 5 days in each city. She visited 4 cities. How many days was she in Alaska?

Multiplication Patterns

What Will I Learn?

In this chapter you will learn to

- multiply by 9 and 10
- explore patterns in a multiplication table
- multiply 3 numbers
- use skills and strategies to solve problems

How Do I Read Math?

When you read a mathematics book, sometimes you read words and symbols, and sometimes you read only symbols.

All of these describe the array of circles shown below:

- **There are 3 rows with 4 circles in each row.**
- **3 × 4 = 12**

VOCABULARY

- Associative Property of Multiplication

Foldables

Use your Foldables to help you with chapter concepts.

1. Fold a 2–inch tab along the long edge of the paper.
2. Fold the paper in half like a hamburger to make two pockets.
3. Glue the outside edges of the pockets together.
4. Label as shown. Record what you learn.
5. Make two and glue them together to form a Foldable with four pockets.
6. Take notes and write facts on index cards.
7. Sort and store cards in your Foldable pocket book.

12.1 Multiply by 10

Learn

This pictograph shows the top choices of 160 third grade students for favorite travel destinations. How many chose an amusement park?

Look at the amusement park row in the graph.

Find: 8 × 10

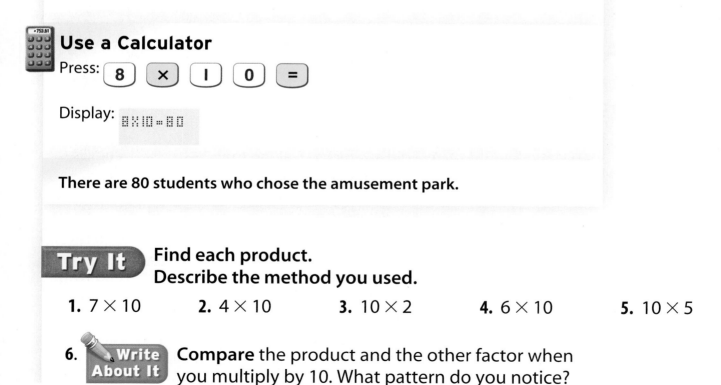

Favorite Travel Destinations

Place	Number of students
Amusement park	🚗🚗🚗🚗🚗🚗🚗🚗
National park	🚗🚗🚗🚗🚗
Movie Studio	🚗🚗🚗

Each 🚗 equals 10 students

There's More Than One Way!

Use Place Value

8 × 1 ten = 8 tens   8 tens = 80 →   So 8 × 10 = 80.

Use Repeated Addition

8 × 10 = 10 + 10 + 10 + 10 + 10 + 10 + 10 + 10 = 80

Use a Calculator

Press: [8] [×] [1] [0] [=]

Display: 8×10=80

There are 80 students who chose the amusement park.

Try It

**Find each product.
Describe the method you used.**

1. 7 × 10   **2.** 4 × 10   **3.** 10 × 2   **4.** 6 × 10   **5.** 10 × 5

6. **Write About It** **Compare** the product and the other factor when you multiply by 10. What pattern do you notice?

Practice and Problem Solving

Find the product.

7.	8.	9.	10.	11.	12.
7 $\times 10$	8 $\times 10$	0 $\times 10$	4 $\times 10$	10 $\times 10$	10 $\times 9$

13. 1×10 **14.** 10×2 **15.** 5×10 **16.** 10×9 **17.** 10×3

18. 10×6 **19.** 8×8 **20.** 7×7 **21.** 5×9 **22.** 4×10

★**23.** 12×10 ★**24.** 10×21 ★**25.** 30×10 ★**26.** 10×32 ★**27.** 50×10

(x) **Algebra** Describe and complete
the skip-counting pattern.

28. 20, 30, 40, ▮, 60, 70, 80, ▮, 100, ▮, 120, 130, 140, 150

Solve. Use data from the pictograph for problems 29–31.

29. How many more people can
ride on the Tram than on the
Super Coaster?

THINK
SOLVE
EXPLAIN

30. Language Arts Write a
paragraph about the number of
people that can fit on the rides.

31. On one ride of the Skywalk, there
are 20 empty seats. How many
people are on the ride?

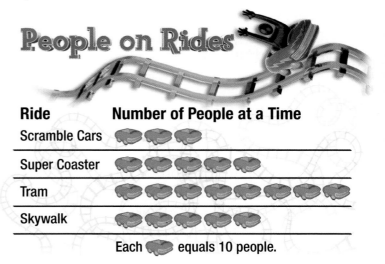

People on Rides

Ride	Number of People at a Time
Scramble Cars	🚗🚗🚗
Super Coaster	🚗🚗🚗🚗🚗
Tram	🚗🚗🚗🚗🚗🚗🚗🚗
Skywalk	🚗🚗🚗🚗🚗

Each 🚗 equals 10 people.

✓ Spiral Review and Test Prep

32. Six bicycles need new tires. How
many tires are there in all? (p. 234)

   A. 12 tires   **C.** 8 tires

   B. 10 tires   **D.** 6 tires

33. What is the missing number in
this skip-counting pattern? (p. 2)

    5, 10, 15, 20, 25, ▮

   F. 26   **H.** 31

   G. 30   **I.** 35

34. $104 - 86$ (p. 114)   **35.** $501 + 321$ (p. 60)   **36.** $2{,}307 + 456$ (p. 72)

12.2 Multiply by 9

Learn

Pablo gives flying lessons. If he gives 7 lessons a day, how many lessons will he give in 9 days?

Find: 9×7

There's More Than One Way!

Subtract from a Known Fact

You can multiply by 10 and subtract to find facts for 9.

$$9 \times 7 = (10 \times 7) - 7$$
$$= 70 - 7 = 63$$

So $9 \times 7 = 63$.

$$9 \times 1 = 9$$
$$9 \times 2 = 18$$
$$9 \times 3 = 27$$
$$9 \times 4 = 36$$
$$9 \times 5 = 45$$
$$9 \times 6 = 54$$
$$9 \times 7 = 63$$
$$9 \times 8 = 72$$
$$9 \times 9 = 81$$
$$9 \times 10 = 90$$

Use Patterns

STEP 1

Look at the pattern in the facts for 9.

Look at the second factor and each product.

The tens digit of the product is always 1 less than the factor you are multiplying with 9.

$9 \times 7 = 63$

Think:
$7 - 1 = 6$

STEP 2

The sum of the digits is always 9.

$9 \times 7 = 63$

Think:
$6 + 3 = 9$

Pablo will give 63 lessons in 9 days.

Try It Find each product.

1. 9×9 **2.** 4×9 **3.** 9×2 **4.** 3×9 **5.** 6×9

6.  **Discuss** with a classmate about which strategy you prefer when multiplying by 9. Explain your reasoning.

Practice and Problem Solving

Find each product.

7. 5×9 **8.** 10×9 **9.** 9×0 **10.** 7×9 **11.** 6×9

12. 9×1 **13.** 2×9 **14.** 8×9 **15.** 9×3 **16.** 9×4

17. 7×8 **18.** 5×10 **19.** 6×7 **20.** 2×7 **21.** 4×8

$\widehat{x}$ **Algebra** Find the rule for each table.

22.

Rule:				
Input	4	5	6	7
Output	36	45	54	63

23.

Rule:				
Input	6	7	8	9
Output	42	49	56	63

Solve for the variable.

★**24.** $(10 \times 8) - g = 72$ ★**25.** $(6 + 5) \times j = 99$ ★**26.** $9 \times (5 + 7) = m$

Solve. Use data from the pictograph for problems 27–28.

27. How many more cartons were delivered to Company D than Company A?

28. ✏️ **Write a problem** that can be solved using the data. Solve it. Ask others to solve it.

THINK
SOLVE
EXPLAIN

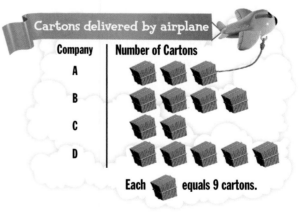

Cartons delivered by airplane

Company	Number of Cartons
A	
B	
C	
D	

Each 📦 equals 9 cartons.

Spiral Review and Test Prep

29. Grace starts school at 8:15 A.M. It is now 7:45 A.M. How much time until school starts? (p. 146)

    A. 15 minutes   **C.** 45 minutes

    B. 1 half-hour   **D.** 1 hour

30. Which number sentence does not have the same sum as the others? (p. 52)

    F. $8 + 4$ **H.** $6 + 6$

    G. $7 + 5$ **I.** $9 + 2$

31. $3{,}430 + 239$ (p. 72)   **32.** 4×4 (p. 210)   **33.** $6{,}392 - 485$ (p. 120)

12.3 Multiplication Table

Learn

A hot air balloon ride travels 8 miles. A guide takes a group on the ride once every weekday. How many miles does the hot air balloon travel in all?

There are 5 weekdays.

Find: 5×8

Use a Multiplication Table

Start at the row for 5. Look at the column for 8. The product is in the box where the row and column meet.

$5 \times 8 = 40$

You can also start at the row for 8, then go to the column for 5. Find the product. You will get the same answer.

$8 \times 5 = 40$

The balloon travels 40 miles in all.

column ↓

×	0	1	2	3	4	5	6	7	8	9	10	11	12
0	0	0	0	0	0	0	0	0	0	0	0	0	0
1	0	1	2	3	4	5	6	7	8	9	10	11	12
2	0	2	4	6	8	10	12	14	16	18	20	22	24
3	0	3	6	9	12	15	18	21	24	27	30	33	36
4	0	4	8	12	16	20	24	28	32	36	40	44	48
5	0	5	10	15	20	25	30	35	40	45	50	55	60
6	0	6	12	18	24	30	36	42	48	54	60	66	72
7	0	7	14	21	28	35	42	49	56	63	70	77	84
8	0	8	16	24	32	40	48	56	64	72	80	88	96
9	0	9	18	27	36	45	54	63	72	81	90	99	108
10	0	10	20	30	40	50	60	70	80	90	100	110	120
11	0	11	22	33	44	55	66	77	88	99	110	121	132
12	0	12	24	36	48	60	72	84	96	108	120	132	144

row →

Try It
Use the multiplication table to find each product.

1. 9×3 **2.** 5×7 **3.** 8×6

4. 9×10 **5.** 4×12 **6.** 11×10

7. **Write About It** **Compare** the products in the rows and columns for 2, 4, and 8. What patterns do you see?

Practice and Problem Solving

Use the multiplication table to find each product.

8. 11×3 **9.** 9×12 **10.** 4×11 **11.** 5×12 **12.** 7×12

★**13.** 13×2 ★**14.** 14×2 ★**15.** 18×2 ★**16.** 15×2 ★**17.** 16×2

18. Which rows have products with either a 0 or 5 in the ones place?

19. Which numbers only have products that are even numbers? What kind of numbers are these?

Solve.

20. A group of 11 people can go in 1 hot air balloon. There are 6 balloons available. How many people can ride in the balloons in all?

THINK SOLVE EXPLAIN **21.** Jason is reading a book about hot air balloons. He reads for 12 minutes each day. Will he read for over an hour in 1 week? Explain.

★**22.** How many days will Jason have to read for a total time of 2 hours?

Spiral Review and Test Prep

23. Mr. Halpern drove 2,457 miles on his trip. What is that number rounded to the nearest hundred? (p. 32)

A. 2,500 **C.** 2,400

B. 2,460 **D.** 2,000

24. Lin must drive 675 miles. So far she has driven 239 miles. How many more miles must she drive? (p. 104)

F. 436 miles **H.** 336 miles

G. 434 miles **I.** 334 miles

Find each missing number.

25. $n \times 4 = 0$ (p. 240) **26.** $432 + t = 690$ (p. 96) **27.** $s - 486 = 394$ (p. 96)

12.4 Algebra: Multiply 3 Numbers

Learn

The Zoo Tours has 2 zoomobiles. Each zoomobile has 5 rows of seats. Each row has 4 seats. How many seats are there in the 2 zoomobiles?

Find: $2 \times 5 \times 4$

VOCABULARY

Associative Property of Multiplication

Use Models

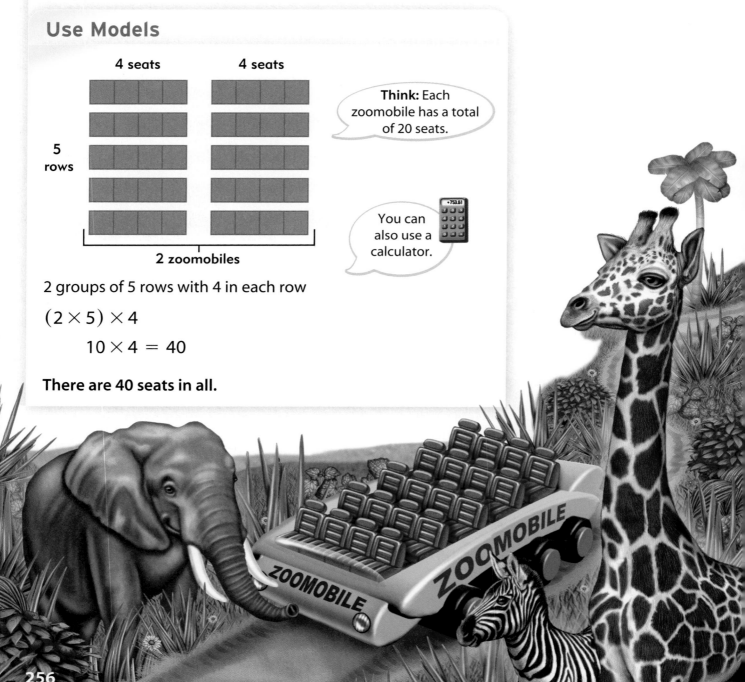

4 seats   4 seats

5 rows

2 zoomobiles

Think: Each zoomobile has a total of 20 seats.

You can also use a calculator.

2 groups of 5 rows with 4 in each row

$(2 \times 5) \times 4$

$10 \times 4 = 40$

There are 40 seats in all.

For 2 weeks, Ms. Gonzales spends $3 a day on bus fares. She takes the bus 5 days a week. How much does she spend on bus fares in all?

Find: 2 × $3 × 5

There's More Than One Way!

Make a Table
Use the table to write an equation.

Number of Weeks	x	Amount Spent Each Day	x	Number of Days	=	Total Amount
2	×	$3	×	5	=	n
		$6	×	5	=	n
				$30	=	n

Use Multiplication Properties
It is easy to multiply numbers by 10. Use parentheses to group the factors to make 10.

Think: Use the Commutative Property of Multiplication to change the order of factors.

2	×	$3	×	5
$3	×	2	×	5
$3	×	(2	×	5)
$3	×		10	= $30

Think: Use the **Associative Property of Multiplication** to group the factors.

Ms. Gonzalez spends $30 in all.

Technology Link

Use the table tool in **Math Tool Chest** to find products of 3 factors.

Try It

Find each product. You may use models.

1. 6 × 2 × 3   **2.** 2 × 3 × 4   **3.** 3 × 3 × 8   **4.** 8 × 4 × 2

5. 5 × 2 × 3   **6.** 4 × 2 × 4   **7.** 2 × 7 × 5   **8.** 3 × 3 × 4

9. **Write About It** **Explain** how you would use properties to make finding 2 × 8 × 5 easier.

Practice and Problem Solving Find each product.

10. $4 \times 5 \times 2$

11. $3 \times 3 \times 3$

12. $4 \times 6 \times 2$

13. $4 \times 2 \times 7$

14. $2 \times 5 \times 8$

15. $7 \times 3 \times 3$

16. $2 \times 4 \times 9$

17. $3 \times 5 \times 3$

★**18.** $2 \times 3 \times 3 \times 3$

★**19.** $3 \times 2 \times 3 \times 2$

★**20.** $5 \times 1 \times 6 \times 2$

(x) Algebra Find the missing numbers.

21. $(n \times 2) \times 3 = 24$

22. $(k \times 3) \times 4 = 48$

23. $(p \times 1) \times (3 \times 2) = 30$

Solve.

24. A small plane has 4 rows of 4 seats. Each seat has room for 2 bags under it. How many bags will fit under the seats in all?

THINK SOLVE EXPLAIN **25.** ✎ **Write a problem** using the number sentence $4 \times 2 \times 5 = 40$.

THINK SOLVE EXPLAIN **26. Make It Right** Here is how Rico multiplied 3 factors. What mistake did he make? Show how to correct it.

$$2 \times 3 \times 4 =$$
$$(2 \times 3) \times 4 =$$
$$5 \times 4 = 20$$

Link to SCIENCE

Many hummingbirds' wings can beat about 55 to 75 times a second.

27. About how many times can a hummingbird's wings beat in 2 seconds?

Spiral Review and Test Prep

28. You traveled 3 hours each day for 5 days. How long did you travel? (p. 204)

A. 8 hours

C. 8 days

B. 15 hours

D. 15 days

29. Which product is equal to the sum of $8 + 7$? (p. 210)

F. 3×4

H. 7×8

G. 4×4

I. 3×5

Find the missing factor. (p. 240)

30. $p \times 3 = 18$

31. $8 \times g = 64$

32. $7 \times s = 63$

33. $t \times 9 = 81$

Extra Practice page 264, Set D

Writing for Math

Jordan babysits 2 hours a day, 3 days a week. If he earns $5 an hour, how much does he earn in a week? Explain your thinking.

Delinda's Response

✓ **THINK** Multiply to find the number of hours Jordan babysits each week. Then multiply to find the amount of money earned.

✓ **SOLVE** $2 \times 3 = 6$ $6 \times \$5 = \$30$
Jordan babysits 6 hours a week.
He earns $30 a week.
Check: $2 \times \$5 = \$10$ $3 \times \$10 = \$30$

✓ **EXPLAIN** First, I multiply 2 by 3 to find the total hours worked each week. The product is 6. Next, I multiply 6 by $5 to find the total amount earned. The product is $30, so Jordan earns $30 a week.

To check, I multiply in a different order. I multiply 2 by $5 to find the amount earned each day. The product is $10. I multiply $10 by 3 to find the 3-day total. The product is $30, so my answer makes sense.

Teacher's Response

← Delinda describes the steps she will use to solve the problem.

← Delinda shows her work.

← Delinda uses appropriate math terms, such as **multiply** and **product**. She clearly explains each step she used to solve the problem.

← Delinda uses the **Commutative** and **Associative Properties** to check her work and explain why her answer makes sense.

Solve. Show your work and tell why your answer makes sense. Use Delinda's work as a guide.

1. A bus has 2 sections of seats. Each section has 4 rows of 5 seats. How many seats are there in all?

2. An album has 3 pages with 3 photos on each page. Each photo shows 4 friends. How many friends are pictured?

12.5 Problem Solving: Strategy
Draw a Picture

Read

Victor has to replace the tires on some old scooters. He has 3 different types of scooters. Each type comes in the colors shown. How many tires does he need to replace?

- **What do you know?**
  3 types of scooters; each type comes in 2 colors; each scooter has 2 tires

- **What do you need to find?**
  the total number of tires

Plan

You can draw a picture to solve the problem.

Use the picture to find the answer.

Solve

Draw 3 groups of scooters. Each group has a red and a green scooter. Each scooter has 2 tires. Count the total number of tires.

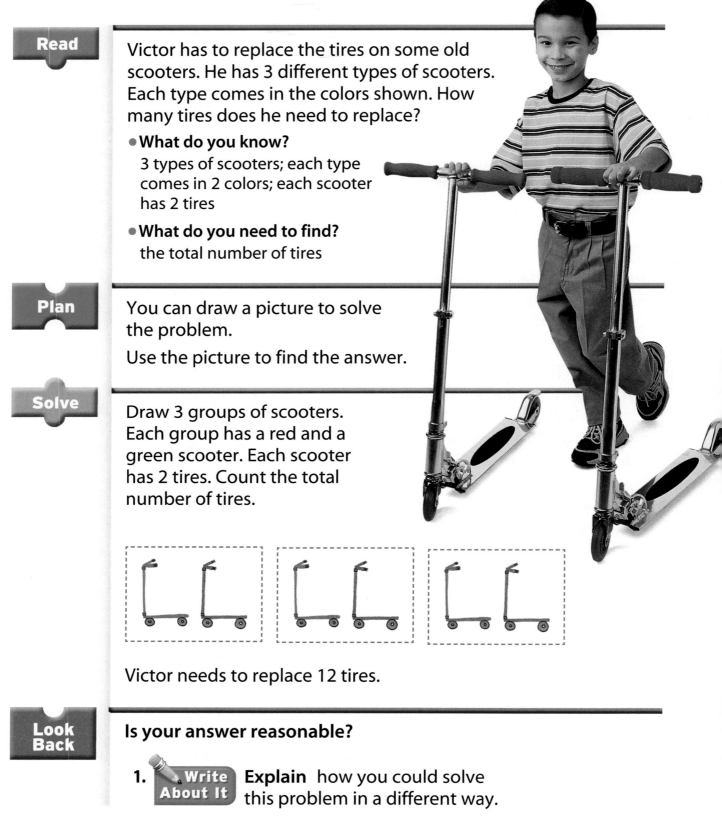

Victor needs to replace 12 tires.

Look Back

Is your answer reasonable?

1. ✏️ **Write About It** **Explain** how you could solve this problem in a different way.

Practice Draw a picture to solve.

2. Dorothy earns $6 an hour. She works 3 hours each day for 4 days a week. How much does she earn in a week?

3. A roller coaster has 6 cars. Each car has 2 wheels. How many wheels are there in all on 4 roller coasters?

4. Mr. Chaney jogs 3 miles a day. He jogs 3 days a week. How many miles does he jog in 4 weeks?

5. The Log Ride makes 7 trips a day. It has 2 cars. Each car holds 4 people. How many people can ride the Log Ride in one day?

Mixed Strategy Review

6. For the field trip, the class is separated into 3 groups. There are 2 groups of 6 students and 1 of 7 students. How many students are in the class?

7. **Collect Data** Survey your classmates about the number of phones their families have. Create a graph using the data. Write a statement about your results.

8.  **Write a problem** that can be solved by drawing a picture. Solve your problem and compare it with other students' problems.

Choose a Strategy
- Logical Reasoning
- Draw a Picture or Diagram
- Make a Graph
- Act It Out
- Make a Table or List
- Find a Pattern
- Guess and Check
- Write an Equation
- Work Backward
- Solve a Simpler Problem

Use the data from the sign for problems 9 and 10.

9. **Mental Math** About how much will 3 monthly passes cost?

★10. You have 2 quarters, 2 dimes, and 2 one-dollar bills. How much more do you need to buy a round-trip ticket on the train?

Train Ticket Prices	
One way	$1.80
Round trip	$3.30
Monthly pass	$49.00

Extra Practice page 264, Set E

Multiplication

1. 4×6 2. 7×1 3. 11×2 4. 6×8 5. 9×2

6. 9×9 7. 7×12 8. 6×6 9. 9×6 10. 8×10

11. 12×0 12. 8×7 13. 7×6 14. 6×5 15. 2×12

16. 9×4 17. 7×7 18. 8×4 19. 7×5 20. 8×8

21. 5×5 22. 3×9 23. 11×0 24. 10×9 25. 1×1

26. $\begin{array}{r} 2 \\ \times 8 \\ \hline \end{array}$
27. $\begin{array}{r} 9 \\ \times 5 \\ \hline \end{array}$
28. $\begin{array}{r} 3 \\ \times 9 \\ \hline \end{array}$
29. $\begin{array}{r} 11 \\ \times 6 \\ \hline \end{array}$
30. $\begin{array}{r} 8 \\ \times 9 \\ \hline \end{array}$

31. $\begin{array}{r} 10 \\ \times 3 \\ \hline \end{array}$
32. $\begin{array}{r} 12 \\ \times 4 \\ \hline \end{array}$
33. $\begin{array}{r} 7 \\ \times 4 \\ \hline \end{array}$
34. $\begin{array}{r} 8 \\ \times 4 \\ \hline \end{array}$
35. $\begin{array}{r} 9 \\ \times 7 \\ \hline \end{array}$

36. $\begin{array}{r} 5 \\ \times 9 \\ \hline \end{array}$
37. $\begin{array}{r} 11 \\ \times 3 \\ \hline \end{array}$
38. $\begin{array}{r} 12 \\ \times 6 \\ \hline \end{array}$
39. $\begin{array}{r} 10 \\ \times 4 \\ \hline \end{array}$
40. $\begin{array}{r} 7 \\ \times 3 \\ \hline \end{array}$

41. $\begin{array}{r} 6 \\ \times 8 \\ \hline \end{array}$
42. $\begin{array}{r} 7 \\ \times 9 \\ \hline \end{array}$
43. $\begin{array}{r} 12 \\ \times 3 \\ \hline \end{array}$
44. $\begin{array}{r} 2 \\ \times 7 \\ \hline \end{array}$
45. $\begin{array}{r} 11 \\ \times 5 \\ \hline \end{array}$

46. $\begin{array}{r} 12 \\ \times 5 \\ \hline \end{array}$
47. $\begin{array}{r} 1 \\ \times 9 \\ \hline \end{array}$
48. $\begin{array}{r} 5 \\ \times 8 \\ \hline \end{array}$
49. $\begin{array}{r} 8 \\ \times 3 \\ \hline \end{array}$
50. $\begin{array}{r} 4 \\ \times 6 \\ \hline \end{array}$

DEAL A FACT

Pick cards to recall basic facts.

Ready

Players: 2
You Will Need: pencil, game board, pennies, Digit Deck (only cards 1–5 from 4 decks)

Set

Use a 6-by-6 grid to make the game board. Players take turns choosing the numbers to fill in across the top and down the side. The teacher chooses the operation, addition or multiplication. Students fill in the answers in the table together. Then the answers are covered with pennies.

GO!

▶ Players take turns choosing 2 cards from the deck. Decide which card is the row, and which card is the column. For example, if 2 and 5 are chosen, find the answer of the 2nd row and 5th column or the 5th row and the 2nd column.

▶ The student says the answer, and picks up the penny to check if correct. If correct, keep the penny.

▶ The player with the most pennies at the end of the game is the winner. If there is no penny covering a square because it has already been taken, then the player loses his or her turn.

Set A Find each product. (pp. 250–251)

1. 10×4
2. 10×1
3. 10×8
4. 10×3
5. 10×2

6. 10×9
7. 10×5
8. 12×10
9. 10×0
10. 6×10

11. 10×7
12. 10×10
13. 11×10
14. 1×10
15. 5×10

Set B Find each product. (pp. 252–253)

16. 7×9
17. 8×9
18. 9×4
19. 9×6
20. 9×2

21. 5×9
22. 3×9
23. 1×9
24. 9×5
25. 9×9

Set C Use a multiplication table to find the missing number. (pp. 254–255)

26. $8 \times g = 88$
27. $y \times 5 = 50$
28. $9 \times 9 = b$
29. $3 \times t = 36$

30. $6 \times s = 48$
31. $a \times 4 = 28$
32. $2 \times 11 = f$
33. $m \times 5 = 60$

34. $10 \times 10 = d$
35. $8 \times n = 72$
36. $12 \times 5 = e$
37. $4 \times 11 = m$

Set D Find each product. (pp. 256–258)

38. $1 \times 9 \times 2$
39. $3 \times 5 \times 2$
40. $2 \times 5 \times 7$
41. $0 \times 9 \times 8$

42. $3 \times 3 \times 7$
43. $8 \times 4 \times 2$
44. $6 \times 7 \times 1$
45. $4 \times 4 \times 2$

Set E Solve. (pp. 260–261)

46. A group of 5 children wants to get on the roller coaster ride. Each person needs 2 tickets. How many tickets does the group need to ride it twice?

47. Jackie pays $6 for bridge tolls each day. He drives across the bridge 3 days a week. How much does he spend in 4 weeks?

48. Ralph bought 2 bus tickets for $2.25 each. He paid for the tickets with a ten-dollar bill. How much change did he get back?

49. On a bus route there are 8 stops. If 4 people get on at each bus stop, and no one gets off, how many people are on the bus at the last stop?

LOG ON www.mmhmath.com
For more practice and Chapter Self-Check Test

Review/Test

Find each product.

1. 12
   × 2

2. 3
   ×9

3. 11
   × 7

4. 7
   ×9

5. 10
   × 5

6. 9
   ×9

7. 10
   × 5

8. 9
   ×0

9. 11
   × 8

10. 9
    ×8

11. 5
    ×12

12. 4
    ×9

13. 4
    ×12

14. 4
    ×10

15. 6
    ×11

16. $(5 \times 2) \times 4$

17. $3 \times (2 \times 4)$

18. $(2 \times 3) \times 9$

19. $3 \times 4 \times 2$

20. $2 \times 3 \times 3$

21. $4 \times 2 \times 7$

Solve.

22. Suppose 3 people can fit in the front seat and 3 people can fit in the back seat of a car. How many people can fit in 5 of these cars added together?

23. Each of the 9 cabins has 3 bedrooms. Each bedroom can sleep up to 3 people. What is the greatest number of people that can sleep there?

24. A train ticket costs $5. You take the train twice a week. How much will you spend in 3 weeks?

25. **Write About It** **Explain** how you would mentally multiply $3 \times 4 \times 5$.

Do I Need Help?

Exercises	Review Concepts	Use Extra Practice Set
1–15	pp. 250–255	Sets A–C
16–21, 24	pp. 256–258	Set D
22, 23, 25	pp. 260–261	Set E

 **Foldables** Use your Foldables to help you review.

Assessment

Applying Math and Science
Make the Best Glue

Carpenters, artists, and dentists all use types of glue when they work.

In this activity, you will make glue with flour and water. Then you will decide how much flour is needed to make the best glue.

Hypothesize

If you start with 1 cup of water, will 1, 2, or 3 spoonfuls of flour make the best glue?

You Will Need

- measuring cup
- 3 bowls
- big spoon
- flour
- water
- paper
- paper clips
- string

Procedure

1. Work with 2 other students. Copy the chart on the next page.

2. Fill a bowl with 1 cup of water.

3. Add 1 big spoonful of flour to the first bowl and stir.

4. Glue a scrap of paper, a paper clip, and a piece of string to a sheet of paper.

5. Repeat with glue made with 2 big spoonfuls of flour.

6. Repeat with glue made with 3 big spoonfuls of flour.

7. Allow the glue to dry completely. Then, test each paper by holding it up with one end of the string.

8. Note which items stick to the paper and which do not. Record your observations of each glue.

Amount of Flour	Observations
One spoonful	
Two spoonfuls	
Three spoonfuls	

Conclude and Apply

1. **Observe** Which glue worked best? Explain your answer.

2. **Use Numbers** How many times more flour is 3 spoonfuls than 1 spoonful? than 2 spoonfuls?

3. What happened to the glue as you multiplied the number of spoonfuls of flour?

Going Further Design and complete an activity to find the amount of water that should be added to 1 spoonful of flour to make the best glue.

Unit Study Guide and Review

Vocabulary

Complete. Use a word from the list.

1. The product of 4×4 is a _____.

2. The _____ shows that $6 \times 2 \times 3 = 6 \times (2 \times 3)$.

3. A _____ is a symbol used to represent an unknown number.

> **VOCABULARY**
> Associative Property of Multiplication
> Commutative Property of Multiplication
> square number
> variable

Skills and Applications

Multiply facts through 12. (pp. 232–239, 250–255)

Find: 7×12

Solution
You can add to a known fact.

$(7 \times 11) + 7$
$\quad 77 \quad + 7 = 84$
$7 \times 12 = 84$

Find each product.

4. 9×2
5. 6×7
6. 8×4

7. 7×7
8. 12×3
9. 11×0

10. 9×8
11. 8×8
12. 5×8

13. $\begin{array}{r} 11 \\ \times\ 8 \\ \hline \end{array}$
14. $\begin{array}{r} 6 \\ \times 3 \\ \hline \end{array}$
15. $\begin{array}{r} 9 \\ \times 4 \\ \hline \end{array}$

Find the missing factor. (pp. 240–242)

Solve for b.

$3 \times b = 18$

Solution
List the 3s facts until you reach 18.

$3 \times 1 = 3 \qquad 3 \times 4 = 12$
$3 \times 2 = 6 \qquad 3 \times 5 = 15$
$3 \times 3 = 9 \qquad \mathbf{3 \times 6 = 18}$

$b = 6$

Find the missing factor.

16. $6 \times p = 54$
17. $8 \times s = 40$

18. $n \times 11 = 77$
19. $w \times 10 = 110$

20. $6 \times j = 72$
21. $l \times 3 = 30$

Foldables Use your Foldables to help you review.

Multiply with 3 numbers. (pp. 256–258)

Find: $3 \times 4 \times 2$

Solution
Use the Associative Property
of Multiplication.

$3 \times 4 \times 2 =$
$3 \times (4 \times 2) =$
$3 \times 8 = 24$

Find each product.

22. $9 \times 3 \times 2$

23. $(2 \times 5) \times 9$

24. $6 \times 0 \times 7$

25. $7 \times (4 \times 2)$

26. $2 \times 3 \times 4$

27. $8 \times 2 \times 3$

28. $2 \times 3 \times 5$

29. $(2 \times 5) \times 4$

Use skills and strategies to solve problems. (pp. 244–245, 260–261)

Chris buys 2 boxes of batteries for his model train. There are 4 packages in each box. Each package comes with 5 batteries.

How many batteries does Chris buy?

Solution
Draw a picture. Then count the total.

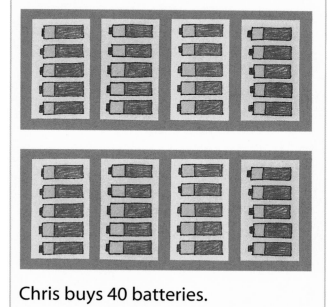

Chris buys 40 batteries.

Solve.

30. It costs $3 a ticket to ride on the cable car. Each cable car has 4 passengers. Is $25 enough to buy tickets for the passengers on 2 cable cars? How can you tell?

31. Suppose you walk 10 minutes each day 3 times a week. How much time do you spend walking in 2 weeks?

32. Jan and Jason each pay $8 on train fare to work each day. They both work 3 days each week. How much do they spend in all each week?

33. Your class has 4 reading groups. There are 3 groups of 8 students and 1 group of 5 students. How many students are in your class?

Unit Review

Enrichment

Using a Shortcut

You can use a shortcut to find the sum of all the numbers from 1 to 10.

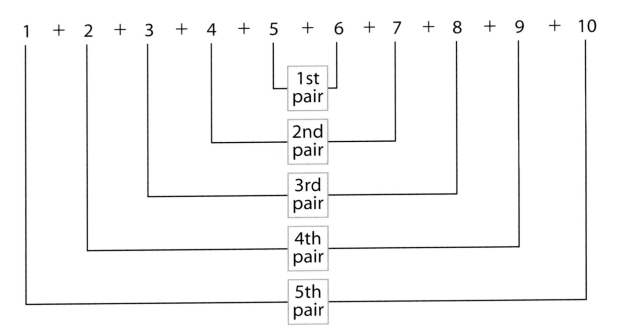

Think of the numbers in pairs connected by the lines.
Look at the first pair of numbers.
What is the sum?
What is the sum of each pair of numbers?

How many pairs are there?

What multiplication sentence shows the sum of all the numbers from 1 to 10?

What is the sum of all the numbers from 1 to 10?

Find the sum using the shortcut.
Use a calculator to multiply.

1. $8 + 9 + 10 + 11 + 12 + 13 + 14 + 15$

2. $54 + 55 + 56 + 57 + 58 + 59 + 60 + 61 + 62 + 63$

3. $12 + 15 + 18 + 21 + 24 + 27 + 30 + 33$

★**4.** How would you find the sum of all the numbers from 1 to 100?

Performance Assessment

What Are Factors and Products?

During Jenn's vacation, she learned a new game.

Here is how you play. You will need a partner. You will also need a pile of number cards numbered from 0 to 12.

Shuffle the cards. Take turns choosing 2 number cards. These are the factors. Find the product by multiplying the 2 factors. The product equals the number of points you get. Add your new points after each turn.

Copy and complete the chart to keep track of you and your partner's points. You will need to decide:

• Who is the winner—the player with the greater or lesser score?

• How long will the game last?

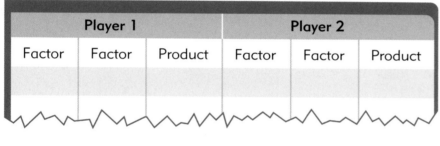

Player 1			Player 2		
Factor	Factor	Product	Factor	Factor	Product

Total Points_____   Total Points_____

Tips For A Good Answer

• Show a score sheet that has factors and products.

• Explain the decisions you made about playing the game.

• Show who won and why.

You may want to save this work in your portfolio.

Assessment

Memory

Vickie is saving 4 pennies a day. How many pennies will she have after 3 days? 30 days? 300 days?

Vickie needs to find 4×3, 4×30, and 4×300.

Using the TI-15

Using the ▸M and MR/MC memory keys can help you solve this problem.

Number of Days	Number of Pennies
3	$4 \times 3 = 12$
30	$4 \times 30 = 120$
300	$4 \times 300 = 1,200$

| 4 | Enter = | ▸M | Enter = | | 4=ᴹ   4. |

| MR/MC | × | 3 | Enter = | | 4×3=ᴹ   12. |

| MR/MC | × | 3 | 0 | Enter = | 4×30=ᴹ   120. |

| MR/MC | × | 3 | 0 | 0 | Enter = | 4×300=ᴹ   1200. |

Complete the multiplication patterns.

1.
$5 \times 4 = \blacksquare$
$5 \times 40 = \blacksquare$
$5 \times 400 = \blacksquare$
$5 \times 4,000 = \blacksquare$

2.
$7 \times 2 = \blacksquare$
$7 \times 20 = \blacksquare$
$7 \times 200 = \blacksquare$
$7 \times 2,000 = \blacksquare$

Solve.

3. Sam is saving $3 a day. How much will he have saved after 6 days? 60 days?

4. Paula collected 8 baseball cards a day. How many cards will she collect in 4 days? 400 days?

For more practice, use Math Traveler™.

Test-Taking Tips

You need to use several steps to solve a **multistep problem.**

Each tour group has 8 people. Four groups ride bicycles. Another 3 groups walk. How many more people ride bicycles than walk?

A. 56 people   **C.** 24 people
B. 32 people   **D.** 8 people

First, find how many people ride bicycles.
$4 \times 8 = 32$ people

Next find how many people walk.
$3 \times 8 = 24$ people

Then subtract to find the difference.
$32 - 24 = 8$ people

The correct choice is D.

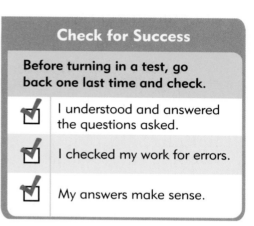

Check for Success

Before turning in a test, go back one last time and check.

- ☑ I understood and answered the questions asked.
- ☑ I checked my work for errors.
- ☑ My answers make sense.

**Read each problem carefully.
Then choose the best answer.**

1. Julia can buy daffodil bulbs in packages of 3 for $5.97, or packages of 2 for $3.90. How much does she save buying 6 bulbs at the better price?

    A. $1.99   **C.** $0.24

    B. $1.95   **D.** $0.04

2. There are 12 students in the third grade and twice that number in the fourth grade. There are 12 boys and 19 girls in the second grade. How many students are in grades 2–4 all together?

    F. 48 students   **H.** 67 students

    G. 55 students   **I.** 87 students

3. Paul and Jim order eggs for $4.75, pancakes for $3.45, and 2 mugs of hot cocoa for $0.80 each. The tax and tip is $2.15. How much change should they get from $15?

    A. $3.05   **C.** $4.65

    B. $3.85   **D.** $11.95

4. Dana saved $1.25 for 2 weeks. He earned another $5. He bought food for $4.66. It cost $1.50 for the subway ride home. How much money did Dana have at the end of the day?

    F. $0.09   **H.** $2.84

    G. $1.34   **I.** $12.41

Test Prep

PART 1 • Multiple Choice

Choose the best answer.

1. What is the value of the underlined digit? (p. 10)

   12,<u>4</u>65

   A. 20,000   **C.** 200

   B. 2,000   **D.** 20

2. Jim started jogging 1 mile on Monday. Every day he jogged 2 more miles than the day before. How many miles did Jim jog on Thursday? (p. 2)

   F. 3 miles   **H.** 7 miles

   G. 5 miles   **I.** 9 miles

3. Which is the same as $\frac{1}{4}$ hour? (p. 144)

   A. 10 minutes

   B. 15 minutes

   C. 25 minutes

   D. 60 minutes

4. Victor has 4 more days of vacation left than Chelsea. Chelsea has 11 days of vacation left. Which equation shows how many days of vacation Victor has? (p. 118)

   F. $11 - 4 = d$ **H.** $11 + 4 = d$

   G. $15 - d = 8$ **I.** $7 + 4 = d$

5. What time will it be in 25 minutes? (p. 146)

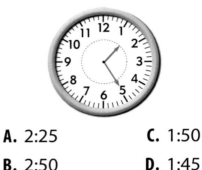

   A. 2:25   **C.** 1:50

   B. 2:50   **D.** 1:45

6. Matthew's new car cost $21,116. Tina paid less for her new car. Which could be the cost of Tina's new car? (p. 24)

   F. $20,999   **H.** $22,009

   G. $21,120   **I.** $30,000

7. Erin jogs 8 miles each day for 5 days each week. Ruben rides his bike 9 miles each day for 4 days each week. Which sentence is true? (p. 244)

   A. Erin travels 4 miles farther each week than Ruben.

   B. Ruben travels 4 miles farther each week than Erin.

   C. Erin travels 5 miles farther each week than Ruben.

   D. Ruben and Erin travel the same distance each week.

Record your answers on the answer sheet provided by your teacher or on a sheet of paper.

8. Identify the rule. (p. 52)

Rule:			
Input	3	12	24
Output	6	15	27

9. Which symbol belongs in the ⬤? (p. 210)

$$3 \times 3 \quad ⬤ \quad 5 + 4$$

10. What number is missing in this pattern? (p. 2)

72, 64, 56, ▮, 40, 32

11. $15 - 8 =$ ▮ (p. 96)

12. What is the range, median, and mode for this set of data? (p. 162)

7, 2, 5, 2, 1, 10, 2, 2, 6

13. **THINK SOLVE EXPLAIN** How can you use multiplication to find the total number of the figure? Explain what you know about the total number. (p. 232)

14. A bus ticket costs $3.65. Leon paid for it with a five-dollar bill. How much change should he get back? (p. 14)

15. Megan started her vacation on June 12. She came home 2 weeks later. On what date did Megan come home? (p. 150)

16. There are 3 people in each of 4 rows of seats in a van. Everyone gets 2 snacks to eat. How many snacks are needed? Show two different strategies to find the answer. (p. 256) **THINK SOLVE EXPLAIN**

17. Tara's vacation is 8 days. Samuel's vacation is 48 hours longer than Tara's vacation. How long is Samuel's vacation? (p. 144)

Record your answer on a sheet of paper. Show your work. **THINK SOLVE EXPLAIN**

18. José fell asleep 2 hours before his plane landed. He woke up 38 minutes before landing. How long did Jose sleep? Explain how you found your answer.

Test Prep

What Do I Need to Know?

You and 2 friends are searching for 9 stars in the sky. You each find the same number of different stars. How many stars do each of you see?

Understand Division

What Will I Learn?

In this chapter you will learn to

- explore the meaning of division
- relate multiplication to division
- divide by 2
- use skills and strategies to solve problems

How Do I Read Math?

When you read a mathematics book, sometimes you read words and symbols, and sometimes you read only symbols.

Here are different ways to describe sharing 10 things between 2 people:

- **ten divided by two equals five.**
- **10 ÷ 2 = 5**

VOCABULARY

- division
- dividend
- divisor
- quotient

Foldables

Use your Foldables to help you with chapter concepts.

1. Fold two sheets of paper in half like hot dogs.
2. Cut one side of each paper to make ten equal tabs.
3. Fold a sheet of construction paper in half like a hot dog, and glue the two 10-tab Foldables inside.
4. Label as shown. Record what you learn.

13.1 Explore the Meaning of Division

Hands On Activity

Division is an operation on 2 numbers that tells how many groups, or how many are in each group. You can use counters to explore division.

Put 16 counters in 2 equal groups.

You Will Need
• two-color counters

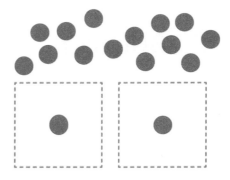

Use Models

STEP 1

To model division, count out 16 counters.

Show 2 groups.

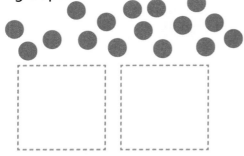

STEP 2

Place a counter in each group.

STEP 3

Continue placing a counter in each group until all the counters are used.

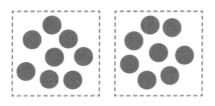

Make a table like the one below. Record the numbers.

Total	Number of Equal Groups	Number in Each Group

Explain Your Thinking

1. How do you model the total?

2. How do you show the number of groups?

3. Are the groups equal? Tell how you know.

4. How many are in each group?

5. **What If** You want 4 counters in each group. How many equal groups can you make using 16 counters?

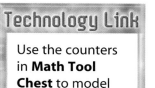

Technology Link

Use the counters in **Math Tool Chest** to model division.

Your Turn

Find the number in each group.

6.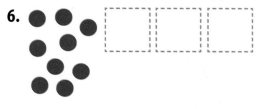

7.

Find the number of equal groups.

8. 2 counters in each group

9. 5 counters in each group

Use counters to complete the table.

	Total	Number of Equal Groups	Number in Each Group
10.	12	n	2
11.	16	4	a
12.	20	t	2

13.  **Write About It** **Analyze** Can you share 18 counters equally between 2 people? 3 people? 4 people? Tell why or why not.

13.2 Algebra: Relate Division and Subtraction

Learn

A scientist takes a total of 12 photographs of 3 parts of space. He takes the same number of photographs for each part. How many photographs of each part does he take?

Find: 12 divided by 3
You can write ÷ for divided by.

$$12 \quad ÷ \quad 3 \quad = \quad n$$

↑	↑	↑
total number of photographs	number of parts	number of photographs of each part

Let's see how to connect models to paper and pencil.

Make Connections

	Models	Paper and Pencil
STEP 1 Start with 12 counters. Show 3 groups.		
STEP 2 Place an equal number of counters in each group.		Use repeated subtraction. Subtract 3 until you reach 0. $\begin{array}{cccc} 12 & 9 & 6 & 3 \\ -3 & -3 & -3 & -3 \\ \hline 9 & 6 & 3 & 0 \end{array}$
STEP 3 Count the number of counters in each group.		Count the number of times you subtract 3. You subtracted 4 times. $\begin{array}{cccc} 12 & 9 & 6 & 3 \\ -3 & -3 & -3 & -3 \\ \hline 9 & 6 & 3 & 0 \end{array}$

He took 4 photographs of each part.

Wanda has collected 10 pictures of the planets. She has 2 pictures of each planet. Of how many planets does Wanda have pictures?

Find: 10 ÷ 2

10	÷	2	=	*a*
↑		↑		↑
total number of pictures		number of pictures of each planet		number of planets

There's More Than One Way!

Use Repeated Subtraction
Start at 10. Keep subtracting 2 until you reach 0.

You subtracted 5 times.

$$10 - 2 = 8 \quad 8 - 2 = 6 \quad 6 - 2 = 4 \quad 4 - 2 = 2 \quad 2 - 2 = 0$$

Use a Number Line
Start at 10. Jump back by 2s until you reach 0.

There are 5 jumps.

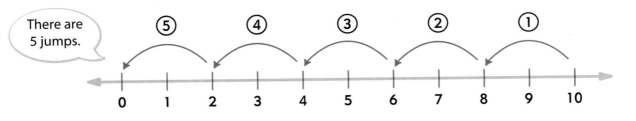

Wanda has collected 5 planets so far.

Try It Write how many times you need to subtract if you use repeated subtraction.

1. $18 \div 9$ **2.** $15 \div 5$ **3.** $20 \div 4$ **4.** $27 \div 3$ **5.** $21 \div 7$

Divide.

6. $18 \div 6$ **7.** $25 \div 5$ **8.** $35 \div 5$ **9.** $8 \div 4$ **10.** $24 \div 3$

11. $35 \div 7$ **12.** $45 \div 5$ **13.** $12 \div 4$ **14.** $36 \div 6$ **15.** $28 \div 7$

Practice and Problem Solving

Write how many times you need to subtract if you use repeated subtraction.

16. $8 \div 4$ **17.** $9 \div 3$ **18.** $32 \div 8$ **19.** $18 \div 6$

Divide.

20. $20 \div 4$ **21.** $10 \div 2$ **22.** $3 \div 3$ **23.** $15 \div 5$

24. $21 \div 7$ **25.** $24 \div 6$ **26.** $6 \div 6$ **27.** $30 \div 5$

$\textcircled{x}$ **Algebra** **Describe and complete each pattern.**

28. 21, 18, ▆, 12, ▆, 6   **29.** 30, 25, ▆, 15, ▆, 5, ▆   **30.** 24, ▆, 16, ▆, ▆, 4

Compare. Write $>$, $<$, or $=$.

★31. $(40 + 2) \div 7 \; \bullet \; 8$ **★32.** $(30 - 5) \div 5 \; \bullet \; 4$ **★33.** $(21 + 7) \div 4 \; \bullet \; 7$

Solve.

THINK SOLVE EXPLAIN **34.** Each of the 4 seasons is about the same number of months. About how many months long is each season? How can you tell?

THINK SOLVE EXPLAIN **35. Analyze** How are division and subtraction alike and different?

36. Carol saves a nickel a day. How much will she have in a week?

Link to SCIENCE

The smallest stars are called neutron stars. Some measure only 6 miles across. The sun is 870,000 miles across.

37. A line of neutron stars each measures 6 miles, for a total of 18 miles across. How many stars are there?

Spiral Review and Test Prep

38. Rita read 3 articles in each of 5 different magazines. How many articles did she read? (p. 210)

    A. 8 articles   **C.** 15 articles
    B. 12 articles   **D.** 16 articles

39. Chris paid $5.00 for a model. Eric bought the same model for $1.45 less. How much did Eric pay? (p. 114)

    F. $3.55   **H.** $4.55
    G. $4.45   **I.** $4.65

40. 8×7 (p. 234)   **41.** $543 + 1{,}007$ (p. 72)   **42.** 7×5 (p. 238)   **43.** 9×0 (p. 214)

BASE IN SPACE

TIME
FOR KIDS

Scientists and astronauts are building the International Space Station. By 2006, the space station will be complete—with enough room to house 7 people at a time.

From 2000 to 2002, 15 astronauts lived in the space station. Their mission was to get the station ready for future explorers. They hooked up electricity, power, and video cables. They also added materials to the space station.

By 2006, the International Space Station will be home to 7 astronauts.

OUT OF THIS WORLD!

How did the astronauts prepare for life in space? They spent time under water. It's the closest thing on Earth to a weightless environment. For every hour spent on a space walk, astronauts trained for 10 hours underwater. They learned how to walk and use machines while floating.

During 5 space trips, astronauts conducted a total of 93 science experiments. While on the space station, they ate 4,000 meals and 3,000 snacks. Space walking sure makes you hungry!

Problem Solving

Reading Skill

Important and Unimportant Information

Which are the most important details in the article?

1. Fifteen astronauts were part of the first 5 missions to the International Space Station. An equal number of astronauts went on each trip. How many astronauts went on each trip?

2. When the International Space Station is complete, it will house 7 astronauts. If 7 astronauts make the trip to the Space Station every year, how many people will have lived in the station in 5 years?

13.3 Algebra: Relate Multiplication to Division

Learn

One week astronauts collected 24 meteorites. They packed the same number of meteorites in 3 boxes. How many meteorites were in each box?

Find: 24 ÷ 3

VOCABULARY

dividend

divisor

quotient

There's More Than One Way!

Use Arrays

Show 24 counters.
Make 3 equal rows.
Count the number in each row.

There are 8 counters in each row.

Use a Related Multiplication Sentence

You know the number of groups and the number in all.
Write a multiplication sentence.

Number of groups		Number in each group		Number in all
3	×	n	=	24
↑		↑		↑
factor		factor		product

Think: 3 × 8 = 24

Multiplication and division are inverse operations. Using multiplication facts can help you with division facts.

Relate the multiplication to division. Write a division sentence.

Number in all		Number of groups		Number in each group
24	÷	3	=	n
↑		↑		↑
dividend		**divisor**		**quotient**

Think: 24 ÷ 3 = 8

There are 8 meteorites in each box.

The astronauts have to store 40 smaller meteorites in trays. Each tray holds the same number of meteorites. How many trays do they need?

Find: 40 ÷ 8

Use a Related Multiplication Sentence

You know the number in each group and the number in all. Write a multiplication sentence.

Number of groups		Number in each group		Number in all
g	×	8	=	40

Think: 5 × 8 = 40

You can also use a calculator.

Now write a division sentence using the same numbers.

Number in all		Number in each group		Number of groups
40	÷	8	=	g

Think: 40 ÷ 8 = 5

The astronauts need 5 trays.

Try It

Write related multiplication and division sentences for each picture.

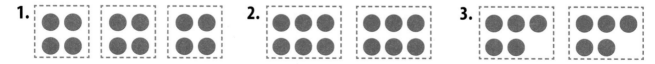

1. 2. 3.

Write related multiplication and division sentences for each group of numbers.

4. 2, 6, 12   **5.** 7, 3, 21   **6.** 5, 8, 40   **7.** 1, 9, 9   **8.** 2, 4, 8

9. **Write About It** **Explain** how a multiplication sentence would help you find 28 ÷ 7.

Practice and Problem Solving

Write related multiplication and division sentences.

10.

11. 2, 7, 14   12. 1, 2, 2   13. 3, 5, 15   14. 5, 6, 30

Ⓧ **Algebra** Write × or ÷ to make each sentence true.

15. 72 ⬤ 9 = 8   16. 8 ⬤ 8 = 64   17. 12 ⬤ 6 = 2   18. 7 ⬤ 6 = 42

★19. (18 + 2) ⬤ 4 = 5   ★20. (27 ⬤ 3) ÷ 9 = 1   ★21. (8 ⬤ 3) ÷ 4 = 6

Solve.

22. In 1969 the Apollo 11 and Apollo 12 missions sent a total of 6 astronauts to the moon. Each Apollo mission carried the same number of astronauts. How many astronauts went on each mission?

23. **Make It Right** Here is how Jamie used multiplication to divide 32 by 8. What mistake did he make? Show how to correct it.

   THINK
   SOLVE
   EXPLAIN

   Find: 32 ÷ 8
   8 × 3 = 32
   32 ÷ 8 = 3

24. **Science** You can see the Tempel 1 comet 3 times in 18 years. The number of years between each sighting is the same. How often can you see the Tempel 1 comet?

25. **Time** A year on Mars lasts 687 Earth days. A year on Earth lasts 365 days. How much longer is a year on Mars than a year on Earth?

✓ Spiral Review and Test Prep

26. Ray can read 9 pages in 1 hour. How many pages can he read in 3 hours? (p. 252)

   A. 12 Pages   **C.** 18 pages
   B. 15 pages   **D.** 27 pages

27. Kim is 3 years younger than Bob. Joe is 4 years older than Bob. Joe is 10 years old. How old is Kim? (p. 244)

   F. 3 years old   **H.** 7 years old
   G. 6 years old   **I.** 14 years old

Solve for the variable. (p. 240)

28. $n \times 4 = 8$ 29. $4 \times y = 4$ 30. $z \times 8 = 16$ 31. $3 \times t = 9$

10. $4 \times 4 = 16$; $16 \div 4 = 4$

Extra Practice page 292, Set B

SENTENCE MAKERS

Toss number cubes to make related number sentences.

Ready

Players: 3

You Will Need: 2 number cubes, paper and pencil

GO!

▶ Two players each roll a number cube.

▶ Player 1 writes 2 multiplication sentences using the numbers rolled.

▶ Player 2 writes 2 related division sentences.

Set

Label each number cube from 1–6.

▶ Player 3 draws a picture for one of the 4 number sentences.

▶ If the picture is correct, player 3 wins a point.

▶ Switch roles writing sentences and drawing pictures.

▶ The first player to reach 5 points is the winner.

13.4 Divide by 2

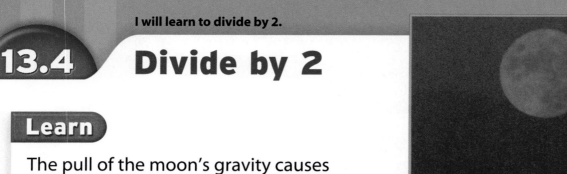

Learn

The pull of the moon's gravity causes oceans to have high and low tides. If there are 14 high tides, how many days have passed?

Find: 14 ÷ 2

> The gravitational pull of the moon produces 2 high tides every day.

There's More Than One Way!

Use Skip-Counting

0 1 2 3 4 5 6 7 8 9 10 11 12 13 14

There are 7 groups of 2 in 14.

> **Think:** How many groups of 2 are in 14?

Use a Related Fact

You can also use multiplication facts to help you divide.

> **Think:** What number times 2 is equal to 14?

> You can also use a calculator.

$$n \times 2 = 14$$
$$7 \times 2 = 14$$

So $14 \div 2 = 7$ or $2\overline{)14}$

7 ← quotient
2)14 ← dividend
↑
divisor

7 days have passed.

Try It   Divide. Write a related multiplication fact.

1. $6 \div 2$ **2.** $8 \div 2$ **3.** $16 \div 2$ **4.** $4 \div 2$ **5.** $10 \div 2$

6. **Write About It** **Discuss** with a classmate about which method you would use to find $56 \div 8$, skip-counting or using a related multiplication fact.

Practice and Problem Solving

Divide. Write a related multiplication fact.

7. $12 \div 2$ **8.** $10 \div 2$ **9.** $18 \div 2$ **10.** $14 \div 2$ **11.** $20 \div 2$

12. $2\overline{)2}$ **13.** $2\overline{)16}$ **14.** $2\overline{)8}$ **15.** $2\overline{)14}$ **16.** $2\overline{)18}$

ⓧ Algebra **Describe and complete the skip-counting patterns.**

17. 20, 16, ▪, 8   **18.** 10, 8, 6, ▪   **19.** 990, ▪, 984, 981

★**20.** Create your own pattern with more than 1 missing number. Ask other students to describe it.

Solve. Use data from the journal for problem 21.

21. Flora keeps track of the tides at the beach. There are 2 low tides each day. How many days has she been at the beach?

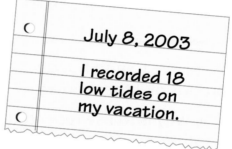

July 8, 2003

I recorded 18 low tides on my vacation.

22. Amy and Joe decide to share a telescope an equal number of months each year. How many months will Amy use the telescope this year?

★**23.** **Analyze** Can Amy and Joe each have the telescope the same number of days each week? Explain.

THINK
SOLVE
EXPLAIN

24. **Write a problem** using the division sentence $12 \div 2 = 6$. Ask other students to solve it.

THINK
SOLVE
EXPLAIN

Spiral Review and Test Prep

25. Sal photographs 3 days a week. How many times does he photograph in 8 weeks? (p. 234)

   A. 15 times   **C.** 32 times

   B. 24 times   **D.** 40 times

26. Which number sentence is equal to 9×4? (p. 256)

   F. $3 \times 2 \times 4$ **H.** $3 \times 3 \times 4$

   G. $6 \times 3 \times 4$ **I.** $2 \times 6 \times 2$

27. $\$2.54 + \$0.78$ (p. 58)   **28.** 4×7 (p. 210)   **29.** $\$8.15 - \$3.95$ (p. 104)

13.5 Problem Solving: Skill
Choose an Operation

Read

Leon is making a model of the solar system. He has 18 pieces of clay. Leon will use 2 pieces of clay for each planet. How many planets will Leon make?

- **What do you know?**
  How much clay Leon has; how much clay used for each planet

- **What do you need to find?**
  How many planets he will make

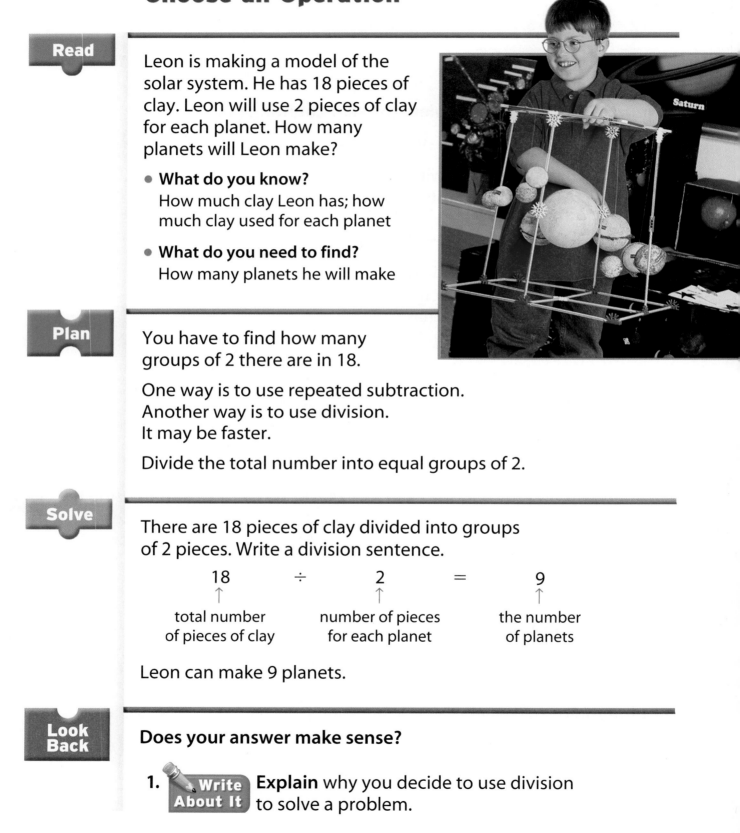

Saturn

Plan

You have to find how many groups of 2 there are in 18.

One way is to use repeated subtraction.
Another way is to use division.
It may be faster.

Divide the total number into equal groups of 2.

Solve

There are 18 pieces of clay divided into groups of 2 pieces. Write a division sentence.

$$18 \div 2 = 9$$

| total number of pieces of clay | number of pieces for each planet | the number of planets |

Leon can make 9 planets.

Look Back

Does your answer make sense?

1. **Write About It** **Explain** why you decide to use division to solve a problem.

Practice

Solve. Tell how you chose the operation.

2. Rico used 18 stars to make a model of the constellation Orion. Then he used 7 stars to make a model of Ursa Minor. How many more stars did Rico use to make Orion than Ursa Minor?

3. Beth uses 12 pieces of wire to make a model of Earth's 3 layers. Each layer will have the same pieces of wire. How many pieces of wire will each layer of her model have?

Mixed Strategy Review

4. A small box holds 4 books. A big box holds 8 books. A store gets 8 small boxes and 5 big boxes of science books. How many books did the store get?

5. Uri has been saving $6 a month. He buys binoculars for $48. How long did it take him to save the money?

Choose a Strategy
- Logical Reasoning
- Draw a Picture or Diagram
- Make a Graph
- Act It Out
- Make a Table or List
- Find a Pattern
- Guess and Check
- Write an Equation
- Work Backward
- Solve a Simpler Problem

Use data from the Supply List for problems 6–11.

6. How many more moon stickers are there than sun stickers?

7. The white paper is divided evenly among 3 students. How many sheets did each student get?

Supply List for Space Poster	
White Paper	15 Sheets
Moon Stickers	14 Stickers
Sun Stickers	8 Stickers
Black Paper	10 Sheets
Blue Paper	12 Sheets

8. What If All the stickers were divided evenly between 2 students. How many stickers would each student get?

9. Emily wants to use 3 sheets of blue paper. How many blue sheets will be left?

10. How many fewer sheets of black paper are there than white paper?

11. **Write a problem** using the data from the Supply list. Solve it. Ask others to solve it.

Extra Practice

Set A Write how many times you need to subtract
if you use repeated subtraction. (pp. 280–282)

1. 9 ÷ 3   **2.** 8 ÷ 2   **3.** 18 ÷ 6   **4.** 20 ÷ 5

Use repeated subtraction to divide.

5. 20 ÷ 4   **6.** 15 ÷ 3   **7.** 16 ÷ 8   **8.** 15 ÷ 5   **9.** 12 ÷ 2

10. 24 ÷ 2   **11.** 18 ÷ 9   **12.** 10 ÷ 5   **13.** 16 ÷ 4   **14.** 21 ÷ 3

Set B Write related multiplication and division
sentences for the picture. (pp. 284–286)

15.

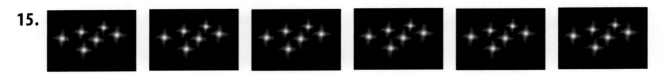

16.

Write related multiplication and division
sentences for each group of numbers.

17. 3, 6, 18   **18.** 5, 6, 30   **19.** 4, 5, 20   **20.** 6, 6, 36   **21.** 2, 8, 16

22. 7, 3, 21   **23.** 2, 9, 18   **24.** 5, 1, 5   **25.** 8, 4, 32   **26.** 10, 2, 20

Set C Divide. (pp. 288–289)

27. 8 ÷ 2   **28.** 12 ÷ 2   **29.** 6 ÷ 2   **30.** 18 ÷ 2   **31.** 2 ÷ 2

32. 2)‾4̅   **33.** 2)‾1̅0̅   **34.** 2)‾1̅4̅   **35.** 2)‾1̅6̅   **36.** 2)‾2̅0̅

Set D Solve. Tell how you chose the operation. (pp. 290–291)

37. Jane has 20 sun stickers and 42
Earth stickers. How many more
Earth stickers does Jane have
than sun stickers?

38. Billy shares 24 moon stickers
equally with 3 friends. How many
stickers does each person get?

Complete.

	Total	Number of Groups	Number in Each Group
1.	45	5	y
2.	18	a	3
3.	16	p	2

Write related multiplication and division sentences for each group of numbers.

4. 3, 7, 21   **5.** 2, 4, 8   **6.** 4, 4, 16   **7.** 5, 7, 35   **8.** 2, 6, 12

Divide.

9. $12 \div 2$ **10.** $15 \div 5$ **11.** $8 \div 2$ **12.** $40 \div 5$ **13.** $12 \div 3$

14. $2\overline{)10}$ **15.** $5\overline{)25}$ **16.** $5\overline{)40}$ **17.** $5\overline{)20}$ **18.** $2\overline{)18}$

Solve.

19. You separate 16 counters into 4 equal groups. How many counters are in each group? Explain how you chose the operation.

20. **Write About It** **Analyze** Which method do you prefer to use to find $20 \div 5$? Why?

Do I Need Help?

Exercises	Review Concepts	Use Extra Practice Set
1–3	pp. 278–279; 280–282	Set A
4–8	pp. 284–286	Set B
9–18	pp. 284–286, 288–289	Sets B and C
19–20	pp. 290–291	Set D

 **Use your Foldables to help you review.**

Assessment

What Do I Need to Know?

There are 14 astronauts going on space shuttle missions. Only 7 astronauts go on each mission. How many missions are there?

Division Facts to 5

What Will I Learn?

In this chapter you will learn to

- divide by 3, 4, and 5

- divide with 0 and 1

- use skills and strategies to solve problems

How Do I Read Math?

When you read a mathematics book, sometimes you read words and symbols, and sometimes you read only symbols.

All of these represent 18 divided by 3 equals 6:

- **eighteen divided by three is six**

- $\mathbf{18 \div 3 = 6}$

- $3\overline{)18}$ with quotient 6

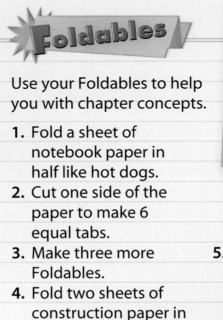

Use your Foldables to help you with chapter concepts.

1. Fold a sheet of notebook paper in half like hot dogs.
2. Cut one side of the paper to make 6 equal tabs.
3. Make three more Foldables.
4. Fold two sheets of construction paper in half like hot dogs.

Glue two 6-tab Foldables inside each one.

5. Record division facts for 0, 1, 3, 4, and 5 on the front tabs. Write related multiplication facts under the tabs.

14.1 Divide by 5

Cassiopeia has 5 major stars.

Learn

There are 30 major stars among Aidan's favorite constellations. Each constellation has the same number of major stars as Cassiopeia. How many favorite constellations does Aidan have?

Find: $30 \div 5$ or $5\overline{)30}$

There's More Than One Way!

Use Skip-Counting

Think: How many groups of 5 are in 30?

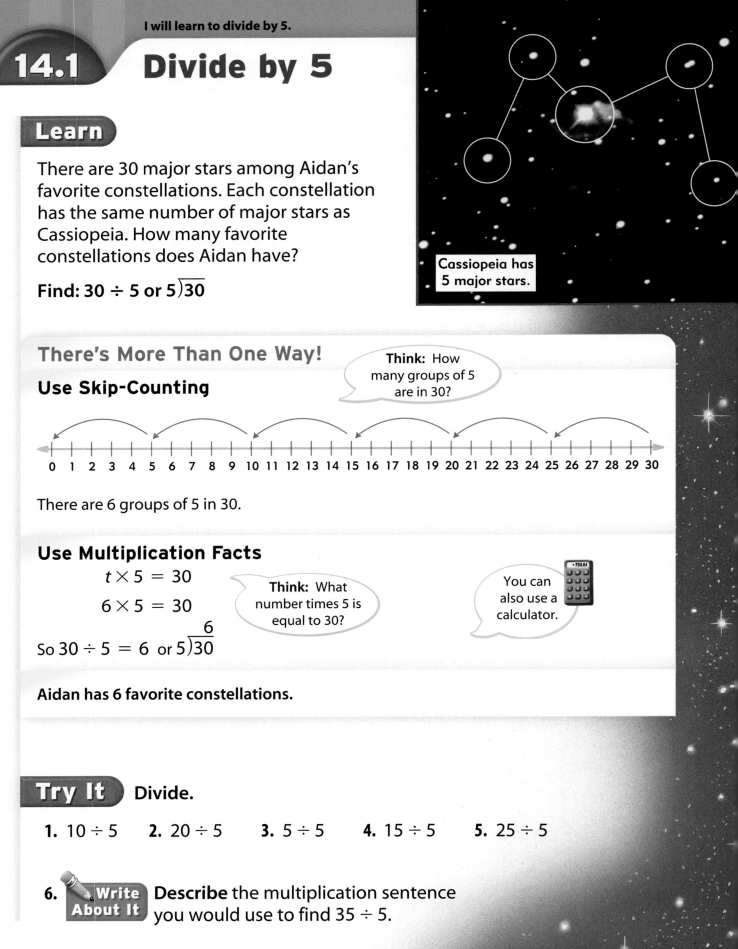

0 1 2 3 4 5 6 7 8 9 10 11 12 13 14 15 16 17 18 19 20 21 22 23 24 25 26 27 28 29 30

There are 6 groups of 5 in 30.

Use Multiplication Facts

$$t \times 5 = 30$$
$$6 \times 5 = 30$$

Think: What number times 5 is equal to 30?

You can also use a calculator.

So $30 \div 5 = 6$ or $5\overline{)30}^{\,6}$

Aidan has 6 favorite constellations.

Try It   Divide.

1. $10 \div 5$ **2.** $20 \div 5$ **3.** $5 \div 5$ **4.** $15 \div 5$ **5.** $25 \div 5$

6. **Write About It** **Describe** the multiplication sentence you would use to find $35 \div 5$.

Practice and Problem Solving

Divide.

7. $35 \div 5$ **8.** $40 \div 5$ **9.** $45 \div 5$ **10.** $50 \div 5$ **11.** $30 \div 5$

12. $5\overline{)5}$ **13.** $5\overline{)30}$ **14.** $5\overline{)20}$ **15.** $5\overline{)10}$ **16.** $5\overline{)15}$

$\widehat{x}$ **Algebra** Solve. Find each missing number.

17. $5 \times d = 15$ **18.** $12 - s = 7$ **19.** $25 \div a = 5$

★**20.** $(8 - 3) \div p = 1$ ★**21.** $(8 + 4) \div c = 6$ ★**22.** $(6 + b) \div 5 = 2$

Solve. Use data from the table for problems 23–25.

23. Allan spent $15.00 to buy each of his sisters a Challenger key chain. How many sisters does he have?

★**24.** Beth spent $30.00 on 1 model of Apollo 12 and some key chains. How many key chains did she buy?

Souvenir	Price
Challenger key chain	$5.00
Model of Apollo 12	$10.00
Astronaut figures	$3.00

THINK SOLVE EXPLAIN

25. ✎ **Write a problem** that can be solved using division. Include data from the table in your problem. Solve it. Ask other students to solve it.

26. Career Jesse is training to be an astronaut. She jogs 8 miles each weekday. If she jogs for 2 weeks, how many miles does she jog in all?

✔ Spiral Review and Test Prep

27. The average distance between Earth and the moon is 238,857 miles. Which digit is in the ten thousands place? (p. 10)

    A. 2   **C.** 5

    B. 3   **D.** 8

28. Karl has 8 times as many planet photos as Tina. Tina has 2 photos. How many photos does Karl have? (p. 204)

    F. 4 photos   **H.** 10 photos

    G. 6 photos   **I.** 16 photos

29. 9×8 (p. 252)   **30.** $7 + 8$ (p. 52)   **31.** $18 - 9$ (p. 96)   **32.** 9×7 (p. 252)

14.2 Divide by 3

It takes Encke 3 years to orbit the sun.

Learn

Sam wants to know how many times the comet Encke has orbited the sun in his lifetime. If Sam is 24 years old, how many times has Encke orbited?

Find: $24 \div 3$ or $3\overline{)24}$

There's More Than One Way!

Use Pictures

STEP 1

Draw 24 objects.

Put 3 objects in each group.

STEP 2

Count the number of equal groups.

There are 8 groups of 3.

Use Multiplication Facts

$3 \times n = 24$

$3 \times 8 = 24$

So $24 \div 3 = 8$ or $3\overline{)24}^{\,8}$

Think: 3 times what number is 24?

You can also use a calculator.

Encke has orbited the sun 8 times so far.

Try It   Divide.

1. $9 \div 3$ **2.** $18 \div 3$ **3.** $3 \div 3$ **4.** $27 \div 3$ **5.** $12 \div 3$

6. **Write About It** Ask a partner about which of the above strategies is better to use to divide.
Explain if you agree or disagree.

Practice and Problem Solving

Divide.

7. $21 \div 3$ **8.** $15 \div 3$ **9.** $6 \div 3$ **10.** $24 \div 3$ **11.** $3 \div 1$

12. $3\overline{)9}$ **13.** $3\overline{)18}$ **14.** $3\overline{)3}$ **15.** $3\overline{)12}$ **16.** $3\overline{)27}$

★17. $(8 + 7) \div 3$ **★18.** $(12 - 9) \div 3$ **★19.** $(3 + 3) \div 3$

ⓧ Algebra Copy and complete.

20.

Rule: Divide by 3			
Input	24	15	27
Output	▢	▢	▢

21.

Rule: Subtract 3			
Input	15	21	9
Output	▢	▢	▢

Solve.

THINK SOLVE EXPLAIN

22. **Write About It** **Compare** Use 2 strategies to find $18 \div 3$. Which do you prefer to use and why?

Link to SCIENCE

There are 9 planets in our solar system.

23. Ms. Wallace teaches her class about 3 different planets each day. How many days will it take to teach all of the planets?

Spiral Review and Test Prep

24. Earth turns on its axis 1 time each day. How many times does it turn in 1 week? (p. 238)

A. 7 times **C.** 30 times

B. 24 times **D.** 365 times

25. Which number is missing?
17, 14, 11, ▢, 5 (p. 2)

F. 8 **H.** 10

G. 9 **I.** 12

Find each missing number.

26. $9 \times n = 72$ (p. 240) **27.** $7 + r = 15$ (p. 52) **28.** $14 - 7 = s$ (p. 96)

14.3 Divide by 4

Learn

A total of 20 students are writing reports about Pluto. How can you show this on the pictograph?

Find: $20 \div 4$ or $4\overline{)20}$

Planet Reports

Planet	Number of Students
Mars	🪐 🪐
Venus	🪐
Pluto	?

Each 🪐 = 4 students

There's More Than One Way!

Use Skip-Counting

Think: How many groups of 4 are in 20?

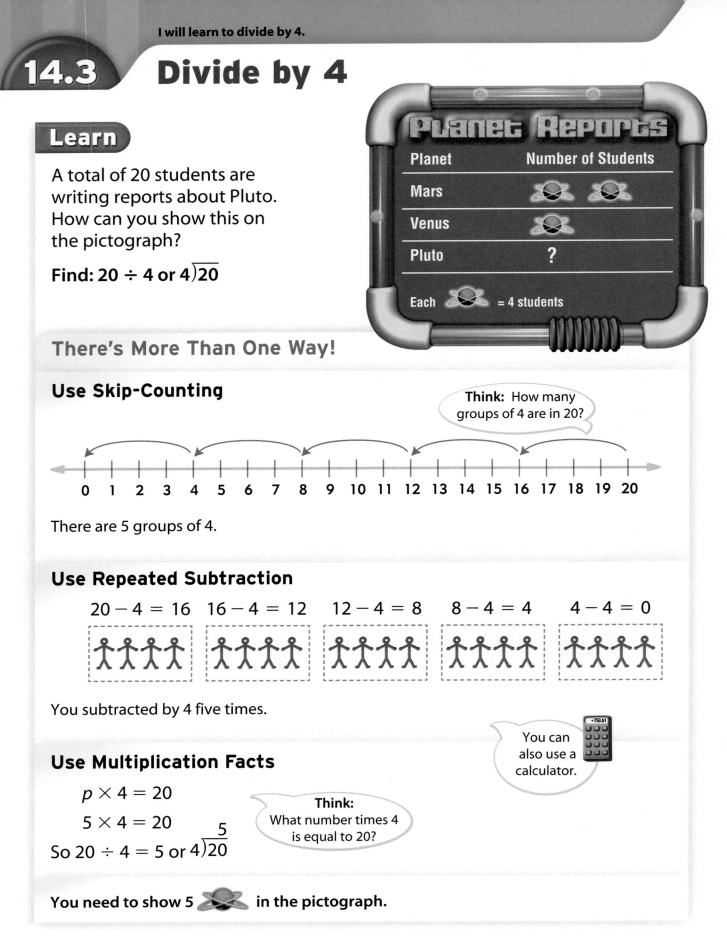

There are 5 groups of 4.

Use Repeated Subtraction

$20 - 4 = 16$ $16 - 4 = 12$ $12 - 4 = 8$ $8 - 4 = 4$ $4 - 4 = 0$

You subtracted by 4 five times.

You can also use a calculator.

Use Multiplication Facts

$p \times 4 = 20$

$5 \times 4 = 20$

So $20 \div 4 = 5$ or $4\overline{)20}$

Think: What number times 4 is equal to 20?

You need to show 5 🪐 in the pictograph.

A class of 28 students will write reports about Saturn. They will be divided into 4 equal groups. How many students will be in each group?

Find: $28 \div 4$ or $4\overline{)28}$

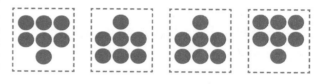

There's More Than One Way!

Use Models

STEP 1

Use 28 counters. Each counter represents 1 student. Draw 4 groups.

STEP 2

Place an equal number in each group. Count how many are in each group.

There are 7 counters in each group.

Use Multiplication Facts

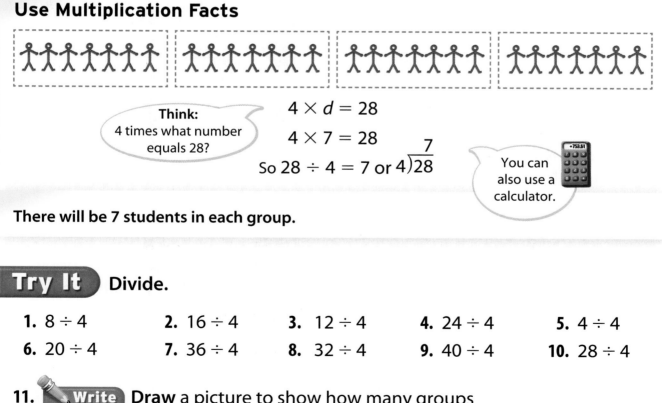

Think: 4 times what number equals 28?

$4 \times d = 28$

$4 \times 7 = 28$

So $28 \div 4 = 7$ or $4\overline{)28}$ with quotient 7

You can also use a calculator.

There will be 7 students in each group.

Try It Divide.

1. $8 \div 4$ 2. $16 \div 4$ 3. $12 \div 4$ 4. $24 \div 4$ 5. $4 \div 4$

6. $20 \div 4$ 7. $36 \div 4$ 8. $32 \div 4$ 9. $40 \div 4$ 10. $28 \div 4$

11. **Write About It** **Draw** a picture to show how many groups of 4 are in 24. **Explain** your drawing.

Practice and Problem Solving Divide.

12. $36 \div 4$ 13. $28 \div 4$ 14. $32 \div 4$ 15. $24 \div 4$ 16. $4 \div 4$

17. $2\overline{)12}$ 18. $5\overline{)15}$ 19. $2\overline{)16}$ 20. $5\overline{)10}$ 21. $3\overline{)21}$ 22. $4\overline{)44}$

★23. $(8 + 8) \div 4$ ★24. $(12 - 4) \div 4$ ★25. $(7 + 5) \div 4$

Ⓧ **Algebra** Copy and complete.

26.

Rule: Divide by 3			
Input	24	15	27
Output	▨	▨	▨

27.

Rule: Add 4			
Input	16	24	12
Output	▨	▨	▨

Solve. Use data from the pictograph for problem 28.

28. There are 32 students on Bus 3. How many figures do you need to show in the pictograph?

29. **Write About It** **Generalize** How can you use skip-counting to find $24 \div 4$?

30. **Make It Right** Here is what Mohammed wrote to find 8 divided by 4. What mistake did he make? Show how to correct it.

$4 + 4 = 8$
so
$8 \div 4 = 4$

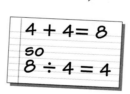

Space Museum Trip

Bus	Number of Students
1	𝟡 𝟡 𝟡 𝟡 𝟡 𝟡
2	𝟡 𝟡 𝟡 𝟡 𝟡
3	?

Each 𝟡 = 4 students

Spiral Review and Test Prep

31. Mel read 4 books. Jill read 12 more books than Mel. Which equation shows how many books Jill read? (p. 118)

   A. $12 - 4 = 8$ **C.** $12 + 4 = 16$

   B. $12 \div 4 = 3$ **D.** $4 \times 3 = 12$

32. There are 8 shelves with 6 books on each shelf. How many books are there in all? (p. 234)

   F. 14 books **H.** 46 books

   G. 24 books **I.** 48 books

33. $325 - 39$ (p. 106) 34. 9×9 (p. 252) 35. $812 - 576$ (p. 106)

Extra Practice page 310, Set C

Writing for Math

The pictograph shows how many groups of children went to the zoo last month. During the fourth week, 24 groups went to the zoo. How can this number be shown on the pictograph? Explain.

Zoo Visits

Weeks	Number of Groups
week 1	☆ ☆ ☆ ☆
week 2	☆ ☆ ☆ ☆ ☆
week 3	☆ ☆ ☆
week 4	

Key: Each ☆ represents 4 groups

Gail's Response

✔ **THINK**

I know each symbol stands for 4 groups. I divide 24 by 4 to find how many symbols to draw.

✔ **SOLVE**

I know 6 × 4 = 24, so 24 ÷ 4 = 6. I need to draw 6 stars.
Check: Skip-count by 4s. 4, 8, 12, 16, 20, 24.

✔ **EXPLAIN**

The graph shows 1 star for every 4 groups. I divided 24 by 4 to find the number of stars to draw. I used the related fact of 6 × 4 = 24 to find 24 ÷ 4. The answer is 6, so I need to draw 6 stars to show 24 groups.

To check, I skip-counted by 4 six times. The result is 24, so my answer makes sense.

Teacher's Response

← Gail explains what she knows about pictographs and symbols. She will divide to solve the problem.

← Gail shows her work.

← Gail uses complete sentences. She uses multiplication to help her solve a division problem.

← Gail uses skip-counting to make sure her answer is reasonable.

Solve. Show your work and tell why your answer makes sense. Use Gail's work as a guide.

1. A classroom is 21 feet long. How many yards long is the classroom?
   3 feet = 1 yard

2. Jen is knitting a scarf. She can knit 4 rows in 1 hour. How long will it take her to knit 20 rows?

14.4 Algebra: Divide with 0 and 1

Learn

Use models to understand dividing with 0 and 1.

Divide with 1

When you divide any number (except 0) by itself, the quotient is 1.

4 ÷ 4 = 1

There are the same number of astronauts and spaceships. 1 astronaut goes in each spaceship.

When you divide any number by 1, the quotient is the original number.

4 ÷ 1 = 4

There are 4 astronauts and only 1 spaceship. So all of the astronauts go in that spaceship.

Divide with 0

When you divide 0 by any number (except 0), the quotient is 0.

0 ÷ 4 = 0

There are no astronauts and 4 spaceships. So there are 0 astronauts in each spaceship.

You **cannot** divide a number by 0. It is not possible to put a number of objects into 0 groups.

4 ÷ ~~0~~ =

If there are 0 spaceships, then you cannot put the 4 astronauts in spaceships. There is **no** answer to this problem.

Try It Divide.

1. 5 ÷ 5   **2.** 0 ÷ 3   **3.** 2 ÷ 1   **4.** 0 ÷ 9   **5.** 7 ÷ 7

6.  **Explain** how you can find 327 ÷ 327.

Practice and Problem Solving

Divide.

7. $1\overline{)8}$ 8. $6\overline{)6}$ 9. $1\overline{)2}$ 10. $4\overline{)0}$ 11. $4\overline{)4}$

12. $6 \div 1$ 13. $2 \div 2$ 14. $3 \div 3$ 15. $0 \div 4$ 16. $8 \div 8$

★17. $0 \div 475$ ★18. $325 \div 325$ ★19. $156 \div 1$

x **Algebra** Write $+$, $-$, $\times$, or $\div$ to make the number sentence true.

20. $12 \bullet 12 = 1$ 21. $9 \bullet 9 = 18$ 22. $6 \bullet 6 = 0$

★23. $(8 \bullet 4) \div 4 = 1$ ★24. $7 \div (14 \bullet 7) = 1$ ★25. $5 \div (5 \bullet 5) = 5$

Solve. Use data from the table for problems 26–27.

26. The shop has 4 shelves to display the Deluxe models. Each shelf will have the same number of models. How many models will be on each shelf?

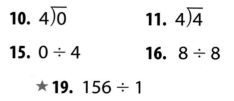

Rocket	Number
Deluxe	4
Standard	12
Basic	8

27. The owner wants an equal number of Standard and Basic models on the shelves. Each shelf will have 4 rockets. How many shelves will he need?

28. **Write a problem** that can be solved using $5 \div 5 = 1$. Solve it. Ask other students to solve it.

THINK
SOLVE
EXPLAIN

Spiral Review and Test Prep

29. Which is the same as 5,603? (p. 6)

    A. $5,000 + 600 + 3$

    B. $5,000 + 600 + 30$

    C. $500 + 60 + 3$

    D. $50 + 60 + 3$

30. Which number sentence, or equation, is in the same fact family as $7 + 6 = 13$? (p. 56)

    F. $7 - 6 = 1$ H. $7 \times 6 = 42$

    G. $13 + 6 = 19$ I. $13 - 6 = 7$

Write the value of each underlined digit. (p. 10)

31. 145,<u>8</u>97   32. 79,9<u>0</u>3   33. 2<u>1</u>3,978   34. 745,<u>3</u>21

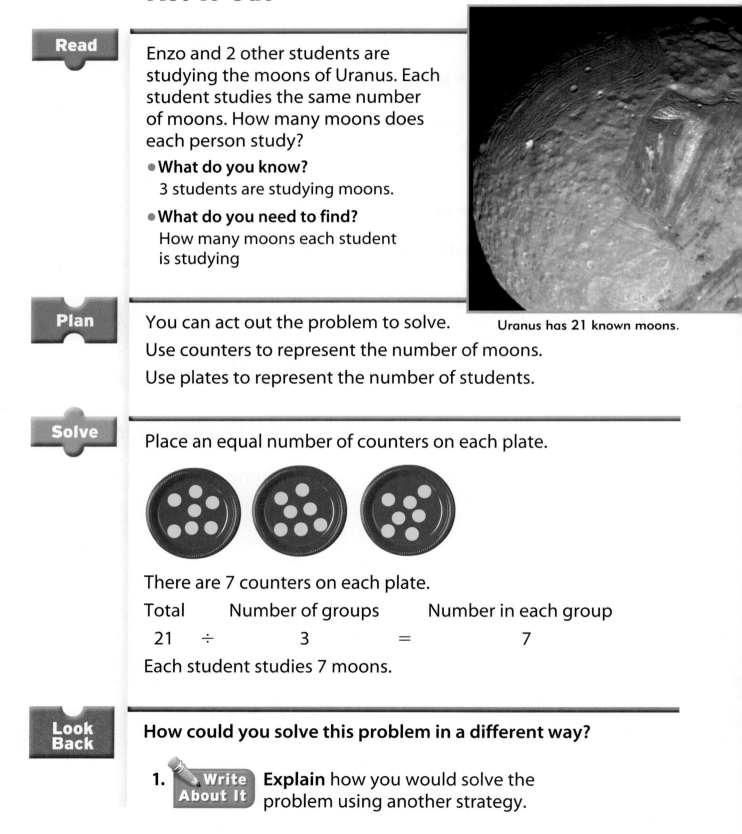

14.5

Problem Solving: Strategy
Act It Out

Read

Enzo and 2 other students are studying the moons of Uranus. Each student studies the same number of moons. How many moons does each person study?

- **What do you know?**
  3 students are studying moons.

- **What do you need to find?**
  How many moons each student is studying

Uranus has 21 known moons.

Plan

You can act out the problem to solve.

Use counters to represent the number of moons.

Use plates to represent the number of students.

Solve

Place an equal number of counters on each plate.

There are 7 counters on each plate.

Total   Number of groups   Number in each group

21   ÷   3   =   7

Each student studies 7 moons.

Look Back

How could you solve this problem in a different way?

1. **Write About It** **Explain** how you would solve the problem using another strategy.

2. Enzo has 10 pictures of Jupiter. He gives the same number of pictures to 2 friends. How many pictures does each friend get?

3. Enzo gets 6 packs of Solar System trading cards. Each pack has 3 cards in it. How many cards does he receive in all?

4. **Music** Eliot can play the song "Fly Me to the Moon" on the piano in 5 minutes. He must practice this song for a half hour. How many times can Eliot play the song during practice?

5. Enzo arrives at the Air and Space Museum at 9:45 A.M. He spends 1 hour looking at airplanes. Then he takes 30 minutes to have a snack. How much time is left until noon?

Mixed Strategy Review

6. **Art** The Hill Street School is making murals. Each mural will be painted on 5 wall tiles. The students can use 15 tiles. How many murals can they paint?

7. ✎ **Write a problem** that can be solved using more than 1 strategy. Solve it at least 2 different ways. Ask others to solve it. Compare strategies.

Choose a Strategy
- Logical Reasoning
- Draw a Picture or Diagram
- Make a Graph
- Act It Out
- Make a Table or List
- Find a Pattern
- Guess and Check
- Write an Equation
- Work Backward
- Solve a Simpler Problem

★8. Look at the prices in the table. You have 2 five-dollar bills, 3 quarters, 2 dimes, and 7 nickels. How much will you have left if you buy a ticket for yourself and an adult on a Saturday?

Space Museum Ticket Prices	
Adult (weekends)	$6.00
Adult (weekdays)	$5.00
Child (weekends)	$3.50
Child (weekdays)	$2.50

Problem Solving

Fast Facts

Division

1. $4 \div 2$
2. $6 \div 3$
3. $10 \div 2$
4. $8 \div 4$

5. $9 \div 3$
6. $12 \div 2$
7. $12 \div 4$
8. $15 \div 5$

9. $0 \div 5$
10. $16 \div 4$
11. $21 \div 3$
12. $32 \div 4$

13. $25 \div 5$
14. $14 \div 2$
15. $10 \div 5$
16. $18 \div 3$

17. $4 \div 4$
18. $12 \div 3$
19. $6 \div 2$
20. $5 \div 1$

21. $27 \div 3$
22. $9 \div 3$
23. $20 \div 4$
24. $15 \div 3$

25. $18 \div 6$
26. $25 \div 5$
27. $7 \div 7$
28. $40 \div 4$

29. $5\overline{)35}$
30. $4\overline{)20}$
31. $2\overline{)8}$
32. $1\overline{)4}$

33. $5\overline{)45}$
34. $3\overline{)15}$
35. $4\overline{)24}$
36. $2\overline{)20}$

37. $5\overline{)20}$
38. $4\overline{)0}$
39. $5\overline{)45}$
40. $2\overline{)16}$

41. $3\overline{)30}$
42. $4\overline{)28}$
43. $4\overline{)48}$
44. $5\overline{)30}$

45. $3\overline{)3}$
46. $3\overline{)33}$
47. $5\overline{)5}$
48. $1\overline{)2}$

49. $4\overline{)24}$
50. $6\overline{)30}$
51. $4\overline{)16}$
52. $3\overline{)36}$

QUOTIENT QUEST

Match quotients to practice your division facts.

Ready

Players: 3
You Will Need: 16 index cards

Set

Write 2 division fact cards for each quotient on 2 index cards. Do not write the quotient.

Mix the cards and place them face down in equal rows.

GO!

▶ Take turns. Each player turns over 2 cards at a time.

▶ If the cards have the same quotient, keep them. Go again.

▶ If the cards do not have the same quotient, put them back. The next player takes a turn.

▶ Continue until all cards have been matched. The winner is the player with the most cards.

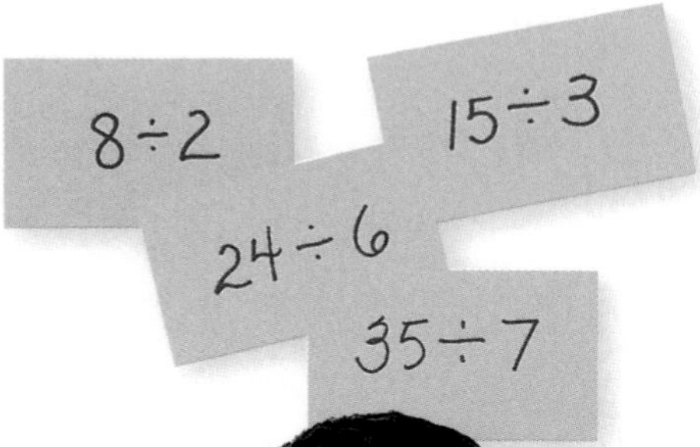

$8 \div 2$ $15 \div 3$
$24 \div 6$
$35 \div 7$

Set A Divide. (pp. 296–297)

1. $10 \div 5$ **2.** $25 \div 5$ **3.** $15 \div 5$ **4.** $40 \div 5$ **5.** $35 \div 5$

6. $5\overline{)20}$ **7.** $5\overline{)30}$ **8.** $5\overline{)45}$ **9.** $5\overline{)50}$ **10.** $5\overline{)5}$

Set B Divide. Write the related multiplication sentence. (pp. 298–299)

11. $9 \div 3$ **12.** $12 \div 3$ **13.** $18 \div 3$ **14.** $27 \div 3$ **15.** $21 \div 3$

16. $3\overline{)3}$ **17.** $3\overline{)30}$ **18.** $3\overline{)24}$ **19.** $3\overline{)21}$ **20.** $3\overline{)15}$

Set C Divide. Write the related multiplication sentence. (pp. 300–302)

21. $4 \div 4$ **22.** $20 \div 4$ **23.** $36 \div 4$ **24.** $32 \div 4$ **25.** $24 \div 4$

26. $4\overline{)16}$ **27.** $4\overline{)12}$ **28.** $4\overline{)28}$ **29.** $4\overline{)40}$ **30.** $4\overline{)8}$

Set D Divide. (pp. 304–305)

31. $5 \div 5$ **32.** $0 \div 3$ **33.** $4 \div 1$ **34.** $3 \div 3$ **35.** $2 \div 2$

36. $1\overline{)4}$ **37.** $4\overline{)0}$ **38.** $12\overline{)12}$ **39.** $1\overline{)2}$ **40.** $4\overline{)4}$

41. $0 \div 5$ **42.** $10 \div 10$ **43.** $3 \div 1$ **44.** $5 \div 1$ **45.** $9 \div 1$

Set E Act out the problem to solve. (pp. 306–307)

46. Marcy cut out 24 stars in art class. She wants to paste them on 4 sheets of paper. If each paper has the same number of stars, how many should she paste on each?

47. The art teacher gave each of 8 students 4 rocket-ship models to build. How many models were given out in all?

48. Tía has 15 moon rocks. She puts the same number of rocks in 5 boxes. How many moon rocks are in each box?

49. Each third grade class made models of 3 of the planets. There are a total of 9 planets. How many third grade classes are there?

LOG ON www.mmhmath.com
For more practice and Chapter Self-Check Test

Review/Test

Divide.

1. $4\overline{)36}$ 2. $3\overline{)18}$ 3. $3\overline{)24}$ 4. $5\overline{)35}$ 5. $4\overline{)12}$

6. $20 \div 4$ 7. $27 \div 3$ 8. $15 \div 3$ 9. $25 \div 5$ 10. $8 \div 4$

11. $5\overline{)20}$ 12. $4\overline{)24}$ 13. $4\overline{)16}$ 14. $2\overline{)16}$ 15. $3\overline{)12}$

Find each missing number.

16. $7 \div 7 = z$ 17. $n \div 6 = 0$ 18. $4 \div t = 4$

19. $y \div 3 = 1$ 20. $s \div 8 = 0$ 21. $0 \div 9 = z$

Solve.

22. There are 35 people on the roller coaster ride. Each car holds 5 people. How many cars are there?

23. Bob tapes 24 cards onto sheets of paper. He puts 3 on each sheet. How many sheets does he use?

24. There are 24 books about our solar system in the library. Ms. Hernandez is dividing them evenly among 6 groups of students. How many books does each group get?

25. **Write About It** **Explain** how you can share equally 12 packs of space food among yourself and 3 friends. How many packs will each of you get?

Do I Need Help?

Exercises	Review Concepts	Use Extra Practice Set
1–15	pp. 296–302	Sets A–C
16–21	pp. 304–305	Set D
22–25	pp. 306–307	Set E

Foldables   **Use your Foldables to help you review.**

Decision Making

At the end of Space Camp, you and your team have to decide between a short or a long trip in the flight simulator. A flight simulator lets you pretend that you are on an actual space flight.

You Decide!

Should you take a long or a short trip?

Data for Flight Simulator	Long Trip	Short Trip
Time	9 days	2 days
Research experiments	9 experiments	5 experiments
Number of people in crew	3 people	5 people

Daily Supplies for Crew	Long Trip	Short Trip
Food	9 pounds	15 pounds
Water	15 pounds	25 pounds
Oxygen	6 pounds	10 pounds

Read for Understanding

1. How many pounds of food are needed daily for each person for the short trip? For the long trip?

2. What is the daily need of oxygen for each person for the short trip?

3. How many pounds of water are needed daily for each person for the long trip?

4. How many experiments will be performed on the long trip? On the short trip?

Make Decisions

5. How many pounds of oxygen are needed in total for the long trip? For the short trip?

6. How many experiments will each person have to do on the long trip? On the short trip?

7. Each team needs at least 18 days of flight simulator time to graduate. How many long trips would have to be made? How many short trips?

8. Now each team must do 15 experiments in the flight simulator to graduate. How many will each person on the long trip have to do? How many more on the short trip?

9. What are some problems that might happen in 9 days in a simulator that might not happen in 2 days?

10. Space Camp runs the simulations for 36 days. What is the greatest number of long trips Space Camp can have? Short trips?

11. What are the advantages of a short trip? The disadvantages?

12. What are the advantages of a long trip? The disadvantages?

Your Decision!

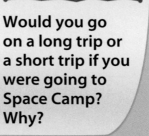

Would you go on a long trip or a short trip if you were going to Space Camp? Why?

Unit Study Guide and Review

Vocabulary

Complete. Use a word from the list.

1. If you need to find how many groups of 5 are in 25, the number 25 is the ___.

2. The answer in a division problem is the ___.

3. The number 4 in the problem $4\overline{)28}$ is the ___.

4. You can use ___ to find the number in each equal group.

> **VOCABULARY**
> dividend
> division
> divisor
> equation
> quotient

Skills and Applications

Divide, using facts through 5. (pp. 278–282; 288–289; 296–305)

Find: $20 \div 5$

Solution
Use repeated subtraction.

$$\begin{array}{cccc} 20 & 15 & 10 & 5 \\ -\ 5 & -\ 5 & -\ 5 & -5 \\ \hline 15 & 10 & 5 & 0 \end{array}$$

You subtracted 4 times until you got to zero, so $20 \div 5 = 4$.

Use a related multiplication sentence.

$\blacksquare \times 5 = 20$

$4 \times 5 = 20$

So $20 \div 5 = 4$.

Divide.

5. $25 \div 5$

6. $24 \div 4$

7. $8 \div 4$

8. $25 \div 5$

9. $4 \div 4$

10. $27 \div 3$

11. $14 \div 2$

12. $0 \div 10$

13. $2\overline{)18}$

14. $5\overline{)45}$

15. $3\overline{)21}$

16. $4\overline{)16}$

17. $2\overline{)20}$

18. $3\overline{)24}$

19. $5\overline{)5}$

20. $1\overline{)4}$

21. $2\overline{)14}$

22. $3\overline{)18}$

Foldables Use your Foldables to help you review.

Relate multiplication and division. (pp. 284–286)

Write related multiplication and division sentences.

5, 6, 30

Solution

$5 \times 6 = 30$
$6 \times 5 = 30$
$30 \div 5 = 6$
$30 \div 6 = 5$

Write related multiplication and division sentences for each group of numbers.

23. 3, 5, 15   **24.** 4, 6, 24

25. 3, 9, 27   **26.** 2, 7, 14

27. 5, 5, 25   **28.** 5, 8, 40

29. 2, 6, 12   **30.** 4, 1, 4

Use skills and strategies to solve problems. (pp. 306–307)

You want to hang 9 pictures of astronauts on a wall.
You want 3 pictures in each row.
How many rows of pictures will you hang?

Solution
Use the Act It Out strategy to solve.

Use shapes to represent pictures. Place 3 pictures in each row.

You will hang 3 rows of pictures.

Use the Act It Out strategy to solve.

31. A ticket to the new outer space movie costs $5.00. Is $16.00 enough money to buy 3 tickets? How can you tell?

32. Tom decorates the walls in his room with stickers of the 9 planets. Each of his 4 walls has 1 sticker of each planet. How many stickers does Tom use?

33. Nina has 32 galaxy pictures. She will divide them evenly among herself and 7 friends. How many pictures will each person get?

Enrichment

Odd or Even Products and Quotients

When you multiply or divide, can you predict if the result will be an odd or even number?

1. Make a table like the one below to find products. Fill in your own examples.

Numbers	Example	Product	Odd or Even?
odd X odd	3 X 5		
odd X odd	1 X 7		
even X even	2 X 6		
even X even	4 X 6		
odd X even	3 X 4		
even X odd	6 X 5		

2. Make a table like the one below to find quotients. Fill in your own examples.

Numbers	Example	Product	Odd or Even?
odd ÷ odd	15 ÷ 3		
odd ÷ odd	25 ÷ 5		
even ÷ even	6 ÷ 2		
even ÷ even	16 ÷ 4		
even ÷ odd	14 ÷ 7		
even ÷ odd	12 ÷ 3		

3. **Generalize** What patterns do you see? Compare your conclusions to those of other students.

4. How can you use these generalizations to check if a product or quotient is reasonable?

5. **Analyze** What happens when you try to divide an odd number by an even number?

316

Performance Assessment

THINK
SOLVE
EXPLAIN

How Do You Divide Evenly?

You and your friends can save money by buying boxes of space figures. Then you can divide the figures evenly among your friends.

Make a chart like the one below to help you.

- Find the total number of figures in each box.

- Find the number of figures each person will get.

- Find numbers that divide evenly.

- Explain how you made your decisions.

Action Figure	Number in Box	Number of Friends (include yourself)	Number Each Gets
Space Kids			
Skywalkers			
Star Travelers			
Martian Monsters			
Space Explorers			

Tips For A Good Answer

- Have a completed chart.

- Show that you used numbers that divide evenly.

- Show your division examples.

- Have a clear explanation of how you decided which numbers to use.

PORTFOLIO

You may want to save this work in your portfolio.

e-Journal www.mmhmath.com
Write about math.   Unit 7   **317**

Assessment

Model Division

Mrs. Jansen is planning a graduation party for her son. There are 7 children coming to the party. She wants to put all 8 children in teams of 2 to play a game. How many teams will be formed?

You can use counters 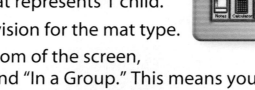 from the *Math Tool Chest* CD-ROM to stamp out a model of the problem.

Each party hat represents 1 child.

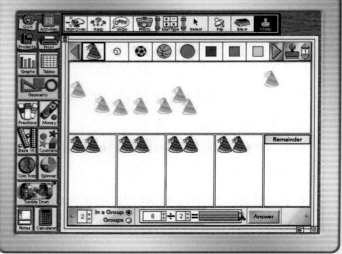

Math Tool Chest CD-Rom

- Choose division for the mat type.
- At the bottom of the screen, choose 2 and "In a Group." This means you are putting the 8 hats in groups of 2.

The number boxes show that you are finding 8 ÷ 2.

How many teams will be formed?

**Use the computer to model each fact.
Then write the quotient.**

1. 14 ÷ 2   **2.** 15 ÷ 5   **3.** 12 ÷ 3   **4.** 20 ÷ 4

Solve.

5. Joel has 28 oatmeal cookies. He wants to give 7 friends the same number of cookies. How many cookies will he give each friend?

6. Sue and her sister have 18 beads in all. They divide the beads into 2 equal groups. How many beads are in each group?

7. **Analyze** How does using the model help you divide?

For more practice, use Math Traveler™.

Test-Taking Tips

You may have taken tests where you need to **show your work.** Those questions are often worth more than multiple-choice questions.

Yoshi and Carol are going to share 18 stickers equally. How many stickers will each of them get?

Show your work by drawing a diagram to solve the problem.

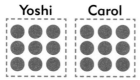

Yoshi   Carol

You can also use division to solve the problem:

$18 \div 2 = 9$

They would each get 9 stickers.

Solve. Show your work.

1. Find the missing number.
$$24 \div x = 12$$

2. There are 24 students in Mr. Ortez's class. The class is divided into 4 equal groups for a trip. How many students are in each group?

3. What number is twice as great as 12?

4. You have 3 pages of photos of your favorite music band. Each page has 8 photos. How many photos do you have in all?

Jeff bought these items.

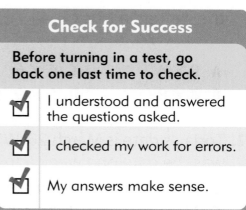

$5.25

$2.90

$1.60

5. How much more did the pad cost than the pen?

6. How much did Jeff spend?

Test Prep

PART 1 • Multiple Choice

Choose the best answer.

1. Which multiplication fact makes the sentence true? (p. 238)
$$7 \times 6 < t$$
   A. 9×4 C. 6×6
   B. 4×8 D. 5×9

2. Today's date is March 20. What was the date one week ago? (p. 150)
   F. March 27   H. March 10
   G. March 13   I. March 7

3. Which equation is true? (p. 118)
   A. $274 + 318 = 582$
   B. $501 - 399 = 101$
   C. $5 \times 8 = 40$
   D. $27 \div 27 = 0$

4. Harry has $35.00 on Monday. He spends $5.00 each day for lunch. On which day does he have $15.00 left? (p. 208)
   F. Thursday   H. Saturday
   G. Wednesday   I. Sunday

5. $8 \times 4 = y$ (p. 234)
   A. 12   C. 32
   B. 24   D. 36

6. Chim practices the piano for 45 minutes. If he starts at 4:30 P.M., what time does he finish? (p. 146)
   F. 3:15 P.M   H. 5:00 P.M
   G. 4:45 P.M.   I. 5:15 P.M

7. Which difference is about 200? (p. 116)
   A. $587 - 135$ C. $1,304 - 691$
   B. $703 - 598$ D. $439 - 210$

8. Find the rule. (p. 204)

Rule:			
Input	3	9	12
Output	6	18	24

   F. Add 3
   G. Multiply by 3
   H. Multiply by 2
   I. Add 6

9. Which number makes the sentence true? (p. 52)
$$(3 + 12) + 35 = 3 + (a + 35)$$
   A. 12   C. 35
   B. 15   D. 0

10. You pay with a five-dollar bill. What is your change? (p. 14)

$3.25

   F. $4.75   H. $2.25
   G. $3.75   I. $1.75

Record your answers on the answer sheet provided by your teacher or on a sheet of paper.

THINK SOLVE EXPLAIN

11. Chris needs to save $435 by December. He has $290. If he saves $15 a month starting in March, will he have $435 by December? Explain. (p. 60)

THINK SOLVE EXPLAIN

12. A tiled floor has 36 tiles in all. The sides of the floor have the same length. How can the tiles be set on the floor? Explain. (p. 324)

13. What sign belongs in the ⬤ ?
12 ⬤ 8 = 4

14. The third grade has 28 students. Each group of 4 is writing 1 planet report. How many reports will there be? (p. 300)

15. Write a multiplication sentence for this array. (p. 196)

16. 16 ÷ 2 = ▊ (p. 288)

Use the bar graph for problems 17–20.

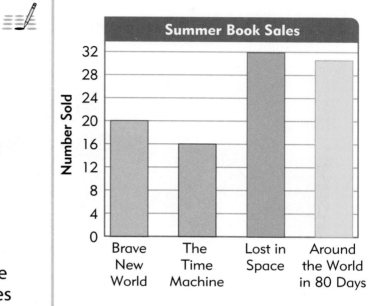

17. How many more copies of *Lost in Space* were sold than copies of *Brave New World*? (p. 168)

18. Which book sold 2 times as many copies as *The Time Machine*? (p. 168)

19. How many books were sold in all? (p. 76)

Record your answer on a sheet of paper. Show your work.

20. How many more copies of *Lost in Space* were sold than *The Time Machine*? Explain how you found your answer. (p. 106)

What Do I Need to Know?

You have 30 rocks and 5 boxes. If you put the same number of rocks in each box, how many rocks are in each box?

Division Facts and Strategies

What Will I Learn?

In this chapter you will learn to

- divide by 6, 7, 8, and 9
- explore dividing by 10
- use skills and strategies to solve problems

How Do I Read Math?

When you read a mathematics book, sometimes you read words and symbols, and sometimes you read only symbols.

All of these represent a fact family of 7, 6, and 42:

- $6 \times 7 = 42$
- $42 \div 7 = 6$
- $7 \times 6 = 42$
- $42 \div 6 = 7$

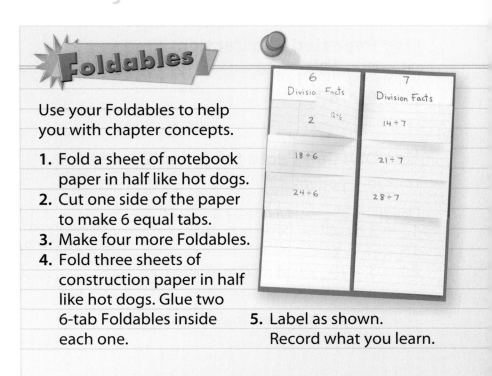

Foldables

Use your Foldables to help you with chapter concepts.

1. Fold a sheet of notebook paper in half like hot dogs.
2. Cut one side of the paper to make 6 equal tabs.
3. Make four more Foldables.
4. Fold three sheets of construction paper in half like hot dogs. Glue two 6-tab Foldables inside each one.
5. Label as shown. Record what you learn.

15.1 Divide by 6 and 7

Learn

To help the environment, some people are planting wildflowers.

If 24 wildflowers are planted in 6 equal groups, how many wildflowers are in each group?

Find: 24 ÷ 6 or 6)‾24

There's More Than One Way!

Use Pictures

Draw 24 flowers. Put flowers in 6 equal groups. Count the number of flowers in each group.

There are 6 groups of 4 in 24.

Use Repeated Subtraction

$24 - 6 = 18 \rightarrow 18 - 6 = 12 \rightarrow 12 - 6 = 6 \rightarrow 6 - 6 = 0$

$24 \div 6 = 4$

Think: You subtracted 4 times.

Use Division Facts for 3 and 2

Look for a pattern.

Divide by 3		Divide by 2
$12 \div 3 = 4$	$\rightarrow$	$4 \div 2 = 2$
$18 \div 3 = 6$	$\rightarrow$	$6 \div 2 = 3$
$24 \div 3 = 8$	$\rightarrow$	$8 \div 2 = 4$

Think: If you divide a number by 3, and then divide by 2, that is the same as dividing by 6.

Divide by 6
$12 \div 6 = 2$
$18 \div 6 = 3$
$24 \div 6 = 4$

There are 4 wildflowers in each group.

The people will be working in groups. If 42 people separate into groups of 7, how many groups will there be?

Find: $42 \div 7$ or $7)\overline{42}$

There's More Than One Way!

Use Skip Counting

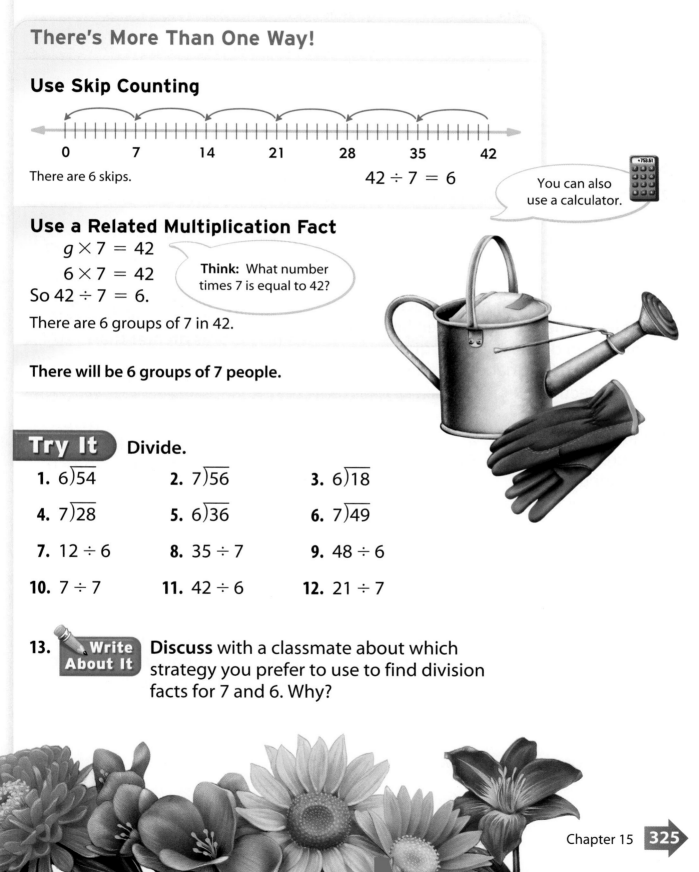

0   7   14   21   28   35   42

There are 6 skips.

$42 \div 7 = 6$

You can also use a calculator.

Use a Related Multiplication Fact

$g \times 7 = 42$

$6 \times 7 = 42$

So $42 \div 7 = 6$.

Think: What number times 7 is equal to 42?

There are 6 groups of 7 in 42.

There will be 6 groups of 7 people.

Try It Divide.

1. $6)\overline{54}$
2. $7)\overline{56}$
3. $6)\overline{18}$

4. $7)\overline{28}$
5. $6)\overline{36}$
6. $7)\overline{49}$

7. $12 \div 6$
8. $35 \div 7$
9. $48 \div 6$

10. $7 \div 7$
11. $42 \div 6$
12. $21 \div 7$

13. **Write About It** **Discuss** with a classmate about which strategy you prefer to use to find division facts for 7 and 6. Why?

Practice and Problem Solving

Divide.

14. $6\overline{)6}$ 15. $7\overline{)14}$ 16. $6\overline{)30}$ 17. $6\overline{)42}$ 18. $7\overline{)21}$

19. $63 \div 7$ 20. $24 \div 6$ 21. $60 \div 6$ 22. $42 \div 7$ 23. $70 \div 7$

ⓧ **Algebra Compare. Write $>$, $<$, or $=$.**

24. $48 \div 6 \bullet 8$ 25. $49 \div 7 \bullet 9$ ★26. $35 \div 7 \bullet 24 \div 6$ ★27. $36 \div 4 \bullet 56 \div 7$

Solve.

THINK SOLVE EXPLAIN
28. **Analyze** When you know that $30 \div 6 = 5$, you also know $30 \div 5 = 6$. Explain why this is true.

★29. Two farmers each have 18 acres of land. They combine their land and then divide it into 6 equal sections. How many acres are in each section?

THINK SOLVE EXPLAIN
30. **Make It Right**
Here's how Jill divided 48 by 6. Tell what mistake she made. Explain how to correct it.

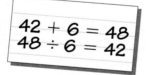
$42 + 6 = 48$
$48 \div 6 = 42$

Link to SCIENCE

Temperatures greater than 120°F were recorded for 43 days in a row in 1917 in Death Valley, California.

31. The average high temperature in Orlando, Florida is 91°F. Compare this temperature to the one given above. What is the difference?

Spiral Review and Test Prep

32. Sid wants to make 8 earthworm boxes with 6 worms in each box. How many worms does he need in all? (p. 234)

   A. 2 worms **C.** 48 worms

   B. 14 worms **D.** 56 worms

33. Lake Tahoe is 1,645 feet deep. What is this number rounded to the nearest thousand? (p. 34)

   F. 1,000 **H.** 1,700

   G. 1,600 **I.** 2,000

34. $18 \div 3$ (p. 298) 35. 6×9 (p. 234) 36. $4\overline{)36}$ (p. 300) 37. 7×5 (p. 238)

Extra Practice page 338, Set A

Problem Solving: Reading for Math
WHERE'S THE WATER?

Quick: Blink! While you blinked, 3 people were added to the world's population. Blink again— another 3 people! That's how quickly Earth's population grows. It adds up to 184 people every minute, 11,040 every hour, 264,960 every day, and almost 97 million every year. That's amazing!

Every new person added to the planet needs water to live. But more water doesn't just appear in the blink of an eye.

KIDS CAN HELP

Bill Ryan of the United Nations Population Fund says kids can help Earth's natural resources. "There are more young people alive now than at any other time in history," he says. "The decisions they make will change the world."

What can you do to save water? It's not hard. Look at the chart to see how much water 1 person uses daily. Think of ways to cut back on your water use.

Problem Solving

DAILY WATER USE

Drinking:
$2\frac{1}{2}$ quarts

Washing 1 load of laundry:
50 gallons

Flushing the toilet once:
24 gallons

Showering for 10 minutes:
25 gallons

Brushing your teeth once: **1 gallon**

Reading Skill **Fact and Opinion** Can you find 3 facts and 1 opinion in this article?

1. The people in 1 family each brush their teeth 3 times a day. They use 18 gallons of water every day for brushing their teeth. How many people are in the family?

2. About how many gallons of water would you use if you did everything in the chart?

15.2 Problem Solving: Skill
Solve Multistep Problems

Read

Jamie raised $8.00 recycling cans, and twice as much recycling bottles. He will split the money equally between 2 charity groups. How much will each group get?

- **What do you know?**
  How much he raised; number of groups

- **What do you need to find?**
  How much money each group will get

Plan

This problem takes more than one step to solve. You must decide how to solve each step and in what order.

First, find the amount raised recycling bottles.

Then, find the total amount raised.

Last, find the amount each group will receive.

Solve

▶ Step 1 $2 \times \$8 = \$16$ ⟶ **Think:** This is twice the amount raised in recycling cans.

▶ Step 2 $\$8 + \$16 = \$24$ ⟶ **Think:** This is the total amount raised in recycling cans and bottles.

▶ Step 3 $\$24 \div 2 = \$12$ ⟶ **Think:** This is the amount each of the 2 groups will get.

Each group will get $12.00.

Look Back

Is your answer reasonable?

1. **Write About It** **Explain** if you could have solved the problem in a different order.

Practice Solve.

2. For 5 days in a row, Kyle bundled 9 bags and Jeff bundled 3 bags. How many bags had the boys bundled after the fifth day?

3. Tala collected 37 cans. Her sister collected 7 fewer cans. How many cans did the girls collect in all?

Mixed Strategy Review

4. Ms. Ping buys 2 boxes of seeds. There are 4 packs in each box. Each pack has 10 seeds. How many seeds did she buy?

5. Jesse has saved $58. He buys soil for $9. He spends the rest of the money on 7 plants. Each plant costs the same amount of money. How much does each plant cost?

Choose a Strategy
- Logical Reasoning
- Draw a Picture or Diagram
- Make a Graph
- Act It Out
- Make a Table or List
- Find a Pattern
- Guess and Check
- Write an Equation
- Work Backward
- Solve a Simpler Problem

Use data from the chart for problems 6–8.

6. What is the range for the least number of cans collected by a grade in a week and the greatest number of cans collected by a grade in a week?

Can Collection Totals			
Grade	Week 1	Week 2	Week 3
1	117	89	53
2	72	113	134
3	109	255	216

7. Which grade collected the greatest number of cans in Week 1? How much greater was this total than that of each other grade?

8. **Write a problem** that is multistep. Use some data from the chart. Solve your problem. Ask others to solve it.

9. Sam collected 6 cans each day for 5 days. Hank collected half as many cans as Sam. At the end of the fifth day, how many cans did the 2 boys collect?

10. Lily walked 4 blocks east, 4 blocks south, 4 blocks west, and 4 blocks north. How many blocks did she walk in all? How far is she from her starting point?

Extra Practice page 338, Set B

Problem Solving

15.3 Divide by 8 and 9

Learn

A group of 8 people are raking leaves. They share 16 trash bags equally. How many trash bags does each person get?

Find: $16 \div 8$ or $8\overline{)16}$

There's More Than One Way!

Use Repeated Subtraction

$16 - 8 = 8$
$8 - 8 = 0$

Think: You subtracted 2 times. So, $16 \div 8 = 2$.

Use a Related Multiplication Fact

$8 \times n = 16$
$8 \times 2 = 16$

Think: 8 times what number is equal to 16?

So $16 \div 8 = 2$.

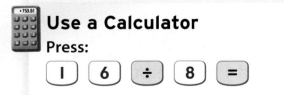

There are 8 groups of 2 in 16.

Use a Calculator

Press:

(1) (6) (÷) (8) (=)

Display:

16÷8=2

Each person gets 2 trash bags.

Mr. Olson surveyed his class to find which types of leaves students have collected. He drew this pictograph to show the results. There are 27 students who have collected oak leaves. How many symbols should he show in the pictograph?

Type of Leaf Collected	Number of Students
maple	🧍🧍
birch	🧍
oak	?

Each 🧍 = 9 students

Find: 27 ÷ 9 or $9\overline{)27}$

There's More Than One Way!

Use an Array

Model the problem using counters.

$$27 \quad ÷ \quad 9 \quad = \quad n$$

↑ number in array   ↑ number of rows   ↑ number in each row

Think: There are 3 counters in each row.

So, 27 ÷ 9 = 3

Use a Related Multiplication Fact

$$n \times 9 = 27$$
$$3 \times 9 = 27$$

Think: What number times 9 is equal to 27?

So, 27 ÷ 9 = 3

Use a Related Division Fact

27 ÷ 9 = n

You know that 27 ÷ 3 = 9.

So, 27 ÷ 9 = 3

Mr. Olson should show 3 🧍 in the pictograph.

Try It Divide.

1. $8\overline{)8}$ 2. $9\overline{)36}$ 3. $8\overline{)40}$ 4. $9\overline{)54}$ 5. $8\overline{)56}$

6. 24 ÷ 8   7. 27 ÷ 9   8. 45 ÷ 9   9. 48 ÷ 8   10. 18 ÷ 9

11. **Write About It** **Explain** how if you know 36 ÷ 9 = 4, you also know that 36 ÷ 4 = 9.

Practice and Problem Solving

Divide.

12. $8\overline{)16}$ **13.** $9\overline{)9}$ **14.** $8\overline{)32}$ **15.** $9\overline{)63}$ **16.** $8\overline{)64}$

17. $72 \div 9$ **18.** $81 \div 9$ **19.** $72 \div 8$ ★**20.** $(9 + 9) \div 9$ ★**21.** $(12 + 12) \div 8$

$\widehat{x}$ **Algebra Copy and complete.**

22.

Rule: Divide by 8				
Input:	24	▪	56	▪
Output:	▪	5	▪	9

23.

Rule:			
Input:	3	5	7
Output:	27	45	63

Solve.

24. Science The shorelines of the world's oceans are being worn away. About 24 feet of the Pacific Ocean shoreline has worn away in 8 years. About how much shoreline is lost each year?

25. Elizabeth travels 63 miles along a river in 9 days. She travels the same number of miles each day. How many miles did she travel each day?

THINK SOLVE EXPLAIN **26.** ✏️ **Write a problem** that can be solved by dividing by 9. Solve it. Ask others to solve it.

27. Make It Right Here's what Teddy used to divide 56 by 8. Tell what mistake he made. Explain how to correct it.

$$64 - 8 = 56$$
$$56 \div 8 = 64$$

THINK SOLVE EXPLAIN

✓ Spiral Review and Test Prep

28. Rico bought a sandwich and a drink that cost $6.35. He paid with a ten-dollar bill. How much change did he get? (p. 14)

   A. $3.65   **C.** $4.35

   B. $3.75   **D.** $4.65

29. Canoe rentals cost $8.75 per hour in the fall. In the summer they cost $0.85 more per hour. How much are canoe rentals per hour in the summer? (p. 58)

   F. $7.60   **H.** $9.60

   G. $7.90   **I.** $9.90

30. $547 + 12 + 689$ (p. 76)   **31.** $4,307 - 768$ (p. 120)   **32.** $\$4.89 + \$9.09$ (p. 60)

Extra Practice page 338, Set C

ROLLING FOR QUOTIENTS

Toss a number cube to get a quotient.

Ready

Players: 3 or more
You Will Need: Number cube, stopwatch, paper and pencil

$$9 \div 3$$
$$12 \div 4$$
$$15 \div 5$$

Set

Label the number cube from 1–6.

Assign 1 player to be the timer.

GO!

► Set the stopwatch to 30 seconds.

► The timer rolls the number cube. Start the clock.

► All players list as many division facts as possible using the number rolled as the quotient.

► After 30 seconds, the timer calls, "Time!"

► The player with the most correct facts gets 1 point.

► The first player with 10 points wins.

► Take turns being the timer and players.

15.4 Explore Dividing by 10

Hands On Activity

You can use place-value models to explore dividing by 10.

You Will Need
- place-value models

Find: 60 ÷ 10

Use Models

STEP 1

Show 60 using tens models.

STEP 2

Separate the models so there is 1 ten in each group.

Count the number of groups.

Explain Your Thinking

1. How did you model the dividend?

2. How did you show the divisor?

3. How many groups are there?

4. What is the quotient?

5. **What If** You need to divide 60 into 10 equal groups. How many will be in each group?

Technology Link

Use the place-value tool in **Math Tool Chest** to divide by 10.

Find: 30 ÷ 10

Let's see how to connect models to paper and pencil.

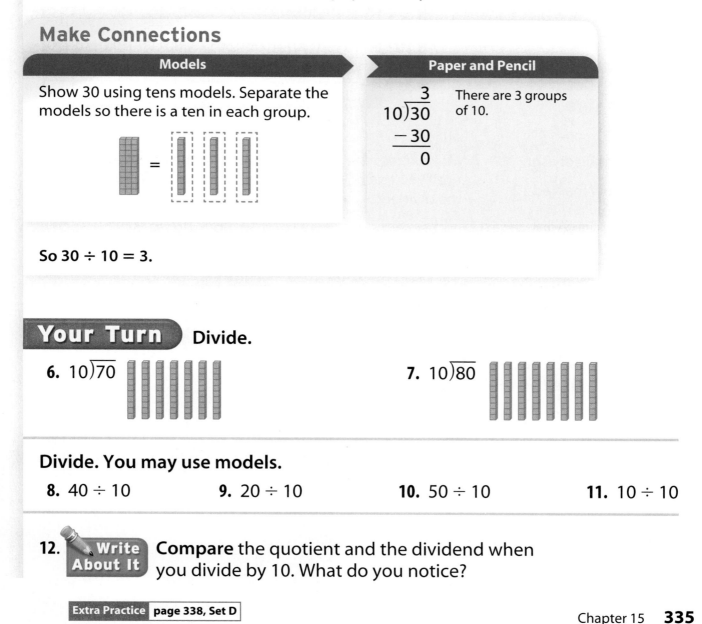

Make Connections

Models	Paper and Pencil

Show 30 using tens models. Separate the models so there is a ten in each group.

$$\begin{array}{r} 3 \\ 10\overline{)30} \\ -30 \\ \hline 0 \end{array}$$

There are 3 groups of 10.

So 30 ÷ 10 = 3.

Your Turn Divide.

6. $10\overline{)70}$

7. $10\overline{)80}$

Divide. You may use models.

8. 40 ÷ 10

9. 20 ÷ 10

10. 50 ÷ 10

11. 10 ÷ 10

12. **Write About It** **Compare** the quotient and the dividend when you divide by 10. What do you notice?

15.5 Use a Multiplication Table

×	0	1	2	3	4	5	6	7	8	9	10	11	12
0	0	0	0	0	0	0	0	0	0	0	0	0	0
1	0	1	2	3	4	5	6	7	8	9	10	11	12
2	0	2	4	6	8	10	12	14	16	18	20	22	24
3	0	3	6	9	12	15	18	21	24	27	30	33	36
4	0	4	8	12	16	20	24	28	32	36	40	44	48
5	0	5	10	15	20	25	30	35	40	45	50	55	60
6	0	6	12	18	24	30	36	42	48	54	60	66	72
7	0	7	14	21	28	35	42	49	56	63	70	77	84
8	0	8	16	24	32	40	48	56	64	72	80	88	96
9	0	9	18	27	36	45	54	63	72	81	90	99	108
10	0	10	20	30	40	50	60	70	80	90	100	110	120
11	0	11	22	33	44	55	66	77	88	99	110	121	132
12	0	12	24	36	48	60	72	84	96	108	120	132	144

Learn

Margo will travel to 12 countries in 36 months. She will stay the same amount of time in each country. How many months will she stay in each country?

Find: $36 \div 12$

Use a Table

STEP 1

Begin with the divisor.

Find the row marked 12.

> **Think:** 12 times what number is equal to 36?
> $12 \times z = 36$

STEP 2

Move across the row until you reach 36, the dividend.

STEP 3

Move to the top of the column. You will reach 3, the quotient.

So $36 \div 12 = 3$.

Margo will spend 3 months in each country.

 Try It Find each missing number. Use the multiplication table.

1. $33 \div 11 = n$
   $11 \times n = 33$

2. $66 \div 11 = y$
   $11 \times y = 66$

3. $48 \div 12 = z$
   $12 \times z = 48$

4. $72 \div 12 = a$
   $12 \times a = 72$

5.  **Explain** how to use the multiplication table to find $60 \div 12$.

Practice and Problem Solving

Find each missing number. Use the multiplication table.

6. $72 \div 12 = t$
$12 \times t = 72$

7. $64 \div 8 = s$
$8 \times s = 64$

8. $56 \div 7 = c$
$7 \times c = 56$

9. $63 \div 9 = d$
$9 \times d = 63$

Divide.

10. $18 \div 6$ **11.** $45 \div 5$ **12.** $32 \div 8$ **13.** $72 \div 9$ **14.** $77 \div 11$

★**15.** $(5 \times 9) \div 9$ ★**16.** $(6 \times 7) \div 7$ ★**17.** $(8 \times 4) \div 4$ ★**18.** $(9 \times 10) \div 10$

ⓧ **Algebra** Write $+, -, \times,$ or $\div$.

19. $30 \bullet 5 = 6$ **20.** $7 \bullet 7 = 14$ **21.** $12 \bullet 6 = 72$ **22.** $55 \bullet 11 = 5$

Solve.

23. Donna walked 28 miles in 7 days. She walked the same amount each day. How many miles did she walk each day?

24. Mindy buys 6 boxes of cat food. Each box holds 6 cans. How many cans does she buy?

25. Number Sense Masud lived in Africa for 12 years. His parents lived there even longer. Is it more likely that they lived there 2 times as long or 12 times as long? How can you tell?

26. ✏️ **Write About It** **Analyze** Why can a multiplication table be helpful in getting answers to division facts?

✓ Spiral Review and Test Prep

27. Adam hiked in the mountains for 2 hours 45 minutes. He began at 4:30 P.M. What time did he finish? (p. 146)

A. 6:15 P.M.   **C.** 7:15 P.M.

B. 6:45 P.M.   **D.** 7:45 P.M.

28. Which number is missing in the skip-counting pattern? (p. 56)

242, 342, _____, 542

F. 352   **H.** 424

G. 362   **I.** 442

29.   9 (p. 234)
   $\times 6$

30. $7.96 (p. 104)
   $- \ 3.07$

31.   6,854 (p. 72)
   $+ \ 693$

32.   5 (p. 238)
   $\times 7$

Extra Practice

Set A Divide. (pp. 324–326)

1. $42 \div 6$ **2.** $28 \div 7$ **3.** $49 \div 7$ **4.** $18 \div 6$ **5.** $24 \div 6$

6. $7\overline{)7}$ **7.** $6\overline{)30}$ **8.** $6\overline{)48}$ **9.** $7\overline{)63}$ **10.** $6\overline{)0}$

11. $28 \div 4$ **12.** $36 \div 6$ **13.** $14 \div 7$ **14.** $0 \div 7$ **15.** $21 \div 7$

16. $6\overline{)12}$ **17.** $7\overline{)35}$ **18.** $6 \div 6$ **19.** $6\overline{)54}$ **20.** $7\overline{)56}$

Set B Solve. (pp. 328–329)

21. There are 31 people on the bus. At the first stop, 9 people get off and 4 people get on. How many people are now on the bus?

22. Fran is on a train traveling 60 miles an hour. The train is 193 miles from Fran's stop. Will she be there in 3 hours? Why or why not?

Set C Divide. (pp. 330–333)

23. $63 \div 9$ **24.** $54 \div 9$ **25.** $27 \div 9$ **26.** $16 \div 8$ **27.** $72 \div 8$

28. $8\overline{)64}$ **29.** $8\overline{)32}$ **30.** $8\overline{)8}$ **31.** $9\overline{)81}$ **32.** $8\overline{)56}$

33. $24 \div 8$ **34.** $9 \div 9$ **35.** $48 \div 8$ **36.** $0 \div 9$ **37.** $72 \div 9$

38. $8\overline{)40}$ **39.** $9\overline{)18}$ **40.** $9\overline{)36}$ **41.** $8\overline{)0}$ **42.** $9\overline{)45}$

Set D Solve. (pp. 334–335)

43. $60 \div 10$ **44.** $30 \div 10$ **45.** $70 \div 10$ **46.** $50 \div 10$

47. $90 \div 10$ **48.** $100 \div 10$ **49.** $10 \div 10$ **50.** $80 \div 10$

51. $20 \div 10$ **52.** $40 \div 10$ **53.** $120 \div 10$ **54.** $110 \div 10$

Set E Divide. Use the multiplication table on page 336. (pp. 336–337)

55. $72 \div 6$ **56.** $12 \div 12$ **57.** $77 \div 11$ **58.** $96 \div 8$ **59.** $121 \div 11$

60. $10\overline{)20}$ **61.** $8\overline{)64}$ **62.** $11\overline{)88}$ **63.** $9\overline{)36}$ **64.** $12\overline{)120}$

65. $9\overline{)18}$ **66.** $66 \div 11$ **67.** $12\overline{)36}$ **68.** $24 \div 12$ **69.** $72 \div 8$

LOG ON www.mmhmath.com
For more practice and Chapter Self-Check Test

Review/Test

Divide.

1. $7\overline{)63}$ 2. $6\overline{)42}$ 3. $8\overline{)32}$ 4. $7\overline{)21}$

5. $7\overline{)42}$ 6. $9\overline{)81}$ 7. $10\overline{)50}$ 8. $7\overline{)49}$

9. $40 \div 8$ 10. $64 \div 8$ 11. $18 \div 6$ 12. $35 \div 7$

13. $56 \div 8$ 14. $36 \div 9$ 15. $36 \div 6$ 16. $27 \div 9$

17. $48 \div 6$ 18. $45 \div 9$ 19. $72 \div 8$ 20. $63 \div 9$

Solve.

21. The science group plants 54 trees in 9 different parks. They plant the same number of trees in each park. How many trees are planted in each park?

22. You spend $70 on 10 tickets for a river raft ride. How much is each ticket?

23. You have 2 packages of pictures. One package has 12 pictures. The other has 24. Each page of your album holds 6 pictures. How many pages will you fill?

24. There are 28 people going on a boat ride. There are 7 boats for the trip. If there are equal groups, how many people can ride in each boat?

25. **Write About It** **Analyze** Which strategy would you use to find $30 \div 6$?

Do I Need Help?

Exercises	Review Concepts	Use Extra Practice Set
1–20, 24	pp. 324–326, 330–332	Sets A and C
23	pp. 328–329	Set B
21, 25	pp. 330–332	Set C
22	pp. 334–335	Set D

 **Use your Foldables to help you review.**

What Do I Need to Know?

Rodney catches 7 fish each day for 5 days. Tamika catches 5 fish each day for 7 days. How many fish does each person catch?

Apply Division: Mean

What Will I Learn?

In this chapter you will learn to

- write multiplication and division fact families

- find the mean

- use skills and strategies to solve problems

How Do I Read Math?

When you read a mathematics book, sometimes you read words and symbols, and sometimes you read only symbols.

All of these are related division facts for $4 \times 6 = 24$:

- $24 \div 6 = 4$

- $24 \div 4 = 6$

VOCABULARY

- mean

Foldables

Use your Foldables to help you with chapter concepts.

1. Fold a sheet of notebook paper in half like hot dogs.
2. Cut one side of the paper to make 6 equal tabs.
3. Record division vocabulary, properties, and fact families on the front tabs. Write definitions, examples,
4. Glue this sheet on the blank page of the Foldable made in Chapter 15.

and notes under the tabs.

Related Fac		Mean
3 x	3,4,12	Definition
4 x 5		
8,7,56		2,3,1,2

16.1 Algebra: Use Related Facts

Learn

The volunteers in the Earth Care Club planted some trees. How many rows of trees are there? How many trees are in each row? How many trees are there in total?

You can use related facts for 3, 6, and 18 to describe the trees.

Use Related Facts

$$3 \times 6 = 18$$

↑ number of rows ↑ number in each row ↑ total

$$6 \times 3 = 18$$

↑ number in each row ↑ number of rows ↑ total

$$18 \div 6 = 3$$

↑ total ↑ number in each row ↑ number of rows

$$18 \div 3 = 6$$

↑ total ↑ number of rows ↑ number in each row

Together, these 4 related facts are called a fact family.

There are 3 rows of trees.
There are 6 trees in each row.
There are 18 trees in total.

Fact Family for 2, 8, and 16

$2 \times 8 = 16 \quad 16 \div 2 = 8$
$8 \times 2 = 16 \quad 16 \div 8 = 2$

Fact Family for 9 and 81

$9 \times 9 = 81 \quad 81 \div 9 = 9$

The club also has volunteers for its clean-up project.
The goal is to raise $20. One volunteer can raise up to $5.
How many volunteers does the club need to reach the goal?

You can use either division or multiplication to solve.
Find: $\$20 \div \$5 = v$ or $v \times \$5 = \$20$

Use Fact Families

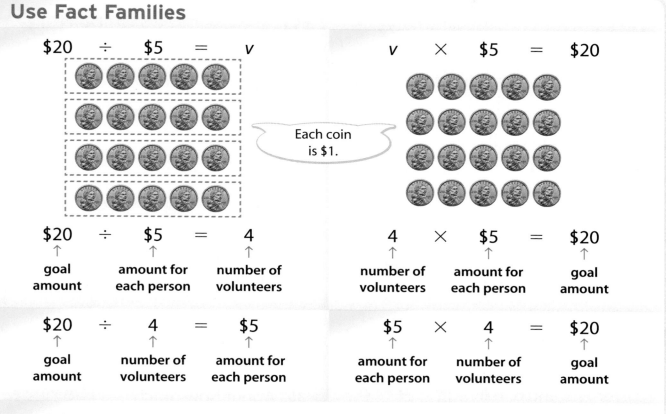

$\$20 \div \$5 = v$

$\$20 \div \$5 = 4$

↑	↑	↑
goal amount	amount for each person	number of volunteers

$v \times \$5 = \$20$

$4 \times \$5 = \$20$

↑	↑	↑
number of volunteers	amount for each person	goal amount

Each coin is $1.

$\$20 \div 4 = \$5$

↑	↑	↑
goal amount	number of volunteers	amount for each person

$\$5 \times 4 = \$20$

↑	↑	↑
amount for each person	number of volunteers	goal amount

The club needs 4 volunteers to reach the goal.

Try It Write a fact family for each picture.

1.

2. ● ● ● ● ● ● ●

Write a fact family for each group of numbers.

3. 6, 8, 48   **4.** 7, 9, 63   **5.** 5, 8, 40   **6.** 4, 9, 36

7. 5, 4, 20   **8.** 7, 7, 49   **9.** 3, 9, 27   **10.** 8, 7, 56

11. **Write About It** **Explain** how you can solve $n \times 8 = 48$ using related multiplication facts.

Practice and Problem Solving

Write a fact family for the pictures.

12. ● ● ● ● ● ● ● ● ● ●
● ● ● ● ● ● ● ● ● ●

13. ☐☐☐☐

Write a fact family for each group of numbers.

14. 4, 6, 24　　　**15.** 8, 9, 72　　　★**16.** 6, 12, 72　　　★**17.** 12, 11, 121

Solve. Write a related fact.

18. 5×4　　　**19.** $35 \div 7$　　　**20.** 7×4　　　**21.** $21 \div 7$　　　**22.** $63 \div 9$

ⓧ Algebra Find each missing number.

23. $3 \times y = 24$　　　**24.** $s \times 7 = 49$　　　**25.** $a \div 4 = 7$　　　**26.** $90 \div f = 9$

Solve.

27. Luisa draws an array of 6 trees. How can she draw them? Then write related facts.

THINK
SOLVE
EXPLAIN

28. Make It Right
David wrote this as the fact family for 2, 3, and 6. Tell what mistake he made. Explain how to correct it.

> 2, 3, 6
> $3 \times 6 = 18$
> $2 \times 6 = 12$
> $18 \div 6 = 3$
> $12 \div 2 = 6$

Link to HEALTH

Humans need about 35 pints of water each week.

29. About how much water do humans need each day?

★**30.** About how much water do humans need in a 4-week period?

Spiral Review and Test Prep

31. Each of the 3 sections of a canoe fits 2 people. How many people can fit in 4 full canoes? (p. 328)

A. 9 people　　　**C.** 24 people

B. 12 people　　　**D.** 30 people

32. Marco starts work at 8:15 A.M. He finishes at 4:00 P.M. How long does he work? (p. 146)

F. 7 h 15 min　　　**H.** 8 h 15 min

G. 7 h 45 min　　　**I.** 8 h 45 min

33. $7\overline{)56}$ (p. 324)　　　**34.** $201 + 37$ (p. 60)　　　**35.** $4\overline{)28}$ (p. 300)　　　**36.** $829 - 13$ (p. 106)

14. $24 \div 6 = 4, 4 \times 6 = 24, 24 \div 4 = 6, 6 \times 4 = 24$

Extra Practice　page 354, Set A

Writing for Math

A group of 9 people hike on a trail. Each hiker drinks 2 bottles of water. How many 6-pack cartons of water are used? Explain your thinking.

David's Response

Teacher's Response

✔ **THINK**

Multiply to find the total number of water bottles. Divide that number by 6 to find how many cartons are used.

← David explains how he will use what he knows to solve the problem.

✔ **SOLVE**

$9 \times 2 = 18$ $18 \div 6 = 3$

Three 6-pack cartons of water are used.

Check: $6 \times 3 = 18$ $18 \div 2 = 9$

← David shows his work.

✔ **EXPLAIN**

Each of the 9 hikers drinks 2 bottles. I multiply 9 by 2 for a product of 18. Next, I divide 18 by 6 to find the number of cartons. The quotient is 3, so 3 cartons are used.

← David uses appropriate math terms such as **multiply**, **product**, **divide**, and **quotient**. He describes each of the 2 steps he needs to solve the problem.

To check, I multiply 6 by 3 to get 18. I divide 18 by 2 to get 9. There are 9 hikers, so the answer makes sense.

← David checks his answer for accuracy and reasonableness.

THINK SOLVE EXPLAIN

Solve. Show your work. Use David's work as a guide.

1. John has 6 packages of 4 stickers to arrange on 2 matching pages of an album. How can he arrange them in equal rows?

2. Anil has tiles arranged in 3 rows of 8. How many flowers made of 6 tiles can he make?

16.2 Problem Solving: Strategy
Guess and Check

Read

Africa is known for its beautiful animals. A group of birds and hippopotamuses roam on the plains of Kenya in Africa. Nine animals are roaming in one area. There is a total of 26 legs. How many birds are there? How many hippopotamuses?

- **What do you know?**
  There are 9 animals total; there are 26 legs in all; birds have 2 legs; hippopotamuses have 4.

- **What do you need to find?**
  How many birds and how many hippopotamuses there are

Plan

Guess the number of birds and hippopotamuses. Try your numbers. Change your guesses if you need to. Record your work.

Solve

Try 2 numbers to see how close to 26 you can get.

Guess: 6 birds; 3 hippopotamuses   **Check:** 24 < 26
$6 \times 2 = 12$ $3 \times 4 = 12$ $12 + 12 = 24$

▶ Try other numbers.

Guess: 5 birds, 4 hippopotamuses   **Check:** 26 legs
$5 \times 2 = 10$ $4 \times 4 = 16$ $10 + 16 = 26$ is correct.

There are 5 birds and 4 hippopotamuses.

Look Back

How could you solve this problem in a different way?

1. **Write About It** How would you adjust your answer to this problem if there were 28 legs? 36 legs?

346

Practice

Use the guess-and-check strategy to solve.

2. There are 2 numbers whose sum is 8 and quotient is 3. What are the 2 numbers?

3. You have 5 coins that total $0.75. What coins do you have?

Mixed Strategy Review

4. A charter boat took 5 people out to fish. They caught a total of 45 fish. If they each caught the same number of fish, how many did each person catch?

5. The Bird Watchers Club has recorded a total of 24 kinds of birds for 6 weeks. They recorded the same number each week. How many kinds of birds did they see in each week?

6. Lila spends $54.00 on a backpack and a canteen. The backpack costs twice as much as the canteen. How much does the backpack cost? The canteen?

★**8. Language Arts** Frank writes this spelling word over and over. When he is finished he has written *e* and *n* a total of 45 times. How many times has he written the word?

9. Ana's science group plants trees to help save forests. There are 9 people in her group. Each planted 7 trees. How many did they plant?

Choose a Strategy
- Logical Reasoning
- Draw a Picture or Diagram
- Make a Graph
- Act It Out
- Make a Table or List
- Find a Pattern
- Guess and Check
- Write an Equation
- Work Backward
- Solve a Simpler Problem

7. A small box holds 5 books. A large box holds 9 books. A bookstore gets a shipment of 7 small boxes and 8 large boxes. How many books are in the shipment?

Environment

10. **Write a problem** that can be solved using the guess-and-check strategy. Use problem 3 as a guide. Solve it. Ask others to solve it.

Extra Practice page 354, Set B

Problem Solving

Fast Facts

Division

1. $6\overline{)12}$ **2.** $7\overline{)49}$ **3.** $9\overline{)45}$ **4.** $12\overline{)84}$ **5.** $8\overline{)64}$

6. $9\overline{)9}$ **7.** $11\overline{)110}$ **8.** $12\overline{)48}$ **9.** $10\overline{)90}$ **10.** $8\overline{)0}$

11. $9\overline{)72}$ **12.** $7\overline{)42}$ **13.** $9\overline{)81}$ **14.** $5\overline{)45}$ **15.** $6\overline{)54}$

16. $8\overline{)48}$ **17.** $12\overline{)96}$ **18.** $11\overline{)77}$ **19.** $10\overline{)100}$ **20.** $12\overline{)12}$

21. $8\overline{)72}$ **22.** $11\overline{)99}$ **23.** $12\overline{)60}$ **24.** $7\overline{)63}$ **25.** $6\overline{)36}$

26. $7\overline{)56}$ **27.** $9\overline{)27}$ **28.** $12\overline{)60}$ **29.** $8\overline{)72}$ **30.** $7\overline{)7}$

31. $6\overline{)54}$ **32.** $11\overline{)88}$ **33.** $12\overline{)24}$ **34.** $10\overline{)40}$ **35.** $6\overline{)30}$

36. $56 \div 8$ **37.** $27 \div 9$ **38.** $36 \div 9$ **39.** $36 \div 12$ **40.** $50 \div 10$

41. $42 \div 6$ **42.** $45 \div 9$ **43.** $121 \div 11$ **44.** $16 \div 8$ **45.** $21 \div 7$

46. $32 \div 8$ **47.** $60 \div 12$ **48.** $72 \div 9$ **49.** $10 \div 10$ **50.** $18 \div 6$

51. $35 \div 7$ **52.** $20 \div 10$ **53.** $54 \div 9$ **54.** $66 \div 11$ **55.** $6 \div 6$

56. $28 \div 7$ **57.** $24 \div 8$ **58.** $14 \div 7$ **59.** $27 \div 3$ **60.** $24 \div 6$

SPIN A FACT

Use spinners to get numbers and operations to write facts.

Ready

Players: 3 or more
You Will Need: 2 spinners, 1 stopwatch, pencil and paper

Set

Make 2 spinners like the ones shown.

Assign 1 player to be the timer.

GO!

▶ Players 1 and 2 each spin a spinner.

▶ Set the stopwatch to 1 minute.

▶ Both players write as many facts as they can, using the number and the operation shown on the spinners. The number on the spinner is the answer of the facts. For example, if you spin a 4 and ÷, one fact is 8 ÷ 2 = 4.

▶ After 1 minute, the timer calls, "Time."

▶ Players get 1 point for each correct fact.

▶ The first player to reach 20 points wins.

16.3 Explore the Mean

Hands On Activity

The **mean** is the number found by dividing the sum of a group of numbers by the number of addends. One way to find the mean is to rearrange groups so they each have the same number.

You can use models to find the mean for 2, 3, 1, and 2.

You Will Need
- connecting cubes

VOCABULARY

mean

Use Models

STEP 1

Make stacks of cubes to show each number.

STEP 2

Rearrange the cubes so that each stack has the same number of cubes.

STEP 3

Count the number of cubes in each stack. This is the mean.

Explain Your Thinking

1. How did you model each number?

2. How did you rearrange the stacks?

3. How many cubes are in each stack?

4. What is the mean for 2, 3, 1, and 2?

Technology Link

Use the counters tool in **Math Tool Chest** to find the mean.

Your Turn

Find the mean.

5. 3, 4, 2

6. 3, 1, 3, 2, 1

7. 2, 2, 4, 4

8. 5, 3

9. 1, 2, 3

10. 1, 3, 0, 2, 4

Find the mean. Use connecting cubes to help.

11. 3, 3, 6   12. 4, 2   13. 4, 0, 4, 4   14. 3, 5, 5, 1, 1

15.  **Write About It** **Explain** how to find the mean for 2, 3, 8, 2, and 0.

16.4 Find the Mean

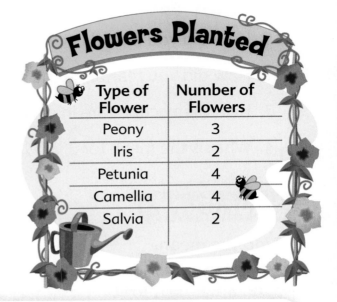

Flowers Planted

Type of Flower	Number of Flowers
Peony	3
Iris	2
Petunia	4
Camellia	4
Salvia	2

Learn

The Garden Club planted flowers on the front lawn of the school. The table shows the number of each type of flower. What is the mean number of flowers planted?

Find the mean for the number of flowers.

Let's see how to connect models to paper and pencil.

Make Connections

	Models	Paper and Pencil
STEP 1 Make stacks of cubes to show each number.	3 2 4 4 2	Add the numbers to find how many in all. $3 + 2 + 4 + 4 + 2 = 15$
STEP 2 Rearrange the cubes into equal stacks.	3 3 3 3 3	Count the number of addends. There are 5 addends. Divide the sum by the number of addends. $15 \div 5 = m$
STEP 3 Count the number of cubes in each stack.		The quotient is 3. That means there are 3 in each group.

You can also use a calculator.

The mean number of flowers planted is 3.

Try It   Find the mean.

1. number of members in each club
   4, 2, 6, 3, 5

2. number of cups of water used
   3, 5, 2, 3, 4, 7

3. **Write About It** **Explain** if the mean will change if the club does not plant peonies.

Practice and Problem Solving

Find the mean.

4. number of birds seen each day
   8, 2, 6, 7, 7

5. number of leaves collected
   5, 2, 4, 3, 1

6. amount of money earned
   $4, $6, $4, $4, $2

7. prices for flowers
   $3, $7, $7, $9, $2, $3, $4

8. 1, 2, 0, 4, 2, 3

9. 9, 11, 7, 5, 6, 10

★ 10. 13, 0, 16, 25, 0, 18

★ 11. 17, 0, 15, 12, 0, 18, 10, 16

★ 12. 24, 17, 6, 36, 17, 12, 28

★ 13. 38, 40, 24, 51, 27, 18

Solve. Use the data from the graph for problems 14–17.

14. Who saw the most flowers?

15. What is the mean number of flowers seen?

16. What is the mode of the number of flowers seen?

THINK
SOLVE
EXPLAIN
17. **Compare** Which is greater, the mean number of flowers or the range? Explain.

Number of Flowers Seen

Miranda
Brian
Gina
Lin

❀ = 2 Flowers

Spiral Review and Test Prep

18. Freddy worked about 20 hours this month. About how many hours could he have worked each week? (p. 300)

    A. 80 hours   C. 5 hours
    B. 40 hours   D. 3 hours

19. The product of 2 numbers is 45. The difference of the 2 numbers is 4. What are the 2 numbers? (p. 328)

    F. 3 and 15   H. 5 and 9
    G. 3 and 7   I. 9 and 13

20. 9×5 (p. 252)   21. 4×7 (p. 210)   22. $81 \div 9$ (p. 330)   23. $48 \div 6$ (p. 324)

Extra Practice

Set A Write a fact family for each group of numbers. (pp. 342–344)

1. 6, 7, 42   **2.** 3, 9, 27   **3.** 5, 8, 40   **4.** 7, 7, 49

5. 6, 8, 48   **6.** 4, 7, 28   **7.** 2, 7, 14   **8.** 5, 9, 45

9. 3, 5, 15   **10.** 3, 7, 21   **11.** 6, 9, 54   **12.** 8, 1, 8

Solve. Write a related fact.

13. 6×9 **14.** 8×4 **15.** 7×3 **16.** 9×8 **17.** 10×8

18. $36 \div 6$ **19.** $45 \div 9$ **20.** $81 \div 9$ **21.** $42 \div 7$ **22.** $48 \div 8$

23. $0 \div 63$ **24.** 7×10 **25.** $35 \div 7$ **26.** $1 \div 1$ **27.** 9×7

Find each missing number.

28. $32 \div d = 8$ **29.** $m \div 4 = 3$ **30.** $v \div 9 = 8$ **31.** $25 \div c = 5$

32. $18 \div g = 3$ **33.** $n \div 7 = 3$ **34.** $30 \div x = 3$ **35.** $64 \div a = 8$

36. $8 \times p = 72$ **37.** $y \times 10 = 80$ **38.** $r \times 8 = 32$ **39.** $7 \times 4 = z$

Set B Use the guess-and-check strategy to solve. (pp. 346–347)

40. Paul is counting tires on cars and motorcycles in the parking lot. If he counts 20 tires, how many motorcycles and cars could there be?

41. Tom and Carol have lived near the shore for a total of 9 years. Tom has lived there 3 years longer than Carol. How many years has each person lived at the shore?

Set C Find the mean. (pp. 350–351, 352–353)

42. 5, 3, 8, 4   **43.** 5, 7, 2, 3, 5, 2   **44.** 3, 7, 0, 3, 2, 4, 2

45. 10, 5, 5, 10, 5   **46.** 7, 6, 7, 2, 6, 7, 7   **47.** 5, 8, 2, 0, 2, 4, 8, 3

Review/Test

Divide.

1. $55 \div 11$ **2.** $24 \div 12$ **3.** $60 \div 10$ **4.** $56 \div 8$ **5.** $72 \div 9$

Write a fact family for each group of numbers.

6. 3, 9, 27 **7.** 7, 5, 35 **8.** 8, 6, 48 **9.** 7, 7, 49

Find each missing number.

10. $48 \div t = 12$ **11.** $72 \div d = 8$ **12.** $36 \div r = 6$ **13.** $v \div 4 = 3$

14. $32 \div a = 4$ **15.** $64 \div a = 8$ **16.** $36 \div y = 4$ **17.** $21 \div z = 7$

Find the mean.

18. 3, 8, 5, 6, 3 **19.** 7, 3, 9, 5, 6 **20.** 7, 4, 4, 6, 4 **21.** 8, 5, 6, 7, 6, 4

Solve.

22. A group of children and dogs is standing on the shore. There are 14 legs in all. How many children and dogs are there?

23. Tara spent a total of 24 hours over 6 days rowing a canoe on the river. If she rowed the same number of hours each day, how many hours each day did she row?

24. The product of 2 numbers is 16. The quotient of these 2 numbers is 4. What are the 2 numbers?

25. **Write About It** **Describe** how you can use a fact family to find the missing factor in $9 \times n = 36$.

Do I Need Help?

Exercises	Review Concepts	Use Extra Practice Set
1–17, 23, 25	pp. 342–344	Set A
18–21	pp. 350–353	Set C
22, 24	pp. 346–347	Set B

 **Use your Foldables to help you review.**

How Fast Are You?

For a 2-legged animal, you may be fast, but the fastest land animals all have 4 legs. The cheetah can run up to 70 miles per hour (mph). That is faster than a car on the highway!

Ostriches are the fastest animals on 2 legs. They can run up to 40 miles per hour. Humans have bodies that are made to run on 2 legs. The fastest a person can run is about 26 miles per hour. That is really fast for a human!

Look at the chart and see which animals are the fastest. These animals need to be fast to survive. The wildebeest lives in Africa and is very fast. It has to outrun a lion. Lions have to catch wildebeests to survive.

How fast are you?

Animal	Speed
Cheetah	70 mph
Wildebeest	50 mph
Lion	50 mph
Ostrich	40 mph
Rabbit	36 mph
Cat	30 mph
Human	26 mph
Elephant	24 mph
Squirrel	12 mph
Spider	Almost 2 mph

Activity

Hypothesize

Predict if you can run faster than a squirrel.

You Will Need
- stopwatch
- tape measure
- calculator

Procedure

1. Work with a partner. Copy the chart.

	Time (in seconds)	Miles per hour
1st Try		
2nd Try		

2. Get help from your teacher to set up a straight track. It should be 88 feet long. If you ran this distance 60 times you would have run a mile.

3. Time how many seconds it takes you to run 88 feet. Try this twice and record both times in the chart.

4. Now find your speed in miles per hour. Use the table below to find it. Record this in your chart.

Time in seconds	3	4	5	6	7	8	9	10
Miles per hour	20	15	12	10	9	8	7	6

Conclude and Apply

1. **Interpret data** Is your hypothesis correct?

2. **Use numbers** You run 6 miles per hour. How much faster is an elephant? Hint: Divide an elephant's speed by 6.

3. You run 12 miles per hour. How many times faster are you than a spider?

Going Further Use division to find out how much faster each animal is than a spider.

Unit Study Guide and Review

Vocabulary

Complete. Use a word from the list.

1. To find the _____ for 2, 3, 7, you divide the sum by 3.

2. If you want to find what number times 8 is equal to 56, then you are finding a _____.

VOCABULARY

factor
mean
product

Skills and Applications

Divide, using facts through 12. (pp. 324–326, 330–332, 334–335)

Find: $48 \div 8$

Solution
Use a related multiplication sentence.

$8 \times n = 48$

$8 \times 6 = 48$

So $48 \div 8 = 6$

Find each quotient.

3. $7\overline{)35}$ 4. $8\overline{)72}$

5. $6\overline{)48}$ 6. $12\overline{)72}$

7. $88 \div 11$ 8. $54 \div 6$

9. $64 \div 8$ 10. $60 \div 10$

11. $24 \div 6$ 12. $72 \div 9$

13. $60 \div 12$ 14. $63 \div 9$

15. $42 \div 7$ 16. $24 \div 4$

Identify fact families. (pp. 342–344)

Find the missing number.
$b \times 7 = 28$

Solution
Use the related division fact in the fact family.

$28 \div 7 = 4$

$4 \times 7 = 28$

So $b = 4$

Write a fact family for each group of numbers.

17. 7, 4, 28   18. 5, 3, 15

19. 9, 6, 54   20. 8, 6, 48

Find each missing number.

21. $54 \div y = 9$ 22. $60 \div t = 6$

23. $k \div 7 = 9$ 24. $a \div 8 = 7$

Foldables   **Use your Foldables to help you review.**

Find the Mean. (pp. 350–351; 352–353)

Find the mean number of hours worked. 3, 5, 4, 5, 3

Solution
Add: $3 + 5 + 4 + 5 + 3 = 20$

Divide the sum by the number of addends:

$20 \div 5 = 4$

The mean number of hours worked is 4.

Find the mean.

25. 6, 3, 4, 6, 7, 4

26. 7, 3, 6, 5, 4

27. 2, 2, 2, 1, 2, 3, 2, 2

28. 5, 10, 5, 10, 10

Use skills and strategies to solve problems. (pp. 328–329, 346–347)

A safety patrol, using motorcycles and trucks, is checking mountain roads for possible rock slides. All 7 vehicles need new tires to make the trip. They need 22 tires in all. How many motorcycles and trucks are there?

Solution
Use the Guess-and-Check strategy:

Guess 1: 5 motorcycles, 2 trucks
5×2 tires $= 10$ tires
2×4 tires $= 8$ tires
$10 + 8 = 18$ tires

Check:
$18 < 22$

Guess 2: 3 motorcycles, 4 trucks
3×2 tires $= 6$ tires
4×4 tires $= 16$ tires
$6 + 16 = 22$ tires

Check:
There are 3 motorcycles and 4 trucks.

Solve.

29. Which 2 numbers have a product of 27 and a quotient of 3?

30. Andie pays $16.75 for film. She gives the clerk a twenty-dollar bill. How much is her change?

31. Judy is counting the birds and cats she sees. She sees a total of 32 legs and 10 animals. How many birds and cats does she see?

32. At a garage sale, hardcover books cost $0.75, and paperback books cost $0.50. If Samantha spent $2.50 and bought both kinds of books, how many of each did she buy?

33. A group of bicycles and wagons needs a total of 16 new tires. There are 6 vehicles in all. How many bicycles and wagons are there?

Unit Review

Enrichment

Egyptian Doubling

Ancient Egyptians used multiplication and addition to divide. Their method is called Egyptian Doubling.

Here is how to use this method to find $32 \div 4$.

Start with 1 group of 4.	1 group → 1	4
Continue doubling each column until you reach 32. The number in the left column is the quotient.	2	8
	4	16
$32 \div 4 = 8$	quotient → 8	32

Sometimes the method requires using addition and doubling. Here is how to use this method to find $96 \div 8$.

Start with one group of 8.	1		8	
Continue doubling each column. Look for numbers that add up to 96. Then find the sum of the corresponding numbers in the left column. This sum is the quotient.	2		16	
	4		32	
$96 \div 8 = 12$	8	**Think:** $\begin{array}{r} 4 \\ +8 \\ \hline 12 \end{array}$	64	**Think:** $\begin{array}{r} 32 \\ +64 \\ \hline 96 \end{array}$

Now you try! Use Egyptian Doubling to complete.

1. Find $24 \div 3$

1	3
2	■
4	■
8	■

2. Find $54 \div 9$

1	9
2	18
4	36
■ + ■ = ■	■ + ■ = ■

Use Egyptian Doubling to find the quotient.

3. $48 \div 8$ **4.** $35 \div 7$ **5.** $42 \div 7$ **6.** $36 \div 3$

7. Summarize Describe how to use Egyptian Doubling to find $108 \div 12$.

Performance Assessment

What Is the Correct Divisor?

For Earth Day last year, a town's schools raised money to plant new trees.

> Leewood School—42 trees
>
> Horizon School—18 trees
>
> Crossroads School—63 trees
>
> Pine Road School—54 trees
>
> Clark School—36 trees

Each school can plant its trees in groups of 6, 7, 8, or 9. The groups must be equal in size with no trees left.

Make a chart like the one below. Use it to show:

- how the trees for each school can be grouped.

- an equation that shows how each school grouped the trees they planted.

School	Number of Trees	Number of Groups	Number in Each Group	Equation
Leewood	42	7	6	$42 \div 7 = 6$

Tips For A Good Answer

- Show a completed chart.

- Show that you chose divisors that would result in equal groups with nothing left.

- Show the correct equation for each grouping.

You may want to save this work in your portfolio.

Assessment

TECHNOLOGY Link

Use Tables to Divide

Students must sign up if they want to help plan the carnival. Each planning group will have 6 students. How many groups will there be if 36 students sign up? If 42 students sign up? If 48 students sign up? If 54 students sign up?

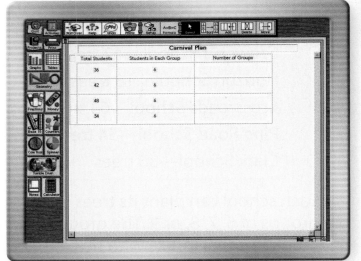

Math Tool Chest CD-ROM

You can use a spreadsheet table to divide.

- Click on the table key ▦ from the *Math Tool Chest* CD-ROM.

- Label the columns *Total Students, Students in Each Group,* and *Number of Groups.*

- In the column labeled *Total Students,* enter the number of students who signed up.

- In the column labeled *Students in Each Group,* enter 6.

- In the column labeled *Number of Groups,* enter a formula to divide *Total Students* by *Students in Each Group.*

How many groups will there be if 36 students sign up? If 42 students sign up? If 48 students sign up? If 54 students sign up?

Use the computer to find each set of quotients. Then complete each equation.

1. $18 \div 6 = $ ▮
   $24 \div 6 = $ ▮
   $36 \div 6 = $ ▮

2. $27 \div 9 = $ ▮
   $36 \div 9 = $ ▮
   $45 \div 9 = $ ▮

3. $56 \div 8 = $ ▮
   $64 \div 8 = $ ▮
   $72 \div 8 = $ ▮

4. $35 \div 7 = $ ▮
   $42 \div 7 = $ ▮
   $49 \div 7 = $ ▮

5. **Analyze** How does using the table help when you have to divide several times?

For more practice, use Math Traveler™.

Test-Taking Tips

For some tests you need to give a **written answer or show your work.** If you make a small mistake, you may get some points if you show you understand how to solve the problem.

Davon has to rent tables for his party for 22 people. He can rent tables that seat 4 people and 6 people. How many tables of each kind will he need if he does not want any empty seats? Show your work.

Show the work to prove your answer.

Try 2 and 3.

$2 \times 6 = 12$ ← 2 tables that seat 6 people each

$3 \times 4 = 12$ ← 3 tables that seat 4 people each

$12 + 12 = 24$ $24 > 22$

Try other numbers, 3 and 1.

$3 \times 6 = 18$ ← 3 tables that seat 6 people each

$1 \times 4 = 4$ ← 1 table that seats 4 people each

$18 + 4 = 22$ people

Davon will need 3 tables that seat 6 people and 1 table that seats 4 people.

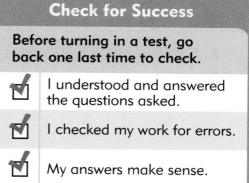

Check for Success

Before turning in a test, go back one last time to check.

✓ I understood and answered the questions asked.

✓ I checked my work for errors.

✓ My answers make sense.

Solve. Show your work.

1. Carl saw 5 people riding bicycles or tricycles. He saw a total of 12 wheels. How many bicycles and tricycles did he see?

2. Lena wants to buy nuts from a vending machine. She must use exact change. The nuts cost $0.85. List 3 different combinations of coins she could use.

3. Write a problem that uses multiplication. The answer must be "64 animals."

Test Prep

PART 1 • Multiple Choice

Choose the best answer.

1. Find $6,743 + 68 + 846$. (p. 76)
   - A. 6,895
   - B. 7,657
   - C. 8,269
   - D. 22,003

2. Ian puts 5 postcards on some album pages. He puts 4 cards on some other pages. He has filled the pages with 31 cards. On how many album pages did he put 5 postcards? (p. 328)
   - F. 3 pages
   - G. 4 pages
   - H. 5 pages
   - I. 6 pages

3. Aaron pays for an atlas with a ten-dollar bill. How much change does he get? (p. 14)

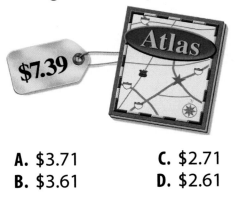

   $7.39 Atlas

   - A. $3.71
   - B. $3.61
   - C. $2.71
   - D. $2.61

4. Find the missing number. (p. 240)
   $$r \times 8 = 8$$
   - F. 0
   - G. 1
   - H. 8
   - I. 64

5. Rico walked along a nature trail 4 miles a day for 3 days. This is 5 miles more than Felix walked. How many miles did Felix walk? (p. 210)
   - A. 2 miles
   - B. 5 miles
   - C. 7 miles
   - D. 12 miles

6. Which number makes the equation true? (p. 256)
   $$(3 \times 4) \times 8 = 3 \times (n \times 8)$$
   - F. 4
   - G. 8
   - H. 12
   - I. 32

7. Alan works from 8:15 A.M. to 12:30 P.M. Jesse works from 12:30 P.M. to 4:30 P.M. How much longer does Alan work than Jesse? (p. 146)
   - A. 1 hour 15 minutes
   - B. 1 hour
   - C. 30 minutes
   - D. 15 minutes

8. Morgan saves $2.00 the first week. Each week after that she saves twice as much money as the week before. How much money did she save the fourth week? (p. 208)
   - F. $8.00
   - G. $16.00
   - H. $20.00
   - I. $24.00

Record your response on the answer sheet provided by your teacher or on a sheet of paper.

Use data from the pictograph for problems 9–12.

Third Grade Students' Votes on Favorite Summer Activity

Activity	Number of Votes
Swimming	☀☀☀☀☀☀☀
Camping	☀☀☀☀☀
Hiking	☀☀
Canoeing	☀☀☀☀
Fishing	☀☀☀

Key: Each ☀ equals 4 votes.

9. How many votes did the activity with the least number of votes get? (p. 166)

10. Which activity got 4 times as many votes as hiking? (p. 210)

11. One activity got 12 more votes than hiking. Which activity is this? (p. 52)

12. Suppose 8 students changed their votes from swimming to fishing. How would this change the pictograph? (p. 166)

THINK SOLVE EXPLAIN

13. Estimate the difference. (p. 116)
912 − 377

14. Which symbol belongs in the ● to make the equation true? (p. 332)
16 ● 8 = 2

15. Carl, Gary, Haley, and Li are in a bicycle race. Carl is ahead of Gary. Haley is right behind Carl. Li is ahead of Carl. Who is first in the race? (p. 150)

16. Find $6 \times 4 \times 2$. (p. 256)

17. Write the number 419,006 in expanded form. (p. 10)

18. Ana wants to buy 3 music CDs. She has $30. Each CD costs $12. Does she have enough money to buy 3 CDs? Explain. (p.254)

THINK SOLVE EXPLAIN

PART 3 • Extended Response

Record your answers on a sheet of paper. Show your work.

THINK SOLVE EXPLAIN

19. Tamika listed the ages of her closest friends: 7, 6, 8, 7, 7, 7, and 7. Find the mean, median, mode, and range of the ages. Show your work and explain the steps you take. (p.163)

Test Prep

What Do I Need to Know?

Ann collects bugs. She has 9 jars. Each jar has 4 bugs. How many bugs did she collect?

Multiplication: Patterns and Estimation

What Will I Learn?

In this chapter you will learn to

- multiply multiples of 10, 100, and 1,000
- estimate products
- use skills and strategies to solve problems

How Do I Read Math?

When you read a mathematics book, sometimes you read words and symbols, and sometimes you read only symbols.

All of these represent 100 multiplied by 5:

- **five times
  one hundred**

- $\begin{array}{r} 100 \\ \times \quad 5 \\ \hline \end{array}$

- **5 × 100**

VOCABULARY

- multiple
- regroup
- estimate
- front-end estimation
- round

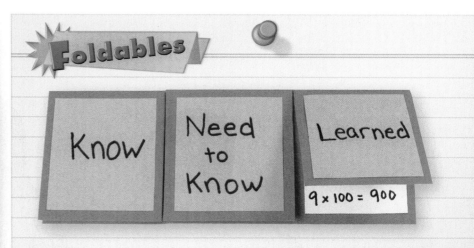

Foldables

Know   Need to Know   Learned

9 × 100 = 900

Use your Foldables to help you with chapter concepts.

1. Fold a large sheet of paper in half like a hot dog.
2. Fold the hot dog into 3 parts.
3. Cut along the folds on one side to form three tabs.
4. Label as shown. Record what you learn.

LOG ON www.mmhmath.com
For Real World Math Activities

17.1 Explore Multiplying Multiples of 10

Hands On Activity

You can use place-value models to multiply 4 × 30.

Use Models

STEP 1

Show 4 groups of 3 tens.

STEP 2

Regroup 10 tens into 1 hundred.

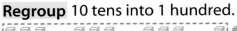

Think: 100 = 10 × 10

STEP 3

Count the total.

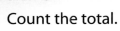

Explain Your Thinking

1. How many groups did you show?

2. How many are in each group?

3. How many tens are there in all?

4. Do you need to regroup? Why?

5. What is the total?

Technology Link

Use place-value models from **Math Tool Chest** to explore multiplying multiples of 10.

Here is how to find products of **multiples** of 10.

Find: 2 × 40

Let's see how to connect models to paper and pencil.

Make Connections

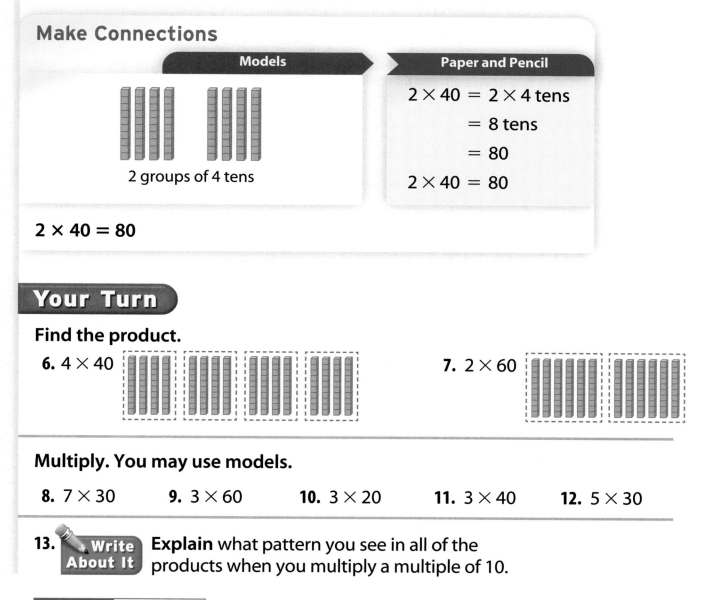

Models

2 groups of 4 tens

Paper and Pencil

2 × 40 = 2 × 4 tens

= 8 tens

= 80

2 × 40 = 80

2 × 40 = 80

Your Turn

Find the product.

6. 4 × 40

7. 2 × 60

Multiply. You may use models.

8. 7 × 30   9. 3 × 60   10. 3 × 20   11. 3 × 40   12. 5 × 30

13. **Write About It** **Explain** what pattern you see in all of the products when you multiply a multiple of 10.

17.2 Algebra: Multiplication Patterns

Learn

Many people collect valuable dolls. A collector has 4 dolls worth $100 each. How much would it cost to buy this collector's set of dolls?

Find: $4 \times \$100$

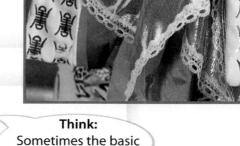

Use Facts and Patterns

$4 \times 1 = 4$

$4 \times 10 = 40$

$4 \times 100 = 400$

> **Think:**
> 4×1 ten $= 4$ tens
> 4×1 hundred $= 4$ hundreds

The collection is worth $400.

More Examples

$9 \times 7 = 63$

$9 \times 70 = 630$

$9 \times 700 = 6,300$

$6 \times 5 = 30$

$6 \times 50 = 300$

$6 \times 500 = 3,000$

> **Think:**
> Sometimes the basic fact has a zero.

Try It Write the number that makes each sentence true.

1. $2 \times 3 = n$
$2 \times 30 = m$
$2 \times 300 = p$

2. $3 \times 6 = y$
$t \times 60 = 180$
$3 \times w = 1,800$

3. $5 \times f = 40$
$5 \times g = 400$
$h \times 800 = 4,000$

Multiply. Use mental math.

4. 8×50

5. 7×300

6. 7×600

7. $3 \times 3,000$

8. **Write About It** **Explain** how to find 7×200.

Practice and Problem Solving

Write the number that makes each sentence true.

9. $4 \times 5 = n$
   $4 \times m = 200$
   $p \times 500 = 2,000$
   $4 \times 5,000 = q$

10. $8 \times 4 = a$
    $8 \times b = 320$
    $8 \times 400 = c$
    $8 \times d = 32,000$

11. $7 \times r = 49$
    $7 \times 70 = s$
    $7 \times t = 4,900$
    $7 \times 7,000 = v$

★**12.** $8 \times (y \times 100) = 3,200$

★**13.** $3 \times (w \times 1,000) = 18,000$

Multiply. Use mental math.

14. 3×80
15. 8×40
16. 70×7
17. 9×30
18. 2×400

19. 500×8
20. 500×7
21. $7 \times 1,000$
22. $5,000 \times 4$
23. $3,000 \times 2$

Solve.

24. A store wants to buy six new collectible dolls. The store will pay the price shown on the right for each doll. How much will the store pay for the dolls?

$40.00

25. **Analyze** Which basic fact will you use to multiply $8 \times 5,000$ mentally?

THINK
SOLVE
EXPLAIN

26. ✎ **Write a problem** multiplying multiples of 10. Solve it. Ask others to solve it.

Spiral Review and Test Prep

27. Jenna has 8 more mystery books than animal books. She has 12 mystery books. How many animal books does she have? (p. 96)

    A. 2 books   **C.** 20 books

    B. 4 books   **D.** 40 books

28. Last month a bookstore sold 1,432 books. What is this number rounded to the nearest thousand? (p. 34)

    F. 2,000   **H.** 1,000

    G. 1,400   **I.** 900

29. $63 \div 7$ (p. 324)
30. 7×4 (p. 210)
31. $64 \div 8$ (p. 330)
32. $400 \div 10$ (p. 334)

Self-Check 9. 20; 50; 4; 20,000 14. 240

17.3 Estimate Products

Learn

Every year 42 basketball cards are made for every team. If José collects all the cards from his 9 favorite teams, about how many cards are in his collection?

VOCABULARY
estimate
front-end estimation
round

Estimate: 9 × 42

Use Rounding

STEP 1

Round the factor that is greater than 10.

9 × 42
↓   ↓
9 × 40

> Remember the rounding rule: 0–4 stay the same. 5–9, round up. Since the ones digit is less than 5, the tens digit stays the same.

STEP 2

Multiply mentally.

9 × 40 = 360

José has about 360 basketball cards.

Round to . . .

Nearest Hundred
Estimate: 3 × 431

3 × 431
↓   ↓
3 × 400 = 1,200

Nearest Thousand
Estimate: 8 × 5,623

8 × 5,623
↓   ↓
8 × 6,000 = 48,000

Abdul has 4 binders of baseball cards, each with 128 cards. About how many baseball cards does he have in all?

Estimate: 4 × 128

Use Front-End Estimation

Front-end estimation uses the "front" digit and zeros for the other digits to estimate.

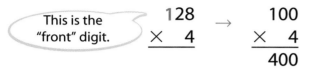

$$
\begin{array}{r} 128 \\ \times\ \ 4 \end{array} \quad \rightarrow \quad \begin{array}{r} 100 \\ \times\ \ 4 \\ \hline 400 \end{array}
$$

This is the "front" digit.

There are about 400 cards in Abdul's binders.

Estimate: 7 × $352

There's More Than One Way!

Use Front-End Estimation

7 × $352

↓   ↓

7 × $300 = $2,100

Use Rounding

7 × $352

↓   ↓

7 × $400 = $2,800

Round to the nearest hundred dollars.

Try It

Estimate each product. Tell how you estimate.

1.   32
   × 7

2.   16
   × 8

3.   123
   × 9

4.   921
   × 3

5.   7,040
   × 8

6.   862
   × 3

7. **Write About It** **Explain** which method is the better one to use when you estimate, front-end estimation or rounding.

Estimate each product. Tell how you estimate.

8. 475
× 9

9. 5,673
× 7

10. 8,765
× 6

11. 8,982
× 7

12. 1,984
× 4

13. $7 \times 8,123$ 14. $3 \times 1,839$ 15. $4 \times 5,290$ 16. $9 \times 1,645$ 17. $9 \times \$641$

18. $8 \times 5,322$ 19. 7×169 20. $8 \times \$78$ 21. $3 \times \$988$ 22. $4 \times \$897$

ⓧ **Algebra Estimate. Write > or < to make each sentence true.**

23. 3×57 ● 210

24. 7×84 ● 560

25. 5×32 ● 200

★26. 7×908 ● 9×778

★27. 8×712 ● 6×829

★28. 7×494 ● 5×328

Solve.

THINK
SOLVE
EXPLAIN

29. **Make It Right** Kelly estimated 4×348. Tell what mistake she made. Explain how to correct it.

348 → 300
× 4 → × 4
1,600

THINK
SOLVE
EXPLAIN

30. **Write About It** **Generalize** how to use basic facts to help you estimate products.

Link to SOCIAL STUDIES ★

Lotta Sjolin of Sweden has a large collection of parking meters. She collected 292 meters from 1989 to 1998.

31. Ove Nordstrom of Sweden has about 12 times more piggy banks than Lotta Sjolin has parking meters. About how many piggy banks does Ove have?

Spiral Review and Test Prep

32. Greg has 72 beads to share equally with 8 friends. How many beads does each person get? (p. 330)
    A. 6 beads   C. 8 beads
    B. 7 beads   D. 10 beads

33. Which is equal to 6×6? (p. 234)
    F. $36 \div 6$ H. $6 + 6$
    G. 12×3 I. 8×4

34. $200 \div 10$ (p. 334)

35. $\$7.21 - \$2.34$ (p. 120)

36. $72 \div 8$ (p. 330)

Extra Practice page 378, Set C

Problem Solving: Reading for Math

FABULOUS FROGS

Sheila Crown is known as the Frog Lady of England—and the world! That's because she has the world's largest collection of frogs. Sheila's frogs croak and jump, but they're not alive. Her collection is made up of more than 10,500 frog-shaped items, such as magnets, stuffed animals, statues, jewelry, and more. The collection landed Sheila a spot in the 2002 *Guinness Book of World Records.*

How long did it take her to collect the frogs? She's been collecting since 1979—and has no plans to stop. Sheila's collection got so huge that she bought a house to keep it in. There she opened the Frogs Galore Museum. People can visit and have a hopping-good time!

Sheila's not the only one crazy for collecting. Take a look at the chart on the right for some other unusual collections.

A small part of Sheila Crown's collection.

Problem Solving

Reading Skill **Make Judgments** Why does it take a long time to build a collection?

1. If Sheila adds 22 frogs to her collection each month, about how many more frogs will she have in 9 months?

2. About how many more neckties are there than coffee mugs?

Amazing Collections

Tom Holmes
11,650 neckties

Kurt Meadows
24,810 key chains

Ted Hoz
69,384 golf balls

Andre Ludwick
505 nail clippers

Marlene Williamson
3,300 coffee mugs

Source: *Guinness Book of World Records*

17.4 Problem Solving: Skill
Find an Estimate or Exact Answer

Read

Matt collects shells. His uncle gives him 6 bags of shells. Each bag has 24 shells. Did Matt's uncle give him more than 100 shells?

- **What do you know?**
  Matt has 6 bags of shells; each bag has 24 shells.

- **What do you need to find?**
  About how many shells are in all 6 bags.

Plan

Sometimes you need to find an exact answer to solve problems. For example, if Matt wanted to know the total number of shells in his collection, he would multiply 6×24 to get an exact answer.

Other times an estimate is enough. Matt wants to know *about* how many shells he has, so he will need to estimate 6×24.

Matt needs to know if the product is greater than a given number. Try an estimate.

Solve

You can round to estimate the product.

$$6 \quad \times \quad 24$$
$$\downarrow \qquad\qquad \downarrow$$
$$6 \quad \times \quad 20 \quad = 120 \qquad 120 > 100$$

Matt's uncle gave him more than 100 shells.

Look Back

Is your answer reasonable? Explain.

1.  **Explain** why an estimate was all that was needed to solve this problem.

376

Practice

Solve. Tell if you found an estimate or exact answer.

2. Cora has 3 bags of shells. Each bag has 98 shells. Does she have over 300 shells in the bags?

3. Trey has 6 jars of shells. Each jar has 12 shells. How many shells are in the jars?

Mixed Strategy Review

4. Kenesha gives away 15 shells. She shares them equally among 5 friends. How many shells does each friend get?

5. Marisol has a bag with dimes and quarters. There are 3 times as many quarters as dimes. There are 28 coins in all. How many of each coin does Marisol have?

Choose a Strategy

- Logical Reasoning
- Draw a Picture or Diagram
- Make a Graph
- Act It Out
- Make a Table or List
- Find a Pattern
- Guess and Check
- Write an Equation
- Work Backward
- Solve a Simpler Problem

Use data from the list for problems 6–13.

6. Are there more or less than 140 nickels in Cody's album?

7. What is the total amount of money on 1 page of Scott's album?

8. About how many quarters are in Pauline's album?

9. About how many more coins does Scott have than Cody?

Coin Collectors Club		
Member	Number of Pages in an Album	Coins on Each Page
Cody	7	22 nickels
Mavis	8	32 dimes
Pauline	5	18 quarters
Scott	9	24 nickels
James	6	34 pennies

10. Erin says that James has fewer than 180 coins. Is she correct? Why?

11. **Write a problem** using the data from the list. Solve it. Ask others to solve it.

★ **12.** What is the total amount of money in Mavis's album?

13. About how many coins do all the collectors have in all?

Problem Solving

Extra Practice

Set A Multiply. (pp. 368–369)

1. 7×60 2. 5×30 3. 8×40 4. 5×70 5. 8×70

6. 4×50 7. 9×30 8. 5×50 9. 9×50 10. 4×70

11. $\begin{array}{r} 60 \\ \times 3 \\ \hline \end{array}$ 12. $\begin{array}{r} 50 \\ \times 6 \\ \hline \end{array}$ 13. $\begin{array}{r} 40 \\ \times 4 \\ \hline \end{array}$ 14. $\begin{array}{r} 60 \\ \times 5 \\ \hline \end{array}$ 15. $\begin{array}{r} 40 \\ \times 9 \\ \hline \end{array}$

Set B Write the number that makes each sentence true. (pp. 370–371)

16.
$8 \times 5 = a$
$8 \times 50 = b$
$8 \times 500 = c$
$8 \times 5,000 = d$

17.
$6 \times 7 = f$
$6 \times 70 = g$
$6 \times h = 4,200$
$6 \times 7,000 = j$

18.
$4 \times 2 = m$
$4 \times 20 = n$
$4 \times 200 = p$
$r \times 2,000 = 8,000$

Set C Estimate each product. (pp. 372–374)

19. $\begin{array}{r} \$852 \\ \times\ \ 3 \\ \hline \end{array}$ 20. $\begin{array}{r} 42 \\ \times\ 6 \\ \hline \end{array}$ 21. $\begin{array}{r} 679 \\ \times\ \ 8 \\ \hline \end{array}$ 22. $\begin{array}{r} 39 \\ \times\ 4 \\ \hline \end{array}$ 23. $\begin{array}{r} 405 \\ \times\ \ 7 \\ \hline \end{array}$

24. $\begin{array}{r} 91 \\ \times\ 5 \\ \hline \end{array}$ 25. $\begin{array}{r} 12 \\ \times\ 3 \\ \hline \end{array}$ 26. $\begin{array}{r} 49 \\ \times\ 6 \\ \hline \end{array}$ 27. $\begin{array}{r} 69 \\ \times\ 7 \\ \hline \end{array}$ 28. $\begin{array}{r} 46 \\ \times\ 8 \\ \hline \end{array}$

29. 3×38 30. 8×59 31. $2 \times \$88$ 32. 4×156 33. 6×572

34. 9×363 35. $7 \times \$412$ 36. 5×255 37. $7 \times \$902$ 38. 3×265

Set D Solve. (pp. 376–377)

39. Cindy has 5 bags of pennies. Each bag holds 87 coins. Does she have over 500 coins in the bags?

40. Roberto has 8 jars of coins. Each jar has 40 coins. How many coins does Roberto have?

41. Rebecca has 3 bags of shells. Each bag holds 45 shells. Does she have over 150 shells in the bags?

42. Jonathon has 8 jars of shells. Each jar has 12 shells. How many shells does Jonathon have?

LOG ON www.mmhmath.com
For more practice and Chapter Self-Check Test

Review/Test

Write the number that makes each sentence true.

1. $8 \times 6 = a$
$8 \times 60 = b$
$8 \times 600 = c$
$8 \times 6,000 = d$

2. $6 \times e = 36$
$g \times 60 = 360$
$6 \times 600 = h$
$6 \times j = 36,000$

3. $m \times 5 = 20$
$4 \times n = 200$
$4 \times 500 = p$
$r \times 5,000 = 20,000$

Multiply. Use mental math.

4. 7×40

5. 6×80

6. $5 \times 4,000$

7. 7×900

8.
$$\begin{array}{r} 500 \\ \times \quad 9 \\ \hline \end{array}$$

9.
$$\begin{array}{r} 600 \\ \times \quad 3 \\ \hline \end{array}$$

10.
$$\begin{array}{r} 8,000 \\ \times \quad 2 \\ \hline \end{array}$$

11.
$$\begin{array}{r} 3,000 \\ \times \quad 6 \\ \hline \end{array}$$

Estimate each product.

12. 3×571

13. 6×89

14. 2×834

15. 4×721

16. 3×679

17. $9 \times 4,391$

18. $6 \times 4,234$

Solve.

19. You have saved $120 to buy gems for your collection. The gems you want are $42 each. Can you buy 3 of them? Why or why not?

20. **Write About It** **Analyze** How can you use estimation to decide if 7×78 is greater than or less than 560?

Do I Need Help?

Exercises	Review Concepts	Use Extra Practice Set
1–3	pp. 370–371	Set B
4–11	pp. 368–369	Sets A and B
12–18	pp. 372–374	Set C
19–20	pp. 376–377	Set D

 **Foldables** Use your Foldables to help you review.

Assessment

What Do I Need to Know?

Jared displays 20 shells in a case. There are 8 cases. How many shells does he have in all?

Multiply by 1-Digit Numbers

What Will I Learn?

In this chapter you will learn to

- multiply multi-digit numbers
- use skills and strategies to solve problems

How Do I Read Math?

When you read a mathematics book, sometimes you read words and symbols, and sometimes you read only symbols.

All of these represent 126 multiplied by 8:

- **eight times one hundred twenty-six**

- **126**
  × 8

- **8 × 126**

VOCABULARY

- Distributive Property

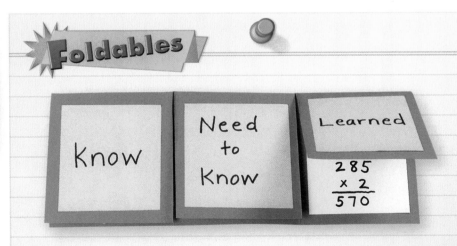

Use your Foldables to help you with chapter concepts.

1. Fold a large sheet of paper in half like a hot dog.
2. Fold the hot dog into 3 parts.
3. Cut along the folds on one side to make three tabs.
4. Label as shown. Record what you learn.

18.1 Explore Multiplying 2-Digit Numbers

Hands On Activity

You can use place–value models to explore 3×14.

You Will Need
- place-value models

Use Models

STEP 1

Show 3 groups. In each group, use 1 ten and 4 ones to show 14.

STEP 2

Combine the tens. Combine the ones.

Regroup 12 ones as 1 ten and 2 ones.

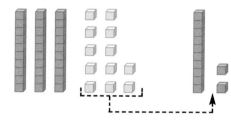

STEP 3

Count the total.

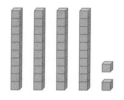

Explain Your Thinking

1. How did you model each factor?

2. Why did you regroup?

3. How many tens and ones are there after you regrouped?

4. What is 3 × 14?

5. **What If** You have 3 groups of 17. What would the product be?

Technology Link

Use the place–value tool in **Math Tool Chest** to multiply 2-digit numbers.

Your Turn

Solve. Then write a number sentence.

6.

7.

8.

9.

10.

11.

Use place-value models to multiply. Record your work.

12. 4 × 18   13. 2 × 23   14. 5 × 16   15. 6 × 21   16. 3 × 19

17.
$$\begin{array}{r} 19 \\ \times\,2 \\ \hline \end{array}$$

18.
$$\begin{array}{r} 24 \\ \times\,3 \\ \hline \end{array}$$

19.
$$\begin{array}{r} 13 \\ \times\,4 \\ \hline \end{array}$$

20.
$$\begin{array}{r} 19 \\ \times\,5 \\ \hline \end{array}$$

21.
$$\begin{array}{r} 17 \\ \times\,3 \\ \hline \end{array}$$

22.  **Write About It** **Explain** a method you can use to multiply a 2-digit number by a 1-digit number.

18.2 Multiply 2-Digit Numbers

Learn

You are going on a field trip with 3 people to collect rocks. Each person gets a kit with 13 tools. How many tools are there in all?

Find: 4 × 13
Estimate: $4 \times 10 = 40$

Let's see how to connect models to paper and pencil.

VOCABULARY
Distributive Property

Make Connections

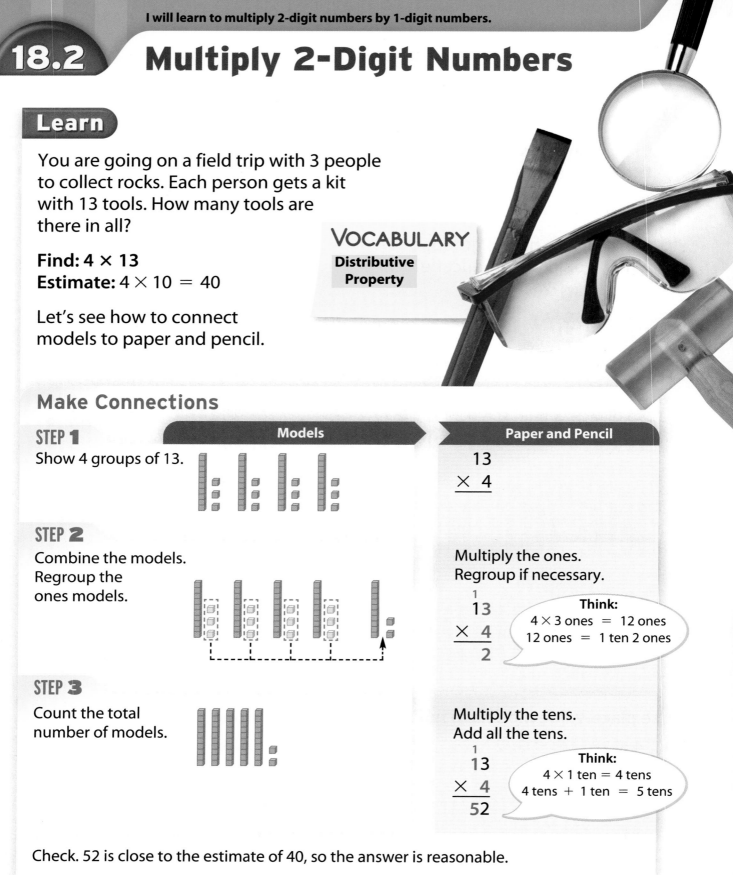

	Models	Paper and Pencil
STEP 1 Show 4 groups of 13.		13 × 4
STEP 2 Combine the models. Regroup the ones models.		Multiply the ones. Regroup if necessary. ¹ 13 × 4 = 2 **Think:** 4 × 3 ones = 12 ones; 12 ones = 1 ten 2 ones
STEP 3 Count the total number of models.		Multiply the tens. Add all the tens. ¹ 13 × 4 = 52 **Think:** 4 × 1 ten = 4 tens; 4 tens + 1 ten = 5 tens

Check. 52 is close to the estimate of 40, so the answer is reasonable.

There are 52 tools in all.

Your team meets 3 times a week to discuss the findings. Each meeting lasts 35 minutes. How many minutes does your team meet each week?

Find: 3 × 35   **Estimate:** $3 \times 40 = 120$

There's More Than One Way!

Use the Distributive Property

You can use the **Distributive Property** to find products.

$$\begin{aligned}
3 \times 35 &= 3 \times (30 + 5) \\
&= (3 \times 30) + (3 \times 5) \\
&= \quad 90 \quad + \quad 15 \\
&= 105
\end{aligned}$$

Think: $35 = 30 + 5$
Think: Multiply each addend by 3.

Use Paper and Pencil

STEP 1

Multiply the ones.
Regroup if necessary.

$$\begin{array}{r} \overset{1}{3}5 \\ \times\ 3 \\ \hline 5 \end{array}$$

Think: 3×5 ones $= 15$ ones
15 ones $= 1$ ten 5 ones

STEP 2

Multiply the tens.
Add all the tens.

$$\begin{array}{r} \overset{1}{3}5 \\ \times\ 3 \\ \hline 105 \end{array}$$

Think: 3×3 tens $= 9$ tens
9 tens $+ 1$ ten $= 10$ tens
10 tens $= 1$ hundred $+ 0$ tens

Check. 105 is close to the estimate of 120, so the answer is reasonable.
Your team meets 105 minutes each week.

Find: 6 × $0.23

> You can also use a calculator.

Multiply Money

Multiply money as you would whole numbers. Write the dollar sign and the decimal point in the product.

$$\begin{array}{r} \overset{1\ \ 1}{\$0.23} \\ \times\ \quad 6 \\ \hline \$1.38 \end{array}$$

Try It Multiply. Estimate to check for reasonableness.

1. 3×39 **2.** 4×62 **3.** 6×27 **4.** $4 \times \$0.72$ **5.** 4×51

6. **Write About It** **Explain** how you can tell if you will need to regroup to solve a multiplication problem.

Practice and Problem Solving

Multiply.

7. $\begin{array}{r} 28 \\ \times\ 4 \\ \hline \end{array}$
8. $\begin{array}{r} \$0.42 \\ \times\quad 2 \\ \hline \end{array}$
9. $\begin{array}{r} 26 \\ \times\ 7 \\ \hline \end{array}$
10. $\begin{array}{r} \$0.71 \\ \times\quad 8 \\ \hline \end{array}$
11. $\begin{array}{r} 58 \\ \times\ 3 \\ \hline \end{array}$

12. $8 \times \$49$
13. 6×32
14. 4×55
15. $3 \times \$0.57$

16. 5×98
★17. $(6 \times 7) \times 4$
★18. $(9 \times 9) \times 8$
★19. $(9 \times 6) \times 5$

Ⓧ **Algebra Match the multiplication with a product in the box.**

Products
612   78   336

20. 4×84
21. 3×26
22. 9×68

Solve

23. **Measurement** Each rock in Paul's rock collection weighs about 3 ounces. If he has 48 rocks in his collection, about how many ounces do all of the rocks weigh?

24. **Make It Right** Nina multiplied 5×67 on the board. What mistake did she make? Show how to solve it.

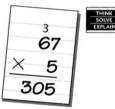

$\begin{array}{r} 3 \\ 67 \\ \times\quad 5 \\ \hline 305 \end{array}$

THINK
SOLVE
EXPLAIN

25. Jane has 56 rocks in her collection. She has them in display boxes. Each box holds 8 rocks. How many boxes does she have filled?

26. **Write About It** How did you decide which product went with which problems in 20–22?

THINK
SOLVE
EXPLAIN

Spiral Review and Test Prep

27. Bert keeps his 28 rocks in small boxes. One box holds 4 rocks, and all the other boxes hold 8. How many boxes does he have that hold 8 rocks? (p. 328)

    A. 2 boxes   **C.** 4 boxes

    B. 3 boxes   **D.** 5 boxes

28. Steve starts with 32 rocks in his collection. He finds 8 more rocks. Which equation shows how many rocks Steve has now? (p. 118)

    F. $32 - 8 = 24$ **H.** $32 \div 8 = 4$

    G. $32 + 8 = 40$ **I.** $32 \times 8 = 256$

Find each missing number.

29. $8 \times n = 40$ (p. 240)
30. $p \times 6 = 42$ (p. 240)
31. $56 \div b = 8$ (p. 324)

Extra Practice   page 396, Set A

Writing for Math

A hamburger at Best Burgers costs $3.25. Is $10.00 enough to buy 3 of them? If so, how much change will you get? Explain.

$3.25

Anita's Response

✓ **THINK** Multiply to find the cost of 3 hamburgers. If it is less than $10.00, find the change.

✓ **SOLVE** 3 × $3.25 = $9.75
$10.00 − $9.75 = $0.25
$10.00 is enough to buy 3 hamburgers with $0.25 change.
Check: $10.00 − $3.25 = $6.75
$6.75 − $3.25 = $3.50
$3.50 − $3.25 = $0.25

✓ **EXPLAIN** The hamburgers cost $3.25 each. I multiply $3.25 by 3. The product is $9.75. I subtract $9.75 from $10.00. The difference is $0.25, so I get $0.25 change.

To check, I subtract $3.25 from $10.00 three times. The final difference is $0.25, which is the change from $10.00. So my answer makes sense.

Teacher's Comments

← Anita explains how she will use what she knows to solve the problem.

← Anita shows her work.

← Anita describes each solution step in complete sentences. She uses appropriate math terms such as **multiply, product, subtract,** and **difference.**

← Anita checks her answer for accuracy and reasonableness.

THINK
SOLVE
EXPLAIN

Solve. Show your work. Use Anita's work as a guide.

1. How much change will Wes get if he buys 3 books for $6.49 each and pays with a $20.00 bill?

2. Jill has 42 caps. Josh has 3 times as many caps as Jill. How many caps does Josh have?

18.3 Problem Solving: Strategy
Make a Graph

Read

A magazine asked its readers what they like to collect. What type of graph can you make to show the most popular type of collection?

- **What do you know?**
  How many people have each type of collection

- **What do you need to find?**
  What kind of graph will help compare the data

Collection	Number of Collectors
Stamps	66
Coins	132
Comics	144
Trains	42
Rocks	120
Dolls	132

Plan

You can make a graph to show the data. You can make a pictograph.

Solve

Make the pictograph. Then compare the number of symbols for each type of collection.

Comics have the most symbols so they are the most popular items to collect.

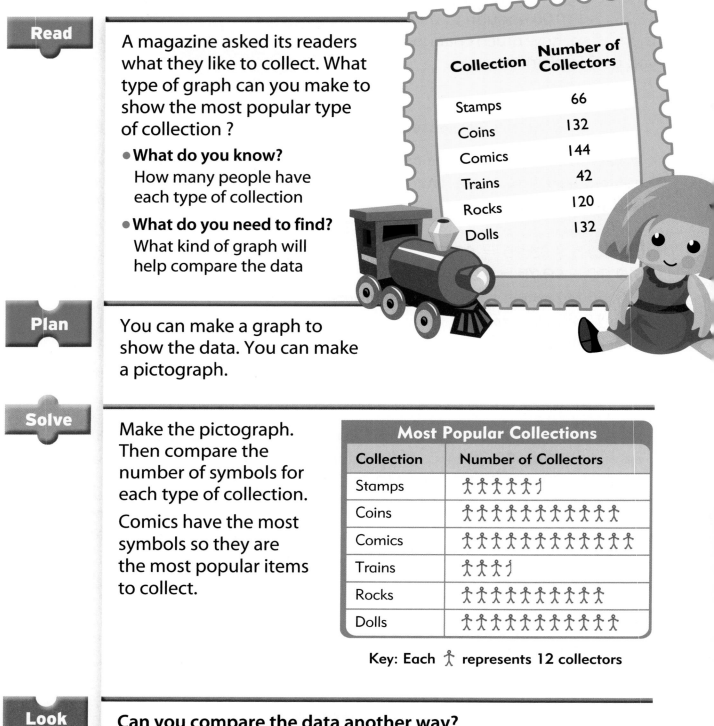

Most Popular Collections	
Collection	Number of Collectors
Stamps	𝅭𝅭𝅭𝅭𝅭𝅭
Coins	𝅭𝅭𝅭𝅭𝅭𝅭𝅭𝅭𝅭𝅭𝅭
Comics	𝅭𝅭𝅭𝅭𝅭𝅭𝅭𝅭𝅭𝅭𝅭𝅭
Trains	𝅭𝅭𝅭𝅭
Rocks	𝅭𝅭𝅭𝅭𝅭𝅭𝅭𝅭𝅭𝅭
Dolls	𝅭𝅭𝅭𝅭𝅭𝅭𝅭𝅭𝅭𝅭𝅭

Key: Each 👤 represents 12 collectors

Look Back

Can you compare the data another way?

1. **Write About It** **Explain** how it is easier to compare the data by looking at a graph instead of a table.

Use data from the table to solve problems 2–6.

2. Make a graph to show the data in the table.

3. Which collection is largest? smallest?

4. **What If** The student with the comic collection got 225 more comics at a yard sale. How would the graph change?

5. Find the range of the data.

Largest Collection in Our School	
Collection	Number of Items
Records	225
Toy Robots	75
Comics	175
Game Cards	350
Dolls	150

6. **Write a problem** using the data from the graph. Solve it. Ask others to solve it.

Mixed Strategy Review

7. Dan and Niko have collected 120 bean bag toys in all. Dan has twice as many as Niko. How many toys does each have?

8. Isaac wants to be at the collector convention when it opens at 9:00 A.M. It takes 50 minutes to drive there. What is the latest Isaac should leave his house?

9. Valerie's 2 most valuable baseball cards are worth $25.50 and $18.50. What is the total value of these 2 cards?

11. **Collect data** from the Internet about a collection. Write a problem based on the data. Solve it. Ask others to solve it.

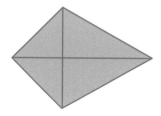

Choose a Strategy
- Logical Reasoning
- Draw a Picture or Diagram
- Make a Graph
- Act It Out
- Make a Table or List
- Find a Pattern
- Guess and Check
- Write an Equation
- Work Backward
- Solve a Simpler Problem

★ 10. **Spatial Reasoning** How many triangles are in the figure below?

Problem Solving

18.4 Multiply Greater Numbers

Learn

Rich has collected 172 different toys. He has 2 of each type of toy. How many toys does Rich have in all?

Find: 2 × 172
Estimate: 2 × 200 = 400

Use Paper and Pencil

STEP 1

Multiply the ones.
Regroup if necessary.

$$\begin{array}{r} 172 \\ \times\ \ 2 \\ \hline 4 \end{array}$$

Think:
2 × 2 ones = 4 ones

STEP 2

Multiply the tens.
Add all the tens.
Regroup if necessary.

$$\begin{array}{r} {}^{1}172 \\ \times\ \ 2 \\ \hline 44 \end{array}$$

Think:
2 × 7 tens = 14 tens
14 tens = 1 hundred 4 tens

STEP 3

Multiply the hundreds.
Add all the hundreds.
Regroup if necessary.

$$\begin{array}{r} {}^{1}172 \\ \times\ \ 2 \\ \hline 344 \end{array}$$

Think:
2 × 1 hundred = 2 hundreds
2 hundreds + 1 hundred = 3 hundreds

Check. 344 is close to the estimate of 400.
The answer is reasonable.

Rich has 344 toys in all.

You can also use a calculator.

Try It

Multiply. Estimate to check the reasonableness.

1. 7 × 162

2. 5 × 278

3. 9 × $50.03

4. 6 × 9,452

5. ✎ **Write About It** **Explain** how multiplying a 3-digit number is the same as multiplying a 4-digit number. Explain how it is different.

390

Practice and Problem Solving

Multiply. Estimate to check the reasonableness.

6. 285
    × 4

7. $236
    × 6

8. 5,087
    × 5

9. 7,950
    × 5

10. 8,445
    × 7

11. 3 × $5.12

12. 9 × $6.57

13. 2 × $97.80

14. 3 × $9,876

Use estimation to find which problems have products less than 1,500 or more than 50,000.

15. 7 × 197

16. 6 × 319

17. 4 × 9,876

18. 7 × 8,006

Solve.

THINK
SOLVE
EXPLAIN

19. **Compare** How is multiplying money like multiplying whole numbers? How is it different?

20. There are 1,245 items on each of 3 floors of a store. How many items are there in all?

★21. What is the mystery number? It is an even number. The number is greater than the product of 4 × 136 but less than the sum of 287 + 261.

Link to ART

Jim Henson's *The Muppet Show*, starring Kermit and Miss Piggy, started in 1976.

22. Jim Henson created Kermit in 1955. How old was Kermit when *The Muppet Show* was created?

Spiral Review and Test Prep

23. Mika went to the Museum of Art at 10:25 A.M. She stayed for $\frac{1}{2}$ hour. What time did she leave? (p. 146)

    A. 10:40 A.M.   C. 11:05 A.M.

    B. 10:55 A.M.   D. 11:35 A.M.

24. Which sign makes the equation true? (p. 204)
    $$12 \bullet 2 = 24$$

    F. ÷   H. +

    G. ×   I. −

25. 5 × 14 (p. 384)

26. 6 × 23 (p. 384)

27. 72 ÷ 8 (p. 330)

28. 72 − 14 (p. 106)

18.5 Choose a Computation Method

Learn

Owen has 225 stamps in each collector's book. He has 5 collector's books. How many stamps does Owen have all together?

Find: 5×225

Estimate: $5 \times 200 = 1,000$

There's More Than One Way!

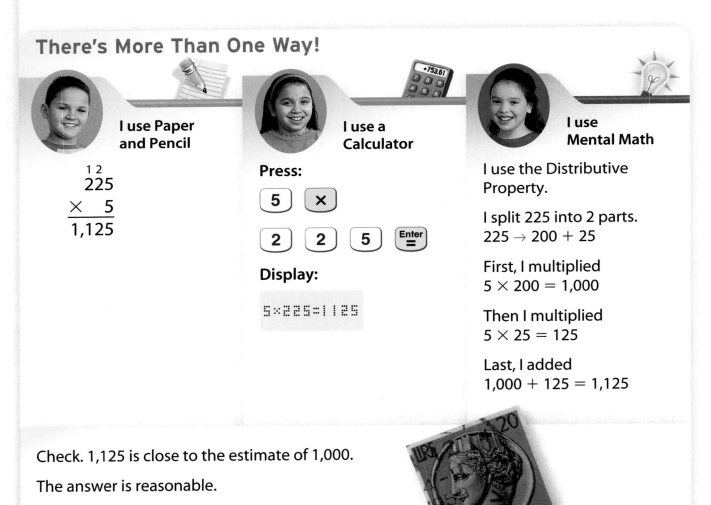

I use Paper and Pencil

$$\begin{array}{r} {}^{1\ 2} \\ 225 \\ \times\ \ \ 5 \\ \hline 1,125 \end{array}$$

I use a Calculator

Press:

| 5 | × |

| 2 | 2 | 5 | Enter = |

Display:

5×225=1125

I use Mental Math

I use the Distributive Property.

I split 225 into 2 parts.
$225 \rightarrow 200 + 25$

First, I multiplied
$5 \times 200 = 1,000$

Then I multiplied
$5 \times 25 = 125$

Last, I added
$1,000 + 125 = 1,125$

Check. 1,125 is close to the estimate of 1,000.

The answer is reasonable.

Owen has 1,125 stamps all together.

What If Owen had a stamp collector's book that had 8 stamps on each page. What is the total number of stamps in a 107-page collector's book?

Find: 8 × 107

Estimate: 8 × 100 = 800

There's More Than One Way!

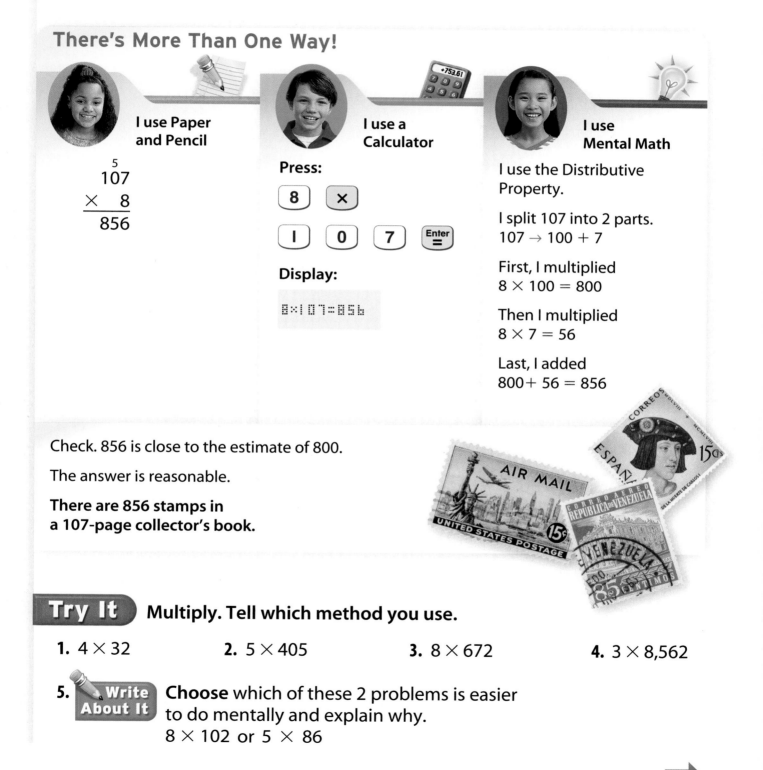

I use Paper and Pencil

$$\begin{array}{r} \overset{5}{107} \\ \times\ \ 8 \\ \hline 856 \end{array}$$

I use a Calculator

Press:

8 ×

1 0 7 Enter =

Display:

8×107=856

I use Mental Math

I use the Distributive Property.

I split 107 into 2 parts.
107 → 100 + 7

First, I multiplied
8 × 100 = 800

Then I multiplied
8 × 7 = 56

Last, I added
800 + 56 = 856

Check. 856 is close to the estimate of 800.

The answer is reasonable.

There are 856 stamps in a 107-page collector's book.

Try It Multiply. Tell which method you use.

1. 4 × 32

2. 5 × 405

3. 8 × 672

4. 3 × 8,562

5. **Write About It** **Choose** which of these 2 problems is easier to do mentally and explain why.
8 × 102 or 5 × 86

Practice and Problem Solving

Pencil/Paper   Calculator   Mental Math

Multiply. Tell which method you use.

6. 8×42

7. 3×615

8. 7×243

9. 2×809

10. 4×425

11. 9×398

12. $5 \times 1,208$

13. $6 \times 3,871$

★14. $3 \times 12,978$

★15. $7 \times 35,000$

★16. $5 \times 45,876$

★17. $4 \times 72,587$

ⓧ **Algebra** Compare. Write $<$ or $>$.

18. 6×34 ⚫ 42×7

19. 2×144 ⚫ 3×78

★20. $6 \times 1,078$ ⚫ $7 \times 1,046$

Solve.

THINK SOLVE EXPLAIN
21. **Compare** When is it easier to use mental math to solve a problem than using paper and pencil?

22. ✏️ **Write a problem** using multiplication of a 3-digit number that is easily solved using mental math.

23. There are 8 large stamps on each page of Hannah's collector's book. She has 64 stamps. How many pages are in the book?

24. Each volunteer donates 3 hours each week. There are 245 volunteers. What is the total number of hours donated by volunteers each week?

THINK SOLVE EXPLAIN
25. **Make It Right** Cathy multiplied 6×103. Tell what mistake she made. Explain how to correct it.

6×103
$(6 \times 100) + (3 \times 100)$
$600 + 300 = 900$
$6 \times 103 = 900$

Spiral Review and Test Prep

26. What is the rule for this function table? (p. 210)

Rule:				
Input	2	4	6	8
Output	6	12	18	24

A. Add 3.

B. Subtract 3.

C. Multiply by 3.

D. Divide by 3.

What is the value of the underlined digit? (p. 6)

27. 2,<u>7</u>08

28. <u>8</u>,673

29. 23,9<u>4</u>1

30. 5,90<u>2</u>

Practice at School ★ Practice at Home

DON'T GO OVER 500

Arrange number cards to get the factors.

Ready

Players: 2 to 6
You Will Need: Digit Deck,
paper and pencil

GO!

▶ The first player draws 3 cards.

▶ Each player arranges those
digits into any 2-digit by
1-digit multiplication problem.

▶ Each player performs the
multiplication on the left side
of the paper. Record the
product on the right side.

▶ The next player draws 3 more
cards and all players repeat
the steps above. Then add
the products from the
2 rounds.

▶ After a round, each player
decides to "continue" or
"stop." When a player
decides to stop, he circles
the final sum of the
products on his paper.

Set

Fold the paper in half. Label the
top left side "multiplication,"
the top right side "addition of
products."

▶ When all players have stopped,
the player closest to 500
without going over is the
winner.

Chapter 18

Extra Practice

Set A Multiply. (pp. 384–386)

1.	41	2.	$0.38	3.	67	4.	$0.54	5.	83
	× 5		× 2		× 7		× 9		× 4

6.	$0.55	7.	32	8.	43	9.	$68	10.	97
	× 9		× 6		× 5		× 7		× 8

Set B Use data from the table for problems 11–13. (pp. 388–389)

11. Make a graph to show the data in the table.

12. How many more items are in the largest group of autographs than in the next largest group?

13. What If Jenny got 5 more men writers' autographs at a book fair. How would the graph change?

Jenny's Autograph Collection	
Type of Autographs	**Number of Autographs**
Women writers	5
Men writers	16
Women actors	11
Men actors	20
Women athletes	13
Men athletes	9

Set C Multiply. (pp. 390–391)

14.	143	15.	$507	16.	346	17.	$4.25	18.	287
	× 2		× 3		× 9		× 4		× 8

19.	2,481	20.	$5,469	21.	$66.65	22.	3,406	23.	7,008
	× 4		× 3		× 9		× 8		× 2

Set D Multiply. Tell which method you used. (pp. 392–394)

24.	56	25.	712	26.	67	27.	1,200
	× 8		× 7		× 6		× 5

28.	168	29.	79	30.	616	31.	1,379
	× 4		× 3		× 9		× 4

LOG ON www.mmhmath.com
For more practice and Chapter Self-Check Test

Review/Test

Multiply.

1. 9×42 2. $5 \times \$63$ 3. 2×89 4. 4×47

5. $6 \times 4{,}000$ 6. $8 \times 6{,}204$ 7. $7 \times 1{,}740$ 8. $3 \times 3{,}009$

9. $9 \times \$4.78$ 10. $5 \times \$0.27$ 11. $8 \times \$9.05$ 12. $6 \times \$83.19$

Multiply. Tell which method you use.

13. 4×51 14. 5×426 15. 8×150 16. $3 \times 5{,}735$

Use data from the table to solve problems 17–18.

Paula's Marble Collection						
Color	Blue	Green	Silver	Black	Yellow	Red
Number of Items	15	12	14	21	7	18

17. Make a graph to show the data in the table.

18. Which color of marbles does Paula have the most of? The least?

19. Lita paid $15.75 for each of 2 dolls. How much did both dolls cost all together?

20. **Write About It** **Analyze** How can estimation help you decide if the exact product for $7 \times \$74.65$ is greater or less than $600?

Do I Need Help?

Exercises	Review Concepts	Use Extra Practice Set
1–4	pp. 382–386	Set A
5–12, 19	pp. 390–391	Set C
13–16, 20	pp. 392–394	Set D
17–18	pp. 388–389	Set B

Foldables Use your Foldables to help you review.

Decision Making

"**W**ow!" Ben thought as he arrived at the Comic Book Trading Show. "I have $25 to spend. What should I buy?"

You Decide!

Which comic books should he buy?

OPTION 1
Super Hero Comics
$1.25 each or 3 comics for $3.50

OPTION 2
Adventure Comics
Bag-o-comics
5 comics in a bag
2 bags in a package
$15.50 for a package

OPTION 3
Outer Space Stories
$1.55 each comic
Buy 6, pay for 5
Buy 9, pay for 8

Read for Understanding

1. If you want to buy only 1 comic book, which kind can you not buy? Why?

2. How much more does 1 Outer Space comic book cost than 1 Super Hero comic book?

3. How many comic books do you get in a package of Adventure Comics?

4. How much do 9 Outer Space comic books cost?

5. How much do 6 Outer Space comic books cost?

6. How much do 6 Super Hero Comics cost?

Make Decisions

7. How much would you pay for 10 Outer Space comic books?

8. How much more do 6 Outer Space comics cost than 6 Super Hero Comics?

9. Write a list of things Ben should know before he decides which comic books to buy.

10. Which comic books should Ben buy if he wants to spend only $5.00 of his money? Why?

11. How many sets of 3 comic books will Ben buy if he decides to buy 9 Super Hero Comic books? How much will it cost him? How can you tell?

12. What If Ben decides to buy a package of Adventure comic books. He pays with a twenty-dollar bill. How much change does he get?

13. What else do you need to consider when making choices of which comic books to buy?

Your Decision!

THINK
SOLVE
EXPLAIN

Which comic books should Ben buy? How many of each? How much money will he have left?

Unit Study Guide and Review

Vocabulary

Complete. Use a word from the list.

1. If you do not need an exact answer, you can round to find an _____.

2. To find 8×35, you can find $(8 \times 30) + (8 \times 5)$. This method uses the _____.

3. Using _____ to estimate 6×259, you multiply 6×200.

> **VOCABULARY**
> Distributive Property
> estimate
> front-end estimation
> round

Skills and Applications

Multiply multiples of 10, 100, and 1,000. (pp. 368–371)

Multiply: 6×700
Use mental math.

Solution
Use basic multiplication facts and patterns.

$6 \times 7 = 42$
$6 \times 70 = 420$
$6 \times 700 = 4{,}200$

Think:
6×7 tens $= 42$ tens
6×7 hundreds $= 42$ hundreds

Multiply. Use mental math.

4. 5×80
5. 4×200
6. $3 \times 4{,}000$
7. $7 \times 5{,}000$
8. 6×900
9. $9 \times 8{,}000$
10. 8×600
11. $5 \times 3{,}000$

Estimate products. (pp. 372–374)

Estimate: 9×78

Solution
Round the factor that is greater than 10. Then multiply mentally.
9×78 Round to the nearest ten.
↓   ↓
$9 \times 80 = 720$
So 9×78 is about 720.

Estimate each product.

12. 4×36
13. 7×91
14. 5×432
15. 8×497
16. $3 \times \$569$
17. $9 \times \$712$
18. $6 \times \$2{,}149$
19. $2 \times \$7{,}832$
20. $6 \times \$726$
21. 3×921

Foldables Use your Foldables to help you review.

Multiply multi-digit numbers. (pp. 382–386, 390–391)

Multiply: 3 × 1,568

Solution
Multiply each place.
Regroup and add if necessary.

$$\begin{array}{r} {\scriptstyle 1\,2\,2} \\ 1{,}568 \\ \times \quad\ 3 \\ \hline 4{,}704 \end{array}$$

Multiply.

22. 4 × 5,307

23. 7 × 2,786

24. 9 × 6,094

25. 3 × $52.69

26. 8 × $66.82

27. 6 × $91.75

28. 5 × $36.43

29. 7 × 4,372

Use skills and strategies to solve problems. (pp. 376–377, 388–389)

Make a graph to show the data in the table.

Collections	Number of Items
Stickers	300
Stuffed Animals	50
Compact Discs	150

Solution
Make a pictograph.

Popular Collections	
Collection	Number of Items
Stickers	☺ ☺ ☺ ☺ ☺ ☺
Stuffed Animals	☺
Compact Discs	☺ ☺ ☺

Key: Each ☺ equals 50 items

Which collection is the largest?
Stickers is the largest collection.

Use data from the table to solve problems 30–32.

Club	Number of Students
Art	33
Chess	12
Computer	24
Music	26
Sports	36

30. Make a graph to show the data in the table.

31. Which club has the greatest number of students?

32. Which club has the least number of students?

33. Janine has 300 stamps. She bought 4 stamp-collecting albums to display her stamps. Each can hold 68 stamps. Did she buy enough albums? Explain.

Enrichment

Hindu Lattice

Here is another way to multiply. Long ago, the Hindu mathematicians in India used this method to multiply large numbers. You can use grid paper to try Hindu Lattice Multiplication.

Find: 7 × 32

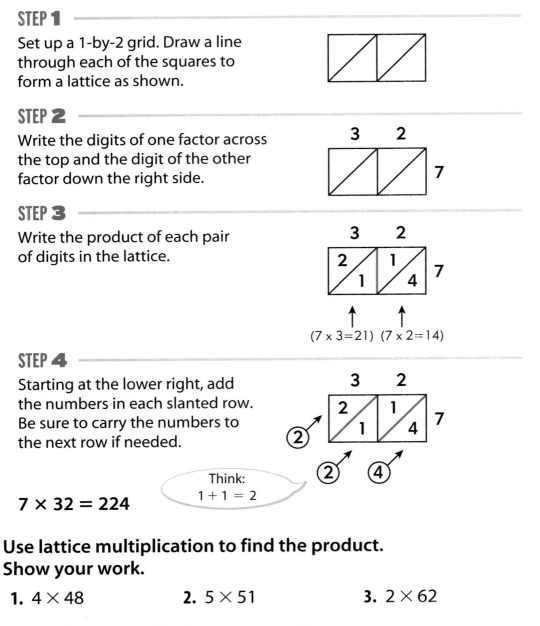

STEP 1

Set up a 1-by-2 grid. Draw a line through each of the squares to form a lattice as shown.

STEP 2

Write the digits of one factor across the top and the digit of the other factor down the right side.

STEP 3

Write the product of each pair of digits in the lattice.

(7 × 3 = 21)   (7 × 2 = 14)

STEP 4

Starting at the lower right, add the numbers in each slanted row. Be sure to carry the numbers to the next row if needed.

Think: 1 + 1 = 2

7 × 32 = 224

Use lattice multiplication to find the product. Show your work.

1. 4 × 48

2. 5 × 51

3. 2 × 62

4. 5 × 387

5. Analyze Describe how you would use the lattice method to find 4 × 1,245.

Performance Assessment

How Big Is Your Collection?

Your family loves to collect things! Your father collects stamps. Your mother collects coins. Your sister collects baseball cards, and you collect stickers. Each person keeps their collection in a special book or album.

How many items can each book hold?

- Stamp books hold 18 stamps on a page. There are 9 pages in a book.

- Coin books hold 12 coins on a page. There are 8 pages in a book.

- Baseball card albums fit 6 cards on a page. There are 45 pages in an album.

- Sticker books hold 9 stickers on a page. There are 25 pages in a book.

Make a chart like the one shown here to help you.

Type of book	Number of items that fit on 1 page	Number of pages	Total number of items

Tips For A Good Answer

- Show a completed chart.
- Include the steps you followed to find the total for each type of book.
- Show the correct total for each type of book.

 You may want to save this work in your portfolio.

e-Journal www.mmhmath.com
Write about math.   Unit 9   **403**

Assessment

TECHNOLOGY Link

Use Place-Value Models to Multiply

Mr. Whitney's class is collecting phone books to recycle. They have filled each of 6 boxes with 12 phone books. How many phone books have they collected so far?

You can build a model of 6 groups of 12 phone books using place-value models in the *Math Tool Chest CD*.

- Choose multiplication as the mat type.

- Stamp out 1 ten and 2 ones in each of the 6 sections at the top of the mat.

The number boxes keep count as you stamp.

How many phone books have they collected so far?

Math Tool Chest CD-ROM

Use the computer to model each multiplication. Then write the product.

1. 4×16 **2.** 6×22 **3.** 7×43 **4.** 3×65

Solve.

5. Raphael is collecting cans to recycle. He has collected 8 bags. There are 36 cans in each bag. How many cans has he collected?

6. Laurel is buying 7 packages of pencils. Each package contains 13 pencils. How many pencils is she buying?

7. **Analyze** How does modeling the problem help you multiply?

For more practice, use Math Traveler™.

Test-Taking Tips

The problems you find on tests sometimes contain extra information that you do not need to use to solve the problem.

It is important to read the problem carefully, decide on the facts you need, and cross out **any extra information** that is not necessary.

The Hat Hut has 195 boxes of hats. Forty-five of the hats are green. Each box holds 3 hats. How many hats are in the boxes?

A. 35 hats   **C.** 375 hats

B. 55 hats   **D.** 585 hats

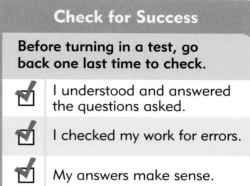

Check for Success

Before turning in a test, go back one last time to check.

☑ I understood and answered the questions asked.

☑ I checked my work for errors.

☑ My answers make sense.

To find the total number of hats, you need to know the number of boxes and the number of hats in each box. You do not need to know the color of any of them.

Find: 3×195

$3 \times 195 = 585$

D is the correct choice.

Read the problem. Identify the extra information you would cross out. Then choose the best answer.

1. Gary bought 2 pens for $1.95 each and a notebook for $2.25. How much did he pay for the pens?

   A. $1.95   **C.** $4.20

   B. $3.90   **D.** $6.15

2. Each bookcase holds books on 2 subjects. There are 14 bookcases with 8 shelves in each bookcase. How many shelves are there in all?

   F. 6 shelves   **H.** 84 shelves

   G. 22 shelves   **I.** 112 shelves

3. Cara practices piano 3 times a week from 3:45 to 5:15. How long is the class?

   A. $2\frac{1}{2}$ hours   **C.** $1\frac{1}{2}$ hours

   B. 2 hours   **D.** 1 hour

4. This year Mrs. Fenway has 8 fewer students in her class than last year. Five students moved away. If she had 32 students last year, how many are there this year?

   F. 14 students   **H.** 42 students

   G. 24 students   **I.** 50 students

PART 1 • Multiple Choice

Choose the best answer.

1. Pearl buys 6 postcards from each city she visits. She visited 18 cities over the last 3 years. How many postcards did she buy? (p. 384)

    A. 21 postcards

    B. 54 postcards

    C. 108 postcards

    D. 680 postcards

2. Kim buys 2 boxes of film on sale. Each box holds 5 rolls of film. How many rolls of film does Kim buy? (p. 204)

    F. 3 rolls   H. 10 rolls

    G. 7 rolls   I. 15 rolls

3. Erin displays her stuffed animals on shelves in her room. She has 4 animals on some shelves and 5 on the others. Erin has 26 stuffed animals in all. How many shelves does she have with 5 stuffed animals? (p. 346)

    A. 2 shelves   C. 4 shelves

    B. 3 shelves   D. 5 shelves

4. What is the mean of this set of numbers? (p. 352)

    4, 8, 3, 7, 9, 5

    F. 3   H. 6
    G. 5   I. 9

Use data from the table for problems 5–6.

Boxes of Trading Cards		
Kind	Number in box	Price
Basketball	25	$22.75
Baseball	125	$75.99
Football	180	$95.00

5. If you buy 3 boxes of football cards, how many cards will you buy? (p. 390)

    A. 360 cards   C. 630 cards

    B. 540 cards   D. 680 cards

6. How much do 2 boxes of basketball cards cost? (p. 390)

    F. $45.50   H. $44.50

    G. $45.25   I. $44.25

7. $6,008 - 1,549$ (p. 120)

    A. 4,451   C. 5,451

    B. 4,459   D. 5,549

8. Len has 6 model boats that are each 12 inches long. He puts them end-to-end on a shelf that is 80 inches long. How many inches of the shelf are empty?

    (p.244)

    F. 72 inches   H. 12 inches

    G. 68 inches   I. 8 inches

PART 2 • Short Response/Grid In

Record your answers on the answer sheet provided by your teacher or on a sheet of paper.

9. Silvio invited some friends for dinner. He ordered 4 pizzas, each with 6 slices. Everyone ate 2 slices of pizza and there were no slices left over. How many people ate pizza? Explain. (p. 328)

10. Tisa sat at her booth at the Coin Collectors' Show from 9:15 A.M. to 2:00 P.M. How long did she sit at the booth? (p. 146)

11. Connie bought 4 basketballs for the team. How much did she spend in all? (p. 390)

$16.85

12. Luke spent $18.90 on a ticket for the amusement park each time he went. Over the summer, he went 5 times. About how much did Luke spend on tickets? (p. 372)

13. What is 9,827 rounded to the nearest hundred? (p. 32)

14. Mr. Rocourt buys 6 T-shirts and a whistle. Each T-shirt costs $9.00 and the whistle costs $0.55. He got back $5.45 in change. How much did he give to pay for the things? Explain. (p. 244)

15. Henri has 56 stamps. He put 8 stamps on each page of his album. How many pages did Henri fill? (p. 330)

16. Selma had 432 coins in her collection. Over 3 years she doubled the size of her collection. How many coins does she now have? (p. 390)

PART 3 • Extended Response

Record your answer on a sheet of paper. Show your work.

17. George and Collin went to the concert in the park . Collin paid $6.75 for his ticket. George paid $2.00 less than Collin. What is the total cost of tickets? Explain how you found your answer. (p. 328)

What Do I Need to Know?

Your school is buying paints for art class. Each color costs $3.00. So far the school has spent $27.00 on different colors. How many colors have they purchased?

Division: Patterns and Estimation

What Will I Learn?

In this chapter you will learn to

- divide multiples of 10 and 100
- estimate quotients
- divide 2-digit numbers
- use skills and strategies to solve problems

How Do I Read Math?

When you read a mathematics book, sometimes you read words and symbols, and sometimes you read only symbols.

All of these represent 240 divided by 6 equals 40:

- **two hundred forty divided by six equals forty**
- $240 \div 6 = 40$
- $6\overline{)240}$ with quotient 40

VOCABULARY

- dividend
- quotient
- compatible numbers
- remainder

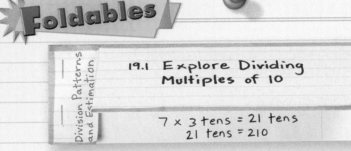

Foldables

19.1 Explore Dividing Multiples of 10

Division Patterns and Estimation

7 × 3 tens = 21 tens
21 tens = 210

Use your Foldables to help you with chapter concepts.

1. Fold the half sheet of paper in half like a hot dog.
2. Place the folded paper in front of you with the fold up. One inch from the left edge, make a cut from the bottom to the top fold.
3. Make six of these and staple them together along the left 1–inch tab.
4. Label as shown. Record what you learn.

19.1 Explore Dividing Multiples of 10

Hands On Activity

You can use place-value models to explore dividing multiples of 10.

Find: 80 ÷ 4

You Will Need
- place-value models

Use Models

STEP 1
Show 80 as 8 tens. Show 4 groups.

STEP 2
Place an equal number of tens in each group.

STEP 3
Find the quotient.

Record your work.

Explain Your Thinking

1. How did you model 80?

2. How did you know to separate the models into 4 equal groups?

3. How many tens models are in each group?

4. What is 80 ÷ 4?

Technology Link

Use the place-value models tool in **Math Tool Chest** to divide multiples of 10.

410

Find: 150 ÷ 5

Let's see how to connect models to paper and pencil.

Make Connections

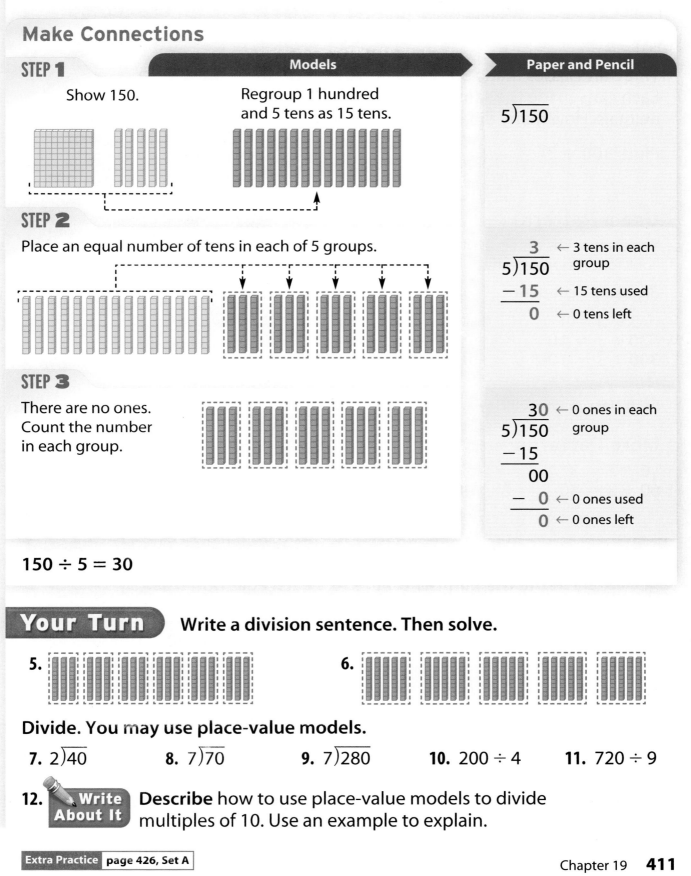

STEP 1

Models

Paper and Pencil

Show 150.

Regroup 1 hundred and 5 tens as 15 tens.

$5\overline{)150}$

STEP 2

Place an equal number of tens in each of 5 groups.

$$\begin{array}{r} 3 \\ 5\overline{)150} \\ -15 \\ \hline 0 \end{array}$$ ← 3 tens in each group
← 15 tens used
← 0 tens left

STEP 3

There are no ones. Count the number in each group.

$$\begin{array}{r} 30 \\ 5\overline{)150} \\ -15 \\ \hline 00 \\ -0 \\ \hline 0 \end{array}$$ ← 0 ones in each group
← 0 ones used
← 0 ones left

150 ÷ 5 = 30

Your Turn Write a division sentence. Then solve.

5.

6.

Divide. You may use place-value models.

7. $2\overline{)40}$　　8. $7\overline{)70}$　　9. $7\overline{)280}$　　10. $200 \div 4$　　11. $720 \div 9$

12. **Write About It** **Describe** how to use place-value models to divide multiples of 10. Use an example to explain.

19.2 Algebra: Division Patterns

Learn

Three art classes made 300 clay animals. Each class made the same number of clay animals. How many did each class make?

Find: 300 ÷ 3

VOCABULARY
dividend
quotient

Use a Pattern

You can use basic facts to divide mentally. Look for division patterns.

dividend   quotient
$3 \div 3 = 1$ **Think:** 3 ones ÷ 3 = 1 one
$30 \div 3 = 10$ 3 tens ÷ 3 = 1 ten
$300 \div 3 = 100$ 3 hundreds ÷ 3 = 1 hundred

Each class made 100 clay animals.

More Patterns

$6 \div 2 = 3$ $40 \div 5 = 8$
$60 \div 2 = 30$ $400 \div 5 = 80$

Try It   Write the number that makes each equation true.

1. $4 \div 2 = n$
   $40 \div 2 = t$
   $400 \div 2 = p$

2. $20 \div 5 = r$
   $200 \div 5 = s$

3. $45 \div 9 = b$
   $c \div 9 = 50$

Divide. Use patterns.

4. $50 \div 5$

5. $90 \div 3$

6. $120 \div 2$

7. $270 \div 3$

8. $200 \div 4$

9. $480 \div 6$

10. $160 \div 4$

11. $400 \div 4$

12. **Write About It** **Explain** how the quotient changes when the number of zeros in the dividend increases.

Practice and Problem Solving

Write the number that makes each equation true.

13. $8 \div 2 = q$
       $80 \div 2 = a$
       $800 \div 2 = d$

14. $18 \div 3 = x$
       $180 \div 3 = w$

15. $30 \div 6 = y$
    $h \div 6 = 50$

Divide. Use patterns.

16. $7\overline{)420}$ 17. $4\overline{)\$280}$ 18. $2\overline{)140}$ 19. $8\overline{)320}$ 20. $9\overline{)540}$

21. $20 \div 2$ 22. $70 \div 7$ 23. $\$150 \div 5$ 24. $350 \div 7$ 25. $560 \div 8$

$\widehat{x}$ **Algebra Describe and complete these skip-counting patterns.**

26. 30, 60, 90, _____ , 150

27. 70, _____ , 50, 40

28. 40, 60, _____ , 100, 120

29. _____ , 80, 120, 160

Solve. Use data from the pictograph for problems 30–31.

30. How many more turtles were made than snakes?

31. **What If** Each ● stands for 100 clay animals. How many ● will represent snails now? Fish?

THINK SOLVE EXPLAIN 32. ✎ **Write About It** **Compare** How is dividing 21 by 7 like dividing 210 by 7? How is it different?

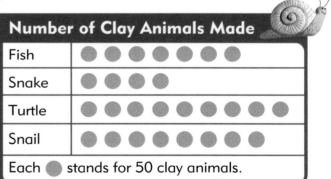

Number of Clay Animals Made

Fish	● ● ● ● ● ● ●
Snake	● ● ● ●
Turtle	● ● ● ● ● ● ● ● ●
Snail	● ● ● ● ● ● ● ●

Each ● stands for 50 clay animals.

Spiral Review and Test Prep

33. Which number does not round to 70? (p. 32)

    A. 74   **C.** 66

    B. 72   **D.** 64

34. What is the product of 5 and 700? (p. 370)

    F. 35   **H.** 3,500

    G. 350   **I.** 35,000

35. 3×658 (p. 390)

36. $8 \times \$24.05$ (p. 390)

37. $315 + 136$ (p. 72)

19.3 Estimate Quotients

Learn

Tony makes these birdhouses to raise money for his youth group. All of the materials are donated. His goal this year is to raise $75. About how many birdhouses does he need to sell?

VOCABULARY

compatible numbers

$4.00

Estimate: $75 ÷ $4

Use Rounding

STEP 1

Round 75 to the nearest ten.

$75 ÷ 4$
↓   ↓
$80 ÷ 4$

STEP 2

Use patterns to divide.

$8 ÷ 4 = 2$
$80 ÷ 4 = 20$

Think: Start with a basic fact.

Tony needs to sell about 20 birdhouses.

More Rounding

Estimate: 52 ÷ 5
Round 52 to the nearest ten.

$52 ÷ 5$
↓   ↓
$50 ÷ 5 = 10$

Estimate: 182 ÷ 9
Round 182 to the nearest ten.

$182 ÷ 9$
↓   ↓
$180 ÷ 9 = 20$

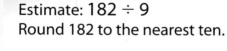

What If Hannah made 155 origami birds to sell for the youth group. She can fit 5 birds in a box. About how many boxes does she need?

Estimate: 155 ÷ 5

There's More Than One Way!

Use Rounding

STEP 1

Round 155 to the nearest hundred.

$$155 \div 5$$
$$\downarrow \qquad \downarrow$$
$$200 \div 5$$

STEP 2

Use patterns to divide.

$$20 \div 5 = 4$$
$$200 \div 5 = 40$$

Use Compatible Numbers

STEP 1

Think of a **compatible number** that is close to 155 and is easy to divide by 5 mentally.

150 is close to 155.

Think:
$15 \div 5 = 3$

STEP 2

Use patterns to divide.

$$15 \div 5 = 3$$
$$150 \div 5 = 30$$

Hannah needs about 30 to 40 boxes.

Estimate.

1. $4\overline{)337}$ 2. $8\overline{)85}$ 3. $3\overline{)165}$ 4. $9\overline{)682}$ 5. $8\overline{)234}$

6.  **Explain** which method gives a closer estimate to the actual answer for $158 \div 5$.

Practice and Problem Solving

Estimate.

7. $3\overline{)260}$ 8. $4\overline{)115}$ 9. $5\overline{)127}$ 10. $7\overline{)502}$ 11. $5\overline{)527}$

12. $533 \div 7$ 13. $170 \div 9$ 14. $400 \div 6$ 15. $329 \div 8$ 16. $220 \div 6$

★17. $5,183 \div 9$ ★18. $5,627 \div 8$ ★19. $8,742 \div 9$ ★20. $1,300 \div 2$

(x) **Algebra Compare. Write > or <.**

21. $126 \div 4$ ● 30 22. $490 \div 7$ ● 60 23. $510 \div 8$ ● 60 24. $400 \div 8$ ● 60

★25. $(2 \times 27) \div 6$ ● 5 ★26. $(128 - 4) \div 2$ ● 31

★27. $(100 - 51) \div 7$ ● 50 ★28. $(300 - 20) \div 7$ ● 60

Solve.

29. Mary Sue earned $210 selling birdhouses. She wants to give the same amount of money to 4 different groups. About how much will she give each group?

30. **Make It Right**
Here is how
Sam estimated 220 ÷ 3. What could Sam have done differently to get a better estimate?

$$220 \div 3$$
$$\downarrow \qquad \downarrow$$
$$300 \div 3 = 100$$

THINK SOLVE EXPLAIN

THINK SOLVE EXPLAIN
31. ✏️ **Write About It Explain** how you could get different estimates for $328 \div 9$.

32. A spool of kite string costs $4. Edwina has $30. Can she buy 7 spools of string? Why or why not?

33. ✏️ **Write a problem** using compatible numbers to estimate $500 \div 7$. Solve it. Ask others to solve it.

34. **Spatial Reasoning** How many triangles of all sizes are in this design?

Spiral Review and Test Prep

35. Which number is missing?
    1, 4, 9, ■, 25, 36, 49 (p. 232)
    A. 10   **C.** 16
    B. 12   **D.** 20

36. Which number is 9 thousands 3 hundreds 6 ones? (p. 6)
    F. 936   **H.** 9,306
    G. 9,036   **I.** 9,360

37. $8,910 - 5,289$ (p. 120)   38. 5×623 (p. 390)   39. $2 \times 1,753$ (p. 390)

Extra Practice page 426, Set C

Practice at School ★ Practice at Home

GETTING CLOSE

Use cards and a number cube to estimate the quotient.

Ready

Players: 2
You Will Need: Digit Deck, number cube, calculator, paper and pencil

Set

Shuffle the cards and place them face down.

Label the number cube 1 to 6.

GO!

▶ Player 1 picks 2 cards and creates the dividend by using the 2 cards in any order.

▶ Each player writes the numbers on paper. The first card is the tens digit and the second card is the ones digit.

▶ Player 2 rolls the number cube for the divisor.

▶ Each player finds the estimated quotient. Record on paper.

▶ Use a calculator to find the actual quotient. The player with the closer estimated quotient gets a point.

▶ Take turns picking the cards and rolling the number cube.

▶ The first player to get 10 points is the winner.

19.4

Explore Division

Hands On Activity

You can use place-value models to divide 75 ÷ 5.

You Will Need
- place-value models

Use Models

STEP 1

Show 75 as 7 tens and 5 ones.   Show 5 groups.

STEP 2

Place an equal number of tens in each group.

STEP 3

Regroup the remaining 2 tens and 5 ones as 25 ones.

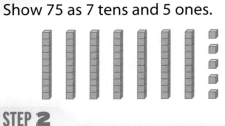

STEP 4

Place an equal number of ones in each group.

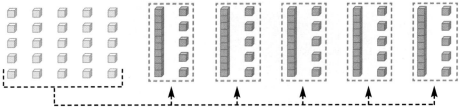

Explain Your Thinking

1. How did you model the dividend and the divisor?

2. How many tens did you put in each group?

3. Why did you need to regroup?

4. How many ones did you have after regrouping?

5. How many ones did you put into each group?

6. What is 75 divided by 5?

Technology Link

Use the place–value models tool in **Math Tool Chest** to explore division by 1-digit number.

Your Turn

Use models to divide.

7. 38 ÷ 2

8. 72 ÷ 6

9. 96 ÷ 4

10. 39 ÷ 3   **11.** 96 ÷ 8   **12.** 44 ÷ 2   **13.** 85 ÷ 5

14.  **Explain** why you should use the models with the greatest place value when you start to divide.

19.5 Divide 2-Digit Numbers

Learn

Rosa makes 57 toy bugs. She gives them to 3 Head-Start classes. How many toy bugs does each class get?

Find: 57 ÷ 3
Estimate: $60 \div 3 = 20$

Let's see how to connect models to paper and pencil.

Make Connections

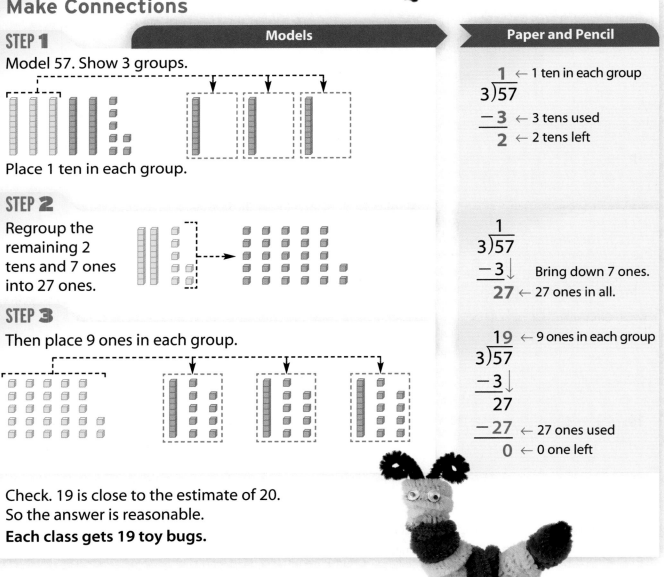

	Models	Paper and Pencil

STEP 1

Model 57. Show 3 groups.

Place 1 ten in each group.

$$\begin{array}{r} 1 \leftarrow \text{1 ten in each group} \\ 3\overline{)57} \\ -\underline{3} \leftarrow \text{3 tens used} \\ 2 \leftarrow \text{2 tens left} \end{array}$$

STEP 2

Regroup the remaining 2 tens and 7 ones into 27 ones.

$$\begin{array}{r} 1 \\ 3\overline{)57} \\ -\underline{3}\downarrow \quad \text{Bring down 7 ones.} \\ 27 \leftarrow \text{27 ones in all.} \end{array}$$

STEP 3

Then place 9 ones in each group.

$$\begin{array}{r} 19 \leftarrow \text{9 ones in each group} \\ 3\overline{)57} \\ -\underline{3}\downarrow \\ 27 \\ -\underline{27} \leftarrow \text{27 ones used} \\ 0 \leftarrow \text{0 one left} \end{array}$$

Check. 19 is close to the estimate of 20. So the answer is reasonable.
Each class gets 19 toy bugs.

Rosa makes 50 toy butterflies. She will pack 4 butterflies in each box. How many boxes will Rosa need? Will she have any butterflies left?

Find: 50 ÷ 4
Estimate: $48 \div 4 = 12$

Use Paper and Pencil

STEP 1

Decide where to place the first digit.

$4\overline{)50}$ **Think:** $4\overline{)5 \text{ tens}}$

Enough tens to divide.

$4\overline{)50}$ ■   The first digit is in the tens place.

STEP 2

Divide the tens.

$$\begin{array}{r} 1 \\ 4\overline{)50} \\ -4 \\ \hline 1 \end{array}$$
← Multiply: 4×1
← Subtract: $5 - 4$
Compare: $1 < 4$

STEP 3

Bring down the ones. Divide the ones.

$$\begin{array}{r} 12\,\text{R2} \\ 4\overline{)50} \\ -4\downarrow \\ \hline 10 \\ -8 \\ \hline 2 \end{array}$$
← Multiply: 4×2
← Subtract: $10 - 8$
Compare: $2 < 4$

The amount left is called the **remainder.**

Check the answer.
Multiply the quotient by the divisor.
Then add the remainder.

quotient → 12 48
divisor → $\times4$ $+2$ ← remainder
$\overline{48}$ $\overline{50}$ ← dividend

Rosa will need 12 boxes. There are 2 butterflies left.

Try It

Divide. Check your answer.

1. $5\overline{)74}$
2. $7\overline{)91}$
3. $4\overline{)65}$
4. $3\overline{)55}$

5. $58 \div 6$
6. $89 \div 8$
7. $78 \div 3$
8. $81 \div 7$

9. **Write About It** Write about the first 2 steps you would take to divide 78 by 4 using paper and pencil.

Practice and Problem Solving

Divide. Check your answer.

10. $4\overline{)72}$ **11.** $2\overline{)32}$ **12.** $3\overline{)96}$ **13.** $6\overline{)75}$ **14.** $5\overline{)86}$

15. $7\overline{)83}$ **16.** $6\overline{)93}$ **17.** $8\overline{)90}$ **18.** $2\overline{)77}$ **19.** $4\overline{)88}$

20. $67 \div 3$ **21.** $62 \div 5$ **22.** $55 \div 4$ **23.** $38 \div 8$ **24.** $78 \div 7$

★**25.** $34 \div 12$ ★**26.** $67 \div 11$ ★**27.** $49 \div 10$ ★**28.** $51 \div 12$ ★**29.** $82 \div 11$

x **Algebra** Copy and complete the table. Describe the pattern.

30.

Rule: Divide by 6.								
Input	78	79	80	81	82	83	84	85
Output	13	13R1						

Solve.

THINK SOLVE EXPLAIN

31. When the divisor is 6, what is the largest possible remainder? Explain.

★**32.** **Write a problem** involving division with an answer of 15 R3. Ask others to solve it.

33. Carmen has 47 straws. She needs 4 straws to make each rectangle. How many rectangles can she make?

34. **Make It Right** Here is how Ron divided 69 by 4. Tell what mistake he made. Explain how to correct it.

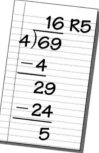

THINK SOLVE EXPLAIN

Spiral Review and Test Prep

35. Which shows the Commutative Property for Addition? (p. 52)

   A. $3 + 5 = 5 + 3$

   B. $3 \times 5 = 5 \times 3$

   C. $2 + (3 + 5) = (2 + 3) + 5$

   D. $3 + (5 - 2) = (5 + 2) - 3$

36. What is the value of the 3 in 234,048 (p. 10)

   F. 3 hundreds

   G. 3 thousands

   H. 3 ten thousands

   I. 3 hundred thousands

37. 5×722 (p. 390)   **38.** $9 \times (293 - 47)$ (p. 390)   **39.** $8 \times 9 \times 3 \times 2$ (p. 390)

Extra Practice page 426, Set E

Problem Solving: Reading for Math
HELPING HANDS

Each day, close to 300 children get a healthful meal through a group called Golden Harvest. Golden Harvest gives free food to hungry people in Georgia and South Carolina.

Since Golden Harvest began in 1982, it has served millions of meals and delivered about 73 million pounds of food. How do they do it? Local supermarkets, food companies, and the United States Department of Agriculture all donate food to Golden Harvest.

HARD WORK

Volunteers are important to Golden Harvest. They pack up groceries and deliver them to elderly people who aren't able to leave their homes. They load hundreds of boxes of food onto trucks and drive them to needy neighborhoods. Volunteers also cook and serve lunch to an average of 183 homeless people every day.

Problem Solving

Reading Skill **Problem and Solution** What problem did Golden Harvest want to help solve? What were some of their solutions?

1. Golden Harvest delivers about 800 grocery boxes each month. About how many boxes are delivered in 1 week?

2. Each month, about 3,000 grocery bags are delivered to seniors. From January to September, how many bags does Golden Harvest deliver?

Here is part of a Golden Harvest report from a January-to-September period:

Number of grocery *bags* delivered each month: **2,784**

Number of grocery *boxes* delivered each month: **804**

Total number of meals served to children: **22,504**

Pounds of food distributed: **16,472,766**

19.6 Problem Solving: Skill
Interpret the Remainder

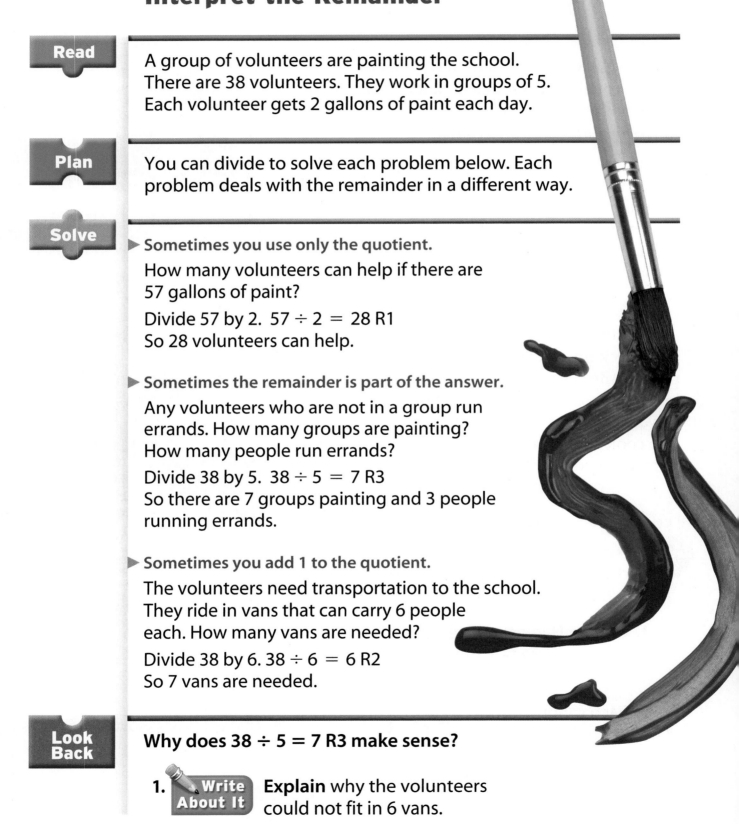

Read

A group of volunteers are painting the school. There are 38 volunteers. They work in groups of 5. Each volunteer gets 2 gallons of paint each day.

Plan

You can divide to solve each problem below. Each problem deals with the remainder in a different way.

Solve

▶ **Sometimes you use only the quotient.**

How many volunteers can help if there are 57 gallons of paint?

Divide 57 by 2. $57 \div 2 = 28$ R1
So 28 volunteers can help.

▶ **Sometimes the remainder is part of the answer.**

Any volunteers who are not in a group run errands. How many groups are painting? How many people run errands?

Divide 38 by 5. $38 \div 5 = 7$ R3
So there are 7 groups painting and 3 people running errands.

▶ **Sometimes you add 1 to the quotient.**

The volunteers need transportation to the school. They ride in vans that can carry 6 people each. How many vans are needed?

Divide 38 by 6. $38 \div 6 = 6$ R2
So 7 vans are needed.

Look Back

Why does $38 \div 5 = 7$ R3 make sense?

1. **Write About It** **Explain** why the volunteers could not fit in 6 vans.

Practice

Solve. Tell how you interpreted the remainder.

2. The committee has $36 for paint. Each can costs $5. How many cans can the committee buy?

3. There are 3 paintbrushes in a bag. The committee needs 11 paintbrushes. How many bags should they buy?

Mixed Strategy Review

Solve.

4. Dimo bought 9 screwdrivers. He paid $2.16 for each screwdriver. How much money did Dimo spend in all?

5. Zoe spent $3.59 on a paint roller and $1.25 on tape. She has $5.75 left. How much money did Zoe start with?

Choose a Strategy

- Logical Reasoning
- Draw a Picture or Diagram
- Make a Graph
- Act It Out
- Make a Table or List
- Find a Pattern
- Guess and Check
- Write an Equation
- Work Backward
- Solve a Simpler Problem

Use data from the Supply List for problems 6–9.

6. The buckets will be shared equally among 36 community members. How many members will share each bucket?

Supply List

4 ladders

9 buckets

6 hammers

5 boxes of nails

7. A total of 18 members need to use the hammers. How many members will share each one?

8. A total of 16 members need to use the ladders. If the ladders are divided evenly among this group, how many members will share each ladder?

9. Name 2 ways that a group of 24 town members could be divided evenly into groups of more than 3 people.

Problem Solving

Chapter 19 Extra Practice

Set A Divide. (pp. 410–411)

1. 4)240   2. 3)210   3. 7)560   4. 5)200   5. 6)480

6. 720 ÷ 9   7. 450 ÷ 5   8. 320 ÷ 8   9. 640 ÷ 8   10. 630 ÷ 7

11. 160 ÷ 4   12. 350 ÷ 7   13. 240 ÷ 3   14. 540 ÷ 9   15. 160 ÷ 2

Set B Write the number that makes each equation true. (pp. 412–413)

16. $32 \div 8 = n$
$320 \div 8 = k$
$3,200 \div 8 = r$

17. $27 \div 9 = t$
$270 \div 9 = r$
$2,700 \div 9 = s$

18. $60 \div 6 = g$
$600 \div 6 = m$
$6,000 \div 6 = n$

19. $x \div 5 = 11$
$y \div 5 = 110$
$z \div 5 = 1,100$

Set C Estimate. Use compatible numbers. (pp. 414–416)

20. 2)59   21. 6)187   22. 9)639   23. 5)295

24. 3)124   25. 5)153   26. 4)358   27. 6)421

Set D Divide. Check your answer. (pp. 420–422)

28. 3)38   29. 6)78   30. 4)78   31. 3)62

32. 47 ÷ 4   33. 53 ÷ 5   34. 69 ÷ 5   35. 44 ÷ 7

36. 280 ÷ 4   37. 420 ÷ 7   38. 350 ÷ 5   39. 300 ÷ 3

40. 300 ÷ 6   41. 320 ÷ 4   42. 210 ÷ 3   43. 90 ÷ 3

Set E Solve. Interpret any remainder. (pp. 424–425)

44. A group of 29 clean-up volunteers are separated into crews of 5. How many complete crews are there?

45. A committee has $26 to buy signs. Each sign costs $4. How many signs can be purchased?

46. An art store receives 89 brushes. They will pack 7 brushes in each box. How many full boxes will they have?

47. Stacey plants 8 flowers in each row. She has 94 flowers. How many complete rows are there?

LOG ON www.mmhmath.com
For more practice and Chapter Self-Check Test

426

Review/Test

Divide.

1. $2\overline{)60}$ 2. $7\overline{)490}$ 3. $5\overline{)300}$ 4. $\$360 \div 4$ 5. $300 \div 3$

Write the number that makes each equation true.

6. $6 \div 2 = o$
    $60 \div 2 = p$
    $600 \div 2 = q$

7. $27 \div 3 = r$
    $270 \div 3 = s$

8. $40 \div 5 = x$
   $y \div 5 = 80$

Estimate.

9. $77 \div 4$ 10. $227 \div 7$ 11. $5\overline{)407}$

Divide.

12. $4\overline{)76}$ 13. $3\overline{)77}$ 14. $9\overline{)59}$ 15. $8\overline{)68}$ 16. $9\overline{)97}$

17. $55 \div 7$ 18. $40 \div 3$ 19. $90 \div 5$ 20. $68 \div 6$ 21. $87 \div 7$

Solve.

22. The 91 members of Kelly's youth group are planting trees. It takes 4 members to plant 1 tree. What is the greatest number of trees they can plant at one time?

23. James earned $364 selling used books. He wants to give the same amount of money to 3 different groups. About how much money will he give to each group?

24. All 53 members of the Historical Society are driving to the town celebration. Each car holds 5 people. How many cars do they need?

25. **Write About It** **Analyze** The quotient in a division problem is 11 and the remainder is 2. If the divisor is 4, what is the dividend? Explain how you got your answer.

Do I Need Help?

Exercises	Review Concepts	Use Extra Practice Set
1–5	pp. 410–411	Set A
6–8	pp. 412–413	Set B
9–11, 23	pp. 414–416	Set C
12–21, 25	pp. 418–422	Set D
22, 24	pp. 424–425	Set E

Foldables Use your Foldables to help you review.

Assessment

What Do I Need to Know?

During the last 3 days, 60 students have helped to paint the mural. The same number of students painted each day. How many students painted each day?

Divide by 1-Digit Numbers

What Will I Learn?

In this chapter you will learn to

- divide 3-digit numbers
- divide numbers with zeros in the quotient
- use skills and strategies to solve problems

How Do I Read Math?

When you read a mathematics book, sometimes you read words and symbols, and sometimes you read only symbols.

All of these represent 300 divided by 3 equals 100:

- $300 \div 3 = 100$

- $3\overline{)300} \atop 100$

VOCABULARY

- unit price
- per

Foldables

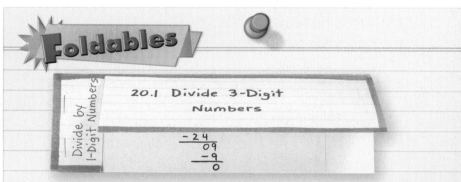

Use your Foldables to help you with chapter concepts.

1. Fold the half sheet of paper in half like a hot dog.
2. Place the folded paper in front of you with the fold up. One inch from the left edge, make a cut from the bottom to the top fold.
3. Make four of these and staple them together along the left 1–inch tab.
4. Label as shown. Record what you learn.

20.1 Divide 3-Digit Numbers

Learn

Some volunteers have 562 fabric squares to make quilts. They use these squares to make 5 quilts. If there are the same number of squares for each quilt, how many squares do they need for each quilt?

VOCABULARY
unit price
per

Find: $562 \div 5$

Estimate: $550 \div 5 = 110$

Use Paper and Pencil

STEP 1

Place the first digit. Divide the hundreds.

$$5\overline{)562}$$

Think: $5\overline{)5\text{ hundreds}}$
Enough hundreds

The first digit is in the hundreds place.

$$\begin{array}{r} 1 \\ 5\overline{)562} \\ -5 \\ \hline 0 \end{array}$$
← Multiply: 5×1
← Subtract: $5 - 5$
Compare: $0 < 5$

STEP 2

Bring down the tens. Divide the tens.

$$\begin{array}{r} 11 \\ 5\overline{)562} \\ -5\downarrow \\ \hline 06 \\ -5 \\ \hline 1 \end{array}$$
← Multiply: 5×1
← Subtract: $6 - 5$
Compare: $1 < 5$

STEP 3

Bring down the ones. Divide the ones.

$$\begin{array}{r} 112 \text{ R2} \\ 5\overline{)562} \\ -5 \\ \hline 06 \\ -5\downarrow \\ \hline 12 \\ -10 \\ \hline 2 \end{array}$$
← Multiply: 5×2
← Subtract: $12 - 10$
Compare: $2 < 5$

112 R2 is close to the estimate of 110. The answer is reasonable.

Check the answer.
$$\begin{array}{r} 112 \\ \times\ \ 5 \\ \hline 560 \end{array} \qquad \begin{array}{r} 560 \\ +\ \ 2 \\ \hline 562 \end{array}$$

They will need 112 squares for each quilt.
There are 2 squares left.

Alina buys 2 spools of thread for $2.54.
What is the unit price?
Unit price is a price given as the cost of a single unit.

Find: $2.54 ÷ 2

There's More Than One Way!

Use Paper and Pencil

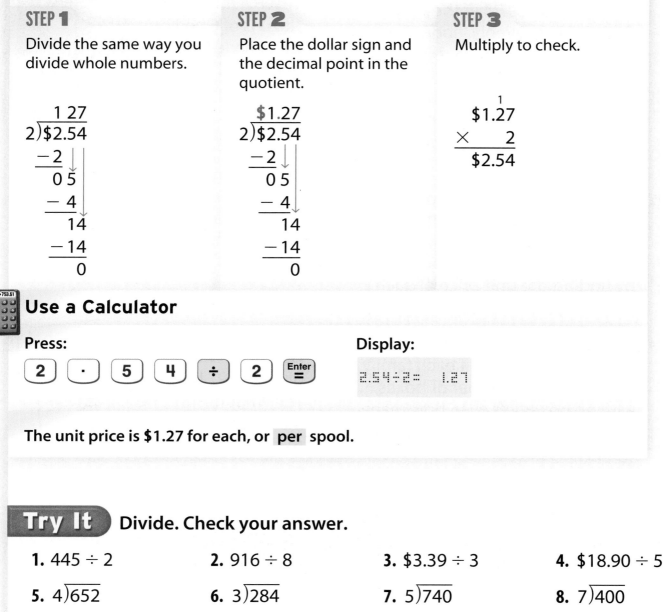

STEP 1

Divide the same way you divide whole numbers.

$$\begin{array}{r} 1\;27 \\ 2\overline{)\$2.54} \\ -2\downarrow \\ \hline 0\;5 \\ -\;4\downarrow \\ \hline 14 \\ -14 \\ \hline 0 \end{array}$$

STEP 2

Place the dollar sign and the decimal point in the quotient.

$$\begin{array}{r} \$1.27 \\ 2\overline{)\$2.54} \\ -2\downarrow \\ \hline 0\;5 \\ -\;4\downarrow \\ \hline 14 \\ -14 \\ \hline 0 \end{array}$$

STEP 3

Multiply to check.

$$\begin{array}{r} \overset{1}{\$1.27} \\ \times2 \\ \hline \$2.54 \end{array}$$

Use a Calculator

Press:

(2) (·) (5) (4) (÷) (2) (Enter =)

Display:

2.54÷2= 1.27

The unit price is $1.27 for each, or **per** spool.

Try It Divide. Check your answer.

1. 445 ÷ 2

2. 916 ÷ 8

3. $3.39 ÷ 3

4. $18.90 ÷ 5

5. 4)652

6. 3)284

7. 5)740

8. 7)400

9. **Write About It** **Describe** how you know where to place the first number in the quotient.

Practice and Problem Solving

Divide. Check your answer.

10. $116 \div 2$ **11.** $368 \div 8$ **12.** $888 \div 9$ **13.** $625 \div 5$ **14.** $362 \div 7$

15. $\$9.84 \div 4$ **16.** $792 \div 5$ **17.** $4\overline{)127}$ ★**18.** $2\overline{)1,244}$ ★**19.** $5\overline{)2,749}$

Solve.

20. Three friends went out to dinner. The bill was $69.74. If they divide the total cost evenly, about how much do they each pay?

21. THINK SOLVE EXPLAIN **Write About It** **Explain** how you can tell that the quotient of $321 \div 7$ is a 2-digit number without working out the whole problem.

22. THINK SOLVE EXPLAIN **Collect Data** Use ads and store flyers to make a chart of items that are sold in groups. Include their prices. Complete your chart by finding the unit price of each kind of item.

★**24.** A food pantry has 115 boxes of cereal for 9 families. If each family gets the same number of boxes, with no boxes left over, how many more boxes of cereal are needed?

Link to ★ **SOCIAL STUDIES** ★

In 1982, the senior citizens of Oberlin, Ohio made this quilt to tell stories of the Underground Railroad.

23. One of the earliest Underground Railroad quilts was made in 1842. How many years later was the Oberlin quilt made?

25. Make It Right Here is how Everett divided 597 by 4. Tell what mistake he made. Show how to correct it.

THINK SOLVE EXPLAIN

Spiral Review and Test Prep

26. Which are compatible numbers for estimating $292 \div 4$? (p. 414)

  A. $210 \div 4$ **C.** $290 \div 4$

  B. $280 \div 4$ **D.** $310 \div 4$

27. The quotient for $487 \div 7$ is closest to (p. 414)

  F. 6   **H.** 60

  G. 7   **I.** 70

28. $5\overline{)45}$ (p. 296)   **29.** $\$2.27 + \$5.95$ (p. 72)   **30.** $\$45.22 - \$4.39$ (p. 120)

Writing for Math

Erasers sell for $0.59 each or in a set of 9 for $4.59. Tell how to persuade someone that buying the set is less expensive. Explain your thinking.

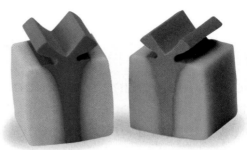

Ben's Response

THINK Divide $4.59 by 9 to find the unit price. Compare that to the cost of 1 eraser.

SOLVE

$$9\overline{)\$4.59} = 0.51$$
$$-45$$
$$09$$
$$-9$$
$$0$$

$0.51 < $0.59

The set of 9 erasers is less expensive.

$9 \times $0.59 = 5.31

Check: $5.31 > $4.59

EXPLAIN It is less expensive to buy the set of 9 erasers than one at a time. I divided $4.59 by 9 to find the unit price of 51¢. That's 8¢ less than the cost of a single eraser. If you buy 9 erasers separately, it will cost $5.31. Getting the set of 9 erasers saves 72¢, so it's less expensive.

Teacher's Response

← Ben explains how he will use what he knows to solve the problem.

← Ben shows his work.

← Ben uses appropriate math terms, such as **divide** and **unit price**.

Ben uses his calculations and his check to persuade the reader to buy the set of 9 erasers rather than one at a time.

Solve. Show your work and tell why your answer makes sense. Use Ben's work as a guide.

1. Muffins are sold for $1.39 each or in a 4-pack for $5.00. Which is the better deal? Why?

2. Neela buys a book of 7 amusement park tickets for $8.75. What is the cost of each ticket?

20.2 Quotients with Zeros

Learn

The students are making sock puppets using 629 buttons. Each puppet uses 6 buttons. How many puppets can the students make?

Find: 629 ÷ 6
Estimate: 600 ÷ 6 = 100

Zeros in the Quotient

STEP 1

Estimate to place the first digit.

6)629

Think: 6)6 hundreds
Enough hundreds to divide.
The first digit is in the hundreds place.

6)629

STEP 2

Divide the hundreds.

```
    1
6)620
 -6      ← 6 × 1      Multiply:
  0      ← Subtract:
            6 − 6
         Compare:
            0 < 6
```

STEP 3

Bring down the tens and divide.

```
   10
6)629
 -6↓
  02
 - 0     ← 6 × 0   Multiply:
   2     ← Subtract:
            2 − 0
         Compare:
            2 < 6
```

Think: Not enough tens to divide. Write zero in the quotient.

STEP 4

Bring down the ones and divide.

```
   104 R5
6)629
 -6 |
  02|
 - 0↓
   29
 -24    ← Multiply: 6 × 4
    5   ← Subtract:
           29 − 24
        Compare:
           5 < 6
```

The amount left is 5.

104 R5 is close to the estimate of 100. The answer is reasonable.

```
Check:   104      624
        ×  6     +  5
        ────     ────
        624      629
```

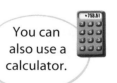
You can also use a calculator.

The students can make 104 puppets. There were 5 buttons left.

Try It   Divide. Check your answer.

1. 7)752

2. 9)$9.09

3. 4)437

4. 3)328

5. **Write About It** Tell where the zero is in the quotient when you divide 552 by 5.

434

Practice and Problem Solving

Divide. Check your answer.

6. $6\overline{)63}$ 7. $9\overline{)724}$ 8. $2\overline{)803}$ 9. $7\overline{)668}$ 10. $3\overline{)927}$

11. $5\overline{)\$5.95}$ 12. $4\overline{)808}$ 13. $2\overline{)\$7.00}$ 14. $8\overline{)187}$ 15. $3\overline{)912}$

16. $416 \div 4$ 17. $749 \div 7$ 18. $981 \div 9$ 19. $527 \div 5$ 20. $864 \div 8$

★21. $3,225 \div 4$ ★22. $7,248 \div 7$ ★23. $2,004 \div 5$

Solve. Use data from the flyer for problems 26–28.

24. The high school has collected 870 books for the local shelter. They will pack them in boxes. Each box holds 8 books. How many boxes do they need?

25. ✏ **Write a problem** whose quotient has 2 digits and a zero in the ones place. Ask others to solve it. THINK SOLVE EXPLAIN

26. **Number Sense** If 300 tickets are sold for the dance, what is the greatest amount of money raised? What is the least amount?

Charity Dance

Date: March 10
Time: 1:30 P.M.
Place: School
Tickets: $6 each or 3 for $15

27. **What If** You buy 3 tickets. How much does each cost? How much do you save in all?

28. How much will a group of 7 people pay for tickets?

Spiral Review and Test Prep

29. Which means the same as 81 divided by 9? (p. 330)

   A. $9 \div 81$ C. $9\overline{)81}$
   B. $81\overline{)9}$ D. 9×81

30. Which is 2 hours earlier than 1:30 P.M.? (p. 146)

   F. 11:00 A.M.   H. 3:30 P.M.
   G. 11:30 A.M.   I. 11:30 P.M.

31. $6\overline{)81}$ (p. 420)   32. 7×62 (p. 384)   33. $\$21.30 + \$11.70$ (p. 72)

20.3 Choose a Computation Method

Learn

Three classes make a total of 156 food faces out of vegetables. Each class made the same number of food faces. How many food faces did each class make?

Find: 156 ÷ 3

Estimate: $150 \div 3 = 50$

There's More Than One Way!

I use Paper and Pencil

$$
\begin{array}{r}
52 \\
3\overline{)156} \\
-15\downarrow \\
\hline
06 \\
-6 \\
\hline
0
\end{array}
$$

I use a Calculator

Press:

[1] [5] [6]

[÷] [3] [Enter =]

Display:

156÷3=   52.

I use Mental Math

I split 156 into 2 parts.

$156 \rightarrow 150 + 6$

First, I divide $150 \div 3 = 50$

Then, I divide $6 \div 3 = 2$

Last, I add $50 + 2 = 52$

Each class made 52 food faces.

Try It   Divide. Tell which method you use.

1. 608 ÷ 2   **2.** 642 ÷ 3   **3.** 465 ÷ 4   **4.** 184 ÷ 8

5. **Write About It**   **Explain** when using a calculator would not be the easiest way to solve a division problem.

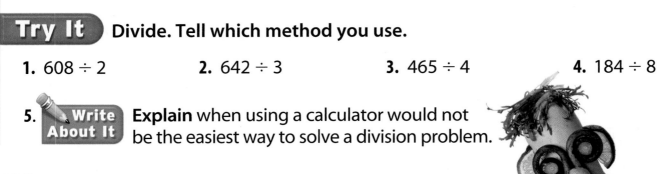

Practice and Problem Solving

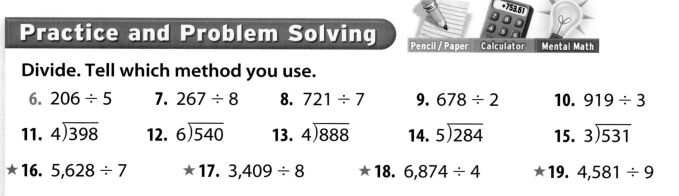

Pencil/Paper   Calculator   Mental Math

Divide. Tell which method you use.

6. $206 \div 5$ **7.** $267 \div 8$ **8.** $721 \div 7$ **9.** $678 \div 2$ **10.** $919 \div 3$

11. $4\overline{)398}$ **12.** $6\overline{)540}$ **13.** $4\overline{)888}$ **14.** $5\overline{)284}$ **15.** $3\overline{)531}$

★**16.** $5{,}628 \div 7$ ★**17.** $3{,}409 \div 8$ ★**18.** $6{,}874 \div 4$ ★**19.** $4{,}581 \div 9$

ⓧ **Algebra** Find each missing number.

20. $625 \div n = 125$ **21.** $b \div 3 = 37$ ★**22.** $8{,}199 \div a = 911$

Solve. Use data from the table for problems 23–24.

23. The table shows data for 4 years. If the same number of dogs were adopted each year, how many dogs were adopted in 1 year?

Animals Adopted from the Shelter	
Dogs	212
Cats	148
Other Animals	87

24. How many animals were adopted from the shelter in 4 years?

★**25. Science** A sea star, also known as a starfish, has 5 arms. How many sea stars are there if 125 arms are counted and all the sea stars have the same number of arms?

26. ✏ **Write About It** **Compare** How is dividing a number with a 2-digit dividend like dividing a number with a 3-digit dividend? How is it different?

THINK
SOLVE
EXPLAIN

Spiral Review and Test Prep

27. Amy bought a book that cost $10.50. She got back a ten-dollar bill in change. How much money did Amy pay with? (p. 72)

   A. $20.00   **C.** $20.50

   B. $20.25   **D.** $20.75

28. Which basic fact can help you solve $200 \div 5$? (p. 412)

   F. $10 \div 5$ **H.** $20 \div 4$

   G. $20 \div 5$ **I.** $25 \div 5$

29. $253 + 893$ (p. 72)   **30.** $8{,}907 - 4{,}888$ (p. 120)   **31.** $2{,}105 + 325$ (p. 72)

20.4 Problem Solving: Strategy
Choose a Strategy

Read

Juan's father makes flowers out of ribbons. He buys a 72-inch-long piece of ribbon and cuts it into 9-inch lengths for each flower. How many flowers can he make?

- **What do you know?**
  The ribbon is 72 in. long; each piece he cuts is 9 in. long.

- **What do you need to find?**
  How many flowers he can make

Plan

Some problems can be solved in more than one way. To solve this problem you can draw a diagram or write an equation.

Solve

▶ Draw a diagram.

Show a 72-inch-long piece of ribbon. Count by 9s to see how many 9-inch pieces will fit.

← —————— 72 in. —————— →

| 9 in. | 9 in. | 9 in. | 9 in. | 9 in. | 9 in. | 9 in. | 9 in. |

There are 8 pieces.

▶ Write an equation.

Each piece is the same length, so you can divide.

Total length		Length of each piece		Number of lengths
72	÷	9	=	8

He can make 8 flowers.

Look Back

Does your answer make sense? Check your answer.

1. **Write About It** **Explain** whether there is another way you can solve this problem.

Practice   Solve. Tell which strategy you choose.

2. **What If** Juan wants to make a bookcase. He cuts a 144-inch-long piece of wood into 8-inch pieces. How many pieces does he have?

3. **Measurement** Tanya makes a square picture frame for her art project. Each side is 15-inches long. How many inches around is the picture frame?

4. The round tables in the library will seat 8 children or 6 adults. How many children can sit at 8 tables? How many adults?

5. One part of the library will have 36 bookcases in 2 equal-sized sections. How many rows of 3 bookcases are in each section?

Mixed Strategy Review

6. Mia has 3 times as many nickels as dimes. She has a total of $1.75. How many nickels and dimes does she have?

★7. **What If** Mia has 25 nickels in her collection of nickels and dimes that totals $1.75. How many more nickels than dimes does she have?

★8. **Social Studies** The Washington Monument in Washington, D.C., opened to the public in 1888, 4 years after the construction was completed. If it took 36 years to build the monument, when did the construction begin?

10. ✎ **Write a problem** that can be solved by drawing a diagram or writing a number sentence. Solve it. Ask others to solve it.

Choose a Strategy
- Logical Reasoning
- Draw a Picture or Diagram
- Make a Graph
- Act It Out
- Make a Table or List
- Find a Pattern
- Guess and Check
- Write an Equation
- Work Backward
- Solve a Simpler Problem

★9. **Art** Keesha wants to put these flower stickers on a picture frame that is 3 inches wide and 6 inches long. How many stickers does she need?

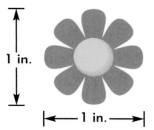

1 in.

1 in.

Extra Practice

Set A Divide. Check your answer. (pp. 430–432)

1. $8\overline{)138}$ 2. $7\overline{)871}$ 3. $3\overline{)\$6.93}$ 4. $5\overline{)582}$

5. $352 \div 6$ 6. $\$9.72 \div 3$ 7. $489 \div 4$ 8. $135 \div 2$

9. $745 \div 9$ 10. $202 \div 8$ 11. $\$6.15 \div 5$ 12. $123 \div 3$

13. $827 \div 5$ 14. $\$7.76 \div 2$ 15. $868 \div 6$ 16. $307 \div 3$

Set B Divide. Check your answer. (pp. 434–435)

17. $2\overline{)407}$ 18. $5\overline{)510}$ 19. $4\overline{)83}$ 20. $6\overline{)542}$

21. $314 \div 3$ 22. $831 \div 8$ 23. $721 \div 7$ 24. $975 \div 9$

25. $426 \div 4$ 26. $620 \div 6$ 27. $322 \div 3$ 28. $816 \div 8$

Set C Divide. Tell which method you use. (pp. 436–437)

29. $707 \div 7$ 30. $275 \div 5$ 31. $346 \div 9$ 32. $96 \div 6$

33. $486 \div 3$ 34. $133 \div 4$ 35. $738 \div 9$ 36. $842 \div 6$

37. $625 \div 5$ 38. $404 \div 3$ 39. $800 \div 5$ 40. $189 \div 7$

Set D Solve. (pp. 438–439)

41. The children's librarian has 75 books about birds, 671 books about mammals, 128 books about fish, and 209 books about other animals. How many books are there in all?

42. The music store has 473 rock CDs, 452 classical CDs, and 475 rap CDs. For which type of music does the store have the most CDs? How many more rap than classical CDs does the store have?

43. A carpenter is making 4-foot shelves for the library. She has 3 boards. Each board is 10 feet long. How many shelves can she make?

44. Harry wants to put no more than 5 apples in each box. There are 108 apples. What is the least number of boxes he can use?

LOG ON www.mmhmath.com
For more practice and Chapter Self-Check Test

Review/Test

Divide. Check your answer.

1. $8\overline{)376}$

2. $3\overline{)\$705}$

3. $4\overline{)419}$

4. $5\overline{)54}$

5. $\$7.76 \div 2$

6. $868 \div 6$

7. $808 \div 9$

8. $\$6.25 \div 5$

9. $967 \div 3$

10. $\$574 \div 7$

11. $\$5.34 \div 6$

12. $307 \div 3$

13. $6\overline{)\$0.24}$

14. $9\overline{)427}$

15. $5\overline{)800}$

16. $4\overline{)668}$

Divide. Tell which method you used.

17. $164 \div 4$

18. $204 \div 4$

19. $7\overline{)147}$

20. $3\overline{)\$31.50}$

21. $542 \div 8$

22. $335 \div 5$

23. $591 \div 6$

24. $\$75.35 \div 5$

25. $9\overline{)819}$

26. $5\overline{)210}$

27. $2\overline{)\$81.54}$

28. $3\overline{)363}$

Solve.

29. The Food Pantry has 144 cans of soup to put into 3 cases. Each case can hold 2 equal layers of cans. How many cans will go in each layer?

30. Large plants are priced at 3 for $8.97. Small plants cost 3 for $3.99. If Lee buys 1 large and 1 small plant, how much does she spend?

31. A 6-pack of juice costs $2.39. About how much are you paying for each can?

32. How many 6-packs of juice do you need for 125 people?

33. **Write About It** **Explain** how you find the unit price.

Do I Need Help?

Exercises	Review Concepts	Use Extra Practice Set
1–16	pp. 430–432, 434–435	Sets A and B
17–28	pp. 436–437	Set C
29–33	pp. 438–439	Set D

 **Use your Foldables to help you review.**

Assessment

Applying Math and Science
Flying Paper Planes

There are many kinds of paper airplanes. Some are small and pointed, while others are large and rounded.

A plane's shape will affect how fast or far it can fly. In this activity, you will compare the flights of 3 paper planes to see which one can fly the farthest.

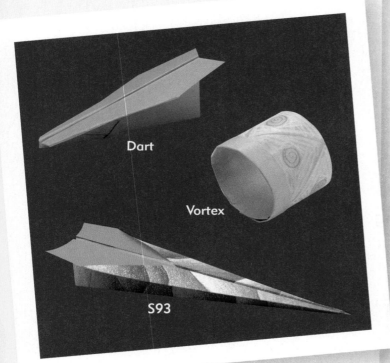

Dart

Vortex

S93

Hypothesize

Look at the picture of the 3 paper planes. Which plane do you think will fly the farthest?

You Will Need

- paper plane instruction sheets
- scissors
- meterstick or tape measure
- tape

Be Careful! **Safety** Be careful when working with scissors.

Procedure

1. Work in a group. Build 3 paper plane models. Copy and complete the chart on the next page to record the distance that each plane traveled.

2. Go to a long hallway or gym. Practice throwing each plane.

3. Throw the S93. Measure how far it traveled.

4. Throw the Dart. Measure how far it traveled.

5. Throw the Vortex. Measure how far it traveled.

6. Round all measurements to the nearest centimeter.

PLANE	DISTANCE
S93	
Dart	
Vortex	

Conclude and Apply

1. Observe Which paper plane flew the farthest? How do you know? Was your hypothesis correct?

2. Use Numbers Divide the greatest distance by each of the two lesser distances to find out how many times farther the first-place plane flew. Round your quotients to the nearest centimeter. Use a calculator to help you.

3. If you could build only 1 plane model, which would you choose? Think about the length of the flight, the overall look of the plane, and how flat or straight the flight was. Explain your choice.

Going Further Design your own paper plane. How does its flight distance compare to that of the other planes?

Unit Study Guide and Review

Vocabulary

Complete. Use a word from the list.

> **VOCABULARY**
> compatible numbers
> dividend
> divisor
> quotient
> remainder
> unit price

1. In $40 \div 5$, 5 is the _____.

2. You divide the total cost by the number of items to find the _____.

3. When you divide compatible numbers there is no _____.

4. Changing numbers to other numbers that form a basic fact to estimate an answer is using _____.

5. When you divide 24 by 4, the _____ is 6.

Skills and Applications

Divide multiples of 10 and 100 mentally. (pp. 410–413)

Find: $810 \div 9$

Solution
Use patterns.
$81 \div 9 = 9$
$810 \div 9 = 90$

Divide. Use mental math.

6. $600 \div 3$ 7. $360 \div 6$ 8. $250 \div 5$

9. $210 \div 7$ 10. $640 \div 8$ 11. $400 \div 4$

12. $360 \div 9$ 13. $100 \div 2$ 14. $240 \div 8$

Divide up to 3-digit numbers. (pp. 420–422, 430–435)

Find: $3\overline{)595}$

Solution
Place the first digit.
Divide each place.

$$
\begin{array}{r}
198R1 \\
3\overline{)595} \\
-3\downarrow \\
\hline
29 \\
-27\downarrow \\
\hline
25 \\
-24 \\
\hline
1
\end{array}
$$

Divide. Check your answers.

15. $7\overline{)\$3.15}$ 16. $6\overline{)\$9.78}$ 17. $9\overline{)\$8.01}$

18. $8\overline{)453}$ 19. $4\overline{)726}$ 20. $53 \div 7$

21. $533 \div 5$ 22. $\$0.54 \div 9$

23. $\$8.64 \div 8$

24. If 616 cans are packed 8 in a box, how many boxes are there?

 Use your Foldables to help you review.

Estimate quotients. (pp. 414–416)

Estimate 435 ÷ 6

Solution
Use compatible numbers.

435 ÷ 6

↓   ↓   435 is about 420.

420 ÷ 6 = 70

435 ÷ 6 is about 70.

Estimate.

25. 627 ÷ 9   **26.** 281 ÷ 3

27. 345 ÷ 7   **28.** 218 ÷ 5

29. Carla wants to divide $552 equally among 6 charities. About how much should she give to each?

30. There are 247 jelly beans to be shared by 4 people equally. About how many will each person get?

Use skills and strategies to solve problems. (pp. 424–425, 438–439)

A piece of wood 36 inches long is cut into 6-inch pieces. How many pieces will there be?

Solution
Draw a diagram or write an equation.

Diagram

Equation

36 ÷ 6 = 6

There will be 6 pieces.

Solve.

31. The Sewing Club sells blankets made of square pieces of cloth. Each blanket has 112 squares with 8 squares in each row. How many rows of squares are there?

32. Another blanket has 16 squares in each row. There are 480 squares made. How many rows are there?

33. Manny and Dee are sewing a blanket using 20 squares in each row. They have 604 squares of cloth to use. How many rows can they make?

Enrichment

Divisibility Rules for 2, 5, and 10

One number is divisible by another number
if there is no remainder when you divide them.
Divisibility rules help you know if a number
is divisible by another number.

A number is divisible by 2 if the ones digit is 0, 2, 4, 6, or 8.

Divisible by 2:	**Not** divisible by 2:
34 80 118 574 546	21 57 93 189 777

A number is divisible by 5 if the ones digit is 0 or 5.

Divisible by 5:	**Not** divisible by 5:
55 15 110 405 900	23 59 276 847 1,362

A number is divisible by 10 if the ones digit is 0.

Divisible by 10:	**Not** divisible by 10:
40 90 550 200 620	65 99 111 208 714

List if each number is divisible by 2, 5, or 10.

1. 75
2. 125
3. 100
4. 42
5. 83

6. 112
7. 86
8. 807
9. 6,330
10. 7,154

11. 31,790
12. 76,538
13. 1,000,000
14. 1,543,265
15. 2,500,003

16. **Analyze** What do you notice about numbers
that are divisible by both 2 and 5?

Performance Assessment

Which Divisor Has the Lowest Remainder?

Different volunteer groups from your town are making flower baskets. They will bring them to places like a Senior Citizens Home.

The baskets are packed in boxes of 4, 5, 7, or 9.

Make a chart like the one below. Record your findings about the kinds of boxes each group should use. Try to have the fewest baskets left.

- Find how many boxes you will need.

- Decide which kind of box to use.

Make this chart to record your data.

Group	Number of Baskets	Box Size	Number of Boxes Needed	Number of Baskets Left
Girl Scouts	254			
Boy Scouts	175			
Helping Hands	196			
Good Neighbors	218			

What If The Good Neighbors group could use 2 different-sized boxes. Could all of the baskets be boxed using only 2 different sizes?

Tips For A Good Answer

- Show a completed chart.

- Show that you tried different-sized boxes to find the best size to use.

- Show the steps you used to divide.

- Show work to determine if the Good Neighbors group can use only 2 different-sized boxes.

PORTFOLIO You may want to save this work in your portfolio.

e-Journal www.mmhmath.com
Write about math.   Unit 10   **447**

Assessment

TECHNOLOGY Link

Use Place-Value Models to Divide

Melissa baked 92 muffins. She plans to place an equal number of them in each of 5 boxes. How many muffins will be in each box?

You can build a model using the place-value tool in the *Math Tool Chest CD-ROM* that shows how Melissa divides the muffins.

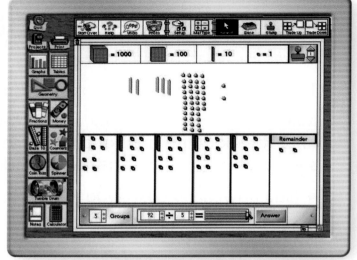

Math Tool Chest CD-ROM

- Choose division as the type of mat.
- Stamp out the number of muffins.
- Group them into 5 equal groups.
- Regroup the models if necessary.

The number boxes keep count as you stamp and group.

- How many muffins will be in each box?
- Are any muffins left?

Use the computer to model each division problem. Then write the quotient.

1. $80 \div 5$ **2.** $72 \div 3$ **3.** $86 \div 7$ **4.** $95 \div 4$

Solve.

5. Mona needs to buy 96 party hats for a party. The party hats come in packages of 6. How many packages does she need to buy?

6. Analyze How does modeling the problem help you divide?

For more practice, use Math Traveler™.

Test-Taking Tips

One way you can be a better test taker is to try and use **mental math** to help you find the answer.

Dawn drove 400 miles in 2 days. She drove the same distance each day. How many miles did she drive each day?

A. 100 miles   **C.** 300 miles

B. 200 miles   **D.** 500 miles

She could not have driven 500 miles. It is more than the 400 total miles she drove. So you know right away that the answer is not D.

Using mental math, think:

$$4 \div 2 = 2$$
$$40 \div 2 = 20$$
$$400 \div 2 = 200$$

Check that 200 is one of the choices. It is. The correct answer is B.

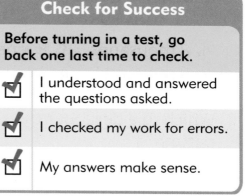

Check for Success

Before turning in a test, go back one last time to check.

- ✓ I understood and answered the questions asked.
- ✓ I checked my work for errors.
- ✓ My answers make sense.

Choose the best answer. Use mental math if possible.

1. A store has 120 bags of marbles. Each bag has 8 marbles. How many marbles are there in all?

   A. 96 marbles   **C.** 800 marbles
   B. 480 marbles   **D.** 960 marbles

2. There are 5 bags of marbles, each holding the same amount. There are 75 marbles in all. How many marbles are in each bag?

   F. 15 marbles   **H.** 35 marbles
   G. 25 marbles   **I.** 40 marbles

3. Matt has $19.75. He buys 2 items for $5.75 each. How much money does he have left?

   A. $8.25   **C.** $14.00
   B. $11.20   **D.** $15.25

4. You can build 4 toys using a building set with 360 pieces. If each toy has the same number of pieces, how many pieces are in each toy?

   F. 8 pieces   **H.** 80 pieces
   G. 9 pieces   **I.** 90 pieces

Test Prep

PART 1 • Multiple Choice

Choose the best answer.

1. What is the value of the underlined digit? (p. 6)

   84,8<u>9</u>8

   A. 8 thousands   C. 8 tens
   B. 8 hundreds   D. 8 ones

2. Which rule describes this pattern? (p. 430)

   243, 81, 27, 9, 3, 1

   F. Multiply by 3.
   G. Divide by 3.
   H. Subtract 162.
   I. Add 162.

3. $381 \div 4 = \blacksquare$ (p. 430)

   A. 96 R1   C. 95 R1
   B. 95 R2   D. 95

4. Which equation describes 80 groups of 3? (p. 368)

   F. $80 \div 30 = 2\ R20$
   G. $80 \times 3 = 240$
   H. $80 \times n = 320$
   I. $80 - 30 = 50$

5. What operation makes this equation true? (p. 420)

   $96 \bullet 6 = 16$

   A. $+$ C. $\times$
   B. $-$ D. $\div$

6. Which is an example of the Associative Property? (p. 53)

   F. $3 + 4 = 4 + 3$
   G. $3 + 0 = 3$
   H. $(3 + 4) + 2 = 3 + (4 + 2)$
   I. $3 \times 0 = 0$

7. The clocks show the times a train leaves Station A and arrives at Station B. How long does it take to go from one station to the other? (p. 146)

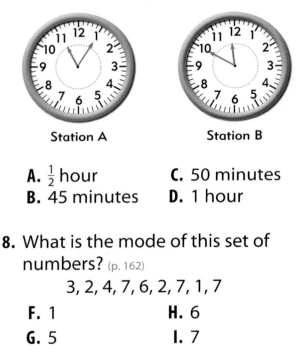

   Station A   Station B

   A. $\frac{1}{2}$ hour   C. 50 minutes
   B. 45 minutes   D. 1 hour

8. What is the mode of this set of numbers? (p. 162)

   3, 2, 4, 7, 6, 2, 7, 1, 7

   F. 1   H. 6
   G. 5   I. 7

9. Kim has 48 inches of ribbon. She uses 8 inches of ribbon to wrap each present. How many presents can she wrap? (p. 330)

   A. 6 presents   C. 4 presents
   B. 5 presents   D. 3 presents

Record your answers on the answer sheet provided by your teacher or on a sheet of paper.

10. Joe had a party on July 3. Mickela had a party on July 31. How many weeks were there between their parties? (p. 150)

11. What is the missing number? Explain how you know. (p. 52)

THINK SOLVE EXPLAIN

$$45 + 23 = 23 + \blacksquare$$

12. Henry read 5 books during February. Each book had 137 pages. How many pages did Henry read during February? (p. 390)

13. The Stokes family spent $45.00 on tickets to a concert. Each ticket cost the same amount. If 3 people went to the concert, how much did each ticket cost? (p. 420)

14. Mrs. Murphy spends 45 minutes a day working outside. About how many minutes does she spend in a week working outside? (p. 372)

15. Thomas has collected 987 bottle caps. What is this number to the nearest hundred? Nearest thousand? (p. 35)

Use data from the bar graph for problems 16–18.

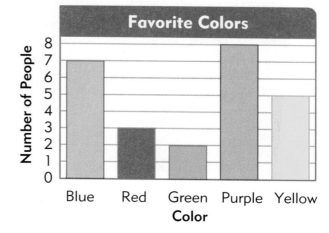

Favorite Colors

Number of People / Color

16. Explain and show how you can find the total number of people who were surveyed. (p. 168)

THINK SOLVE EXPLAIN

17. How many more people like purple than green? (p. 168)

18. The total number of people who like red and green equals the number of people who like which color? (p. 168)

Record your answer on a sheet of paper. Show your work.

THINK SOLVE EXPLAIN

19. The sum of 2 numbers is 320. The difference between the 2 numbers is 40. What are the 2 numbers? Explain how you know. (p. 346)

Test Prep

What Do I Need to Know?

In-line skates are usually 3 inches longer than your shoes. Measure your shoe to the nearest inch. How long would your in-line skates be?

Measurement: Customary Units

What Will I Learn?

In this chapter you will learn to

- measure with nonstandard units
- estimate and measure length, capacity, and weight in customary units
- convert customary units
- use skills and strategies to solve problems

How Do I Read Math?

When you read a mathematics book, sometimes you read words and symbols, and sometimes you read only symbols.

Here are some abbreviations of customary units:

- **Length: in., ft, yd**
- **Capacity: c, pt, qt, gal**
- **Weight: oz, lb**

VOCABULARY

- length
- capacity
- weight

Foldables

Use your Foldables to help you with chapter concepts.

1. Fold the short side of a large sheet of paper into 4 parts.
2. Open the paper and refold into 3 parts along the long side.
3. Unfold and draw lines along the folds.
4. Label as shown. Record what you learn.

Chapter 21 Measurement: Customary Units	Non-Standard	Customary
Length	Line up paper clips end to end to measure the length of a book. How many paper clips did you use? other non standard units - crayons, connecting cubes	units - inches feet yards tools - inch ruler yardstick tape measure
Capacity		
Weight		

21.1 Explore Lengths

Learn

Length is the measurement of distance between two endpoints.

You can use a nonstandard unit, such as a paper clip, to estimate the length of a pencil.

You Will Need
- small paper clips
- pencil

VOCABULARY
length

Use Models

STEP 1

Copy the table.

Estimate how many paper clips long the pencil is.

Record your estimate in the table.

Object	Estimate	Number of Paper Clips

STEP 2

Lay paper clips end to end along the pencil.

Record the number of paper clips in the table.

STEP 3

Choose other objects in your classroom.

Estimate and record their measurements in the table.

Use another nonstandard unit to measure.

454

Explain Your Thinking

1. What is your estimate for the length of the pencil?

2. How many paper clips long is the pencil?

3. How close is that to your estimate?

Find the length of the pencil.
Let's connect measuring with nonstandard units to standard units.

Make Connections

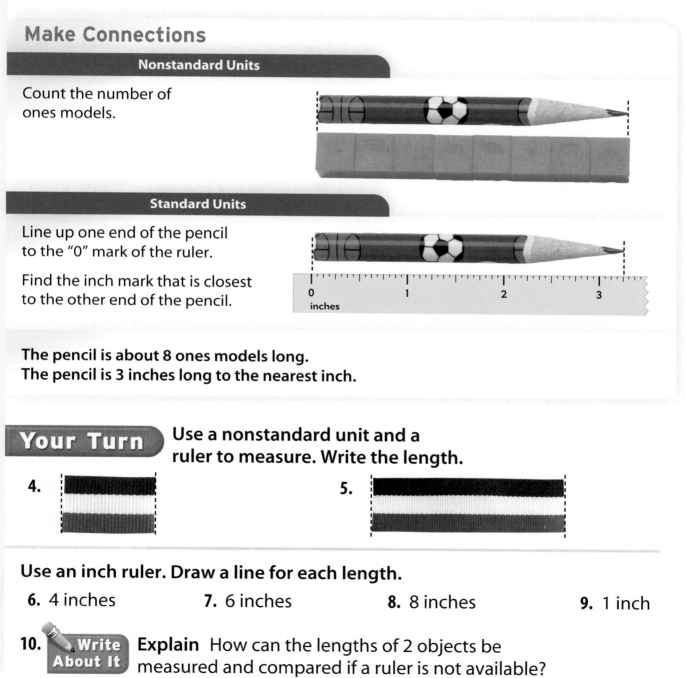

Nonstandard Units

Count the number of ones models.

Standard Units

Line up one end of the pencil to the "0" mark of the ruler.

Find the inch mark that is closest to the other end of the pencil.

The pencil is about 8 ones models long.
The pencil is 3 inches long to the nearest inch.

Your Turn Use a nonstandard unit and a ruler to measure. Write the length.

4.

5.

Use an inch ruler. Draw a line for each length.

6. 4 inches   7. 6 inches   8. 8 inches   9. 1 inch

10. **Write About It** **Explain** How can the lengths of 2 objects be measured and compared if a ruler is not available?

21.2 Explore Customary Units of Length

Learn

You can use a ruler to explore lengths measured in customary units.

You Will Need
- inch ruler
- eraser

Table of Measures	
1 foot (ft)	= 12 inches (in.)
1 yard (yd)	= 36 inches or 3 feet
1 mile (mi)	= 1,760 yards or 5,280 feet

Use Models

STEP 1

Copy the table.

Estimate the length of the eraser in inches. Record your estimate in the table.

Object	Estimate	Length

STEP 2

Line up one end of the eraser to the 0 mark on the ruler.

Find the closest $\frac{1}{2}$ inch mark to the other end of the eraser.

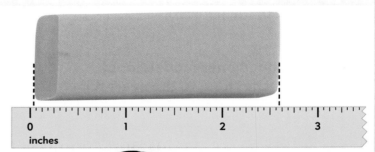

STEP 3

Choose other objects. Estimate and record their lengths to the nearest half inch in the table.

After completing the table, list the objects in order from shortest to longest.

Explain Your Thinking

1. What is your estimate for the length of the eraser?

2. How long is the eraser to the nearest $\frac{1}{2}$ inch?

3. Is this measurement exact? Explain.

There are other customary units used to measure lengths. Let's connect objects to measuring tools and units.

Make Connections

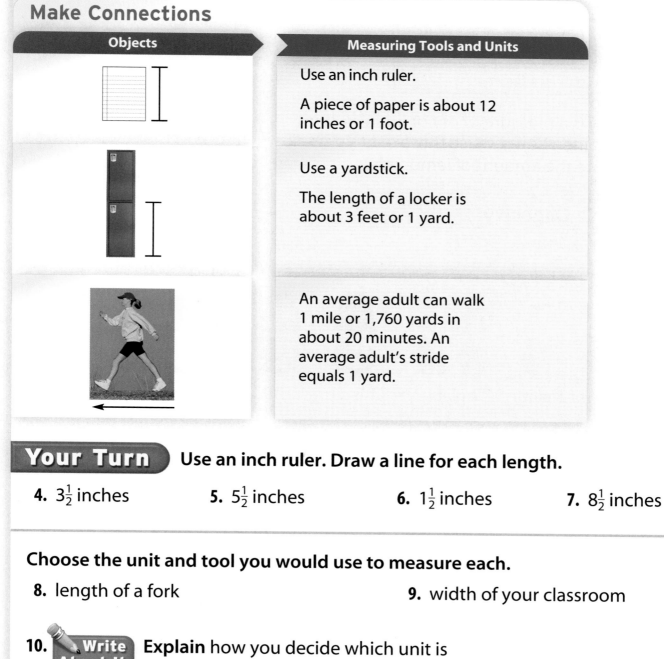

Objects	Measuring Tools and Units
	Use an inch ruler. A piece of paper is about 12 inches or 1 foot.
	Use a yardstick. The length of a locker is about 3 feet or 1 yard.
	An average adult can walk 1 mile or 1,760 yards in about 20 minutes. An average adult's stride equals 1 yard.

Your Turn Use an inch ruler. Draw a line for each length.

4. $3\frac{1}{2}$ inches

5. $5\frac{1}{2}$ inches

6. $1\frac{1}{2}$ inches

7. $8\frac{1}{2}$ inches

Choose the unit and tool you would use to measure each.

8. length of a fork

9. width of your classroom

10. **Write About It** **Explain** how you decide which unit is best to use to measure an object.

21.3 Customary Units of Capacity

Learn

Jena is at the lemonade stand. She has poured some lemonade for customers. About how much lemonade has Jena poured?

Customary Units of Capacity
1 pint (pt) = 2 cups (c)
1 quart (qt) = 4 cups or 2 pints (pt)
1 gallon (gal) = 4 quarts

Capacity is a measure of dry or liquid volume of a container. You can use these containers to estimate the amount of lemonade.

Estimate Capacity

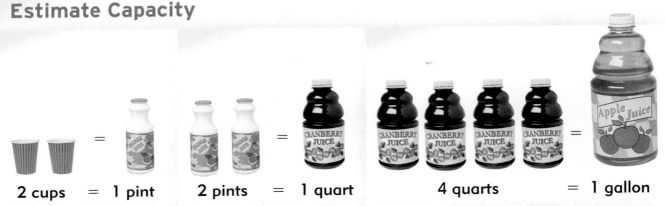

2 cups = 1 pint   2 pints = 1 quart   4 quarts = 1 gallon

Jena has poured about 2 cups, or 1 pint, of lemonade.

Try It Choose the best estimate.

1. **A.** 1 gal
   B. 1 qt
   C. 1 c

2. **A.** 1 gal
   B. 1 pt
   C. 1 c

3. **A.** 1 gal
   B. 1 c
   C. 1 qt

4. **Write About It** **Explain** how you choose which unit to use to measure the capacity of a container.

458

Practice and Problem Solving

Choose the better estimate.

5.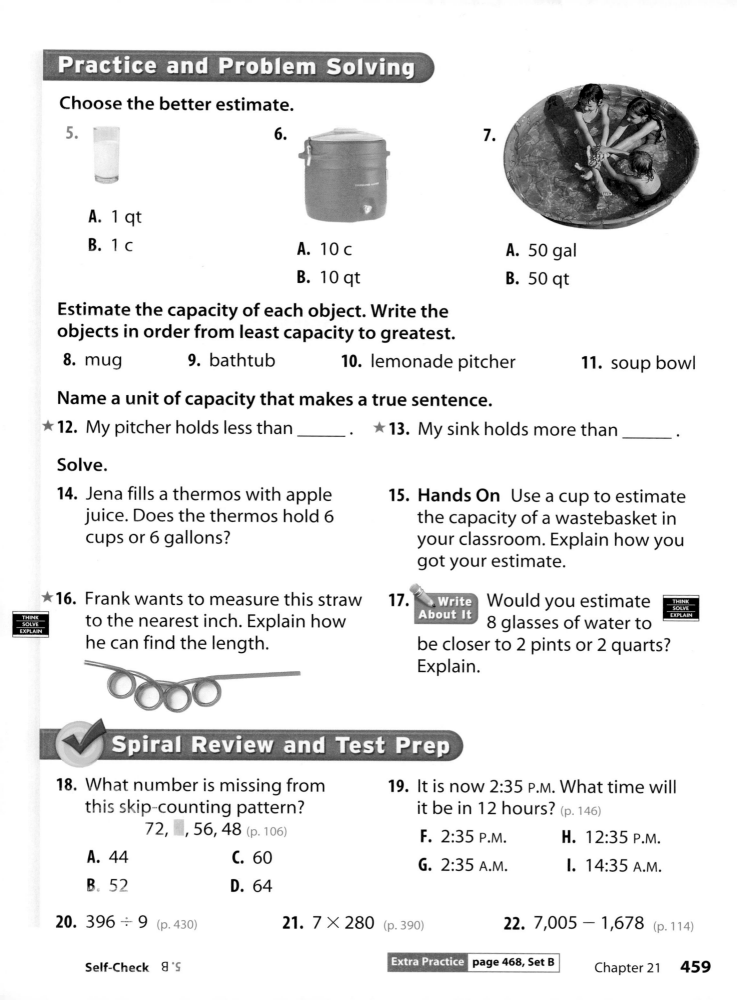

   A. 1 qt
   B. 1 c

6.

   A. 10 c
   B. 10 qt

7.

   A. 50 gal
   B. 50 qt

Estimate the capacity of each object. Write the objects in order from least capacity to greatest.

8. mug   9. bathtub   10. lemonade pitcher   11. soup bowl

Name a unit of capacity that makes a true sentence.

★12. My pitcher holds less than _____ .   ★13. My sink holds more than _____ .

Solve.

14. Jena fills a thermos with apple juice. Does the thermos hold 6 cups or 6 gallons?

15. **Hands On** Use a cup to estimate the capacity of a wastebasket in your classroom. Explain how you got your estimate.

★16. Frank wants to measure this straw to the nearest inch. Explain how he can find the length.

17. **Write About It** Would you estimate 8 glasses of water to be closer to 2 pints or 2 quarts? Explain.

THINK SOLVE EXPLAIN

Spiral Review and Test Prep

18. What number is missing from this skip-counting pattern?
    72, ▮, 56, 48 (p. 106)
    A. 44   **C.** 60
    B. 52   **D.** 64

19. It is now 2:35 P.M. What time will it be in 12 hours? (p. 146)
    F. 2:35 P.M.   **H.** 12:35 P.M.
    G. 2:35 A.M.   **I.** 14:35 A.M.

20. 396 ÷ 9 (p. 430)   21. 7 × 280 (p. 390)   22. 7,005 − 1,678 (p. 114)

21.4 Customary Units of Weight

Learn

How can Crystal estimate and measure a whistle and a ball to see how heavy each object is?

Weight is a measurement that tells how heavy an object is.

VOCABULARY
weight

Customary Units of Weight
16 ounces (oz) = 1 pound (lb)

Estimate Weight

about 1 ounce

about 1 pound

16 1-ounce whistles have about the same weight as a 1-pound ball.

One whistle weighs about 1 ounce.
One ball weighs about 1 pound.

Try It Choose the better estimate.

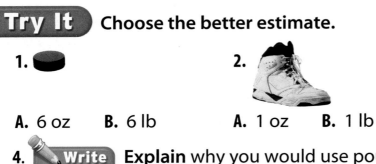

1. **A.** 6 oz   **B.** 6 lb

2. **A.** 1 oz   **B.** 1 lb

3.  **A.** 2,500 oz   **B.** 2,500 lb

4. **Write About It** **Explain** why you would use pounds to measure the weight of a bicycle.

Practice and Problem Solving

Choose the better estimate.

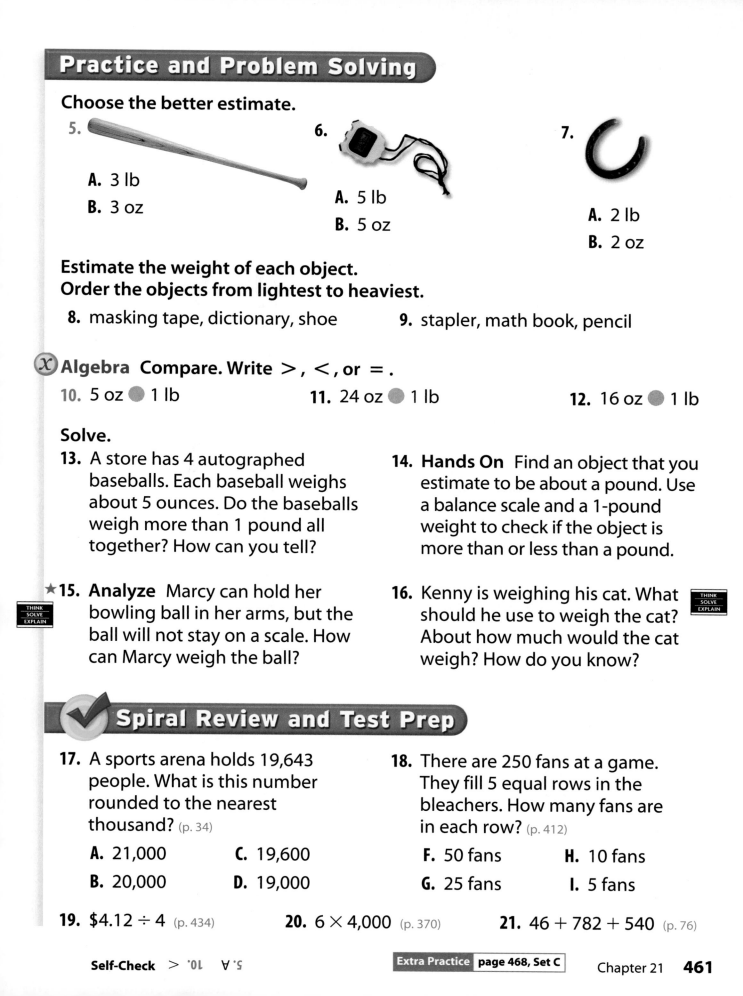

5.
A. 3 lb
B. 3 oz

6.
A. 5 lb
B. 5 oz

7.
A. 2 lb
B. 2 oz

Estimate the weight of each object.
Order the objects from lightest to heaviest.

8. masking tape, dictionary, shoe

9. stapler, math book, pencil

X **Algebra Compare. Write >, <, or = .**

10. 5 oz ● 1 lb

11. 24 oz ● 1 lb

12. 16 oz ● 1 lb

Solve.

13. A store has 4 autographed baseballs. Each baseball weighs about 5 ounces. Do the baseballs weigh more than 1 pound all together? How can you tell?

14. **Hands On** Find an object that you estimate to be about a pound. Use a balance scale and a 1-pound weight to check if the object is more than or less than a pound.

★15. **Analyze** Marcy can hold her bowling ball in her arms, but the ball will not stay on a scale. How can Marcy weigh the ball?

16. Kenny is weighing his cat. What should he use to weigh the cat? About how much would the cat weigh? How do you know?

THINK
SOLVE
EXPLAIN

Spiral Review and Test Prep

17. A sports arena holds 19,643 people. What is this number rounded to the nearest thousand? (p. 34)

A. 21,000   C. 19,600

B. 20,000   D. 19,000

18. There are 250 fans at a game. They fill 5 equal rows in the bleachers. How many fans are in each row? (p. 412)

F. 50 fans   H. 10 fans

G. 25 fans   I. 5 fans

19. $4.12 ÷ 4 (p. 434)

20. 6 × 4,000 (p. 370)

21. 46 + 782 + 540 (p. 76)

21.5 Convert Customary Units

Learn

The pins in bowling are set in the shape of a triangle. How many inches is each side of the triangle?

3 feet

3 feet   3 feet

Convert, or change, larger units to smaller units. Change feet into inches.

There's More Than One Way!

Think: 1 foot = 12 inches

Use Repeated Addition

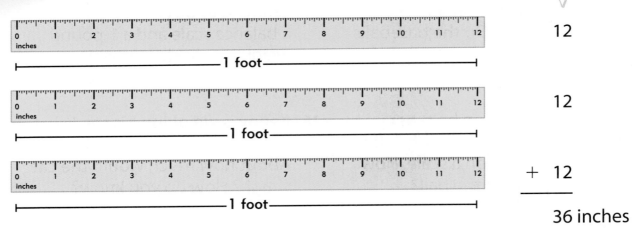

12

12

+ 12
_____

36 inches

Use Patterns

1 foot = 12 inches

2 feet = 24 inches

3 feet = 36 inches

Use Multiplication

3 feet = ▓ inches

3 × 12 inches = ▓ inches

3 × 12 inches = 36 inches

3 feet = 36 inches

Think: Since 1 foot = 12 inches, you multiply 3 feet by 12 inches.

Each side of the triangle is 36 inches.

The coach needs to have 24 cups of sports drink for the players. How many quarts of sports drink does the coach need to buy?

Convert smaller units to larger units. Change cups to quarts.

There's More Than One Way!

Use Repeated Subtraction

$24 - 4 - 4 - 4 - 4 - 4 - 4 = 0$

You subtracted 6 times. There are 6 quarts in 24 cups.

Use a Table

Think: 4 cups = 1 quart

Cups	4	8	12	16	20	24	28
Quarts	1	2	3	4	5	6	7

The table shows that 24 cups equals 6 quarts.

Use Division

Think: Since 4 cups = 1 quart, you divide 24 cups by 4 cups.

You can also use a calculator.

24 cups = ▮ quarts

24 cups ÷ 4 = ▮ quarts

24 cups ÷ 4 = 6 quarts

24 cups = 6 quarts

The coach needs to buy 6 quarts of sports drink.

Try It Write the number that makes each sentence true.

1. 2 gal = ▮ qt   **2.** 2 ft = ▮ in.   **3.** 2 lb = ▮ oz   **4.** 4 yd = ▮ ft

5. 4 lb = ▮ oz   **6.** 16 qt = ▮ gal   **7.** 6 ft = ▮ in.   **8.** 3 gal = ▮ qt

9. **Write About It** **Compare** when you multiply and divide to change units.

Practice and Problem Solving

Copy and complete.

10.

Quarts		8		16	
Gallons	1		3		5

11.

Pounds			2	3		5
Ounces	16				64	

Write the number that makes each sentence true.

12. 7 gal = ▪ qt   **13.** 3 ft = ▪ in.   **14.** 16 oz = ▪ lb   **15.** 3 lb = ▪ oz

16. ▪ oz = 6 lb   ★**17.** 2 ft 6 in. = ▪ in.   ★**18.** 18 qt = ▪ gal   ★**19.** 6 ft 7 in. = ▪ in.

ⓧ Algebra Compare. Write >, <, or = .

20. 5 ft ● 48 in.   **21.** 5 lb ● 32 oz   **22.** 2 gal ● 12 qt

Solve. Use data from the picture for problems 23–25.

23. Tani is exercising with 2 of the red weights. How many ounces is she lifting all together?

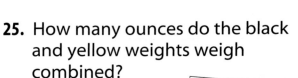

2 lb   3 lb   4 lb

24. How many ounces more is a yellow weight than a black weight?

25. How many ounces do the black and yellow weights weigh combined?

THINK SOLVE EXPLAIN **26.** ✏ **Write a problem** that can be solved by changing feet to inches. Solve it. Ask others to solve it. Compare solutions.

27. Make It Right
Harry drew a picture and wrote about a fish he caught. Tell what mistake he made. Explain how to correct it. THINK SOLVE EXPLAIN

30 inches

The fish is 2 feet.

Spiral Review and Test Prep

28. Three tickets to a high school football game cost $18.00. How much is each ticket? (p. 298)

    A. $24.00   **C.** $6.00

    B. $21.00   **D.** $5.00

29. Each of 12 members gives 4 cans of food to the food drive. How many cans are given? (p. 254)

    F. 3 cans   **H.** 40 cans

    G. 16 cans   **I.** 48 cans

30. 320 ÷ 4 (p. 410)   **31.** 78 ÷ 6 (p. 420)   **32.** 5,321 − 467 (p. 120)

Extra Practice page 468, Set D

GOING, GOING, GONE!

With the help of science and technology—and lots of practice—professional athletes are becoming world-wide record breakers.

Take baseball, for example. In 1927, Babe Ruth set a record of 60 home runs in a season. It took 34 years for the record to be broken by Roger Maris, who hit 61 home runs. In 1998, Mark McGwire topped Maris by 9, setting a new record. Three years later, San Francisco Giants outfielder Barry Bonds smacked 73 homers!

Some people say science plays a big part in helping athletes break records. Sports scientists create and test new equipment to help athletes win big. Today, baseball players use light bats made out of ash wood. The lighter bat makes it easier for a batter to swing faster. An ash bat weighs about 2 pounds. Babe Ruth used a hickory bat that weighed more than 3 pounds!

Problem Solving

 Reading Skill **Make Predictions** Could athletes get better in the future? Why or why not?

1. Babe Ruth's bat weighed over 3 pounds. How many ounces did his bat weigh?

2. How many more home runs did Barry Bonds hit than Mark McGwire?

21.6 Problem Solving: Skill
Check for Reasonableness

Read

Kia is practicing her long jump. She jumps 48 inches. Kia says that she jumped 10 feet. Is her statement reasonable?

- **What do you know?**
  Kia jumped 48 inches

- **What do you need to find?**
  If she jumped 10 feet

Plan

Check for Reasonableness

A reasonable answer fits with the facts in a problem.

You can use what you know about units of length to check whether Kia's statement is reasonable.

Solve

▶ Convert inches to feet.

Kia jumped 48 inches.

Find what number of feet multiplied by 12 that equals 48.

> **Think:**
> 12 inches = 1 foot

$n \times 12 = 48$ $n = 4$

4 feet $<$ 10 feet

Kia did not jump 10 feet.

So Kia's statement is not reasonable.

Look Back

How could you check your answer?

1. **Write About It** **Describe** a reasonable statement about the distance Kia jumped.

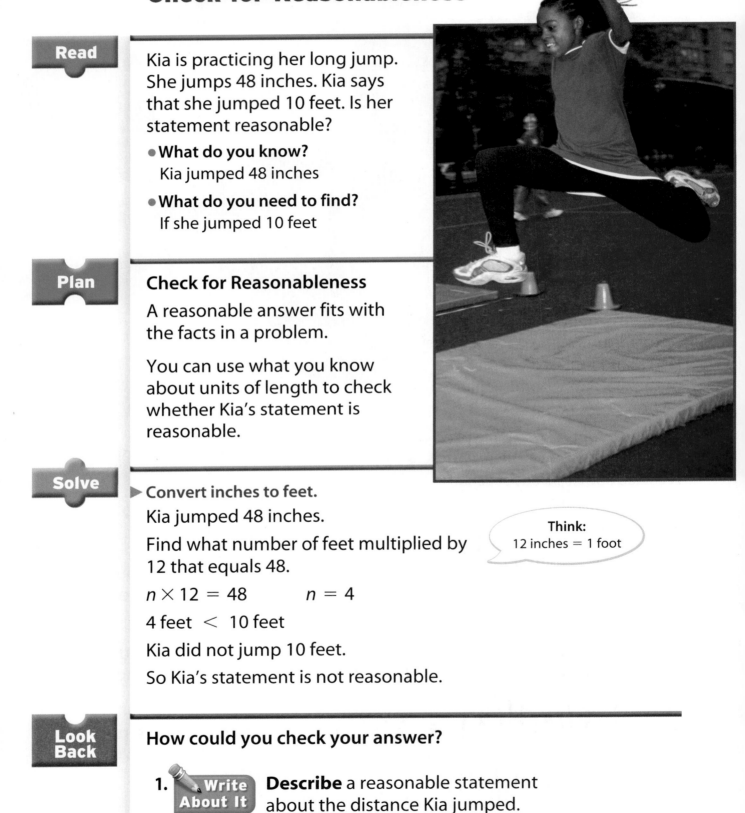

Practice

Solve. Explain your answer.

2. Dave high jumped 32 inches. Tyler high jumped 1 yard. Tyler claims he jumped the farthest. Is he correct? How many inches was Tyler's jump?

3. Liv jumps 26 inches. Jake jumps 2 feet 3 inches. Liv says she jumped the greater distance. Is she correct?

Mixed Strategy Review

4. Maya got home from school at 4:45 P.M. It took her 15 minutes to ride her bike home. She played hockey for 1 hour right after school. What time did school end?

5. There were 57 people in all at the track meet. There were twice as many fans as athletes. How many fans were at the track meet?

Choose a Strategy
- Logical Reasoning
- Draw a Picture or Diagram
- Make a Graph
- Act It Out
- Make a Table or List
- Find a Pattern
- Guess and Check
- Write an Equation
- Work Backward
- Solve a Simpler Problem

Use data from the chart for problems 6–11.

6. Ling says that her jump was greater than Trixie's. Is her statement correct?

7. Hal says that his jump was greater than Jim's. Is his statement reasonable?

8. Convert the distance that Hal threw to feet and inches.

9. Who threw farther, Ling or Trixie? How much farther?

Longest Distance		
Student	**Long Jump**	**Ball Throw**
Hal	48 inches	78 inches
Jim	2 feet 2 inches	1 yard 5 inches
Ling	3 feet 1 inch	1 yard
Trixie	38 inches	3 feet 3 inches

10. ✏ **Write a problem** using the data from the chart. Solve it. Ask others to solve it.

★**11.** What is the distance in inches that Jim threw the ball?

Extra Practice

Set A For problems 1–3, draw a line segment of each length. (pp. 454–455, 456–457)

1. 4 paper clips   **2.** 10 paper clips   **3.** 7 paper clips

Choose the best estimate.

4. A bicycle's wheel is about 24 ▮ wide.

    A. inches   **B.** feet   **C.** yards

5. A shoe is about 1 ▮ long.

    A. inch   **B.** foot   **C.** yard

Set B Choose the better estimate. (pp. 458–459)

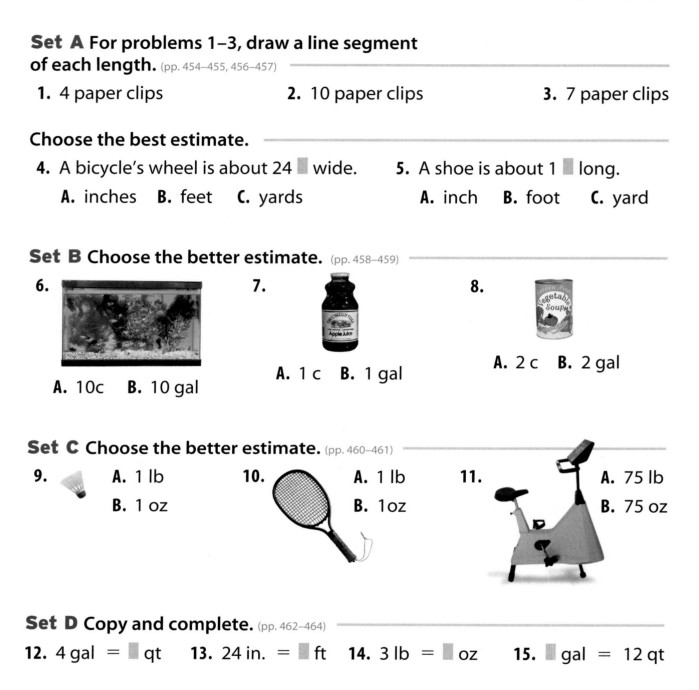

6.   **A.** 10c   **B.** 10 gal

7.   **A.** 1 c   **B.** 1 gal

8.   **A.** 2 c   **B.** 2 gal

Set C Choose the better estimate. (pp. 460–461)

9.   **A.** 1 lb   **B.** 1 oz

10.   **A.** 1 lb   **B.** 1oz

11.   **A.** 75 lb   **B.** 75 oz

Set D Copy and complete. (pp. 462–464)

12. 4 gal = ▮ qt   **13.** 24 in. = ▮ ft   **14.** 3 lb = ▮ oz   **15.** ▮ gal = 12 qt

Set E Check for reasonableness. Solve. (pp. 466–467)

16. Matthew is 50 inches tall. He says he is about the same height as his cousin, Fred. If Fred is 4 feet tall, is Matthew's statement reasonable? Why or why not?

17. Wendy's best high jump is 42 inches. Ellen's best is 3 feet. Ellen says that she jumped higher. Is this reasonable? Why or why not?

LOG ON   **www.mmhmath.com**
For more practice and Chapter Self-Check Test

Review/Test

Measure the length in paper clips and to the nearest inch.

1.

Choose the best estimate.

2. A tennis racket is about 2 ▮ long.
   A. in.   **B.** ft   **C.** yd

3. A basketball hoop is about 3 ▮ high.
   A. in.   **B.** ft   **C.** yd

Choose the better estimate.

4.
   A. 1 gal   **B.** 1 c

5.
   A. 12 oz   **B.** 12 lb

Write the number that makes each sentence true.

6. 36 in. = ▮ ft

7. 2 lb = ▮ oz

8. 4 gal = ▮ qt

Solve.

9. Mr. Costa jogs from his house to the park several times each day. He says he jogs over 1,000 yards. Is this reasonable? Explain.

10. **Write About It** **Generalize** Tell how you decide which unit to use when making a measurement.

Do I Need Help?

Exercises	Review Concepts	Use Extra Practice Set
1–3	pp. 454–455; 456–457	Set A
4–5	pp. 458–459; 460–461	Sets B and C
6–8	pp. 462–464	Set D
9–10	pp. 466–467	Set E

 **Use your Foldables to help you review.**

Assessment

What Do I Need to Know?

How long is the eraser?

Measurement: Metric Units

What Will I Learn?

In this chapter you will learn to

- estimate and measure length, capacity, and mass in metric units
- convert metric units
- estimate temperature in degrees Fahrenheit and degrees Celsius
- use skills and strategies to solve problems

How Do I Read Math?

When you read a mathematics book, sometimes you read words and symbols, and sometimes you read only symbols.

Here are some abbreviations of metric units:

- **Length: cm, dm, m**
- **Capacity: mL, L**
- **Mass: g, kg**

VOCABULARY

- mass
- degrees Celsius
- degrees Fahrenheit

Foldables

Use your Foldables to help you with chapter concepts.

1. Fold the short side of a large sheet of paper into 4 parts.
2. Open the paper and refold into 3 parts along the long side.
3. Unfold and draw lines along the folds.
4. Label as shown. Record what you learn.

Chapter 22 Measurement: Metric Units	Customary	Metric
Length	12 inches (in.) = 1 foot (ft) 3 feet = 1 yard (yd)	100 centimeters (cm) = 1 meter (m) 1 decimeter (dm) = 10 centimeters
Capacity		
Weight		

22.1 Explore Metric Units of Length

Hands On Activity

You can use a centimeter ruler to explore metric units of length.

You Will Need
- centimeter ruler
- meterstick or measuring tape
- classroom objects

Metric Units of Length

1 meter (m) = 100 centimeters	
1 decimeter (dm) = 10 centimeters (cm)	
1 meter = 10 decimeters	
1 kilometer (km) = 1,000 meters	

Use Models

STEP 1

Copy the table.

Estimate the length of the golf tee.

Record your estimate in the table.

Object	Estimate	Length

STEP 2

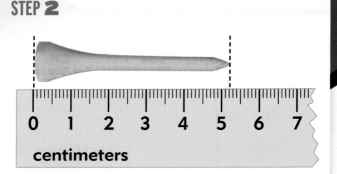

centimeters

Line up the left end of the golf tee to the 0 mark on the ruler.
Find the closest centimeter mark to the right end of the golf tee.
Record the length in the table.

STEP 3

Choose other objects. Estimate and record their lengths to the nearest centimeter in the table.

List the objects in order from longest to shortest.

Explain Your Thinking

1. What is your estimate for the length of the golf tee?

2. What is the actual length of the golf tee?

3. How do your estimates of other objects compare with the actual measurements?

There are other metric units used to measure lengths. Let's connect objects to measuring tools and units.

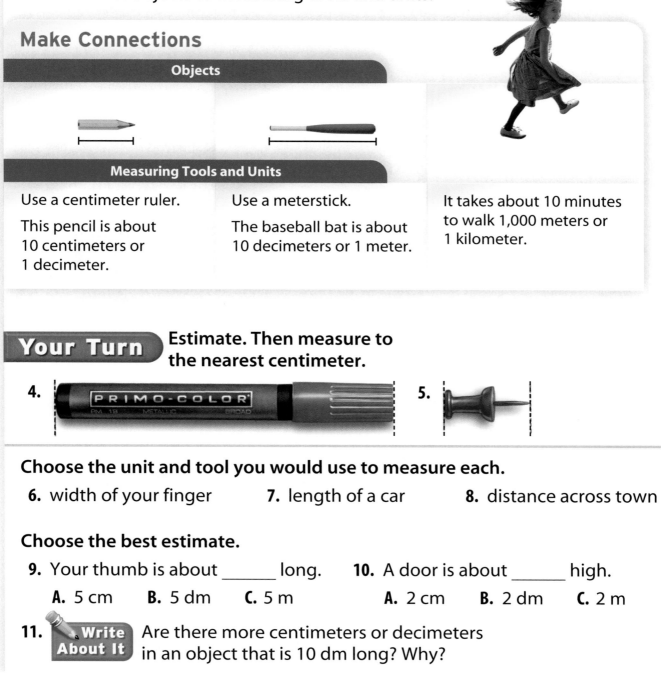

Make Connections

Objects		
Measuring Tools and Units		
Use a centimeter ruler.	Use a meterstick.	It takes about 10 minutes to walk 1,000 meters or 1 kilometer.
This pencil is about 10 centimeters or 1 decimeter.	The baseball bat is about 10 decimeters or 1 meter.	

Your Turn — Estimate. Then measure to the nearest centimeter.

4. PRIMO·COLOR
PM_18   METALLIC   BROAD

5.

Choose the unit and tool you would use to measure each.

6. width of your finger

7. length of a car

8. distance across town

Choose the best estimate.

9. Your thumb is about _____ long.

    A. 5 cm   **B.** 5 dm   **C.** 5 m

10. A door is about _____ high.

    A. 2 cm   **B.** 2 dm   **C.** 2 m

11. **Write About It** Are there more centimeters or decimeters in an object that is 10 dm long? Why?

22.2 Metric Units of Capacity

Learn

After tennis, Jason sips a bottle of sports drink. How much liquid does the bottle hold?

Metric Units of Capacity
1 liter (L) = 1,000 milliliters (mL)

You can use these containers to estimate the capacity.

Estimate Capacity

This dropper holds about 1 milliliter of liquid.

This glass holds about 250 milliliters of liquid.

This bottle holds about 1 liter, or 1,000 milliliters, of liquid.

The bottle holds about a liter of sports drink.

Try It   Choose the better estimate for problems 1–3.

1.   **A.** 2 mL
        B. 2 L

2.   **A.** 200 mL
        B. 200 L

3.   **A.** 20 mL
        B. 20 L

4. List the containers in problems 1–3 in order from least to greatest capacity.

5.  **Write About It** **Explain** whether you would choose milliliters or liters to measure the amount of liquid a spoon can hold.

Practice and Problem Solving

Choose the better estimate.

6.  **A.** 100 mL
   B. 100 L

7. **A.** 50 mL
   B. 50 L

8.  **A.** 2 mL
   B. 2 L

Estimate. Decide if the container holds more than, less than, or about the same as 1 liter.

9.

10.

11.

12. List the items in problems 6–11 in order from least to greatest capacity.

Estimate the capacity of each object. Write the objects in order from least capacity to greatest.

13. a cup

14. a bucket

15. a bowl

16. a lid from a jar

Solve.

17. **Hands On** Use a dropper to estimate the capacity of a small glass. Compare your results with your classmates.

★18. **Science** Rob mixes 75 milliliters of orange concentrate into 750 milliliters of water. Does he make more than, less than, or 1 liter of mixture? Explain.

THINK
SOLVE
EXPLAIN

Spiral Review and Test Prep

19. All 5 starters on a basketball team take the same number of practice shots. They take 75 shots in all. How many does each player take? (p. 420)

   A. 12 shots   **C.** 20 shots
   B. 15 shots   **D.** 25 shots

20. Michael jogged 120 yards 5 times to warm up for a game. How far did he jog in all? (p. 390)

   F. 500 yards   **H.** 600 yards
   G. 570 yards   **I.** 605 yards

Write the number that makes the sentence true. (p. 462)

21. 4 ft = ▮ in.

22. 2 lb = ▮ oz

23. ▮ qt = 3 gal

22.3 Metric Units of Mass

Learn

Wanda carries her ice skates as she leaves practice. About how much mass do you think Wanda is carrying?

VOCABULARY
mass

Metric Units of Mass
1 kilogram (kg) = 1,000 grams (g)

Mass is the amount of matter in an object. **You can use these objects to estimate the mass.**

Estimate Mass

This paper clip is about 1 gram.

One skate is about 1 kilogram.

1,000 paper clips have about the same mass as one skate.

Wanda is carrying about 2 kilograms.

Try It

Choose the best estimate. Then list the items in problems 1–3 from least to greatest mass.

1.    **A.** 1 g   **B.** 1 kg

2.   **A.** 2 g   **B.** 2 kg

3.   **A.** 15 g   **B.** 15 kg

4. **Write About It** **Explain** how many grams of mass an item can have, to the nearest gram, and still be less than a kilogram.

Practice and Problem Solving

Choose the better estimate.

5. 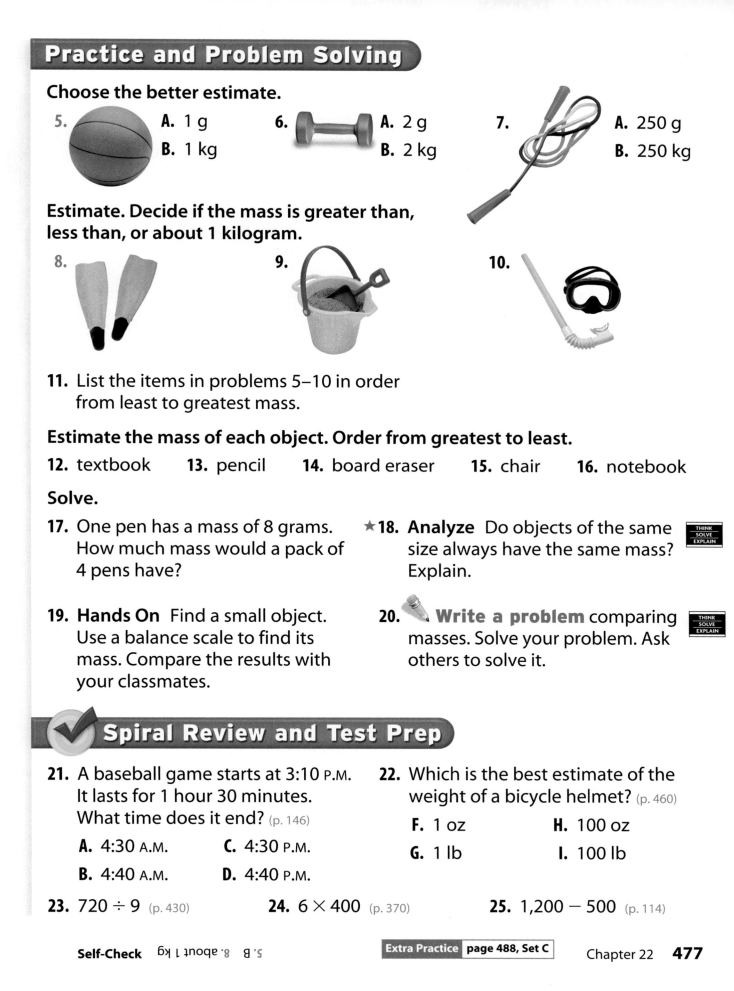 **A.** 1 g
   B. 1 kg

6. **A.** 2 g
   B. 2 kg

7. **A.** 250 g
   B. 250 kg

Estimate. Decide if the mass is greater than, less than, or about 1 kilogram.

8.

9.

10.

11. List the items in problems 5–10 in order from least to greatest mass.

Estimate the mass of each object. Order from greatest to least.

12. textbook   13. pencil   14. board eraser   15. chair   16. notebook

Solve.

17. One pen has a mass of 8 grams. How much mass would a pack of 4 pens have?

★18. **Analyze** Do objects of the same size always have the same mass? Explain. THINK SOLVE EXPLAIN

19. **Hands On** Find a small object. Use a balance scale to find its mass. Compare the results with your classmates.

20. **Write a problem** comparing masses. Solve your problem. Ask others to solve it. THINK SOLVE EXPLAIN

✓ Spiral Review and Test Prep

21. A baseball game starts at 3:10 P.M. It lasts for 1 hour 30 minutes. What time does it end? (p. 146)

    A. 4:30 A.M.   **C.** 4:30 P.M.
    B. 4:40 A.M.   **D.** 4:40 P.M.

22. Which is the best estimate of the weight of a bicycle helmet? (p. 460)

    F. 1 oz   **H.** 100 oz
    G. 1 lb   **I.** 100 lb

23. $720 \div 9$ (p. 430)   24. 6×400 (p. 370)   25. $1,200 - 500$ (p. 114)

22.4 Convert Metric Units

Learn

Jen and her family are playing croquet. Jen hits the ball 5 meters. How many centimeters are in 5 meters?

Convert meters into centimeters.

There's More Than One Way!

Use Repeated Addition

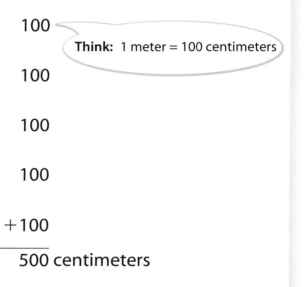

$$
\begin{aligned}
&100 \\
&100 \\
&100 \\
&100 \\
+&100 \\
\hline
&500 \text{ centimeters}
\end{aligned}
$$

Think: 1 meter = 100 centimeters

Use Patterns

1 meter = 100 centimeters
2 meters = 200 centimeters
3 meters = 300 centimeters
4 meters = 400 centimeters
5 meters = 500 centimeters

Use Multiplication

5 meters = ▮ centimeters
5 × 100 centimeters = ▮ centimeters
5 × 100 centimeters = 500 centimeters
5 meters = 500 centimeters

Think: Since 1 meter = 100 centimeters, you multiply 5 meters by 100 centimeters.

There are 500 centimeters in 5 meters.

Here are the mallet and the croquet ball. The mallet has a mass of 700 grams. The ball has a mass of 1,300 grams. What is the combined mass in kilograms?

700 grams + 1,300 grams = 2,000 grams

Convert grams to kilograms.

There's More Than One Way!

Use Repeated Subtraction

> **Think:** 1,000 grams = 1 kilogram.

$2,000 - 1,000 = 1,000$ $1,000 - 1,000 = 0$

You subtracted 2 times. There are 2 kilograms in 2,000 grams.

Use a Table

Kilograms	1	2	3	4
Grams	1,000	2,000	3,000	4,000

The table shows that 2,000 grams equals 2 kilograms.

Use Division

> You can also use a calculator.

$$2,000 \text{ grams} = \blacksquare \text{ kilograms}$$
$$2,000 \text{ grams} \div 1,000 = \blacksquare \text{ kilograms}$$
$$2,000 \text{ grams} \div 1,000 = 2 \text{ kilograms}$$
$$2,000 \text{ grams} = 2 \text{ kilograms}$$

> **Think:** Since 1,000 grams = 1 kilogram, you divide 2,000 grams by 1,000 grams. Use patterns.

The combined mass is 2 kilograms.

Try It **Write the number that makes each equation true.**

1. 2 m = ▊ cm
2. 3 L = ▊ mL
3. 3 kg = ▊ g
4. 5 kg = ▊ g

5. 6 m = ▊ cm
6. 2 L = ▊ mL
7. 7 kg = ▊ g
8. 9 m = ▊ cm

9. **Write About It** **Compare** How is changing liters to milliliters like changing kilograms to grams?

Practice and Problem Solving

Copy and complete.

10.

Liters		2	
Milliliters	1,000		3,000

11.

Kilograms		2		4
Grams	1,000		3,000	

Write the number that makes each equation true.

12. $3\text{ m} = \blacksquare \text{ cm}$ **13.** $8\text{ L} = \blacksquare \text{ mL}$ **14.** $4\text{ kg} = \blacksquare \text{ g}$ **15.** $3\text{ L} = \blacksquare \text{ mL}$

★**16.** $\blacksquare \text{ kg} = 12,000\text{ g}$ ★**17.** $30\text{ m} = \blacksquare \text{ cm}$ ★**18.** $10\text{ L} = \blacksquare \text{ mL}$

Ⓧ **Algebra Compare. Write >, <, or =.**

19. 5 kg ⬤ $4,800\text{ g}$ **20.** 12 cm ⬤ 1 m **21.** $1,300\text{ mL}$ ⬤ 1 L

Solve.

22. Hands On Have several friends each broad jump once. Measure and record the length of each jump in centimeters. What distance in meters is each jump closest to?

23. Make It Right This is how Marco converted kilograms to grams. Tell what mistake he made. Explain how to correct it.

$$7kg = \blacksquare\ g$$
$$7 \times 100 = 700$$
$$7kg = 700g$$

Link to SOCIAL STUDIES ★

In the Olympics, women discus throwers use a disc that is 18 centimeters wide.

★**24.** Several discs are lined up side by side. They take up about a meter of space. How many discs could there be?

Spiral Review and Test Prep

25. Vera's gym bag weighs 4 pounds. How many ounces does it weigh? (p. 462)

   A. 16 oz   **C.** 64 oz

   B. 32 oz   **D.** 400 oz

26. Which number makes the equation true? (p. 420)
$$14 \div 3 = \blacksquare$$

   F. 42   **H.** 4 R2

   G. 5   **I.** 3 R2

Write the value of each underlined digit. (p. 10)

27. 512,<u>3</u>41 **28.** 1<u>6</u>,421 **29.** 123,6<u>3</u>7

< .91   00ε,21

Extra Practice page 488, Set D

MEASUREMENT MATCH

Match the measurement card with the correct object.

Ready

Players: 2
You Will Need: index cards, marker, glue

Set

Make up pairs of index cards. Find pictures of objects and paste 1 on each card. On a separate card, write the measurements for each object.

16 ounces

GO!

► Mix up the cards and arrange them in an array, face down.

► Match the picture card with the correct measurement.

► Each player takes turns picking the cards.

► If the cards match, keep the cards and take another turn.

► Continue until all pairs are matched. The player with more pairs of cards wins.

16 ounces

22.5

Problem Solving: Strategy
Logical Reasoning

Read

Coach Paul needs to fill the water cooler at the game with 4 gallons of water. He has a 3-gallon bottle and a 5-gallon bottle. How can he use the bottles to get exactly 4 gallons of water into the cooler?

- **What do you know?**
  4 gallons needed; 3-gallon and 5-gallon bottles available

- **What do you need to find?**
  How to use the bottles to measure 4 gallons of water

Plan

One way to solve the problem is to think about the difference in the capacities of the 2 bottles. Use this difference to find how to fill the cooler.

Solve

▶ **Step 1** Fill the 5-gallon bottle.

▶ **Step 2** Pour the water into the 3-gallon bottle.

▶ **Step 3** Pour what remains in the 5-gallon bottle into the water cooler.

▶ **Step 4** You now have 2 gallons in the cooler. Empty the 3-gallon bottle and repeat steps 1 to 3 to get 2 more gallons into the cooler.

Look Back

What other strategies could you use to solve the problem?

1. 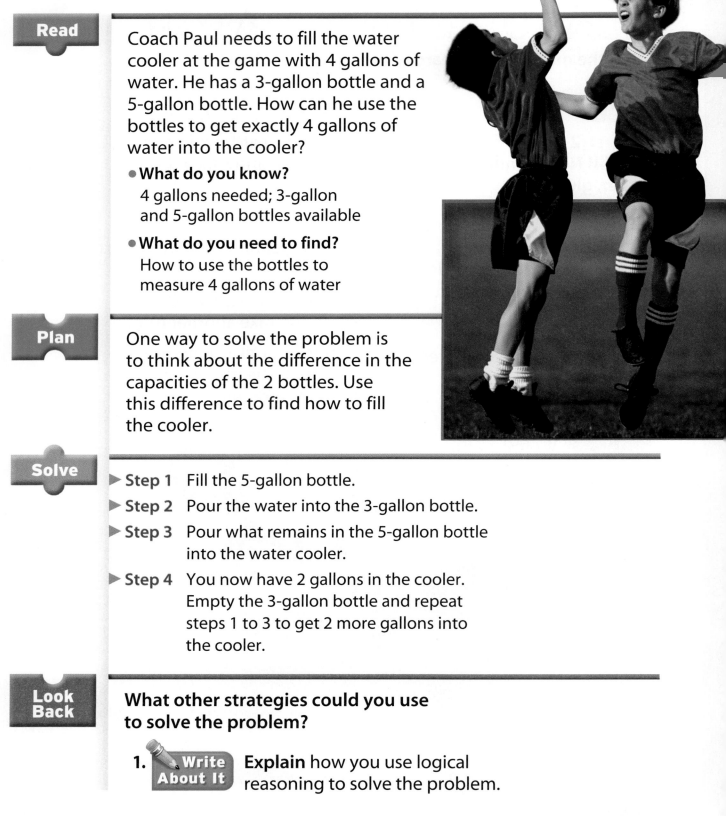 **Write About It** **Explain** how you use logical reasoning to solve the problem.

Practice   Use logical reasoning to solve.

2. Coach Betty wants 11 liters of water in a cooler; she has a 5-liter bottle and an 8-liter bottle. How can she use them to measure exactly 11 liters?

3. Kevin leaves his office and goes up 3 floors to run an errand. Then he goes down 1 floor. Later he goes down 4 more floors and up 3. He is now on the fifth floor. On which floor is Kevin's office?

4. After the soccer game, Paula, Fran, and Ivy go out to eat. One has pizza, another has a hamburger, and the third has salad. Fran and Paula do not eat pizza. Fran does not eat meat. Who eats the hamburger?

5. Max, Nick, Ruth, and Pam are standing in line for tickets to a baseball game. Nick is not first. Ruth is ahead of Pam, but not ahead of Nick. The first person in line is a boy. List the names in order from first to last in line.

Mixed Strategy Review

Use data from the table for problems 6–7.

Baseball Pitchers with Most Career Wins	
Player	Wins
Cy Young	511
Walter Johnson	416
Christy Mathewson	
Grover Alexander	

Choose a Strategy
- Logical Reasoning
- Draw a Picture or Diagram
- Make a Graph
- Act It Out
- Make a Table or List
- Find a Pattern
- Guess and Check
- Write an Equation
- Work Backward
- Solve a Simpler Problem

6. The combined number of wins for the last 2 players on the table is 746. Each won the same number of games. How many games did Grover Alexander win?

7. How many less games did Christy Mathewson win than the pitcher with the most wins?

8. **Write a problem** that can be solved using logical reasoning. Solve it. Ask others to solve it.

Problem Solving

22.6 Temperature

Learn

In summertime, Key West, Florida is known for having high temperatures. The temperature for a summer day is shown. What is the temperature?

This thermometer measures temperature in degrees Fahrenheit (°F).

VOCABULARY
degrees Celsius
degrees Fahrenheit

Use a Fahrenheit Thermometer

STEP 1

Find the top of the red line.

STEP 2

Read the number next to the end of the red line.

The temperature is 90 degrees Fahrenheit, or 90°F.

Degrees Fahrenheit are customary units of temperature.

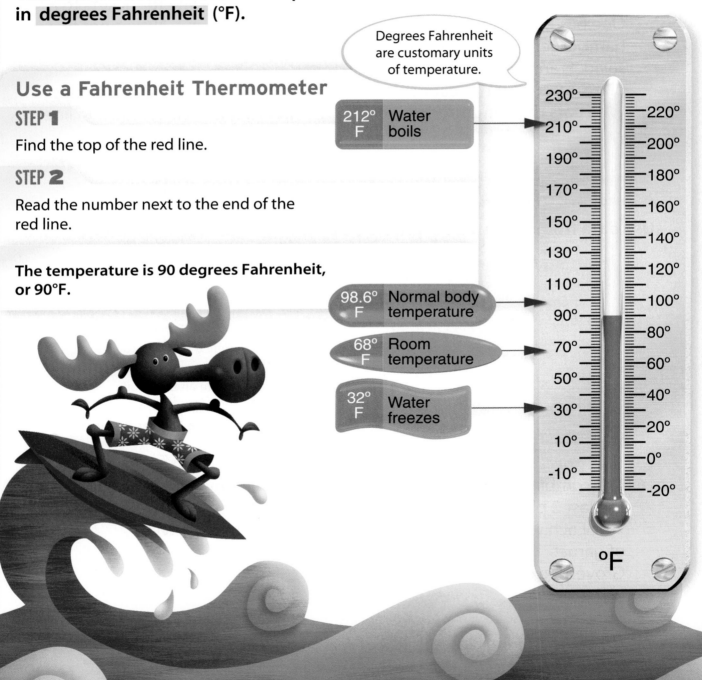

212° F Water boils

98.6° F Normal body temperature

68° F Room temperature

32° F Water freezes

What If You traveled to Indianapolis, Indiana, in the wintertime. The temperature shown is for a day in December. What kind of clothing would you wear?

This thermometer measures temperature in degrees Celsius (°C).

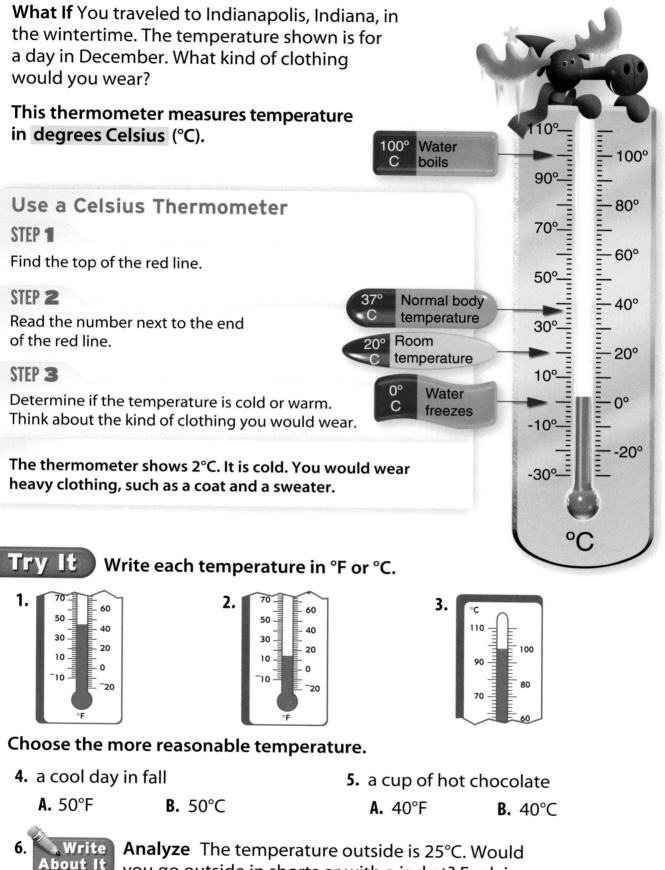

100° C — Water boils

37° C — Normal body temperature

20° C — Room temperature

0° C — Water freezes

Use a Celsius Thermometer

STEP 1

Find the top of the red line.

STEP 2

Read the number next to the end of the red line.

STEP 3

Determine if the temperature is cold or warm. Think about the kind of clothing you would wear.

The thermometer shows 2°C. It is cold. You would wear heavy clothing, such as a coat and a sweater.

Try It Write each temperature in °F or °C.

1.

2.

3.

Choose the more reasonable temperature.

4. a cool day in fall

   A. 50°F   **B.** 50°C

5. a cup of hot chocolate

   A. 40°F   **B.** 40°C

6. **Write About It** **Analyze** The temperature outside is 25°C. Would you go outside in shorts or with a jacket? Explain.

Practice and Problem Solving

Write each temperature in °F or °C.

7.

8.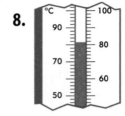

9.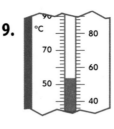

10.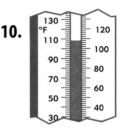

Choose the more reasonable temperature.

11. a hot summer day
    A. 35°F **B.** 35°C

12. an ice pack
    A. 0°C **B.** 32°C

13. a bowl of hot soup
    A. 25°F **B.** 25°C

Decide which kind of clothing you should wear.
Write *shirt, sweater,* or *heavy coat.*

14. 36°C

15. 56°F

16. 93°F

17. 28°F

Solve.

18. **Hands On** Estimate the temperature outside in degrees Fahrenheit and degrees Celsius. Then use thermometers to measure. Compare your estimates and the actual temperatures.

19. **Make It Right**
    This is what Missy listed for clothes to wear when the temperature is 31°F. Tell what mistake she made. Explain how to correct it.

THINK SOLVE EXPLAIN

20. Chuck's temperature is 101°F. Is this above or below normal body temperature? Explain.

THINK SOLVE EXPLAIN

21. The temperature was 15°C at noon. It dropped to 10°C at 11 P.M. How many degrees did the temperature fall?

Spiral Review and Test Prep

22. Herman drinks 4 pints of milk in 1 day. How many quarts is this? (p. 462)
    A. 1 quart **C.** 3 quarts
    B. 2 quarts **D.** 4 quarts

23. Rita pays for a $5.79 baseball cap with a ten-dollar bill. How much change does she get? (p. 120)
    F. $15.79 **H.** $4.31
    G. $5.21 **I.** $4.21

24. 108 ÷ 4 (p. 430) 25. 3)81 (p. 420) 26. 3 × 206 (p. 390) 27. 321 + 45 + 678 (p. 76)

7. 32°F 11. B

Extra Practice page 488, Set F

Writing for Math

The thermometer shows the temperature at noon. It is predicted to be 6°C colder by midnight. What will the temperature be at that time? Explain your thinking.

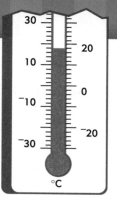

Erin's Response

✓ **THINK** Read the temperature shown on the thermometer. Subtract 6 degrees.

✓ **SOLVE** The temperature at noon is 18°C.
$18° - 6° = 12°$.
The temperature will be 12°C at midnight.

✓ **EXPLAIN** First, I read the thermometer. It shows a temperature of 18°C. It is getting colder, so I subtract 6 from 18. The difference is 12, so the temperature will be 12°C by midnight.

To check, I begin at 12°C and add 6°. The sum is 18°C, which matches the temperature shown on the thermometer. My answer makes sense.

Teacher's Response

← Erin shows what she knows and tells how she will solve the problem.

← Erin shows her work.

← Erin clearly describes her thinking. She uses appropriate math terms, such as **temperature**, **thermometer**, **subtract**, and **difference**.

← Erin checks her answer by using addition.

THINK SOLVE EXPLAIN

Solve. Show your work and tell why your answer makes sense. Use Erin's work as a guide.

1. It is 25°C outside. Is it appropriate to wear a coat, a hat, and mittens? Explain.

2. The temperature shown is 5°C colder than it will be by 2:00 P.M. What will the temperature be then?

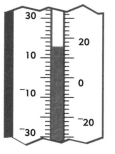

Extra Practice

Set A Choose the better estimate. (pp. 472–473)

1. A bike is about _____ long.

   A. 2 cm   **B.** 2 m

2. A cat is about _____ tall.

   A. 24 cm   **B.** 24 dm

3. A door is about _____ wide.

   A. 1 m   **B.** 1 cm

Set B Choose the better estimate. (pp. 474–475)

4. **A.** 2 mL
   B. 2 L

5. **A.** 100 mL
   B. 100 L

6. **A.** 120 mL
   B. 120 L

Set C Choose the better estimate. (pp. 476–477)

7. **A.** 20 g   **B.** 20 kg

8. **A.** 2 g   **B.** 2 kg

9. **A.** 250 g   **B.** 250 kg

Set D Write the number that makes each equation true. (pp. 478–480)

10. 2 L = ▓ mL

11. 4 m = ▓ cm

12. 2 kg = ▓ g

Set E Use logical reasoning to solve. (pp. 482–483)

13. Coach Hal wants 7 liters of water in a water cooler. He has a 3-liter container and a 5-liter container. How can he measure exactly 7 liters into the cooler?

14. Ian moves the football 3 yards forward. Pete loses 8 yards. On the next play, Ian gains 12 yards forward to the 24-yard line. At which yard line did they begin?

Set F Decide which kind of clothing you should wear for each temperature. Write *shirt*, *sweater*, or *heavy coat*. (pp. 484–486)

15. 29°C

16. 55°F

17. 91°F

18. 18°F

Review/Test

Estimate and measure to the nearest centimeter.

1.

2.

Choose the best estimate.

3. A tennis racquet is about ▊ long. **A.** 8 cm **B.** 8 dm **C.** 8 m

4. A basketball hoop is about ▊ high. **A.** 3 cm **B.** 3 dm **C.** 3 m

5. A table tennis net is about ▊ high. **A.** 8 cm **B.** 8 dm **C.** 8 m

6. **A.** 30 mL **B.** 30 L

7. **A.** 1 g **B.** 1 kg

8. **A.** 250 g **B.** 250 kg

Write the number that makes each equation true.

9. $3 \text{ m} = $ ▊ cm

10. $2 \text{ kg} = $ ▊ g

11. $4 \text{ L} = $ ▊ mL

12. ▊ $\text{m} = 700 \text{ cm}$

13. $3 \text{ kg} = $ ▊ g

14. $80 \text{ m} = $ ▊ cm

15. $5 \text{ dm} = $ ▊ cm

Choose the more reasonable temperature.

16. a comfortable room **A.** 72°F **B.** 72°C

17. ice cream **A.** 0°C **B.** 32°C

18. a cup of hot tea **A.** 48°F **B.** 48°C

Solve.

19. You have a 4-liter jug and a 6-liter jug. You want to pour exactly 8 liters of water into a tank. How can you use the jugs to do this?

20. **Write About It** **Generalize** Would you be wearing a heavy jacket or a shirt if the temperature was 39°C? Why?

Do I Need Help?

Exercises	Review Concepts	Use Extra Practice Set
1–8	pp. 472–477	Set A–C
9–15	pp. 478–480	Set D
16–18, 20	pp. 484–487	Set F
19	pp. 482–483	Set E

Foldables Use your Foldables to help you review.

Decision Making

You and your family are planning your vacation for next year. Which of these places would you want to visit?

You Decide!

Where and when will you go and what will you take?

Shore Resort and Beach Hotel

Weather:
June 1–August 31:
Sunshine 5 out of 7 days

Average temperature: 85°F

Cost:
$125 each person

Includes:
Room and breakfast each day

at the New Jersey Shore

Ski Super Mountain

AT SNOW LODGE IN VERMONT

Weather: December 1–January 31: About 3 inches of snow each day

Average temperature: 20°F

Cost: $225 each person

Includes: Room and 3 meals each day

Collingsboro Campsite

in the Virginia Woods

Weather:
September 30–November 1:
Sunshine 4 out of 7 days

Average Temperature: 12°C

Cost: $40 each day

Includes: Campsite and use of utilities

1. Which vacation spot will be the warmest? The coldest?

2. Where would you go if you want to go on vacation in July? Why?

3. How much will it cost a family of 3 to go on the skiing vacation for 3 days?

4. If you go skiing for 4 days, about how many inches of snow would you expect?

5. If you stay at the beach for 14 days, about how many days of sunshine might you expect?

6. Where does it probably rain more, at the shore resort or at the Collingsboro Campsite?

Make Decisions

7. You spend $75 a day on meals. How much less would it cost to stay at the campsite for a week than at the ski lodge?

8. **What If** You decide to go skiing for a week. What date would you leave for your vacation? What date would you return? What kind of clothes should you pack?

9. How much does it cost a family of 4 to stay for 3 days at the shore resort?

10. How much would it cost to stay at the Collingsboro Campsite for 1 week?

11. Write a list of things you should think about before deciding where to go on vacation.

12. You have $1,000 to spend on your vacation. Where will you go? For how long? How will you spend the money?

Your Decision!

THINK
SOLVE
EXPLAIN

Which vacation will you go on? When will you go? How long will you stay? What clothing will you take?

Problem Solving

Unit Study Guide and Review

Vocabulary

Complete. Use a word from the list.

1. To measure temperature in customary units, use ___.

2. The amount of matter in an object is its ___.

3. Centimeter and meter are measures of ___.

4. If you want to know how much liquid a container holds, you need to measure its ___.

VOCABULARY
capacity
degrees Celsius
degrees Fahrenheit
length
mass

Skills and Applications

Estimate and measure length. (pp. 454–457, 472–473)

Estimate and measure the length to the nearest inch and centimeter.

Solution
The ribbon is about 1 inch long or about 3 centimeters long.

Estimate and measure the length to the nearest inch and centimeter.

5.

Choose the best estimate.

6. Your foot is about ▮ long.

   A. 40 cm   **B.** 40 dm   **C.** 40 m

7. Your math textbook is about ▮ wide.

   A. $8\frac{1}{2}$ in.   **B.** $8\frac{1}{2}$ ft   **C.** $8\frac{1}{2}$ yd

Estimate and measure weight, mass, and capacity. (pp. 458–461, 474–477)

Choose the better estimate.

A. 1 oz   **B.** 1 lb

Solution
The bike helmet is about 1 pound.

Choose the best estimate.

8.   **A.** 20 oz
      B. 20 lb
      C. 2 oz

9. a glass of milk

   A. 1 c   **B.** 1 gal   **C.** 1 qt

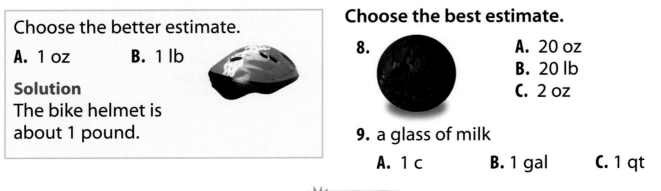 Foldables Use your Foldables to help you review.

Convert units of length, weight, mass, and capacity. (pp. 462–464, 478–480)

Complete.

■ qt = 2 gal

Solution

You can convert gallons into quarts by multiplying.

Think: 1 gal = 4 qt   2 × 4 = 8

8 qt = 2 gal

Complete.

10. ■ inches = 3 feet

11. 2 pounds = ■ ounces

12. 4 meters = ■ centimeters

13. 5 quarts = ■ pints

14. ■ feet = 4 yards

15. 5 liters = ■ milliliters

Estimate temperature in degrees Fahrenheit and degrees Celsius. (pp. 484–486)

Choose the reasonable temperature of an ice cube.

A. 25°F   **B.** 25°C

Solution

An ice cube is frozen water. The reasonable temperature is 25°F.

Choose the reasonable temperature.

16. freezer   **A.** 30°F   **B.** 30°C

17. cool water   **A.** 12°F   **B.** 12°C

18. snowball   **A.** 15°F   **B.** 15°C

Use skills and strategies to solve problems. (pp. 466–467, 482–483)

Joe is 52 inches tall. Sam is 3 inches shorter than Joe. Greg is 4 feet tall. Sal is taller than Joe. Who is the shortest?

Solution

Use logical reasoning.

Think: Joe is 52 in.
Sam is 52 in. − 3 in. = 49 in.
Greg is 4 ft = 48 in.
Sal is taller than 52 in.

Greg is the shortest.

Solve.

19. Bev jumped 38 inches. Carol jumped 3 feet. Did Carol jump farther than Bev? Explain.

20. How can you use a 2-liter bottle and a 3-liter bottle to pour exactly 4 liters of liquid into a large tub?

Enrichment

Benchmarks

Most countries use the **metric system** of measurement.

The United States uses the **customary system** of measurement.

You can use benchmarks to help you compare measures using different measurement systems.

Length

$2\frac{1}{2}$ centimeters is about 1 inch.

2 inches is about 5 centimeters.

Copy and complete. Use your ruler to help.

1. There are about ____ in. in 10 cm.

2. There are about ____ cm in 5 in.

3. There are about ____ cm in 8 in.

4. There are about ____ in. in 25 cm.

Weight and Mass

One kilogram is about 2 pounds.

Capacity

Four liters is about one gallon.

Copy and complete.

5. About_____ kg = 6 lb

6. About_____ lb = 4 kg

7. About_____ gal = 8 L

8. About_____ L = 5 gal

9. **Analyze** When do you think you would need to convert between measurement systems?

Performance Assessment

What's My Object?

Work with a partner. Choose an object in your classroom. Describe the object by using 3 to 5 attributes. See the list for ideas.

Make a chart like the one below to record your measurements. Use any attributes you want.

- Work alone so your partner doesn't know the object you chose.

- Measure your object using the correct measurement tools.

- Fill in your chart, using the correct units of measurement. Fold your chart over at the first column, so your partner cannot see the name of the item.

- Show your partner the chart. He or she gets 3 chances to guess the object. After each guess, you may give your partner another clue by answering a yes or no question.

- Take turns choosing an object and guessing which object your partner chose.

Attributes Chart	
Color	Temperature
Length	Capacity
Perimeter	Width
Area	Depth
Volume	Height
Weight or Mass	Texture (Rough or Smooth)

Item	Length	Width	Weight	Guess 1	Guess 2	Guess 3

Fold your paper here.

A Good Answer

- Show a correctly filled-in chart.

- Use the correct tool to measure.

- Use correct units of measurement.

 You may want to save this work in your portfolio.

Assessment

TECHNOLOGY Link

Use a Table to Convert Measurements

Zena has boards that are 3 feet, 6 feet, and 7 feet long. How many inches long is each board?

You can use a spreadsheet table in the *Math Tool Chest CD-ROM* program to convert measurements.

- Click on the table key ▦ in *Math Tool Chest* CD-ROM.

- Label the columns *Feet* and *Inches*.

- In the column labeled *Feet,* enter the measurements of the three boards.

- In the column labeled *Inches,* enter a formula to convert feet to inches.

How many inches long is each board?

Math Tool Chest CD-ROM

Use the computer to convert each measurement to inches.

1. 8 feet   **2.** 9 feet   **3.** 11 feet   **4.** 15 feet

Solve.

5. Juan has 2 pounds of chicken. He needs to convert this amount to ounces. How many ounces of chicken does he have?

6. The cafeteria serves 15 gallons of apple juice each day. How many quarts of apple juice do they serve?

7. Analyze How does using the table help you convert feet to inches?

For more practice, use Math Traveler™.

Test-Taking Tips

When taking a test with many questions, it is important not to rush. Read carefully and make sure you use the **correct measurements.**

Look at this picture. The dog ran to bury the bone. How many inches long is the trail from the doghouse to the hole?

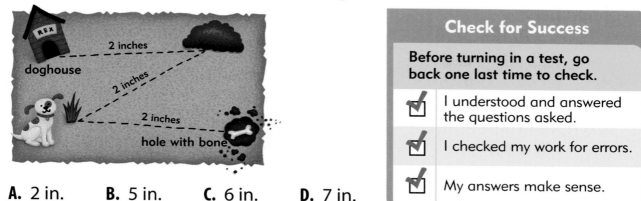

2 inches

doghouse

2 inches

2 inches

hole with bone

A. 2 in.　　**B.** 5 in.　　**C.** 6 in.　　**D.** 7 in.

Check for Success

Before turning in a test, go back one last time to check.

☑ I understood and answered the questions asked.

☑ I checked my work for errors.

☑ My answers make sense.

First, look at the top part of the trail. It is 2 inches.

Then, look at the next part of the trail. It is 2 inches.

Next, look at the bottom part of the trail. It is 2 inches.

Add: $2 + 2 + 2 = 6$.

The correct choice is C.

Use the map at right to solve the problems. Choose the best answer.

1. Jodi needs to get to the library. How far is the path from her apartment building to the library?

   A. $2\frac{1}{2}$ inches　　**C.** 4 inches

   B. $3\frac{1}{2}$ inches　　**D.** $4\frac{1}{2}$ inches

2. Jodi is traveling from the library to the store. How far is the path from the library to the store?

   F. $\frac{1}{2}$ inch　　**H.** 2 inches

   G. 1 inch　　**I.** $2\frac{1}{2}$ inches

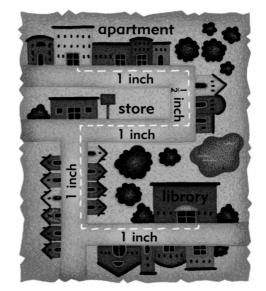

apartment

1 inch

$\frac{1}{2}$ inch

store

1 inch

1 inch

library

1 inch

PART 1 • Multiple Choice

Choose the best answer.

1. What is the range of this set of numbers? (p. 162)
   14, 3, 4, 12, 2, 7, 8
   A. 14   **C.** 8
   B. 12   **D.** 2

2. Which is the best estimate? (p. 372)
   4 × $18.37
   F. $64   **H.** $84
   G. $80   **I.** $160

3. There are 467 students in Fort Lee Elementary school. Each of the 6 different grades has about the same number of students. About how many students are in each grade at the school? (p. 414)
   A. 20 students
   B. 40 students
   C. 50 students
   D. 80 students

4. Matt was 45 inches tall last year. Now he is 1 inch taller. If Matt grows 2 more inches next year, how tall will he be then? (p. 462)
   F. 4 ft   **H.** 50 in.
   G. 5 ft   **I.** 51 in.

5. Which number makes this equation true? (p. 241)
   $9 \times n = 36$
   A. 2   **C.** 6
   B. 4   **D.** 9

6. Beth's skates each weigh 16 ounces. How many pounds do her skates weigh in all? (p. 462)
   F. 32 lb   **H.** 2 lb
   G. 16 lb   **I.** 1 lb

7. James bought 2 T-shirts for his family while he was on vacation. How much money did he spend in all? (p. 390)

   A. $4.45   **C.** $17.80
   B. $10.90   **D.** $22.80

8. Pete fills a 3-quart bottle with water and pours it into a tub. He does this 4 times. Which equation shows how many quarts he has in the tub? (p. 438)
   F. $4 + 3 = 7$ **H.** $4 \times 12 = 48$
   G. $4 \times 3 = 12$ **I.** $12 - 3 = 9$

Record your answers on the answer sheet provided by your teacher or on a sheet of paper.

THINK SOLVE EXPLAIN **9.** Which number makes the sentence true? Explain. (p. 238)

$$7 \times w = 8 + 6$$

10. Look at the clock below. What time will it be in 25 minutes?

(p. 146)

THINK SOLVE EXPLAIN **11.** Collin is going outside on a 33°F day. What type of clothing should he wear? Explain. (p. 484)

12. The auditorium can hold 4,000 people. If each row of seats holds 50 people, how many rows of seats are in the auditorium? (p. 412)

13. What is the mean of the numbers 4, 9, 3, 5, and 4? (p. 162)

14. Mrs. Martin bought pizzas for the youth club. Each pizza had 8 slices in it. How many pizzas did she buy if there were 120 slices of pizza total? (p. 430)

Solve. Use data from the graph for problems 15–17.

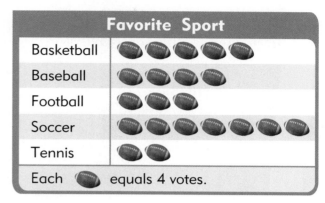

Favorite Sport

Basketball
Baseball
Football
Soccer
Tennis

Each 🏈 equals 4 votes.

15. Which sport got 4 more votes than football? (p. 166)

16. How many people voted for baseball and tennis? (p. 166)

17. How many people were surveyed? (p. 384)

Record your answer on a sheet of paper. Show your work.

18. Lisa's long jump measured 45 inches. Tyra's long jump measured 4 feet. Julia's long jump measured 52 inches. Write the order of the jumps from greatest to least. Explain how you solved the problem. (p. 482)

Test Prep

What Do I Need to Know?

Look at the buildings in this picture.
Find as many shapes as you can.

2- and 3-Dimensional Figures

What Will I Learn?

In this chapter you will learn to

- identify 2- and 3-dimensional figures
- identify lines, line segments, rays, and angles
- identify polygons, triangles, and quadrilaterals
- use skills and strategies to solve problems

How Do I Read Math?

When you read a mathematics book, sometimes you read words to identify figures.

These are both polygons:

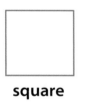

square   **triangle**

VOCABULARY

- 3-dimensional figure
- 2-dimensional figure
- ray
- angle
- right angle
- open figure
- closed figure
- polygon
- quadrilaterals

Foldables

Use your Foldables to help you with chapter concepts.

GEOMETRY

3-dimensional figure is a figure that has length, width, and height.

2-Dimensional Figures

3-Dimensional Figures

1. Fold a large sheet of paper in half like a hot dog, but make one side 1 inch longer than the other. This will form a 1 inch tab that you can write on.

2. Fold the hot dog in half like a hamburger.

3. Open and cut along the fold on the short side to form two tabs.

4. Label as shown. Record what you learn.

23.1 3-Dimensional Figures

Learn

This model is made up of 3-dimensional figures. A **3-dimensional figure** is a figure that has length, width, and height. Which figures were used to build the model?

VOCABULARY

3-dimensional figure	**cube**
	vertex
rectangular prism	**cone**
	base
cylinder	**pyramid**
edge	**sphere**
face	**net**

You can compare the blocks used in the model with these 3-dimensional figures.

3-Dimensional Figures

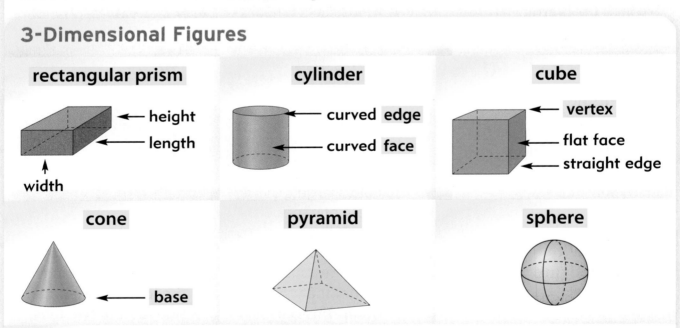

rectangular prism — height, length, width

cylinder — curved edge, curved face

cube — vertex, flat face, straight edge

cone — base

pyramid

sphere

Cubes, rectangular prisms, pyramids, a cone, and cylinders were used to build the model.

You can sort 3-dimensional figures by characteristics.

Compare 3-Dimensional Figures

Figure	Name	Number of Curved Sides	Number of Flat Faces	Number of Edges	Number of Vertices
	Cube	0	6	12	8
	Rectangular Prism	0	6	12	8
	Sphere	1	0	0	0
	Cylinder	1	2	2	0
	Cone	1	1	1	1
	Pyramid	0	5	8	5

You can make models of 3-dimensional figures out of paper.

Make Models

Each **net** can be cut out and folded to make the figure shown next to it.

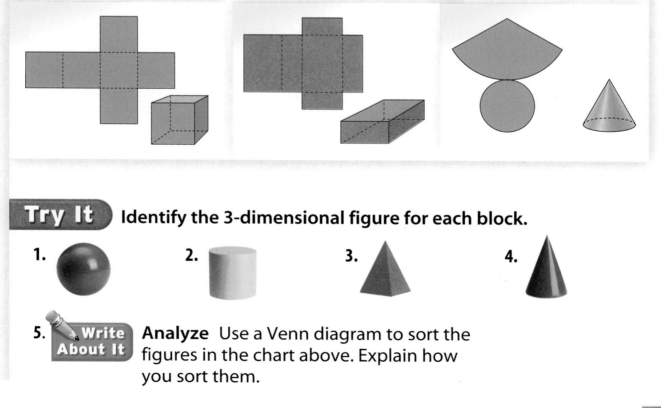

Try It Identify the 3-dimensional figure for each block.

1.

2.

3.

4.

5. **Write About It** **Analyze** Use a Venn diagram to sort the figures in the chart above. Explain how you sort them.

Practice and Problem Solving

Name the 3-dimensional figure each object looks like.

6.

7.

8.

9.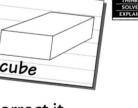

Solve. Use data from the table for problems 10–11.

10. How would you complete the chart for a rectangular prism?

11. ✎ **Write a problem** using the data from the table. Solve it. Ask others to solve it.

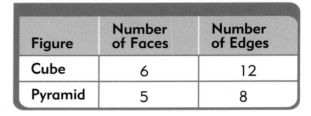

Figure	Number of Faces	Number of Edges
Cube	6	12
Pyramid	5	8

12. **Collect Data** Find objects in your classroom that look like 3-dimensional figures. Make a chart that lists the objects. Identify the figures they look like.

13. Katharine, Cory, and Rosendo have 342 pom-poms for an art project. If they each get the same number of pom-poms, how many pom-poms will each have?

14. **Art** You have blocks that are shaped like these figures. Build a house using blocks.

cube   cone   pyramid

15. **Make It Right** Tim drew and labeled this figure. Tell what mistake he made. Then show how to correct it.

cube

Spiral Review and Test Prep

16. Which weighs about 1 pound? (p. 460)

    A. A tree   **C.** A watch

    B. A football   **D.** A lightbulb

17. A puppy weighs 48 ounces. How many pounds is this? (p. 462)

    F. 2 lb   **H.** 3 lb

    G. 2 lb 2 oz   **I.** 3 lb 2 oz

18. ■ h = 60 min (p. 144)

19. 1m = ■ cm (p. 478)

20. 1gal = ■ qt (p. 462)

6. rectangular prism

Extra Practice page 520, Set A

BUILDING HISTORY

TIME FOR KIDS

Many buildings in Indiana hold a special place in U.S. history. That's because this state has more than 1,000 sites on the National Register of Historic Places, a list of important historical buildings and sites.

The Historic Landmarks Foundation of Indiana buys historic buildings and raises money to fix them. Each year, the group lists the 10 Most Endangered Buildings in Indiana.

KIDS PITCH IN

The Foundations runs a yearly competition called "Create a Landmark." Students work together to learn about and build 3-dimensional models of Indiana's historic structures.

First, students learn about the building. Then they study pictures of it. Finally, they gather materials—from pasta to toothpicks—to make a smaller model of it.

The models are displayed at the Children's Museum of Indiana. The work brings attention to the state's endangered buildings.

This hotel is an Indiana landmark.

Reading Skill

Make Inferences What kinds of information do the Indiana students have to learn before building a model?

1. Look at the photo. What shapes can you see?

2. Ten classes entered the Create a Landmark competition. There are 18 students in each class. How many students in all entered the competition?

Problem Solving

23.2 2-Dimensional Figures

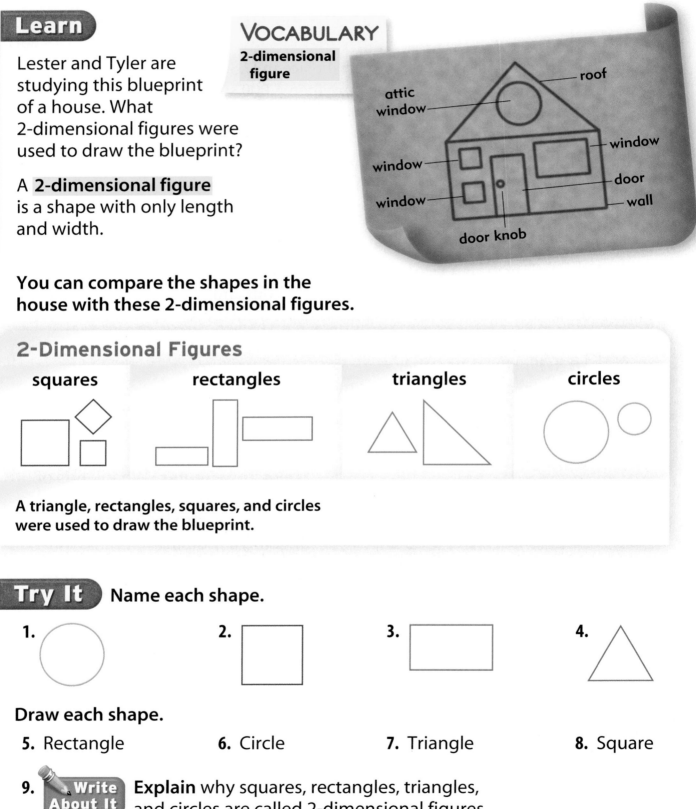

Learn

Lester and Tyler are studying this blueprint of a house. What 2-dimensional figures were used to draw the blueprint?

A **2-dimensional figure** is a shape with only length and width.

VOCABULARY

2-dimensional figure

You can compare the shapes in the house with these 2-dimensional figures.

2-Dimensional Figures

squares	rectangles	triangles	circles

A triangle, rectangles, squares, and circles were used to draw the blueprint.

Try It Name each shape.

1.   2.   3.   4.

Draw each shape.

5. Rectangle **6.** Circle **7.** Triangle **8.** Square

9. **Write About It** **Explain** why squares, rectangles, triangles, and circles are called 2-dimensional figures.

Practice and Problem Solving

Copy and complete the table.

	Figure	Number of Sides	Number of Angles
10.		3	
11.	Rectangle		4
12.	Circle	0	

Identify each 2-dimensional figure. Sort by sides and angles.

13. ◯

14. ◿

15. ▭

16. ◇

Solve.

17. Name a figure that has 3 sides and 3 angles.

THINK SOLVE EXPLAIN

18.  **Write About It** **Generalize** Are all squares rectangles? Are all rectangles squares? Explain.

★19. Draw a picture of a figure that has no angles and a curved edge. Is there more than one such shape?

Link to SOCIAL STUDIES ★

 Sir Christopher Wren designed the Sheldonian Theatre in Oxford, England. This was Oxford's first classical building.

20. What 2-dimensional figure is seen here in the Sheldonian Theatre?

Spiral Review and Test Prep

21. Mr. Fox got 4 prices for a car. Which was the least? (p. 26)

    A. $17,000   **C.** $16,580

    B. $16,900   **D.** $16,200

22. Find the missing number.
$$n \times 7 = 7 \text{ (p. 214)}$$

    F. 0   **H.** 2

    G. 1   **I.** 7

23. $567 \div 7$ (p. 430)

24. 9×630 (p. 390)

25. $3,041 - 1,289$ (p. 114)

26. $\$3.80 + \$9.44$ (p. 58)

23.3 Lines, Line Segments, Rays, and Angles

Learn

The Brooklyn Bridge in New York City has hundreds of wires. The wires hold up the bridge. What kind of lines do you see in the photo?

VOCABULARY

line	intersecting lines
horizontal lines	parallel lines
line segment	vertical lines
endpoint	angle
ray	right angle

Lines

line

A **line** is straight. It goes in 2 directions. It does not end. This line is horizontal. **Horizontal lines** are lines that go from left to right.

line segment

A **line segment** is straight. It has 2 **endpoints**.

ray

A **ray** is straight. It has 1 endpoint and goes on without end in 1 direction.

intersecting lines

Intersecting lines meet, or cross, at a common point.

parallel lines

Parallel lines do not cross. These lines are vertical. **Vertical lines** are lines that go up and down.

The bridge has parallel lines, intersecting lines, vertical lines, and line segments.

An **angle** is formed by 2 rays with the same endpoint. Here are 3 types of angles.

Angles

A **right angle** forms a square corner.

← right angle symbol

This angle is greater than a right angle.

This angle is less than a right angle.

Try It

Name each figure.

1.

2.

3.

4.

Draw each figure.

5. An angle less than a right angle

6. horizontal parallel lines

7. line segment

8. An angle greater than a right angle

9. **Write About It** **Describe** the lines formed by the rails on a straight section of railroad tracks using some vocabulary words.

Practice and Problem Solving

Decide whether the angle is less than, equal to, or greater than a right angle.

10.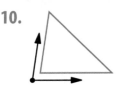

11.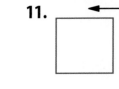

12.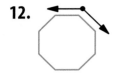

13.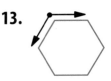

Draw each figure.

14. vertical line   **15.** ray   **16.** intersecting lines   **17.** parallel lines

Solve.

★ **18.** Manuel's apartment building is shaped like a rectangular prism. There are 74 windows on each side of the building. If 2 window washers each wash the same number of windows, how many will each wash?

19. Make It Right Ellen drew and identified this figure. Tell what mistake she made. Then show how to correct it.

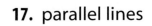
These 2 lines intersect.

THINK SOLVE EXPLAIN

20. **Write About It** **Compare** How is a line different from a line segment? How are they the same?

21. Hands On Use the edge of a piece of paper to find right angles in your classroom. Discuss the results with your classmates.

Spiral Review and Test Prep

22. What is the value of the 4 in the number 38,495? (p. 6)

    A. 40   **C.** 4,000

    B. 400   **D.** 40,000

23. Yori built a house for his pet. His pet has a mass of about 250 grams. Which animal could be his pet? (p. 476)

    F. A flea   **H.** A dog

    G. A hamster   **I.** A horse

24. $23 (p. 384)
    × 4

25. 6)708 (p. 430)

26. 5,478 (p. 72)
    + 767

27. 600 (p. 114)
    − 58

10. less than

Extra Practice page 520, Set C

COORDINATE FIGURES

Find coordinate pairs to create geometric figures.

Ready

Players: 2
You Will Need: Digit Deck, graph paper, a ruler, paper and pencil

Set

Make a game board out of graph paper like the one below. Shuffle the deck. Place cards face down.

GO!

▶ Player 1 picks 3 cards. Use 2 of them to make a coordinate pair. Record the pair on the game sheet and as a dot on the grid. Keep your unused card. Place your used cards face down.

▶ Player 2 takes a turn.

▶ Next, Player 1 picks 2 new cards. Using any of your 3 cards, make a new coordinate pair. Record the pair on the game sheet, and as a dot on the grid. Then connect the dots. Extend the segment in both directions to reach to the edges of the grid.

▶ Continue until a player has 1 pair of parallel lines, 1 pair of lines that do not intersect, and 1 pair of lines that intersect within the borders of the grid.

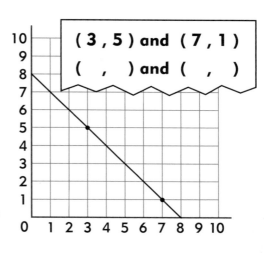

(3 , 5) and (7 , 1)
(,   ) and (,   )

23.4 Polygons

Learn

This screen door is made of many different figures. What types of figures do you see?

You can compare the figures in the screen door with the shapes below.

VOCABULARY
open figure
closed figure
polygon
pentagon
hexagon
octagon

Open Figures

Open figures have ends that do not meet.

Closed Figures

Closed figures begin and end at the same point.

Polygons

Polygons are closed figures with straight sides.

side →

A **pentagon** has 5 sides and 5 angles.

A **hexagon** has 6 sides and 6 angles.

An **octagon** has 8 sides and 8 angles.

The screen door shows a pentagon, triangles, and hexagons.

Try It
Write *yes* or *no* to tell if each figure is a polygon. If it is, identify the polygon.

1.

2.

3.

4.

5.  **Explain** if a circle is a polygon.

Practice and Problem Solving

Write yes or no to tell if each figure is a polygon. If it is, identify the polygon.

6.

7.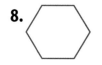

8.

9.

Draw and identify each polygon.

10. It has 3 sides.

11. It has 4 sides. All are equal.

12. It has 8 sides.

13. It has 5 sides.

Solve. Use data from the picture for problem 14.

14. **Logical Reasoning** Ray made 3 polygons using a total of 17 toothpicks. Here is one of his polygons. What other 2 polygons could Ray make using one toothpick for each side?

THINK SOLVE EXPLAIN

15. **Spatial Reasoning** All of the sides of a triangle and a square are the same length. What polygon can you make by putting the triangle on top of the square? Draw a picture to show your answer.

★16. A tile worker has 5 tiles. Some are rectangles and some are pentagons. They have a total of 23 sides. How many are pentagons?

Spiral Review and Test Prep

17. Mr. Wallace moved into his house 3 years ago. In how many years will Mr. Wallace have lived in his house for 10 years? (p. 96)

   A. 7 years   C. 30 years
   B. 13 years   D. 300 years

18. A builder buys 3 stacks of lumber. Each stack weighs 125 pounds. How much does the lumber weigh in total? (p. 390)

   F. 128 pounds   H. 375 pounds
   G. 275 pounds   I. 3,125 pounds

19. 3 m = ▌ cm
   (p. 478)

20. 2 wk = ▌ d
   (p. 144)

21. 2 lb = ▌ oz
   (p. 462)

22. 1 pt = ▌ c
   (p. 462)

23.5 Triangles

Learn

This building is called a dome. It is made up of many **triangles**. Triangles can be classified by their sides or by their angles. What types of triangles make up this dome?

VOCABULARY

triangles
equilateral
scalene
isosceles
acute
obtuse

Types of Triangles

equilateral triangle

2 cm   2 cm
2 cm

Three sides are the same length.

isosceles triangle

3 cm   3 cm
2 cm

Two sides are the same length.

scalene triangle

1 cm   2 cm
3 cm

No sides are the same length.

acute triangle

All angles are less than a right angle.

right triangle

One angle is a right angle.

obtuse triangle

One angle is greater than a right angle.

The dome has acute equilateral triangles.

Try It

Identify each triangle as equilateral, isosceles, or scalene. Then identify each as acute, right, or obtuse.

1.

2.

3.

4.

5. 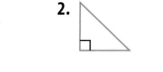 **Write About It** Can a triangle be both scalene and isosceles? Explain.

Practice and Problem Solving

Identify each triangle as equilateral, isosceles, or scalene.

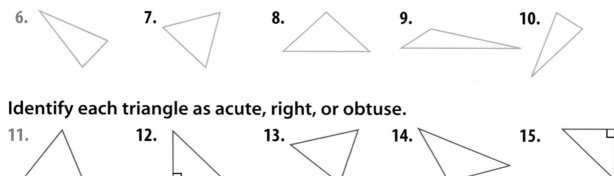

6.   7.   8.   9.   10.

Identify each triangle as acute, right, or obtuse.

11.   12.   13.   14.   15.

Solve. Use the picture for problems 16–17.

16. The edges of the front part of the roof form a triangle. Classify the triangle in 2 different ways.

★ 17. The height of the doghouse is 50 inches. How many feet is this?

18. **Write a problem** using classification of triangles. Solve it. Ask others to solve it.

THINK SOLVE EXPLAIN

19. **Spatial Reasoning** Stand a sphere, a cylinder, and a pyramid on their bases. Then slice each 3-dimensional figure straight down the middle. What 2-dimensional figures will the edges of each piece form?

20. **Art** An artist used 2 identical right triangles to create part of a sculpture. What polygon could be formed with these 2 pieces?

Spiral Review and Test Prep

21. Which makes the sentence true?
    4 gallons = ▆ quarts (p. 462)

     A. 1   **C.** 16

     B. 12   **D.** 24

22. Which number sentence does not belong in the fact family? (p. 342)

     F. $4 \times 3 = 12$ **H.** $4 + 3 = 7$

     G. $12 \div 4 = 3$ **I.** $3 \times 4 = 12$

23. $85 - 37$ (p. 106)   24. $826 + 8{,}832$ (p. 72)   25. $126 \div 6$ (p. 324)   26. 3×907 (p. 390)

23.6 Quadrilaterals

Learn

Frank Lloyd Wright, a famous architect, used geometric shapes in new ways. He designed this window. Are there any **quadrilaterals** in the window? A quadrilateral is a closed figure with 4 sides.

You can compare the shapes in the window to these figures.

Quadrilaterals

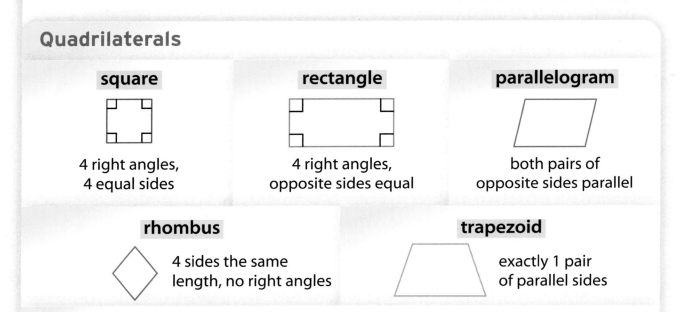

square
4 right angles, 4 equal sides

rectangle
4 right angles, opposite sides equal

parallelogram
both pairs of opposite sides parallel

rhombus
4 sides the same length, no right angles

trapezoid
exactly 1 pair of parallel sides

The window is made of parallelograms and rectangles.

Diagonal Lines

A **diagonal line** connects one vertex to another vertex, but is not a side.

Try It Identify each quadrilateral.

1.

2. [square]

3. [rhombus/diamond]

4. [parallelogram]

5.  **Write About It** **Explain** how all quadrilaterals are alike. Then tell about some differences.

Practice and Problem Solving

Identify each quadrilateral. Draw diagonal lines for each figure.

6. [rectangle]

7. [trapezoid]

8. [parallelogram]

9. [rhombus/diamond]

10. It has opposite sides that are parallel and no right angles.

11. It has 4 sides of equal length with 2 angles less than right angles.

Solve. Use data from the table for problems 12–14.

12. Choose a poster. Draw a picture to show what it might look like.

13. **Write a problem** using the data from the table.

★**14.** Which poster could have squares in it?

15. THINK SOLVE EXPLAIN **Write About It** **Explain** how a square is like a rhombus.

Geometric Art Posters in Ms. Lorenzo's House		
Posters	Figures	Number of Figures
A	Rhombus	8
B	Trapezoid	6
C	Parallelogram	10
D	Rectangle	9

✓ Spiral Review and Test Prep

16. A builder uses 12,075 bricks. What is this number rounded to the nearest hundred? (p. 32)

A. 12,000 **C.** 12,100

B. 12,080 **D.** 12,200

17. Miguel is 5 feet tall. How many inches tall is Miguel? (p. 462)

F. 55 inches **H.** 62 inches

G. 60 inches **I.** 66 inches

18. 12 yd = ■ ft (p. 462)   **19.** 12 qt = ■ gal (p. 462)   **20.** 4 lb = ■ oz (p. 462)

23.7 Problem Solving: Skill
Use a Diagram

Read

Kito made a diagram of a swimming pool, but he forgot to label 2 sides of the pool. What labels are missing?

- **What do you know?**
  Length of 4 sides

- **What do you need to find?**
  The length of 2 missing sides

Plan

A diagram is an illustration that shows how parts join to form a whole. The labels help identify the parts.

Use what you know about polygons to find the missing labels.

16 ft

14 ft

25 ft

32 ft

Solve

One unlabeled side plus 14 feet equals 25 feet.

Think: 25 feet − 14 feet = 11 feet

Another side is labeled 32 feet. The unlabeled side plus 16 feet is equal in length to the longer side.

Think: 32 feet − 16 feet = 16 feet.

The missing labels are 11 feet and 16 feet.

Look Back

Is your answer reasonable?

1. **Write About It** How did you use the diagram to help you solve this problem?

Use data from the illustration to solve problems 2–3.

2. The diagram shows a special window Kito designed for his house. Write all you know about the shape of this window. What kind of triangle is it?

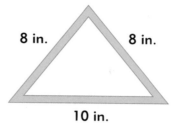

8 in.   8 in.

10 in.

3. How would this window be different if it were an equilateral triangle?

Mixed Strategy Review

4. Trish had 39 baseball cards. She traded some with her friend Lou. She gave him 12 cards and got 9 cards from Lou. How many cards did she have then?

5. Dante, Sophie, and Kate collect different kinds of puzzles. Kate does not collect picture puzzles. Dante collects crossword puzzles. One of them collects picture puzzles. Who collects number puzzles?

Choose a Strategy
- Logical Reasoning
- Draw a Picture or Diagram
- Make a Graph
- Act It Out
- Make a Table or List
- Find a Pattern
- Guess and Check
- Write an Equation
- Work Backward
- Solve a Simpler Problem

6. Lee uses 48 red and black blocks to make a house. He uses 3 times as many red blocks as he does black blocks. How many of each color block does he use?

7. Marlon is setting up his model train. The black car is between the yellow car and the orange car. The orange car is between the red car and the black car. The yellow car is in front of the black car. Which car is last?

8. Alex made a diagram of a triangular garden with 2 sides of 8 feet and a third side of 12 feet. What type of triangle is this?

Problem Solving

Extra Practice

Set A Identify each figure. (pp. 502–504)

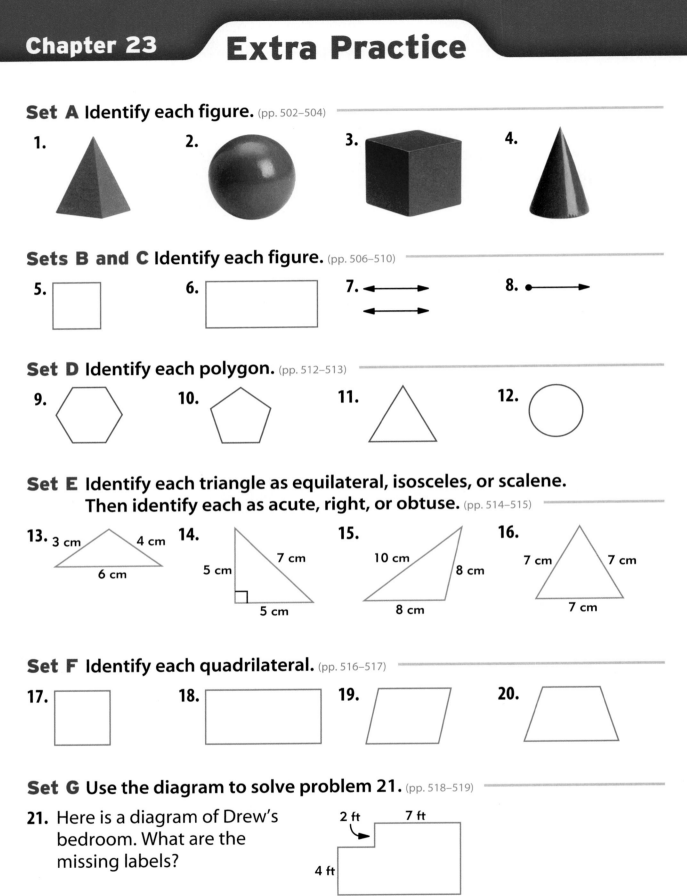

1.
2.
3.
4.

Sets B and C Identify each figure. (pp. 506–510)

5.
6.
7.
8.

Set D Identify each polygon. (pp. 512–513)

9.
10.
11.
12.

Set E Identify each triangle as equilateral, isosceles, or scalene. Then identify each as acute, right, or obtuse. (pp. 514–515)

13. 3 cm 4 cm 6 cm
14. 7 cm 5 cm 5 cm
15. 10 cm 8 cm 8 cm
16. 7 cm 7 cm 7 cm

Set F Identify each quadrilateral. (pp. 516–517)

17.
18.
19.
20.

Set G Use the diagram to solve problem 21. (pp. 518–519)

21. Here is a diagram of Drew's bedroom. What are the missing labels?

2 ft   7 ft
4 ft
10 ft

LOG ON www.mmhmath.com
For more practice and Chapter Self-Check Test

Identify each figure.

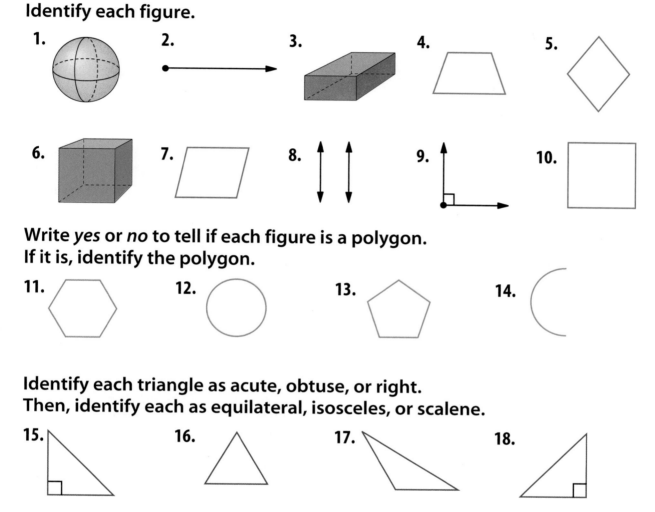

1.

2.

3.

4.

5.

6.

7.

8.

9.

10.

Write *yes* or *no* to tell if each figure is a polygon. If it is, identify the polygon.

11.

12.

13.

14.

Identify each triangle as acute, obtuse, or right. Then, identify each as equilateral, isosceles, or scalene.

15.

16.

17.

18.

Solve.

19. Mario's wall design has 3 different triangles and 3 different open figures. Draw a design that Mario could have painted.

20. **Write About It** **Analyze** Is a pentagon a polygon? Is it a quadrilateral? Explain.

Do I Need Help?

Exercises	Review Concepts	Use Extra Practice Set
1–10	pp. 502–510	Sets A, B, and C
11–14, 20	pp. 512–513, 516–517	Sets D and F
15–18	pp. 514–515	Set E
19	pp. 518–519	Set G

Use your Foldables to help you review.

Assessment

Look at the windows of this house. Look at their shapes and sizes. What do you notice?

Geometry

What Will I Learn?

In this chapter you will learn to

- identify congruent and similar figures
- explore translations, reflections, and rotations
- explore symmetry
- find the perimeter and area
- explore volume
- use skills and strategies to solve problems

How Do I Read Math?

When you read a mathematics book, sometimes you read words and symbols, and sometimes you read only symbols.

These words all mean congruent:

- **same size, same shape**
- **equal**

VOCABULARY

- similar
- congruent
- translation
- reflection
- rotation
- symmetrical figure
- line of symmetry
- perimeter
- area
- cubic unit
- volume

Foldables

Use your Foldables to help you with chapter concepts.

1. Fold a large sheet of paper in half like a hot dog, but make one side 1 inch longer than the other. This will form a 1 inch tab that you can write on.
2. Fold the hot dog into 3 parts, and then fold it in half.
3. Open to find the hot dog divided into six sections.
4. Cut along the five folds on the short side to form six tabs.
5. Label as shown. Record what you learn.

24.1

Congruent and Similar Figures

Learn

Look at the 2 windows. What do you notice about their size and shape? Compare the windows to the door. What do you notice about the sizes and shapes?

VOCABULARY

congruent
similar

Use Models

congruent figures

Congruent figures are figures that have the same shape and same size. The rectangles above are congruent.

similar figures

Similar figures are figures that have the same shape but not the same size. The rectangles above are similar, but not congruent.

Try It

Write whether the figures are congruent or only similar.

1.

2.

3.

4.  **Explain** why you think this statement is true or false: All congruent figures are similar.

Practice and Problem Solving

Write whether the figures are congruent, only similar, or neither.

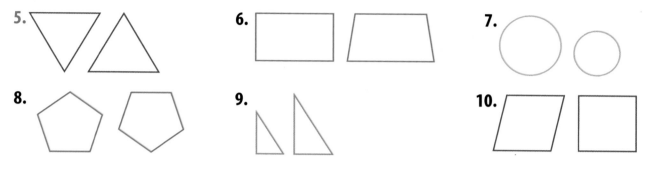

5.

6.

7.

8.

9.

10.

Copy each figure on dot paper. Then draw one congruent figure and one similar figure.

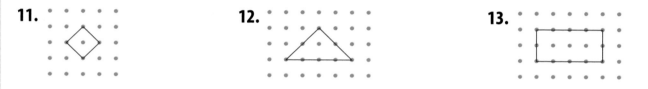

11.

12.

13.

Solve.

14. Are all figures that are the same shape congruent?

15. Do figures have to be in the same position to be congruent?

THINK
SOLVE
EXPLAIN

16. Kelly draws a triangle with sides 3cm, 4cm, and 3cm. Is the triangle scalene? How do you know?

17. A rectangle has 2 sides labeled, 8 ft and 4 ft. What are the measurements of the other 2 sides? Explain.

THINK
SOLVE
EXPLAIN

Spiral Review and Test Prep

18. Which figure has 8 sides? (p. 512)

    A. pentagon   **C.** octagon

    B. hexagon   **D.** trapezoid

19. Jason needs a total of 72 feet of fencing for his yard. Each fence section is 8 feet. How many sections does Jason need? (p. 330)

    F. 80 sections   **H.** 9 sections

    G. 64 sections   **I.** 8 sections

20. 3×744 (p. 210)   **21.** $345 \div 5$ (p. 296)   **22.** $378 + 21 + 444$ (p. 76)

24.2 Explore Translations, Reflections, and Rotations

Hands On Activity

Use models to explore how you can move figures.

You Will Need
- cardboard
- scissors
- graph paper

VOCABULARY
translation
reflection
rotation

Slide, flip, and turn the triangle.

Use Models

Trace the triangle shape and dot. Then move it by sliding, flipping, or turning it. Trace the shape after each move.

Slide

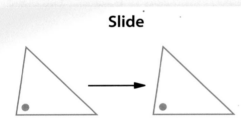

Flip

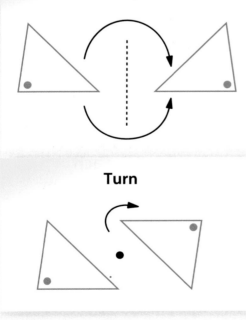

Turn

Explain Your Thinking

1. Tell what happens to each figure if you slide, flip, or turn it.

2. Can you always tell how a figure was moved? Why or why not?

3. Does the shape of a figure change when you move it? Why or why not?

Let's see how to make and describe translations, reflections, and rotations.

Make Connections

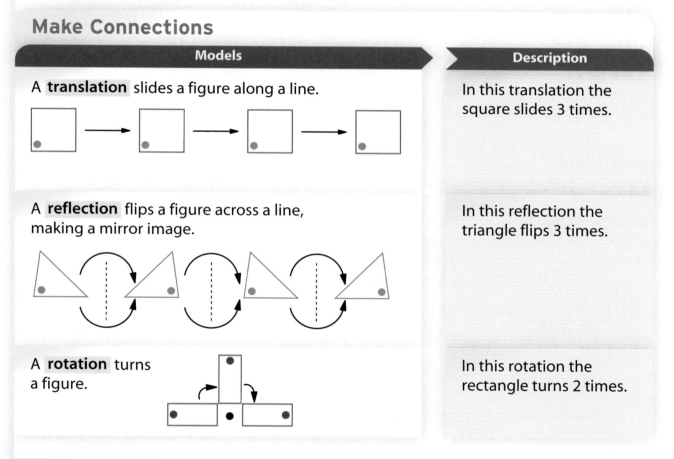

Models	Description
A **translation** slides a figure along a line.	In this translation the square slides 3 times.
A **reflection** flips a figure across a line, making a mirror image.	In this reflection the triangle flips 3 times.
A **rotation** turns a figure.	In this rotation the rectangle turns 2 times.

Your Turn

Write *reflection, rotation,* or *translation* to describe how each figure was moved.

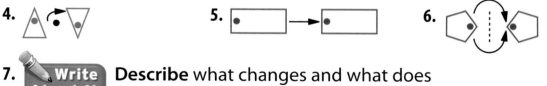

4.   5.   6.

7. **Write About It** **Describe** what changes and what does not change when a figure is moved.

Extra Practice page 540, Set B

24.3 Explore Symmetry

Hands On Activity

A **symmetrical figure** is a shape where one half of the shape is the mirror image of the other.

You can use paper shapes to explore symmetry.

You Will Need
- colored paper
- scissors

VOCABULARY
symmetrical figure
line of symmetry

Use Models

STEP 1

Fold a piece of paper in half. Make sure the fold leaves a line.

STEP 2

Cut out a shape from the paper which includes the folded edges.

STEP 3

Unfold your shape. The fold line is a **line of symmetry**.

The 2 sides are exactly the same.

Explain Your Thinking

1. Look at the 2 parts of the tree. Are they congruent? How do you know?

2. Fold the tree in many different ways. Can you find other lines of symmetry? How many?

3. **What If** The figure was a rectangle. How many lines of symmetry would there be?

528

Let's describe figures with different lines of symmetry.

Make Connections

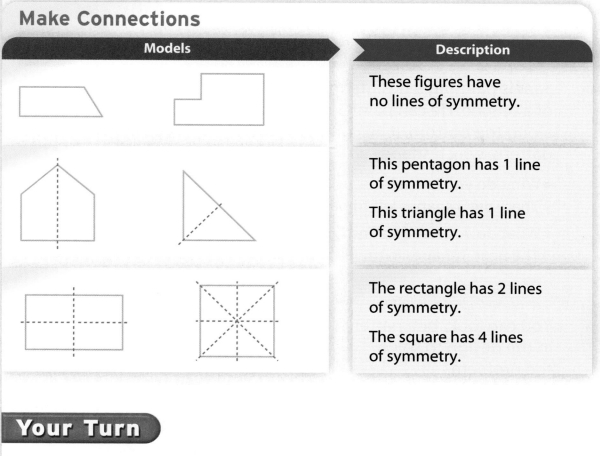

Models	Description
	These figures have no lines of symmetry.
	This pentagon has 1 line of symmetry. This triangle has 1 line of symmetry.
	The rectangle has 2 lines of symmetry. The square has 4 lines of symmetry.

Your Turn

Write *yes* or *no* to tell if each line is a line of symmetry.

1.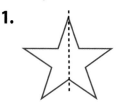

2.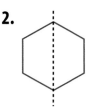

3.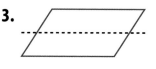

Trace, cut out, and draw all the lines of symmetry for each figure.

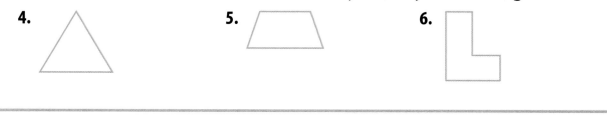

4.

5.

6.

7. **Write About It** **Explain** how a line of symmetry is related to a reflection.

24.4 Problem Solving: Strategy
Find a Pattern

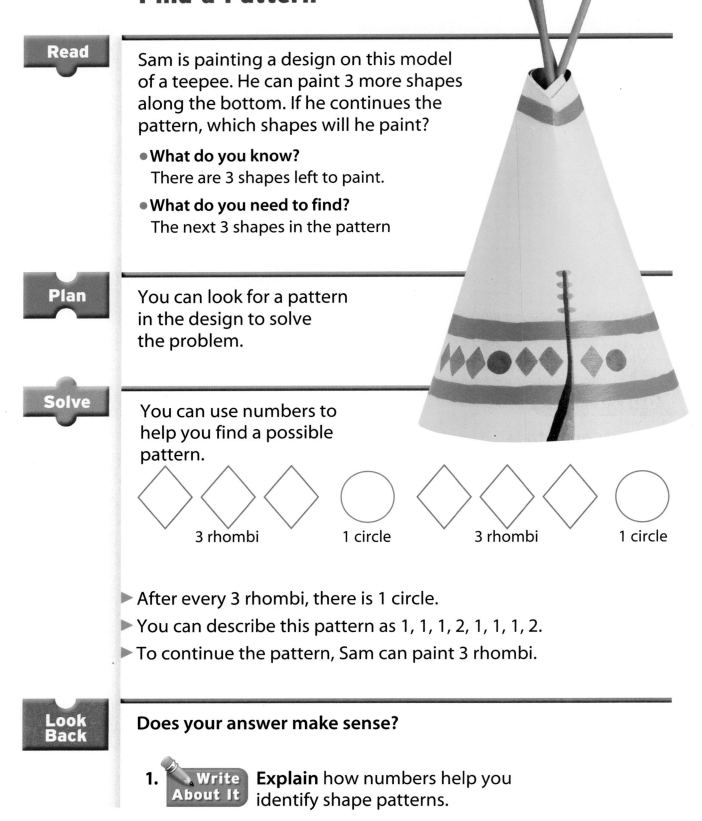

Read

Sam is painting a design on this model of a teepee. He can paint 3 more shapes along the bottom. If he continues the pattern, which shapes will he paint?

- **What do you know?**
  There are 3 shapes left to paint.

- **What do you need to find?**
  The next 3 shapes in the pattern

Plan

You can look for a pattern in the design to solve the problem.

Solve

You can use numbers to help you find a possible pattern.

3 rhombi   1 circle   3 rhombi   1 circle

▶ After every 3 rhombi, there is 1 circle.

▶ You can describe this pattern as 1, 1, 1, 2, 1, 1, 1, 2.

▶ To continue the pattern, Sam can paint 3 rhombi.

Look Back

Does your answer make sense?

1. **Write About It** **Explain** how numbers help you identify shape patterns.

Practice Find a pattern to solve.

2. Sam paints a different pattern on another teepee. What shape do you think he paints next?

3. How can you use numbers to describe the pattern Sam uses on this teepee?

4. Tami is making a design as part of a beaded belt. There are 3 beads in the first row, 6 beads in the second row, and 9 beads in the third row. If this pattern continues, how many beads will she use in the sixth row?

5. Peter is designing a pattern for a tile wall. He puts 2 red tiles in the first row, 4 red tiles in the second row, and 8 red tiles in the third row. How many tiles are in each of the next 2 rows?

Mixed Strategy Review

★ **6.** Dean is making a pattern that repeats 2 squares and 3 triangles. He has room for 30 shapes. How many squares will he draw? How many triangles?

7. ✏ **Write a problem** that shows shapes and can be solved by finding a pattern. Solve it. Ask others to solve it.

Choose a Strategy
- Logical Reasoning
- Draw a Picture or Diagram
- Make a Graph
- Act It Out
- Make a Table or List
- Find a Pattern
- Guess and Check
- Write an Equation
- Work Backward
- Solve a Simpler Problem

Use data from the table for problems 8–9.

8. How many more students are making pueblos than teepees?

9. How many more students will have to make teepees to have the same number as those who make log cabins?

Model Home Project	
Project	**Number**
Teepee	🧍 🧍 🧍
Pueblo	🧍 🧍 🧍 🧍
Log cabin	🧍 🧍 🧍 🧍 🧍

Each 🧍 equals 2 students.

Problem Solving

24.5 Perimeter

Learn

Lisa drew a picture of this house. She wants to cut strips of paper to make a frame for it. Lisa estimates that she needs about 20 centimeters of paper strips. Will this be enough?

Find the perimeter of the picture to solve this problem.

VOCABULARY
perimeter

Use a Ruler

STEP 1

Perimeter is the distance around an object or shape.

Measure the lengths of the sides.

The picture is 5 centimeters long and 4 centimeters wide.

STEP 2

Add the lengths of the 4 sides to find the perimeter:
4 cm + 5 cm + 4 cm + 5 cm = 18 cm

Think: The opposite sides of a rectangle are equal.

Lisa needs 18 centimeters of paper strips. Her estimate is reasonable.

Try It   Use a centimeter ruler to find the perimeter.

1.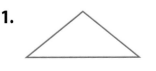

2.

3.  **Explain** how you can find the perimeter of a rectangle by measuring only 2 sides.

Practice and Problem Solving

Use a centimeter ruler to find the perimeter.

4. ☐

5. ☐

6. ⬡

Find the perimeter.

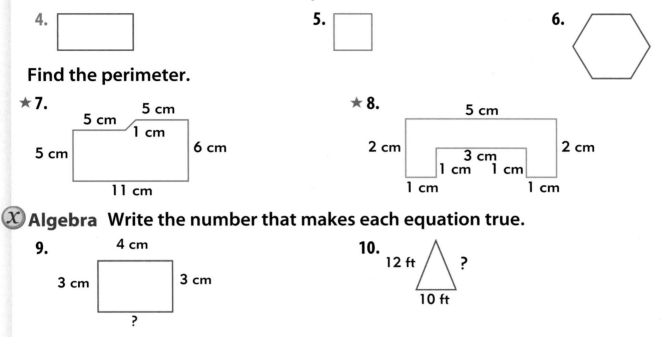

★**7.**
5 cm
5 cm
1 cm
5 cm
6 cm
11 cm

★**8.**
5 cm
2 cm
3 cm
2 cm
1 cm 1 cm
1 cm
1 cm

ⓧ **Algebra** Write the number that makes each equation true.

9.
4 cm
3 cm
3 cm
?

$P = 3 + 3 + 4 + \blacksquare = 14$ cm

10.
12 ft
?
10 ft

$P = 12 + \blacksquare + 10 = 34$ ft

Solve. Use data from the picture for problems 11–12.

11. Jeff swims laps in this square pool. In each lap he swims the length of the pool. How many feet does he swim in 4 laps?

12. Each pool chair cost $89.25. What was the total cost for the 3 pool chairs?

27 ft

Spiral Review and Test Prep

13. Mr. Gomez has to replace 3 windows in his house. Each window costs $34.95. How much does he pay in all? (p. 210)

   A. $94.85   **C.** $105.85

   B. $104.85   **D.** $106.85

14. A carpenter builds 24 doors for 6 houses. Each house gets the same number of doors. How many doors are there for each house? (p. 300)

   F. 2 doors   **H.** 30 doors

   G. 4 doors   **I.** 144 doors

Write the number of sides for each figure. (p. 512)

15. pentagon

16. octagon

17. triangle

24.6 Area

Learn

Area is the number of square units needed to cover a region or figure. Part of a floor is covered with a square tile design. What is the area of the tiled part of the floor?

You can use graph paper to find the area.

Find the number of tiles covering the floor.

Use Models

▶ Use graph paper to draw the floor. Show 1 square unit for each square tile. There are 5 rows and 8 columns.

▶ Shade the square units to show the floor.

▶ Count the total number of square units that are shaded.

▶ There are 40 tiles, so there are 40 square units.

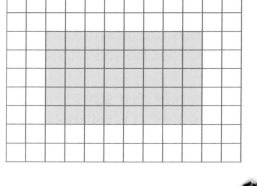

The area of the tiled part of the floor is 40 square units.

Mrs. Ramos wants to put carpet on the floor in her home office. This is a diagram of the office. How much carpet does she need?

Find the area of the figure.

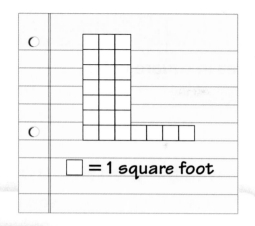

$\square$ = 1 square foot

Irregular Polygon

STEP 1

Separate the irregular figure into 2 rectangles. Count the number of tiles in the larger rectangle.

There are 21 square feet.

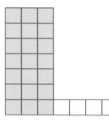

STEP 2

Count the number of tiles in the smaller rectangle.

There are 4 square feet.

STEP 3

Add the area of each rectangle to find the area of the irregular figure.

21 + 4 = 25 square feet

The area of the office is 25 square feet.
Mrs. Ramos needs 25 square feet of carpet.

Try It Find each area in square units.

1.

2.

3.

4. **Write About It** **Explain** how you can use multiplication to find the area of the shape in problem 1.

Practice and Problem Solving

Find each area in square units.

5.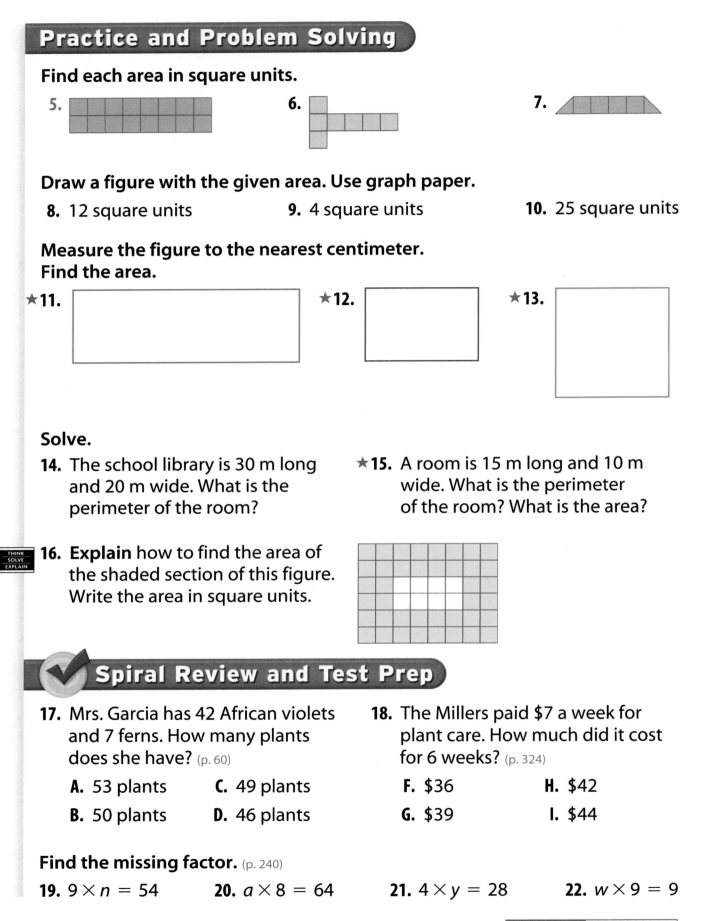

6.

7.

Draw a figure with the given area. Use graph paper.

8. 12 square units

9. 4 square units

10. 25 square units

Measure the figure to the nearest centimeter. Find the area.

★11.

★12.

★13.

Solve.

14. The school library is 30 m long and 20 m wide. What is the perimeter of the room?

★15. A room is 15 m long and 10 m wide. What is the perimeter of the room? What is the area?

16. **Explain** how to find the area of the shaded section of this figure. Write the area in square units.

THINK
SOLVE
EXPLAIN

17. Mrs. Garcia has 42 African violets and 7 ferns. How many plants does she have? (p. 60)

   A. 53 plants   C. 49 plants

   B. 50 plants   D. 46 plants

18. The Millers paid $7 a week for plant care. How much did it cost for 6 weeks? (p. 324)

   F. $36   H. $42

   G. $39   I. $44

Find the missing factor. (p. 240)

19. $9 \times n = 54$

20. $a \times 8 = 64$

21. $4 \times y = 28$

22. $w \times 9 = 9$

Writing for Math

A medium-size square has an area between that of the small and large squares. On graph paper, draw the medium-size square and give its area. Explain your thinking.

Todd's Response

Teacher's Response

✓ **THINK** Find the areas of the small and large squares. Draw a square with an area between those areas.

← Todd explains what he knows and how he will solve the problem.

✓ **SOLVE**

← Todd shows his work.

Size	Small	Medium	Large
Area	4	9	16

✓ **EXPLAIN** The diagrams help me see a pattern. The small square has 2 units on each side. The large square has 4 units on each side. The medium square has 3 units on each side, so its area is 9 square units.

← Todd uses diagrams to help him see and continue a pattern.

To check, I count units in each square. The medium-size square has an area of 9 square units, which is between 4 square units and 16 square units.

← Todd uses counting strategies to check his answer.

Solve. Use Todd's work as a guide.

1. On graph paper, draw a rectangle with an area of 12 square units. Tell how you know its area is 12 square units.

2. On graph paper, draw a rectangle that has 6 rows with 5 units in each row. Find its area.

e-Journal www.mmhmath.com
Write about math.
Chapter 24 **537**

24.7 Explore Volume

Hands On Activity

Volume is the number of cubes it takes to fill a space.

What is the volume of a rectangular prism that is 4 cubes long, 3 cubes wide, and 2 cubes high?

You can use cubes to explore volume.

VOCABULARY
volume
cubic unit

You Will Need
• cubes

Use Models

STEP 1

Connect 4 cubes.

STEP 2

Add 2 more rows of 4 cubes to make one layer.

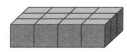

STEP 3

Repeat steps 1 and 2 to make one more layer. Now count the total number of cubes to find the volume.

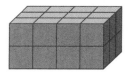

Explain Your Thinking

1. What is the volume of the rectangular prism?

2. Can different figures have the same volume? Why or why not?

3. Can you use the same number of cubes to make different figures that have different volumes? Why or why not?

Find the volume of a box that is 5 units long, 3 units wide and 2 units high.

Let's see how to make and describe the volume of a box.

Make Connections

	Description
Count the cubic units in the shape. The number of **cubic units** in the rectangular prism is the volume. 	There are 3 rows of cubes with 5 cubes in each row. There are 15 cubes in each layer. There are 2 layers. There are 30 cubes in all.

The volume is 30 cubic units.

Your Turn

Find each volume in cubic units.

4.

5.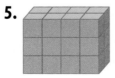

6.

7.  **Write About It** **Explain** why all shapes with the same volume are not congruent. Give an example.

Extra Practice

Set A Identify each as congruent or only similar. (pp. 524–525)

1. 2. 3. 4.

Set B Tell whether each is a translation, rotation or reflection. (pp. 526–527)

5. 6. 7.

Set C Tell whether each figure has a line of symmetry. (pp. 528–529)

8. 9. 10.

Set D Use this pattern for problem 11. (pp. 530–531)

11. Describe this pattern using words and numbers. Which shape should come next?

Set E Find each perimeter. (pp. 532–533)

12. 35 in. / 30 in. / 30 in. / 35 in. / 30 in.

13. 15 cm

14. 12 m / 12 m / 9 m

Set F Find each area in square units. (pp. 534–536)

15. 16. 17.

Set G Find each volume in cubic units. (pp. 538–539)

18. 19. 20.

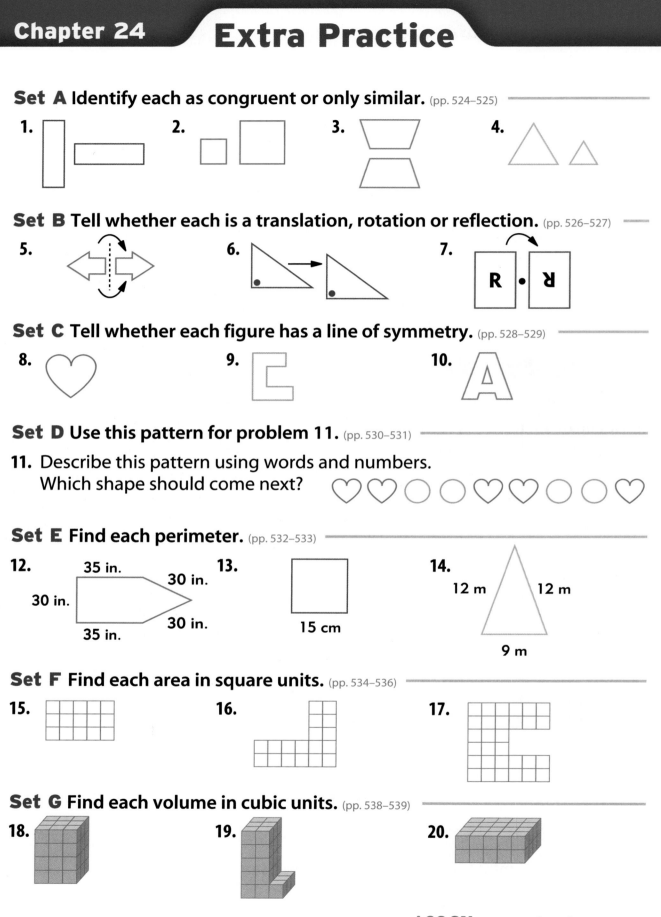

Write whether the figures are congruent or only similar.

1.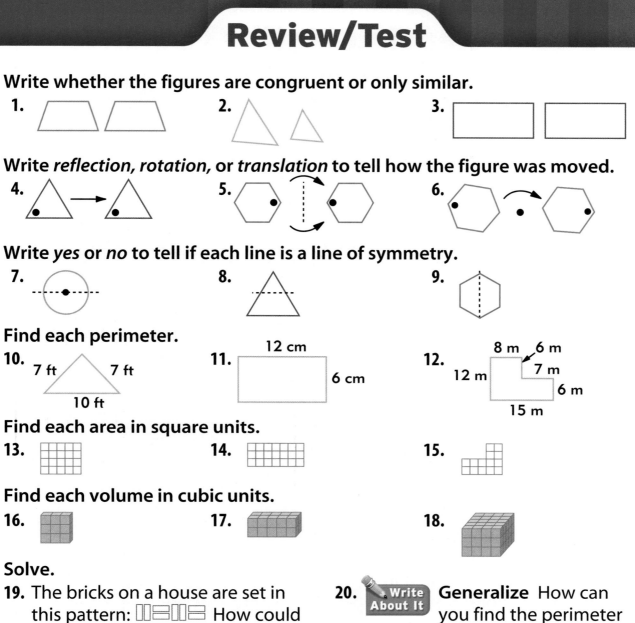

2.

3.

Write *reflection*, *rotation*, or *translation* to tell how the figure was moved.

4.

5.

6.

Write *yes* or *no* to tell if each line is a line of symmetry.

7.

8.

9.

Find each perimeter.

10. 7 ft   7 ft
    10 ft

11. 12 cm
    6 cm

12. 8 m   6 m
    12 m   7 m
            6 m
    15 m

Find each area in square units.

13.

14.

15.

Find each volume in cubic units.

16.

17.

18.

Solve.

19. The bricks on a house are set in this pattern: ⏸⏸▭⏸⏸▭ How could the next 2 bricks look in the pattern?

20. **Write About It** **Generalize** How can you find the perimeter of a rhombus if you know the length of only 1 side?

Do I Need Help?

Exercises	Review Concepts	Use Extra Practice Set
1–3	pp. 524–525	Set A
4–6	pp. 526–527	Set B
7–9	pp. 528–529	Set C
10–12, 20	pp. 532–533	Set E
13–15	pp. 534–536	Set F
16–18	pp. 538–539	Set G
19	pp. 530–531	Set D

Foldables **Use your Foldables to help you review.**

Shapes in the Stars

For thousands of years people have told stories about the stars. Different cultures looked at the night sky. They connected stars together to form pictures. For each picture they told a story. These pictures in the stars are called constellations.

The constellations shown are called Sagittarius, or "the archer," Libra, "the scale," and Cancer, "the crab."

Each constellation is made of 2-dimensional shapes. What shapes can you find in the constellations?

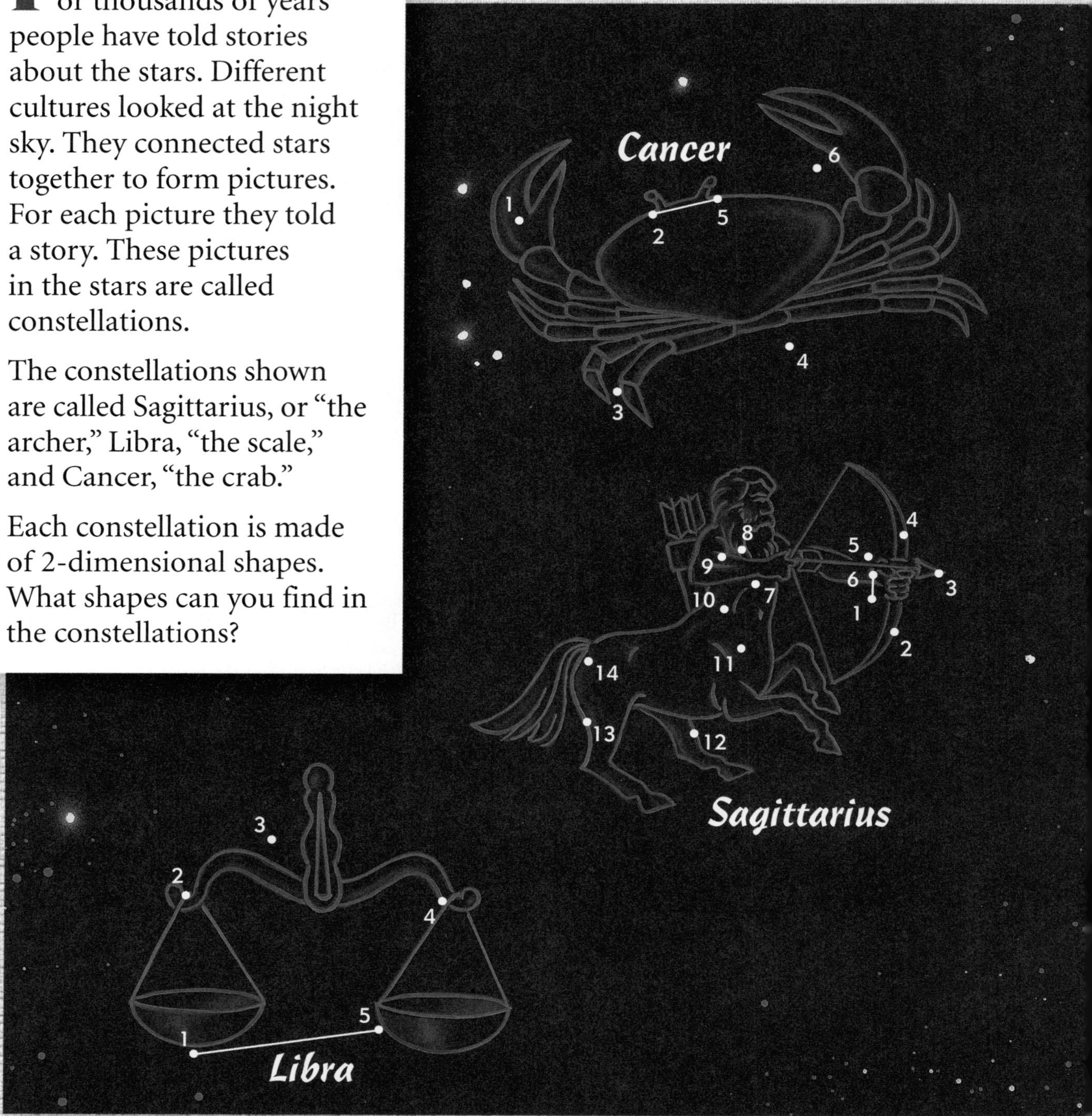

Cancer

Sagittarius

Libra

Activity

You Will Need
- tracing paper

Hypothesize

Predict whether you will make more quadrilaterals or triangles by drawing the lines of these 3 constellations.

Procedure

1. Copy the outline of stars of these 3 constellations on a sheet of tracing paper.

2. On your copy of Libra, connect the following stars with straight lines. Do so in this order: 1-2-3-4-5. What shape do you see?

3. On your copy of Cancer, connect the following stars with straight lines. Do so in this order: 1-2-3-4-5-6. What shape do you see?

4. On your copy of Sagittarius, connect the following stars with straight lines. Do so in this order: 1-2-3-4-5-6. And: 7-8-9-7. What shapes do you see? Now connect: 10-11-12-13-14-10. What shape do you see?

Conclude and Apply

1. **Classify** Did you find more triangles or quadrilaterals?

2. **Observe** What shapes did you not find in the stars?

3. Suppose you can only draw straight lines between the stars. What shape do you think cannot be drawn?

Going Further Make your own constellation. Plot stars on a piece of paper and make shapes from them. Write a story about your constellation.

Problem Solving

Vocabulary

Complete. Use a word from the list.

1. The number of cubic units that fit inside a 3-dimensional figure is called its ___.

2. Two figures that are the same shape but not the same size are ___.

3. The distance around an object is its ___.

4. A figure with 4 straight sides is a ___.

VOCABULARY
congruent
perimeter
quadrilateral
similar
volume

Skills and Applications

Identify and classify 2- and 3-dimensional figures. (pp. 502–513)

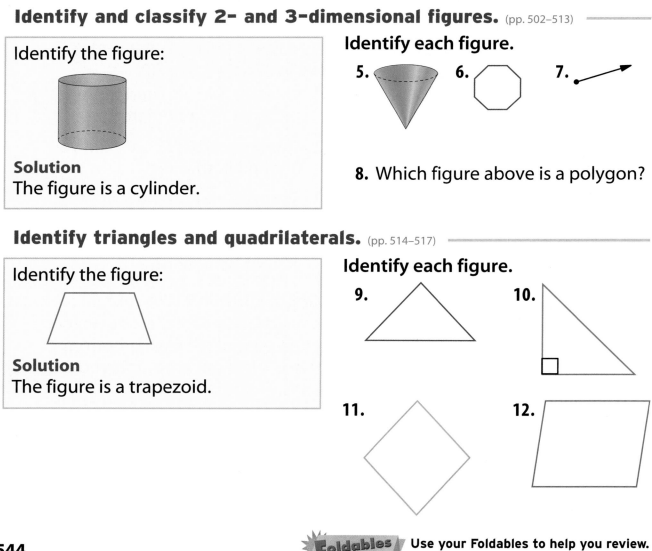

Identify the figure:

Solution
The figure is a cylinder.

Identify each figure.

5. 6. 7.

8. Which figure above is a polygon?

Identify triangles and quadrilaterals. (pp. 514–517)

Identify the figure:

Solution
The figure is a trapezoid.

Identify each figure.

9. 10.

11. 12.

Foldables Use your Foldables to help you review.

Identify congruent, similar, or symmetrical figures. (pp. 524–529)

Write whether the figures are congruent. Tell whether each line is a line of symmetry.

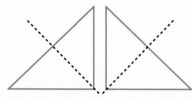

Solution
The triangles are congruent.
Each line is a line of symmetry.

Identify each as congruent or similar. Show whether each figure has a line of symmetry.

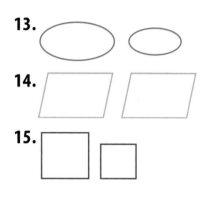

13.

14.

15.

Find the perimeter, area, and volume. (pp. 532–539)

Find the perimeter of a face.

Solution
Perimeter of a face
$= 4 + 4 + 4 + 4 = 16$ units

Find the perimeter and area.

16.

17.

Find the volume.

18.

Use skills and strategies to solve problems. (pp. 518–519, 530–531)

What could the next shape be?

Solution
Find a pattern.
Use numbers to describe the pattern: 1, 2, 2, 2, 1, 2, 2, 2, 1.

The square comes next.

Use the figures below for problems 19–20.

19. Describe the pattern in words, and numbers.

20. What could the next shape be?

Enrichment

Tessellation

When repeated 2-dimensional figures cover a flat surface without overlapping or leaving any space between them, those figures **tessellate.** The repeating pattern formed by the figures is called a **tessellation**.

These figures do tessellate.

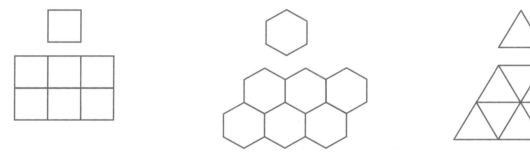

These figures do not tessellate.

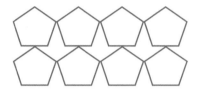 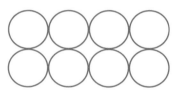

Tell if each figure will tessellate. Write *yes* or *no*.

1. 2. 3. 4.

5. Use this pentagon to create a tessellation.

6. Write About It **Explain** whether this is a tessellation.

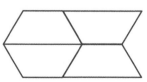

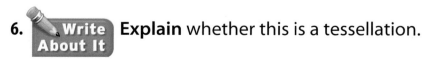

Performance Assessment

What Are the Perimeter and the Area?

Draw a floor plan of your home with rectangular rooms on grid paper. Label each room of the house. Find the perimeter and area for each room.

Make a chart like the one below for each room. Use the chart to answer these questions:

- What is the perimeter of each room?

- What is the area of each room?

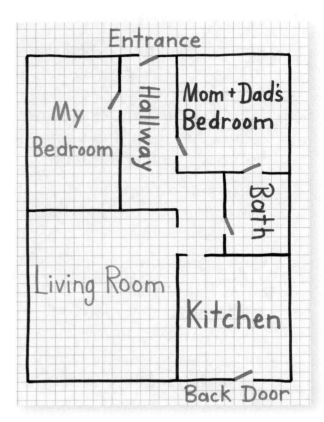

Room	Area	Perimeter
Kitchen		
Living Room		
Bedroom 1		
Bedroom 2		
Bedroom 3		

Tips For A Good Answer

- Show a floor plan.

- Have a completed chart with each perimeter and area showing.

You may want to save this work in your portfolio.

e-Journal www.mmhmath.com
Write about math.   Unit 12   **547**

Assessment

TECHNOLOGY Link

Draw and Identify a Figure

Pablo is designing a deck. He needs to draw a regular hexagon to use in his sketch of the deck. A regular figure has all equal sides. Draw a regular hexagon. Show that the figure is a regular hexagon.

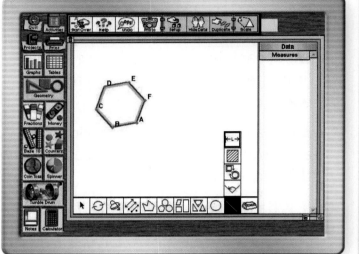

Math Tool Chest CD-ROM

You can use a drawing program with geometry tools to draw geometric figures.

- Click on Geometry Tools ◣▉○ from the *Math Tool Chest* CD-ROM.

- Choose the polygon tool. Draw a hexagon.

- Use the measurement tool ▨ to find the length of each side.

How do you know the figure is a regular hexagon?

Use the computer to draw each figure. Show that the Math Tool Chest CD-ROM figure you have drawn is correct.

1. equilateral triangle   **2.** regular pentagon   **3.** regular octagon

Solve.

4. Garin is drawing plans for his garden. He wants to draw a scalene triangle to show the shape of his garden. Draw a scalene triangle.

5. Analyze How do the geometry and measurement tools help you draw correct figures?

For more practice, use Math Traveler™.

Test-Taking Tips

For some types of test questions, you need to use **information from a picture** to find the answer.

Which 2 pieces in this puzzle are congruent?

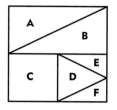

A. A and D **C.** A and B

B. B and E **D.** E and D

You can trace the shapes to find which have the same shape and size.

The correct choice is C.

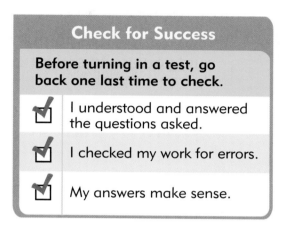

Check for Success

Before turning in a test, go back one last time to check.

✓ I understood and answered the questions asked.

✓ I checked my work for errors.

✓ My answers make sense.

Choose the best answer.
Use the information in the pictures.

1. Which shape has 4 square corners and 4 equal sides?

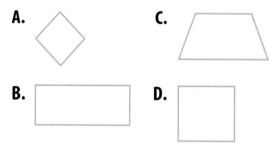

2. Which shape can be folded in half so that the 2 parts match exactly?

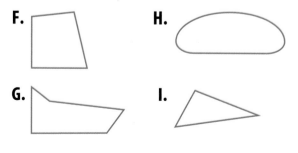

3. Which figure has a face shaped like a triangle?

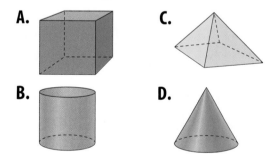

4. The perimeter of the rectangle is 20 inches. What is the length of side A?

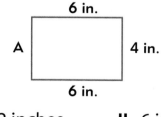

6 in.

A   4 in.

6 in.

F. 2 inches   **H.** 6 inches

G. 4 inches   **I.** 8 inches

Test Prep

PART 1 • Multiple Choice

Choose the best answer.

1. Which compatible numbers would you use to estimate $558 \div 9$? (p. 414)

   A. $640 \div 8$ **C.** $630 \div 9$
   B. $450 \div 9$ **D.** $540 \div 9$

2. Which weighs about 8 pounds? (p. 460)

   F. An apartment building
   G. A bird's nest
   H. A birdhouse
   I. A tree

3. Jayne has a 3-gallon container and a 5-gallon container. She pours 5 gallons of water in a fish tank. Then she uses the 5-gallon container to fill the 3-gallon container. Finally she pours what is left in the 5-gallon container in the fish tank. How much water did Jayne pour into the fish tank? (p. 482)

   A. 10 gallons   **C.** 7 gallons
   B. 8 gallons   **D.** 6 gallons

4. Which equation is not correct? (p. 204)

   F. $5 \times 4 = 9$ **H.** $12 \div 1 = 12$
   G. $12 \times 1 = 12$ **I.** $8 \times 0 = 0$

5. Haley's address is a 3-digit number. The hundreds digit is 2 times the ones digit. The sum of the hundreds digit and ones digit is 12. The tens digit is the same as the ones digit. What number is Haley's address? (p. 244)

   A. 622   **C.** 824
   B. 633   **D.** 844

6. Which angle is less than a right angle? (p. 508)

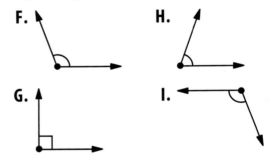

7. The blue house has 6 rooms with 3 windows in every room. The white house has 7 rooms with 2 windows in every room. Which shows how to compare the number of windows in the houses? (p. 238)

   A. $9 = 9$ **C.** $18 > 14$
   B. $14 > 18$ **D.** $18 - 9$

8. 7×34 (p. 384)

   F. 2,128   **H.** 238
   G. 288   **I.** 218

Record your answers on the answer sheet provided by your teacher or on a piece of paper.

9. What is the perimeter of this figure? (p. 532)

10. How many quarts equal the same amount as 3 gallons? (p. 462)

11. Which number makes the equation true? Explain your reasoning. (p. 256)

$$(7 \times \blacksquare) \times 4 = 7 \times (2 \times 4)$$

12. In Essex County 678 houses were built last year. What is this number rounded to the nearest ten? (p. 32)

13. This diagram shows the floor pattern on a newly tiled floor. Will the next column of tiles be squares or triangles? Explain. (p. 530)

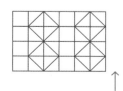

14. Identify the rule. (p. 204)

Input	3	5	8
Output	6	10	16

15. Building 5 has 175 apartments. Building 6 has 30 more apartments than Building 5. If Building 4 has 160 apartments, how many apartments do Buildings 4, 5, and 6 have in all? (p. 76)

16. The window in Mr. Draddy's living room is 120 inches long. How many feet long is the window? (p. 462)

Record your answer on a sheet of paper. Show your work.

17. Which green figure will cover the hexagon if you have 6 of them? Draw a picture and explain why your answer is correct. (p. 512)

Test Prep

What Do I Need to Know?

Kyle shares a 4-slice pizza with 3 friends. Each person ate 1 slice. What fraction of the pizza did Kyle eat?

Understand Fractions

What Will I Learn?

In this chapter you will learn to

- read, identify, and write fractions
- explore equivalent fractions
- compare and order fractions
- explore finding parts of a group
- use skills and strategies to solve problems

How Do I Read Math?

When you read a mathematics book, sometimes you read words and symbols, and sometimes you read only symbols.

All of these show fractions:

- **picture:** △
- **number:** $\frac{1}{2}$ ← **1 part shaded**
  ← **2 equal parts**
- **words: one half**

VOCABULARY

- fraction
- numerator
- denominator
- equivalent fractions
- simplest form

Foldables

Use your Foldables to help you with chapter concepts.

1. Stack four sheets of paper about an inch apart.
2. Roll up the bottom edges of the paper. Stop them 1 inch from the top edges.
3. Crease the paper to hold the tabs in place.
4. Staple along the fold.
5. Label as shown. Record what you learn.

Understand Fractions

25.1 Parts of a Whole
that name the same amount. $\frac{3}{6} = \frac{1}{2}$

25.2 Explore Equivalent Fractions

25.3 Fractions in Simplest Form

25.4 Compare and Order Fractions

25.5 Parts of a Group

25.6 Explore Finding Parts of a Group

25.7 Problem Solving: Check for Reasonableness

25.1 Parts of a Whole

Learn

This carrot cake is cut into 5 equal parts. How much of the cake does not have icing?

A **fraction** is a number that names part of a whole or group.

Find: the fraction of the cake that does not have icing

VOCABULARY
fraction
numerator
denominator

There's More Than One Way!

Use Fraction Models

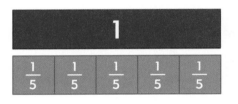

The cake is divided into 5 equal parts. $\frac{5}{5}$ represents the whole cake. $\frac{1}{5}$ represents one piece of cake. One piece out of 5 pieces, $\frac{1}{5}$, does not have icing.

Use Paper and Pencil

numerator → **1** ← part without icing
denominator → **5** ← total number of parts

Read: one fifth   **Write:** $\frac{1}{5}$

Think: The fraction models show how a whole can be divided into 5 equal parts, or fifths.

One fifth, or $\frac{1}{5}$, of the cake does not have icing.

How much of the cake has icing?

Find: the fraction of the cake that has icing

There's More Than One Way!

Use a Number Line

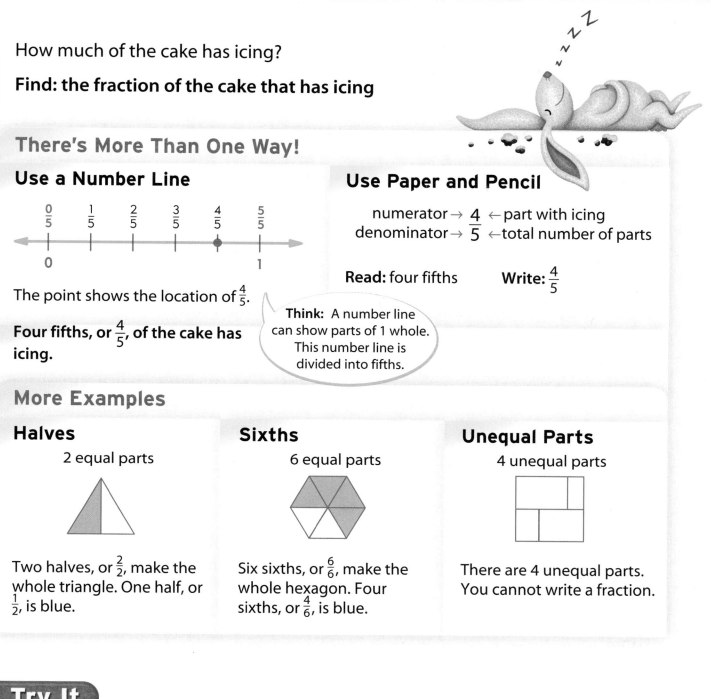

$$\frac{0}{5} \quad \frac{1}{5} \quad \frac{2}{5} \quad \frac{3}{5} \quad \frac{4}{5} \quad \frac{5}{5}$$

0   1

The point shows the location of $\frac{4}{5}$.

Four fifths, or $\frac{4}{5}$, of the cake has icing.

Use Paper and Pencil

numerator → $\underline{4}$ ← part with icing
denominator → 5 ← total number of parts

Read: four fifths   **Write:** $\frac{4}{5}$

Think: A number line can show parts of 1 whole. This number line is divided into fifths.

More Examples

Halves
2 equal parts

Two halves, or $\frac{2}{2}$, make the whole triangle. One half, or $\frac{1}{2}$, is blue.

Sixths
6 equal parts

Six sixths, or $\frac{6}{6}$, make the whole hexagon. Four sixths, or $\frac{4}{6}$, is blue.

Unequal Parts
4 unequal parts

There are 4 unequal parts. You cannot write a fraction.

Try It

Tell if the figure shows equal parts. If yes, write a fraction for the part that is shaded.

1.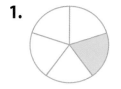

2.

3.

4.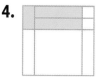

5. **Write About It** **Explain** how you write a fraction to describe the shaded parts of a whole.

Practice and Problem Solving

Tell if the figure shows equal parts. If yes, write a fraction for the part that is shaded.

6.
7.
8.
9.

Draw a picture and write a fraction for each.
Make sure your parts are equal.

10. one fourth   **11.** two thirds   **12.** three eighths   **13.** five twelfths

Write a fraction that names the point on the number line.

14.

0   1

15.

0   1

Link to HEALTH

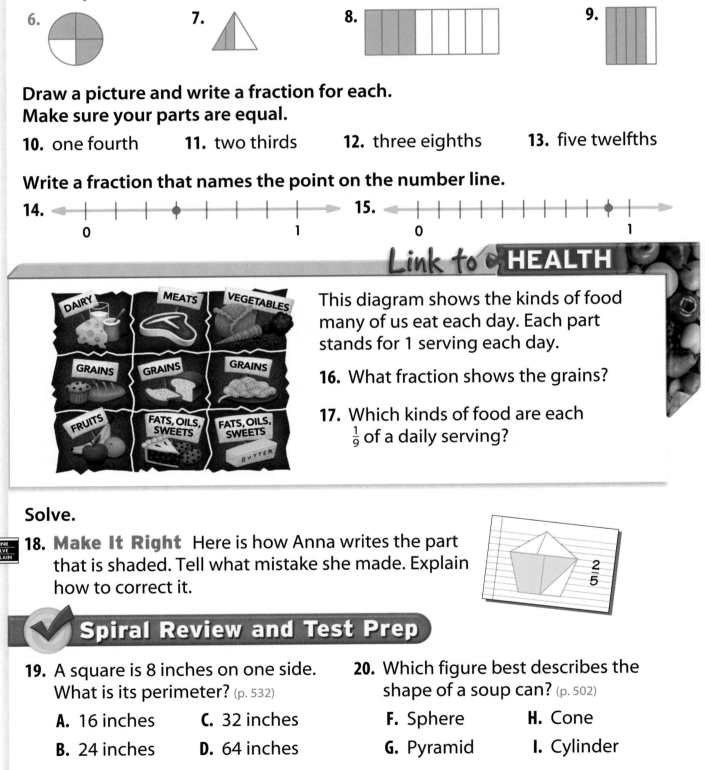

This diagram shows the kinds of food many of us eat each day. Each part stands for 1 serving each day.

16. What fraction shows the grains?

17. Which kinds of food are each $\frac{1}{9}$ of a daily serving?

Solve.

THINK
SOLVE
EXPLAIN

18. Make It Right Here is how Anna writes the part that is shaded. Tell what mistake she made. Explain how to correct it.

$\frac{2}{5}$

Spiral Review and Test Prep

19. A square is 8 inches on one side. What is its perimeter? (p. 532)

   A. 16 inches   **C.** 32 inches

   B. 24 inches   **D.** 64 inches

20. Which figure best describes the shape of a soup can? (p. 502)

   F. Sphere   **H.** Cone

   G. Pyramid   **I.** Cylinder

21. $566 \div 8$ (p. 330)   **22.** 3×78 (p. 384)   **23.** $1,835 + 906$ (p. 72)

6. yes; $\frac{3}{4}$

Extra Practice page 572, Set A

Problem Solving: Reading for Math

HOW ABOUT THEM APPLES?

If an apple a day keeps the doctor away, then people from Virginia don't have anything to worry about! Virginia ranks number 6 in the states that produce the most apples. What do people do with all of these fruits? They put them in lunch boxes, bake them in pies, turn them into applesauce, squeeze them into apple juice, and much more. Here's a recipe from an orchard in Virginia. Eat up!

VIRGINIA APPLE SQUARES

1 large egg
1 tsp. baking powder
1 tsp. cinnamon
$\frac{1}{2}$ cup brown sugar
1 tsp. vanilla
$\frac{1}{2}$ cup chopped pecans

1 cup flour
$\frac{1}{4}$ tsp. salt
$\frac{1}{2}$ cup margarine
$\frac{1}{2}$ cup white sugar
1 cup apples, diced

Melt the margarine. Then mix it with the egg, brown sugar, vanilla, and white sugar. In another bowl, mix the flour, baking powder, salt, and cinnamon. Pour the sugar mixture into the flour mixture and beat until smooth. Next, mix in the pecans and apples. Pour into an 8-inch square glass pan and bake at 350°F for 35 to 40 minutes. Makes 8 squares.

Reading Skill **Steps in a Process** How many different steps do you follow to make apple squares?

1. You ate 2 of the squares. What fraction of the whole did you eat?

2. You want to make 24 squares. How many cups of apples will you need?

Problem Solving

25.2 Explore Equivalent Fractions

Hands On Activity

You can use fraction models to find fractions that name the same amount, or **equivalent fractions**.

Find 2 fractions that are equivalent to $\frac{1}{2}$.

You Will Need
• fraction models

Use Models

STEP 1

Start with the model for 1 whole. Use one $\frac{1}{2}$ fraction piece to show one half.

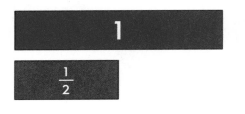

STEP 2

Use $\frac{1}{4}$ fraction pieces to equal the length of the $\frac{1}{2}$ piece. Count the number of $\frac{1}{4}$ fraction pieces.

STEP 3

Use $\frac{1}{8}$ fraction pieces to equal the length of the $\frac{1}{2}$ piece. Count the number of $\frac{1}{8}$ fraction pieces.

Explain Your Thinking

1. How many $\frac{1}{4}$ fraction pieces are equal to the length of the $\frac{1}{2}$ fraction piece?

2. How many $\frac{1}{8}$ fraction pieces are equal to the length of the $\frac{1}{2}$ fraction piece?

3. What are the 2 equivalent fractions for $\frac{1}{2}$?

4. **What If** You use $\frac{1}{10}$ fraction pieces. How many pieces will be equal to $\frac{1}{2}$?

Technology Link

Use the fractions tool in **Math Tool Chest** to explore equivalent fractions.

Here is how to show equivalent fractions for $\frac{1}{3}$.

Let's see how to connect models to pencil and paper.

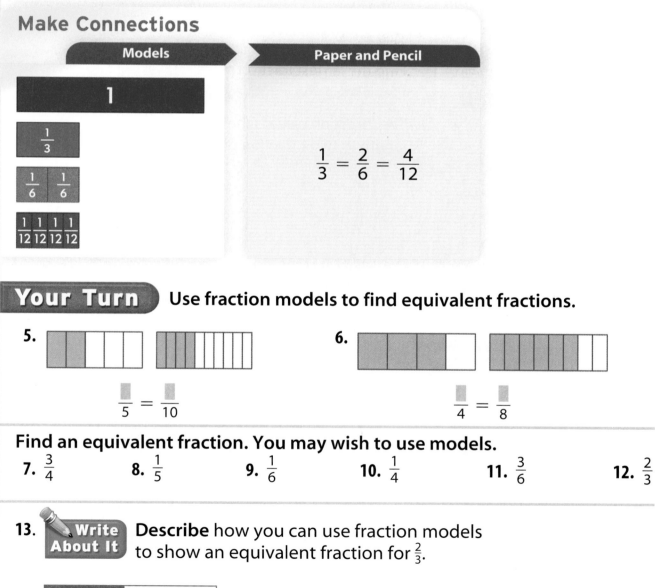

Make Connections

| Models | Paper and Pencil |

$$\frac{1}{3} = \frac{2}{6} = \frac{4}{12}$$

Your Turn Use fraction models to find equivalent fractions.

5. $\dfrac{}{5} = \dfrac{}{10}$

6. $\dfrac{}{4} = \dfrac{}{8}$

Find an equivalent fraction. You may wish to use models.

7. $\frac{3}{4}$
8. $\frac{1}{5}$
9. $\frac{1}{6}$
10. $\frac{1}{4}$
11. $\frac{3}{6}$
12. $\frac{2}{3}$

13. **Write About It** **Describe** how you can use fraction models to show an equivalent fraction for $\frac{2}{3}$.

25.3 Fractions in Simplest Form

Learn

VOCABULARY

simplest form

June made a pizza with 8 equal pieces. She put mushrooms on $\frac{2}{8}$ of the pizza. How can you write this fraction in simplest form?

A fraction is in **simplest form** when it is expressed using the largest fraction piece possible.

Find: $\frac{2}{8}$ in simplest form

Use Models

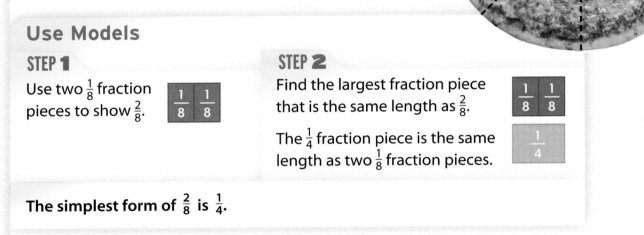

STEP 1

Use two $\frac{1}{8}$ fraction pieces to show $\frac{2}{8}$.

| $\frac{1}{8}$ | $\frac{1}{8}$ |

STEP 2

Find the largest fraction piece that is the same length as $\frac{2}{8}$.

| $\frac{1}{8}$ | $\frac{1}{8}$ |

The $\frac{1}{4}$ fraction piece is the same length as two $\frac{1}{8}$ fraction pieces.

| $\frac{1}{4}$ |

The simplest form of $\frac{2}{8}$ is $\frac{1}{4}$.

Try It   Write each fraction in simplest form.

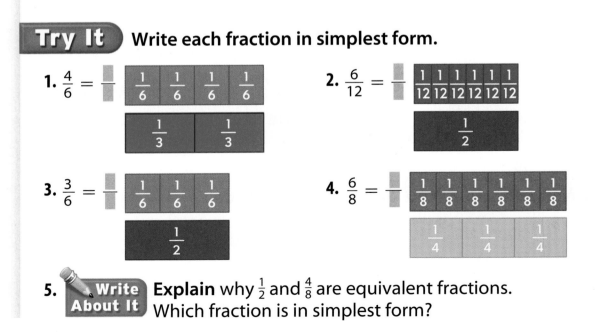

1. $\frac{4}{6} = \frac{\ }{\ }$

| $\frac{1}{6}$ | $\frac{1}{6}$ | $\frac{1}{6}$ | $\frac{1}{6}$ |

| $\frac{1}{3}$ | $\frac{1}{3}$ |

2. $\frac{6}{12} = \frac{\ }{\ }$

| $\frac{1}{12}$ | $\frac{1}{12}$ | $\frac{1}{12}$ | $\frac{1}{12}$ | $\frac{1}{12}$ | $\frac{1}{12}$ |

| $\frac{1}{2}$ |

3. $\frac{3}{6} = \frac{\ }{\ }$

| $\frac{1}{6}$ | $\frac{1}{6}$ | $\frac{1}{6}$ |

| $\frac{1}{2}$ |

4. $\frac{6}{8} = \frac{\ }{\ }$

| $\frac{1}{8}$ | $\frac{1}{8}$ | $\frac{1}{8}$ | $\frac{1}{8}$ | $\frac{1}{8}$ | $\frac{1}{8}$ |

| $\frac{1}{4}$ | $\frac{1}{4}$ | $\frac{1}{4}$ |

5. **Write About It** **Explain** why $\frac{1}{2}$ and $\frac{4}{8}$ are equivalent fractions. Which fraction is in simplest form?

Practice and Problem Solving

Write each fraction in simplest form.

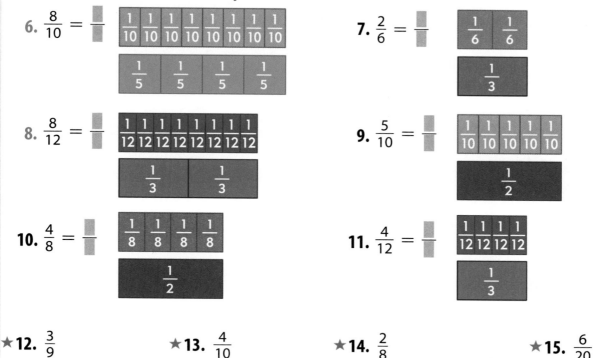

6. $\frac{8}{10} = \frac{\blacksquare}{\blacksquare}$

7. $\frac{2}{6} = \frac{\blacksquare}{\blacksquare}$

8. $\frac{8}{12} = \frac{\blacksquare}{\blacksquare}$

9. $\frac{5}{10} = \frac{\blacksquare}{\blacksquare}$

10. $\frac{4}{8} = \frac{\blacksquare}{\blacksquare}$

11. $\frac{4}{12} = \frac{\blacksquare}{\blacksquare}$

★12. $\frac{3}{9}$

★13. $\frac{4}{10}$

★14. $\frac{2}{8}$

★15. $\frac{6}{20}$

Solve.

16. Reggie eats 2 pieces of a pie. The pie has 6 equal pieces. How much of the pie does he eat? How can you write this fraction in simplest form?

17. Dana folds a piece of paper in fourths. She colors 2 parts blue. How can she write the blue parts as a fraction? What is this fraction in simplest form?

Spiral Review and Test Prep

18. Jessie puts her carrot cake in the oven at 2:20 P.M. It must bake for 45 minutes. What time will the cake be ready? (p. 146)

   A. 1:45 P.M.   **C.** 2:45 P.M.

   B. 2:55 P.M.   **D.** 3:05 P.M.

19. Adam needs to find the area of a square. He knows that 1 side is 8 inches. What is the area of the square? (p. 534)

   F. 58 sq in.   **H.** 64 sq in.

   G. 62 sq in.   **I.** 68 sq in.

Write the number to make each equation true. (p. 462)

20. 4 gal = $\blacksquare$ qt

21. 2 lb = $\blacksquare$ oz

22. 15 ft = $\blacksquare$ yd

23. 3 ft = $\blacksquare$ in.

25.4 Compare and Order Fractions

Learn

Jenna and Martha are using fruit to make smoothies. Jenna pours in $\frac{1}{4}$ cup of orange juice, and Martha pours in $\frac{3}{4}$ cup of orange juice. Who pours in more orange juice?

Compare: $\frac{1}{4}$ and $\frac{3}{4}$

There's More Than One Way!

Use Models

Use fraction pieces to model and compare $\frac{1}{4}$ and $\frac{3}{4}$.

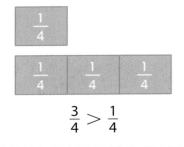

$$\frac{3}{4} > \frac{1}{4}$$

Use a Number Line

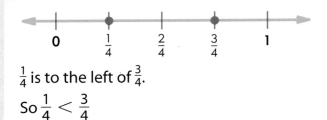

$\frac{1}{4}$ is to the left of $\frac{3}{4}$.

So $\frac{1}{4} < \frac{3}{4}$

So Martha uses more orange juice than Jenna.

Boris uses $\frac{5}{6}$ cup of fruit juice to make his fruit smoothie. Lana uses $\frac{2}{3}$ cup of fruit juice, and Garry uses $\frac{3}{4}$ cup of fruit juice. Who uses the most fruit juice in their fruit smoothie?

Compare and order: $\frac{5}{6}, \frac{2}{3}, \frac{3}{4}.$

There's More Than One Way!

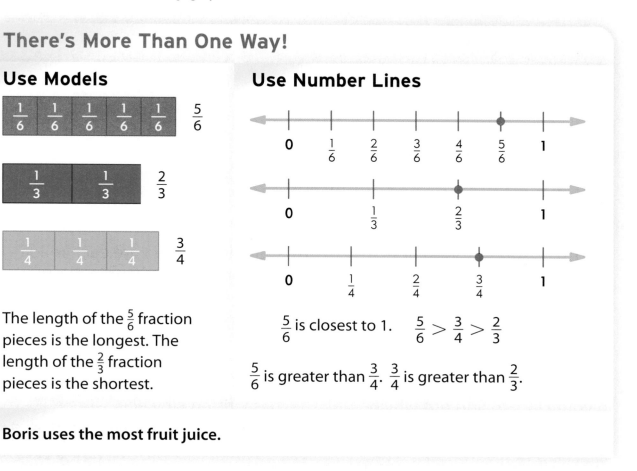

Use Models

$\frac{5}{6}$

$\frac{2}{3}$

$\frac{3}{4}$

The length of the $\frac{5}{6}$ fraction pieces is the longest. The length of the $\frac{2}{3}$ fraction pieces is the shortest.

Use Number Lines

$\frac{5}{6}$ is closest to 1. $\frac{5}{6} > \frac{3}{4} > \frac{2}{3}$

$\frac{5}{6}$ is greater than $\frac{3}{4}$. $\frac{3}{4}$ is greater than $\frac{2}{3}$.

Boris uses the most fruit juice.

Try It Compare. Write $>$, $<$, or $=$. Use models.

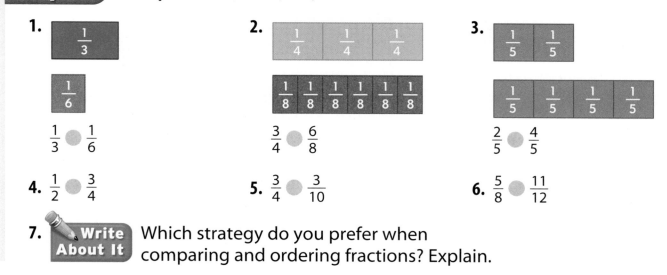

1. $\frac{1}{3}$

$\frac{1}{6}$

$\frac{1}{3}$ ⬤ $\frac{1}{6}$

2. $\frac{1}{4}$ $\frac{1}{4}$ $\frac{1}{4}$

$\frac{1}{8}$ $\frac{1}{8}$ $\frac{1}{8}$ $\frac{1}{8}$ $\frac{1}{8}$ $\frac{1}{8}$

$\frac{3}{4}$ ⬤ $\frac{6}{8}$

3. $\frac{1}{5}$ $\frac{1}{5}$

$\frac{1}{5}$ $\frac{1}{5}$ $\frac{1}{5}$ $\frac{1}{5}$

$\frac{2}{5}$ ⬤ $\frac{4}{5}$

4. $\frac{1}{2}$ ⬤ $\frac{3}{4}$

5. $\frac{3}{4}$ ⬤ $\frac{3}{10}$

6. $\frac{5}{8}$ ⬤ $\frac{11}{12}$

7. **Write About It** Which strategy do you prefer when comparing and ordering fractions? Explain.

Practice and Problem Solving

Compare. Write >, <, or = . Use models.

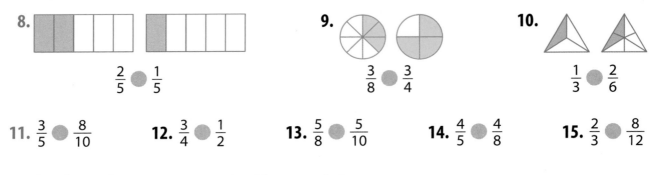

8. $\frac{2}{5} \bullet \frac{1}{5}$

9. $\frac{3}{8} \bullet \frac{3}{4}$

10. $\frac{1}{3} \bullet \frac{2}{6}$

11. $\frac{3}{5} \bullet \frac{8}{10}$

12. $\frac{3}{4} \bullet \frac{1}{2}$

13. $\frac{5}{8} \bullet \frac{5}{10}$

14. $\frac{4}{5} \bullet \frac{4}{8}$

15. $\frac{2}{3} \bullet \frac{8}{12}$

Order from least to greatest. Use models.

16. $\frac{1}{8}, \frac{5}{8}, \frac{3}{8}$

★17. $\frac{2}{3}, \frac{2}{9}, \frac{2}{5}$

★18. $\frac{1}{4}, \frac{3}{8}, \frac{2}{3}$

Solve.

19. **Health** A survey found that about $\frac{2}{5}$ of the women surveyed choose foods for a healthy diet. Does this fraction represent most of the group? Explain.

20. Claudio and Tara are each reading the same book. Claudio has read $\frac{3}{5}$ of the book. Tara has read $\frac{1}{2}$ of the book. Who has read more?

THINK SOLVE EXPLAIN

21. **Collect Data** Survey students in your class to find out which is their favorite food—pizza, hamburger, or hot dog. Make a bar graph. Compare your results.

22. **Make It Right** Justin has written why he thinks $\frac{5}{8} > \frac{2}{3}$. Tell what mistake he made. Write the correct answer.

THINK SOLVE EXPLAIN

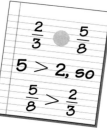

$\frac{2}{3} \bullet \frac{5}{8}$

$5 > 2$, so

$\frac{5}{8} > \frac{2}{3}$

Spiral Review and Test Prep

23. What is the volume? (p. 538)
    - **A.** 6 cubic units
    - **B.** 8 cubic units
    - **C.** 12 cubic units
    - **D.** 14 cubic units

24. The Martins buy a pizza. It has 8 slices. All 4 members of the Martin family each eat 2 slices. How many slices are left? (p. 244)
    - **F.** 64 slices
    - **G.** 12 slices
    - **H.** 6 slices
    - **I.** 0 slices

Name each figure.

25. (p. 502)

26. (p. 512)

27. (p. 502)

28. (p. 516)

Extra Practice page 572, Set C

Practice at School ★ Practice at Home

MAKE IT WHOLE

Use models to show fractions.

Ready

Players: 2

You Will Need: a set of fraction models, 2 number cubes (one numbered from 1 through 6; the other numbered with even numbers 2 through 12)

Set

Make the number cubes.

GO!

▶ Player 1 tosses the number cubes and calls out the fraction tossed—the greater number is the denominator and the lesser number is the numerator. The player then finds the fraction models for the named fraction.

▶ Now player 2 tosses the number cubes to get a fraction.

▶ Players can trade in fractions to get equivalent pieces to help make their wholes. For example, if you have $\frac{3}{4}$ and you toss a $\frac{1}{2}$, you can trade $\frac{1}{2}$ for $\frac{2}{4}$ to make 1 whole and $\frac{1}{4}$.

▶ Players have the option to pass. The first player who makes exactly 5 wholes is the winner.

25.5 Parts of a Group

Learn

Ants are carrying berries. What part of the group of berries is raspberry? What part of the group of berries is blueberry?

You can use a fraction to describe part of a group.

Use Paper and Pencil

number of raspberries → 1 ← numerator
total number of berries → 6 ← denominator

One-sixth, or $\frac{1}{6}$, of the group are raspberries.

number of blueberries → 5 ← numerator
total number of berries → 6 ← denominator

Five-sixths, or $\frac{5}{6}$, of the group are blueberries.

One-sixth and five-sixths make up the whole group.

More Examples

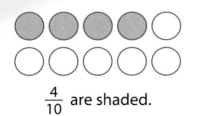

$\frac{4}{10}$ are shaded.

$\frac{5}{8}$ are shaded.

Try It
Write a fraction for the part of each group that is shaded.

1.  2. 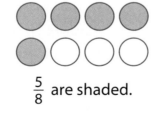 3.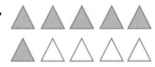

4. **Write About It** **Explain** how you write a fraction to describe the shaded parts of a group.

566

Write a fraction for the part of each group that is shaded.

5.

6.

7. △ △ △ △ △

Copy and shade the part of each group to show the fraction.

8. $\frac{3}{4}$ ▢ ▢ ▢ ▢

9. $\frac{1}{3}$ ○ ○ ○

10. $\frac{5}{6}$ △ △ △ △ △ △

$\widehat{x}$ **Algebra** Write a fraction for the part of the group that is shaded. What could the next shape be? Explain.

11. ○ ▢ ● ▦ ○ ▢ ●

Solve. Use the picture for problems 12–13.

12. **Art** In this painting, 3 of the pieces of fruit in the top bowl near the pitcher are apples and 2 are oranges. What fraction tells the part of this group that is apples?

Still Life with Apples and Oranges by Paul Cézanne

★ 13. **Language Arts** Write a few sentences involving fractions to describe the painting.

14. Mara's ticket to the museum costs $6.95 and Milo's ticket costs $2.35 more than Mara's ticket. How much did they spend in all?

✓ Spiral Review and Test Prep

15. What is the area of this figure? (p. 534)

   A. 24 sq units   **C.** 12 sq units

   B. 16 sq units   **D.** 7 sq units

16. Kyle has 15 small boxes of cereal. If he divides them evenly among his 5 friends, how many boxes will each friend get? (p. 296)

   F. 2 boxes   **H.** 11 boxes

   G. 3 boxes   **I.** 21 boxes

17. $432 \div 6$ (p. 324)

18. 6×754 (p. 390)

19. $2 \times \$12.14$ (p. 390)

25.6 Explore Finding Parts of a Group

Hands On Activity

You can use 2-color counters to explore finding parts of a group.

Find: $\frac{1}{4}$ **of 12**

You Will Need
- 2-color counters

Use Models

STEP 1

Use 12 counters.

STEP 2

Make 4 equal groups.

STEP 3

Count the number of counters in one group.

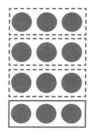

Explain Your Thinking

1. Why do you use 12 counters?

2. Why do you make 4 equal groups?

3. Why do you find the number of counters in 1 group?

4. How many counters are in one group?

5. What is $\frac{1}{4}$ of 12?

568

Find: $\frac{2}{3}$ of 15

Let's see how to connect models to paper and pencil.

Use the counters tool in **Math Tool Chest** to find parts of a group.

Technology Link

Make Connections

	Models	Paper and Pencil
STEP 1 Use 15 counters.		$\frac{2}{3}$ of 15
STEP 2 Make 3 equal groups.		Divide 15 by the denominator to find how many are in each group. $\frac{2}{3}$ of 15 $15 \div 3 = 5$ There are 5 in each group.
STEP 3 Count the number of counters in 2 groups.		Multiply the numerator by 5 to find how many in 2 groups. $\frac{2}{3}$ of 15 $2 \times 5 = 10$ There are 10 in 2 groups.

$\frac{2}{3}$ of 15 = 10

Your Turn

Use counters to solve.

6. $\frac{1}{2}$ of 8

7. $\frac{1}{3}$ of 9

8. $\frac{3}{4}$ of 8

9. **Write About It** **Explain** how you decide how many equal groups to make with counters to find the fraction of a number.

25.7 Problem Solving: Skill
Check for Reasonableness

Read

Lani baked 36 cookies. She put chocolate chips in $\frac{1}{4}$ of the cookies.

Her younger sister, Karen, says 18 of the cookies have chocolate chips. Is 18 a reasonable number?

- **What do you know?**
  Chocolate chips are in $\frac{1}{4}$ of the 36 cookies. Karen says 18 of the cookies have chocolate chips

- **What do you need to find?**
  How many cookies have chocolate chips

Plan

An answer is reasonable if it makes sense.

You need to find $\frac{1}{4}$ of 36. Use what you know about fractions.

Solve

$\frac{1}{4}$ of 36

$36 \div 4 = 9$
4 groups of $9 = 36$.

Chocolate chips are in 1 of the groups.

1 group of 9 cookies $= 9$ cookies

Check the reasonableness of your answer.
$18 > 9$

18 is not a reasonable number.

Look Back

How could you check your answer?

1. **Write About It** How does checking for reasonableness help solve problems?

Practice

Solve. Check for reasonableness.

2. Al bought a loaf of banana bread. He cut the banana bread into 8 slices. Al's friends ate $\frac{3}{4}$ of the bread. Is it reasonable to say that his friends ate 4 slices?

3. Wayne made 12 slices of carrot cake. He put coconut frosting on $\frac{2}{3}$ of the carrot cake slices. Is it reasonable to say that 8 slices had coconut frosting?

4. Erin made 12 cupcakes. Her brother ate $\frac{1}{6}$ of the cupcakes. Are there 5 cupcakes left?

5. Ms. Baker brought 20 items for the bake sale. Of those items $\frac{2}{5}$ were pies. Are there 12 pies?

Mixed Strategy Review

6. One side of an equilateral triangle is 6 centimeters. What is its perimeter?

Use data from the graph for problems 7–10.

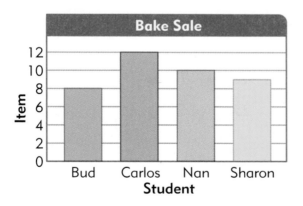

Choose a Strategy

- Logical Reasoning
- Draw a Picture or Diagram
- Make a Graph
- Act It Out
- Make a Table or List
- Find a Pattern
- Guess and Check
- Write an Equation
- Work Backward
- Solve a Simpler Problem

7. Mr. Burns bought $\frac{1}{3}$ of Carlos' bags of munchie mix. How many bags of munchie mix did he buy?

8. A customer bought $\frac{3}{5}$ of Nan's granola squares. How many squares did the person buy?

9. How many items were brought in for the bake sale?

10. **Write a problem** using the data from the graph. Solve it. Ask others to solve it.

Chapter 25

Extra Practice

Set A Write a fraction for the part that is shaded. (pp. 554–556)

1.
2.
3.
4.

Set B Write one equivalent fraction for each. (pp. 558–559)

5. $\frac{2}{3}$
6. $\frac{1}{8}$
7. $\frac{2}{5}$
8. $\frac{1}{9}$
9. $\frac{3}{5}$

Write each fraction in simplest form. (pp. 560–561)

10. $\frac{4}{10}$
11. $\frac{3}{9}$
12. $\frac{8}{20}$
13. $\frac{2}{14}$
14. $\frac{5}{25}$

Set C Compare. Write $>$, $<$, or $=$. Use models. (pp. 562–564)

15. $\frac{1}{3} \bullet \frac{1}{2}$
16. $\frac{3}{5} \bullet \frac{1}{5}$
17. $\frac{4}{5} \bullet \frac{1}{3}$
18. $\frac{1}{2} \bullet \frac{4}{8}$
19. $\frac{2}{3} \bullet \frac{3}{5}$

Set D Write a fraction for the part of each group that is shaded. (pp. 566–567)

20.
21.
22.

Set E Find the fraction of a number. (pp. 568–569)

23. $\frac{1}{8}$ of 16
24. $\frac{1}{3}$ of 9
25. $\frac{3}{8}$ of 8
26. $\frac{1}{2}$ of 18

Set F Solve. (pp. 570–571)

27. Katherine has a set of twin brothers and Jace has 4 sisters. One half of their brothers and sisters are students in third grade. Is it reasonable to say that 3 of them are in third grade?

28. Wanda made a dozen muffins. Her family ate $\frac{1}{3}$ of the muffins. Did her family eat 8 muffins?

LOG ON www.mmhmath.com
For more practice and Chapter Self-Check Test

Write a fraction for the shaded part.

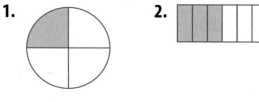

1.
2.
3.
4.

Find an equivalent fraction. Use models.

5. $\frac{1}{2}$
6. $\frac{1}{4}$
7. $\frac{2}{3}$
8. $\frac{1}{3}$
9. $\frac{2}{5}$

Compare. Write $>$, $<$, or $=$. Use models.

10. $\frac{3}{4}$ ⬤ $\frac{3}{10}$
11. $\frac{1}{3}$ ⬤ $\frac{1}{2}$
12. $\frac{2}{3}$ ⬤ $\frac{6}{12}$
13. $\frac{4}{10}$ ⬤ $\frac{2}{5}$

Find each fraction of a number.

14. $\frac{1}{8}$ of 8
15. $\frac{2}{3}$ of 9
16. $\frac{1}{2}$ of 10
17. $\frac{3}{4}$ of 12

Solve.

18. Morgan and Wes eat a box of raisins. Morgan eats $\frac{1}{2}$ of the raisins. Wes eats $\frac{1}{3}$ of the raisins. Did Morgan eat more raisins than Wes? Explain.

19. There are 12 students in line for lunch. One fourth of them choose a salad. Did 5 students choose salad?

20. **Write About It** **Explain** how to find $\frac{1}{4}$ of 20.

Do I Need Help?

Exercises	Review Concepts	Use Extra Practice Set
1–4	pp. 554–556, 566–567	Sets A and D
5–9	pp. 558–561	Set B
10–13	pp. 562–564	Set C
14–17, 20	pp. 568–569	Set E
18–19	pp. 570–571	Set F

Foldables Use your Foldables to help you review.

What Do I Need to Know?

You have 6 oranges and 3 pears. What part of the group of fruit is oranges? Write the amount as a fraction.

Fractions and Probability

What Will I Learn?

In this chapter you will learn to

- read and write mixed numbers
- add and subtract fractions
- determine the probability
- use skills and strategies to solve problems

How Do I Read Math?

When you read a mathematics book, sometimes you read words and symbols, and sometimes you read only symbols.

All of these represent one whole plus one half:

- ◐ ◑
- $1\frac{1}{2}$

- **One and one half**

VOCABULARY

- mixed numbers
- probability
- equally likely
- possible outcomes

Foldables

Use your Foldables to help you with chapter concepts.

1. Stack four sheets of paper about an inch apart.
2. Roll up the bottom edges of the paper. Stop them 1 inch from the top edges.
3. Crease the paper to hold the tabs in place.
4. Staple along the fold.
5. Label as shown. Record what you learn.

> Fractions and Probability
>
> $\frac{8}{12} = \frac{2}{3}$ ← simplest form
>
> Add Fractions
>
> Subtract Fractions
>
> Probability

26.1

Mixed Numbers

Learn

Ron and Kevin use $\frac{1}{2}$ glass of milk for cake batter. They also use 1 glass of milk for pudding. How much milk did they use all together?

Show the amount of milk as a mixed number.

A **mixed number** is a number that has a whole number part and a fraction part.

Use Pictures

1 whole glass and $\frac{1}{2}$ glass

Write: $1\frac{1}{2}$

Read: one and one half

$1\frac{1}{2}$ means 1 whole plus $\frac{1}{2}$.

More Examples

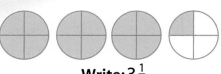

Write: $2\frac{2}{3}$
Read: two and two thirds

Write: $3\frac{1}{4}$
Read: three and one fourth

Try It Write as a mixed number.

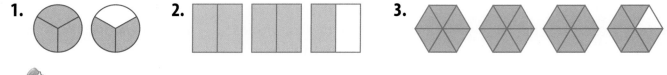

1. 2. 3.

4. **Write About It** **Explain** why you think $1\frac{1}{2}$ is called a mixed number.

576

Practice and Problem Solving

Write as a mixed number.

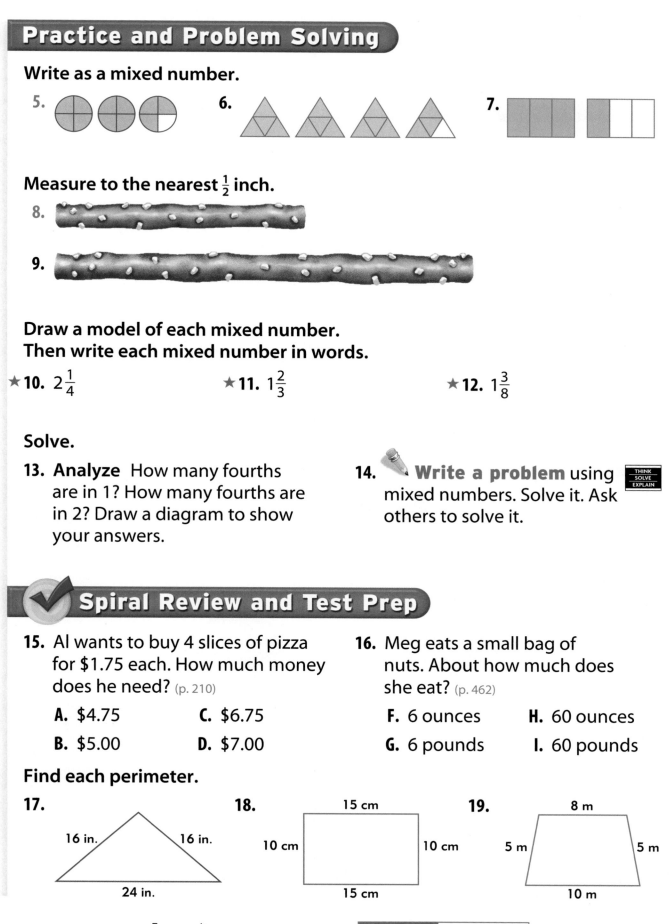

5.

6.

7.

Measure to the nearest $\frac{1}{2}$ inch.

8.

9.

Draw a model of each mixed number.
Then write each mixed number in words.

★ **10.** $2\frac{1}{4}$

★ **11.** $1\frac{2}{3}$

★ **12.** $1\frac{3}{8}$

Solve.

13. Analyze How many fourths are in 1? How many fourths are in 2? Draw a diagram to show your answers.

14. ✎ **Write a problem** using mixed numbers. Solve it. Ask others to solve it.

THINK
SOLVE
EXPLAIN

Spiral Review and Test Prep

15. Al wants to buy 4 slices of pizza for $1.75 each. How much money does he need? (p. 210)

   A. $4.75   **C.** $6.75

   B. $5.00   **D.** $7.00

16. Meg eats a small bag of nuts. About how much does she eat? (p. 462)

   F. 6 ounces   **H.** 60 ounces

   G. 6 pounds   **I.** 60 pounds

Find each perimeter.

17.
16 in.   16 in.
24 in.

18.
15 cm
10 cm   10 cm
15 cm

19.
8 m
5 m   5 m
10 m

26.2 Explore Adding Fractions

Hands On Activity

You can use fraction models to explore adding fractions.

Find: $\frac{2}{8} + \frac{3}{8}$

Use Models

STEP 1

Use two $\frac{1}{8}$ fraction pieces to show $\frac{2}{8}$.

STEP 2

Add three $\frac{1}{8}$ fraction pieces to show $\frac{3}{8}$.

STEP 3

Combine the pieces. Count the total number of $\frac{1}{8}$ fraction pieces.

Explain Your Thinking

1. How do you model the first addend?

2. How do you model the second addend?

3. When you combine the pieces to show addition, how many $\frac{1}{8}$ fraction pieces are there?

4. What is the sum of $\frac{2}{8} + \frac{3}{8}$?

Find: $\frac{1}{5} + \frac{3}{5}$

Let's see how to connect models to paper and pencil.

Make Connections

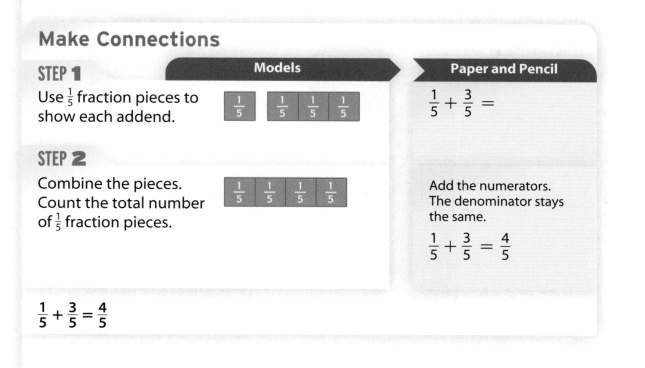

STEP 1
Use $\frac{1}{5}$ fraction pieces to show each addend.

| $\frac{1}{5}$ | $\frac{1}{5}$ | $\frac{1}{5}$ | $\frac{1}{5}$ |

Paper and Pencil

$\frac{1}{5} + \frac{3}{5} =$

STEP 2
Combine the pieces. Count the total number of $\frac{1}{5}$ fraction pieces.

| $\frac{1}{5}$ | $\frac{1}{5}$ | $\frac{1}{5}$ | $\frac{1}{5}$ |

Add the numerators. The denominator stays the same.

$\frac{1}{5} + \frac{3}{5} = \frac{4}{5}$

$\frac{1}{5} + \frac{3}{5} = \frac{4}{5}$

Your Turn

Add.

5. $\frac{1}{4}$ $\frac{1}{4}$ $\frac{1}{4}$

$\frac{1}{4} \quad + \quad \frac{2}{4}$

6. $\frac{1}{5}$ $\frac{1}{5}$ $\frac{1}{5}$

$\frac{1}{5} \quad + \quad \frac{2}{5}$

7. $\frac{1}{10}$ $\frac{1}{10}$ $\frac{1}{10}$ $\frac{1}{10}$ $\frac{1}{10}$ $\frac{1}{10}$ $\frac{1}{10}$

$\frac{2}{10} \quad + \quad \frac{5}{10}$

8. $\frac{1}{6}$ $\frac{1}{6}$ $\frac{1}{6}$ $\frac{1}{6}$ $\frac{1}{6}$

$\frac{3}{6} \quad + \quad \frac{2}{6}$

9. $\frac{1}{8}$ $\frac{1}{8}$ $\frac{1}{8}$ $\frac{1}{8}$ $\frac{1}{8}$ $\frac{1}{8}$ $\frac{1}{8}$

$\frac{4}{8} \quad + \quad \frac{3}{8}$

10. $\frac{1}{12}$ $\frac{1}{12}$ $\frac{1}{12}$ $\frac{1}{12}$ $\frac{1}{12}$

$\frac{2}{12} + \frac{3}{12}$

11.  **Write About It** **Describe** how you could use fraction models to find a sum and then express it in simplest form.

26.3 Explore Subtracting Fractions

Hands On Activity

You can use fraction models to subtract fractions.

Find: $\frac{7}{12} - \frac{2}{12}$

You Will Need
- fraction models

Use Models

STEP 1

Use seven $\frac{1}{12}$ fraction pieces to show $\frac{7}{12}$.

STEP 2

Take away two $\frac{1}{12}$ fraction pieces.

| 1/12 | 1/12 | 1/12 | 1/12 | 1/12 | 1/12 | 1/12 |

STEP 3

Count the number of remaining $\frac{1}{12}$ fraction pieces to find the difference.

Explain Your Thinking

1. How do you show the number you are subtracting from?

2. How do you show the number you are subtracting?

3. How many fraction pieces are left?

4. What is the difference of $\frac{7}{12}$ and $\frac{2}{12}$?

Find: $\frac{7}{10} - \frac{4}{10}$

Let's see how to connect models to paper and pencil.

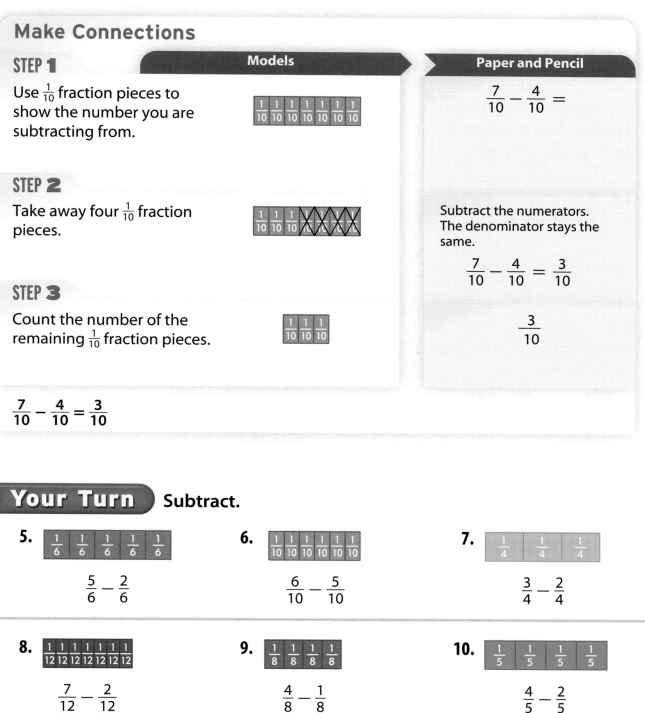

Make Connections

	Models	Paper and Pencil
STEP 1 Use $\frac{1}{10}$ fraction pieces to show the number you are subtracting from.	$\boxed{\frac{1}{10}\ \frac{1}{10}\ \frac{1}{10}\ \frac{1}{10}\ \frac{1}{10}\ \frac{1}{10}\ \frac{1}{10}}$	$\frac{7}{10} - \frac{4}{10} =$
STEP 2 Take away four $\frac{1}{10}$ fraction pieces.	$\boxed{\frac{1}{10}\ \frac{1}{10}\ \frac{1}{10}\ \cancel{\frac{1}{10}}\ \cancel{\frac{1}{10}}\ \cancel{\frac{1}{10}}\ \cancel{\frac{1}{10}}}$	Subtract the numerators. The denominator stays the same. $\frac{7}{10} - \frac{4}{10} = \frac{3}{10}$
STEP 3 Count the number of the remaining $\frac{1}{10}$ fraction pieces.	$\boxed{\frac{1}{10}\ \frac{1}{10}\ \frac{1}{10}}$	$\frac{3}{10}$

$\frac{7}{10} - \frac{4}{10} = \frac{3}{10}$

Your Turn Subtract.

5. $\boxed{\frac{1}{6}\ \frac{1}{6}\ \frac{1}{6}\ \frac{1}{6}\ \frac{1}{6}}$

$\frac{5}{6} - \frac{2}{6}$

6. $\boxed{\frac{1}{10}\ \frac{1}{10}\ \frac{1}{10}\ \frac{1}{10}\ \frac{1}{10}\ \frac{1}{10}}$

$\frac{6}{10} - \frac{5}{10}$

7. $\boxed{\frac{1}{4}\ \frac{1}{4}\ \frac{1}{4}}$

$\frac{3}{4} - \frac{2}{4}$

8. $\boxed{\frac{1}{12}\ \frac{1}{12}\ \frac{1}{12}\ \frac{1}{12}\ \frac{1}{12}\ \frac{1}{12}\ \frac{1}{12}}$

$\frac{7}{12} - \frac{2}{12}$

9. $\boxed{\frac{1}{8}\ \frac{1}{8}\ \frac{1}{8}\ \frac{1}{8}}$

$\frac{4}{8} - \frac{1}{8}$

10. $\boxed{\frac{1}{5}\ \frac{1}{5}\ \frac{1}{5}\ \frac{1}{5}}$

$\frac{4}{5} - \frac{2}{5}$

11.  **Write About It** **Explain** why the denominator does not change when you find the difference for $\frac{3}{5} - \frac{1}{5}$.

26.4 Add and Subtract Fractions

Learn

The Bayview Elementary School is publishing a cookbook. What part of the 8 chapters has recipes for breakfast and dinner?

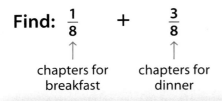

Find: $\frac{1}{8}$ + $\frac{3}{8}$

    ↑   ↑

chapters for   chapters for
breakfast   dinner

All You Need
Cookbook
1 Quick Breakfasts
2 Quick Lunches
3 Hot Lunches
4 Cold Lunches
5 Quick Dinners
6 Hot Dinners
7 Cold Dinners
8 Easy Desserts

Add Fractions

STEP 1
Add the numerators and use the same denominator.

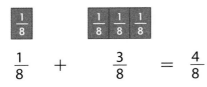

$\frac{1}{8}$ + $\frac{3}{8}$ = $\frac{4}{8}$

STEP 2
Write the sum in simplest form.

$\frac{4}{8} = \frac{1}{2}$

There are breakfast and dinner recipes in $\frac{4}{8}$ or $\frac{1}{2}$ of the chapters.

Find: $\frac{4}{10} + \frac{6}{10}$

Another Example

STEP 1

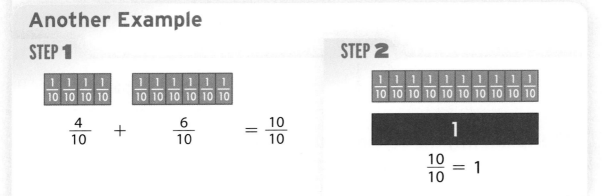

$\frac{4}{10}$ + $\frac{6}{10}$ = $\frac{10}{10}$

STEP 2

$\frac{10}{10} = 1$

Stacy finds a recipe for enchiladas in Chapter 3 of the cookbook. The recipe for enchiladas calls for $\frac{1}{4}$ cup of grated cheese. She has $\frac{3}{4}$ cup of grated cheese. How much cheese will she have left after making the enchiladas?

Find: $\frac{3}{4}$ — $\frac{1}{4}$

↑ amount of cheese Stacy has

↑ amount of cheese the recipe calls for

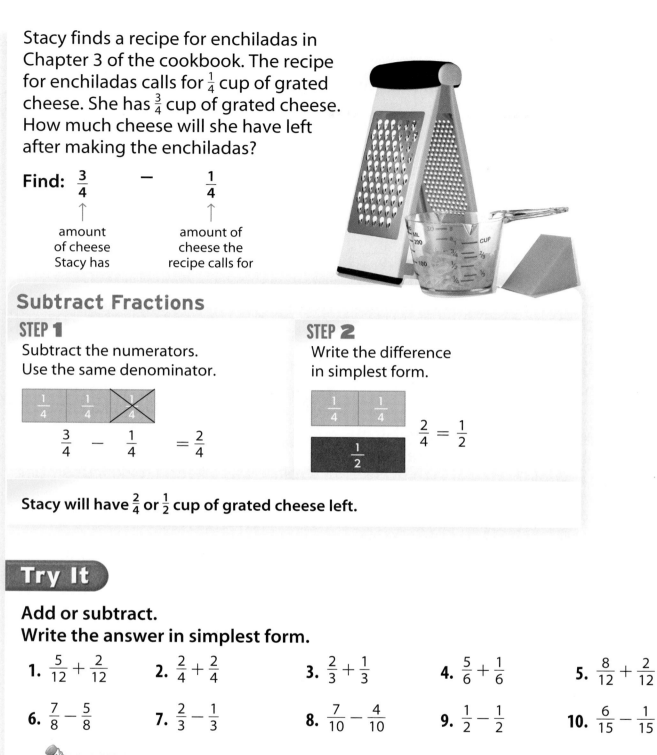

Subtract Fractions

STEP 1
Subtract the numerators. Use the same denominator.

$$\frac{3}{4} - \frac{1}{4} = \frac{2}{4}$$

STEP 2
Write the difference in simplest form.

$$\frac{2}{4} = \frac{1}{2}$$

Stacy will have $\frac{2}{4}$ or $\frac{1}{2}$ cup of grated cheese left.

Try It

Add or subtract.
Write the answer in simplest form.

1. $\frac{5}{12} + \frac{2}{12}$
2. $\frac{2}{4} + \frac{2}{4}$
3. $\frac{2}{3} + \frac{1}{3}$
4. $\frac{5}{6} + \frac{1}{6}$
5. $\frac{8}{12} + \frac{2}{12}$

6. $\frac{7}{8} - \frac{5}{8}$
7. $\frac{2}{3} - \frac{1}{3}$
8. $\frac{7}{10} - \frac{4}{10}$
9. $\frac{1}{2} - \frac{1}{2}$
10. $\frac{6}{15} - \frac{1}{15}$

11. 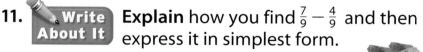 **Write About It** **Explain** how you find $\frac{7}{9} - \frac{4}{9}$ and then express it in simplest form.

Practice and Problem Solving

Add or subtract. Write the answer in simplest form.

12. $\frac{7}{10} + \frac{1}{10}$ 13. $\frac{1}{7} + \frac{4}{7}$ 14. $\frac{1}{4} + \frac{3}{4}$ 15. $\frac{3}{8} + \frac{4}{8}$ 16. $\frac{3}{6} + \frac{4}{6}$

17. $\frac{4}{10} - \frac{2}{10}$ 18. $\frac{4}{6} - \frac{1}{6}$ 19. $\frac{4}{5} - \frac{1}{5}$ 20. $\frac{8}{11} - \frac{5}{11}$ 21. $\frac{5}{8} - \frac{1}{8}$

$\textcircled{x}$ **Algebra** **Compare. Write** $>$, $<$, **or** $=$.

22. $\frac{6}{8} + \frac{2}{8} \, \bullet \, \frac{5}{8} + \frac{1}{8}$ 23. $\frac{8}{9} - \frac{2}{9} \, \bullet \, \frac{2}{3} - \frac{1}{3}$ 24. $\frac{3}{4} - \frac{2}{4} \, \bullet \, \frac{7}{8} - \frac{1}{8}$

Solve.

25. **Health** A chef uses $\frac{1}{8}$ of a pound of tuna for each serving of a dish. If the chef makes 3 servings, how much tuna does the chef use?

★26. **Generalize** How can you tell if the sum of 2 fractions is greater than 1 whole?

27. **Make It Right** Here is how Emily subtracted 2 fractions. Tell what mistake she made. Explain how to correct it.

$$\frac{8}{10} - \frac{5}{10} = \frac{13}{10} = 1\frac{3}{10}$$

THINK
SOLVE
EXPLAIN

Link to ★ SOCIAL STUDIES ★

Six hundred members of the Nikopaka Festa Committee made the largest sushi roll. It was a kappa maki (cucumber roll) that was 1,093 yards long in Yoshii, Japan, on October 12, 1997.

★28. **Measurement** How many feet was the kappa maki?

Spiral Review and Test Prep

29. Sally sold 320 cheese sticks. Each serving has 4 cheese sticks. How many servings were sold? (p. 412)

    A. 80 servings   **C.** 40 servings

    B. 60 servings   **D.** 20 servings

30. A large muffin pan has 4 rows of 6 muffin holders. How many muffins can the pan hold? (p. 210)

    F. 10 muffins   **H.** 24 muffins

    G. 14 muffins   **I.** 36 muffins

Find an equivalent fraction. (p. 558)

31. $\frac{4}{12}$ 32. $\frac{8}{10}$ 33. $\frac{6}{12}$ 34. $\frac{1}{3}$ 35. $\frac{1}{4}$

Writing for Math

You use $\frac{3}{12}$ of the lemons on Monday and $\frac{5}{12}$ of the lemons on Tuesday. How many lemons did you use all together? Write the sum in simplest form. Explain your thinking.

Marc's Response

✓ **THINK** Add to find the total fraction of lemons used. Find an equivalent fraction in simplest form.

✓ **SOLVE**

$\frac{1}{12}$	$\frac{1}{12}$	$\frac{1}{12}$	$\frac{1}{12}$	$\frac{1}{12}$	$\frac{1}{12}$	$\frac{1}{12}$	$\frac{1}{12}$

$$\frac{3}{12} + \frac{5}{12} = \frac{8}{12}$$

$\frac{1}{3}$	$\frac{1}{3}$

$$\frac{8}{12} = \frac{2}{3}$$

$\frac{2}{3}$ of the lemons are used.

Check: $\frac{5}{12} + \frac{3}{12} = \frac{8}{12}$

✓ **EXPLAIN** I used $\frac{3}{12}$ of the lemons on Monday and $\frac{5}{12}$ of the lemons on Tuesday. When I added the fractions, the sum was $\frac{8}{12}$. I found that $\frac{2}{3}$ was the equivalent fraction in simplest form by using fraction models.

I added the fractions in reverse order to check my addition.

Teacher's Response

← Marc explains how he will use what he knows to solve the problem.

← Marc shows his work.

← Marc uses appropriate math terms such as **added, fractions, sum, equivalent,** and **simplest form.** He explains and justifies his answer.

← Marc checks his answer for accuracy and reasonableness.

Solve. Show your work and tell why your answer makes sense. Use Marc's work as a guide.

1. Jane eats $\frac{5}{8}$ of a small pizza at dinner and $\frac{3}{8}$ of it the next day for lunch. How much of the pizza does Jane eat in all?

2. Daniel has $\frac{3}{4}$ cup of trail mix. He eats $\frac{1}{4}$ cup for a snack. How much trail mix is left? Write your answer in simplest form.

26.5 Probability

Learn

There are 6 yellow raisins and 1 brown raisin left in the box. Latisha is about to pick one. What is the likelihood that she will pick a raisin from the box? A yellow raisin? A brown raisin? A green raisin?

Find the likelihood, or probability, of an outcome.

Probability is the chance that an event will occur.

VOCABULARY
probability
certain
likely
unlikely
impossible

Use a Picture

It is **certain** that Latisha will pick a raisin. There are only raisins in the box.

It is **likely** that she will pick a yellow raisin. Six out of 7 raisins are yellow.

It is **unlikely** that she will pick a brown raisin. Only 1 out of 7 raisins is brown.

It is **impossible** that she will pick a green raisin. None of the raisins are green.

Try It
Write *certain, likely, unlikely,* or *impossible* to describe the probability of picking each item.

1. piece of fruit

2. banana

3. green apple

4. red apple

5. **Write About It** **Explain** how you decide if picking an item of a certain color is likely or unlikely.

Practice and Problem Solving

PEPPERS

Write *certain, likely, unlikely,* or *impossible* to describe the probability of picking a:

6. green pepper   7. pepper   8. raisin   9. red pepper

Draw a spinner for each probability.

★10. Likely but not certain to land on a 4

★11. Unlikely but not impossible to land on an even number

Solve. Use data from the spinner for problems 12–15.

THINK SOLVE EXPLAIN

12. Whenever you buy a child's lunch at Burger World, you get to spin the spinner for a prize. Is it likely that you will win a teddy bear when you spin? Explain.

13. What fraction of the spinner has the teddy bear on it?

JOKES

14. Sofia hopes she will get a poster for a prize. What word could describe the probability that she will get what she wants?

15. **Compare** Which is more likely, getting a basketball or getting a joke book? Explain. **THINK SOLVE EXPLAIN**

Spiral Review and Test Prep

16. Which polygon has 6 sides? (p. 512)

   A. pentagon
   B. hexagon
   C. octagon
   D. rectangle

17. A floor has 5 rows and 7 columns of square tiles. How many square tiles make up the area of the floor? (p. 534)

   F. 12 square tiles
   G. 24 square tiles
   H. 30 square tiles
   I. 35 square tiles

18. $6 \times 1{,}258$ (p. 234)

19. $3{,}408 - 476$ (p. 120)

20. $468 + 329$ (p. 60)

26.6 Explore Finding Outcomes

Hands On Activity

You can use a 2-color counter to explore the results of probability experiments.

VOCABULARY
equally likely
possible outcomes

Find out what the results would be if you flipped a counter 20 times.

Use Models

It is **equally likely** to get red or yellow. You can show the probability as a fraction.

$\dfrac{1}{2}$ ← number of chances it will be red
← total number of possible outcomes

STEP 1

Copy the table. Predict the possible outcomes if you toss the counter 20 times. **Possible outcomes** are any of the results that could occur in an experiment. Record in the table.

> There are 2 possible outcomes: landing on red or landing on yellow.

Outcomes		
Counters	Prediction	Tallies

STEP 2

Toss 1 counter 20 times. Record the outcome each time.

STEP 3

Write the total results for each outcome.

Explain Your Thinking

1. How many times did the counter land showing red?

2. How many times did the counter land showing yellow?

3. How does your prediction compare to the actual result?

4. **What If** You repeated the experiment. Would you change your prediction?

A number cube with the numbers 1–6 was tossed 25 times.

Here are 2 ways you can record the outcomes.

Make Connections

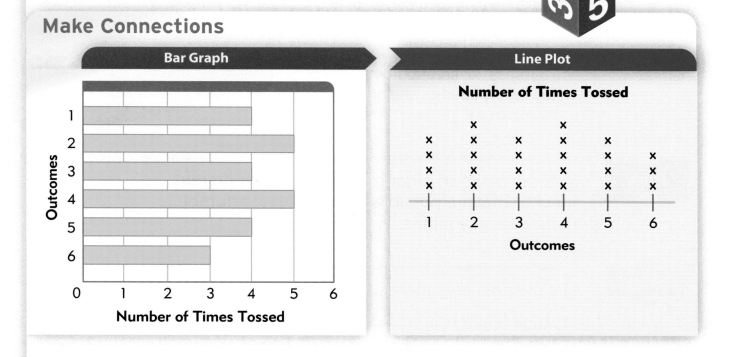

Your Turn

**List the possible outcomes for each.
Then do the experiment and record the
outcomes in a line plot and a bar graph.**

5. Toss a coin 10 times.

6. Toss a 1–6 number cube 20 times.

7. **Write About It** **Explain** There are 2 white cubes, 6 red cubes, and 1 blue cube in a bag. Which color cube are you most likely to pull from the bag?

26.7

Problem Solving: Strategy
Make an Organized List

Read

Donna wants to buy lunch. She has a choice of a sandwich, a fruit, and a drink. How many different lunches does she have to choose from? What are the possible combinations?

- **What do you know?**
  Her choices are tuna or chicken, apple or banana, milk or chocolate milk.

- **What do you need to find?**
  How many lunches she has to choose from

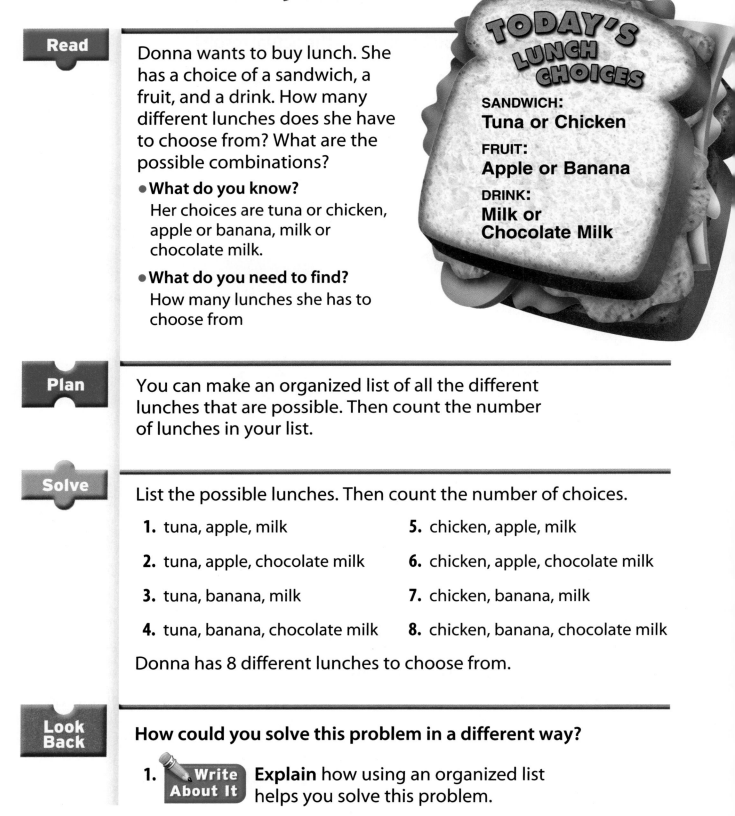

TODAY'S LUNCH CHOICES

SANDWICH: Tuna or Chicken

FRUIT: Apple or Banana

DRINK: Milk or Chocolate Milk

Plan

You can make an organized list of all the different lunches that are possible. Then count the number of lunches in your list.

Solve

List the possible lunches. Then count the number of choices.

1. tuna, apple, milk
2. tuna, apple, chocolate milk
3. tuna, banana, milk
4. tuna, banana, chocolate milk

5. chicken, apple, milk
6. chicken, apple, chocolate milk
7. chicken, banana, milk
8. chicken, banana, chocolate milk

Donna has 8 different lunches to choose from.

Look Back

How could you solve this problem in a different way?

1. **Write About It** **Explain** how using an organized list helps you solve this problem.

Practice

Use an organized list to solve.
Use the data from the sign for problems 2–5.

2. You have a choice of a main dish and a drink. How many different combinations are possible?

3. List 3 possible combinations of breakfast specials.

4. **What If** For 50¢ more you could add a side dish. How many possible combinations do you have now?

BREAKFAST SPECIALS

ONLY **$2.50**

Includes
Main Dish and Drink

MAIN DISH:
Eggs, Pancakes or Waffles

SIDE DISH:
Potatoes, Sausage or Bacon

DRINK:
Milk or Juice

Mixed Strategy Review

5. How much would 3 breakfast specials cost?

6. There are 36 eggs in several cartons on a store shelf. Some cartons hold 6 eggs and others hold 8. How many of each carton are there?

7. ✎ **Write a problem** that you can solve by using an organized list. Solve it. Ask others to solve it.

8. Mr. Ling is getting 5 bags ready so his students can conduct a probability experiment. He wants to put 6 of 1 fruit card and 2 of another fruit card in each bag. How many fruit cards does he need?

Choose a Strategy
- Logical Reasoning
- Draw a Picture or Diagram
- Make a Graph
- Act It Out
- Make a Table or List
- Find a Pattern
- Guess and Check
- Write an Equation
- Work Backward
- Solve a Simpler Problem

★9. Rachel uses a spinner to conduct an experiment. The spinner lands on red 75 times, white 15 times, and black 15 times. Draw a picture to show what the spinner probably looks like.

Problem Solving

Set A Write as a mixed number (pp. 576–577)

1.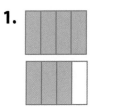

2.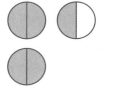

3.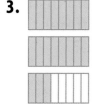

4.

Set B Add or subtract. Write each answer in simplest form. (pp. 578–584)

5. $\frac{1}{5} + \frac{3}{5}$ **6.** $\frac{5}{12} + \frac{5}{12}$ **7.** $\frac{3}{4} + \frac{1}{4}$ **8.** $\frac{3}{8} + \frac{7}{8}$

9. $\frac{11}{12} - \frac{6}{12}$ **10.** $\frac{5}{6} - \frac{1}{6}$ **11.** $\frac{8}{9} - \frac{2}{9}$ **12.** $\frac{4}{5} - \frac{2}{5}$

Set C Write *likely*, *unlikely*, *certain*, or *impossible* to describe the probability of picking. (pp. 586–587)

13. a number 7   **14.** an odd number

15. a number 5   **16.** a number 3

17. an even number   **18.** a number 9

Set D List the possible outcomes. (pp. 588–589)

19. Spinning a spinner with odd numbers from 1 through 7

20. Writing the letters of your first name on slips of paper and picking a letter from a bag

Set E Make an organized list to solve. (pp. 590–591)

21. For a snack, Robert can choose 1 fruit and 1 drink. The fruit choices are peach, orange, or pear. The drink choices are milk, juice, or water. How many possible snack combinations does he have?

22. Phil wants to buy a new pair of skates. He can buy roller skates or in-line skates. Both kinds of skates come in silver and black. How many choices does he have? What are the choices?

LOG ON www.mmhmath.com
For more practice and Chapter Self-Check Test

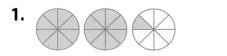

Write as a mixed number.

1.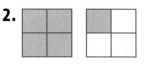

2.

Add or subtract. Write each answer in simplest form.

3. $\frac{2}{8} + \frac{4}{8}$

4. $\frac{7}{12} + \frac{5}{12}$

5. $\frac{7}{11} - \frac{4}{11}$

Use the words *likely, unlikely, certain,* **or** *impossible* **to describe the probability.**

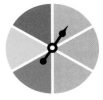

6. a color
7. blue

8. List the possible outcomes.

Solve.

9. To make a sandwich, Sandy can choose from white or whole wheat bread, chicken or cheese, with mustard or without. How many different choices does she have? What are they?

10. **Write About It** **Explain** how to conduct an experiment to predict the number of red counters in a bag that has 30 counters in it.

Do I Need Help?

Exercises	Review Concepts	Use Extra Practice Set
1–2	pp. 576–577	Set A
3–5	pp. 578–584	Set B
6–7	pp. 586–587	Set C
8, 10	pp. 588–589	Set D
9	pp. 590–591	Set E

Foldables **Use your Foldables to help you review.**

Assessment

Decision Making

You are planning a party for 6 people. You can make your own food platter or order one that is already prepared.

You Decide!

Which platter will you use for your party?

OPTION 1
Prepared Platter

$\frac{3}{4}$ pound American Cheese
$\frac{3}{4}$ pound Swiss Cheese
1 pound Ham
$\frac{7}{8}$ pound Turkey
1 pound pickles
6 cups of pasta salad
12 sandwich rolls
2-quart bowl of lettuce and tomato salad

Price: $40.00

OPTION 2
Self-Made Platter

American Cheese	$4.00 per pound
Swiss Cheese	$4.00 per pound
Ham	$8.00 per pound
Turkey	$8.00 per pound
1 dozen rolls	$2.39
Head of lettuce	$1.29
1 pound of tomatoes	$2.00
Pickles	$4.00 per jar

Ingredients for about 6 cups of pasta salad

1 pound pasta	$2.00 per pound
$\frac{1}{2}$ cup Italian dressing	$2.75 per jar

Read for Understanding

1. How many pounds of meat do you get in the prepared platter?

2. How many pounds of cheese do you get in the prepared platter?

3. How is the prepared platter the same as a self-made platter? How are they different?

4. How many sandwiches can each guest have if you choose the prepared platter?

5. Which is there more of on the prepared platter, ham or turkey?

6. How much pasta salad will you have if you make $\frac{1}{2}$ as much as is on the prepared platter?

7. **What If** You buy a pound of American cheese, a pound of Swiss cheese, a pound of ham, and a pound of turkey. How much money will you spend?

8. **What If** You buy $2\frac{1}{2}$ pounds of turkey, 1 pound of pasta, 1 pound of tomatoes, and a jar of pickles. How much will you spend?

Make Decisions

9. How much will rolls cost if you make your own platter and have the same number as the prepared platter?

10. About how much will the same amount of meats and cheeses that are in the prepared platter cost if you make your own platter?

11. How much will it cost if you make 6 cups of your own pasta salad?

12. You decide to buy $\frac{3}{4}$ of the number of rolls that come with the prepared platter. Will that be enough for your party? Explain.

13. Make a list of what you need to know to decide which platter is better for your party.

Your Decision!

THINK
SOLVE
EXPLAIN

Which platter did you choose for your party? Why?

Vocabulary

Complete. Use words from the list.

1. The number below the bar in a fraction is called the _____.

2. You can tell that $\frac{2}{3}$ and $\frac{6}{9}$ are the same amount because they are _____.

3. A number made up of a whole number and a fraction is called a(n) _____.

4. If you are sure an event will occur, you can say the _____ for the event is certain.

5. The _____ for tossing a coin are heads and tails.

VOCABULARY
denominator
equivalent fractions
mixed number
numerator
possible outcomes
probability

Skills and Applications

Identify, read, and write fractions and mixed numbers. (pp. 554–556, 566–567, 576–577)

Write a fraction for the part that is shaded.

Solution

parts shaded → $\frac{5}{8}$ ← numerator
total parts → ← denominator

So $\frac{5}{8}$ of the rectangle is shaded.

Write a fraction for the part that is shaded.

6.

7. △ △ △ ▲ ▲

8.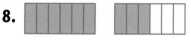

Compare and order fractions and find equivalent fractions. (pp. 558–564)

Compare. Write $>$, $<$, or $=$.

$\frac{4}{5}$ ● $\frac{1}{5}$

| $\frac{1}{5}$ | $\frac{1}{5}$ | $\frac{1}{5}$ | $\frac{1}{5}$ |

$\frac{1}{5}$

Solution

$\frac{4}{5} > \frac{1}{5}$

Compare. Write $>$, $<$, or $=$.

9. $\frac{3}{5}$ ● $\frac{4}{5}$

10. $\frac{1}{3}$ ● $\frac{1}{4}$

11. $\frac{6}{12}$ ● $\frac{1}{2}$

12. $\frac{3}{8}$ ● $\frac{7}{8}$

13. $\frac{3}{6}$ ● $\frac{3}{9}$

Foldables Use your Foldables to help you review.

Add and subtract fractions. (pp. 578–584)

Find the sum. $\frac{1}{6} + \frac{2}{6}$

Solution

Step 1
Add. $\frac{1}{6} + \frac{2}{6} = \frac{3}{6}$

Step 2
Simplify. $\frac{3}{6} = \frac{1}{2}$

Find the sum or difference in simplest form.

14. $\frac{1}{7} + \frac{4}{7}$ **15.** $\frac{3}{8} + \frac{3}{8}$

16. $\frac{5}{6} + \frac{4}{6}$ **17.** $\frac{9}{10} - \frac{6}{10}$

18. $\frac{5}{8} - \frac{3}{8}$ **19.** $\frac{7}{9} - \frac{1}{9}$

Find the number of outcomes and the probability. (pp. 586–589)

List the possible outcomes. Which is most likely?

Solution
Think:
Which numbers could the spinner possibly land on?

Possible outcomes: 1, 2, 3, 4, or 5
Most likely: 3

List the possible outcomes. Which is most likely to be picked?

20. Picking a card from six cards numbered 2 through 6 and two with number 3

21. Tossing a number cube numbered 1 through 6

22. Tossing a 2-color green and white counter

23. Picking a raisin from a mixed box of 20 yellow and 30 brown raisins

Use skills and strategies to solve problems. (pp. 590–591)

Jodi wants to buy a pair of shoes. Black and brown are her color choices. Leather and canvas are her material choices. How many different choices does she have?

Solution
Make a list of the choices:
  1. black, leather
  2. black, canvas
  3. brown, leather
  4. brown, canvas
She has 4 choices.

Solve.

24. Sean wants to buy an ice cream cone. They come in vanilla, chocolate, or strawberry. They also come with or without sprinkles. How many choices does he have?

25. Terry can choose a hamburger or cheeseburger, with fries, salad, or chips for lunch. How many choices does she have? What are the possible combinations?

Enrichment

Dependent Events

Dependent events are 2 events in which the result of the first affects the result of the second.

Without looking, you pick a cube from the bag at the right. You pick a red cube. The probability of picking a red cube is 1 out of 4, or $\frac{1}{4}$.

You do not put the red cube back in the bag. You pick another cube without looking. You pick yellow. The probability of picking yellow is 1 out of 3, or $\frac{1}{3}$.

You do not put the yellow cube back in the bag.

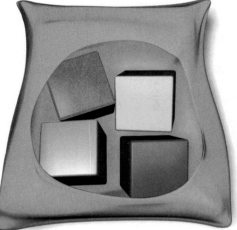

1. What is the probability that you will pick the purple cube?

Use the bag of cubes to the right for problems 2–3.

2. What is the probability that you will pick a purple cube?

3. **What If** You pick a purple cube and do not put it back. What is the probability that you will pick purple now?

4. Design your own experiment. Choose the cubes to put in the bag. Describe the probability for each color of cube that is picked and not put back in the bag.

5. **Generalize** How does the probability change when you do not put the cube back in the bag?

Performance Assessment

What Is the Probability?

Use connecting cubes in different colors to find the probability of picking a certain fruit from a bag.

- Yellow represents banana.
- Red represents apple.
- Orange represents peach.
- Green represents lime.

Use 10 cubes: 3 yellow, 2 red, 1 orange, and 4 green.

What is the probability for picking each type of fruit? Copy and complete the chart. Write a fraction to show the answer.

Write a fraction to show what part of the total number of cubes each color is.

Now put the cubes into a bag. Without looking, pick a cube. Record your results in the chart. Put the cube back in the bag. Repeat. Take 100 turns. Then fill in the probability column. Compare the 2 results.

Fruit	Color Cube	Probability	Number of Times Picked
Banana	Yellow	$\frac{30}{100}$	
Apple	Red		
Peach	Orange		
Lime	Green		

Tips For A Good Answer

- Show a completed chart.
- Show the correct probabilities and fractions.

You may want to save this work in your portfolio.

Assessment

TECHNOLOGY Link

Model Equivalent Fractions

Sergio and his friends are sharing a pizza. The pizza is cut into 6 slices, so each slice is $\frac{1}{6}$ of the pizza. If Sergio ate $\frac{1}{2}$ of the pizza, how many slices did he eat?

You can model the number of slices of pizza Sergio ate using fraction models 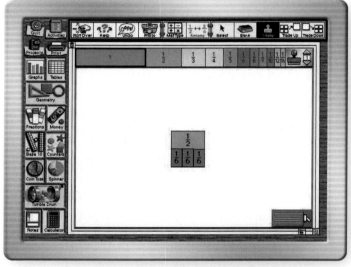 from the *Math Tool Chest* CD-Rom.

Math Tool Chest CD-ROM

- Stamp out a $\frac{1}{2}$ fraction piece.

- Stamp out three $\frac{1}{6}$ fraction pieces under the $\frac{1}{2}$ fraction piece.

- The model shows that $\frac{1}{2} = \frac{3}{6}$.

How many slices of pizza did Sergio eat?

Use the computer to model each fraction. Then find one equivalent fraction.

1. $\frac{1}{3}$ 2. $\frac{4}{8}$ 3. $\frac{3}{9}$ 4. $\frac{3}{12}$

5. **Analyze** How do fraction models help you find equivalent fractions?

Solve.

6. Maria made a carrot cake. She cut it into 12 pieces, so each piece is $\frac{1}{12}$ of the cake. She gave $\frac{1}{3}$ of the cake to her brother. How many pieces did she give to her brother?

7. Mrs. Arnez cut a ribbon into 8 smaller pieces. Each piece is $\frac{1}{8}$ of the long piece. She gave 2 of the smaller pieces to Sue. What fraction of the long piece of ribbon did she give to Sue?

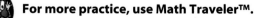

For more practice, use Math Traveler™.

Test-Taking Tips

Sometimes you need to use information from a chart to answer questions on a test.

Type of Pizza	Amount Eaten
Mushroom	$\frac{5}{8}$
Sausage	$\frac{3}{8}$
Onion	$\frac{1}{8}$
Pepperoni	$\frac{6}{8}$

Which kind of pizza was eaten the most?

A. Mushroom   C. Onion

B. Sausage   D. Pepperoni

Look at the column in the chart called "Amount Eaten." Each pizza was cut into 8 slices. The greatest fraction tells you which pizza was eaten the most.

The correct choice is D.

Check for Success

Before turning in a test, go back one last time to check.

☑ I understood and answered the questions asked.

☑ I checked my work for errors.

☑ My answers make sense.

Use information from the chart to choose the best answer.

1. Who read for the longest amount of time?

   A. Lou   C. Kirk

   B. Cora   D. Sam

2. Who read for the shortest amount of time?

   F. Lou   H. Sam

   G. Kim   I. Kirk

3. Who read exactly twice as long as Kim?

   A. Cora   C. Kirk

   B. Lou   D. Sam

Name	Time Spent Reading
Cora	$\frac{3}{4}$ hour
Kim	$\frac{1}{3}$ hour
Sam	$\frac{2}{3}$ hour
Lou	$\frac{1}{4}$ hour
Kirk	$\frac{1}{2}$ hour

Test Prep

PART 1 • Multiple Choice

Choose the best answer.

Use data from the graph for problems 1–3.

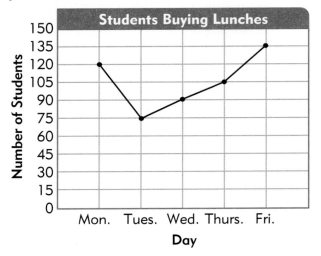

Students Buying Lunches

1. How many more students bought lunch on Friday than on Monday? (p. 106)

   A. 1 more   **C.** 25 more

   B. 15 more   **D.** 35 more

2. On which day did 15 more students buy lunch than on Wednesday? (p. 60)

   F. Monday   **H.** Thursday

   G. Tuesday   **I.** Friday

3. On which day did the fewest students buy lunches? (p. 174)

   A. Monday   **C.** Wednesday

   B. Tuesday   **D.** Thursday

4. Janine buys 12 muffins. She buys twice as many corn muffins as bran muffins. There are only 2 types of muffins. How many corn muffins does she buy? (p. 346)

   F. 2 corn muffins

   G. 4 corn muffins

   H. 8 corn muffins

   I. 10 corn muffins

5. Mel bought roast beef, ham, turkey, a loaf of white bread, and rye bread. How many different kinds of sandwiches can he make if he only puts 1 kind of meat on 1 kind of bread? (p. 590)

   A. 3 sandwiches

   B. 4 sandwiches

   C. 6 sandwiches

   D. 10 sandwiches

6. Lily leaves home and drives 10 blocks to the store. She walks north 2 blocks to the post office, then 3 more blocks north to the florist. How many blocks must she walk to get to her car? (p. 532)

   F. 8 blocks   **H.** 6 blocks

   G. 7 blocks   **I.** 5 blocks

PART 2 • Short Response/Grid In

Record your answers on the answer sheet provided by your teacher or on a sheet of paper.

7. Which number would make the sentence true? (p. 462)

4 pounds = ▮ ounces

[THINK SOLVE EXPLAIN] 8. Explain how you could use mental math to find the product of 6 x $11.99. (p. 390)

9. What is 4,595 rounded to the nearest hundred? (p. 324)

10. What symbol makes the sentence true? (p. 582)

$$\frac{1}{5} + \frac{2}{5} \quad \bullet \quad \frac{9}{10} - \frac{3}{10}$$

11. Apples are 3 for $1.08. How much does each apple cost? (p. 431)

12. A square playground has a side that is 158 feet long. What is the perimeter of the playground? (p. 532)

[THINK SOLVE EXPLAIN] 13. Tyrone is getting dressed for the playground. He knows that it is 85°F outside. What type of clothing should he wear? Explain. (p. 484)

14. How much of the pizza is left? Write a fraction. (p. 554)

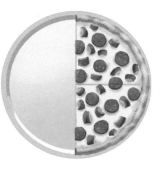

15. What number makes the equation true? (p. 336)

$$36 \div ▮ = 3$$

16. What is the perimeter? (p. 532)

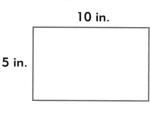

10 in.

5 in.

PART 3 • Extended Response

Record your answer on a sheet of paper. Show your work. **[THINK SOLVE EXPLAIN]**

17. In Store A a box of Fruity O's cereal costs $1.75. In Store B you can buy 3 boxes of Fruity O's for $5.10. How much less does 1 box of Fruity O's cost in the store that sells it for less? Explain your method.

Test Prep

What Do I Need to Know?

During 10 days at the beach, Allison swam in the ocean 9 days. What fraction represents the number of days she did not go swimming?

Relate Fractions and Decimals

What Will I Learn?

In this chapter you will learn to

- relate fractions to decimals
- understand tenths and hundredths
- understand decimals greater than one
- compare and order decimals
- use skills and strategies to solve problems

How Do I Read Math?

When you read a mathematics book, sometimes you read words and symbols, and sometimes you read only symbols.

Both of these represent three-tenths:

- ▢▢▢▢▢▢▢▢▢▢
- **0.3**

VOCABULARY

- decimal
- decimal point
- equivalent decimals
- hundredths
- tenths

Foldables

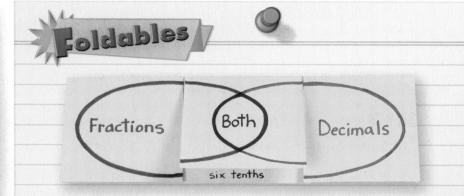

Use your Foldables to help you with chapter concepts.

1. Fold a sheet of paper like a hot dog.
2. Fold the folded paper into 3 parts.
3. Unfold and cut along the two fold lines on one side to form three tabs.
4. Draw overlapping ovals to form a Venn diagram. Label as shown. Record what you learn.

27.1 Explore Fractions and Decimals

Hands On Activity

A **decimal** is a number that uses place value and a decimal point to show tenths and hundredths.

You can use graph paper to explore fractions and decimals.

VOCABULARY
decimal
decimal point

You Will Need
- graph paper
- colored pencils

Use Models

STEP 1
Make a 10–column grid so there are 10 equal parts. Shade 4 parts.

STEP 2
Make a 10–row by 10–column grid so there are 100 equal parts. Shade 40 parts.

STEP 3
The same number can be written different ways.

Copy and complete the table. Write each shaded part as a fraction and a decimal.

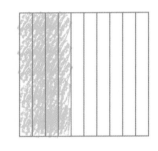

Fraction	Decimal	Word
$\frac{4}{10}$	0.4	four tenths
$\frac{40}{100}$		

A **decimal point** is a period separating the ones and the tenths in a decimal.

Explain Your Thinking

1. How many tenths are shaded in the whole grid? How many hundredths?

2. How do you write the shaded part in Step 1 as a fraction? As a decimal?

3. How do you write in words the shaded part in Step 1?

4. How do you write the shaded part in Step 2 as a fraction? As a decimal?

5. How do you write in words the shaded part in Step 2?

Technology Link

Use the fraction tool in **Math Tool Chest** to explore fractions and decimals.

Your Turn

Write a fraction and a decimal for each shaded part.

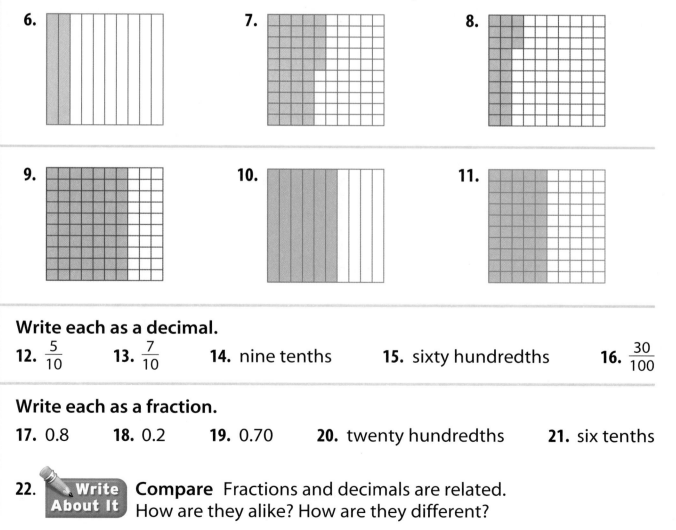

6.

7.

8.

9.

10.

11.

Write each as a decimal.

12. $\frac{5}{10}$ 13. $\frac{7}{10}$ 14. nine tenths   15. sixty hundredths   16. $\frac{30}{100}$

Write each as a fraction.

17. 0.8   18. 0.2   19. 0.70   20. twenty hundredths   21. six tenths

22. **Write About It** **Compare** Fractions and decimals are related. How are they alike? How are they different?

27.2 **Fractions and Decimals**

Learn

Martin's camp sells postcards for 50¢ each. What part of a dollar is 50¢? How can you write this amount as a decimal?

Show 50¢ as a fraction and decimal.

Let's see how to connect fractions and decimals to money.

VOCABULARY
equivalent decimals
hundredths
tenths

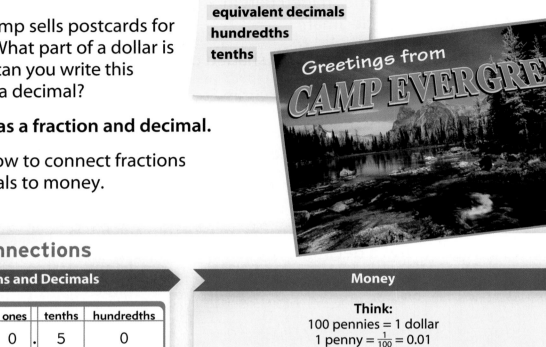
Greetings from CAMP EVERGREEN

Make Connections

Fractions and Decimals	Money

Fractions and Decimals

ones	tenths	hundredths
0	. 5	0

$\frac{50}{100} = 0.50$
fifty **hundredths**

ones	tenths	hundredths
0	. 5	

$\frac{5}{10} = 0.5$
five **tenths**

ones	tenths	hundredths
0	. 5	

$\frac{2}{4} = \frac{1}{2}$

Money

Think:
100 pennies = 1 dollar
1 penny = $\frac{1}{100}$ = 0.01

50 pennies = $\frac{50}{100}$ = $0.50

Think:
10 dimes = 1 dollar
1 dime = $\frac{1}{10}$ = 0.1

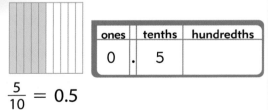

5 dimes = $\frac{5}{10}$ = $0.50

Think:
4 quarters = 1 dollar
1 quarter = $\frac{25}{100}$ = 0.25

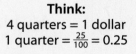

2 quarters = $\frac{50}{100}$ = $0.50

50¢ is $\frac{1}{2}$ of a dollar. To write 50¢ as a decimal is $0.50.

The camp counselors spend about 60¢ to make each lanyard. How can you write this amount in different ways?

There's More Than One Way!

Use Models
Use coins to show 60¢.

$0.60

Use Fractions
You can write this amount as a fraction.

Write: $\frac{60}{100}$

$\frac{60}{100} = \frac{6}{10}$

$\frac{60}{100}$ and $\frac{6}{10}$ are equivalent fractions.

Use Decimals
You can write this amount as a decimal.

ones	tenths	hundredths
0 .	6	
0 .	6	0

0.60 and 0.6 are **equivalent decimals**, or decimals that name the same number.

Try It Write a decimal for each.

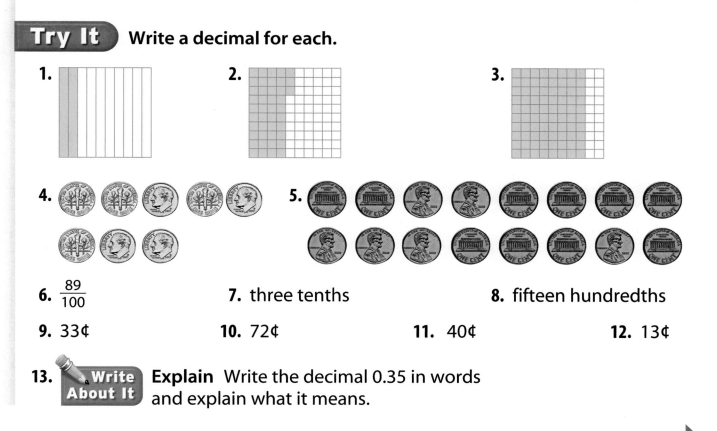

1.

2.

3.

4.

5.

6. $\frac{89}{100}$

7. three tenths

8. fifteen hundredths

9. 33¢

10. 72¢

11. 40¢

12. 13¢

13. **Write About It** **Explain** Write the decimal 0.35 in words and explain what it means.

Practice and Problem Solving

Write a decimal for each.

14.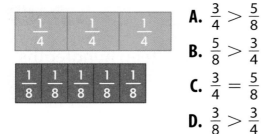

15.

16.

17.

18. $\frac{5}{10}$

19. one tenth

20. $\frac{26}{100}$

21. 71¢

22. five hundredths

★**23.** $\frac{2}{5}$

★**24.** three fourths

★**25.** $\frac{1}{25}$

★**26.** $\frac{3}{20}$

Solve. Use the grid for problems 27–28.

27. Art An artist made this design for the Young Campers newsletter. How many parts of the grid are shaded? Write a decimal to show the shaded part.

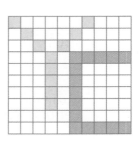

28. How many parts of the grid are yellow? Green? Write these as decimals.

29. It costs 60¢ to make and mail the newsletter. How much would it cost for 10 newsletters? For 100?

★**30. Collect data** from your classmates about how far they live from school, using tenths of a mile.

31. Make It Right Cindy wrote $\frac{1}{10}$ as a decimal. Tell what mistake she made. Explain how to correct it.

0.01 is $\frac{1}{10}$

THINK
SOLVE
EXPLAIN

Spiral Review and Test Prep

32. Which is true? (p. 562)

| $\frac{1}{4}$ | $\frac{1}{4}$ | $\frac{1}{4}$ |

| $\frac{1}{8}$ | $\frac{1}{8}$ | $\frac{1}{8}$ | $\frac{1}{8}$ | $\frac{1}{8}$ |

A. $\frac{3}{4} > \frac{5}{8}$

B. $\frac{5}{8} > \frac{3}{4}$

C. $\frac{3}{4} = \frac{5}{8}$

D. $\frac{3}{8} > \frac{3}{4}$

33. Which describes the likelihood of picking a peach from a bag of apples? (p. 586)

F. Certain

H. Unlikely

G. Likely

I. Impossible

34. 5×32 (p. 382)

35. $9\overline{)68}$ (p. 420)

36. $\$8.47 + \$4.76$ (p. 72)

Extra Practice page 620, Set A

Problem Solving: Reading for Math
WHEELED WONDER

Move over, car. There's a new people mover in town, and it's called Segway. The Segway Human Transporter is hitting the streets nationwide—and causing lots of talk.

The 2-wheeled Segway "will be to the car what the car was to the horse and buggy," inventor Dean Kamen says. Segway looks like a cross between a scooter and a lawnmower. It uses batteries to travel as fast as 17 miles an hour—great for zipping around town. The scooter needs only 10 cents worth of electricity for 6 hours of use.

Kamen hopes his invention will replace cars in big cities. He hopes it will help the environment by cutting down on car use and pollution. Segway may just change the way we live—and drive.

A postal worker on a Segway

Other Inventions that Changed Our Lives

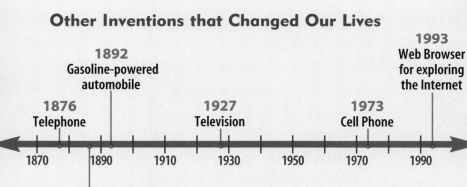

- 1993 Web Browser for exploring the Internet
- 1892 Gasoline-powered automobile
- 1876 Telephone
- 1927 Television
- 1973 Cell Phone
- 1870 1890 1910 1930 1950 1970 1990
- 1888 Ballpoint Pen

Problem Solving

Reading Skill **Problem and Solution** What types of problems could the Segway help to solve?

1. Look at the time line. What fraction of the inventions listed were created in the 1800s? Write your answer in fraction and then in decimal form.

2. How much would it cost to power up the Segway for 9 hours of use every day for 5 days?

27.3 Decimals Greater Than One

Learn

Pedro keeps his fishing lures in 2 boxes. Each box has 10 equal parts. One box is completely filled. The other is partially filled with 6 lures. What part of the 2 boxes is filled with fishing lures? Show the amount in different ways.

There's More Than One Way!

Use Models

Think: 1 whole and 6 out of 10

$1\frac{6}{10}$

Use a Place-Value Chart

ones		tenths
1	.	6

Write: 1.6
Read: one and six tenths

One and six tenths of the boxes is filled.

Use Money

Use decimals to write money amounts.

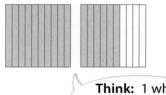

Write: $1.40
Read: One dollar and forty cents

Try It Write each decimal.

1.

2.

3.

4. $1\frac{62}{100}$

5. $3\frac{8}{10}$

6. $5\frac{1}{100}$

7. **Write About It** **Explain** how to write $2\frac{23}{100}$ as a decimal.

Practice and Problem Solving

Write each decimal.

8.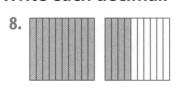

9.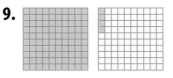

10.

11. seven and one tenth

12. nine and thirty hundredths

13. two dollars and five cents

14. nine dollars and eighteen cents

15. $4\frac{3}{10}$

16. $6\frac{72}{100}$

17. $5\frac{36}{100}$

★ 18. $1\frac{1}{2}$

★ 19. $3\frac{3}{4}$

ⓧ Algebra Describe and complete the following skip-counting patterns.

20. 3.20, 3.2▮, 3.22, 3.2▮, 3.24

21. 2.15, 2.25, 2.▮5, 2.▮5, 2.55

Solve.

THINK
SOLVE
EXPLAIN

22. ✎ **Write About It** **Analyze** Do 3.5 and 0.35 name the same number? Draw models with your explanation.

★ 23. Pedro bought a yo-yo for $7.89 and string for $1.29. How much change did he get from a ten-dollar bill?

Link to ★ SOCIAL STUDIES ★

An average pineapple weighs about 1.5 kg. In 1978, the world's largest pineapple was harvested in Brazil. It weighed 7.96 kg.

24. Write 7.96 kg in words.

✔ Spiral Review and Test Prep

25. Which group is in order from least to greatest? (p. 562)

A. $\frac{2}{9}, \frac{6}{9}, \frac{4}{9}$

C. $\frac{2}{9}, \frac{4}{9}, \frac{6}{9}$

B. $\frac{6}{9}, \frac{4}{9}, \frac{2}{9}$

D. $\frac{4}{9}, \frac{2}{9}, \frac{6}{9}$

26. What is the perimeter of a square that is 4 meters on a side? (p. 532)

F. 8 meters

H. 16 meters

G. 12 meters

I. 32 meter

27. 5×133 (p. 390)

28. $6\overline{)213}$ (p. 430)

29. $\frac{3}{5} - \frac{2}{5}$ (p. 582)

27.4 Compare and Order Decimals

Learn

An ERA, or earned run average, is a decimal that tells how many earned runs a pitcher allows his opponent to score in 9 innings. Which pitcher has the lower ERA?

Earned Run Average (2002 Season)

Player	ERA
Randy Johnson	2.32
Pedro Martinez	2.26

There's More Than One Way!

Use Models

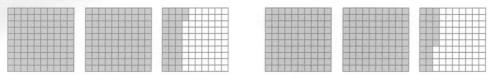

2.32 > 2.26

Use a Place-Value Chart

Compare each place.

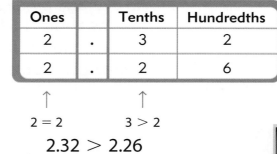

Ones		Tenths	Hundredths
2	.	3	2
2	.	2	6

↑ ↑
2 = 2   3 > 2
2.32 > 2.26

Use Place Value

Line up the decimal points. Compare each place, starting at the greatest place.

2 . 3 2
2 . 2 6
↑ ↑
2 = 2   3 > 2   2.32 > 2.26

Pedro Martinez has a lower ERA than Randy Johnson.

The table shows the ERAs for 3 pitchers in the American League.

Write their ERAs in order from least to greatest.

AMERICAN LEAGUE PITCHERS ERA
(2002 season)

PLAYER	ERA
MARK MULDER	3.47
PEDRO MARTINEZ	2.26
DAVID WELLS	3.75

There's More Than One Way!

Use a Number Line

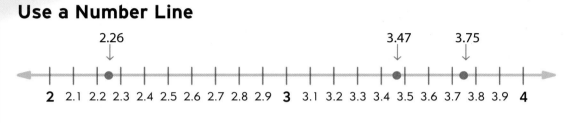

2.26   3.47   3.75

2   2.1   2.2   2.3   2.4   2.5   2.6   2.7   2.8   2.9   **3**   3.1   3.2   3.3   3.4   3.5   3.6   3.7   3.8   3.9   **4**

2.26 < 3.47   2.26 < 3.75   3.47 < 3.75

Use Place Value

STEP 1

Line up the decimal points. Compare the greatest place first.

3.47

2.26

3.75

Think: 2 < 3

So 2.26 is the least.

STEP 2

Compare the the next greatest place.

3.**4**7

3.**7**5

Think: 4 < 7

So 3.47 < 3.75.

STEP 3

Order the decimals from least to greatest.

2.26, 3.47, 3.75

The order of the ERAs from least to greatest is 2.26, 3.47, 3.75.

Try It

Compare. Write >, <, or = .

1. 0.70 ⚫ 0.73   **2.** 3.21 ⚫ 3.02   **3.** 0.56 ⚫ 1.09   **4.** 0.9 ⚫ 0.86

5. **Write About It** **Explain** how you can tell when a decimal is greater than or less than another decimal.

Practice and Problem Solving

Compare. Write >, <, or = .

6. 0.6 ● 0.8

7. 0.71 ● 0.78

8. 0.44 ● 0.35

9. $1.45 ● $1.54

10. 0.40 ● 0.4

11. 0.6 ● 0.3

12. 0.37 ● 0.62

13. $0.75 ● $0.90

★14. 3.58 ● 4.1

★15. 3.91 ● 3.8

★16. 4.08 ● 4.1

★17. 4.4 ● 4.38

Write in order from greatest to least.

18. 0.9, 0.3, 0.6

19. 0.52, 0.25, 0.75

20. 4.55, 4.45, 4.85

Solve. Use data from the table for problems 21–22.

21. Which pitcher had the lowest earned run average?

22. The pitcher with the highest earned run average played for Houston. Who is he?

National League Pitchers (2002 Season)	
Player	**ERA**
Tom Glavine	2.62
Randy Johnson	2.32
Greg Maddux	2.96
Roy Oswalt	3.01

23. **Write About It** **Compare** How is comparing and ordering decimals like comparing and ordering whole numbers? How is it different?

24. **Make It Right** Aaron compared 3.8 and 5.4. Tell what mistake he made. Explain how to correct it.

3.8 ● 5.4
8 > 4
So 3.8 > 5.4

Spiral Review and Test Prep

25. Linda is working on a science project. She adds $\frac{1}{4}$ cup of one liquid to $\frac{1}{4}$ cup of a different liquid. How much is this in all? (p. 578)

   A. $\frac{1}{2}$ cup   C. $\frac{2}{8}$ cup

   B. $\frac{1}{4}$ cup   D. $\frac{1}{8}$ cup

26. Which describes this shape? (p. 514)

   F. Right triangle
   G. Obtuse triangle
   H. Acute triangle
   I. Equilateral triangle

27. $\frac{5}{8} - \frac{1}{8}$ (p. 580)

28. $\frac{1}{6} + \frac{5}{6}$ (p. 578)

29. 42 ÷ 6 (p. 324)

30. 59 ÷ 8 (p. 420)

Extra Practice page 620, Set C

Practice at School ★ Practice at Home

99¢ OR LESS!

Pick number cards to create money amounts.

Ready

Players: 2 or more
You Will Need: Digit Deck, paper, pencil

Set

Each player creates a sheet like the one shown here.

GO!

▶ On the first round, players take turns drawing 3 cards from the Digit Deck.

▶ Each player chooses 2 of the 3 digits to make the least possible money amount. For example, cards 3, 2, and 7 would be $0.23.

▶ The players each record the money amount on the start line.

▶ For the next round each player draws 3 new cards. Choose 2 to make a money amount that is as low as possible but **greater** than the previous one. Record this amount on the next line.

▶ A player may pass at any time. Play continues with each player making amounts that are greater than the previous one. The first player to fill the lines and have less than $0.99 for the total amount is the winner.

27.5 Problem Solving: Skill
Choose an Operation

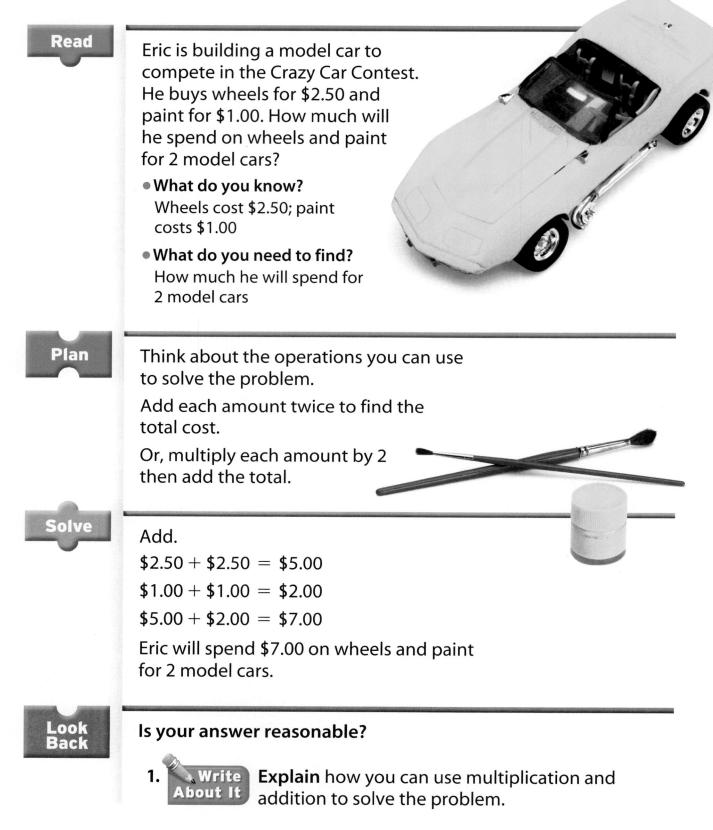

Read

Eric is building a model car to compete in the Crazy Car Contest. He buys wheels for $2.50 and paint for $1.00. How much will he spend on wheels and paint for 2 model cars?

- **What do you know?**
  Wheels cost $2.50; paint costs $1.00

- **What do you need to find?**
  How much he will spend for 2 model cars

Plan

Think about the operations you can use to solve the problem.

Add each amount twice to find the total cost.

Or, multiply each amount by 2 then add the total.

Solve

Add.

$2.50 + $2.50 = $5.00

$1.00 + $1.00 = $2.00

$5.00 + $2.00 = $7.00

Eric will spend $7.00 on wheels and paint for 2 model cars.

Look Back

Is your answer reasonable?

1. **Write About It** **Explain** how you can use multiplication and addition to solve the problem.

Practice Solve. Tell how you chose the operation.

2. Rosa spent $3.76 on model parts. Emma spent $2.89. Who spent more on model parts? How much more?

3. Bob sold a model car he made for $45.85. Jedd sold his model car for $23.37 more than Bob's car. How much did Jedd sell his car for?

Mixed Strategy Review

4. Joanne makes shelves to store her model cars. She buys a 66-inch-long piece of wood and cuts it into 11-inch lengths for each shelf. How many shelves can she make?

5. Chad can choose red or blue decals to decorate his car. He can paint his car one color—yellow, white, or green. How many different ways can Chad decorate his car? What are they?

Choose a Strategy

- Logical Reasoning
- Draw a Picture or Diagram
- Make a Graph
- Act It Out
- Make a Table or List
- Find a Pattern
- Guess and Check
- Write an Equation
- Work Backward
- Solve a Simpler Problem

Use data from the list for problems 6–11.

6. In May, the Crazy Car Club had 19 members. In June, 12 more people joined the club and 5 members dropped out of the club. How many members did the club have at the end of June?

7. Beth bought decals and wheels. How much did she spend?

8. Cal bought 3 paintbrushes. How much did he spend?

10. Carla bought every item on the list. How much did she spend?

Cost of Equipment

Item	Cost
Decals	$2.75
Paint	$1.89
Paintbrush	$3.35
Wheels	$2.39
Wire	$1.25

9. What is the difference in the cost between paint and wire?

11. ✎ **Write a problem** using the data from the list. Solve it. Ask others to solve it.

Problem Solving

Extra Practice

Set A Write a decimal for each. (pp. 606–610)

1. **2.** **3.** **4.**

5. $\frac{3}{10}$ **6.** $\frac{70}{100}$ **7.** $\frac{54}{100}$ **8.** Eighty cents

Set B Write each decimal. (pp. 612–613)

9. **10.** **11.**

12. $9\frac{3}{10}$ **13.** $4\frac{34}{100}$ **14.** $9\frac{78}{100}$ **15.** two and nine tenths

Set C Compare. Write >, <, or =. (pp. 614–616)

16. 0.4 ● 0.6   **17.** 0.5 ● 0.4   **18.** 4.1 ● 1.4   **19.** 2.86 ● 2.68

20. 0.80 ● 0.8   **21.** 4.19 ● 4.09   **22.** 0.87 ● 1.01   **23.** 0.87 ● 0.78

Write the decimals in order from least to greatest.

24. 0.26, 0.62, 0.52   **25.** 0.37, 0.24, 0.46   **26.** 2.23, 1.23, 1.32

Write the decimals from greatest to least.

27. 0.89, 0.98, 9.80   **28.** 4.18, 4.81, 4.80   **29.** 0.79, 7.97, 9.70

Set D Solve. Tell what operation you used. (pp. 618–619)

30. Bud's model car costs $3.40. Tom's car costs $1.90. How much do the cars cost in all? Which operation did you use?

31. Jan's supplies cost $2.80. Sue's supplies cost $1.70 less than Jan's. How much do Sue's supplies cost? Which operation did you use?

Review/Test

Write a decimal for the part that is shaded.

1. **2.** **3.** **4.** **5.**

Write a decimal.

6. $\frac{23}{100}$ **7.** 9¢   **8.** $\frac{75}{100}$ **9.** $8\frac{44}{100}$ **10.** $6\frac{62}{100}$

11. three hundredths **12.** two and one tenth **13.** four and eighteen hundredths

Compare. Write $>$, $<$, or $=$.

14. 0.6 ⬤ 0.5   **15.** 0.36 ⬤ 0.63   **16.** 3.1 ⬤ 3.10   **17.** 5.54 ⬤ 5.45

Write the decimals in order from least to greatest.

18. 0.2, 0.4, 0.1   **19.** 0.26, 0.16, 0.46   **20.** 1.8, 1.5, 1.6   **21.** 3.35, 3.04, 2.37

Solve.

22. Nora's raft cost $7.65. How much change should she receive from a ten-dollar bill?

23. Kerri's CD has 10 songs. Seven songs are jazz. Write a decimal to show the number of jazz songs.

24. Bruce finds 2 shells at the beach. One shell is 16.5 centimeters wide. The other is 16.2 centimeters wide. Which measurement is greater?

25. Write About It **Explain** how to order 0.64, 0.39, and 0.62 from greatest to least.

Do I Need Help?

Exercises	Review Concepts	Use Extra Practice Set
1–13	pp. 606–613	Set A and B
14–21, 25	pp. 614–616	Set C
22–24	pp. 618–619	Set D

Foldables **Use your Foldables to help you review.**

Assessment

What Do I Need to Know?

A group of 10 people built this sand castle. Seven of them are girls. Write the part of the group that is girls as a decimal.

Add and Subtract Decimals

What Will I Learn?

In this chapter you will learn to

- add and subtract decimals

- use skills and strategies to solve problems

How Do I Read Math?

When you read a mathematics book, sometimes you read words and symbols, and sometimes you read only symbols.

Both of these represent 0.91 minus 0.23 equals 0.68:

- $0.91 - 0.23 = 0.68$

- $$\begin{array}{r} 0.91 \\ -0.23 \\ \hline 0.68 \end{array}$$

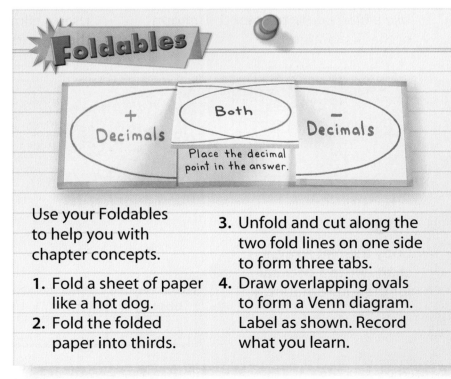

Use your Foldables to help you with chapter concepts.

1. Fold a sheet of paper like a hot dog.

2. Fold the folded paper into thirds.

3. Unfold and cut along the two fold lines on one side to form three tabs.

4. Draw overlapping ovals to form a Venn diagram. Label as shown. Record what you learn.

28.1 Explore Adding Decimals

Hands On Activity

You can use graph paper to explore adding decimals.

Find: 0.48 + 0.57

You Will Need
- graph paper
- colored pencils or crayons

Use Models

STEP 1

Use a blue pencil to color the amount of the first addend.

STEP 2

Use a yellow pencil to color the amount of the second addend.

STEP 3

Copy the place-value chart. Write a decimal for the total amount.

ones	.	tenths	hundredths

Explain Your Thinking

1. How did you model each addend?

2. After coloring the second addend, how many whole grids are colored?

3. What part of the second grid is colored?

4. What is 0.48 + 0.57?

Your Turn

Add. You may wish to use models.

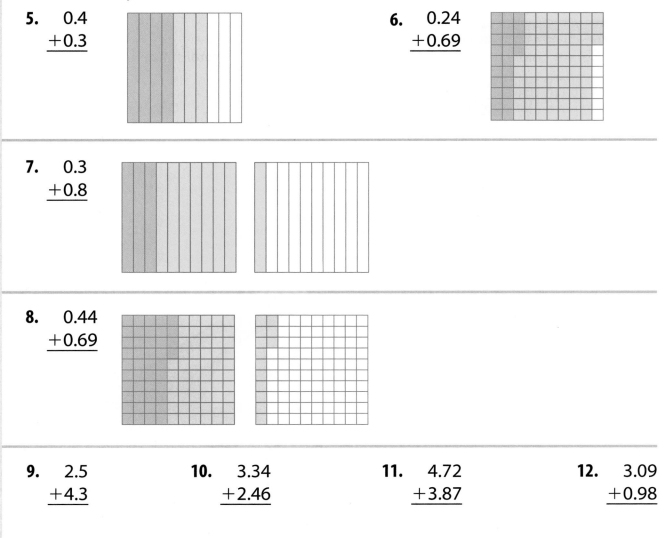

5. 0.4
   +0.3

6. 0.24
   +0.69

7. 0.3
   +0.8

8. 0.44
   +0.69

9. 2.5
   +4.3

10. 3.34
    +2.46

11. 4.72
    +3.87

12. 3.09
    +0.98

13. **Write About It** **Explain** how you use models to add 1.04 and 0.97. Then solve.

28.2 Add Decimals

Learn

In the morning show, the whale eats 1.7 kilograms of food. In the afternoon show, it eats 1.5 kilograms. How many kilograms of food does the whale eat in all?

Find: 1.7 + 1.5

Let's see how to connect models to paper and pencil.

Make Connections

Models

▼ Use different colors to show each addend. Count to find the total shaded.

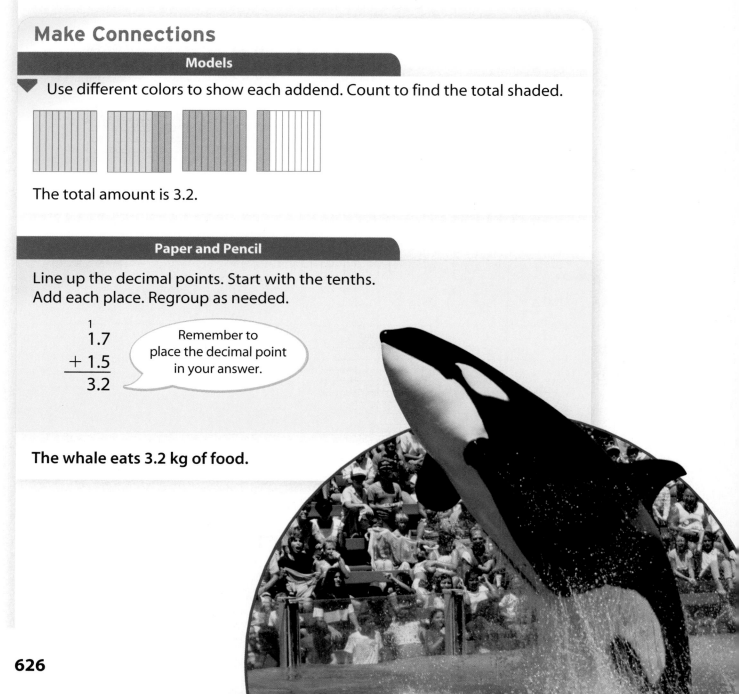

The total amount is 3.2.

Paper and Pencil

Line up the decimal points. Start with the tenths. Add each place. Regroup as needed.

$$
\begin{array}{r}
{}^{1} \\
1.7 \\
+\ 1.5 \\
\hline
3.2
\end{array}
$$

> Remember to place the decimal point in your answer.

The whale eats 3.2 kg of food.

At the souvenir shop, Harold buys a key chain for $2.45 and stickers for $0.98. How much did he spend in all?

Find: $2.45 + $0.98

There's More Than One Way!

Use Paper and Pencil

STEP 1

Line up the decimal points. Add as you would whole numbers. Regroup if necessary.

$$
\begin{array}{r}
^{1\ 1}\\
\$2.45\\
+\ \ 0.98\\
\hline
3\ 43
\end{array}
$$

STEP 2

Place the decimal point and dollar sign in the sum.

$$
\begin{array}{r}
^{1\ 1}\\
\$2.45\\
+\ \ 0.98\\
\hline
\$3.43
\end{array}
$$

Use a Calculator

Press: [2] [·] [4] [5] [+] [0] [·] [9] [8] [Enter =]

Display: 2.45+0.98=
                3.43

Write the dollar sign in the sum.

Harold spent $3.43 in all at the souvenir shop.

Try It   Add.

1. 1.4
   +3.7

2. 5.4
   +2.5

3. $0.78
   + 0.13

4. 6.35
   +3.39

5. $6.06
   + 4.20

6. **Write About It** **Explain** how adding decimals is like adding whole numbers and how it is different.

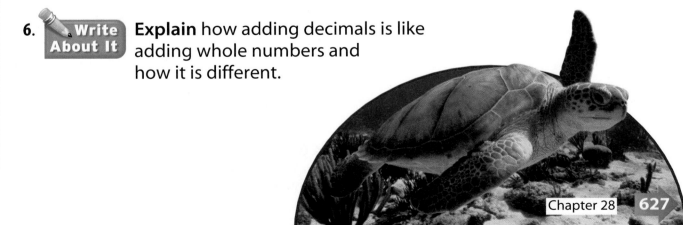

Practice and Problem Solving

Add.

7. 2.59
+4.82

8. 6.74
+6.38

9. 1.3
+7.2

10. 7.3
+8.8

11. $0.84
+ 0.27

12. $6.05 + $7.49 **13.** 0.6 + 0.9 **14.** $1.34 + $5.93 **15.** 8.04 + 3.52

16. 0.48 + 0.27 **17.** 3.98 + 2.36 **18.** 0.68 + 3.84 **19.** 7.63 + 4.45

★**20.** 0.23 + 1.22 + 0.63 ★**21.** 1.6 + 5.4 + 0.2 ★**22.** 0.52 + 0.24 + 3.22 + 4.51

Solve.

23. Scott buys a book on beaches. It costs $9.56. How much does he spend for 2 of these books?

24. Admission to the park is $6.95. How much does it cost for 4 people to go to the park?

25. Ian buys 6 bags of rolls. Each bag holds 5 rolls. How many rolls does Ian buy?

26. **Write a problem** where you have to add using decimals. Solve it. Ask others to solve it.

★**27.** **Language Arts** The name *crayon* comes from French words for "oily chalk." If 8 crayons in a box of 64 are different shades of red, what fraction of all the crayons are red?

28. **Make It Right**
Here is how Jenny added money amounts. Tell what mistake she made. Explain how to correct it.

$2.45
+ 1.94
$439

THINK
SOLVE
EXPLAIN

Spiral Review and Test Prep

29. 123 feet = ▓ yards (p. 462)

   A. 10   **C.** 159

   B. 41   **D.** 369

30. Find: $\frac{1}{4}$ of 32 (p. 568)

   F. 8   **H.** 24

   G. 12   **I.** 28

31. 900 − 548 (p. 114)

32. 7 × 613 (p. 390)

33. $\frac{5}{10} + \frac{3}{10}$

Extra Practice page 636, Set A

Writing for Math

A 3-day walkathon covers 96.0 km. Walkers travel 37.6 km the first day, and 32.7 km the second day. How many km must they walk the third day to reach the finish line? Explain your thinking.

Stacey's Response

✓ **THINK** Add to find the 2-day total walked. Subtract the sum from 96.0 km to find the distance remaining on the third day.

✓ **SOLVE**

$37.6 + 32.7 = 70.3$ $96.0 - 70.3 = 25.7$
Walkers will travel 25.7 km on the third day.
Check: $25.7 + 32.7 + 37.6 = 96.0$

✓ **EXPLAIN** First, I added the amounts for the first two days. The sum is 70.3 km. Then I subtracted the sum from 96.0 km, the total 3-day distance. The difference is 25.7 km.

To check, I added all 3 distances. The sum is 96.0, which matches the 3-day total. My answer makes sense.

Teacher's Response

← Stacey describes the steps she will use to solve the problem.

← Stacey shows her work.

← Stacey uses appropriate math terms, such as **add**, **sum**, **subtract**, and **difference**. She explains both steps she used to solve the problem.

← Stacey uses addition, the **inverse operation of subtraction**, to check her answer.

Solve. Show your work. Use Stacey's work as a guide.

1. On a school trip, a class travels 117.7 km by train and 28.9 km by bus. How far did the class travel?

2. Grace buys 1.4 lb of raisins and 2.5 lb of peanuts. She wants 5 lb of trail mix. How many pounds of granola should Grace buy?

28.3 Problem Solving: Strategy
Solve a Simpler Problem

Read

Mr. and Mrs. Li take 3 children to the museum. How much do the Lis spend on admission and parking?

- **What do you know?**
  There are 3 children and 2 adults.

- **What do you need to find?**
  The total cost of admission and parking

Plan

You need to find 3 things to solve the problem.

- How much do they pay for admission?

- How much do they pay for parking?

- How much do they pay for everything all together?

The Science Museum

$7.95 . . . . Adults
$5.95 . . . . Children
$5.95 . . . . Senior Citizens
$5.25 . . Each for groups of 25 or more
$4.50 . . . . Parking

Solve

First round the amounts to the nearest dollar.
These numbers are easier than the original numbers.

	Cost for adults	+	Cost for children	+	Cost for parking
	$2 \times \$8$	+	$3 \times \$6$	+	$5
Total Cost	$16	+	$18	+	$5 = \$39$

Now that you know how to solve the problem, use the original numbers.

	$2 \times \$7.95$		$3 \times \$5.95$		$4.50
Total Cost	$15.90	+	$17.85	+	$4.50 = \$38.25$

Look Back

Is your answer reasonable?

1. **Write About It** **Explain** how using simpler numbers can help you solve a problem.

630

Practice   Solve.

2. Look back at the admission prices. How much money would the family save if they went to the museum as part of a group of 30 people?

3. The family has lunch in the museum cafeteria. Lunches cost $3.65 and drinks are $0.95. How much do they pay in all for lunch?

4. The museum is 0.4 miles away from the train station. A diner is 1.7 miles beyond that. How far is it from the train station to the museum, then to the diner?

5. The family takes the train to the museum. Each train ticket is $4.75. How much do they pay for admission and train tickets?

Mixed Strategy Review

6. The museum is 42 miles away. It costs about $0.32 each mile to drive and $4.50 to park. The train tickets are $4.75 each way. Is it cheaper to drive or take the train? How much cheaper?

7. **Measurement** The museum wants to rope off a space that is under construction. It is a rectangular space with sides that measure 12 feet and 14 feet. How much rope do they need?

Use the data in the graph for problems 8–10.

8. The museum took a survey to see which exhibits guests liked most. How many people did they survey in all?

9. How many more people liked It's Electric than World of Magnets?

Choose a Strategy
- Logical Reasoning
- Draw a Picture or Diagram
- Make a Graph
- Act It Out
- Make a Table or List
- Find a Pattern
- Guess and Check
- Write an Equation
- Work Backward
- Solve a Simpler Problem

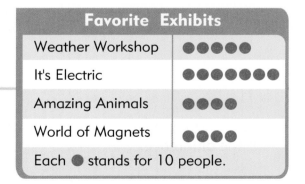

Favorite Exhibits	
Weather Workshop	●●●●●
It's Electric	●●●●●●●
Amazing Animals	●●●●
World of Magnets	●●●●
Each ● stands for 10 people.	

10. **Write a problem** using the data in the pictograph. Solve it. Ask others to solve it.

Problem Solving

28.4 Explore Subtracting Decimals

Hands On Activity

You can use graph paper to explore subtracting decimals.

Find: 1.6 − 0.9

You Will Need
- graph paper
- colored pencils or crayons
- scissors

Use Models

STEP 1

Use a colored pencil to color a model for 1.6.

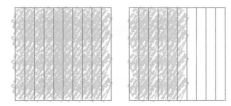

STEP 2

Show taking away by cutting 9 columns away.

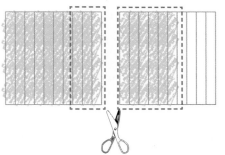

STEP 3

Find the amount left.
This is the difference.

Explain Your Thinking

1. How did you model 1.6?

2. How did you show 0.9 being subtracted?

3. What part of the grid is left?

4. What is 1.6 − 0.9?

Your Turn

Subtract. You may wish to use models.

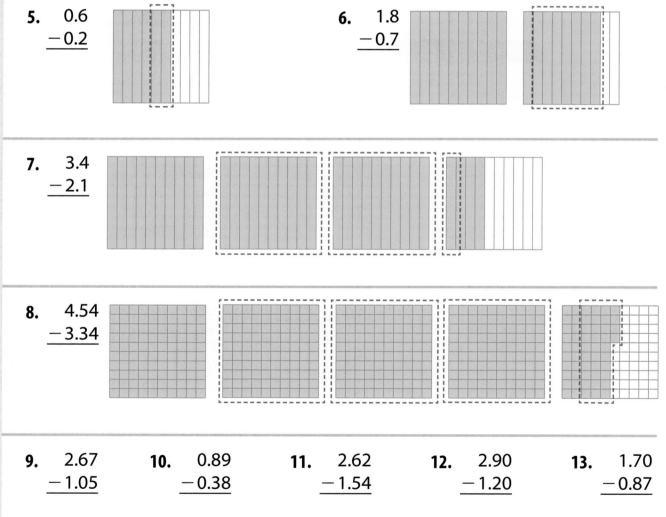

5. 0.6
   − 0.2

6. 1.8
   − 0.7

7. 3.4
   − 2.1

8. 4.54
   − 3.34

9. 2.67
   − 1.05

10. 0.89
    − 0.38

11. 2.62
    − 1.54

12. 2.90
    − 1.20

13. 1.70
    − 0.87

14. 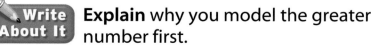 **Write About It** **Explain** why you model the greater number first.

28.5 Subtract Decimals

Learn

Miguel's go-cart is 2.50 yards long. Sam's go-cart is 1.75 yards long. How much longer is Miguel's go-cart than Sam's go-cart?

Find: 2.50 − 1.75

Let's see how to connect models to paper and pencil.

Make Connections

	Models	Paper and Pencil
STEP 1 Shade to show 2.50.		Line up the decimal points. $$\begin{array}{r} 2.50 \\ -\,1.75 \\ \hline \end{array}$$
STEP 2 Cut 1 whole and 75 small squares to show taking 1.75 away.		Start with the hundredths. Subtract each place. Regroup as needed. $$\begin{array}{r} {}^{1}\ {}^{4}\ {}^{10}\\ 2.\cancel{5}\cancel{0} \\ -\,1.75 \\ \hline 0\,75 \end{array}$$
STEP 3 Count to find the difference.	You can also use a calculator.	Place the decimal point in the difference. $$0.75$$

Miguel's go-cart is 0.75 yards longer than Sam's go-cart.

Try It — Subtract.

1. 3.4 − 1.7   **2.** 6.8 − 2.7   **3.** 0.76 − 0.37   **4.** 6.52 − 1.29

5.  **Explain** how you can check the answer when subtracting decimals.

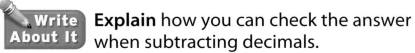

Practice and Problem Solving

Subtract.

6.
$$\begin{array}{r} 6.7 \\ -3.4 \\ \hline \end{array}$$

7.
$$\begin{array}{r} 6.36 \\ -5.58 \\ \hline \end{array}$$

8.
$$\begin{array}{r} \$0.77 \\ -\$0.58 \\ \hline \end{array}$$

9.
$$\begin{array}{r} 8.90 \\ -6.86 \\ \hline \end{array}$$

10.
$$\begin{array}{r} \$8.15 \\ -\$2.39 \\ \hline \end{array}$$

11.
$$\begin{array}{r} 8.3 \\ -5.2 \\ \hline \end{array}$$

12.
$$\begin{array}{r} 0.9 \\ -0.5 \\ \hline \end{array}$$

13.
$$\begin{array}{r} \$7.54 \\ -\$3.92 \\ \hline \end{array}$$

★14. $(5.3 + 1.3) - 3.8$ ★15. $(3.4 + 7.6) - 4.2$ ★16. $(8.2 + 1.1) - 3.3$

ⓧ **Algebra** Copy and complete.

17.
$$\begin{array}{r} 7.3\blacksquare \\ -3.25 \\ \hline 4.09 \end{array}$$

18.
$$\begin{array}{r} 8.9 \\ -\blacksquare.4 \\ \hline 3.5 \end{array}$$

19.
$$\begin{array}{r} 5.87 \\ -2.26 \\ \hline \blacksquare.61 \end{array}$$

20.
$$\begin{array}{r} \blacksquare.65 \\ -4.24 \\ \hline 5.41 \end{array}$$

21.
$$\begin{array}{r} 4.53 \\ -3.1\blacksquare \\ \hline 1.35 \end{array}$$

Solve. Use data from the table for problems 22–24.

22. How much more power does the Roamer have than the Runner?

23. How much does it cost to buy the Runner and the Extreme?

Scooters		
Model	Horsepower	Price
Roamer	5.5	$369.00
Runner	4.75	$299.95
Extreme	6.5	$395.95

24. ✏️ **Write a problem** using the data in the table. Solve it. Ask others to solve it.

25. ✏️ **Write About It** **Compare** How is subtracting decimals like subtracting money? How is it different? `THINK SOLVE EXPLAIN`

Spiral Review and Test Prep

26. Which is a certain event? (p. 586)

    A. Spin 3

    B. Spin 4

    C. Spin 5

    D. Spin red

27. Jody uses $\frac{3}{8}$ teaspoon of garlic powder and $\frac{5}{8}$ teaspoon of pepper in a recipe. How much spice is this? (p. 582)

    F. 1 teaspoon   **H.** $\frac{8}{16}$ teaspoon

    G. $\frac{2}{8}$ teaspoon   **I.** $\frac{1}{2}$ teaspoon

28. $\frac{1}{2} + \frac{1}{2}$ (p.582)

29. $68.42 + $5.21 (p. 72)

30. $3\overline{)\$1.26}$ (p. 430)

Extra Practice

Set A Add. (pp. 626–628)

1. 5.7 +6.5	**2.** 0.91 +0.19	**3.** $7.25 + 3.19	**4.** 4.55 +5.69
5. 2.4 +4.8	**6.** 0.4 +0.8	**7.** $3.48 + 4.98	**8.** 6.02 +4.79
9. 0.37 +0.46	**10.** 2.76 +3.43	**11.** 0.93 +2.66	**12.** 6.18 +3.42

13. $0.29 + $0.82   **14.** 4.60 + 3.78   **15.** 8.58 + 5.47   **16.** 4.85 + 6.33

Set B Solve. Use the data from the table for problems 17–19. (pp. 630–631)

17. Mrs. Hira's summer school class is inventing games. She buys some supplies for the project. She buys 4 bags of marbles and 2 boxes of plastic chips. How much does she spend?

Project Supplies	
Bag of Marbles	$1.79
Box of Plastic Chips	$2.29
Box of Markers	$5.99
Box of Index Cards	$3.49

18. How much would it cost to buy 2 bags of marbles and 1 each of the other items?

19. How much would she spend for 2 boxes of index cards and 2 boxes of markers?

Set C Subtract. (pp. 634–635)

20. 7.1 −4.6	**21.** 8.3 −4.6	**22.** $7.80 − 3.94	**23.** 7.74 −3.89
24. 6.4 −4.1	**25.** 0.8 −0.3	**26.** $6.37 −2.14	**27.** 9.09 −4.36
28. 0.67 −0.39	**29.** 5.46 −2.72	**30.** 0.93 −0.44	**31.** 4.56 −2.73

LOG ON   www.mmhmath.com
For more practice and Chapter Self-Check Test

Add.

1.   3.63
    +4.37

2.   2.85
    +8.19

3. $8.08
    + 4.22

4.   9.2
    +7.4

5.   5.47
    +3.21

6.   2.4
    +5.8

7.   0.5
    +0.2

8.   3.45
    +2.62

9. $0.32 + 1.48$

10. $0.3 + 0.4 + 0.7$

11. $0.2 + 0.7 + 0.9$

Subtract.

12.   8.8
    −4.3

13.   4.79
    −3.25

14. $7.95
    − 3.49

15.   6.03
    −4.56

16.   5.50
    −1.48

17.   0.79
    −0.28

18.   3.84
    −3.18

19.   0.95
    −0.46

20. $5.07 − 3.68$

21. $0.32 − 0.11$

22. $2.38 − 1.24$

Solve.

23. A fruit tray had 2.8 pounds of melon, and 3.2 pounds of berries. How many pounds of fruit were on the tray?

24. Heather uses 2.6 kilograms of clay to make a sculpture. Arlen uses 3.5 kilograms of clay. Who uses more clay? How much more?

25. **Write About It** **Analyze** How can you use addition to check the answer to $1.96 − 1.89$?

Do I Need Help?

Exercises	Review Concepts	Use Extra Practice Set
1–11	pp. 624–628	Set A
12–22	pp. 632–635	Set C
23–25	pp. 630–631	Set B

 **Use your Foldables to help you review.**

Applying Math and Science
How Does Distance Affect Your Aim?

A basketball player can score 2 or 3 points by making a basket. In professional basketball, the players make an average of about 44 baskets for every 2-point shot per game. From farther away, however, they make fewer shots.

In this activity, you will discover how much harder it is to make baskets as you get farther away from the basket.

Hypothesize

Out of 10 tries, how many baskets will you make from 1 meter away? From 4 meters away?

You Will Need

- paper ball
- ruler or meterstick
- trash can

Procedure

1. Work with a partner. Take turns. Copy and complete the chart on the next page. Record the number of baskets you made at each distance. Write your answer as a decimal.

2. Stand 1 meter from an empty trash can.

3. Try 10 shots. Record how many go in.

4. Repeat step 3 from 2 meters, 3 meters, and 4 meters.

Distance	Attempts	Number of shots made	Fraction of shots made	Decimal equivalent
1 m	10		$\frac{\blacksquare}{10}$	
2 m	10			
3 m	10			
4 m	10			

Conclude and Apply

THINK SOLVE EXPLAIN

1. **Interpret data** At which distance was it easiest to make baskets? Explain.

2. **Use numbers** Put the decimals in the table in order from least to greatest.

3. Compare the number of shots you made at 1m and at 4m.

4. Make a bar graph to display your data. Talk about what it shows.

Going Further Design and complete an activity to find the longest distance you can be from the basket and still make at least 1 shot in 10.

Unit Study Guide and Review

Vocabulary

Complete. Use a word from the list.

1. In the number 9.4, the 4 is in the ___ place.

2. A ___ has a numerator and denominator.

3. A ___ always has a number to the right of the decimal point.

4. In the number 4.92, the 2 is in the ___ place.

VOCABULARY
decimal
decimal point
fraction
hundredths
tenths

Skills and Applications

Identify fraction and decimal equivalents. (pp. 606–607)

Write a fraction and a decimal for the model.

Solution
Think: 72 out of 100 squares are shaded.

Fraction	**Decimal**
$\frac{72}{100}$	0.72

Write a fraction and a decimal for each model.

5.
6.

Write a decimal.

7. 1 quarter of a dollar

8. $1\frac{7}{10}$

9. $3\frac{35}{100}$

Read and write decimals to hundredths. (pp. 608–613)

Write a decimal for the part that is shaded.

Solution
Think: 3 out of 10 parts are shaded.

Read: three tenths

Write: 0.3

Write a decimal for the part that is shaded.

10.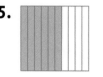

Write a decimal.

11. $\frac{9}{10}$

12. $\frac{89}{100}$

13. $\frac{1}{4}$

14. Nine and fifteen hundredths

 **Use your Foldables to help you review.**

Compare and order decimals. (pp. 614–616)

Write $>$, $<$, or $=$.

3.45 ⬤ 3.68

Solution
Line up the decimals.
Compare each place.

Ones		Tenths	Hundredths
3	.	4	5
3	.	6	8

3.45 $<$ 3.68

Compare. Write $>$, $<$, or $=$.

15. 0.3 ⬤ 0.6   **16.** 0.64 ⬤ 0.46

17. 1.23 ⬤ 1.43   **18.** 3.6 ⬤ 3.60

19. 5.49 ⬤ 5.42   **20.** 2.35 ⬤ 2.38

Order from least to greatest.

21. 4.2, 4.1, 3.7   **22.** 6.8, 6.5, 6.0

23. 5.84, 5.48, 5.68   **24.** 7.21, 7.12, 7.11

Add and subtract decimals. (pp. 624–628, 632–635)

Add or subtract.

3.5 + 2.6   6.74 − 3.45

Solution

```
  1
  3.5
+ 2.6
-----
  6.1
```

```
    6 14
  6.7̸4̸
- 3.45
------
  3.29
```

Add or subtract.

25.
```
  5.92
+ 3.40
```

26.
```
  6.30
− 3.22
```

27. 7.13 + 2.96   **28.** 4.0 − 0.85

29. 2.27 + 4.54   **30.** 7.33 − 2.59

31. 0.9 + 0.3 + 0.6

Use skills and strategies to solve problems. (pp. 618–619, 630–631)

In 2 races, Ana's car went 6.5 feet and 7.75 feet. Burt's car went 6.75 feet and 7.25 feet. Whose car had the greater total distance?

Solution
Use simpler numbers first.
7 + 8 = 15   7 + 7 = 14   15 > 14

Now use the original numbers.
6.5 + 7.75 = 14.25
6.75 + 7.25 = 14.00   14.25 > 14.00

Ana's car had the greater total distance.

Use data from the chart for problems 32–33.

Rainfall Amounts (in inches)					
March	April	May	June	July	August
4.2	5.3	2.6	2.1	0.6	0.8

32. How much more rain did March and April have than May and June?

33. How much more rainfall did March, April, and May have than June, July, and August?

Enrichment

Russian Abacus

You may have seen a Japanese abacus before. The Russian abacus is a little different—it lets you show decimals.

A Russian abacus is called a *schoty* (SHOH-tee). The picture shows what a schoty looks like. The schoty is showing 36.5.

The beads have been moved to the left to show the correct number. For example, there are 3 tens, 6 ones, and 5 tenths in 36.5.

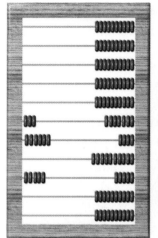

thousands
hundreds
tens
ones
decimal point
tenths
hundredths

Write the number shown by each abacus.

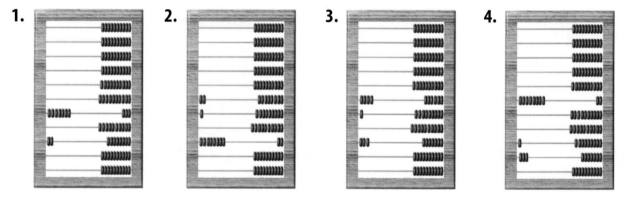

1.
2.
3.
4.

Describe how you could show these numbers on a schoty.

5. 2.05   **6.** 104.1   **7.** 67.52   **8.** 921.4

9. Generalize Do you think a schoty would be better to use than a calculator? Explain.

Performance Assessment

How Will You Spend Your Money?

Your aunt gives you $25 to spend on your new puppy. With this amount, you need to buy a collar, a tag, and grooming tools, such as a brush or comb. You can use the amount left over to buy more puppy items.

Choose your items from this catalog. Add up your 3 main purchases. Record how much money is spent and how much money is left over. Then decide what you will buy with the leftover money.

PUPPY PRODUCTS

Plastic Collar $6.71

Nylon Collar $5.49

Gold Tag $4.98

Silver Tag $3.98

Comb $2.56

Brush $3.73

Ball $0.79

Box Treats $2.64

Chew Toy $4.26

Tips For A Good Answer

- Show a complete list.
- Include a collar, a tag, and grooming tools.
- Show what was purchased with the leftover money.

You may want to save this work in your portfolio.

e-Journal www.mmhmath.com
Write about math.
Unit 14 **643**

TECHNOLOGY Link

Change Fractions to Decimals

Lois wants to buy a candy bar. The clerk told her it cost $\frac{3}{4}$ of a dollar. How can you write this amount using a dollar sign and a decimal point?

To answer this question, you have to change $\frac{3}{4}$ into a decimal.

Using the TI-15

To change a fraction to a decimal, enter the following:

3 **n** 4 **d** **Enter =** **F→D**

So, Lois has $0.75.

Mitchell has $0.10. What fraction of a dollar does he have? To change a decimal to a fraction, enter the following:

0 **.** 1 0 **Enter =** **F→D**

So, Mitchell has $\frac{1}{10}$ of a dollar.

Change each fraction to a decimal.

1. $\frac{1}{2}$ 2. $\frac{1}{4}$ 3. $\frac{2}{5}$ 4. $\frac{7}{10}$ 5. $\frac{4}{5}$

Change each decimal to a fraction.

6. 0.2   7. 0.85   8. 0.15   9. 0.47   10. 0.3

Solve.

11. Jeremy has saved $0.63 in pennies. What fraction of a dollar has he saved?

12. Tosha has $\frac{9}{20}$ of a dollar in her pocket. How much money does Tosha have?

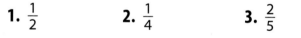

For more practice, use Math Traveler™.

Test-Taking Tips

Sometimes the numbers in a problem make it seem harder than it actually is. It may be helpful to **use simpler numbers.**

Josh ran 3.25 miles today and 1.75 miles yesterday. How far did he run all together?

A. 1.75 miles   **C.** 6 miles

B. 5 miles   **D.** 6.75 miles

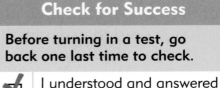

Check for Success

Before turning in a test, go back one last time to check.

☑ I understood and answered the questions asked.

☑ I checked my work for errors.

☑ My answers make sense.

Round to the nearest whole number to make it easier to solve the problem.

Josh ran 3 miles and then 2 miles. You can add to find the total.
Now go back and add the original numbers.
$3.25 + 1.75 = 5.00$ or 5

The correct choice is B.

Solve each problem. Use simpler numbers to help you. Then choose the best answer.

1. Phil ate $\frac{5}{8}$ of a pie. John ate $\frac{3}{8}$ of another one. Each pie was the same size. How much more did Phil eat than John?

   A. $\frac{2}{8}$ **C.** $\frac{3}{4}$

   B. $\frac{2}{4}$ **D.** $\frac{8}{8}$

2. Kayla had $2.75 last month. She saved $5.35 this month. How much does she have now?

   F. $7.00   **H.** $8.10

   G. $7.05   **I.** $8.35

3. Which number makes the equation true?

   $$3.44 + \blacksquare = 6.24$$

   A. 1.80   **C.** 3.85

   B. 2.80   **D.** 4.80

4. Jenna bought $2\frac{1}{2}$ pounds of apples, $1\frac{1}{2}$ pounds of cherries, and 3 pounds of pears. How many pounds of fruit did she buy in all?

   F. 6 pounds   **H.** $7\frac{1}{2}$ pounds

   G. 7 pounds   **I.** $8\frac{1}{2}$ pounds

Test Prep

PART 1 • Multiple Choice

Choose the best answer.

1. Cody ate $\frac{3}{8}$ of a pizza. Donna ate $\frac{2}{8}$ of the same pizza. How much of the pizza did they eat in all? (p. 582)

   A. $\frac{1}{8}$

   B. $\frac{2}{8}$

   C. $\frac{5}{8}$

   D. $\frac{7}{8}$

2. Which sum is about 1,200? (p. 64)

   F. $408 + 621$

   G. $678 + 733$

   H. $567 + 632$

   I. $488 + 534$

3. Rudy lives 0.82 mile from school. She has walked 0.23 mile so far. How much farther does she need to walk to get to school? (p. 634)

   A. 0.59 m

   B. 0.69 m

   C. 1.05 m

   D. 1.25 m

4. There are 32 members in the art class. They will work in groups to make a new model car. How could they make equal groups?

   (p. 300)

   F. 2 groups of 15

   G. 8 groups of 4

   H. 4 groups of 9

   I. 6 groups of 6

5. Identify the rule: (p.210)

Rule:	
Input	Output
4	12
6	18
8	24

   A. Add 3.

   B. Multiply by 3.

   C. Add 8.

   D. Multiply by 4.

6. Millie is building a rectangular pen for her dog. Two sides are each 10 feet long and the other 2 sides are each 8 feet long. What is the perimeter of the pen? (p. 532)

   F. 80 feet

   G. 36 feet

   H. 20 feet

   I. 18 feet

7. Which is not true? (p. 511)

   A. A square has 4 equal sides.

   B. A circle has 2 equal sides.

   C. A square is a rectangle.

   D. A triangle has exactly 3 sides.

8. How many quarts are in 3 gallons? (p. 462)

   F. 4 quarts

   G. 8 quarts

   H. 12 quarts

   I. 16 quarts

Record your answers on the answer sheet provided by your teacher or on a sheet of paper.

Use data from the chart for problems 9–11.

Here are rates from 4 different cellular telephone companies.

Price for 1-Minute Call		
Company	Daytime	Nighttime
A	$0.42	$0.32
B	$0.45	$0.25
C	$0.33	$0.28
D	$0.35	$0.35

9. What is the difference between the daytime and nighttime price for Company B? (p. 634)

10. How much would Company C charge for a 2-minute daytime call? (p. 624)

11. Which company has the greatest difference between daytime and nighttime calls? (p. 632)

12. Sean is watching a movie that is 80 minutes long. If the movie ends at 5:20 P.M., what time did the movie begin? (p. 146)

13. Ruth says she has shaded 0.5 of this square. Tyrone says she has shaded $\frac{1}{2}$ of this square. Who is correct? Explain. (p. 608)

THINK SOLVE EXPLAIN

14. Owen studied the growth of a plant. At the beginning of the experiment, the plant was 4 inches tall. It grew 2 inches each week. How tall was the plant after 5 weeks? (p. 208)

15. Describe this pattern in words and numbers. (p. 530)

THINK SOLVE EXPLAIN

16. There are 8 cubes in a bag. Three cubes are red. What is the probability of picking a red cube? (p. 586)

PART 3 • Extended Response

Record your answers on a sheet of paper. Show your work.

THINK SOLVE EXPLAIN

17. Marco drinks a total of 5 pints of water in one day. Danielle drinks a total of 8 cups. Carl drinks a total of 2 quarts. Who drinks the most water in 1 day? (p. 458)

Test Prep

Glossary

(Italicized terms are defined elsewhere in this glossary.)

A

acute triangle A *triangle* with all *angles* less than a *right angle*. (p. 514)

addend A number to be added. (p. 52)

addition An operation on two or more numbers that gives a *sum*. (p. 52)

A.M. A name for the time from 12 midnight to 12 noon. (p. 140)

angle A figure formed when two *rays* or *lines* meet at the same *endpoint*. (p. 509)

area The number of *square units* needed to cover a region or figure. (p. 534)

array Objects or symbols displayed in rows and columns. (p. 196)

Associative Property of Addition When adding, the grouping of *addends* can change but the *sum* is the same. (p. 53)

Example: $(4 + 5) + 2 = 11$
$4 + (5 + 2) = 11$

Associative Property of Multiplication When multiplying, the grouping of the *factors* does not change the *product*. (p. 257)

Example: $3 \times (6 \times 2) = 36$
$(3 \times 6) \times 2 = 36$

B

bar graph A graph that shows data by using bars of different lengths. (p. 168)

base The flat *face* on which a *3-dimensional figure* can rest. (p. 502)

benchmark number A number used to estimate the number of objects without counting them. (p. 30)

C

capacity A measure of dry or liquid *volume* of a container. (p. 458)

centimeter (cm) A *metric unit* for measuring *length*. (p. 472) (See Table of Measures.)

certain An event that will definitely happen. (p. 586)

circle A *closed, 2-dimensional figure* having all points the same distance from a given point. (p. 506)

closed figure A figure that starts and ends at the same point. *(p. 512)*

Commutative Property of Addition When adding, the order of the *addends* can change but the *sum* is the same. *(p. 53)*

Example: 12 + 15 = 27
15 + 12 = 27

Commutative Property of Multiplication When multiplying, the order of *factors* does not change the *product*. *(p. 197)*

Example: 7 x 2 = 14
2 x 7 = 14

compatible numbers Numbers that are close to the numbers in a problem and easy to divide mentally. *(p. 414)*

cone A pointed *3-dimensional figure* with a circular *base*. *(p. 502)*

congruent figures Figures that have the same shape and same size. *(p. 524)*

cube A *3-dimensional figure* with six *congruent* square *faces*. *(p. 502)*

cubic unit The *volume* of a *cube*, one of whose sides is the given unit of *length*. *(p. 539)*

cup (c) A *customary unit* for measuring *capacity*. *(p. 458) (See Table of Measures.)*

customary units Units of measure that include *inches*, *quarts*, and *pounds*. *(p. 456) (See Table of Measures.)*

cylinder A *3-dimensional figure* with two *congruent faces* that are circular. *(p. 502)*

D

decimal A number that uses *place value* and a *decimal point* to show *tenths* and *hundredths*. *(p. 606)*

decimal point A period separating the ones and the *tenths* in a *decimal*. *(p. 606)*

Examples: 0.8, 2.1, 27.64
↑   ↑   ↑
decimal point

decimeter (dm) A *metric unit* for measuring *length*. *(p. 472) (See Table of Measures.)*

Glossary **649**

Glossary

Glossary

degrees Celsius (°C) Unit for measuring *temperature*. *(p. 485)*

degrees Fahrenheit (°F) Customary unit for measuring *temperature*. *(p. 484)*

denominator The number below the bar in a *fraction*. It tells the number of equal parts in all. *(p. 554)*

Example: $\dfrac{5}{6}$ ← *denominator*

difference The answer in a *subtraction* problem. *(p. 96)*

digit Any of the symbols used to write numbers—(0, 1, 2, 3, 4, 5, 6, 7, 8, 9). *(p. 6)*

Distributive Property of Multiplication To multiply a *sum* by a number, you can multiply each *addend* by the number and add the *products*. *(p. 384)*

Example: $4 \times (1 + 3) =$
$4 \times 1 + 4 \times 3 = 16$

dividend A number to be divided. *(p. 284)*

division An operation on two numbers that tells how many groups or how many in each group. *(p. 278)*

Example:
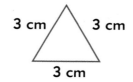
2 ← *quotient*
3)6 ← *dividend*
↑
divisor

divisor The number by which the *dividend* is divided. *(p. 284)*

E

edge A *line segment* where two *faces* of a *3-dimensional figure* meet. *(p. 502)*

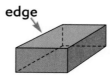
edge

elapsed time The amount of time it takes to go from start to finish. *(p. 146)*

endpoint The point at either end of a *line segment*. The beginning point of a *ray*. *(p. 508)*

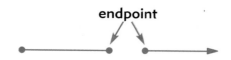
endpoint

equally likely An event that is just as likely to happen as not to happen. *(p. 588)*

equation A number sentence that shows 2 amounts are equal. *(p. 97)*

equilateral triangle A *triangle* with three *sides* of the same *length*. *(p. 514)*

3 cm   3 cm
3 cm

equivalent decimals *Decimals* that name the same number. *(p. 609)*

Examples: 0.3 and 0.30
1.2 and 1.20

equivalent fractions Two or more different *fractions* that name the same amount. *(p. 558)*

Examples: $\frac{1}{2}$ and $\frac{2}{4}$

$\frac{4}{6}$ and $\frac{2}{3}$

estimate To find an answer that is close to the exact answer. *(p. 64)*

even number A number that has 0, 2, 4, 6 or 8 in the ones place. *(p. 2)*

expanded form A way of writing a number as the *sum* of the values of its *digits*. *(p. 7)*

Example: 536 can be written as 500 + 30 + 6.

F

face A flat *side* of a *3-dimensional figure*. *(p. 502)*

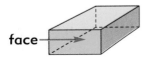
face

fact family A group of *related facts* using the same numbers. *(p. 96)*

Example: 5 + 3 = 8   3 + 5 = 8
8 − 3 = 5   8 − 5 = 3

factors Numbers that are multiplied to give a *product*. *(p. 193)*

Example: 5 x 6 = 30
↑   ↑
factors

foot (ft) A *customary unit* for measuring *length*. *(p. 456) (See Table of Measures.)*

fraction A number that names part of a whole or group. *(p. 554)*

Examples: $\frac{1}{2}, \frac{3}{4}, \frac{5}{6}$

front-end estimation A way of estimating a number using zeros and the *digit* in the greatest place. *(p. 373)*

G

gallon (gal) A *customary unit* for measuring *capacity*. *(p. 458) (See Table of Measures.)*

gram (g) A *metric unit* for measuring *mass*. *(p. 476) (See Table of Measures.)*

H

half hour Amount of time equal to 30 *minutes*. *(p. 144)*

hexagon A *polygon* with six *sides* and six *angles*. *(p. 512)*

hour (h) Unit of time equal to 60 *minutes*. *(p. 144)*

hundredths One of one hundred equal parts. *(p. 608)*

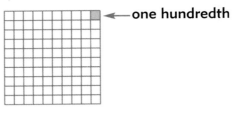
one hundredth

Glossary

Glossary

I

Identity Property of Addition When one *addend* is zero, the *sum* is the same as the other *addend*. *(p. 53)*

Identity Property of Multiplication When one is multiplied by a number, the *product* is that number. *(p. 214)*

impossible An event that cannot happen. *(p. 586)*

inch (in.) A *customary unit* for measuring *length*. *(p. 456) (See Table of Measures.)*

intersecting lines *Lines* that meet or cross each other. *(p. 508)*

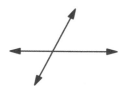

inverse operations Operations that are opposite, such as *addition* and *subtraction* or *multiplication* and *division*. *(p. 96)*

is greater than (>) Symbol to show that the first number is greater than the second. *(p. 24)*

   Example: 5 > 3

is less than (<) Symbol to show that the first number is less than the second. *(p. 24)*

   Example: 3 < 5

isosceles triangle A *triangle* with two *sides* of the same *length*. *(p. 514)*

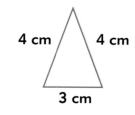

K

key Tells how many items each symbol stands for. *(p. 166)*

kilogram (kg) A *metric unit* for measuring *mass*. *(p. 476) (See Table of Measures.)*

L

length The measurement of distance between two *endpoints*. *(p. 454)*

likely An event will probably happen. *(p. 586)*

line A straight path that goes in two directions without end. *(p. 508)*

line graph A graph that uses a *line* to show how something changes over time. *(p. 174)*

line of symmetry A *line* on which a figure can be folded so that both sides match. *(p. 528)*

line plot A graph that uses Xs above a *number line* to show data. *(p. 160)*

line segment A straight path that has two *endpoints*. *(p. 508)*

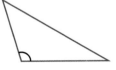

liter (L) A *metric unit* for measuring *capacity*. *(p. 474) (See Table of Measures.)*

M

mass The amount of matter in an object. *(p. 476)*

mean The number found by dividing the sum of a group of numbers by the number of *addends*. *(p. 350)*

median The middle number in a group of numbers arranged in numerical order. *(p. 162)*

> Example: The median of 3, 6, and 8 is 6.

meter (m) A *metric unit* for measuring *length*. *(p. 472) (See Table of Measures.)*

metric units Units of measure that include *centimeters, grams* and *liters*. *(p. 472) (See Table of Measures.)*

milliliter (mL) A *metric unit* for measuring *capacity*. *(p. 474) (See Table of Measures.)*

minute (min) Unit of time equal to 60 seconds. *(p. 140)*

mixed number A number that has a *whole number* part and a *fraction* part. *(p. 576)*

> Example: $6\frac{3}{4}$

mode The number or numbers that occur most often in a set of *data*. *(p. 162)*

> Example: 3, 5, 4, 6, 7, 4, 2, 3, 4
> The mode is 4.

month A unit for measuring time equal to about 30 days. *(p. 150)*

multiple The *product* of a number and any *whole number*. *(p. 193)*

multiplication An operation on two numbers to find a total. It can be thought of as repeated *addition*. *(p. 190)*

multiplication sentence A math statement that shows a product. *(p. 193)*

N

net A flat *pattern* that can be folded to make a *3-dimensional figure*. *(p. 503)*

numerator The number above the bar in a *fraction*. It tells the number of parts. *(p. 554)*

> Example: $\frac{4}{5}$ ← *numerator*

O

obtuse triangle A *triangle* with one angle greater than a *right angle*. *(p. 514)*

Glossary

Glossary

octagon A *polygon* with eight sides and eight *angles*. (p. 512)

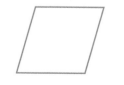

odd number A number that has a 1, 3, 5, 7 or 9 in the ones place. (p. 2)

open figure A figure that has ends that do not meet. (p. 512)

ordered pair A pair of numbers that gives the location of a point on a map or grid. (p. 172)

ordinal number A number used to tell order or position. (p. 150)

ounce (oz) A *customary unit* for measuring *weight*. (p. 460) (See Table of Measures.)

P

parallel lines *Lines* that stay the same distance apart from each other. They do not cross (p. 508)

parallelogram A *quadrilateral* with both pairs of opposites *parallel*. (p. 516)

pattern A series of numbers or figures that follows a rule. (p. 56)

Examples: Numbers: 2, 4, 6, 8, 10

Patterns:

pentagon A *polygon* with five *sides* and five *angles*. (p. 512)

per For each. (p. 430)

perimeter The distance around an object or shape. (p. 532)

period Each group of three *digits* in a *place-value* chart. (p. 10)

Example: 639,271

Thousands Period			Ones Period		
Hundred Thousands	Ten Thousands	Thousands	Hundreds	Tens	Ones
6	3	9	2	7	1

pictograph A graph that shows data by using symbols. (p. 166)

pint (pt) A *customary unit* for measuring *capacity*. (p. 458) (See Table of Measures.)

place value The value given to a *digit* by its place in a number. (p. 4)

Example: In 5,349, the 3 is in the hundreds place and has a value of 300.

P.M. A name for the time from 12 noon to 12 midnight. (p. 140)

polygon A *closed figure* with straight sides. *(p. 512)*

possible outcomes Any of the results that could occur in an experiment. *(p. 588)*

pound (lb) A *customary unit* for measuring *weight*. *(p. 460) (See Table of Measures.)*

probability The chance that an event will occur. *(p. 586)*

product The answer in *multiplication*. *(p. 193)*

Example: 6 x 3 = 18 ◂ *product*

pyramid A *3-dimensional figure* that is shaped by *triangles* on a *base*. *(p. 502)*

Q

quadrilateral A *closed figure* with four sides. *(p. 516)*

quart (qt) A *customary unit* for measuring *capacity*. *(p. 458) (See Table of Measures.)*

quarter hour Amount of time equal to 15 minutes. *(p. 144)*

quotient The answer in *division*. *(p. 284)*

Example: 15 ÷ 3 = 5 ◂ *quotient*

R

range The *difference* between the greatest and the least numbers in a set of numbers. *(p. 162)*

ray A figure that has one *endpoint* and goes without end in one direction. *(p. 508)*

rectangle A *polygon* with four sides. The opposite sides are the same *length*. *(p. 516)*

rectangular prism A *3-dimensional figure* with six rectangular sides. *(p. 502)*

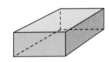

reflection (flip) A movement of a figure across a *line*, producing a mirror image. *(p. 527)*

regroup To rename a number in a different way. *(p. 58)*

Example: 42 can be regrouped as 4 tens and 2 ones or as 3 tens and 12 ones.

related facts Basic facts using the same numbers. *(p. 96)*

Glossary

Glossary

remainder The number left after dividing. *(p. 420)*

Example: $22 \div 7 = 3\,R1$

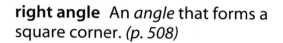

remainder

rhombus A *quadrilateral* with four *sides* of the same *length* and no right *angles*. *(p. 516)*

right angle An *angle* that forms a square corner. *(p. 508)*

right triangle A *triangle* with one *right angle*. *(p. 514)*

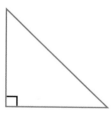

rotation (turn) A movement of a figure that is rotated around a point. *(p. 527)*

round To find the value of a number based on a given *place value*. *(p. 32)*

Example: 27 rounded to the nearest 10 is 30.

scale Marks that are equally spaced along a side of a graph. *(p. 168)*

scalene triangle A *triangle* with no sides the same *length*. *(p. 514)*

side One of the *line* segments in a *polygon*. *(p. 512)*

similar figures Figures that have the same shape but may have different sizes. *(p. 524)*

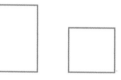

simplest form A *fraction* that is expressed using the largest fraction piece possible. *(p. 560)*

skip-count To count by twos, fives, tens, and so on. *(p. 2)*

sphere A *3-dimensional figure* that has the shape of a ball. *(p. 502)*

square A *polygon* that has four equal sides. *(p. 512)*

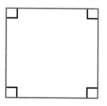

square number The *product* of multiplying two of the same *factors*. (p. 233)

square units A *square*, one of whose sides is a given unit of *length* that is used to measure *area*. (p. 534)

standard form A way of writing a number that shows only its *digits*. (p. 6)

subtraction An operation on two numbers that tells how many are left (*difference*) when some are taken away. (p. 96)

Example: 9 − 4 = 5
↑
difference

sum The answer in *addition*. (p. 52)

Example: 6 + 4 = 10 ← *sum*

survey A method of gathering data by asking people questions. (p. 160)

symmetrical figure A figure in which both sides of the *line* match exactly. (p.528)

T

tally A way of counting by making a mark for each item counted. (p. 160)

Example: 卌 stands for 5.

temperature A measurement that tells how hot or cold something is. (p. 484)

tenths One of ten equal parts. (p. 608)

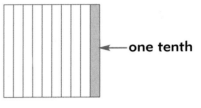
← one tenth

tessellation Repeated shapes that cover a flat surface without leaving any gaps. (p. 546)

3-dimensional figure A figure that has *length*, width, and height. (p. 502)

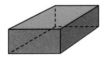

time line A drawing that shows the date and order in which events occurred. (p. 152)

translation (slide) A movement of a figure along a *line*. (p. 527)

trapezoid A *quadrilateral* with exactly one pair of *parallel* sides. (p. 516)

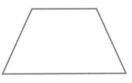

triangle A *polygon* with three sides. (p. 514)

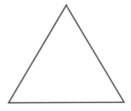

Glossary

2-dimensional figure A figure that has only *length* and width. *(p. 506)*

week A unit for measuring time equal to seven days. *(p. 150)*

weight A measurement that tells how heavy an object is. *(p. 460)*

whole number Numbers in the set 0,1,2,3,4, and so on. *(p. 4)*

unit price A price given as the cost for a single unit. *(p. 430)*

word form A way of writing a number using words. *(p. 6)*

unlikely An event that is not *likely* to happen. *(p. 586)*

yard (yd) A *customary unit* for measuring *length*. *(p. 456)* *(See Table of Measures.)*

variable A letter used to represent an unknown quantity. *(p. 241)*

vertex The common point where three or more *edges* of a *3-dimensional figure* meet. *(p. 502)*

Zero Property of Multiplication
When zero is multiplied by a number, the *product* is zero. *(p. 214)*

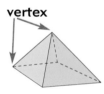

vertex

Example: $0 \times 5 = 0$

volume The amount of space that a *3-dimensional figure* encloses. *(p. 538)*

Table of Measures

CUSTOMARY

Length

1 foot (ft) = 12 inches (in.)

1 yard (yd) = 3 feet or 36 inches

1 mile (mi) = 5,280 feet or 1,760 yards

Weight

1 pound (lb) = 16 ounces (oz)

Capacity

1 pint (pt) = 2 cups (c)

1 quart (qt) = 2 pints or 4 cups

1 gallon (gal) = 4 quarts

METRIC

Length

1 meter (m) = 100 centimeters (cm)

1 decimeter (dm) = 10 centimeters

1 meter = 10 decimeters

1 kilometer (km) = 1,000 meters

Mass

1 kilogram (kg) = 1,000 grams (g)

Capacity

1 liter (L) = 1,000 milliliters (mL)

TIME

1 minute (min) = 60 seconds

1 hour (h) = 60 minutes

1 day = 24 hours

1 week = 7 days

1 year = 12 months (mo)

TEMPERATURE

32° Fahrenheit (°F) ... Water freezes

212° Fahrenheit ... Water boils

0° Celsius (°C) ... Water freezes

100° Celsius ... Water boils

SYMBOLS

<	is less than	¢	cent	↔	ray
>	is greater than	°	degree	∠	angle
=	is equal to	↔	line	∟	right angle
$	dollar	⟶	line segment	(5, 3)	ordered pair

Index

A

Act It Out, as problem-solving strategy, 306–307

Activities. *See* Cross-curricular problems, Decision Making, Enrichment, Game Zone, Hands On Activities, Math and Science, Problem Solving, Writing.

Acute triangle, 514–515

Addend, 52–54, 56–57, 60–62, 64–65, 72–74, 76–77, 80–81, 90, 96–98, 192–194, 350–351, 352–353, 578–579, 624–625

Addition, 52–54, 56–57, 58–59, 60–62, 64–65, 72–74, 76–77, 80–81, 88, 90, 96–98, 132, 192–194, 234, 250, 532–533, 578–579, 582–584, 624–625, 626–628
Associative Property of, 52–54
choosing a computation method for, 80–81
Commutative Property of, 52–54
estimating sums, 64–65, 88
facts, 56–57
Identity Property of, 52–54
mental math, 57, 80–81
modeling properties of, 90
odd or even sums, 132
of decimals, 624–625, 626–628
of dollar amounts, 61–62
of fractions, 578–579, 582–584
of greater numbers, 72–74
of length of sides, 532–533
of more than two numbers, 76–77
of whole numbers, 60–62, 72–74
patterns, 56–57
properties, 52–54
regrouping in, 58–59, 60–62, 72–74, 76–77, 626–627
related to multiplication, 192–194
related to subtraction, 96–98
repeated, 192–194, 234, 250, 462, 478

Algebra, 11, 33, 52–54, 56–57, 62, 65, 74, 77, 81, 96–98, 102–103, 108, 115, 117, 125, 142, 192–194, 206, 214–215, 239, 240–242, 251, 253, 256–258, 280–282, 284–286, 289, 297, 299, 302, 304–305, 326, 332, 337, 342–344, 370–371, 374, 394, 412–413, 416, 422, 437, 461, 464, 480, 533, 567, 613, 635
addition patterns, 56–57
addition properties, 52–54
divide with 0 and 1, 304–305
multiply 3 numbers, 256–258
relate division and subtraction, 280–281
relate multiplication to division, 284–286
subtraction patterns, 102–103
use related facts, 342–343

A.M., 140–142, 146–148

Analog clocks, 140–142, 144, 146–148

Analyzing, 28, 33, 46, 54, 57, 65, 77, 90, 117, 163, 164, 173, 175, 182, 184, 201, 219, 226, 247, 279, 289, 293, 316, 318, 326, 337, 339, 362, 371, 379, 397, 402, 404, 427, 446, 448, 461, 494, 496, 577, 600, 613

Angles, 507–510, 514–515
right, 508–510, 514–515

Area, 534–536, 537

Arrays, 196–197, 204, 211, 224, 284, 331

Art, 307, 391, 439, 504, 515, 567

Assessment, Performance, 45, 89, 133, 183, 225, 271, 317, 361, 403, 447, 495, 547, 599, 643

Associative Property of Addition, 52–54

Associative Property of Multiplication, 256–258

B

Balance scale, 461, 476

Bar graphs, 168–169, 179, 183, 184, 185, 589, 639

Base, 502–504

Benchmark numbers, 30–31

Benchmarks, 494

Bills, 12–13, 14–16

C

Calculator, using, 61, 73, 76, 77, 80–81, 107, 121, 124–125, 162, 167, 210, 235, 250, 256, 270, 288, 330, 385, 390, 392–394, 431, 434, 436, 437, 439, 463, 627, 644

Calendars, 150–151

Capacity, 458–459, 474–475
customary, 458–459
metric, 474–475

Careers, 54, 62, 103, 297

Celsius (C), 484–486, 487

Centimeter (cm), 472–473, 478–479, 494, 514, 532, 533

Certain, 586–587

Change, 12–13, 14–16, 61, 387
adding, 61
making, 14–16

Charts, 2, 6, 10, 24, 26, 89, 133, 160–161, 271, 317, 361, 403, 447, 495, 547, 601, 612, 614, 624
hundreds, 2
place value, 6, 10, 26, 612, 614, 624
tally, 160–161

Circle, 506–507

Circle graphs, 182

Clocks
analog, 140–142, 143, 144, 146–148
digital, 140–142, 146–148

Closed figure, 512–513, 516–517

Coins, 12–13, 14–16, 608–609, 612–613

Combinations, 590–591

Commas, using in math, 7

Commutative Property of Addition, 52–54

Commutative Property of Multiplication, 196–197, 200, 234, 257

Comparing, 24–25, 26, 27, 142, 152, 160, 224, 254, 299, 335, 353, 388–389, 391, 394, 413, 437, 463, 464, 479, 480, 494, 510, 587, 607, 614–616, 635
data and graphs, 160, 388–389
dates and events, 152
decimals, 614–615
measurements, 463, 464, 479, 480, 494
money, 24–25, 27
multiplication models, 224
numbers, 24–25
time, 142

Comparing and contrasting, 149

Compatible numbers, 414–416

Computation methods, choosing, 26, 34, 73, 80–81, 124–125, 193, 204, 205, 210, 211, 234–235, 238, 250, 252, 257, 281, 284–285, 288, 296, 298, 300, 301, 324, 325, 330–331, 373, 385, 390, 392–393, 415, 430, 431, 436–437, 462–463, 478–479, 554, 555, 562, 563
adding on to known facts, 238
Commutative Property, 234
compatible numbers, 415
Distributive Property, 385, 392–393
doubling known facts, 210, 234–235, 238
front-end estimation, 373
making a table, 257
mental math, 80–81, 124–125, 392–393, 436–437
repeated addition, 193, 234, 250, 462, 478
repeated subtraction, 281, 300, 324, 330, 463, 479
rounding, 373, 415
skip-counting, 204, 210, 288, 296, 300, 325
subtracting from known facts, 252
using arrays, 204, 211, 284, 331
using calculators, 73, 80–81, 124–125, 250, 330, 385, 392–394, 431, 436, 463
using division, 463, 479
using division facts, 324, 331
using equations, 205
using fraction models, 554, 562, 563
using models, 205, 301, 554, 562, 563
using multiplication, 462

Index

Index

Index

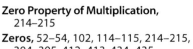

Index

Credits